ARTISANS *in* EARLY IMPERIAL CHINA

Anthony J. Barbieri-Low

University of Washington Press · *Seattle & London*

PUBLISHED WITH THE ASSISTANCE OF THE GETTY FOUNDATION.

THIS PUBLICATION IS ALSO SUPPORTED BY THE PUBLICATIONS COMMITTEE, DEPARTMENT OF ART AND ARCHAEOLOGY, PRINCETON UNIVERSITY, AND BY A GRANT FROM THE MILLARD MEISS PUBLICATION FUND OF THE COLLEGE ART ASSOCIATION.

MM

Printed in Italy
Designed by Ashley Saleeba
25 24 23 22 21 5 4 3 2 1

University of Washington Press
uwapress.uw.edu

The paper used in this publication meets the minimum requirements of American National Standard for Information Sciences—Permanence of Paper for Printed Library Materials, ANSI Z39.48-1984.

LIBRARY OF CONGRESS
CATALOGING-IN-PUBLICATION DATA

Barbieri-Low, Anthony J. (Anthony Jerome), 1967–
Artisans in early imperial China /
Anthony Barbieri-Low. — 1st ed.
p. cm.
Includes bibliographical references and index.
ISBN: 978-0-295-98713-2 (hardback : alk. paper)
ISBN: 978-0-295-74938-9 (paperback : alk. paper)
1. Artisans—China—History.
2. Artisans—China—Social life and customs.
or social conditions. I. Title.
HD2346.C6B37 2007
331.7'94—dc22 2007002327

Artisans in Early Imperial China

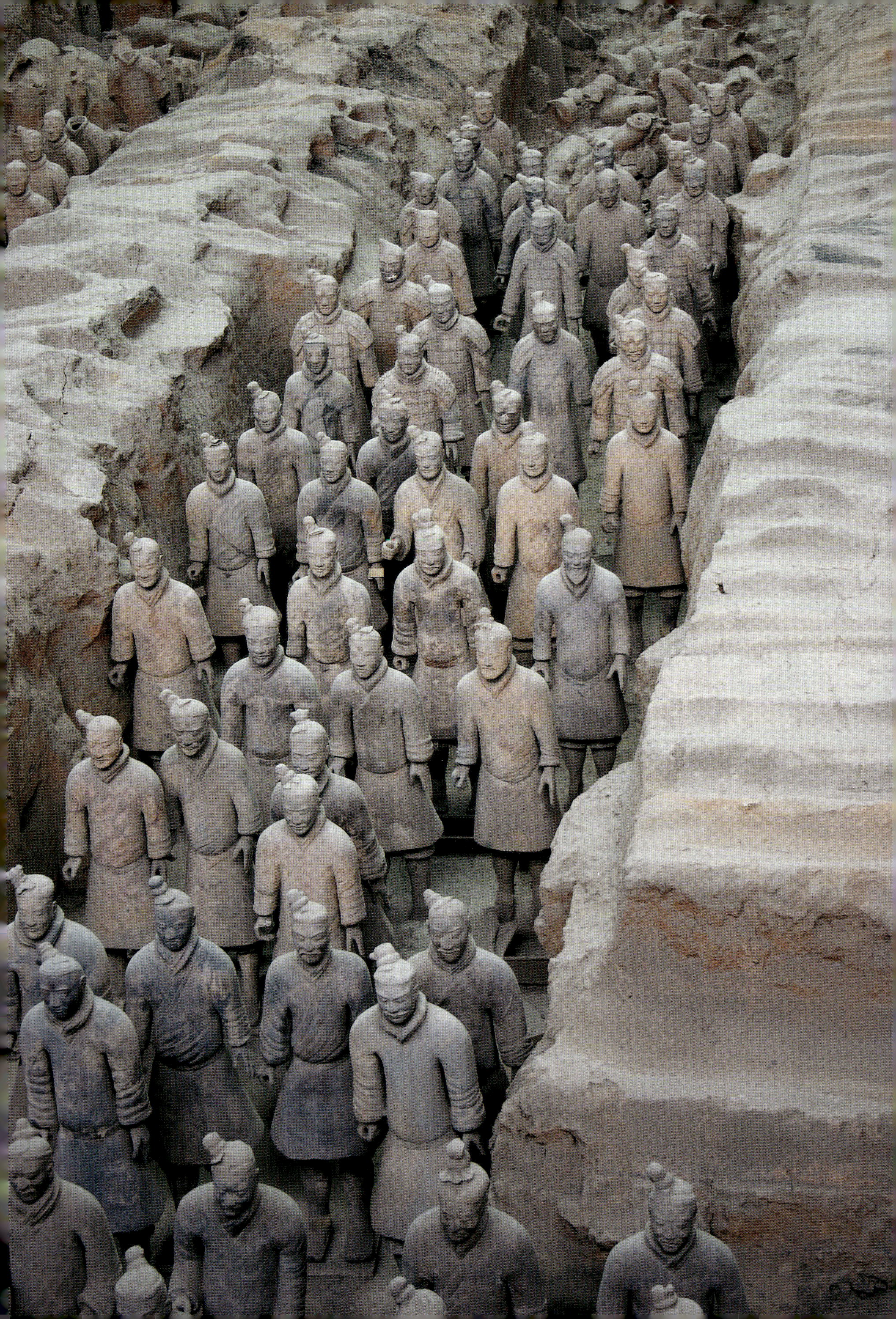

To

JEANNIE AND THE LITTLE ONES

CONTENTS

ACKNOWLEDGMENTS

A book of this scope and complexity necessarily requires much gestation time. I first conceived the idea for this book when I was completing a dissertation on the organization of imperial workshops during the Han period. By looking at inscriptional materials, surviving objects, and received texts, I was able to uncover significant details concerning not only the macro-organization of imperial workshops within the structure of the state and upon the landscape but also the micro-organization at one particular lacquer factory, including its management structure and division of labor. As I neared completion of that project, however, I became keenly aware that what my findings lacked was a human dimension. Who were all these men and women who toiled for the emperor in small workshops and larger factories? What was their place in society? Because of limitations of time and experience, I was not able to tackle those issues at the dissertation stage. Thus, this book was born.

My research for this book benefited early on from my involvement in a multiyear, interdisciplinary research project to study the famous Wu Family Cemetery in northeast China. As one of my contributions to the research effort, I chose to study the stone carvers of the Shandong area, who created the intricate pictorial scenes and decorative borders that adorned the tombs and shrines of the aspiring middle-income class during the Han. My findings in regard to the stone carvers nicely complemented my earlier work on lacquer artisans and provided valuable material for several chapters in this book. Some of this material was published previously in the catalog for the Wu Family Cemetery exhibition, *Recarving China's Past: Art, Archaeology, and Architecture of the "Wu Family Shrines"* (Princeton: Princeton University Art Museum; New Haven: Yale University Press, 2005), and is reprinted here with permission. I would like to express thanks to my colleagues on that project, Cary Liu, Michael Nylan, Susan Beningson, and David A. Sensabaugh, for their stimulating ideas and pleasant travel companionship.

This book was primarily written during a leave from teaching provided by the School of Arts and Sciences at the University of Pittsburgh and a Fellowship for University Teachers from the National Endowment for the Humanities. Of course, any views, findings, conclusions, or recommendations expressed in this book do not necessarily reflect those of the National Endowment for the Humanities. The research was also funded by travel grants and grants for research materials from the Asian Studies Center and the Office of Research at the University of Pittsburgh and from the J. Paul Getty Trust. The generous use of color illustrations was made possible by subventions from the Department of Art and Archaeology, Princeton University, the Millard Meiss Publication Fund of the College Art Association, the Asian Studies Center of the University of Pittsburgh, the Metropolitan Center for Far Eastern Art Studies, and the Richard D. and Mary Jane Edwards Endowed Publication Fund of the School of Arts and Sciences, University of Pittsburgh.

Throughout the writing and research phase, I benefited from suggestions and critical feedback offered by colleagues and friends throughout the world, including Robert W. Bagley, David N. Keightley, Michael Puett, Lothar von Falkenhausen, Katheryn Linduff, Hsu Cho-yun, Robin D. S. Yates, Jerome Silbergeld, Klaas Ruitenbeek, Zheng Yan, Xin Lixiang, Jiang Yingju, Xing Yitian, Susan Naquin, Martin Kern, Evelyn Rawski, Dora C. Y. Ching, Seymour Drescher, Donald S. Sutton, William Chase, Rob Ruck, and the Working Class History Seminar of the University of Pittsburgh.

I would also like to express my gratitude to the diligent and helpful staff of the East Asian Library at the University of Pittsburgh, especially Zhang Haihui, Agnes Wen, Hong Xu, Shen Zhijia, and Zou Xiuying, who all provided support for this project and helped me to track down elusive sources.

I would also like to thank the three anonymous reviewers commissioned by the University of Washington Press, who offered helpful criticisms on the first manuscript draft of this book.

And, finally, I want to express my heartfelt gratitude to Michael Loewe, who was University Lecturer at Cambridge University and whose detailed reading of the entire manuscript resulted in innumerable corrections and suggestions. His generous efforts have saved me from several blunders and have improved the usefulness of this book to early China scholars. It almost goes without saying, however, that any errors that remain are entirely my own.

Artisans in Early Imperial China

1

INTRODUCTION

Artisans and Their Art in Context

Objects can truly fascinate us.

When people encounter an ancient artifact in a museum case, they often report experiencing a tangible sense of contact with the remote past. Nevertheless, no matter how much a glittering cultural relic may dazzle the eye with its opulent decoration or intrigue the mind with its intricate design, whatever connection one might feel through this artifact is actually quite shallow. Hanging on a gallery wall or sitting in a museum display case, the material object has been stripped of two important types of context. The first is the context of use. No ancient object was ever designed to sit in a museum case, and placing it there removes almost any clue as to how an object was used and what meaning it held within a larger system of material culture. Archaeologists consider the restoration of use-context one of their primary missions. When archaeologists recover objects, they meticulously record the location of the object and its relationship to assemblages of other artifacts in the vicinity. Through comparative analysis and textual research they hope to reconstruct how the object was used in the past and what it might have meant to its user and to other members of society.

The other type of context stripped from ancient artifacts is even more difficult to recover, namely the social and economic context of the object's creation. Who made it? What place in society did this person occupy? Why did he or she make it? How was it made? How was the creator trained? How was the object sold or transferred into the hands of its ultimate owner? These are questions we would like to answer, and should try to answer, if we want to truly appreciate our encounter with the material relics of the past. Sadly though, an object's creative context is often lost long before it is discarded in the ground. Recovering this information often requires piecing together scattered clues from received texts, inscriptions, and archaeological sites, combined with an intensive study of the object itself.

Let us look at two famous artifacts from early imperial China and see how the partial restoration of their creative context alters our perception of them. Nearly everyone is familiar with the famous army of terracotta warriors found in pits near the necropolis at the foot of Mount Li, the final resting place of Ying Zheng, the First Emperor of Qin (see figure 1.1). Discovered in 1974 and hailed as one of the greatest archaeological discoveries of the twentieth century, the terracotta-warrior pits were just one element of an enormous funerary complex designed to be a microcosm of the First Emperor's palace and empire. The terracotta army was meant to occupy a total of four burial pits, but only three were completed and outfitted with terracotta figures. Excavations are still ongoing, but it is estimated that approximately 6,000–8,000 life-size human and equine figurines reside in the pits. Infantry figures are the most common, but archers, charioteers, cavalrymen, officers, and generals are also represented.

Chinese reports on the figures and popular Western accounts tend to stress the fact that, among those figures uncovered thus far, no two have been found that are exactly alike. Some authors even suggest that the figures were portraits of actual soldiers and that the facial variety reflected the ethnic diversity of the new empire. For example, Arthur Cotterell, in his 1981 popular account *The First Emperor of China,* declared that "each head is a personal portrait, and so far the excavators have not discovered two faces which are the same. Unlike the stereotyped funerary statues of other ancient rulers, these soldiers are modeled on living men."[1] While it is true that each figure is somewhat unique, recent research has debunked the fanciful notion that all the figures are individual portraits of living soldiers. Lothar Ledderose, in his book *Ten Thousand Things,* explained how the figures were made using techniques of mass production, enabling many units to be made quickly. The production scheme was deployed using combinations of modular units, giving the army the "credible variety" it needed to have magical efficacy.[2]

Researchers who have examined the terracotta figures closely have outlined the procedures used to fashion them.[3] Each warrior consists of seven major components (plinth, feet, calves, torso, arms, hands, and head), constructed separately or in stages

(opposite) 1.1 *Terracotta Army Pit 1.* Qin period (221–207 BCE). Museum of the Qin Emperor's Terracotta Warriors and Horses, Lintong County, Shaanxi. Photo by Anthony Barbieri-Low, August 4, 2005.

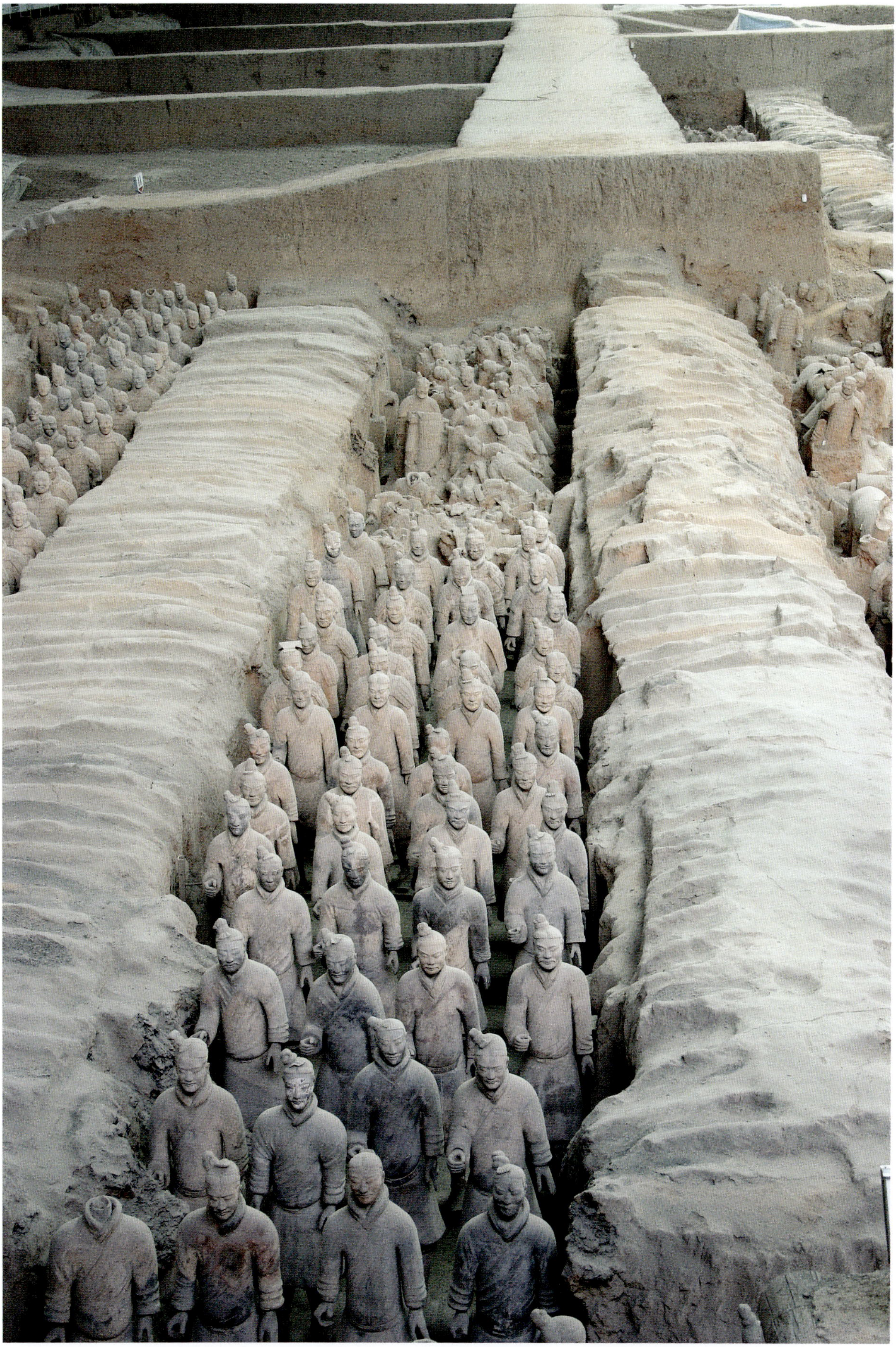

and fitted together with wet clay. Starting at the base, the plinth was likely molded in a rectangular (or sometimes pentagonal) box. To this, the craftsmen attached the feet, usually before air-drying the combined base unit. The legs below the knee could be solid or hollow but were usually built up from coils or panels of clay to form the basic shape, then covered with another layer of clay that was modeled with the features of the pants. The torso was the most schematic component in its basic construction. The hollow, columnar torso of standing figures was formed by first building up coils of clay, supported by internal buttresses and external cords. A further layer of clay was then applied to the exterior, and this was sculpted to form the details of the torso. A third, thin layer of clay was then applied and carved to fashion the scales and cords of the mail armor. Arms came in both flexed and extended types and were similarly fashioned of clay coils and inserted into the torso. The hands were made in molds for either open or gripping poses and inserted into the cuff of the arms. The thumbs were usually formed separately and attached in custom poses to hold specific bronze weapons. The basic shape of the head was formed in a two-part mold, divided just in front of the ear. Further layers of clay were then added, and the face was sculpted to individuate the features, indicating expression, hair, mustache, eyebrows, etc. Finally, the figures were coated with raw lacquer and painted in bright colors of red, green, blue, purple, orange, black, and white.

Ledderose brought our attention to the fact that the terracotta warriors were built up from a limited repertoire of basic component types, which were then recombined in different ways to simulate the infinite nature of human variation. In reality, there were only eight basic types of head, eight types of torso, seven types of shoes, and two types of hand.[4] Even the seemingly individualistic faces are made up of what one scholar has called "aggregates of prefabricated expressive and representational units."[5] Many of the components were made to standardized sizes or types, often in molds, but because every molded part was later worked by hand, incised, and painted, the whole work begins to take on the appearance of a custom manufacture. Because they were constructed from modules, and not as an organic whole, the terracotta figures simply cannot be considered complete portraits of individuals.[6] That is not to preclude the possibility that the facial features of some figures were not modeled on generic facial types or even individual traits of specific persons.

In the last few years, the ongoing excavations at the Mount Li necropolis have revealed new life-size terracotta figures, some startlingly different from the static, programmed mannequins in the terracotta army pits. One newly discovered pit contained ceramic figures of civil officials and other bureaucrats who would assist the emperor in the next life.[7] Another contained an assortment of life-size figures of entertainers, strongmen, and storytellers who would entertain him in his underworld realm.[8] The natural pose and stunning realism of the strongman in figure 1.2 has no precedent in the extant art of the Warring States or Qin periods and has prompted more than one scholar to conjure up the old argument of Western influence to explain its apparently revolutionary style. One prominent scholar has even suggested that the

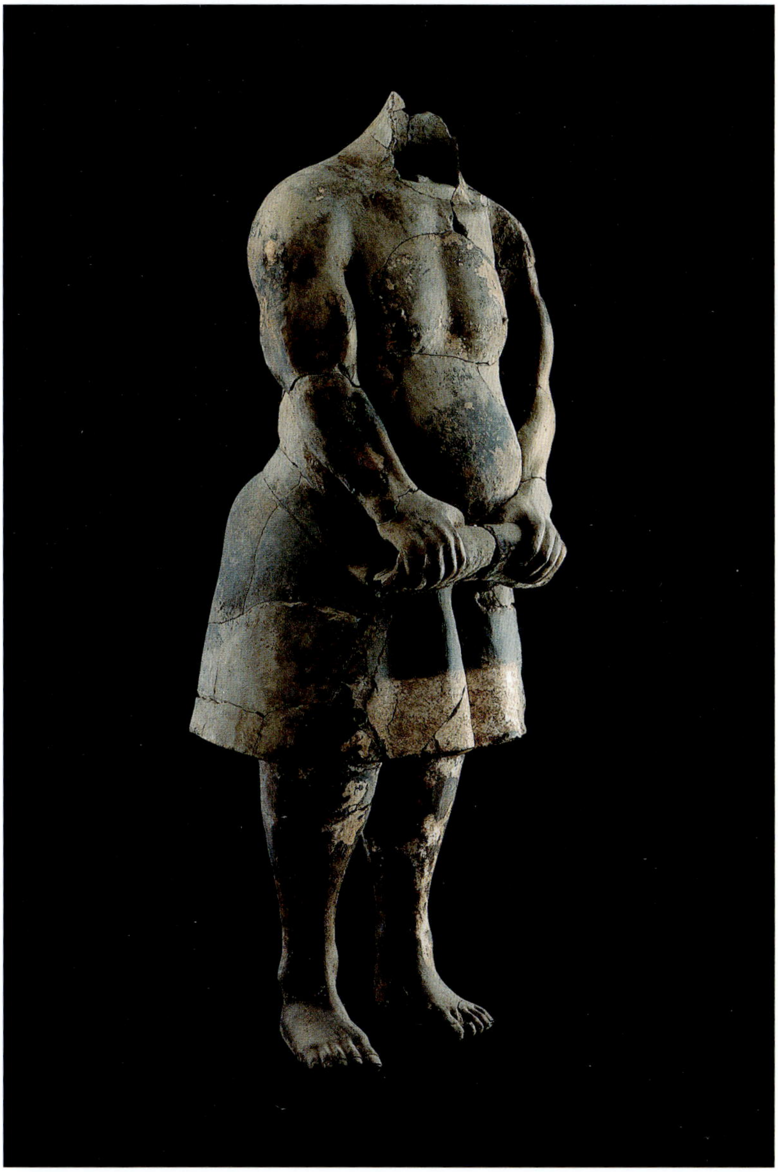

1.2 *Strongman*. Qin period (221–207 BCE). Terracotta with polychrome paint. H. 1.72 m. Museum of the Qin Emperor's Terracotta Warriors and Horses, Lintong County, Shaanxi. O. Louis Mazzatenta/ National Geographic Image Collection.

strongman figure was made by foreign-born craftsmen, but strong continuities in construction techniques and workshop labeling strongly argue that he and his cohort of entertainers were fashioned by indigenous, ethnic-Han artisans.[9]

Let us now turn our attention to the artisans who made the terracotta army. A number of the terracotta figures carry stamped or incised inscriptions, placed in unobtrusive locations, that indicate the name and affiliation of the foreman or the master potter responsible for their manufacture (see figure 1.3). To date, eighty-seven different names have been found on the thousands of reconstructed human and equestrian figures.[10] These names can be broken down into two distinct categories of artisans. The first group encompasses those state artisans employed by palace ceramic

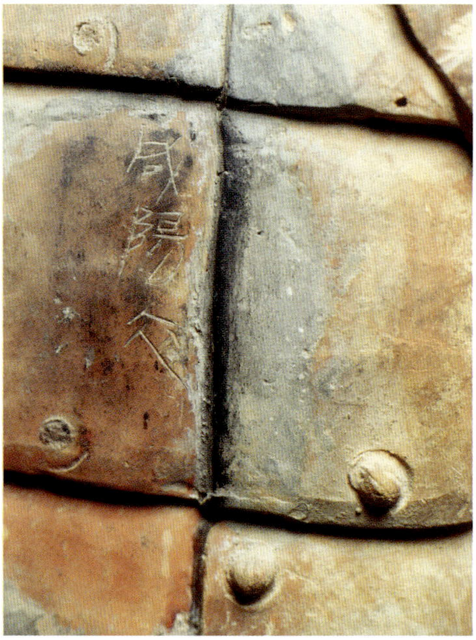

1.3. *Artisan-foreman name, "Yi of Xianyang City," inscribed on terracotta figure.* Qin period (221–207 BCE). Museum of the Qin Emperor's Terracotta Warriors and Horses, Lintong County, Shaanxi. Photo courtesy of Cultural Relics Publishing House.

workshops. Their names are usually affixed to the figurine by means of stamp blocks. These names include De (Acquire), Jiang (Frontier), and Xi (Connected). Most of these given names seem to be either male names or androgynous names of indeterminate gender. The given names are usually prefixed by the word *gong* (palace), which according to Yuan Zhongyi (b. 1932) is likely an abbreviation of Gongshui (Palace Water Factory), a Qin palace bureau in charge of making water pipes, hollow architectural bricks, and ceramic roof tiles. Ledderose has observantly pointed out that the legs of the terracotta warriors do look very similar to the water pipes excavated from Qin palace sites![11] The seals of all three persons listed earlier (De, Jiang, and Xi) have also been found on ceramic roof tiles or bricks from the Qin palace area. Thus, some of the makers of the terracotta army, or at least those masters supervising the artisan teams, were not master sculptors but ceramic artisans skilled at fitting pipes and mass-producing bricks or roof tiles. At least one other official bureau contributed skilled workers to the project. The seals prefixed by the word *da* (large) probably indicate an affiliation with the Chamberlain for the Palace Buildings (Jiangzuo **Da**jiang), who was the court official responsible for palace and tomb construction.

The second group of names recorded on the terracotta warriors seems to have belonged to artisans normally employed in private ceramic workshops in Xianyang or the surrounding counties. Their names are usually inscribed with a stylus into the clay of the figurine (as in figure 1.3) and not affixed with official stamps, like those used by the palace artisans. Some of the given names of these artisans include Ye (Wilderness), Jing (Respect), Zhong (Heavy), and Yue 㜓(Beautiful). The last name mentioned is written with a graph that contains a female semantic classifier and is used only in phrases describing female beauty. Thus, the name possibly belonged to a female master potter.[12] The inscribed given names are occasionally prefixed by the county of residence of the master potter, such as Xianyang (the Qin capital), Yueyang, Linjin, or Anyi. Most potters, in fact, were from the Xianyang area, as was the master who inscribed his name on the warrior's armor seen in figure 1.3. Those master potters who came from the county of Linjin had to travel about one hundred kilometers to reach the tomb site, and those from Anyi County had to travel nearly two hundred kilometers.

It seems that the independent artisans from private ceramic workshops were probably conscripted to contribute work to the First Emperor's tomb project as part of their annual tribute labor to the throne. They were likely assembled together at kiln sites near the terracotta army pits, working under nominal supervision from palace officials. They were likely provided with basic shelter and food and probably returned to their normal workplaces after one month's rotation. The fact that they could incise these brief inscriptional texts also tells us something about their level of literacy.

Yuan Zhongyi has analyzed the stylistic differences between those terracotta warriors made by artisans conscripted from private workshops and those made by palace artisans. Predictably, his research shows that those warrior figures made in the palace workshops were of a consistently higher quality and made with finer clay. Their postures were uniformly upright, martial, and strong, and the shapes and sizes of the molded body parts show little variation. Those figures made by persons from the private regional workshops, in contrast, tended to be more uneven in quality; some were masterpieces of detail and others were quite shoddy and full of defects. There were minor variations in the methods of construction between the two groups as well. Of note is the fact that the pieces made by conscripted artisans tended to show more genuine human variation in height, weight, age, and expression, with much more variation in hairstyle. The human facial types and models for these pieces may have been drawn from among the common people of the potters' daily experience. The inspiration for the palace artisans may have been the guards and warriors who worked in the palace compounds.

Yuan's stylistic analysis tends to show that the artisans conscripted from private workshops enjoyed more freedom of personal expression in their sculpture, especially in the finishing details of the faces. They had also been trained under a variety of sculptural traditions, and this consciously or unconsciously manifested itself in their work. The stylistic variation of these pieces probably also resulted from decentralized training and less stringent supervision of these workers at the construction site. Those pieces made in the palace workshop, in contrast, were uniformly of the same stiff and formal style. All the palace artisans had probably undergone the same artistic training and all worked in the same location.

The ultimate fate of the ceramic craftsmen who worked on the terracotta army was probably quite different from that of the convicts and children of slaves who dug the pits for the magic army and heaped the earth on the tomb mound of the First Emperor.

Hundreds or even thousands of those unfortunate young men died of exhaustion and disease in the course of the work and were buried in shallow graves just west of the worksite (see chapter 6). Those who managed to survive had their sentences commuted in exchange for military service in the desperate attempt to hold off the organized popular rebellion which brought down the Qin Empire. Most were probably slaughtered on the battlefield between 209 and 206 BCE.

Our second famous artifact may not be as familiar to the general reader as the terracotta warriors, but devotees of Asian art will quickly recognize this image as the Changxin Palace lamp, arguably one of the most beautiful and evocative objects to survive from early imperial China (see figure 1.4). Archaeologists discovered the lamp, actually more properly labeled a candlestick, in 1968 in the tomb of a Han dynasty prince's consort.[13]

The candlestick was a featured piece in several traveling exhibits of masterworks from ancient China, including the Great Bronze Age of China show, which traveled to the Metropolitan Museum of Art and four other venues during 1980–1, and the Golden Age of Chinese Archaeology exhibit, which toured the country in 1999 and 2000. Learned commentators all concur that the Changxin Palace lamp is an object of extreme beauty, a masterpiece of human ingenuity and artistic expression. The entry for the lamp in the *Great Bronze Age of China* catalog claims, "It ranks among the finest of early Chinese sculptures, whether in bronze, terracotta, or wood," and it displays "a relaxed ease and a psychological realism entirely lacking in [the earlier Qin figurines]."[14] Jessica Rawson, writing for the *Golden Age* catalog, praised the lamp for its "elegance and the aura of serenity it conveys."[15] For his recent book *Women in Early Imperial China*, Bret Hinsch selected extreme facial close-ups of the Changxin Palace lamp for his book jacket, suggesting that this figure could represent the appearance and status of women during the Qin and Han periods. In China itself, the lamp has become a popular icon and in some ways a symbol of China's glittering past.[16]

The gilded-bronze lamp is nearly half a meter high and takes the form of a kneeling palace servant girl who holds aloft the base of a candlestick (for a tallow candle) with her left hand while steadying its crown with her right. Under her thick outer robe, which is fastened with a sash, she wears a padded scarf and an inner silk robe with generous, billowing sleeves that cascade over the top of the candle chamber. Her hair is tied up in a chignon, and most of her head is covered by a square cloth, the corner of which trails slightly over her left shoulder.

The Changxin Palace lamp is, indeed, a clever mechanical device. The lamp pan itself carries a projecting handle (once with a longer wooden insert), which could be used to rotate the base to direct light toward different areas of the room. Two sliding,

(opposite) 1.4 *Changxin Palace lamp.* Former Han period, ca. 170–151 BCE. Gilded bronze. H. 48 cm. Hebei Provincial Museum. Photo courtesy of Cultural Relics Publishing House.

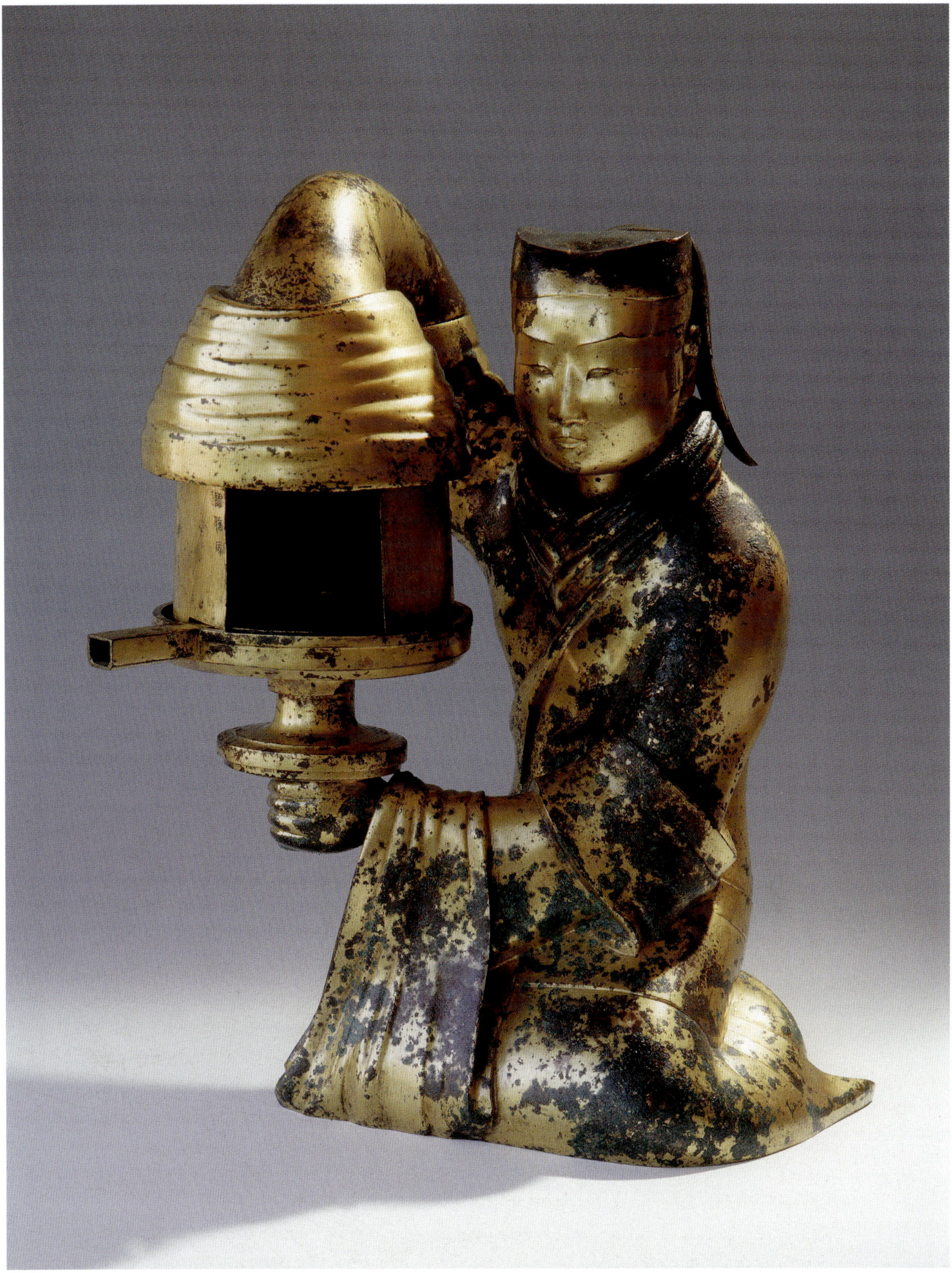

semicylindrical panels are set into the lamp base. These can be opened or closed to regulate the intensity of light. The right sleeve of the palace girl conveniently serves as the chimney for the candle, drawing all the smoke up into her arm. Though, to my knowledge, no one has ever tested this assumption, it is thought that the soot from the candle would end up in the base of the figure and could be easily cleaned from a removable container.

Ingeniousness aside, what really strikes all who encounter this lamp are the physical and psychological details. The girl's face reveals a complex tapestry of emotional expression. At first glance, she seems to exude a placid beauty and centered focus worthy of a classical Greek bust or a Gandharan Buddha in meditative bliss. Yet her eyes are slightly downcast to avoid our direct gaze. Her partially opened mouth is as enigmatic as the Mona Lisa's smile. Does this girl really exude inner contentment, or does she merely ingratiate her masters and submissively harbor her pain in silence? Dwelling over her face even longer we can perceive layers of awe, resolve, resentment, and resignation. Thus, like any great sculptural face, hers is a mirror onto our own souls.

Her posture also reveals remarkable balance and tension. Walking around to the back of this figure (see figure 1.5), we see that her spine is mostly erect and that she sits on the backs of her heels. Yet her shoulders seem to droop just slightly from weariness, and her arches are taut, as much of her weight rest on the balls of her feet.

What we seem to be experiencing is a direct window onto the past. We perceive the sensitivity of the artist, the beauty and pain of the model, and the poignant fate of palace servitude. But contrary to these perceptions, the Changxin Palace lamp is not a unique sculptural creation by some unnamed Chinese Praxiteles. Investigating this object closer we find that formal and aesthetic impressions, informed by our post-Renaissance eyes, can be quite misleading.

Let us begin by examining when this lamp was made and which persons were fortunate enough to own it. The Changxin Palace lamp was inscribed in nine places by different artisans and bureaucrats, on at least three different occasions. These texts can give us insight into the history of manufacture and ownership of the piece (see table 1.1).

There are two schools of thought regarding the history of ownership of this beautiful lamp, based on different interpretations of the phrase "Yangxin Jia" (House of Yangxin).[17] The most plausible explanation places the manufacture of the piece at an imperial atelier within the Former Han capital of Chang'an, sometime late in the reign of Emperor Wen (r. 180–157 BCE) or early in the reign of his son Emperor Jing (r. 156–141 BCE). Our gilt-bronze palace servant first saw service in what was apparently the Imperial Bathhouse within the Palace of Lasting Trust (Changxin Gong), the residence of empresses and empress dowagers during the Former Han dynasty.[18] Later, she appears to have been transferred to the imperial bedchambers and came under the control of the Palace Servant Bureau (Neizhe), a small cadre of twenty eunuchs who managed the clothing and other personal items for the imperial family. In 150

TABLE 1.1. INSCRIPTIONS CARVED ONTO THE CHANGXIN PALACE LAMP

Location of Inscription	*Transcription and Translation*
1. Underside of upper candlestick support	長信尚浴，容一升少半升，重六斤，百八十九，今內者臥。 The Controller of the Imperial Bath of the Palace of Lasting Trust Capacity [for tallow candle] a little under 1.5 *sheng* (265 ml) Weight: 6 *jin* (1.497 kg)[1] [Number] 189 Currently located in the bedchambers [supervised by] the Palace Servant Bureau
2. Outer rim of candlestick support	陽信家 The House of Yangxin
3. Outer rim of lower candlestick support (held in left hand)	陽信家，並重二鈞十二斤，七年，第一。 The House of Yangxin Combined weight [of entire lamp]: 2 *jun* and 12 *jin* (15.78 kg) Seventh year Number one
4. Outer rotating sleeve	陽信家。並重二斤二兩。 The House of Yangxin Combined weight [of both sleeves]: 2 *jin* and 2 *liang* (490 g)
5. Inner rotating sleeve (left side)	陽信家。 The House of Yangxin
6. Inner rotating sleeve (right side)	並二斤二兩。 Combined weight [of both sleeves]: 2 *jin* and 2 *liang* (490 g)
7. Outer rim of candlestick pan	陽信家 The House of Yangxin
8. Right shoulder	陽信家 The House of Yangxin
9. Lower corner of hem	今內者臥。 Currently located in the bedchambers [supervised by] the Palace Servant Bureau

1. For each component of the candlestick, I have given the declared weight in Han measure, followed by the actual current weight in modern metric measure. Excavated standard weights for the Former Han period vary between 238 g/*jin* to 258 g/*jin* (average = 248), though sometimes bronze corrosion may have altered the weight of some of those pieces (or our piece under examination here). It appears that three different standard weights were used to assess the components of the Changxin Palace lamp, with weights varying from 219.2 g/*jin* to 230.5 g/*jin* to 249.5 g/*jin*. This suggests that the various parts may have been made (or at least weighed) in at least three different locations. Whether or not the candlestick was originally weighed with tallow in place may have also affected these results.

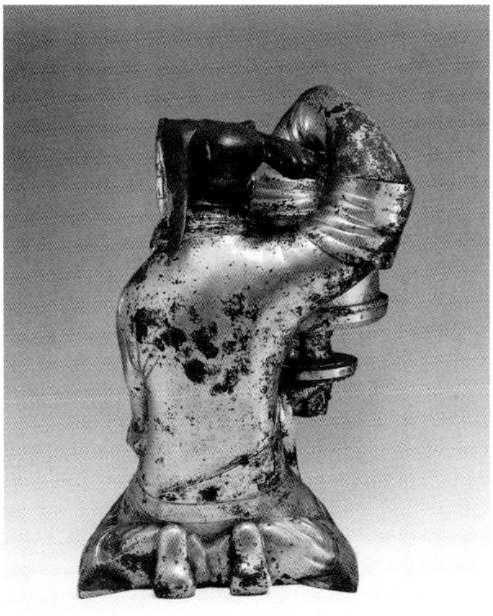

1.5 *Back of Changxin Palace lamp.* Former Han period, ca. 170–151 BCE. Gilded bronze. H. 48 cm. Hebei Provincial Museum. From Yang Xiaoneng, no. 137.

BCE, in the seventh year of his reign, Emperor Jing (or perhaps his influential mother, Empress Dowager Dou, d. 135 BCE) gave the lamp to his eldest daughter, the Elder Yangxin Princess (Yangxin Zhang Gongzhu) (ca. 160 BCE–ca. 110 BCE), at which time it was once again weighed and labeled.[19] Some years later, the princess gave the lamp to her younger half brother, the fabulously dissolute Liu Sheng, Prince of Zhongshan, possibly as a present to celebrate his marriage to Dou Wan, thought to be an offspring of a powerful collateral branch of the imperial family. When Dou Wan died sometime between 118 and 113 BCE, the lamp was placed in the main chamber of her tomb, where it lay until it was excavated in 1968, its parts scattered by earthquakes and partially corroded by encroaching water. Thus, we see that this pretty object changed hands many times but always remained as a prized treasure within the imperial family. It began its service lighting the bathing quarters of an empress's palace and ended its service lighting the "eternal palace" of Dou Wan. As a tomb lamp, it may have also served the ritual function of lighting the path of the deceased's soul on its journey to the otherworld.[20]

The inscriptions in table 1.1 also reveal something of the obsessive nature of Han bureaucratic and factory practice. The lamp is assembled from eight separate components, and seven of these (all except the head) are marked with either the Yangxin household or Palace Servant Bureau tag, brands of control and ownership to be sure. If any recognizable part of the lamp became separated from the rest, one could still be certain that its proper owner was indicated. One is reminded of the barcode labels that present-day companies place on material assets like computers to track their whereabouts. In addition, the weight of several of the lamp's subassemblies and the unit as a whole were recorded, both by the initial workshop clerks, who were required to keep track of expended materials, and by later bureaucrats who just wanted to know. The volume of the lamp pan was recorded as well, so that properly sized

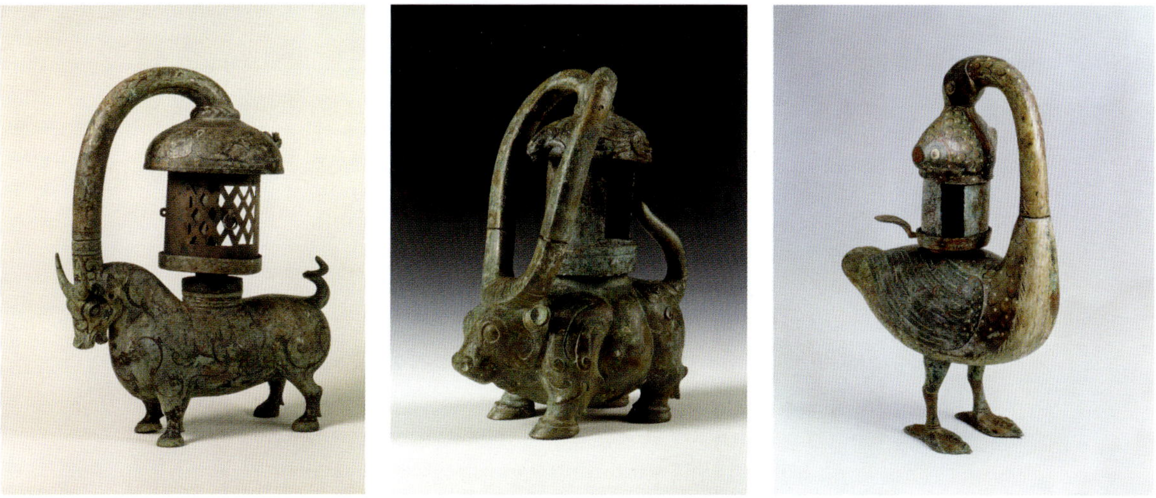

(a) (b) (c)

1.6 *Bronze zoomorphic lamps*

(a) *Bull.* Latter Han period, ca. 24–100 CE. Bronze with inlaid silver. H. 46 cm. Nanjing Museum. Photo courtesy of Cultural Relics Publishing House. Unearthed from Hanjiang, Jiangsu.

(b) *Water buffalo.* Latter Han period, ca. 24–100 CE. Bronze. H. 27 cm. Nanjing Museum. Photo courtesy of Cultural Relics Publishing House. Unearthed from Jiangsu.

(c) *Goose.* Former Han period, ca. 50 BCE–8 CE. Bronze with polychrome paint. H. 53 cm. Pingshuo Archaeological Station. Photo courtesy of Cultural Relics Publishing House. Excavated from Shuo County, Shanxi.

replacement candles could be ordered from storage and so that the expenditure of tallow could be tracked. Though it seemed to carry sentimental value for its various imperial owners, the Changxin Palace lamp was treated by workshop clerks, eunuchs, and accountants merely as a physical asset to be recorded and tracked.

The ingenious design of the lamp, as described above, also strikes the casual observer. However, the curious features of the two-piece rotating lampshade (that adjusts the direction and intensity of light) and the ash-disposal system are not unique to this lamp. They can be found on several other bronze lamps and incense burners from the same period (see figure 1.6). In one, a waterfowl bends its neck to grasp a fish; in others, horns of bovids arch to meet the candlestick top, just as the hand of our maiden steadies this lamp while her sleeve conveniently serves as a broad smoke hood. These are all variations on the same modular design. Though measurements are not readily available for the components of all these examples, certain parts like the lamp pan and shutters were probably made to standardized dimensions and could be exchanged between different submodels. Thus, it appears that even the form and posture of the Changxin Palace lamp was dictated in some way by the demands of a standardized, modular design.

Our palace lady cannot even claim to be a unique production, even as a specific variation on the adjustable room-lamp design. Two of the nine inscriptions carved on her parts include numbers that were probably serial numbers within a larger production run. The oldest of these inscriptions mentions the number 189.[21] So it appears our diffident lady was merely one of an extensive batch of similar or possibly identical palace lamps. We will probably never know how many pieces were produced. A single one likely did not produce much light, so several were probably arrayed at the foot of a sleeping platform, in the bathing area, or throughout the quarters of the highborn women who owned them.

Unfortunately, the inscriptions that tell us so much about who owned the Changxin Palace lamp and how it was created tell us nothing about *who* made it and under what working conditions. To uncover some of that story, we need to supplement our object analysis by looking at historical records, inscriptions on other objects, and archaeological remains. The lamp is cast in bronze and gilded over its entire surface. During the Former Han period, government workshops were supplied with copper for making bronze from mines in the south of the empire. The primary demand for copper came from the government mints at Chang'an, which cast over 600,000 bronze coins per day (total weight 2.1 metric tons/day),[22] but bronze also was used to cast millions of crossbow mechanisms, arrows, containers, and other objects. A highly placed public official informs us that state iron and copper mines employed almost exclusively unfree labor, both convicted criminals and conscripted peasants, totaling more than 100,000 men (see detailed discussion in chapter 6).[23] Thus, at the first stage of production, the raw materials for the Changxin lamp were mined and processed by heavily exploited labor, probably with great loss of life. Once these materials arrived at the imperial workshop or factory, they were cast into the finished lamp. Many of the master artisans who crafted the molds for such objects appear to have been "free" men, either commissioned for money by the state or conscripted from artisan families in exchange for a family tax break. Some government factories, however, employed skilled slaves to instruct others in the complex processes of casting. Without belaboring here the dangers endured by the miners, smelters, and casters who made this piece, we cannot ignore the trail of sweat and tears that lead to such apparent beauty. The gilder who finished the Changxin Palace lamp unknowingly faced his own dangers. Gilders during the early imperial period were called "gold paint artisans" because they gilded metal objects by smearing on a viscous amalgam of gold leaf and liquid mercury. When the object was roasted in a low-temperature oven, the mercury was driven off as a highly toxic gas, and the gold was left bonded to the surface metal. Gilders, like the one who finished this lamp, probably suffered from the irreversible nerve and organ damage characteristic of mercury poisoning.

Thus, by combining formal and object analysis with an investigation of inscriptions, historical texts, and manufacturing traces, we now have a much more comprehensive picture of the Changxin Palace lamp. Far from a unique masterpiece of artistic genius, the Changxin lamp was actually a mass-produced, decorative palace item based on a modular design. It was commissioned by the imperial family, who extracted the labor of conscripts, convicts, and slaves to cast its finished form, and who later tossed it around among themselves like a precious bauble.

Such knowledge should not detract from our ultimate appreciation of the artifact but should enhance it immeasurably. No longer a shiny curiosity in a glass case, an artifact of the remote past can truly come alive and satisfy our craving for a visceral connection to our long-dead human kin. I still remember the heart-pounding thrill of examining an ancient ceramic pot and suddenly noticing the thumbprint of the potter impressed on the interior wall. Placing my large thumb over the tiny impression instantly gave me a somewhat disturbing sense of intimate, intrusive knowledge. This "pretty thing" was no longer just a thing; it was the dedicated project of a human artisan, probably a woman, who once held the piece in exactly the same manner as I did.

In figure 1.7, you will find a similar, though more intentional, imprint of an artisan. This ceramic brick once formed part of the wall of a tomb in Shandong, dated to the Latter Han period (25–220 CE) or slightly later.[24] While the artisan was producing hundreds of identical, undecorated tomb bricks, he playfully impressed his left hand deeply into the soft clay of some of the unfired pieces. On one side of the brick he also stamped his surname, Zhang, just as he did with his more elaborate creations, such as the hollow architectural brick displaying the Green Dragon of the East (see figure 1.8). The handprint looks like an ordinary male hand, though the build is somewhat muscular, befitting someone who kneaded clay from dawn to dusk. There are no missing fingers, no swollen joints, or deeply scarred flesh that would indicate a brutal work environment. We are glad that Mr. Zhang felt at ease enough with the demands of his work to experiment with his own handprint in clay. I have reproduced the image to scale, so that the reader can place his or her left hand in the imprint left by Brickmaker Zhang.

The goal of this book is to restore something of this sense of human awareness to the so-called art objects from ancient China. Terracotta figures, gilt-bronze lamps, and other artifacts of the Chinese past are often viewed without regard to the social and economic contexts of their creation, yet they were made by real individuals who contributed greatly to the early Chinese society and economy. Through this book, I hope to refocus our gaze from the glittering objects and monuments of China to the men and women who made them. Understanding these lives and the complex social, commercial, and technological networks in which they participated will allow us to humanize the material remains of the past.

The methodology I have followed in this book mirrors somewhat my own academic training.[25] I would not call myself exclusively a historian, an archaeologist, or an art historian, though my training has been in all these disciplines. If pressed to pin a label on myself, I would probably call myself a material-culture historian. I realized early on in my study of early China that any comprehensive understanding of the subject would have to be informed by a variety of sources that are normally the exclusive domain of separate academic disciplines.

The historian chiefly relies on received texts and collected commentaries to reconstruct his account of this past. His sources may also include philosophical works, stories, poetry, dramas, polemics, law codes, and imperial decrees. In general, the artisan

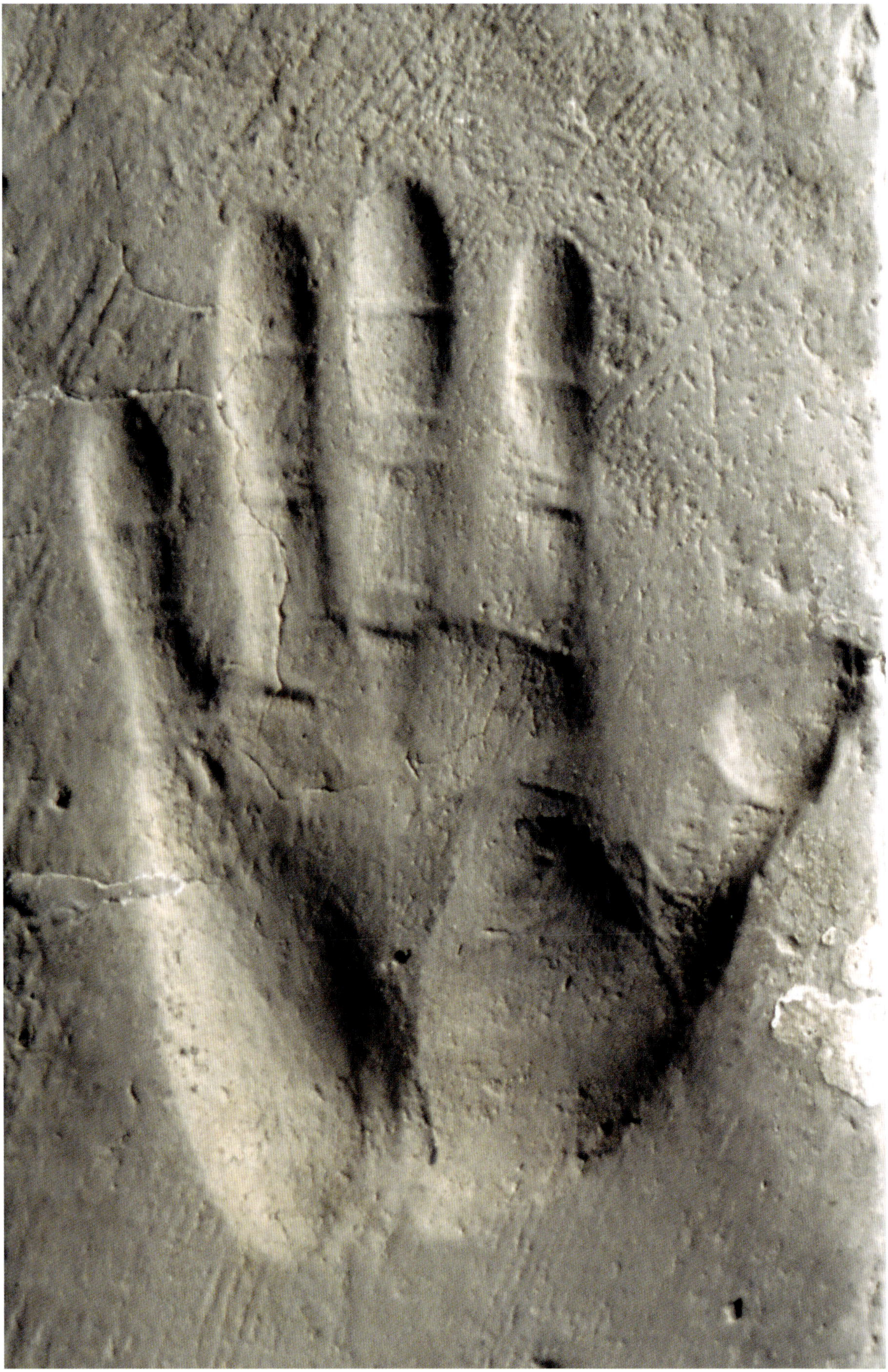

(opposite) 1.7 *Hollow architectural brick.* Latter Han period (25–220 CE). Terracotta. H. 33.5 cm. W. 16 cm. Linyi Municipal Museum, Shandong. Photo courtesy of Shandong Provincial Museum and China Institute Gallery, Providing for the Afterlife exhibition, spring 2005.

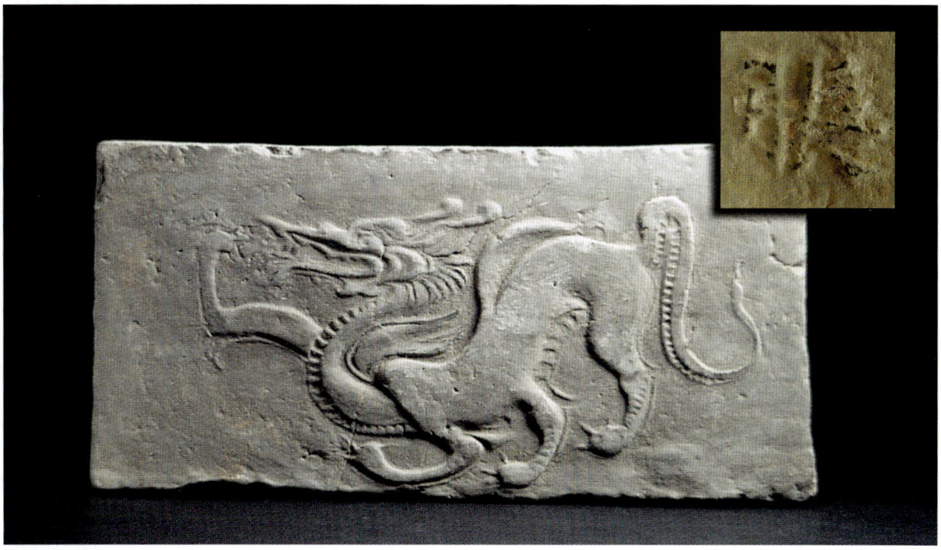

1.8 *Hollow architectural brick.* (Inset) Rubbing of name stamp from side of brick, "Zhang." Latter Han period (25–220 CE). Terracotta. H. 17 cm. W. 33.7 cm. Linyi Municipal Museum, Shandong. Photo courtesy of Shandong Provincial Museum and China Institute Gallery, Providing for the Afterlife exhibition, spring 2005.

and his workshop receive scant attention in these works. Written histories tend to focus on the exploits of cultural heroes and political leaders. If artisans are mentioned, it is only incidentally, in relation to major building projects or as the creators of individual works of artistic genius. The philosopher mentions artisans only when he wishes to use a workshop analogy to explain some loftier concept like the creation of human culture or when he wants to lay out a scheme for the proper relations of the classes. Received texts were copied perhaps dozens of times before they assumed their current printed form and were subjected to innumerable corruptions and interpolations. Occasionally, portions of known texts have been excavated by archaeologists. Upon comparison, it is often revealed that the excavated text differs significantly from the received text in both order and content.

Modern archaeology has opened up a way to supplement and correct these received texts. By careful excavation of workshop areas such as kiln sites, foundries, and quarries, archaeology can paint a vivid picture of the lives and work of ancient artisans. But archaeological data are also subject to strong biases. Some workshops leave more obvious traces than others. An iron foundry leaves a mountain of slag, whereas a painter's studio will disappear almost without a trace. Furthermore, where one digs and what one is looking for are often decided by nationalist aims or modern construction agendas. For example, despite the declared Marxist focus of Chinese archaeology, the greatest funding for planned archaeological digs is concentrated on elite tombs that yield objects suitable to fill museums with tourists. Chinese archaeologists rarely intentionally seek out habitation sites or workshop complexes. When these types of site are uncovered, it is often through sheer accident, when new construction churns up ancient ground levels. Nearly 90 percent of all Chinese archaeological digs are this type of salvage operation, hastily carried out to make way for construction. There are also biases in the interpretation of archaeological data, involving the gender and social class of the author and the subject. Problems of artifact dating and the questionable use of unprovenanced pieces held in private collections and public museums also beset the field.

The objects produced in the workshops can speak directly to us in a way that is more tangible than the discourse of texts. A few rare pieces have been handed down since antiquity, but most have been excavated by scientific archaeology or other means in the last two centuries. Scientific analysis of the structure of an object can reveal a great deal about the methods of production and the sources of the raw materials. Technical examination of objects, however, reveals much more about fabrication methods than it does about the lives and careers of the people who made them. Stylistic analysis of form and decoration can reveal the hand of individual artists or workshops and suggest cultural interactions.

In some cases, objects are inscribed with words or symbols related to their manufacture or distribution. Sometimes these are simple symbols such as a maker's mark or a studio sign. In other cases, objects carry an official stamp from an organ of government control. Occasionally, inscriptions relate the name of the patron and the circumstances of the object's creation and dedication. Inscriptions are often difficult to transcribe and interpret, not only because of wear and tear, but also because they tend to use phrases that are obscure and are open to varying punctuation and interpretation. Inscriptions are harder to interpret than received texts, which have been handed down with a steady stream of commentaries and dictionaries.

Thus, the sources of the historian, the archaeologist, and the art historian all have their strengths and weaknesses. It is my express aim to draw on all of these sources to paint a more complete picture of the lives and careers of artisans in early imperial China. Employing an interdisciplinary approach is not wholly unusual in this field, for many scholars of early China often find themselves using some sources outside their primary field of expertise to supplement admittedly fragmentary data. Often, the historian will use archaeological data to illustrate, supplement, or even correct the received account of the past, while the art historian will frequently cite received texts to illustrate the historical background that influenced the style of the artist whom he or she is studying. What I hope to accomplish in this study is to draw *equally* on all the sources of these fields and combine them in such a way that their strengths will be mutually complementary while their inherent biases will be somewhat mitigated.

The uneven nature of the different sources has enabled me to fill some sections of this book with rich detail concerning the lives and work of certain artisan groups, while others are given only cursory mention. This is regrettable, but I am restricted by the available material. For example, more than a dozen Han iron foundries have been scientifically excavated, and the location and scale of iron works are mentioned in received texts. Furthermore, some iron objects carry inscriptions detailing their type, dimensions, and place of manufacture. Thus, we know quite a bit about iron production and ironworkers during the Han. On the other side of the coin, we know painfully little about women artisans in early imperial China. They are mentioned in only a few places in the received literature, even though their work was apparently crucial to the textile and lacquer industries. We know a few of their names, from inscriptions left on lacquer or clay vessels, but no workshop definitely employing women has ever been excavated. As a result, dozens of pages can be devoted to male ironworkers, whereas women artisans receive only a few pages of coverage.

No study like the one before us has ever been attempted for early China, and for good reason. It is not that previous scholars simply ignored a potentially interesting topic of research but rather that, until recently, the accumulated body of relevant information was simply too small to support any reasonable inferences. Outside the realm of Chinese civilization, scholars have produced several admirable studies of ancient craftsmen and their place in society. In Egypt, excavations at the site of Deir el-Medina, the village occupied for centuries by the craftsmen who built the tombs in the Valley of the Kings, have enabled Egyptologists to study their lives and careers in stunning detail. We now know about lineages of master craftsmen, work methods, payment schedules, bread riots, personal animosities among neighbors—a complete world of real human drama.[26] Even though the time focus of the present book is one thousand years later than New Kingdom Egypt, nothing approaching that level of detail is possible for early imperial China. In many ways, I hope my study is comparable to Alison Burford's classic work *Craftsmen in Greek and Roman Society,* which was published more than thirty years ago.[27] The amount of information concerning artisans that is available from transmitted texts, archaeology, and inscriptions is roughly similar for the Greco-Roman world and for early imperial China and is qualified by the same types of limitations. By the late imperial period in China, a truly detailed personal study of artists is possible, and James Cahill has written an admirable study of how painters really lived and worked in Ming and Qing China, based on diaries, colophons, and other minor texts.[28]

Recent finds in Chinese archaeology and some reinterpretations of older data have finally made a study of early Chinese artisans more feasible. New archaeological discoveries are constantly infusing early Chinese studies with new objects and previously unknown texts for study. In recent years, the sheer volume of excavated texts from tombs has become quite overwhelming. The closest analogy I can formulate is with the Dead Sea Scrolls, found at Qumran in the Judean Desert between 1947 and 1956. In the intervening half century of study by hundreds of scholars around the

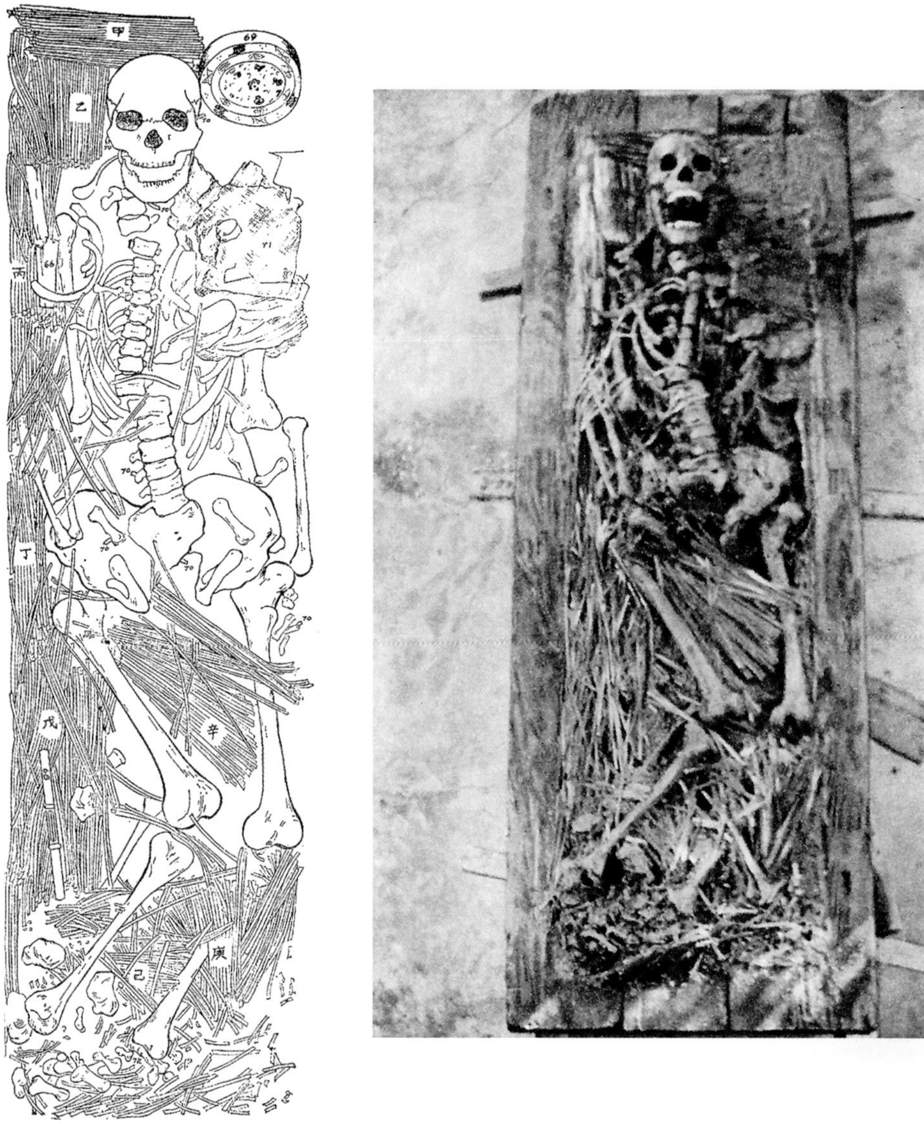

1.9 *Tomb of the minor official Xi.* Qin period, ca. 216 BCE. (Left) Coffin contents with labeled groups of bamboo slips. (Right) Photo of skeleton, coffin floor, and contents. From Yunmeng Shuihudi Qin Mu Bianxiezu, fig. 15, pl. 8.1. Photos courtesy of Cultural Relics Publishing House.

globe, those documents have revolutionized our knowledge of Old Testament textual history, postbiblical Jewish law and ritual, and the views and practices of premessianic Jewish sects. It is no exaggeration to proclaim that, in China, a textual find with the impact of the Dead Sea Scrolls is made by archaeologists every few years, and scholars must race to keep ahead of the flood of new information.

Two recent textual finds, in particular, inform significant portions of this study. In 1975, archaeologists excavated a tomb in the Shuihudi area of Yunmeng County, Hubei, that belonged to a minor official of the Qin Empire named Xi (Happy), who died in 217 or 216 BCE (see figure 1.9).[29] Apparently, Happy dutifully carried some of his former office documents and personal books into his tomb. The tomb contained over eleven hundred bamboo slips inscribed with passages from and commentary on Qin laws of the late third century BCE, a separate bamboo book of case law, two different versions of a divination manual, a letter from a regional governor dated 227 BCE, a composite text of maxims, and a chronicle with dates ranging from 306 to 217 BCE.

The second discovery came in December 1983, when archaeologists working at the site of Zhangjiashan, near Jiangling, Hubei, discovered 1,236 bamboo slips in a medium-size vertical-pit tomb.[30] Judging by the calendar and tomb inventory found among the texts, it appears that the tomb belonged to an unnamed local official who retired due to illness in 194 BCE. The Zhangjiashan tomb (no. 247) contained portions of Han statutes and ordinances in a collection apparently dated 186 BCE, a book of case law, a mathematical primer, medical texts, a chronicle (202–186 BCE), and a political-military dialogue.[31]

The legal documents from these two sites do not represent the entire law codes of the Qin and Han dynasties. Rather, they appear to represent digests copied from the larger legal corpus by local officials, who needed to have reference only to clauses that concerned their particular jobs. Legal codes, and Chinese legal codes in particular, are normative proscriptions on behavior. The Chinese legal tradition, unlike the Western legal tradition, grew out of a desire to suppress anarchy and disorder, not to safeguard individual rights and liberties. We have no way of knowing how strictly the detailed Qin and Han legal statutes were enforced, for the surviving body of case law is quite meager, but we can learn much about the attitudes and priorities of the ruling elite who wrote these codes. Indirectly, the legal texts can also be a gold mine of data on social status and mores, labor organization, economic structure, and many other topics. From these two invaluable collections of bamboo slips, we learn something of how artisans were trained in imperial factories and how they were punished for shoddy work. We learn how markets were organized and taxed by the state, and how sales contracts were drawn up and enforced. We also discover how the state acquired and managed several pools of unfree artisan labor, including conscripts, convicts, and slaves. The information is heavily biased toward state-employed artisans, but we must accept our apples where they fall.

And still, even more texts keep pouring forth. In the mid-1980s, archaeologists discovered another cache of documents on 829 bamboo slips from another tomb at the Zhangjiashan cemetery, tentatively dated to around 170 BCE.[32] The writings include calendars, medical texts, philosophical anecdotes, and a digest (372 slips) of fifteen statutes from the Han code. These texts remain unpublished at present, but since the legal extracts probably copy different portions of the Han code than those from tomb 247, they will undoubtedly provide the raw material for further study of these topics.

There are several alternative ways this book could have been structured. I could have organized it chronologically, tracing the social role of artisans in early China over several centuries. Such an approach might have given us an insight into the evolution of artisans from endogamous groups of craft specialists, attached to the ruling clans, to free-market actors whose services were requisitioned or taxed by the state. I have tried to include a little of this story in different sections of the book, but if such a course were followed exclusively, we still might not know much about the lives of artisans in any one period.

I might have attempted to follow a traditional "masterpiece" approach, examining individual artisans and their great works, but, as one can surmise from my analysis of the Changxin Palace lamp, what modern critics label as a masterpiece may have had a very different significance to the people of early imperial China. Further, the ravages of war and time have destroyed all the original works of the truly famous painters, calligraphers, and architects of early China. All that we possess are some assessments by ancient critics and a handful of poorly produced second- and third-hand copies made in later centuries. Finally, even if a masterpiece approach were possible, it would surely not tell us much of real interest.

I decided to structure this book contextually, with each chapter examining a different aspect of the lives and careers of artisans. In some ways, this approach parallels that of Craig Clunas, who in his groundbreaking book *Art in China* looks at the audience for and uses of art in different contexts like the temple, the court, and the marketplace.[33] Clunas's book, however, ranges over the whole history of Chinese artistic endeavor and rarely considers how artisans were treated in society, how they were trained, or how they carried out their craft.

Chapter 2, "Artisans in Society," analyzes the position of artisans within early Chinese society and economy. In China, an artisan was defined as a man or woman who made or decorated things with their hands. This label incorporated painters, sculptors, founders, masons, wood-carvers, and many other nonagricultural laborers. Ancient philosophers and social critics agreed that artisans constituted a major class in society, but because they worked with their hands, artisans were looked down upon by those men who "toiled with their minds." This chapter seeks to answer a series of questions. What was the artisan's social status and how was he or she viewed by others? What qualities made a particular artisan admired or despised? What social and occupational mobility did they have, and what was their level of literacy? What role did artisans play in the economy?

Chapter 3, "Artisans in the Workshop," delves deeper into the practical life of artisans by stepping into their places of work. It describes how artisans were trained and what special tools and techniques they used to fashion objects. This is followed by an investigation of working hours and workplace hazards or diseases. The unique religious practices of artisans and the role of women in the shops are also briefly addressed.

In this and subsequent chapters, it may seem at times that I have burdened the reader with digressions into technical processes merely for the sake of thoroughness, but my ultimate aim has always been to uncover the social and economic environment in which *gong* artisans (craftsmen and nonagricultural laborers) lived and worked. For example, when I detail the chemistry and technical processes of lacquer production or the steps involved in quarrying and stone carving, my true purpose is to use this information to reveal the fine division of labor among the artisans and the economic rationale for their techniques of mass production. When I detail the various stages of the metallurgical process (in chapter 3 and continuing in chapter 6), my goal is to use this account to underscore the physical hazards to the workers and to uncover the government decision-making processes behind labor mobilization. The benefit of this indirect approach to the study of artisans is that objects stripped from their original context can now come alive, even if we cannot pin an exact name on their maker.

Chapter 4, "Artisans in the Marketplace," follows the artisan into the bazaar and investigates how his or her goods were advertised and sold. The chapter opens with a review of the early Chinese marketing structure, following a Skinnerian macroregional model. This is followed by a detailed look at the organization of official markets and the fees, taxes, and legal responsibilities of merchants. After a brief section on the marketing territory of artisans, the chapter closes with an examination of the startlingly "modern" marketing techniques used to hawk goods in a competitive environment. These included rhyming jingles, knockoffs of royal products, and the use of family trademarks.

Chapter 5, "Artisans at Court," elevates the reader from the dirt and din of the marketplace to the rarefied air of the palace and looks at the lives of court artisans. The chapter is divided into two complementary parts. The first part contains a discussion of the nature and purpose of visual and material culture at court and introduces a representative sample of palace objects and images, from painted murals with political and didactic content to room furnishings and tableware. The second part of this chapter investigates the artisans who actually made this material and visual culture for the court and opens with an examination of the bureaucratic structure of palace workshops, focusing on two of the most important workshop units. To personalize the art of the court, three men who created some of this palace visual culture are singled out for further examination. One is Ding Huan, an almost mythical craftsman whose life story falls outside the traditional historical accounts. He is credited with inventing mechanical gadgets of great ingenuity and embellishing palace salons to an almost unimaginably opulent degree. Zhang Heng was a great poet, cartographer, and astronomer at the Latter Han court who designed ingenious scientific instruments. Cai Yong was a famous scholar, poet, and official at court, who also happened to be an accomplished painter and calligrapher. His role in the art produced for the court almost anticipates the great scholar-official artists of much later imperial times.

Chapter 6, "Artisans in Irons," ends the book on a sobering note, descending into the labor camps and slave markets to look at the most abject classes of artisans. These men and women were the conscripts, convicts, and slaves who constructed and decorated many of the great palaces, temples, and tombs of early China. The chapter looks at their legal status, their living and dying conditions, and the tasks they were assigned.

The justification for this book and its principal argument can be simply stated. I argue that one cannot truly understand the visual and material cultural remains of early imperial China without understanding something about how they were made, who made them, and under what social and economic circumstances they were fashioned. By learning how objects were made, we learn not only about ancient technology and materials but also about how labor and materials were measured, valued, and economized. We also learn to temper our appreciation of "works of art" that may turn out to be mass-produced objects. By uncovering the name, gender, and social status of the artisan who made an object, we begin to humanize the cultural remains of the distant past. We learn which objects were made by women and which by men and can begin to theorize the reason behind the gendered division of labor. We might also learn which objects were made by free artisans, working for their own benefit, and which objects are tainted by the exploitation of slave or convict labor. Only once we learn some of this, can we truly comprehend and appreciate the material-culture remains of early China.

In addition to this primary thesis, which is implicit throughout the entire book, I have also ventured to include two supplementary arguments that situate the case of early imperial China within larger debates in the fields of economic history and labor history. Chapter 6 presents a self-contained argument concerning the nature of the early imperial state's mobilization of coerced labor. I argue that the government made conscious cost-benefit analyses when employing various pools of hired or coerced labor for a given project, taking into account the nature of the work, the season of the year, and the overall cost to the peasant-based economy. Ideally, the state endeavored to optimally exploit each of these sources of labor without upsetting the balance of the economy or fostering revolt.

In chapters 3–5, I draw early imperial China into one of the most contentious debates in economic history. For most of the last fifty years, scholars in ancient history and economic anthropology have engaged in a spirited battle over the nature of pre-state and ancient state economies. In the most simplistic, polarizing terms, this has been framed as a struggle between the Primitivists and the Modernists. In the first half of the twentieth century, the Modernists, led by the classical historian Michael Ivanovitch Rostovtzeff (1870–1952), drew a bit too uncritically on the uneven written and archaeological sources for the ancient economies of Greece and Rome and argued that ancient economic life was very much like a budding version of our own, ruled by market-driven prices, high levels of monetization, productive cities, and far-flung trade—all the hallmarks of incipient capitalism.[34]

The first volleys from the Primitivist camp came in the 1950s from the pen of Karl Polanyi (1886–1964), a man deeply disgusted with the excesses of modern capitalism.[35] Polanyi argued that the economies of ancient and pre-state societies were fundamentally different from that of our modern market-driven world, and that our outlook had been so distorted by our capitalist environment that we unconsciously projected our view of the world onto a structurally different past. Briefly summarized, Polanyi argued for a return to a *substantive* definition of the economy, which defined it as the materialist means-producing sphere of society (production, exchange, consumption).[36] For Polanyi, the economy could not be viewed as an entity separate from society but was deeply embedded within and interrelated to the institutional framework of that society. He laid out three different forms of integration of economic life, which in varying degrees have determined the allocation of resources in all human societies: reciprocity, redistribution, and exchange. The mutual gift-giving mechanism of reciprocity, which was embedded in the kinship structure, was seen to dominate in many primitive, egalitarian societies, where profit-driven trade was (according to Polanyi) nonexistent. In chiefdom-level societies and in many early states, the dominant transactional mode was said to be redistribution, in which the authorities of a central place appropriated the productive resources of society through taxation or tribute and redistributed them as rations and transfers to the population at large. According to Polanyi, market exchange, driven by rational, economizing behavior and supply and demand mechanisms, was nonexistent in prestate societies and did not become the dominant transactional mode until the nineteenth century in the West. Thus, for Polanyi, true fluctuating prices or profit-driven trade did not exist to any appreciable degree in the premodern world. Prices were set by law, custom, or royal edict, and exchanges involved no true risk to the merchant. Merchants and traders were more motivated by gaining prestige and rank than with "base" profit-seeking motives.

The eminent ancient historian Moses I. Finley (1912–86) was deeply influenced by the skepticism of Polanyi and by the growing pessimism of the late 1960s. In a series of lectures later published as *The Ancient Economy* (1973), Finley mounted an eloquent and concerted offensive for the Primitivist camp that would become the orthodox view for nearly two decades.[37] Finley stressed that agriculture, and not commerce, was the dominant form of economic activity in Greece and Rome. He argued that private trade was carried out only on a minimal scale, and usually only in luxuries. Finley viewed Roman towns and cities as parasitic centers of consumption and redistribution and not as productive industrial centers. Individuals were most concerned with gaining status, and loans and investment were not made for productive purposes.

In the 1980s the pendulum began to swing back to the Modernist camp, not coincidentally at a time of greater economic growth and optimism in the West. Morris Silver systematically refuted Karl Polanyi's assertions concerning the nonexistence of price-setting markets in the ancient Near East.[38] In Finley's cherished heartland of the Roman Empire, Kevin Greene's survey of the archaeological evidence revealed far stronger market elements in the Roman economy than the Primitivist model would have ever allowed. It now appears that Roman commerce was more highly monetized than previously thought and that trade in luxury goods like *terra sigillata* (Arretine ware) was very widespread and penetrated even into rural and peripheral areas.[39]

Recent surveys have demonstrated the usefulness of viewing ancient state economies as a set of variables operating on continuous scales rather than trying to force them into the ill-fitting universal stages or modes of Marx or Polanyi or into the polarizing debates of *same* and *other*.[40] Many scholars now recognize that all economies since the rise of state-level societies display some level of commercialization, craft specialization, and market integration, alongside varying amounts of reciprocity, redistributive allocations, and state control. At different times, and under different historical circumstances, these variables might be located at different positions on a scale, though in no sense is the history of past economies a determined, unilinear trajectory.

The position I take in this book insinuates early imperial China into the debate for the first time and comes down squarely in the camp of the Modernists. To be fair, it should be noted that Polanyi and Finley never made any attempt to include China in their theories of ancient and premodern economies, for the Far East was far beyond their realm of expertise. In the end, that oversight prevented them from realizing an important counterpoint to their arguments. Early imperial China provides an example of an economy that, while still strongly agrarian and redistributive, was also home to burgeoning commercial activity. More than any other civilization in the ancient world, early imperial China operated under a money economy, where nearly everything could be purchased with standardized coins produced in vast quantities by state mints. Official salaries were paid half in coins and half in grain (mostly as a buffer against inflation of either commodity), and even peasants had to pay a portion of their taxes in cash each year. Though, in theory, the Chinese state wished to suppress commercialization in favor of agriculture, they nevertheless established market laws and regulations that greatly facilitated commerce. Recently unearthed legal texts now show that the early imperial Chinese state possessed a developed body of enforceable contract law that ensured market reliability, protected property rights, and lowered the kind of transaction costs that Douglass North has written were a hindrance to greater market activity in other premodern economies.[41]

Beginning in chapter 3, I approach the debate from a different angle, through an investigation of the methods of mass production used by lacquer artisans and stonemasons. These male and female artisans used a variety of methods, including stencils, pattern books, modular designs, and standardized tools, in an effort to produce more product with fewer labor inputs. The skilled labor of master artisans was economized in search of maximum profits. The artisans appear to have understood that custom-manufactured products were very highly prized, so they invested their works with a veneer of customization which belied their programmed modularity. Such methods of mass production were stimulated by a scarcity of skilled labor, increasing demands from clients, and price pressure from the competitive marketplace. In chapter 4, the precociously modern economic world of early imperial China is revealed through an investigation of market structure and regulation. The strongest evidence for a competitive market environment comes from a study of the commercial slogans, family brands, and jingles used to sell everything from lacquer vessels to bronze mirrors to axle bushings.

The mere presence of some degree of mass production, quality control, modular design, price-setting markets, and advertising slogans may not make early imperial China a modern world, but it is certainly not the archaic realm that Polanyi would have characterized it as. We recognize elements of our own market economy in this world, not because (as Polanyi and Finley would have argued) our minds are so biased that we project our capitalist thinking onto a structurally different past, but because the past of two thousand years ago already did possess some elements, in nascent form, that are omnipresent in our modern world.

This brief introductory chapter is not really the place to give a complete overview of the history and society of early imperial China. For that, there are many excellent works available to the general reader and the specialist scholar.[42] What I would like to present here is just a quick sketch of the bounds of the time period under study. When I say "early imperial China," I am referring to the Qin (221–207 BCE) and Han dynasties (206 BCE–220 CE), the first two unified empires occupying most of the territory we now recognize as the nation of China. At times, I will venture into the preceding Warring States period (ca. 453–222 BCE), when the economic and philosophical foundation for the early imperial period was laid.

The founding of the Qin Empire in 221 BCE is arguably the single most important event in Chinese history. After a series of economic and legal reforms carried out in the mid–fourth century BCE, the Qin state began to surpass its rival states in agricultural productivity and military might. One by one, the Qin conquered and annexed each of the other six major states of the Warring States period, until the last holdout fell in 221 BCE. The imperial bureaucratic state that was established by the Qin and solidified during the Han was to form the basic blueprint for all the political formations to rule China until the collapse of the Qing dynasty in the early twentieth century.

The Han period is usually divided into three subperiods. The Former (or Western) Han begins in 206 BCE, when the founder, Liu Bang, was named king of Han, and ends early in the year 9 CE. That was when a collateral relative of the royal house named Wang Mang usurped the Han throne and declared his short-lived Xin dynasty (9–23 CE). Wang Mang was killed by rebels in 23 CE, and during a protracted civil war, Liu Xiu reasserted the Liu family line and restored the Han dynasty. This restoration is typically known as the Latter (or Eastern) Han and dates from 25 to 220 CE.

It is logical and defensible to treat the Qin and Han dynasties (221 BCE–220 CE) as one period for study. The Han government adopted many of the legal, fiscal, and administrative policies of the Qin, with very minor modifications. The key point of political continuity from the Qin to the Han was in the institution of emperor, which the Han bolstered with a coherent ideological justification. Throughout the time period under study there were many significant social, economic, and intellectual developments. Starting around 2 CE, there began a noticeable migration of population away from the traditional heartlands of the north and northwest into the central and southern provinces. This was the beginning of the trend that would finally see the south surpass the north in population around 850 CE. In the domain of labor, it appears that slave labor began to decrease somewhat in importance toward the middle of the period, accompanied by a rise in wage labor. Commercialization appears to have been pronounced in the Qin and early Han periods, followed by a marked decline toward the middle of the Former Han and a gradual increase throughout the remainder of the period. Peasant landholdings suffered constant erosion over the whole period, falling inexorably into the hands of large landlords. Conceptions of the supernatural and notions of personal immortality also underwent fundamental development during the Qin and Han periods, as did the structure of state cults. Finally, an increase in patrilineal rhetoric, especially during the Latter Han, began to redefine the acceptable roles for women in society. But despite all these changes, there was also a general continuity in the basic patterns of life, labor, and economy over the more than four hundred years of the period.

The year 220 CE marks a convenient closing date for this study. Broadening this work to include the vast Wei-Jin Nan-Bei Chao period (222–589 CE) would have been very impractical. That long and unsettled period of history saw the rise of Buddhism, the development of calligraphy as a privileged art form, and a whole new literature on aesthetics and literary criticism. Many more famous painters are known from this period, and some early copies of their works have even survived the ravages of time. Some significant research has been done on painters and calligraphers from this period, but a detailed study of professional craftsmen working in other, non-elite fields during this subsequent era will have to await further research.

2

ARTISANS IN SOCIETY

Working at mean tasks bears witness, in itself, to a person's indifference towards excellence: the labour he expends on things of no value demonstrates this. No promising youth is moved to want to be [the sculptor] Phidias by the sight of the statue of Zeus in Pisa, or to be [the sculptor] Polyclitus by the sight of the Hera in Argos. . . . Enjoying a product and finding it pleasing do not necessarily mean that the person who made it deserves serious consideration.

—PLUTARCH (CA. 46–CA. 120 CE), LIFE OF PERICLES[1]

THE *GONG* ARTISAN: DEFINITIONS AND ETYMOLOGIES

At the first, we should be clear what we mean by the word "artisan." In most modern works, an artisan is defined as a general category for craftspeople, encompassing all those who either make or decorate objects as their primary occupation. Their products can be as utilitarian as pots and tools or as ornamental as paintings, sculpture, and jewelry. Regular artisans are often distinguished from so-called true artists, who are thought to make something called "art" based on lofty aesthetic and moral motivations and are assumed (quite erroneously) to be above groveling for monetary remuneration.

The term "artisan" in this study is offered as a translation of the Chinese word *gong* 工. In early texts, the word *gong* encompasses all those who engage in a broad range of activities from jade working to iron casting to mural painting. It seems to indicate any craftsman (or woman) who made objects, regardless of whether or not the objects were decorated, and thus closely approximates the modern English connotations of the word "artisan." It should also be made quite clear that early China possessed no word to indicate an "artist" in the modern Western sense of the word. Even the portrait painters to the emperor were lumped together with common potters under the same term, *gong*.

During the period under study (221 BCE–220 CE), prefixes were commonly added to the word *gong* to indicate the specific craft undertaken. Some of the compound phrases we will encounter in this book include

hua-gong 畫工 (design painter; figure painter)
shi-gong 石工 (mason; stone carver)
huangtu-gong 黃塗工 (amalgam gilder)
su-gong 素工 (core carver for lacquer vessels)
mu-gong 木工 (joiner; carpenter; woodworker)
lian-gong 湅(鍊)工 (metalsmith)
xi-gong 舄工 (shoemaker)

In its broadest application, the label *gong* was even applied to ditchdiggers, construction workers, and other manual laborers, though it was never applied to farmers, foresters, huntsmen, or fishermen. In its customary sense, however, it indicated nonagricultural laborers, male or female, who made or decorated things with their hands.

The oldest surviving etymological Chinese dictionary, *Explaining the Graphs and Analyzing the Characters* (Shuowen jiezi), completed in 121 CE by the Latter Han lexicographer Xu Shen (30–124 CE), defines the word *gong* quite tersely:

> 工,巧飾也.
> *gong* artisan: [one who] skillfully decorates.[2]

Xu Shen chose to focus on the decorative aspect of the artisan's craft, overlooking the manufacturing aspect that was basically at the core of the artisan's usefulness to society. After his brief definition, Xu then offers us an intriguing etymology for the word *gong*:

> 象人有規矩.
> [The character] is a pictograph of a person with a [combined(?)] compass and carpenter's square.

Xu Shen, whose etymologies for Chinese graphs are only occasionally correct, was probably correct in his analysis that the graph *gong* is a simple pictographic logogram for a tool. It accords with common sense that the picture of a tool could be extended in meaning to represent the workers who used such a tool. For an analogous scenario, consider that in ancient Egypt the collective term for "craftsmen" was *hmwt* (conventionally pronounced "hemut"). This word is etymologically related to the word *hmw* , which means "skilled," and ultimately derives from the word *hmt* , which signifies a stone carver. The principal hieroglyphic element in each of these words (to the left of the groupings) is a pictographic representation of the type of drill used to bore stone vases, key status objects at the time of the creation of the hieroglyphic script (ca. 3100–3000 BCE). Figure 2.1 is a detail from a Fifth Dynasty tomb carving showing these drills in use. Note that the form of the hieroglyphic caption *hmt* (stone-vase craftsman) to the left of the thigh of each craftsman is nearly identical to the representation of the tool being used by the men. Thus, we see that a word that originally signified a particular tool was extended in stages to first denote the craftsmen who used that tool and later to signify all craftsmen regardless of material.[3]

Figure 2.2 shows one of the earliest appearances of the Chinese graph *gong*. It is a Period I oracle-bone inscription (ca. 1300–1200 BCE) that refers to the ritual activities of the *duogong* (many artisans).[4] Though the forms of many Chinese graphs have evolved dramatically since their first known appearance during the Anyang period (ca. 1300–1100 BCE), the simple form of *gong* has not changed much, a fact that made it one of the first graphs to be confidently transcribed by scholars.[5] Most paleographers basically agree with Xu Shen that the graph for *gong* originally represented some sort of tool or device, but they give little credence to his theory that it represents a man holding a combined compass and carpenter's square.[6]

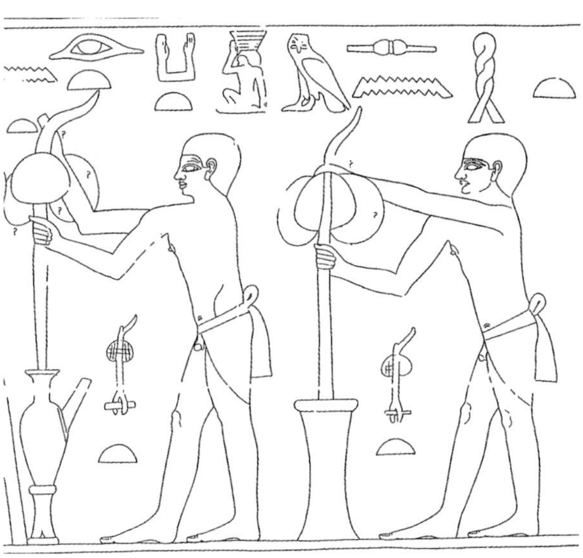

2.1 *Craftsmen at work boring stone vases.* Egyptian, Fifth Dynasty, ca. 2500–2400 BCE. From Wild, pl. 173. Section of the relief on the south wall of the chapel of the tomb of Ti, at Saqqara.

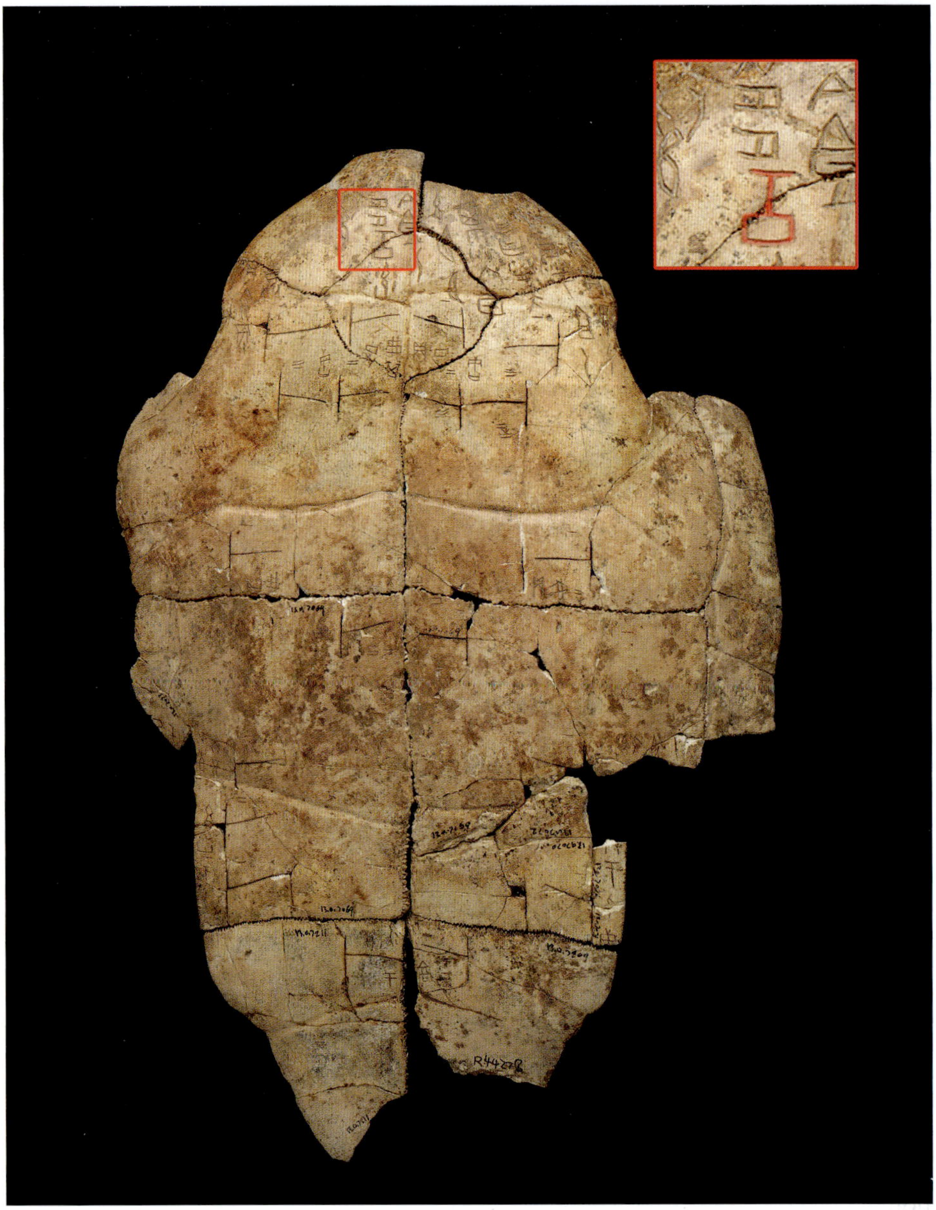

2.2 *Inscribed turtle plastron.* (Inset) Character for "artisan" highlighted in red. Anyang period, ca. 1300–1200 BCE. Turtle shell. Collection of the Institute of History and Philology, Academia Sinica. Photo courtesy of Academia Sinica. Excavated from pit YH127, Xiaotun, Anyang, Henan.

Scholars critical of Xu's reading all point to the early form of the graph *gong*, highlighted in red in figure 2.2, which appears as a handle and shaft connected to some sort of weight or box. Based on this boxlike structure at the base of the graph, some scholars have proposed that it might represent the kind of weighted tamper

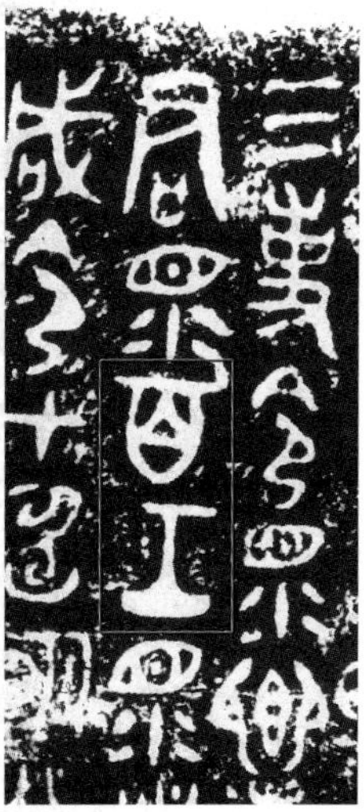

2.3 *Inscription on cover of the "Ling fangyi" (detail).* Highlighted area: *baigong,* "the hundred artisans." Western Zhou period, ca. early tenth century BCE. Ink rubbing of bronze vessel. Freer Gallery of Art, 30.54. From Guo Moruo, vol. 1, rubbing 3.

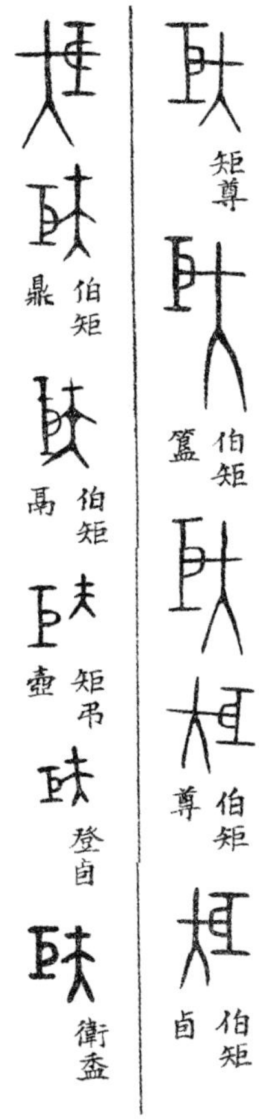

2.4 *Bronze inscriptional forms of* ju, *"carpenter's square."* Western Zhou period (ca. 1045–771 BCE). From Rong Geng, *Jinwen bian,* no. 0731.

commonly used to build rammed-earth foundations and city walls in ancient China. Pointing to this same feature, others have advanced the theory that the graph depicts some type of stringed musical instrument, where the box represents the sounding chamber. Another scholar, pointing to the rather bladelike shape of the same lower feature in the bronze inscriptional form of the graph (figure 2.3), believes that it originally represented a woodworker's axe.[7]

Amid this confusion of interpretations, philologist Li Xiaoding (b. 1918) advanced a simple theory that actually brings us back to the Latter Han scholar Xu Shen.[8] Li pointed to the form of the graph *ju* 矩 (carpenter's square) seen in several Western Zhou bronze inscriptions (see figure 2.4). Here, we clearly see a man holding a tool. Since the word indicated by the graph has always meant a carpenter's square, we can safely assume that a carpenter's square is the tool represented in the pictograph. Li rightly points out that the form of the tool the man is holding is identical to the graph *gong* in its abbreviated form. So maybe the much-maligned Xu Shen was correct after all, and the graph *gong* originally represented a carpenter's square.

Xu's cryptic statement that the graph *gong* shows a man *holding* a carpenter's square might be explained if we suppose that the etymological entries for *gong* (artisan) and *ju* (carpenter's square) in the current text of *Explaining the Graphs and*

Analyzing the Characters had become conflated or corrupted during the transmission of the text. The graph *ju* really does show a man holding a carpenter's square, and that entry follows shortly after the entry for *gong* in all editions of Xu Shen's dictionary.

To sum up, it appears on current evidence that the Chinese word for "artisan" (*gong*) was originally a pictographic logogram indicating a tool, possibly a carpenter's square.[9] The term was later extended in meaning to signify the workers (and ritual practitioners) who used that tool. By the time of its first appearance in the extant written record (ca. 1200–771 BCE), the term *gong* already encompassed a broad spectrum of artisans, regardless of specialty. To round off our discussion of the etymology and scope of the word *gong*, we should also note that another character derived from the depiction of a tool, *jiang* 匠, was used in early China to indicate carpenters and architects. In this case, the graph depicts an axe inside a box or built enclosure.[10] The distinction between *gong* and *jiang* is not always clear in early texts, and the two terms were sometimes used in combination, as *gong-jiang* 工匠, to form an all-inclusive term for craftspeople. This compound is still widely used in the Chinese language today as a collective term for craftspeople.

SOCIAL STATUS OF ARTISANS

Just as in many other traditional societies, artisans in early imperial China were said to form a specific social class. Class structure in Qin and Han society was fairly complex, and social groups were often evaluated and ranked along multiple axes. Following Ch'ü T'ung-tsu (Qu Tongzu),[11] a defined social class should fit the following criteria:

1. Members are judged and ranked based on commonly accepted values.
2. Persons of similar status think of themselves as equals belonging to the same group.
3. Members of a class have a similar lifestyle.
4. Members of the same class are acceptable for social interaction and marriage.
5. Privileges are granted and legal restrictions are imposed on the group as a whole.

The emperor and the imperial family occupied the highest social class in Qin and Han society, followed at ever-increasing distances by the enfeoffed princes (*zhuhou wang*), the nobility (*liehou*), government officials, commoners, convicts, and slaves, in that order. The large mass of commoners, those free persons who did not hold a title with hereditary privileges, were customarily subdivided into four further classes, based upon occupation. These are the traditional *simin* (four peoples). The traditional ordering is *shi, nong, gong, shang* 士, 農, 工, 商 (scholars, farmers, artisans, and merchants). The Han historian Ban Gu (32–92 CE) summed up the social role of each of the four peoples in his "Treatise on Food and Money" (Shihuozhi) in the *History of the Former Han* (Hanshu): "Scholars, farmers, artisans, and merchants; each of the four peoples had their respective profession. Those who studied in order to occupy positions of rank were called the *shi* (scholars). Those who cultivated the soil and propagated grains were called *nong* (farmers). Those who manifested skill (*qiao*) and made utensils were called *gong* (artisans). Those who transported valuable articles and sold commodities were called *shang* (merchants)."[12]

Obviously, Ban Gu and other authors intended the classification of the four commoner groups to be a hierarchy of value. Ban Gu was describing the social situation he believed existed in an ancient golden age (before 700 BCE), but as Derk Bodde has shown, the traditional ranking of the *simin* actually reached its current form only in the second century BCE. During the preceding Warring States period (453–222 BCE), when the concept of commoner rankings was first employed, the ordering was more erratic, though in most texts, artisans and merchants still occupied the two lowest positions. Scholars were almost always on top, and farmers usually ranked second.[13]

It has been argued that the classification of the "four peoples" was merely a rhetorical device and did not directly affect government policy or accurately reflect popular attitudes. While it is true that there is no known statute from the Qin and Han law codes that uses the classification of the *simin* as criteria for legal distinctions or administrative policy, the practical effect of many of the laws was to solidify that exact four-level classification. The people occupying each group could hardly have escaped the feeling that they were being treated as a unit. For example, the law separated out merchants for special sumptuary laws and taxes, yet required certain services and taxes of land-based peasants that merchants and urban artisans could avoid. Furthermore, artisans appear to have been subject to a special labor corvée that might have lasted longer than the customary one month served by other groups. I would argue, therefore, that the law codes of the Qin and Han reinforced the rhetoric of the *simin* and made these groups realize some level of class consciousness.

Since our artisans resided among its ranks, let us look at the commoner classification in more detail. During the late Zhou period, when the term first appeared in the commoner rankings, the word *shi* 士 did not mean "literary scholar," as it would later. Instead, it usually indicated the sons of peripheral branches of noble families who had to gain official position based on skills and merit. By the Han period, the term had come to mean both book scholars and members of influential landed families, the types of men who filled the new imperial bureaucracy. The Han term could denote those who merely sat as pupils of known scholars such as the academicians (*boshi*), those who studied specifically to enter officialdom, or those who had already entered government service. Though scholars were ranked as having the highest prestige among the commoners, they were not universally wealthy. While it is true that the majority of scholars came from wealthy backgrounds, a circumstance that gave them the leisure time to study, others came from humbler circumstances and had to work at manual occupations to earn the money for study.

The term *nong* 農 generally referred to anyone who worked the land as their primary means of support. This included landowning peasants, tenant farmers, and hired agricultural laborers. Though they were often looked down upon by other commoners because of their poverty and the unceasing toil of their occupation, peasants were highly valued by moralist writers and by the state, primarily because these privileged groups knew that their idle existence could not continue without the common farmer and his taxes paid in grain.

Ranked below our *gong* artisans, with whom we shall become very familiar, were the *shang* 商, the merchants and traders of the empire. The *shang* category actually included shopkeepers, traders, industrial-scale manufacturers, moneylenders, and even large-scale animal breeders. Though many merchants probably struggled to eke out a living, several became scandalously wealthy, and therein lies the greatest contradiction in the social hierarchy of the Han world. Though they were consistently criticized as being parasites on the economy, men who reaped but did not sow, merchants could rise in the estimation of their fellow commoners by simply getting rich. And while it was true that political power trumped all other factors when determining social prestige, wealth came a close second. A rich man was envied by most, regardless of the source of his wealth. At times, wealth could buy political office, which brought power and all its attendant prestige. From the beginning of the Han period, merchants were supposedly barred from becoming officials. This rule was not always followed, however, and at times was openly ignored.

Artisans have rarely, if ever, been considered an honored class in any traditional society; they were tolerated, despised, feared, and sometimes envied, but never truly respected or revered. Some of the reasons for their shabby treatment in the written sources are quite easy to fathom. The people who wrote the moralistic accounts that ranked the classes were aristocrats, politicians, and philosophers, not manufacturers or laborers. To justify their own position at the apex of society, they necessarily had to denigrate the other classes. Both in the mind-set of early China and in that of its contemporary, the Roman West, the nature of one's labor formed the primary criterion for deciding which occupations were worthy of praise and which were not. To demonstrate this point, let us compare the views of the Chinese philosopher Mencius (fourth century BCE) and the great Roman orator and politician Marcus Tullius Cicero (106–43 BCE). Mencius's famous dictum on the subject reads: "Some labor with their brains and some labor with their brawn. Those who labor with their brains govern others; those who labor with their brawn are governed by others. Those governed by others, feed them. Those who govern others are fed by them. This is a universal principle of the world."[14]

Mencius made this statement, which he claimed was an old maxim, in the context of a dialogue concerning the division of labor. The follower of another teacher who greatly honored agriculture asked Mencius why the ruler of a state should not share in the work of tilling fields with his people. Mencius replied by saying that inequality among men was both a natural and a necessary situation. Some things (and people) were just naturally worth more than others, just as certain parts of the body were more important than others. Since the mind (literally, "heart," *xin*) was more important than the arms, a man who worked with his mind (i.e., a ruler or a philosopher) was naturally better and more important than a man who relied on the work of his arms.[15] Mencius also pointed out the necessity of the class-based division of labor, arguing that each person in society could not possibly be wholly self-sufficient. Just as the farmer could not till his fields and have time to make all his tools and clothing, so, Mencius argues, the ruler could not practice agriculture and rule the people well. Thus, there exists a necessary division of labor between artisan labor and mental pursuits, lest neither be successful.

The Roman elite denigrated craftsmen as well, though their reasoning was slightly different from that employed by Mencius. In one section of an extended letter to his son, known to us by the title *De officiis* (On duties), Cicero discusses what is considered "fitting" or "seemly" (Latin, *decorum*) in dealings with men, in personal appearance, and in one's occupation. Regarding the latter, he states:

> Now in regard to trades and employments, which are to be considered liberal and which mean, this is the more or less accepted view. First, those employments are condemned which incur ill-will, as those of collectors of harbor taxes and moneylenders. Illiberal, too, and mean are the employments of all who work for wages, whom we pay for their labor and not for their art; for in their case their very wages are the warrant of their slavery. We must also consider mean those who buy from merchants in order to resell immediately, for they would make no profit without much outright lying . . . *and all craftsmen are engaged in mean trades, for no workshop can have any quality appropriate to a free man.*[16]

In Cicero's valuation of labor, the key distinction was not between manual labor and mental pursuits but between the liberal arts, which were carried out for sheer mental pleasure, and any occupation which sought practical application, including fields like mathematics and medicine.[17] Furthermore, Cicero considered the workshop environment to be inherently debasing, probably due to the vulgar clothing, ill manners, and coarse language one might encounter there. But for Cicero, the "wage slavery" involved in working for money was the greatest point of condemnation against craftsmen, for it precluded loftier motivations for creation.

Though Mencius did not bring the curse of wages to bear in denigrating Chinese artisans, many later Chinese writers certainly would. During the Northern Song period (960–1126 CE), a new class of scholar-artists emerged who did not possess the trompe l'oeil skills of the academy painters nor even the proficiency of common marketplace painters. The literati's painting was simpler and at times quite unschooled, yet they would criticize these other two groups as mere professionals, since they relied on paid commissions for their livelihood and did not paint merely for enjoyment or self-expression. The scholar-artists considered that painters who concentrated on realistic depictions, who employed a colorful palette, or, worst of all, who accepted monetary payment for their work were no better than butchers or tinkers in the marketplace. They were not to be considered real artists.

ECONOMIC ROLE AND STATUS OF ARTISANS

When referring to the role of the artisan in the ancient economy, Romanist Jean-Paul Morel declared that "because the crafts were disdained in ancient times, we tend to underestimate their economic importance."[18] This statement could easily apply to early China as well, where the importance of agriculture was stressed by all writers, almost to the exclusion of every other sector of the economy. The ancient Chinese writers slighted the economic role of artisans, and we tend to follow their biases uncritically.

No matter how artisans were ranked on the imagined ladder of social status, no reasonable author in early China thought that artisans were entirely superfluous. All except the most strident of the "guns and grain" type of Legalist or the "back to nature" breed of Daoists would agree that artisans fulfilled a vital role in the functioning of the state and its economy and could not be eliminated without dire consequences. Specifically, certain sections of the Legalist polemic *Book of Lord Shang* (Shangjunshu) seem to suggest that the world needed only farmers and soldiers and could do without artisans and merchants entirely. Similarly, portions of the *Classic of the Way and Its Power* (Daodejing) insinuate that crafty artisans only bred deceit and thievery. The ideal world presented in that work was one in which people remained in their self-sufficient villages and never ventured abroad for commerce. Beyond these two extreme positions, most other writers agreed that artisans were a necessary, productive group in the economy, though their views differed significantly as to what proportion of society they thought should be engaged in handicrafts and what type of products those artisans should produce.

One of the few beliefs held in common by the Confucians and the Legalists was that agriculture should be the fundamental occupation of the people and that handicrafts should be discouraged as being of secondary importance. Farming in North China was a precarious enterprise. The best land was located on the river alluvium and was intensively farmed, but mountains and wastelands dominated the remainder of the landscape. In good years, the benefits of irrigation and fertilizer could generate large yields, even with relatively primitive cultivation techniques. In bad years, however, droughts and floods could lead to wide-scale crop failure and famine. The state relied on the taxable surplus from agriculture to fund its wars and enterprises and realized that if the people did not retain enough food for themselves, rebellions would arise. This meant that to prevent disaster, the state needed to store up grain in good years and had to keep the vast majority of the population on the land as farmers.

After the economic boom of the middle Warring States period (ca. 400–300 BCE), there appears to have been a movement of some of the rural population into the bustling new urban centers. As people in increasing numbers abandoned the traditional livelihood of agriculture for careers as artisans and traders, the margin of safety for the state continued to shrink. It is at this time that the arguments concerning the "root" and "branch" occupations begin to appear in contemporary writings.[19] Farming, and the traditionally related occupation of sericulture, were called the *ben* 本, literally, the "root of the tree."[20] Handicrafts and trading were referred to as the *mo* 末, "tips of the branches." The obvious implication of this metaphor is that the roots of a tree must be strong for it to remain standing. If the branch ends become heavier than the roots, the tree must surely topple. Many of the economic measures of the early empires were designed to stimulate agricultural production and discourage craft production and commerce. Tax burdens were frequently shifted from the farming population onto the merchants and artisans, in an attempt to make the latter occupations less profitable and less desirable. Sumptuary laws that were targeted solely against the merchant class, such as the prohibition against wearing silk or riding in carriages, were also designed to make that profession less prestigious and to drive the people back to the land.

Time and time again, we hear complaints that an alarming number of people were engaged in the secondary *mo* occupations and that disaster was imminent. We hear it in 178 BCE in the memorials encouraging an increased emphasis on agriculture that were sent to Emperor Wen (r. 180–157 BCE) by Jia Yi (ca. 201–169 BCE) and Chao Cuo (d. 155 BCE). They claimed that everywhere in the empire people were turning away from the fundamental occupation. While the merchants lived like kings, farmers were destitute and starving and would soon turn to cannibalism and rebellion. They warned that the empire was "like a boat about to capsize."[21] We hear it in 81 BCE, during the famous debate that resulted in the *Discourses on Salt and Iron* (Yantielun), when the Scholars and Worthies claimed that, because the government had sanctioned greed by nationalizing the salt and iron industries, all the common peasants were following suit and abandoning their farms.[22] We hear it again around 150 CE, when the reclusive, sociopolitical critic of the Latter Han Wang Fu (ca. 90–165 CE), in his *Criticisms of a Hidden Man* (Qianfulun), made the exaggerated claim that each productive farmer had to support the idle ways of one hundred urban residents in the capital.[23] Yet advances in agricultural technique and the opening of new land must have kept pace with the proportional decrease in the farming population, for beyond the usual famine years, the universal cataclysm predicted by these writers never occurred.

The role of artisans in the ancient Chinese economy appears to have changed significantly over time. During the Bronze Age (ca. 1800–600 BCE), the archaeological and written sources suggest that most specialized artisans were attached to the royal or noble lineages. Very few, if any, were independent entrepreneurs. Certainly, all production of status markers like bronze vessels and jade objects was tightly controlled. Some men and women may have made their living apart from the support and control of kings and lords, as specialist potters or weavers, but we cannot discern their traces. After the revolutionary changes brought about by the introduction of iron tools and the birth of the autocratic state with its tax-paying peasantry (ca. 600–300 BCE), independent artisans finally appear in the sources alongside their royally patronized comrades.

The *Record of the Scrutiny of Crafts* (Kaogongji) is a curious, idealizing text that purports to be a description of the products and processes of different artisans attached to a ruling house.[24] When the *Ritual System of the Zhou* (Zhouli) text was rediscovered during the second century BCE, it was found that the sixth division of that work, concerning the offices under the Overseer of Public Works, was missing, so the text of the *Record of the Scrutiny of Crafts* was inserted as a suitable replacement. Judging by the style and grammar of the text, the deployment of newly emergent concepts like Yin and Yang, and the mention of certain place-names, the *Record of the Scrutiny of Crafts* appears to have been composed sometime in the late Warring States period, possibly around 300 BCE. The presence of a certain number of words in the Qi dialect has led scholars to conclude that the author was from that state, located in what is present-day Shandong.[25]

According to the anonymous author of the *Record of the Scrutiny of Crafts*, the *baigong* (hundred artisans) constituted one of the six key elements in the operation of the state:

> There are six major tasks in the state, and the hundred artisans occupy one of those. . . . Those who sit and deliberate governance are called the king and his nobles. Those who arise and carry out policy are called the high ministers. Those who examine curvature and surface qualities in order to work the five raw materials [metal, wood, leather, jade, and clay] and fashion the utensils of the common people are called the hundred artisans. Those who circulate the precious commodities of the four directions so that the articles may become the wealth [of the state] are called the merchant-traders. Those who expend their strength to nourish the wealth of the land are called farmers. Those who work silk and hemp into finished articles are said to do women's work.[26]

Though his book concerns mostly state artisans who made articles for the court, the author of *Record of the Scrutiny of Crafts* acknowledges in this passage that other artisans also made the vessels and tools of the common people. The author has apparently not yet made any economic linkage, however, between the artisans and the merchants.[27] This is probably because the author was living in a time, or at least referring to a past time, when merchants merely dealt in exotics and high-value commodities for court patrons. It was not really until the end of the Warring States period that free artisans and independent merchants would integrate their production and distribution roles to spur the first great economic boom in Asia and the first genuine cash-based market economy in the Far East.

For many idealist Warring States and Han period authors, the proper economic role of artisans was only to fashion simple tools and vessels, and the proper role of merchants was to distribute these to people who needed them. Artisans should not carve rafters with intricate tracery, embellish cups with gold mounts or jade inlay, or fashion realistic figurines to bury with the dead. Such productions were viewed by moralists as a waste of human labor and material wealth and as a potential distraction for the sovereign from his duties of governance.

In his *Criticisms of a Hidden Man,* Wang Fu extended the *ben* and *mo* arguments made by earlier authors and claimed that each profession also had its own fundamental "root" and its peripheral "branches." "For the hundred artisans, usefulness is the root (*ben*), whereas artful decoration constitutes the branches (*mo*). For merchants and traders, the circulation of goods occupies the root, whereas selling curiosities comprises the branches. If these groups stay with the fundamental and shun the secondary, then the common people can become enriched."[28]

Thus, if Wang Fu could not convince artisans and merchants to return to the fundamental occupation of agriculture, at least maybe he could encourage them to produce and distribute only undecorated items of practical use. Such a scenario was clearly not realistic during the Han period, during which private, luxury workshops flourished like never before to satisfy an almost insatiable demand for greater conspicuous display. Wang Fu and other moralist writers describe intricate lacquer screens and hardwood coffins which employed the labor of hundreds or even thousands of men to construct. Markets were filled with curious and wonderful items from all reaches of the empire and beyond. Idealist writers believed such craft production caused grave harm to the agricultural basis of society.[29]

The great historian Sima Qian (ca. 145–86 BCE), the most perceptive and prescient of all economic writers, was also a true pragmatist. He saw no need to regulate what artisans could make or what merchants could sell. On the economic roles of the commoner classes, he writes:

> Society obviously must have farmers before it can eat; foresters before it can extract timber resources; artisans before it can have manufactured goods; and merchants before they can be distributed. But once these exist, what need is there for government directives, mobilizations of labor, or periodic assemblies? Each man has only to be left to utilize his own abilities and exert his strength to obtain what he wishes. Thus, when a commodity is cheap, it invites a rise in price; when it is very expensive, it invites a reduction. When each person works away at his own occupation and delights in his own business then, like water flowing downward, goods will naturally flow forth ceaselessly day and night without having been summoned, and the people will produce commodities without having been asked. Does this not tally with reason? Is it not a natural result?[30]

Sima Qian was able to see not only that all economic groups in society were interdependent but that they could be self-regulating under market forces and could integrate smoothly without government intervention. What each man accomplished, out of his own self-interest, benefited the economy as a whole. In this idea, Sima Qian anticipated Adam Smith's formulation of the "invisible hand" by almost two thousand years.

What was the income potential of regular artisans, and how rich could an illustrious artisan become? Sima Qian was of the opinion that handicrafts were the second-fastest way for a poor man to obtain wealth (and thus honor). He quotes from a popular saying to the effect that, "if a man is trying to work his way up from poverty to riches, then farming is not as good as handicrafts, and handicrafts are not as good as trade; embroidering lovely patterns at home is not as good as relying upon the market gate."[31] It appears from texts and inscriptions that the vast majority of artisans were just able to maintain a subsistence-level standard of living and could hardly be considered wealthy or even middle class. A crew of masons making a stone offering hall in Donge County in present-day Shandong between 152 and 154 CE were paid the generous sum of 25,000 coins for their work. But since this amount had to be split among more than ten men, each mason barely received enough to feed himself and pay his taxes.[32] Famous artisans (*minggong*) probably received much higher commissions for their work.[33] Nevertheless, it seems that very few artisans, even those of the illustrious set, ever entered into the stratosphere of wealth that Sima Qian called "untitled nobility" (*sufengzhe*), that is, those who could enjoy the luxurious life of a lord without ever having received a hereditary title or significant income from official salaries.[34] Among his list of thirty famous moneymakers of Han and pre-Han times, most of the fabulously rich made their money in urban trading networks or in large-scale iron and salt manufacture.[35] A few others made their fortune by smaller-scale production and regional trading in commodities like animal fat, dried sheep stomachs, and condiments. Only one true artisan family was said to have become rich through handicrafts. This was the Zhi family,[36] who cornered a regional market sharpening knives. It was said that they ate from "cauldrons of food," an idiom meaning they could eat the five major varieties of meat on a regular basis.

THE IDEALIZED ARTISAN

Even though artisans may not have held a very elevated social standing compared to the nobles, officials, and scholars at the top of the social ladder, members of those honored classes could still appreciate the qualities of an artisan who perfectly fulfilled the potential of his or her role. Many writers did, in fact, voice opinions about what the perfect artisan would be like, how his or her skill would manifest itself, and what processes would be used to create works of sublime beauty. However, the idealized artisan was a person who did not really exist, except as a kind of Platonic mental construct in the mind of the philosopher, the poet, or the historian. Some famous historical or legendary artisans were said to approach the ideal, and we shall meet some of them in this chapter and throughout the rest of the book.

QIAO, THE DOUBLE-EDGED SWORD

The great artisan was thought to possess a quality known as *qiao*. This is an extremely ambivalent term, packed with both positive and negative connotations. On the positive side, the word indicates the great skillfulness of an artisan who has mastered his craft. It sometimes also indicated skill at other pursuits, such as archery or military strategy. To have simple competence or ability in handicrafts was called *ji* or *shouji* (hand skills), but to possess *qiao* was a far higher attainment. A statute in the Han law code concerning the training of state artisans declares that after a period of time those novices whose *qiao* was not perfected would be barred from becoming state artisans.[37] The term *qiao* also suggests ingenuity, cleverness, and the ability to invent new contraptions or methods. The semilegendary court artisan Ding Huan, discussed in chapter 5, was a man who created ingenious mechanical devices and decorated palaces to unimaginable levels of opulence. He was said to be "one of the artisans with the greatest *qiao* in the whole world."[38]

The term *qiao* also carried many negative connotations. It could signify the ability and the inclination to use skill for deceit and trickery. To Confucian moralists, *qiao* deployed in handicrafts and decoration represented the kind of extravagance that could bankrupt the treasury or distract the ruler. When used as a modifier with *yan* (speech), as in *qiaoyan* (artful speech), it signified the flowery speech of sycophants and sophists that could deceive with its cleverness. In the *Analects* (Lunyu), Confucius is quoted as saying that "*qiao* speech and a pretentious manner can hardly lead to benevolence."[39] To the author of the *Classic of the Way and Its Power*, the artisan's *qiao* represented an unnatural exercise of human ingenuity that, along with the quest for profit, led to the presence of thieves and bandits in the world.[40]

In the English language, the words "artful" and "crafty" have historically carried the same double connotations of skill at handicrafts, with a potential for trickery and deception, as the Chinese term *qiao*. In the translations for this book, when the meaning is ambiguous or the negative connotation is intended, I have chosen "crafty" as the translation for *qiao*. When the positive connotation is intended, I have translated *qiao* as "skillful" or "clever."

REALISM AND SPIRIT

From the late Warring States period until several centuries after the Han, writers all concurred that *mimesis* was the highest goal of painting, sculpture, and even, in some cases, architecture. The greatest praise was reserved for those artisans who were able to realistically simulate their subjects. It was not until nearly a thousand years later that the literati painters of the Song and Yuan periods would define self-expression as the ultimate aim of the arts, especially in painting and calligraphy, and denigrate realism as a mannered trick of professionals and academy painters.

But during early imperial China, realism was still paramount. The most frequently used terms to describe this quality were *zhen* (real) and *si* (resemblance). It was said in praise of Mao Yanshou, the semihistorical Han court portrait painter to Emperor Yuan, that "ugly or beautiful, old or young, he was always able to capture the real likeness of his subject (*de qi zhen*)."[41] Lie Yi, the wholly legendary painter and jade carver employed by the First Emperor of Qin, was said to paint and carve figures "so true to life" (*ruo zhen*) that he never dared to dot their pupils for fear the images would get up and run away.[42]

It was recognized, however, that some subjects were easier to portray than others because they lacked actual models with which to stand in comparison. A famous story from the *Master Han Fei* (Han Feizi) (composed ca. 240 BCE), which was recycled or alluded to many times in later works, has a king of Qi asking one of his court painters:

> "What are the most difficult things to paint?"
>
> He replied, "Dogs and horses are the most difficult."
>
> "Which are the easiest?"
>
> He replied: "Demons and goblins are easiest. Since dogs and horses are things known by man, visible before us the day through, they cannot be completely simulated and thus are difficult. Demons and goblins are without [fixed] form (*xing*) and are not visible before us; hence they are easy."[43]

Even architectural creations were subject to an assessment of their level of realistic simulation. In one of the most delightful stories from early China, recorded in the *Miscellaneous Notes on the Western Capital* (Xijing zaji),[44] we hear of the exploits of the architect Hu Kuan and the extraordinary village re-creation he built for the first Han emperor's (Gaozu's) father:

> When Gaozu's father, the Honorary Grand Supreme Emperor, had moved to the new capital of Chang'an and resided deep in the palace, he was quite melancholy and unhappy. Gaozu surreptitiously had his father's friends ask the reason for this. It turns out that of the things he most enjoyed about his commoner life—[scenes of] butchers and other young men selling in the marketplace, buying liquor, selling pancakes, watching cockfights, and playing soccer—none of these were present in the palace. Therefore, he was unhappy.
>
> Gaozu then constructed New Feng (Xin Feng) and transplanted all of the former residents [of his hometown of Feng] there to complete it. The emperor's father was then happy, because New Feng housed more rascally characters and did not have any aspiring officials. Even the old Altar of the Soil from Fenyu Village, at which Gaozu had often sacrificed when he was younger, was moved to New Feng and set up there. When Gaozu had completed New Feng and had moved the old altar there, all that he had constructed, the lanes and alleys, the

roof beams and eaves, all appeared just like their old counterparts. Every man and woman, young or old, as they stood at the head of the road, leading each other arm in arm, each recognized their dwellings. When the dogs, sheep, chickens, and ducks were released into the main street, they fought with each other to identify their old homes.

This had all been built by Gaozu's architect (*jiang*) Hu Kuan. All those who had been relocated were greatly pleased with the close resemblance (*si*) of his creation and considered it his great virtue. Thus, they all competed with each other in heaping rewards and gifts upon him. In little over a month, this had amounted to more than a hundred *jin* of gold.[45]

The *Historical Records* (Shiji) of Sima Qian records the naming of New Feng in honor of Gaozu's father but does not record this story.[46] Also, the town's builder, Hu Kuan, is not known from any other contemporary textual source. In some editions of the *Miscellaneous Notes on the Western Capital* his name is given as Wu Kuan. The variability in the transcription of this man's name suggests that this story was orally transmitted for some time before it was first written down, probably in the fourth century CE. Evidently, the story had already coalesced into something similar to its current form by the mid–third century CE, because it is reported that Cao Mao, the ill-fated Emperor Shao of the Wei (r. 254–60 CE) once painted a scroll on this theme called *Setting Free the Chickens and Dogs in Xinfeng* (Xinfeng fang jiquan tu), a work still extant during the Tang.[47] It is quite immaterial whether this fanciful tale actually happened or not. What is important for our purposes is the attitude toward Hu Kuan's creation that the author attributes to the residents. Hu's greatest accomplishment was not how beautifully, how flamboyantly, or how quickly he built his Epcot-style re-creation of Gaozu's old home village, but how realistically he simulated the appearance of the original buildings and their settings. Even the chickens, rather unbiased critics, approved of his work.

For the more metaphysically minded critic and philosopher, perfect realism of form was not enough. The *Lord of Huainan* (Huainanzi) authors (ca. 122 BCE) were concerned also with how a work conveyed the *shen* (spirit/soul) of a subject. For them, there was a fundamental dichotomy between the body and the spirit. The spirit of a being conditioned its outward physical form (*xing*).[48] To faithfully portray a subject, an artist had to also convey something of its spirit in the work. To illustrate this concept, they give a specific example from the field of painting: "If one paints an outline of [the legendary beauty] Xishi's face so that it is beautiful yet not pleasing, or uses a compass to define [the famous warrior] Meng Ben's eyes so they are large yet not terrifying, the master of form [i.e., spirit], will be lacking [in the work.]"[49] They declare in another section that, "seeking that which is beyond the usual, a painter will take pains with every hair, but miss the total appearance."[50] In other words, an ultrarealist painter can get lost in the details and fail to capture the essence of the subject. Such concerns anticipate what would become a key debate among art critics of later times in China. For centuries to come, there would be an ongoing discourse concerning the relationship between *xingsi* (formal likeness) and *qiyun* (spirit resonance) in painting.

THE PHILOSOPHY AND RHETORIC OF ARTISAN CREATIVITY

The *Lord of Huainan* authors, and other early Chinese philosophers, had no real abiding concern for artisans or their crafts. However, they often used artisans in analogies to illustrate moral and philosophical concepts.[51] One might recall the famous dictum attributed to Confucius in the *Analects* that says, "If an artisan wants to be good at his craft, he must first make sharp his tools."[52] Confucius was constructing an analogy between the craftsman, perhaps a woodworker, and the gentleman who wishes to cultivate *ren* (benevolence). Just as the woodworker must sharpen his tools to achieve his goal, Confucius tells his disciple Zigong that the gentleman must become a client of worthy officials and cultivate friendships with men who already manifest benevolence. Numerous philosophical texts contain even more detailed anecdotes concerning both the mechanical and the intangible aspects of the master artisan's creative genius.

But are such analogies constructed by philosophers of any use to us? What insights can philosophers, most of whom probably never dirtied their hands with physical work, give us concerning the creative psychology and artistic processes of manual laborers and skilled artisans? The sad truth is that we do not have the benefit of a text written from the perspective of a real, practicing artisan who lived during the early imperial period that explains his or her creative process. Even if some artisans were literate enough to write such an account down, and it is probable that many were, it is very unlikely that any ever did. Craft techniques were often kept as family secrets in traditional societies and were the guarantee of a family's livelihood. Writing them down would be considered foolhardy in the extreme. It is only in the post-Han period that we see the first tracts written by artists, nearly all painters, explaining how they worked and evaluating what qualities made a work special.[53]

So, all we are left with for the late Warring States and early imperial period are the anecdotes and theoretical models of philosophers. In some way, the philosopher shares the same relationship with the craftsman as the art critic in our society does with the artist or that the literary critic does with the novelist. The creators themselves do not always realize the more profound meanings of their own works or the deep psychological influences that inform them. Thus, it is appropriate for the critic or the philosopher to construct a theory that can explain how and why an artist has created something of special value. We would love to hear the perspective of both the artist and the critic, but in this case, we will have to be satisfied with the words of the critic alone.

How did philosophers and other elite authors conceptualize an artisan's creative process? What factors were involved in the making of a high-quality piece or even a masterpiece? Could such methods be transmitted to others? Who ultimately invented the useful crafts?

To begin our investigation, let us first look at the view of creativity espoused in the *Record of the Scrutiny of Crafts.* The author of that text was clearly not a craftsman himself, but he does seem to have had some role in the supervision or observation of artisans. His descriptions of parts and object types are very detailed, but his formulas for metallurgical processes and his measurements of various artifacts have been rationalized and idealized to such an extent that they do not accord with reason or correlate well with excavated objects. Nevertheless, the opening paragraphs of the work, which precede the more detailed sections, provide us with some of our only philosophical musings on the mechanics of artistic creation. They state, in part: "Timing in accord with the seasons, an environment with a suitable configuration of vital energy (*qi*), excellent raw materials, and skillful (*qiao*) artisans; if one is able to combine all these qualities, only then can he make something that is good."[54]

After this simply elegant but quite abstract statement, the *Record* author then goes on to describe in more detail the interaction of these four factors. He makes it clear that, even if an artisan had the requisite skill and excellent materials, if he or she tried to work out of tune with the seasons or in the wrong geographic location, the product would turn out poorly. It was thought in early China that certain regions were ideally suited to produce certain types of object. For example, it is stated in the *Record* that only in the lands of Wu (present-day Jiangsu, plus parts of Zhejiang and Anhui) and Yue (present-day Zhejiang, Shaoxing area) could one produce the best swords. This was thought to be the result of a particular *qi* (configuration of vital energy) present in those locations. If one attempted to make a sword outside those regions, the finished result would not be perfect. The author uses an analogy to the habitats of living things to further his point. Outside their natural habitats, plants wither and animals die. He cites the specific example of citrus trees, saying that orange trees from the Yangzi area produce sweet fruit, but if one planted the same tree species north of the Huai River (i.e., in Shandong), the fruit of the same plant would taste bitter.[55] This is because the *qi* of the northern lands is unsuitable for growing sweet oranges. Though the author of the *Record* does not mention the subject, it is also true that the quality of lacquer vessels is very dependent on geography. To properly cure the paper-thin coating of lacquer vessels, the painted pieces must be placed in conditions of high temperature (25–30°C) and high humidity (75–85 percent). These conditions are ideally found year-round in the humid belt of the Yangzi River valley, especially in what is now Sichuan, Hubei, and Hunan. Lacquer from these areas was greatly admired during the Han, and its luster owed much to the proper *qi* under which it was produced. When we try to explain why certain regions are better suited to make particular products, we use words like "temperature" and "humidity," or we point to differing qualities of ore sources or timber. But, to the early Chinese artisans, the concept of suitable *qi* explained the phenomenon quite adequately.

As perceived by more philosophically minded authors, especially those of the Daoist "school," an idealized artisan in his most transcendent state partook of something supernatural in his acts of creativity. To these authors, artistic production was not just a mechanical convergence of factors of environment, materials, and skill such as was suggested by the author of the *Record of the Scrutiny of Crafts*. Something intangible must also be present to create truly incredible objects. Numerous anecdotes in the *Master Zhuang* (Zhuangzi), *Master Lie* (Liezi), and *Lord of Huainan* texts tell of artisans "in the zone," men who could perform flawless acts of creation without strain or overt thought.

As Confucius said, an artisan, at a minimum, must first have the proper tools and the basic skill set. But truly excellent work is produced only by those who are not just qualified but greatly experienced, having internalized the process of creation so completely that the act is almost without conscious thought. This is the meaning of the story of the master buckle maker found in chapter 22 of the *Master Zhuang*.[56]

> The grand marshal's belt-hook maker was eighty years old, but he had not lost the tiniest part of his old dexterity. The grand marshal said, "What skill (*qiao*) you have! Is there a special way to this?"
>
> "I have a way. From the time I was twenty I have loved to forge belt-hooks. I never look at other things—if it's not a belt-hook, I don't bother to look at it. Using this method of deliberately *not* using other things [i.e., extreme specialization], I was able in the long run to get some *use* out of it."[57]

Assuredly, the buckles of our figurative master belt-hook maker were probably excellent pieces, but they were not considered masterpieces. The greatest masterpieces are not made in quantities large enough for the creator to develop the unconscious internalization of craft that comes through single-minded repetition and minute specialization. To illustrate the making of an almost-supernatural masterwork, the *Master Zhuang* relates the story of Woodworker Qing:[58]

> Woodworker Qing carved a piece of wood and made a bell-rack support, and when it was finished, everyone who saw it marveled, for it seemed to be the work of the gods or spirits. When the Marquis of Lu saw it, he asked, "What clever technique (*shu*) is it you have?" Qing replied, "I am only a craftsman (*gong ren*)—how would I have any clever technique? There is one thing, however. When I am going to make a bell-rack support, I never let it deplete my energy. I always fast in order to still my mind. When I have fasted for three days, I no longer have any thought of congratulations or rewards, of titles or stipends. When I have fasted for five days, I no longer have any thought of praise or blame, of skill or clumsiness. And when I have fasted for seven days, I am so still that I forget I have four limbs and a form and body. By that time, the ruler and his court no longer exist for me. My skill (*qiao*) is concentrated and all outside distractions fade away. After that, I go into the mountain forest and examine

> the Heavenly nature of the trees. If I find one of superlative form, and I can visualize a bell-rack support within my mind's eye, I put my hand to the job of carving; if not, I let it go. This way I am simply matching up the Heavenly nature of the tree with my Heaven-given talents. That's probably the reason that people wonder if the results were not made by the spirits."[59]

Thus, according to the *Master Zhuang* author, a true masterpiece (a work seemingly made by the gods) can be created only when the artist forgets his patron, forgets his commission, and even forgets himself in his process of attuning with the Dao and becoming one with his materials. In his forgetting, he is actually remembering his natural, spontaneous self. Upon reading the story of Woodworker Qing, one is reminded of the way Michelangelo conceived of working marble. In one sonnet he wrote that "the best of artists never has a concept [which] a single block of marble does not contain inside its husk; / But to it may attain, only if hand follows the intellect."[60] Michelangelo's view was Neoplatonic, in that the finished piece, like the perfected soul, was trapped in a rough husk, waiting only to be freed by the hand of higher creative power (the artist as God the creator). The *Master Zhuang* author's Daoist view held that the perfect form could be freed from the raw material by the artisan only if he freed himself from artificiality and conscious thought, realizing the heavenly, spontaneous nature within both the material and himself.

The Daoist philosophers also make it clear that the *shu* (knack or clever technique) of making great objects cannot be transmitted through words or observation. The *Master Zhuang* and the *Lord of Huainan* both recount the story of Wheelwright Pian. When asked by Duke Huan of Qi (r. 685–643 BCE) why he has denigrated the books of the sages, Pian tells the duke about his craft. "When I chisel a wheel, if the blows of the mallet are too gentle, the chisel slides and won't take hold. But if they are too hard, it bites in and won't budge. Not too gentle, not too hard—you can get it in your hand and feel it in your mind. You can't put it into words, and yet there's a knack to it somehow. I can't teach it to my son, and he can't learn it from me."[61] Thus, for the *Master Zhuang* author, just as the master craftsman cannot transmit the intangible "knack" (*shu*) of his art, the thing that can be gained only by hard-won experience and insight, the teachings of the ancient sages cannot be transmitted through the imperfect medium of language.

Obviously, the creative process seen in these *Master Zhuang* anecdotes cannot have applied to all levels of craftsmen. The local potter who cranked out dozens of chamber pots each day probably did not fast for days or commune with the Dao before he sat down to work at his wheel. Such preparations would have been a frivolous waste of time in the real world of the artisan economy. Rank-and-file artisans may not have had the leisure for time-consuming mental preparation and ritual, but they also rarely produced what would be considered masterpieces. On the other hand, it is possible that these stories do reveal some of the creative process of master court artisans, men who did have sufficient time to focus their minds and who were expected to produce flawless objects. Also, these are probably the only type of artisans that elite authors such as Confucius, Mencius, or Zhuang Zhou might have deigned to observe at work, in either a royal or a noble workshop environment. Stories of this type are just too prevalent throughout the philosophical and historical traditions to be complete fantasy. Looking to more recent times, we are reminded of the similar rituals performed by master Japanese and Javanese sword makers even today.

To many authors in early China, what the sage kings and wise ministers of the past had created in the way of political institutions and objects of material culture was already perfect. The role of the latter-day practitioner was more properly to transmit and protect this knowledge, not to wantonly create new forms. Thus, while some authors might praise the appropriate display of skillfulness in the execution of a craft, they will not credit the artisan with the ultimate invention of the craft or its products. Some culture hero or sage, a man far more noble than a lowly artisan, must have been responsible for the initial stage of invention. As stated in the preface to the *Record of the Scrutiny of Crafts:* "It is the sages (literally, "the knowledgeable ones") who invent things. The skillful ones who preserve this knowledge and pass it on from generation to generation are called the artisans. Thus, all the occupations of the hundred artisans are really the creation of the sages. Smelting metal to make a sharp blade, hardening clay to make vessels, fashioning carts to travel on land, making boats to travel on water, these are all creations of the sages."[62] According to this passage, artisans merely transmit technical knowledge imparted to them by the sages and cultural heroes of the legendary past, demigods like Shen Nong, who invented the plow, or ministers to the legendary emperors like Xi Zhong, who invented the wheeled cart.

ARTISANS AND THE AGE

Let us lay one final metaphysical burden on the idealized artisan, who would probably have laughed quite heartily if he could have understood the high-sounding words used to describe his productive activities. Just as today, when environmental scientists consider the health and size of the frog population to be an early-warning barometer for the health of the environment, so too did some writers in early China consider that the quality of artisans' products reflected the stability and moral quality of the age in which the objects were created.

At the close of the Imperial Annals of the reign of Emperor Xuan (r. 74–49 BCE) in the *History of the Former Han*, the historian Ban Gu inserted his customary eulogy summarizing the qualities of the entire reign. The reign of Emperor Xuan was considered by Ban and other authors to have been a glorious age, the very renaissance of the Han dynasty after the near ruinous reign of Emperor Wu (r. 141–87 BCE). Ban writes, in part:

In eulogy we say:

. . . Even [Emperor Xuan's] skillful artisans and craftsmen, and the vessels and utensils they created, could seldom be matched by those from the time of Emperors Yuan [r. 48–33 BCE] or Cheng [r. 33–7 BCE]. This fact is indeed sufficient to indicate that his officials were worthy of their positions and that the common people were satisfied in their occupations.[63]

In early China, it was also thought that the music of a particular time reflected the zeitgeist of the era. In the "Great Preface" to the *Book of Songs* (Shijing), attributed to the Han scholar Wei Hong (fl. 25–57 CE), it is said: "The music of the era of good government is quiescent and [therefore] joyous, for the governing is harmonious. The music of the period of confusion is resentful and [therefore] wrathful, for the governing is discordant. The music of the country running to ruin is mournful and nostalgic, for the people are in misery."[64] In the traditional Confucian views of Ban Gu and Wei Hong, the moral superiority of the good ruler suffuses through the entire populace by means of his conduct, his policies, and the intangible power of his charisma. Musicians and artisans alike were said to pick up on this spirit and be so contented in their occupations that their products were correspondingly splendid, restrained, balanced, and even joyful. The music, poetry, and products of the decadent age reflected a negative spirit through the same mechanism. Many a similar argument has been advanced by art historians of our time to explain the idealism and rationalism of classical Greek statuary or the angst of modern art, but I doubt they are aware that this method of reasoning was already employed by writers in ancient China.

THE DESPISED ARTISAN

Philosophers and historians might praise the idealized artisan as a person transmitting the work of the sages or reflecting the virtue of the ruler, but their idealized artisan was just a mental construct, an ideal form used for the purpose of discourse, and it is doubtful that the common people viewed artisans in those terms. The popular perception of artisans clearly seems to have been a negative one. As we saw in the quotation from Plutarch heading this chapter, one can praise the graceful and even sublime creation of an artisan without respecting the person who made the work.

First of all, the people of early China seem always to suspect that artisans were trying to pass off shoddy goods in the marketplace or attempting to cheat them in some way. The Legalist thinker Han Fei (d. 233 BCE) classified artisans and traders who "disguise worthless, broken articles as proper goods" as one of the *wudu* (five vermin) that eat away at the strength of the state.[65] The Qin and Han governments wrote detailed legal provisions designed to curb such unethical activities. The Legalist philosophical basis of the Qin and Han statutes assumed that all artisans were deceitful by nature and would take advantage of any opportunity to profit illegally, if not restrained by harsh deterrents. Some of these laws were recovered from the Zhangjiashan site. The Han "Statute on [Passes] and Marketplaces" from 186 BCE stated:

> If someone [in the marketplace] attempts to sell plain silk cloth (*zeng*) whose width is not a full 2 *chi* and 2 *cun* (50.6 cm), the material shall be seized. Those who report an infraction that leads to the arrest of the culprits shall receive the confiscated goods.[66]

> All those who acquire goods through deception or who sell, trade, or buy with an intent to cheat others will be adjudicated under the "Statute on Robbery" for the full illegal value of the transaction.[67]

The first clause is specifically targeted at silk intentionally woven or cropped to substandard widths. Silk was sometimes used as currency in transactions, and it was important to regulate the quality and width of the commodity. The second clause was more general in scope and could apply to any deception or fraud in the marketplace. The "Statute of Robbery" mentioned in the second clause was very severe. Prosecution was based on the value of the stolen or counterfeited items, and conviction related to a moderately priced item could result in mutilating punishments and five or six years in a labor camp (see table 6.2).

The government had one further reason to mistrust privately employed artisans, for unlike the land-bound peasants, who were tied to a specific district through the household registration system, artisans were potentially more mobile on the landscape. States tend to be suspicious of those members of society whom they are unable to track reliably or tax efficiently. Mobile merchant-traders were viewed in Qin and Han China with the same suspicious gaze.

Even government artisans in state factories were viewed with strong suspicion. The Qin statutes contained numerous quality-control and inspection provisions to keep tabs on the artisans' work. Qin state artisans were not allowed to inspect their own weights and measures for accuracy.[68] Theft of raw materials or finished products by state artisans was also treated very harshly, with brutal canings for even the smallest infraction. By the end of the Han, deceitful state artisans had colluded with corrupt officials, seriously compromising military preparedness by producing shoddy weapons. The official Cui Shi (ca. 110–170 CE) remarked in his political critique, *Discourses on Administration* (Zhenglun) (written ca. 150 CE):

> Ravenous officials compete to reduce the amount of resources expended [by the state artisans], while cunning and deceitful state artisans compound the problem by stealing or adulterating those same resources. It has even come to the point that some artisans use nettle-hemp to bind up bows and crossbows and adulterate lacquer fluid with rice porridge. They take the red-hot iron plates used

for armor and quench them in vinegar to make the iron stiffer and easier to work, but then the finished armor suit will shrink to the point that a person can no longer fit in it. Moreover, the knives and spears they make are all blunt. Therefore, the brave young men who dare to fight in the border regions all have to make their own weapons; they are not willing to use government-issued arms.[69]

His proposed solution was an even more rigorous application of the harsh laws for artisans already on the books.

One of the most famous cases of artisan greed and corruption is found in the illuminating and apocryphal story of the court painters to Emperor Yuan (r. 48–33 BCE) of the Former Han, found in the *Miscellaneous Notes on the Western Capital*:

Since Emperor Yuan of the Han had so many women in his harem, he was not able to see them very frequently. Thus, he commissioned his painters to paint portraits [of all the women], and basing his choices on the portraits, the emperor summoned the women and bestowed his favors on them. All the women of the harem bribed the artists [to paint them favorably]. Some gave as much as 100,000 cash, and none gave less than 50,000 cash. Only Wang Qiang [Wang Zhaojun] was not willing to do such a thing. Thus, she was not able to be seen by the emperor. It came about that a Xiongnu [envoy] came to court seeking a woman to become the queen of the *shanyu*, his *yanzhi*.[70] So the emperor judged according to the portraits and ordered Zhaojun to go. When it came time for her to leave and he summoned her into his presence, he realized that she was the most beautiful [woman] in all the harem. Her replies and deportment were genteel and decorous. The emperor regretted the choice, but her name had already been entered into the treaty [along with those of four other women]. The emperor valued his trustworthiness among foreign states and thus could not change the selection. Later, he fully investigated the matter and had all the painters executed and their bodies exposed in the marketplace. When their families' confiscated assets were recorded, the value totaled many millions. Among the painters, there was Mao Yanshou from Duling. He was a portrait painter. Ugly, beautiful, old, or young, he was always able to achieve true likeness. Chen Chang from Anling, and Liu Bo and Gong Kuan from Xin Feng, drew cows, horses, and flying birds. They also painted portraits, but they could not keep up with Mao Yanshou in the representation of the beautiful and the ugly. Yang Wang of Xiadu was also good at painting. He was especially good at painting textiles. Fan Yu also was skilled at textile painting. On one and the same day all of them were executed in the marketplace. From that point on, the number of painters in the capital dwindled.[71]

We see in this story that the court portrait painters were caught accepting large bribes from harem ladies to paint them with a favorable stroke of the brush. The women did this so that they might have a chance to procreate with the emperor, who selected his bedmates only by consulting a portrait gallery.

In another anecdote from the *Miscellaneous Notes on the Western Capital,* artisans are portrayed as lewd and gossiping busybodies.[72] Late in his reign, Emperor Cheng (r. 33–7 BCE) ignored his empire and reportedly killed some of his own male offspring, all for the love of two women, Zhao Feiyan and her younger sister Zhao Zhaoyi. It was said that when the infamous sisters walked along a palace pathway, the *you gong* (notorious artisans), who were allowed to work in the inner quarters, snickered at Zhaoyi and made comments about her. Zhao Feiyan was said in this passage to be slim-waisted and slight of build, whereas her sister was quite plump and could not keep up with her on the path.

In some cases, the activities of artisans might have even evoked feelings of anxiety and fear among the population, not just derision and suspicion. Lydia Thompson has recently argued that stone carvers and other artisans were viewed as akin to magicians or sorcerers because they were able to produce objects with talismanic properties, transform materials, and bring out latent cosmic energies in seemingly inert substances.[73] As we shall see in the next chapter, metalsmiths and lacquer workers also performed detailed rituals and called on tutelary deities to assist them in their work. As pseudosorcerers, artisans were not to be toyed with, for they could potentially wreak supernatural vengeance upon anyone who crossed them. Even their own patrons seem to have been careful to retain the good favor of the artisans they commissioned for tombs or other projects.[74] If a disgruntled stone carver chose to sabotage or curse a family tomb, the entire future of a patriline could be placed in jeopardy.

SOCIAL AND OCCUPATIONAL MOBILITY

Earlier in this chapter, I defined artisans in early imperial China as a distinct social class. Since much of their class identity, however, was based upon their occupation, might not our artisans be more properly defined as an occupational caste instead? According to the *International Encyclopedia of the Social Sciences*, the anthropologist A. L. Kroeber defined a caste as "an endogamous and hereditary subdivision of an ethnic unit occupying a position of superior or inferior rank in comparison with other such subdivisions."[75] The key features of his definition are that caste membership is ascribed at birth and that marriages are allowed only to other members of the same caste. Thus, unlike under a class system, no mobility is possible into or out of a caste unit. Furthermore, anthropologists note that castes are often culturally distinct, economically interdependent, and occupationally specialized.[76]

Some scholars have suggested that artisans in the Chinese Bronze Age (ca. 1800–600 BCE) were organized into occupationally specialized, endogamous clans that fit all the definitions of a true caste.[77] They point to evidence from oracle-bone texts, the so-called clan emblems on bronze vessels, and the names of clans mentioned in some

Zhou period texts that suggest affiliation with crafts like metallurgy, weaving, or pot throwing. The evidence currently available is far from conclusive, but the notion of occupational clans in the Shang and Western Zhou periods does find collateral support in ethnographic analogies to traditional societies elsewhere in which so-called craft clans were prevalent.[78]

Moving closer to our period of study, we see that several philosophical texts of the late Warring States, all dated to the third century BCE, contain some variation on the phrase "the child of an artisan will always become an artisan." For example, in the "Xiao kuang" (Lesser Basket) chapter of the *Master Guan* (Guanzi), Duke Huan (r. 685–643 BCE) is made to ask his minister Guan Zhong (d. 645 BCE) how to "settle the people," meaning how can he keep the various classes (gentry, peasants, artisans, and merchants) in their place.[79] Guan Zhong argues that the sage ruler would make all the artisans live and work together, isolated from other classes, preferably in government workshops. Because of this concentration, they could enjoy each other's company to their mutual benefit and instruction, and sons would naturally follow their fathers' occupations, since they would have seen nothing else growing up. The fact that the real historical figure of Duke Huan of Qi is fictitiously made to ask Guan Zhong how to settle the people in their occupations suggests that this was not the social situation when this story was written around 300 BCE.

In fact, a variety of other textual sources indicate that this scenario of caste-bound artisans living in segregation did not reflect the contemporary reality of the late Warring States period (300–222 BCE) but was a nostalgic plea to restore a vanished social world. In his study *Ancient China in Transition,* Hsu Cho-yun argued that the Warring States period was a time of dramatic social mobility when aristocrats could be made paupers, and paupers could rise to become dictators or kingmakers.[80] Personal and military merit began to count as much or more than birth station in determining one's social potential.

The expectation that one's life occupation was open to variable fates and not solely determined by the mother's or father's profession is also reflected in the newly discovered *rishu*, literally, "daybooks," found in several late Warring States, Qin, and Han tombs. The daybooks were divination manuals that indicated the auspicious or inauspicious days for carrying out various activities such as marriage, travel, and even cutting cloth. According to the research of Poo Mu-chou, these divination texts were used by a broad spectrum of society and can be taken to represent some of the shared religious and social beliefs of the general population.[81]

The tomb of the minor official Xi at the site of Shuihudi, which was described in chapter 1, contained two different editions of daybooks in addition to the now-famous legal texts.[82] The most extensive daybook is referred to as Daybook Text A and was found near the head of the deceased. The first part of this text lists days that were generally lucky or unlucky, according to different systems of numeration. The latter half of the text relates the auspiciousness of different days in the context of specific activities like marriage or childbirth.

The section with the heading "Giving Birth to Children" (Sheng zi) is particularly fascinating.[83] It lists the sixty days of the Chinese cyclical calendar and informs the reader of the fate of a child born on each day (see figure 2.5).[84] Consideration is given to temperament, health, prosperity, and future occupation. Here is a sample of ten different listings from the sixty-day almanac. (Letters in parentheses indicate the placement of the passage in the original slips, as shown in figure 2.5.)

- If one gives birth on an *yihai* day: the child will be fine and become rich. (a)
- If one gives birth on a *dingchou* day: the child will be good at using words but may have a milky film over his corneas [i.e., be a blind bard]. (b)
- If one gives birth on a *gengyin* day: if a girl, she will become a merchant; if a boy, he will enjoy fine clothes and jewels and be wealthy. (c)
- If one gives birth on an *yiwei* day: the child will be sickly, will be orphaned young, but will later become wealthy. (d)
- If one gives birth on a *renyin* day: it will not be auspicious, for the child will be a girl. (e)
- If one gives birth on a *bingwu* day: the child will grow up to be fond of alcohol and [because of this] will become sickly. Later he will become wealthy. (f)
- If one gives birth on a *dingwei* day: it will not be auspicious. The child will have no mother and will certainly be bound and imprisoned one day. (g)
- If one gives birth on a *shenyin* day: the child will certainly become a minor official. (h)
- If one gives birth on a *jiazi* day: the child will be orphaned young and will wear filthy clothes. (i)
- If one gives birth on a *jisi* day: the child will be of base status and will certainly be a bondservant to someone else. (j)

On two specific days in the cycle of sixty, the Shuihudi daybook says that the child will likely become an artisan, or at least be born with superior craft skills.

- If one gives birth on a *dinghai* day: the child will be a crafty artisan and will be filial in character.[85] (k)
- If one gives birth on an *yichou* day: the child will be skilled at the martial arts and be a crafty artisan.[86] (l)

Approximately half of the sixty birth outcomes in the divination text are positive or neutral, while the other half involve predominantly negative fates.[87] In comparison to other Chinese divination genres, this is surprisingly optimistic. The childbirth text is almost as informative for what it does not say as for what it does say. It *does not* say that a male child will become a peasant farmer just like his father or become an official by birthright. What it *does say* is that a child might become an artisan, a soldier, an official, a beggar, a female shaman, a female merchant, or a slave, all depending upon

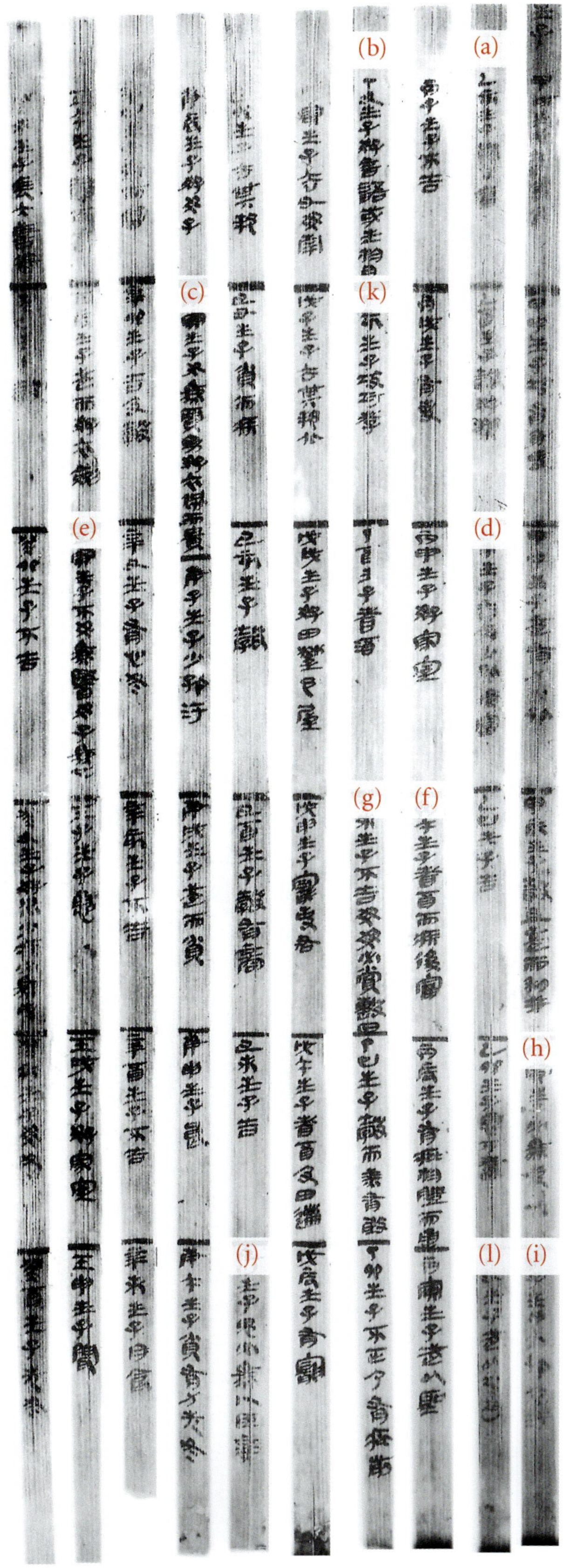

2.5 *Text of "Giving Birth to Children" from Daybook Text A.* Qin period, ca. 216 BCE. Ink on bamboo. L. 25 cm. Photo courtesy of Cultural Relics Publishing House.

astrological fate. There is no suggestion, of course, that free will could enter into career selection. It is also obvious that most mothers cannot choose freely to bear a child on a particularly favorable day or avoid ill-omened days. Yet even though one's profession was not perceived as freely chosen, these texts do suggest that occupation was not commonly thought to be determined by being born into a particular family or caste in society. Thus, the son of a peasant or soldier might be blessed at birth with craft skill and hence be destined to become an artisan.

While it is probably fruitless to try to find any consistent logic behind these astrological fates, it might be possible that the diviners were using sympathetic word magic and sound puns to arrive at some of their predictions.[88] Arbitrary selection was probably more fundamental to the creation of these fate tables than any fixed criteria or regular correlation, since different editions sometimes pronounce remarkably different outcomes for the same date. For example, compare the two days from the Shuihudi text on which one might give birth to an artisan (*dinghai, yichou*) to the days listed in a similar table from the Six Dynasties text *Classic of Obstetrics* (Chanjing).[89]

> *dinghai:* Will be of base status.
> *yichou:* Will be gallant in nature but will labor bitterly.

Clearly, there was no fixed tradition among diviners as to the days on which a woman was likely to give birth to a future artisan.

What have we learned from this digression into early Chinese astrology? What we now know is that by at least 216 BCE, the general population seems to have believed that one's profession was not necessarily determined by the father's or mother's occupation at all. Many avenues were open to a newborn. Though the daybooks say that one's occupational fate was determined by the date of birth, the fact that various options were possible proves that there was significant opportunity for and acceptance of occupational mobility within society.

Now, let us leave the astrologer's tent and come back to the real world. What textual and inscriptional evidence is there to support the view that artisans were not fixed in their professions but could become socially mobile? Obviously, even though artisans were already near the bottom of the social ladder to begin with, they could quite easily slip into the still lower ranks of unfree persons (convicts and slaves) through any of the mechanisms discussed in chapter 6. What we are more interested in here, however, is finding out how easily artisans could climb up onto the more rarefied rungs of the social ladder and become scholars, officials, or even nobility.

Throughout the Warring States period (ca. 453–222 BCE) and during the rebellion and civil war at the end of the Qin (ca. 209–202 BCE), upward social mobility was achieved most quickly through military merit. According to a Qin legal statute from Shuihudi, a *gong lichen* (male bondservant artisan) could earn his freedom and become a regular artisan (*gong*) by fighting for the Qin army and cutting off the head of one enemy combatant.[90] In fact, even a family member or other individual sympathetic to the bondservant artisan could kill an enemy in battle and use the trophy head to free him. If the artisan had been previously castrated as part of his punishment, he was made a eunuch artisan (*yinguan gong*) within the palace. Female bondservant artisans do not seem to have been eligible under this military statute for any change in status.

The case of Zhou Bo (d. 169 BCE) presents the most remarkable instance of a lowly craftsman vaulting up the social ladder through military merit.[91] During the Qin dynasty, Zhou Bo scratched out a living as an artisan in eastern China, making the bamboo frames that support silkworms as they feed on mulberry leaves. On occasion, he earned some extra money playing the flute at funerals, and he also served in the local militia as a bowman. When a man from his district named Liu Ji (later, the founder of the Han dynasty) rose up in rebellion against the Qin, Zhou Bo joined him. Zhou Bo was instrumental in several key victories against the Qin armies and later against Liu Ji's powerful rival, Xiang Yu. After the establishment of the Han dynasty, Zhou Bo was enfeoffed as a noble and given the title of Defender in Chief (Taiwei), the highest military post in the land. Later, he had a key role in suppressing the coup d'état planned by the Lü clan (180 BCE), for which he was given a huge bounty of gold and named chancellor of the empire, making him the most powerful man in the country after the emperor.

For the Latter Han period (25–220 CE), the rich biographical sources of stele inscriptions and the *History of the Latter Han* (Hou Hanshu) relate stories concerning two types of artisans who achieved high social standing. The first type was a new breed of Renaissance man, the scholar-artist. These were men like the great calligrapher and sometime painter Cai Yong, along with the painters Zhao Qi and Liu Bao, who were officials and scholars first and foremost but who happened to have artistic talent as well. Their artistic endeavors seemed to have played no major role in their rise to fame, but those activities did not hinder or stigmatize them either. Their lives will be discussed at length in chapter 5.

The Latter Han sources also tell us of several other talented craftsmen who eventually became noted literary scholars or respectable officials in the government bureaucracy. Their stories are more of the rags-to-riches type we saw in the life of Zhou Bo. They form part of a larger body of similar biographies of scholar-officials from the Latter Han, framed with the same literary motifs: A boy from a poor family, who typically lost his father early in life, has an innate love of scholarship and a talent for understanding the Classics. He is compelled by circumstance to work at menial jobs (day laborer, pig breeder, artisan, bookseller) to earn money for study, but eventually his talent and virtue are recognized and he is summoned to enter the ranks of the Imperial Academy or the bureaucracy.[92]

One man whose life story fits this type was Shentu Pan, whose "career" occupied the tumultuous final half century of the Latter Han.[93] Shentu Pan was born around 120 CE in Chenliu Commandery in the east. His father died when he was only nine years old, plunging his family into deep poverty. His biography states that, "because his family was so poor, he hired himself out as a lacquer artisan (*qi gong*)." The term translated here for "hire," *yong*, might in this context actually mean that Shentu sold himself into indentured servitude for a period of up to two years, at a prearranged price.[94] Later, Shentu was able to resume his studies and eventually came to the attention of Guo Tai (127–69 CE), one of the student leaders of the Imperial Academy. Shentu also greatly impressed Cai Yong, who was a native of the same province. Shentu received numerous summonses to enter the bureaucracy, all of which he turned down. The more positions he refused, the more offers he received, and the greater his fame spread. He went into seclusion in the mountains, working for two more years at menial jobs, just around the time the Great Proscription was first announced in 166 CE.[95] Thus, he managed to escape that disaster unscathed. During the disastrous civil wars at the end of the Han, he also managed to avoid the invitations of the general He Jin and the warlord Dong Zhuo (d. 192 CE) to take a position in government. The historian's greatest praise for Shentu Pan was that he succeeded at something that few scholars or officials of that treacherous era managed to accomplish: he died in his own bed at a ripe old age (ca. 194 CE).

Outside the standard historical sources, Han inscriptions can also shed some light on artisan mobility. A Han period stele, which is no longer extant but was recorded during the Song dynasty, contained a eulogy to a certain Master Guo who lived in northeast China during the second century CE.[96] Master Guo's stele biography is similar to others from this period and contains the usual praise for his ancestors and his personal character. The text relates that, before he entered officialdom, Master Guo "undertook the work of a blacksmith, and in all his work was not neglectful."[97] At some point after his smithing career, he was appointed to a series of clerkly and administrative positions in the commandery bureaucracy and finished his career with a brief stint as Acting Regional Inspector of Jizhou, a moderately important position. His eulogist bemoans the tragic fact that just as Master Guo was being groomed for the national stage and was about to make a real difference, merciless Heaven struck him down during an extended famine. He died in 179 CE.

It is clear from the sources that, although manual professions such as those relied on by men like Shentu Pan and Master Guo were considered humble and somewhat demeaning, there was nothing about any of these jobs that would have legally barred these men from public service. To later biographers, their decision to stoop to manual labor in order to continue their studies was even considered a badge of honor. Only merchant-traders were legally barred from becoming officials during the Han. It certainly did not help to be poor, nor to spend time away from study working at artisan jobs, but so long as a young male artisan avoided being officially registered as a *shang* merchant, there always remained the possibility, however slight, that he could enter officialdom or become a famous scholar.

Having surveyed the situation from the late Warring States period to the end of the Latter Han, we see that artisans during these five centuries do not appear to have been caste-bound to their professions but seemed to enjoy at least some possibility of upward social mobility. That does not deny the fact than many children of artisans did indeed become artisans as a matter of tradition. Nor does it preclude the possibility that, at different times before and after the period under study, artisans in China indeed formed something like an occupational caste. For example, there is some suggestion that skilled Chinese artisans during the Three Kingdoms and Jin periods (220–420 CE) became relatively scarce, due to demographic and economic pressures, and were then classified into hereditary units to ensure their continued service to the state.[98] This seems to be analogous to the situation in the last century of the Roman Empire, when a shortage of artisans in state factories and urban centers, caused by plagues and barbarian invasions, forced lawmakers to attempt to bind the remaining workers into hereditary castes.[99]

LEVEL OF LITERACY

It is difficult to assess the general level of literacy in early imperial China and quite impossible to arrive at any valid numbers for the percentage of men or women of any class who could read and write. The written word was valued in early China more so than in almost any other ancient society. Literacy was considered a proper and desirable goal by more than just the professional scribal class or the leisured aristocracy. Literary scholarship, focusing on the memorization and interpretation of Classical texts, was viewed as rigorous mental training for the gentleman and as a means to enter the official bureaucracy. We know that books were sold in the metropolitan marketplaces and that local governments sometimes maintained primary and secondary schools to teach reading and writing, often limited in duration to the agricultural slack seasons. Even so, the vast majority of peasants were probably not literate beyond recognizing their own names in written form. When commoners required binding contracts in the marketplace, the documents were usually drawn up by professional scribes, and the contract text read to the transacting parties and witnesses for verification.

The level of literacy among those employed in government service was far higher than among the peasant population. The Qin and Han empires were run by massive, hierarchical bureaucracies that relied on the collation and dissemination of millions of pieces of written data for their smooth operation. Written census records were maintained at the local level for every household unit in the empire, and theoretically these files were updated on an annual basis. Records of grain in storage, land use figures, military and civilian labor conscription rolls, job performance evaluations, sighted omens and prodigies: all of these were meticulously written down, copied, and disseminated throughout the bureaucracy. Nearly every civilian or military work unit employed at least one professional scribe (*shi*) for bureaucratic correspondence, and some employed hundreds. During the Former Han period scribes-in-training had to pass a written test for recognition, pronunciation, and reproduction of five thousand Chinese characters, taken after three years of study, to qualify for an actual post.[100] In 5 BCE, the government directly employed 130,285 literate officials. At least twice that many literate scribes and functionally literate runners were probably employed by local administrations for the labor-intensive tax and census collection activities.[101]

What percentage of Qin and Han craftsmen were literate, and what was the nature of their literacy? Experts in the field of ancient literacy make distinctions for many different levels and types of literacy, ranging from simple recognition and reproduction of one's name to the ability to understand and communicate profound thoughts through reading and writing. Classicist W. V. Harris has used the term "craftsman's literacy" to describe the situation in which a sizable proportion of skilled craftsmen gain and transmit a functional level of literacy to carry out their craft and its related business functions.[102] On a historical continuum, craftsman's literacy follows the more limited scribal literacy and precedes any kind of mass literacy. In classical Greece and Rome, and up until the nineteenth century in the West, a far greater percentage of craftsmen than members of the general population were functionally literate.[103]

There is abundant material evidence that many artisans in early imperial China possessed this level of craftsman's literacy. The master of an artisan work crew in an imperial workshop was required by law to inscribe his name, work unit, and the year of manufacture on finished pieces to guarantee quality control and to enable accountants to track production quotas and materials. Master artisans in private workshops occasionally inscribed their names, auspicious slogans, or other information on bronze mirrors, lacquer vessels, iron tools, pottery, and textiles. The names inscribed on these articles are our chief source for the identity of common artisans, men and women whose names and lives would be lost to history were it not for their ability to write.

As we will see in the next two chapters, Han stone carvers left behind a particularly large number of durable monuments inscribed by their hands, and these products provide us with an opportunity to investigate the nature of their literacy in more detail. In one case, more than one hundred masons conscripted for a royal tomb project carved brief texts onto stone blocks, including their names, their native places, and the source of the quarried stone.[104] Dozens of carved epitaphs and memorial stelae, dating from the Latter Han period and made by crews of independent masons, have been preserved aboveground or uncovered by archaeologists. In the Shandong/Jiangsu area, numerous pictorial-stone monuments have been found that display short text-labels used to identify narrative scenes. These clues suggest that at least one person on a stone-carving crew was literate. Yet the literacy of the master mason in Han China seems to have been categorically different from the literacy possessed by the bureaucratic clerk in Han ministries or by the literary scholar of Classical texts.

For example, the graphs in many stone inscriptions are riddled with "errors." Numerous characters are missing strokes or contain nonstandard additional strokes. Determinatives are routinely swapped or absent, and phonetic loans, in which a particular graph is replaced by a homophone, are exceedingly common.[105] A rather humorous loan, shared by many Han stone inscriptions, is the substitution of *zao* (flea) for *zao* (early), such as in the line "He took leave of his parents and siblings early."[106] Similar phonetic loans and nonstandard orthography can also be seen in the inscriptions on privately produced Han bronze mirrors.[107] In the world of craftsman's literacy, perfect accuracy in character form was not as crucial as it was in the account book of the official clerk or in the belles lettres of the literati. For the artisan, and apparently for his low-ranking clientele, close enough was usually good enough. The official clerk had to ensure that laws were understood literally, and the Classical scholar desired the words of the sages to be transmitted accurately. Mistakes and phonetic loans do occur in pre-Han bureaucratic documents and literary texts, but their presence diminishes greatly during the Han period.[108] William Boltz has argued that the early Chinese language as a whole was drifting toward the kind of loose "phonetic and asemantic" writing practiced by Han artisans, until the meticulous bureaucrats clamped down on the linguistic evolution.[109]

A distinction should be made between the epitaphs carved on moderately inexpensive monuments and those carved on commemorative stelae dedicated to deceased scholars and officials. Stele texts were elegantly composed by fellow scholars and were often carved to reproduce accomplished brush calligraphy (see figure 2.6). Apparently, the text was brushed or traced onto the stone by an accomplished literatus, and the carver merely engraved each character. These texts contain very few errors and the graphs are sometimes quite beautiful. The graphs of epitaphs on modest monuments are quite unattractive by comparison (see figure 2.7) and the texts contain many errors. These were clearly carved in the hand of the mason and were not tracings of masterful brush calligraphy.

Looking at the literary structure of epitaphs on moderately inexpensive stone offering halls, we see that they are clearly generic texts, full of stock phrases and trite sentiments about death and mourning: ("Wu-hu—the Sorrow!" "He returned to the Yellow Springs." "We shouldered the soil to make the tomb mound.") These clues lead me to the conclusion that the long epitaph inscriptions carved onto stone monuments were mostly composed by the carvers themselves, after only minimal biographical input from the family.[110] I envision a scenario similar to the use of model legal forms during the Tang dynasty, in which blanks were left within model texts for personal details (name, date, official positions held, cause of death), and the poetic phrases and boilerplate language were prepackaged around them.[111] After the family provided these facts, the carvers could immediately set to work without a second thought. Thus, we see that some Han carvers were indeed quite literate, but only to the extent that they could perform their jobs effectively.

What then were artisans in early imperial China, and what social and economic role did they play? Menial laborer, key economic engine, parasite on society, transmitter of sagely knowledge, genius, sorcerer, forger, and cheat; the early Chinese artisan could be any or all of these things; the label one employed merely depended on one's perspective and one's dealings with that class. From our historical vantage point, we should look upon them as akin to the working classes of the Industrial Age, human beings full of honor and full of flaws but uniquely trained and suited to their specialized crafts. Early Chinese artisans are eminently worthy of our attention, so let us now step into their shops and see how they worked.

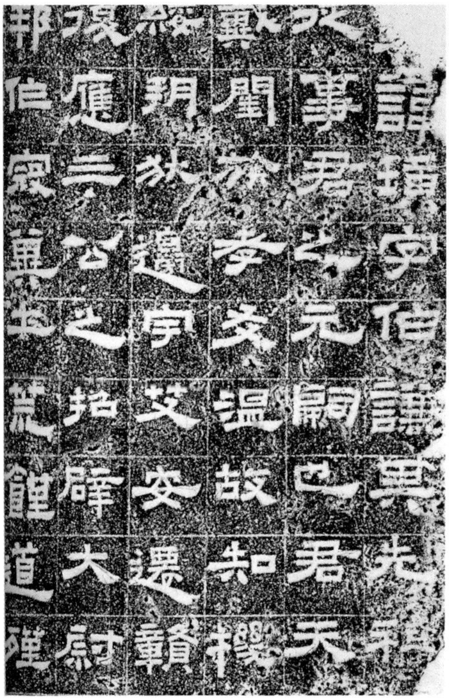

2.6 *Detail of inscription dedicated to the former governor Xianyu Huang.* Latter Han period, dated January 7, 166 CE. Ink rubbing on paper. Tianjin Municipal Museum of History. From Tani and Hiroshi, vol. 2, pl. 81. Excavated from Lanchengcun, Tianjin City.

2.7 *Detail of inscription dedicated to the clerk An Guo.* Latter Han period, dated February 2, 158 CE. Ink rubbing on paper. Royal Ontario Museum. Photo by Klaas Ruitenbeek. Excavated from Songshan, Jiaxiang, Shandong.

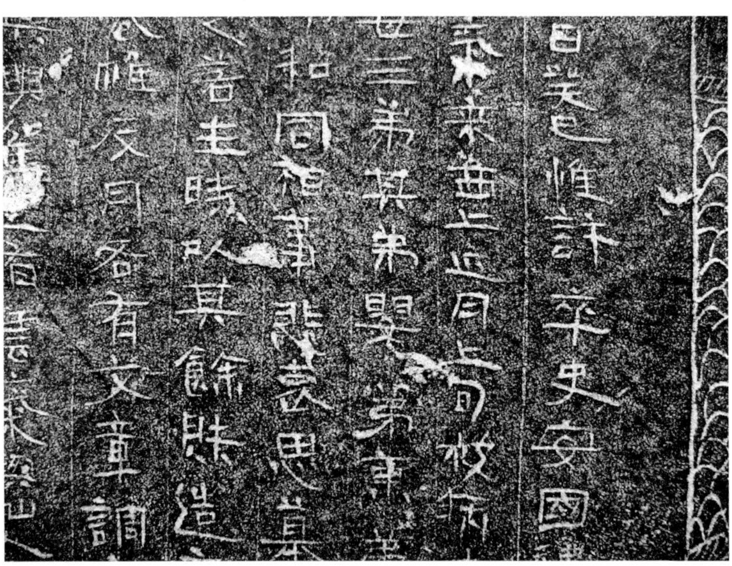

3

ARTISANS IN THE WORKSHOP

An artisan carried out his or her craft in a workshop. Practically, the workshop is a mobile concept, since it existed wherever the requisite materials and labor were gathered, be it in a dedicated building or at a temporary jobsite. During the Qin and Han periods, the commonplace word for an artisan's workshop was *zuoshi* (fabrication chamber). For example, the entrance into the production quarter of the main Weiyang Palace (Weiyang Gong) at the Han capital of Chang'an was commonly referred to as the Workshop Gate (Zuoshimen).[1] It was literally the side door to the palace, well beyond the site of the royal gates and the sight of the royal gaze. The official, bureaucratic term for a state-run workshop during the Qin and early Former Han periods was *gongshi* (artisan chamber).[2] Often, this was shortened in titles to simply *gong*, which we might translate as "workshop" or "factory," depending on the scale of production and the internal organization of the facility.[3] A famous imperial factory repeatedly referred to in this book is the Western Workshop of Shu Commandery (Shu Jun Xigong) located in the city of Chengdu, in present-day Sichuan.[4] Another older and less commonly encountered term for an official workshop was *zuofu* (fabrication treasury). The word still resonates with connotations of the hoarding of ritual bronzes and jades produced therein.[5]

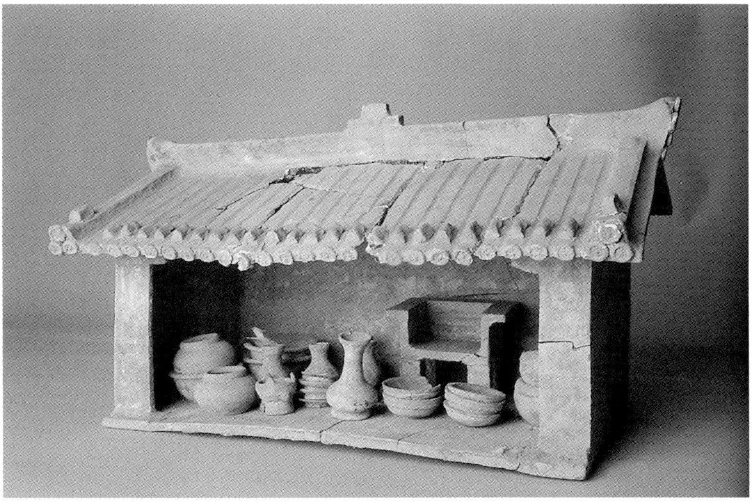

3.1 *Beer-making shop.* Latter Han period, ca. 100–220 CE. Terracotta. L. 48.4 cm. H. 32 cm. Henan Provincial Museum. From Henan Bowuyuan, pl. 61.

Workshops came in many types. Some, like the massive government-run iron foundries we will encounter in chapter 6, were open-air facilities, while other types of shop were clearly located indoors, as implied by the word *shi* (chamber) appended to the common terms for workshop. Obviously, no workshop building survives intact from early imperial China for us to examine. Depictions of early Chinese workshops are also quite rare, but a few terracotta models and pictorial-stone carvings from the Han period do seem to represent, with some faithfulness, what an actual workshop might have looked like. A clay model, found undisturbed in a Latter Han tomb near Luoyang, seems to portray a small beer-making shop (see figure 3.1).[6] The shop model consists of a single-bay, gable-roofed structure, open on one side. Shelves, low tables, vats, a mortar and pestle set, amphora, and other tools of the trade were arranged both inside and outside the structure. The open-sided structure this model simulates would have allowed the workers to spread out into the open area during good weather and retreat under the eave to escape the elements. One could also infer that the finished product might be sold directly from the open shop-front. The general layout of the shop is corroborated by low-relief representations of liquor shops on impressed bricks from Sichuan.[7] While it is true that a brewery is not properly a "workshop" for object fabrication, the general layout of both was similar in many ways.

Figure 3.2 shows a group of three terracotta models found in a late Former Han tomb near Luoyang. The excavators have interpreted this group as comprising a suite of workshops for dyeing fabric.[8] All the buildings are somewhat schematic in design, and the structure in figure 3.2a seems quite simple and unspecialized in function. The other two buildings, however, do possess some features that support such an interpretation. The trough with free-spinning wheel in figure 3.2b appears to be intended for grinding pigments, while the stoves seen in figures 3.2b and 3.2c might have been used for boiling vegetable dyes and soaking fabric. Note, once again, that all three structures are open on one side.

3.2 *Fabric-dyeing workshops*. Former Han period, ca. 50 BCE–8 CE. Terracotta. (a) H. 50 cm. W. 46 cm. (b) H. 43 cm. W. 52 cm. (c) H. 46 cm. W. 34.5 cm. Henan Provincial Museum. From Henan Bowuyuan, pls. 58–60.

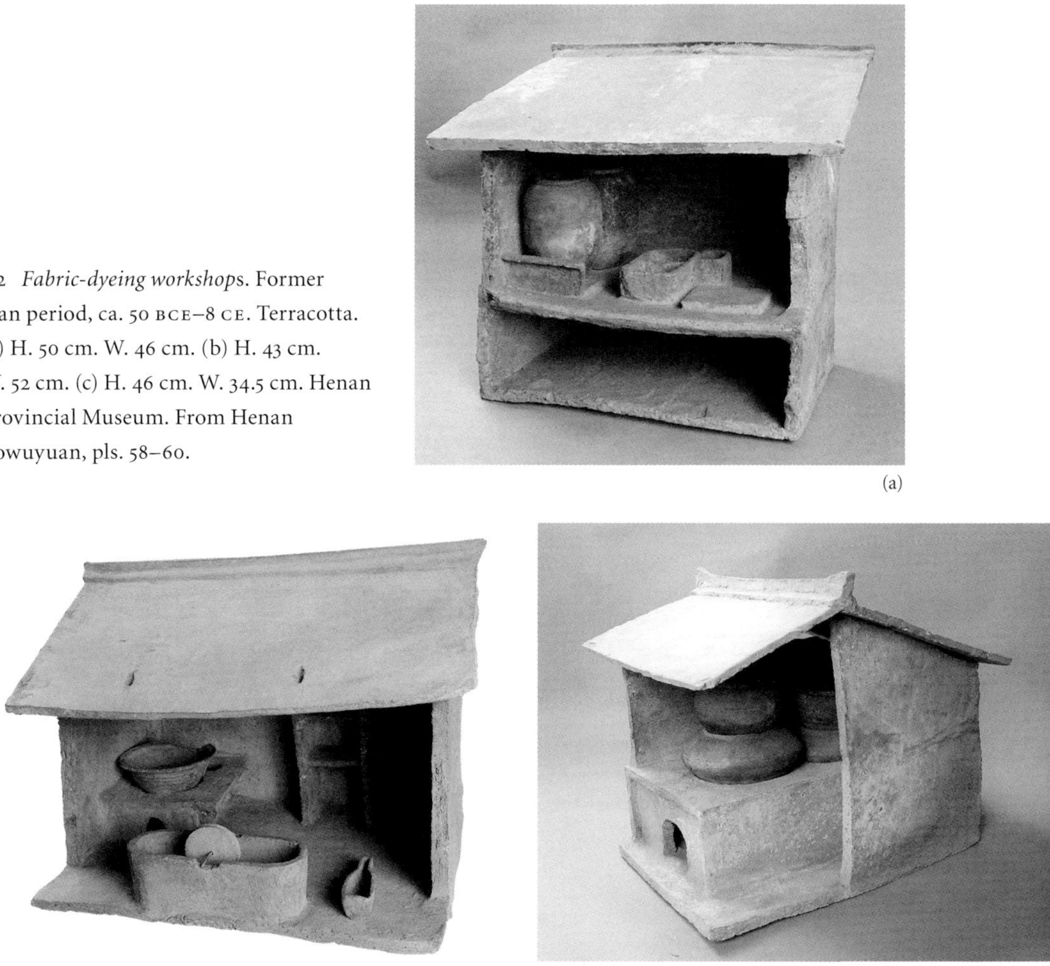

(a) (b) (c)

Figure 3.3 is a rubbing from a Latter Han carved stone that depicts a workshop for making iron swords.[9] At the left, two or more men are operating what appears to be the bellows of a fining hearth. The bellows seems to be suspended from above, so we could conclude that the workshop was covered by a roof or at least an awning. To their immediate right, four men are hammering something at an anvil. Further right, a man is sighting the trueness of a sword blade, while a group to his right appear to be working with other tools. Some tools are seen hanging from pegs on the wall, so we can infer that the workshop was walled on at least one side. At the far right, two men are standing in a doorway, which may represent the entrance to the workshop. The absence of other architectural features in this carving prevents us from drawing any further inferences concerning the size and layout of the smith's shop. I doubt that blacksmiths' workshops were completely enclosed, because of the dangers of heat and toxic smoke. Like the brewer's shop in figure 3.1, a blacksmith's shop was probably open to the air on at least one side.

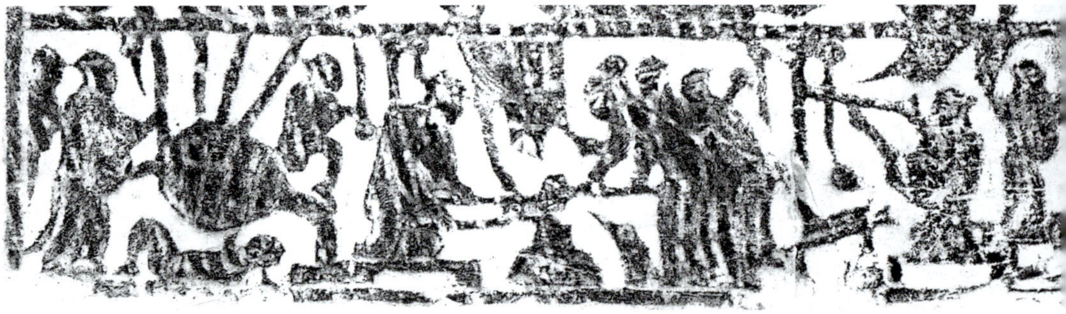

3.3 *Sword smith's workshop.* Latter Han period, ca. 147–89 CE. Ink rubbing on paper (detail). Original stone in National Museum of Chinese History, Beijing. Photo courtesy of Shandong Fine Arts Publishing House.

ARTISAN TRAINING

Boys and girls might have followed one of several paths to become artisans. They might have been born into a family of artisans and merely continued the family occupation, or they might have been recommended by family members or acquaintances for training under a master. As you will read in chapter 6, one might also be assigned artisan activities after enslavement, criminal conviction, or corvée labor conscription.

We are largely uninformed about how artisans were trained in their craft. Most workshops were probably run by one, or perhaps two, resident master artisans, supervising a number of apprentices and hired hands. Judging by inscriptional and textual evidence, the master artisan was referred to in honorific contexts as Master or Teacher (*shi*), a form of address common in other master/disciple contexts. Sometimes the title of Master was suffixed to the field of craft specialization. Thus, a master painter or draftsman was referred to as a *hua-shi* (drawing master).[10]

It seems that the master's apprentices were called *di* or *dizi* (disciples), as these were the customary terms for followers of a master teacher in other contexts.[11] A Han period inscription on a stone pillar-gate dated 147 CE mentions the participation of two stone carvers, one named Meng Ji and another referred to as Ji *di* Mao, thus "Apprentice Mao of Master Stone Carver Meng Ji."[12] This interpretation is rendered less certain by the fact that the graph *di* can also mean "younger brother."

It is possible, in some cases, to differentiate the work of a master from that of his apprentices in the output of particular workshops and sometimes even on the same piece. It appears that the master often completed the preliminary composition for a piece and rendered the important details of figural representations, while apprentices were often left to perform repetitive and unimaginative tasks, such as carving out decorative borders or painting broad areas.

Figure 3.4 is a lacquer platter made in the city of Chengdu (Sichuan) in the first half of the third century CE. The scene of two boys fighting with sticks that occupies the central roundel is sensitively executed, probably by a master lacquer figure painter.

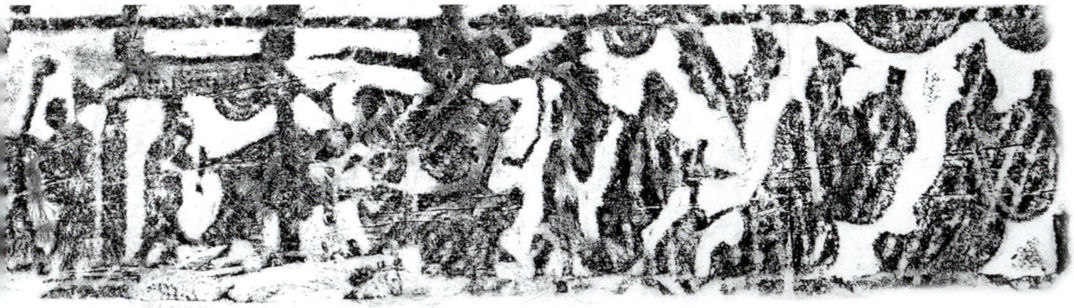

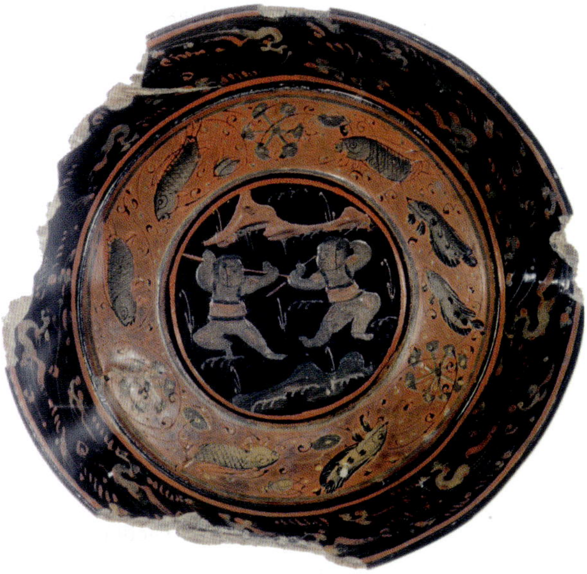

3.4 *Lacquer platter.* Early third century, ca. 200–49 CE. Lacquer on wooden core. D. 14 cm. Ma'anshan Municipal Museum. Photo courtesy of Cultural Relics Publishing House. Excavated from the tomb of Zhu Ran (d. 249 CE), Ma'anshan City, Anhui.

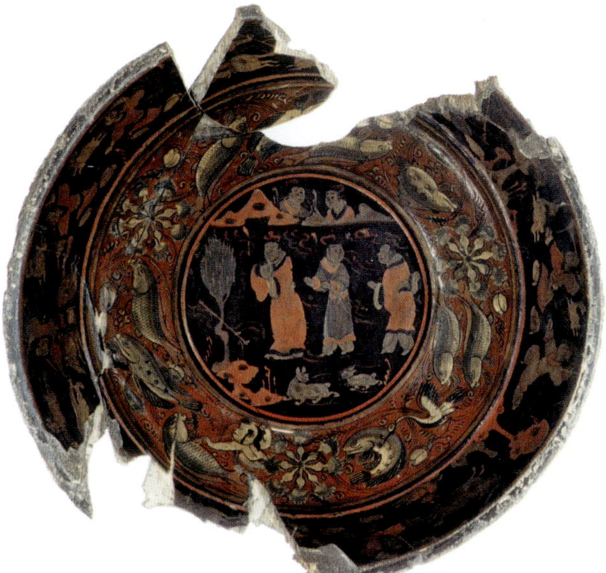

3.5 *Lacquer platter.* Early third century, ca. 200–49 CE. Lacquer on fabric-reinforced wooden core, with gilded-bronze mount. D. 24.8 cm. Ma'anshan Municipal Museum. Photo courtesy of Cultural Relics Publishing House. Excavated from the tomb of Zhu Ran (d. 249 CE), Ma'anshan City, Anhui.

The design of fish amid scrolling kelp vines in the band around this roundel, however, is a poorly executed interpretation of the type of Roman inhabited-scroll motifs seen on Western silver vessels brought into China along the Silk Road.[13] Compare the treatment of a similar scene, wholly painted by a more experienced hand, in figure 3.5. Clearly, the platter in figure 3.4 was a collaborative effort between a master painter, who executed the central scene, and his apprentices, who completed the less-crucial elements of the design.

The disciples of a master artisan were charged with transmitting the master's craft models and techniques to later generations within their workshop tradition. These often-secret methods were referred to as the *fa* (model, method) of the master. If the master had no sons or other disciples to carry on his tradition, his tradition was said to be *jue* (cut off).[14]

Our sources do not tell us the number of months or years that were required for an apprentice in a private workshop to learn the craft and become a full-fledged artisan in his or her own right. We do, however, have much more detailed information concerning the normative training periods for state-employed artisans. Once again, our chief sources are the unearthed extracts from the Qin statutes from Shuihudi and the Han statutes from Zhangjiashan.[15] Judging by the relevant statutes, it appears that during the Qin and Han periods, state artisans were selected from promising candidates through a screening procedure where only the top 30 percent were chosen for training. These men and women were expected to apprentice for two years before achieving full artisan status. No differentiation was made in the statutes to account for the varying difficulty levels of different arts. The first year of training was a probationary period, during which time the *xingong* (literally, "new artisan") was expected to learn the basics of the craft from the craft master who supervised his or her state-run workshop. During the late Warring States and Qin periods, the person who held this teaching and supervisory workshop post was referred to as the Master of Artisans (Gongshi), whereas Han workshops seem to have used the title Artisan in Charge of Fabrication (Zaogong).[16] During the probationary year, an apprenticed state artisan was expected to produce half the output of an experienced full-fledged artisan. Only after he or she passed an examination following the first year would the artisan's family receive the tax break given to the families of government artisans (for details, see chapter 6 under "The Conscripted Artisan").

By the end of the second year, the apprentice was expected to complete the same work quota as an experienced hand. If he or she attained mastery over the craft before the two-year period was up, this news was to be reported to the superiors in the state-factory organization, and the newly enrolled artisan could be monetarily rewarded. However, if after two years, he or she still had not attained complete mastery (*qiao bu cheng*), this was duly recorded in their files and, according to the Han statute, the person was not allowed to become a state artisan.

These Qin and Han training regulations seem idealistic and rather inflexible. In contrast, the Tang period training regulations, as preserved in the *Six Statutes of the Tang* (Tang liudian) (completed 739 CE) and in the "Treatise on Bureaucratic Posts" (Baiguan zhi) in the *New History of the Tang* (Xin Tangshu) (completed 1060 CE), take into account that all crafts are not equally difficult to master.[17] The Assistant Supervisors of the Directorate for Imperial Manufactories (Shaofu Cheng), who were in charge of most Tang palace workshops, established a training scale with at least nine gradations, depending on the difficulty of the craft and the number of tasks to be learned. It was recognized that metalwork in gold, silver, and bronze, including casting, engraving, openwork, and inlay decoration, required the most training. Apprentices in those fields were given a full four years to learn their assigned craft. Training for complex woodcrafts such as fashioning wheeled carriages or musical instruments encompassed three years. What the Tang authors called *pingman* (regular) crafts were allotted the same two years for training stipulated in the Qin and Han statutes for all types of craft. Many crafts, including those using bamboo, lacquer, and wood, required one year. Below this, the Tang statutes mention "miscellaneous crafts," with training periods ranging from nine months down to only forty or fifty days. Such short training periods were probably reserved for simple, repetitive tasks and reflect an advanced stage in the evolution of workshop specialization.

OBJECT FABRICATION

Once the status of full-fledged *gong* artisan was achieved, how did these men and women carry out their craft in a workshop? Ideally, we would like to know the basic tool kit of each artisan field and all the procedures used to make and decorate objects. Unfortunately, the limitations of space and the fragmentary state of our knowledge prevent such a comprehensive approach here. Instead, I will make some general observations about production strategies and then focus at greater length on the production processes within two key crafts: lacquering and stone carving.

Early legal and mathematical texts suggest that the estimation of required materials and manpower was an important first consideration for the government procurer and the independent artisan alike. The government official in charge of a construction project had to be able to calculate the number of person-days required, the amount of materials needed or earth to be moved, and the amount of grain required to feed the corvée laborers or convicts. When a private contractor was faced with a task such as building a well, he wanted to know similar quantities: how much earth had to be moved, how many stone blocks would be needed, and, ultimately, what price he should contract for the project.

To solve such contract estimation problems, government officials made use of mathematical rules contained in calculation texts (*suanshu shu*). Two examples of these have been handed down from antiquity: the *Arithmetical Classic of the Gnomon and the Circular Paths of Heaven* (Zhoubi suanjing) and the *Nine Chapters on the Mathematical Arts* (Jiuzhang suanshu), both compiled into their current form around the first century BCE.[18] Another calculation text, recently unearthed from tomb 247 at Zhangjiashan (ca. 186 BCE), shows strong similarities to the *Nine Chapters on the Mathematical Arts*. The majority of the mathematical "word problems" contained in these books are practical rather than theoretical in nature and address issues commonly faced in the administrative work of officials, the deliberations of master builders, and the commerce of merchants. Topics include:

1. Calculation of the area of irregularly shaped farm fields
2. Determination of the amount of earth to be moved for walls, moats, and canals
3. Fair distribution of labor service taxes across several counties
4. Conversion of various types of grain
5. Determination of the unit price of an object when one knows the total amount of a commodity and its total cost
6. Calculation of return on investments and proportional division of proceeds

One genre of problem found in these texts also reveals something of interest concerning the division of labor within Qin and Han workshops:

> Now, a person can straighten fifty arrow shafts in one day, or he can pack feathers for thirty arrows, or he can install fifteen arrowheads. Assume: he straightens shafts, packs feathers, and installs arrowheads, all by himself. Tell: How many arrows can he make in one day?
>
> Answer: 8 $\frac{1}{3}$ arrows.[19]

Clearly, judging by this problem, arrow production normally involved the work of at least three specialized artisans, working along a kind of assembly line. It was so unusual for one artisan to make an arrow from start to finish that it became a subject for mathematical calculation. Much more will be said about this precocious division of workshop labor in the following sections.

The statutes and ordinances of the Qin and Han legal codes laid out further guidelines for the officials concerned with the estimation of manpower and materials. Officials were held responsible for their initial estimates of labor and materials and could be fined severely or dismissed if the project ran over budget. The regulations provided normative ratios for the amount of work that different ages and classes of men and women could perform, conversion factors for person-hours expected under different seasonal conditions, and grain-ration tables categorized by worker age, gender, and status.

It is no coincidence that the minor official buried in Zhangjiashan tomb 247 took with him into the grave both an arithmetical primer and a collection of Han legal statutes. After all, he wanted to be well prepared for his future job. Both types of text would be required to correctly estimate the labor and materials needed for work projects in his parallel underworld post, lest he suffer supernatural fines and punishments at the hands of the lords of the underworld.

The complementary traditions of mass production and quality control were a second noteworthy feature of early Chinese production, especially in state-run workshops. Early Chinese techniques of mass production were revealed to scholars only during the twentieth century, through the work of archaeology and epigraphy. It now appears clear that Chinese workshops, since at least the third century BCE, widely employed labor- and material-saving methods that we more commonly associate with the First Industrial Revolution or even with the later industrialist Henry Ford. Fine specialization of labor, standardization of parts, modular construction, inventory accounting, and professional management were instituted on an empire-wide scale during the Qin and Han periods to produce more objects using relatively less material and fewer labor inputs.[20] Specific implementations of these methods to lacquering and stone carving will be described in the following pages.

When an object is made from start to finish under the hands of one master craftsman, he or she comprehends the object and the process as an organic whole. Any flaws in design or execution will be caught and corrected by him or her in the natural process of creation. However, when an object is made on an assembly line, each artisan concentrates on only one step of the process. He or she cannot anticipate larger problems with coherence, symmetry, or overall aesthetic effect that may develop at some point in the disjointed procedure. That is why quality-control procedures to catch defects usually evolve alongside mass-production techniques.

In China, the widespread use of quality-control inspections begins during the mid–Warring States period, in a growing climate of personal and group responsibility. Within the context of the coalescing bureaucratic state, it was viewed that all people within the state, regardless of rank, should be held accountable for their actions, and only those with demonstrated merit should be rewarded. Many of these techniques of administration were later called Legalism and were associated with Shang Yang (d. 338 BCE) and the state of Qin, but contemporary inscriptions demonstrate that they were quite commonly deployed by other states of the period as well.[21] The Qin state should be given credit, however, for perfecting bureaucratic systems of responsibility and refining them to an almost-unimaginable degree. The digest of Qin legal statutes found at Shuihudi reveals an administrative system in which all workshop and factory procedures were supposedly under constant scrutiny. The law required that weights and measures be standardized and regularly checked by traveling inspectors, and that raw materials and finished products be inspected for quality and standardized dimensions.

All along the chain of production, individual state artisans were held personally responsible for their work and were compelled by law and bureaucratic procedure to mark their names and work units on the finished products. Early legal provisions also mandated that artisans in private workshops who wanted to produce lacquer vessels for sale in the market first had to notify local authorities. They then had to inscribe their complete name and the date of manufacture on each completed piece.[22] In state workshops, defective workmanship resulted in monetary fines for free artisans and floggings for convicts and slaves. Good work was also rewarded, but it does seem that the Qin "stick" engineered by Shang Yang and his cohort was far larger than its "carrot." The inscriptions on objects produced in state workshops also aided in the process of material accounting. Each product was given a standardized size and name and was ordered from the factory under a strict quota from the state. Strict accounting of materials within the system allowed for the control of waste and embezzlement.

The Han inherited the Qin system of factories and quality-control inscriptions and maintained it with only minor changes. If anything, they elaborated the tradition, requiring ever-longer quality-control inscriptions on products, some recording as many as eight artisans and five officials. Toward the end of the Han period, however, we start to hear complaints that the quality-control measures at imperial and private workshops were being circumvented through government negligence or outright corruption. Government procurers, in collusion with dishonest factory officials and private artisans, sought to skim money off government contracts by using substandard materials. As we saw in the last chapter, even government-issued weapons were said to be too blunt for soldiers to use at the front.

The government critic Cui Shi's proposed solution to this alarming problem was to suggest that the state enforce the system of punishments for shoddy work that had apparently fallen into disuse. He writes in *Discourses on Administration:*

> The *Monthly Ordinances* (Yueling)[23] says, "Inscribe the objects with the artisans' names in order to ensure their honesty. If their work is not up to par, then they must be punished in order to put an end to such deception." Nowadays, even though the goods are inscribed with the artisans' names, one is not able to reward or punish them. Also, there are so many amnesties proclaimed and redemptions allowed, and those in charge are so lax, that there is no punishment for the artisans to fear. Now, metal weapons and leather articles are of great concern to the state. It is thus fitting to give special attention to these matters and increase the penalties related to [weapons] manufacture. For those who dare to artfully make shoddy goods or engage in corrupt behavior, if they are guilty, do not let them get off with amnesties or redemption fines. Then, officials will indeed be respectful in their duties, and artisans will be careful in their work.[24]

Despite pleas by Neo-Legalists like Cui Shi to reinforce the old system of punishments for shoddy work, the corruption continued to spiral out of control during the death throes of the Han dynasty. Now, let us turn to specific implementations of production strategies and see how two different groups of Han artisans really worked and what methods they used to increase production efficiency.

LACQUERWORK

Their multitude of vessels are carved and polished.
First, [the artisan] incises the imminent stars,
then paints the vermilion bands; colorful and dazzling patterns!
Writhing dragons and serpents are incised between the vermilion bands, while birds and beasts, both strange and wondrous, are scattered among the hills and forests

. . . .

Their lacquer vessels with metal mounts are polished and incised, made by a thousand artisans marshaling a hundred different skills.

—YANG XIONG (53 BCE–18 CE), "SHU CAPITAL RHAPSODY"[25]

Lacquer is a natural, botanically derived polymer that was used in early China to beautify, waterproof, and protect eating vessels, clothing, household objects, and weapons. In the eyes of socially conscious individuals, lacquer vessels were considered portable, displayable wealth and the classiest tableware upon which to eat. They were viewed in much the same way that silver plate was viewed during the Roman Empire or how Chinese porcelain was viewed during the seventeenth and eighteenth centuries in Europe. Qin and Han elite tombs might contain hundreds of lacquer vessels of the highest quality, while tombs of lower-status individuals might still contain one or two inferior-quality examples. According to one contemporary Han account, a fine lacquer cup could cost as much as ten bronze cups.[26] Inscriptions on lacquer objects and recorded prices reveal a broad spectrum of cash values for lacquer objects, primarily based on quality. A single lacquer platter of high quality might cost as much as 1,200 coins, enough money to buy thirty live chickens, while a crudely carved and painted red lacquer cup might still cost a relatively pricey fifty coins in the local market.[27]

Lacquered objects are created through a time-consuming and labor-intensive process that begins with the extraction of sap from the lacquer tree (*Rhus verniciflua*) or one of its botanical cousins.[28] The fluid was collected into containers from small notches cut into the trunk of the tree during the summer months, similar to the extraction processes for latex or maple syrup. The lacquer fluid was kept in airtight containers until final processing to avoid premature desiccation. Once it arrived at the workshop, the fluid was heated to remove most of the remaining water and mixed with additives and mineral pigments in different formulations. Meanwhile, a vessel core was prepared that would accept the lacquer coating. Cores were often chiseled out of cured light woods (chestnut or poplar), but for even lighter, more-expensive pieces they might be fashioned out of ramie fabric lined into a mold.[29]

The lacquering process itself required several days or weeks to complete, because each of the several layers of lacquer could be only microns thick and might take a few days to cure. First, a relatively thick, black priming layer consisting of lacquer fluid mixed with ash was applied to even out the surface irregularities of the core. This was followed by one or more thinner layers of unpigmented lacquer, preparing the ground for painted decoration. Adhering to a millennia-old tradition, the interior ground of vessels was always painted red, while the exterior ground was always painted black. Finally, the ground layers were emblazoned with angular, swirling, or figurative designs, predominantly in red or black lacquer paint. Luxurious pieces might be further adorned with mounts and handles of gilded or silvered bronze.

Pressed by the ever-increasing demand for lacquer vessels and constrained by the time and labor requirements of this production process, lacquer artisans of early imperial China developed a body of tools and techniques to improve precision and increase material and labor efficiency in the workshop while preserving at least the appearance of high-quality, custom manufacture. Today, we would call these techniques of mass production. A remarkably refined division of labor was central to the mass production of lacquer objects in Han China. For example, within the lacquer bureau of the state-run Western Workshop of Shu Commandery, the production process was divided into a number of discrete, sequential steps performed by specialized artisans who rarely worked outside their assigned roles. This division of labor seems to have increased over the course of the first century BCE, until as many as eight distinct artisans were named in the production of one lacquer cup (see chart 3.1). In addition to the regular assembly-line crew, many Han factories also employed several *ronggong* (scattered artisans), odd-job men or women who had no fixed task but instead floated among several different stages of the production process as needed. If you include the unnamed men and women who gathered and processed the lacquer, ground the pigments, and cast the metal mounts, as many as twenty or thirty artisans might have collaborated in making one cup. Han period critics of the profligate use of nonagricultural labor claimed that making a single decorated cup actually consumed the labor of a hundred artisans.[30]

For want of a more appropriate term, we could call this a premodern assembly line.[31] In an assembly line, each worker performs only one step in the production process. This task can be performed quickly and repetitively, without switching locations, tools, or even thought processes. Fine division of labor in an assembly line also avoids wasting the valuable labor of skilled artisans on simple or menial tasks. In an assembly line, there is no time to think, to experiment, or to create. Innovation is suppressed in favor of uniformity and speed.

This sophisticated, seemingly modern division of labor in Han lacquer workshops was encouraged by a fortuitous conjuncture of technological and cultural factors. The first factor was the physical properties of lacquer itself. Unlike a hammered-gold bowl, a lacquer vessel cannot be made in one continuous operation, for each thin layer requires up to two days to dry before the next layer can be applied. Further, some stages in the process are far simpler to complete than others. It requires much less skill to coat a lacquer bowl with primer than to paint the elaborate vermilion designs on the upper layers. These conditions encouraged a divided production process in which each artisan performed the same repetitive operation (one stage or one layer) on a large batch of vessels each day. Skilled labor was conserved for the most elaborate steps, separated from the mass of unskilled or medium-skilled laborers who performed the preliminary steps. A second factor that reinforced this division of labor was a millennia-old workshop tradition inherited from bronze casting that encouraged specialization of workers and standardization of parts. The third factor, especially in state-run workshops, was the influence of the well-entrenched bureau-

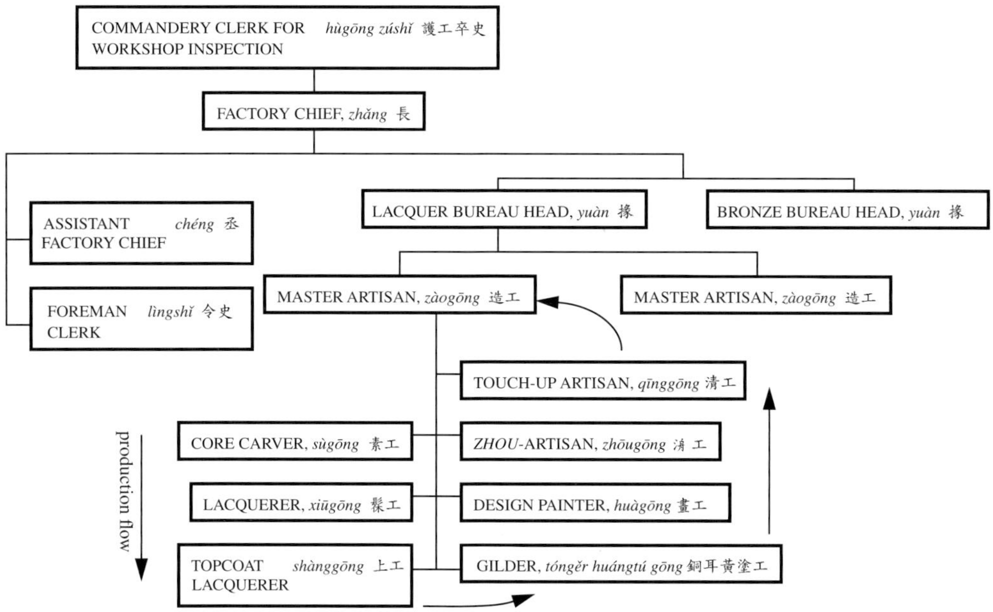

Chart 3.1 *Organizational structure and division of labor at the Western Workshop of Shu Commandery,* 2 BCE

cratic culture that insisted that each person (and each object) have a proper title and defined role.

Standardization of vessel types and sizes was another method used to streamline lacquer production. The same set of tools and molds could be used continually, and parts produced by different workers (such as metal mounts) could fit together on final assembly without adjustments. This also corresponded well with the bureaucratic state's program of standardizing all aspects of life and culture, such as writing, weights and measures, axle widths, and bureaucratic posts. According to the Qin "Statute on Artisans," "all vessels of the same type must have the same dimensions."[32] Though this idealizing statute was obviously impossible to enforce for all manufactured objects, there does appear to have been a high degree of uniformity in the size of lacquer platters and cups from both imperial and private workshops. Han platters came in three standard size groupings. Surviving examples of the most common type all measure within a few millimeters of 27.0 centimeters in diameter. According to their label headers, such platters were constructed to hold a standardized capacity of one *dou* (2000 milliliters) of food.[33] Only by maintaining a uniform diameter on these platters could the gilded-metal mount, which had been produced in another workshop, be guaranteed to fit the rim perfectly.

Uniform dimensions, at least within each workshop, were probably achieved by the use of standardized molds (for fabric-cored vessels) and jigs (for wood-cored vessels). Stacking-cup sets like the one shown in figure 3.19 would have been nearly impossible to produce efficiently without some sort of jig system to ensure standardization of size. It also appears that the wooden cores of large, circular pieces like basins and beer jugs were turned on a wood lathe rather than carved out by hand. On some pieces, one can still see the traces of concentric bands left by the lathe process. Using a lathe not only increased the overall speed of core production by multiplying human labor but also allowed for greater standardization of vessel-wall thickness and overall shape, since the lathe operator probably used calipers or profile gauges.

Potentially, the painting of the decorative designs on a lacquer piece could be very time-consuming, especially if an artisan spent time conceiving of a unique pattern and experimented with it sufficiently to ensure success. However, the demands for more product at competitive prices did not allow him or her this luxury. Lacquer vessels in Qin and Han China were usually decorated using a modular design system in which a limited repertoire of design elements were recombined and resized to produce seemingly infinite variation. This system was utilized in China by artisans working in all media for thousands of years and was described and analyzed by Lothar Ledderose in his book *Ten Thousand Things*.[34]

The early Chinese lacquer artisan needed to decorate certain recurring shapes: roundels of varying size, circular and oval bands, and, more rarely, rectangular panels. Since, by this period, most lacquer painting was still largely ornamental and not strongly representational, the lacquer artisan typically filled these spaces with swirling cloud scrolls, lozenges, zigzags, and other elements derived from textile patterns. Each of these design units could be enlarged, multiplied, rotated, or distorted to fit nearly any space. Though constrained by certain unwritten design conventions as to how motifs could be juxtaposed, it does appear that each artisan was free to combine these standard units into new compositions. This apparent variety, however, masked an inherent regularity. Further, since some modules took less skill to execute than others, the modular system also allowed less-skilled apprentices to paint simpler elements like zigzags, leaving the more demanding cloud scrolls or figural elements to the master.

At the Western Workshop of Shu Commandery and other Han imperial lacquer factories, the increasing yearly demands for more palace tableware eventually suppressed even the limited creativity allowed by the modular design system. Sometime around 30 BCE, one fixed pattern was selected as the official design for all imperial platters (see figure 3.6a), and another one was chosen for all imperial cups (see figures 3.6b–c). State-employed lacquer painters would slavishly copy these patterns for nearly five decades and evidently no longer had any opportunity to shape the design process. In the case of the lacquer cups, amazing uniformity was achieved through a sequence of simple and easily remembered brush strokes which followed the same order, regardless of the design painter named on the cup.

The method by which artisans painted the pattern seen under the handles of these imperial cups highlights another way in which copying techniques were meant to simulate custom manufacture. At first glance, the designs under the left and right handles seem to be complementary mirror images (see figure 3.6c). Close examination reveals, however, that the designs are exactly the same, but that one has been rotated 180° from the other. Apparently, the design painter held the cup in his left hand and completed the design under one handle, then rotated the cup 180° and painted the exact same sequence of strokes under the other handle. Using the same design twice ensured that the painter did not have to master two complex sequences of mirror-reversed strokes. Since the design was complex, and hidden away under the handles, it was unlikely that even the most discerning patron would notice the breach in the rules of symmetry.

One could surmise that the painters at the imperial workshops enforced this design uniformity with official pattern sheets. The stylistic evidence, however, strongly suggests that the painters were using vessels painted months or years previously as visual models on the workbench. When one compares the designs on imperial lacquers over the period from 16 BCE to 14 CE, one notices that the imperial pattern begins to degrade considerably over time, through a process of replicative degeneration, much in the same way that college class handouts will gradually become illegible as a teacher uses last year's handout as the master for copying rather than using the ultimate original. By copying last year's model without referring to an original pattern sheet, the lacquer painters drifted farther and farther from the original idea without realizing it.[35]

At times, the art of the lacquer painter crossed the boundary from rote human automation into the realm of true mechanical replication. First, there is evidence that lacquer painters at the Western Workshop of Shu Commandery used a turntable to execute the red lacquer bands that encircle the interior and exterior of platters. Two pieces of evidence point in this direction. A minute hole is still visible in the very center on some platters. Usually, it was covered up cosmetically by a dollop of red lacquer, as in the platter in figure 3.6a. The hole was probably placed over a pin attached to a turntable. To paint a perfect circle, the artisan needed only to spin the turntable slowly and hold his lacquer-laden brush against the surface of the vessel. A similar device is still used by porcelain painters in English factories to apply bands of gold paint around the rims of plates. A second piece of evidence is the circular bands themselves, flawlessly executed with no sign of the brush having been lifted more than once.

One of the most distinctive decorative flourishes on Qin and Han period lacquers is the small, tight spiral. This versatile design module was deployed in many different zones. Sometimes it appears independently amid larger cloud scrolls to fill up blank space. Other times, it is attached to the ends of scrolls or figural elements to provide visual complexity and balance. On expensive lacquers made for the imperial table or on pieces custom-ordered by elite patrons, these tiny spirals (less than 1 centimeter in diameter) were painted by hand with a delicate, rabbit-hair brush, requiring a steady hand and virtuoso technique (see cup in figure 3.6b). In contrast, on many mediocre-quality lacquers, even some made by second-tier government workshops, the spirals were printed onto the vessel with a transfer stamp (or in some cases

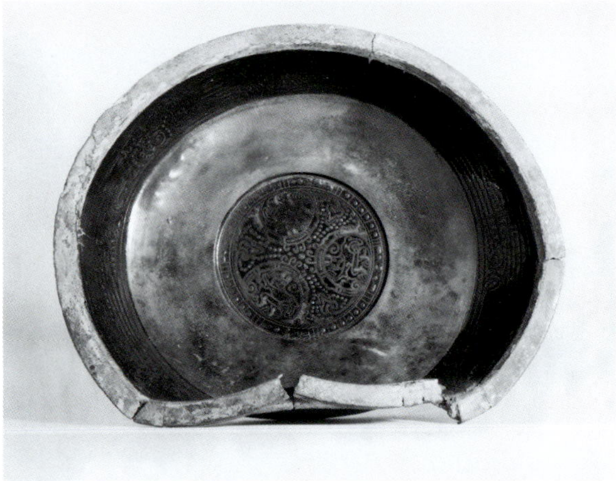

3.6 *Imperial patterns for lacquerware*
(a) *Food platter.* Former Han period, dated 1 CE. Fabric-cored lacquer platter with gilded-bronze mount. D. 27 cm. Asian Art Museum of San Francisco, B62M60. Photo courtesy of Asian Art Museum of San Francisco. This platter was made at the Office of Workmen of Guanghan Commandery and was looted from a Han tomb in the Lelang cemetery, North Korea.

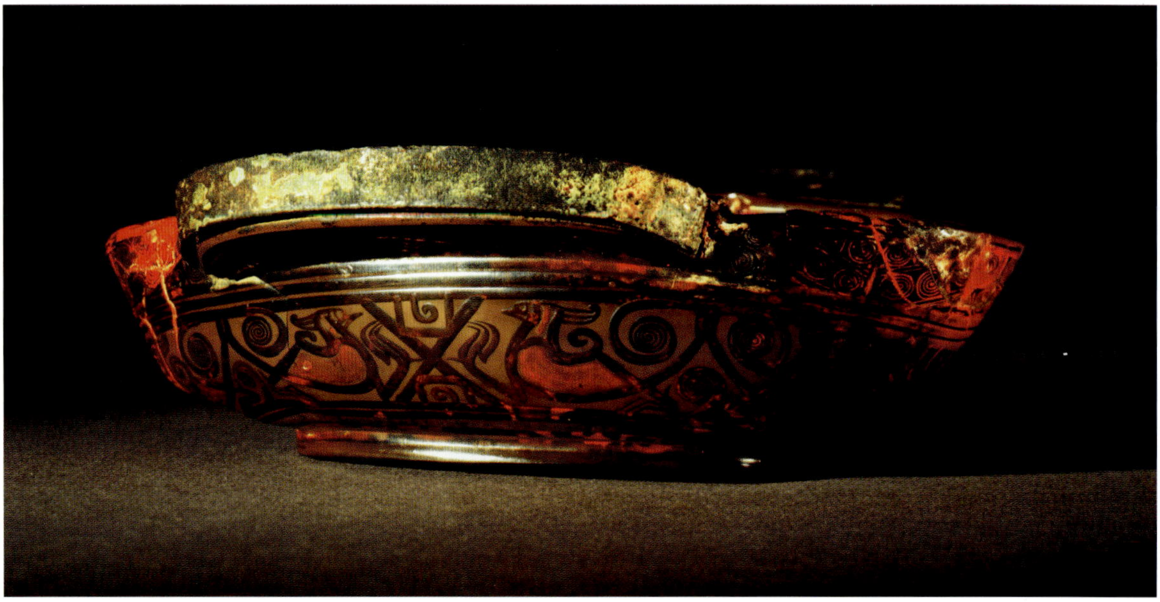

(b) *Beer cup.* Former Han period, dated 4 CE. Lacquer over wood core with gilded-bronze mount. L. 17.7 cm. British Museum, OA 1955.10-24.1. Photo courtesy of Trustees of the British Museum. This cup was made at the Western Workshop of Shu Commandery and was looted from a tomb in the Lelang cemetery around 1937–8.

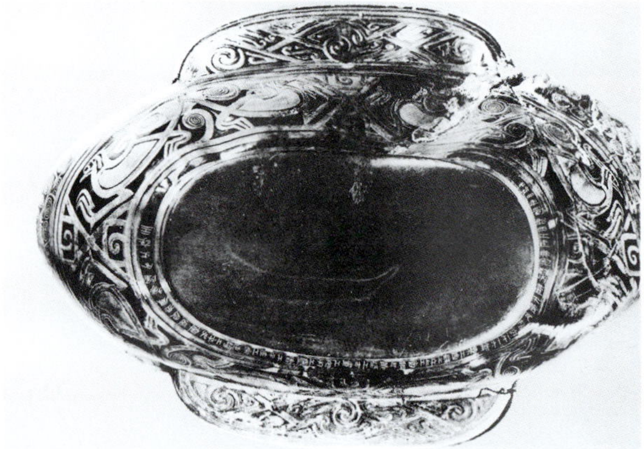

(c) *Underside of* (b). From Umehara, *Shina Kandai,* pl. 22.

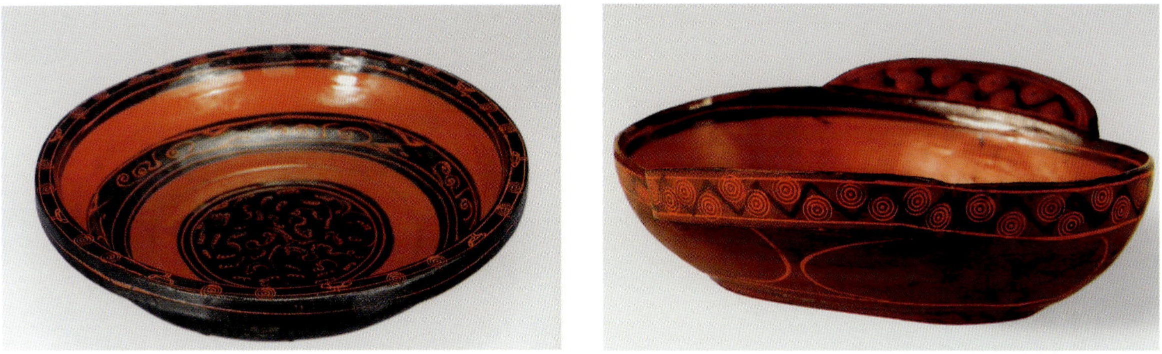

(a) (b)

3.7 *Lacquer vessels with printed spirals*
(a) *Lacquer platter*. Former Han period, ca. 50 BCE–8 CE. Lacquer on wood core. D. 21 cm. H. 4.5 cm. Yangzhou Municipal Museum. Photo courtesy of Yangzhou Municipal Museum. Excavated from a tomb near Yangzhou City, Jiangsu.
(b) *Lacquer eared cup*. Former Han period, ca. 50 BCE–8 CE. Lacquer on wood core. L. 15.7 cm. H. 5.6 cm. Nanjing Municipal Museum. Photo courtesy of Nanjing Municipal Museum. Excavated from a tomb in Yizheng County, Jiangsu.

a stencil). Printing of spirals leaves several diagnostic traces. Either all the spirals on a piece are perfectly identical or a portion of the stamp fails to transfer, leaving the image of a partially eaten pie (see figure 3.7). Using transfer stamps for a small but intricate portion of the design served to streamline one of the most skill-demanding and time-consuming stages of the painting process while retaining the overall appearance of quality, custom workmanship. Transfer patterns were never used for the larger, more obvious parts of the design. The varied surface contours of different vessel types would have made this impractical with the contemporary technology. We know that transfer printing was already widely used in Han textile production by the second century BCE to simulate the much more time-consuming art of embroidery.[36] Transfer stamps were also ubiquitous in the mass production of hollow, decorated bricks for tombs.

STONE FUNERARY MONUMENTS

Exhausting their savings, [An Guo's family] hired famous masons from Gaoping, named Wang Shu, Wang Jian, and Jiang Hu, to build this small [offering] hall. Tirelessly they carted the unhewn stones from a small hill southwest of the county town Yangshan. They cut, ground, and polished the slabs. They measured and built the hall. On the eaves and outer walls, they carved different designs. And [inside the hall] they engraved decorations and pictorial scenes: interlocking dragons and winding serpents; fierce tigers stretching forward their heads, gazing into the distance; black apes ascending heights; lions and bears roaring, strewn everywhere like clouds. There are towers and pavilions of unequal heights;

great processions of chariots set forth. Above, there are clouds and immortals; below, figures of filial piety, excellent virtue, and benevolence. Superiors are dignified, and their attendants are respectful. Inferiors are obedient and look agitated as well as joyous. For many months, the craftsmen worked on this hall, expending an incalculable amount of labor. The hall cost 27,000 coins.

EPITAPH ON A STONE FROM THE OFFERING HALL DEDICATED TO AN GUO, FEBRUARY 2, 158 CE[37]

The use of stone for monumental sculpture and buildings was never central to Chinese art or architecture before the arrival of Buddhism. However, as early as the Han period, stone had become a popular medium in some regions for lining tombs and for constructing aboveground funerary monuments. This cultural phenomenon reached its pinnacle in the century from about 84 CE to 184 CE[38] in several areas of northeast China and in the Chengdu Plain to the southwest.[39] Above all other regions, the stone-carving tradition of the Shandong Peninsula area was most prominent. In fact, by one count, 60 percent of all extant decorated stones datable to the Han period come from this region.[40] Why this one area developed such a market for stone funerary monuments has much to do with an intertwining of geography and cultural history. The low hills of the area are filled with easily quarried limestone, transportable on a network of waterways. Stone monuments also have a deep history in this area of northeast Asia, with the stones themselves sometimes treated as objects of worship.[41] Lastly, the area was a zone of concentrated population and wealth from agriculture and manufacturing, with few equals in the Han Empire.

By analyzing the working traces remaining on carved stones and aided by clues from a few Han period inscriptions,[42] we can now reconstruct much of the process of carving stone funerary monuments during the Han.[43] Unfortunately, this reconstruction is still sketchy and pales in comparison to the more complete picture we have of the process and organization of New Kingdom (1550–1070 BCE) Egyptian tomb decoration.[44] By necessity, it is a composite sketch that is also somewhat normative, subsuming regional workshop variation and chronological developments.

The preferred stone for carving, in the Shandong area at least, was a hard, fine-grained limestone quarried from the surrounding hills.[45] Even today, the area remains a bustling center for limestone quarries, limekilns, and stone-carving workshops. Han period inscriptions claim that only the finest, illustrious stone materials (*mingshi*) were used, and that they were "free of veins or brown streaks." They were always said to be quarried from the south-facing slopes of hills found to the south or southwest.[46] It is unclear looking at modern maps precisely which limestone-bearing hills were intended by these phrases, but the actual quarry location was probably less important than the auspicious connotations expressed by the figurative location.

To extract limestone blocks from the hillside, a mason wielded a heavy iron sledgehammer (*chui*), whose head alone could weigh five to seven kilograms, and directed

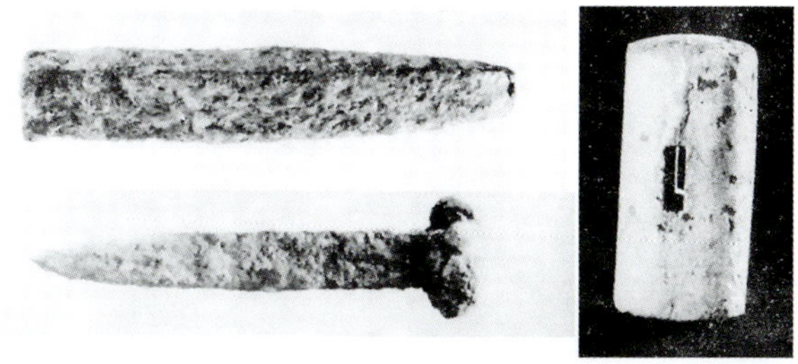

3.8 *Flat-bladed and pointed chisels (left) and hammerhead (right).* Qin period, ca. 209 BCE. Iron. From Qin Yong Keng Kaogudui, pls. 12.5, 13.1, 13.2. Excavated from the stone-dressing site near the First Emperor of Qin's necropolis at Lintong, Shaanxi.

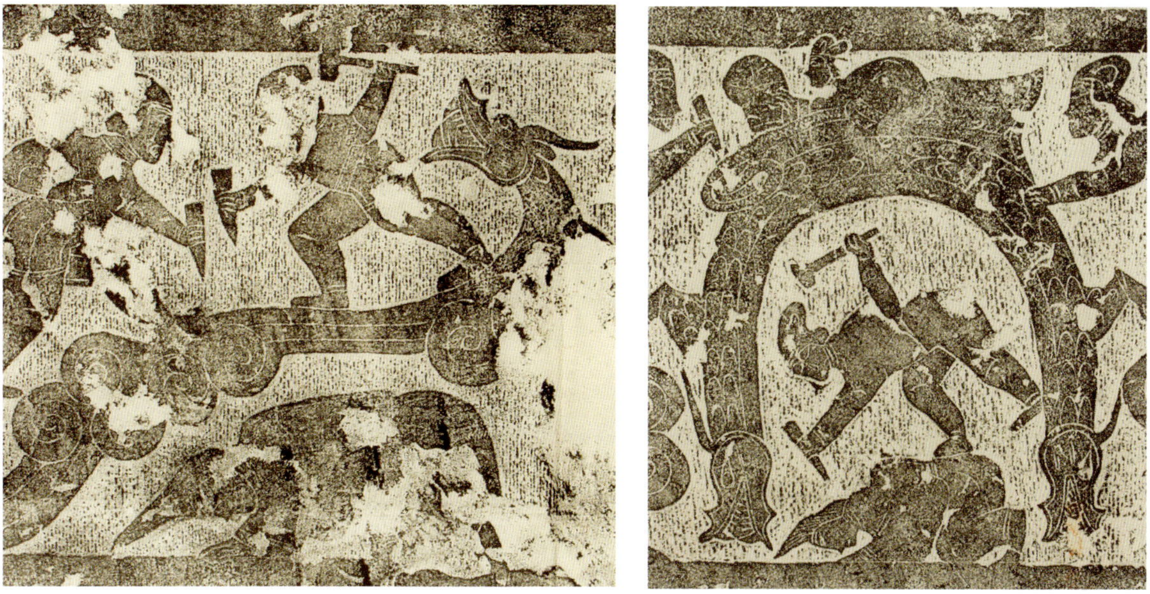

(a) (b)

3.9 *Servants of the Thunder God wielding sledgehammers and iron chisels.* (a) Detail of ceiling stone of Offering Hall 1 at Wuzhaishan, Jiaxiang County, Shandong. (b) Detail of ceiling stone of Offering Hall 2 at Wuzhaishan. Latter Han period, ca. second century CE. Ink-on-paper rubbings. Princeton University Art Museum. Far Eastern Seminar Collection, 2002-307.16, 2002-307.31. Photos by Bruce M. White.

it at a pointed chisel (*zan*). Once a slot was opened up in the rock, he forced one or more iron wedges (*juan*) into the crevice and pounded them forcefully to cleave off a huge chunk of limestone. Archaeologists have uncovered numerous examples of these tools from quarries and stone-dressing sites (see figure 3.8).[47] Though we possess no contemporary depiction showing quarrymen at work, the stone carvers who decorated the offering halls found at the Wuzhaishan site in Jiaxiang County, Shandong, cleverly alluded to their own profession when they depicted the minions of the Thunder God (Lei Gong) wielding hammer and chisel to smite the heads of thunderstruck earth-dwellers (see figure 3.9).

Once quarried, the stones were probably at least crudely dressed near the pit before transport to the masons' workshop. Judging by working traces remaining on the

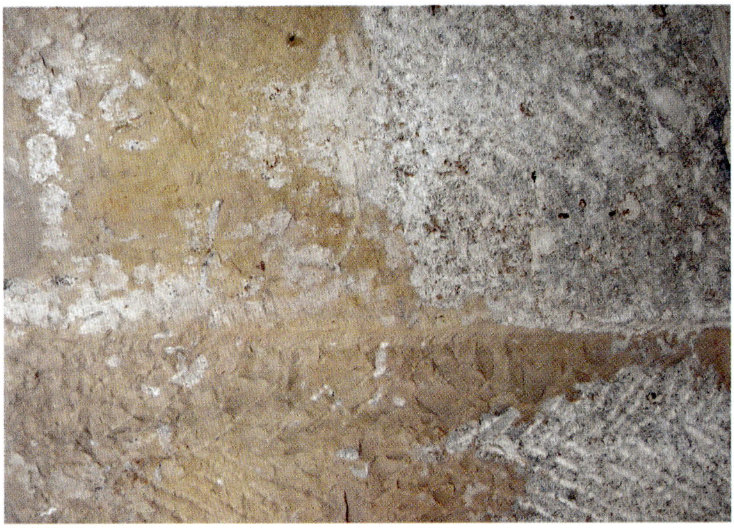

3.10 *Working traces on the undecorated side of a pictorial stone.* Latter Han period, ca. second century CE. Mencius Temple Museum, Zoucheng City, Shandong. Photo by Anthony Barbieri-Low, June 22, 2002.

undecorated backs of stones from Shandong (see figure 3.10), it appears that a mason worked down the surface of the stone by chiseling numerous parallel trenches, first in one direction and then in rows roughly perpendicular to these, enabling him to easily hack off the stone nodules at the intersections of the furrows. This process continued, using finer and finer chisels, until the desired slab thickness was achieved. In some geographic regions, this distinctive cross-hatching was not completely smoothed during the finishing of the decorated face but was retained as a background texture to highlight the pictorial carvings. The masons counted the stones using the measure word *tou* (head), saying they completed so many *tou* of stones.[48]

The next stage in the process was to move the stone slabs from the quarry to the workshop site for planing and decoration. Stone is difficult to transport great distances overland, especially in an era of unpaved roads, but one Han inscription suggests that the stones for a particular monument were indeed bound up and carted overland.[49] Conveniently, the Shandong area was crisscrossed by numerous rivers and canals, making waterborne transport far more efficient. The stones from a Han tomb in present-day Liangshan County, weighing more than eight thousand kilograms, were quarried from a source identified by present-day local carvers as being twenty-four kilometers north of the site.[50] Though overland transportation of such a mass of stone would have been feasible, reconstructed maps of the area suggest that there was indeed a river course running from the quarry toward the tomb site.[51]

Once at the workshop, the stones were squared off with the aid of a carpenter's square (*ju*) (see figure 3.11, object in left figure's hand), given a final dressing (*zhuoli*), and ground smooth (*mozhi*).[52] A few mason's titles carved on stones from a Han prince's tomb suggest that the workers who performed this task were called *zhishi* (stone levelers).[53] Usually, just one or two surfaces of a given stone would be worked

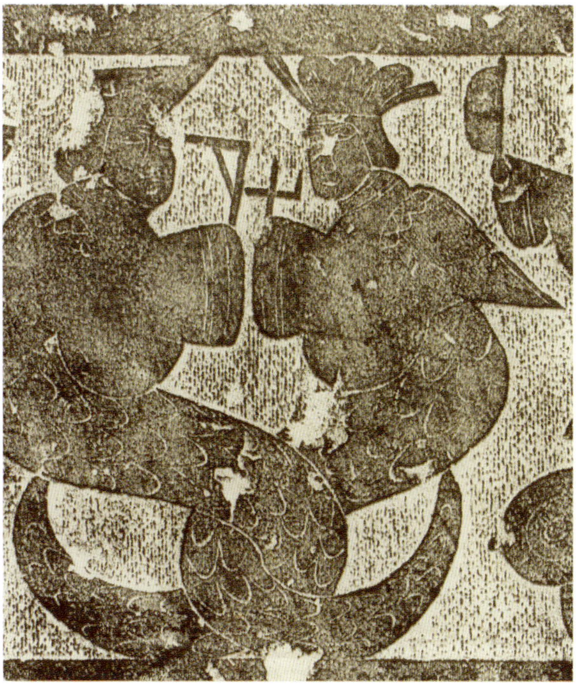

3.11 *Fuxi holding the carpenter's square and Nüwa holding the compass.* Detail of Offering Hall 1 at Wuzhaishan, Jiaxiang County, Shandong. Latter Han period, ca. second century CE. Ink-on-paper rubbing. Princeton University Art Museum. Far Eastern Seminar Collection, 2002-307.17. Photo by Bruce M. White.

completely smooth, only those that were to be exposed to view in the final monument. The remaining surfaces were left with the rough, quarry finish (see figure 3.10). It appears from a fragmentary marginal inscription on one stone that Han carvers referred to the face that carried the decoration as the *biao* (exposed surface).[54]

After the stones were dressed, the masons called in the master draftsman (*huashi*). On the inscribed doorpost from the stone offering hall dedicated to Xiang Tajun, a former official of Donge County who died in 150 CE, the master draftsman is named as a certain Master Dai Sheng from Gaoping Town. Master draftsmen like Dai Sheng would compose the pictorial program, divide the surface into registers, and lay down the borders, figures, and other pictorial elements using brush and black ink. Some stones still display traces of these original drafts (see figure 3.12, center bottom).[55] Using the master's sketch as a guide, sculptors would then carve the pictorial groups and decorative borders into low relief, processes described in two inscriptions as "engraving the ornaments" (*diaowen*) and "chiseling the illustrations" (*kehua*).[56] In some stylistic traditions this involved lowering the stone ground around each pictorial group, while in others it entailed lowering the pictorial surface relative to a striated background. Also at this stage, smooth, rectangular scene labels were prepared for later, optional use by more literate artisans.

Once the pictorial surface was separated from the ground, a line carver would finish the scene by engraving lines on the figures, indicating facial features and clothing. An examination of the rubbings from the Wuzhaishan site in Shandong demon-

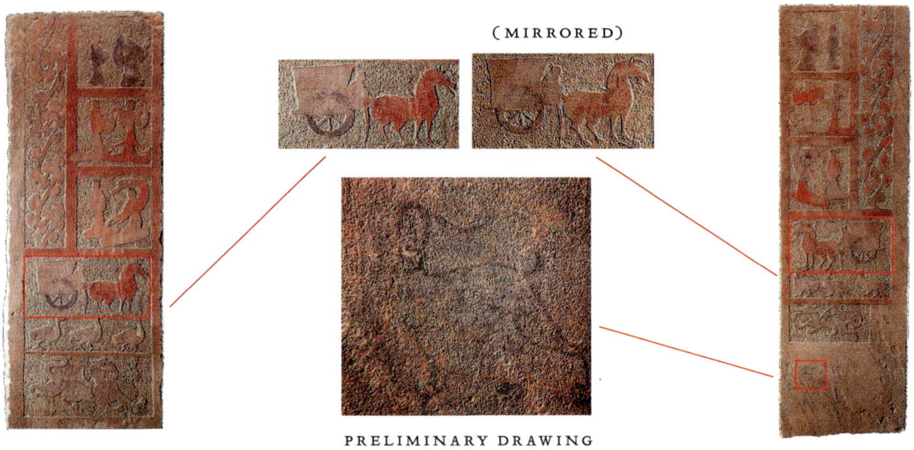

3.12 *Tomb doorposts.* Artist's preliminary sketch at lower right expanded at center bottom; horse-drawn carriage on right doorpost mirror-reversed to center middle for comparison with identical image on left doorpost. Latter Han period, ca. second century CE. Carved limestone with polychrome pigments. Shaanxi Provincial Archaeological Institute. Photo courtesy of Shaanxi Provincial Archaeological Institute. Excavated from tomb 1 at Dabaodang, Shaanxi.

strates that some facial features were executed distinctively on each of the three reconstructed stone chambers from the site. On each monument, noses of figures in three-quarter profile were carved in one consistent fashion, suggesting that only one line carver finished the facial details for each structure and, by extension, that the three halls were each made by a different work crew (see figure 3.13).

The last stages of the process began with moving the decorated stones to the cemetery site for final assembly. Then, final adjustments could be made to the mortise-and-tenon joinery for gabled roofs and to the door pivots for tombs. If desired, labels could now be filled with appropriate captions or epitaphs. In many regions of Han China, the tomb artisans completed the project by adding brightly colored painted accents to the carvings using black, red, blue, orange/brown, and white mineral pigments.[57] The paint originally applied to most stones has long since fallen away, but the brightly colored traces found on recently excavated examples should serve as a reminder that the classical starkness of Han pictorial stones might be as much an illusion as the once-axiomatic classical whiteness of Greek statuary and architecture (see figure 3.12).

Further analyzing the organization of this process, it appears from inscriptions that a funerary-monument work crew was supervised by two types of master artisan: one or more master masons, called *shi* (master) or *shigong* (stone [master] artisan), who coordinated the quarrying and carving, and one or more master draftsmen (*huashi*), who laid out the composition and executed the preliminary sketches.[58] A similar work flow and division of labor was seen among Egyptian New Kingdom

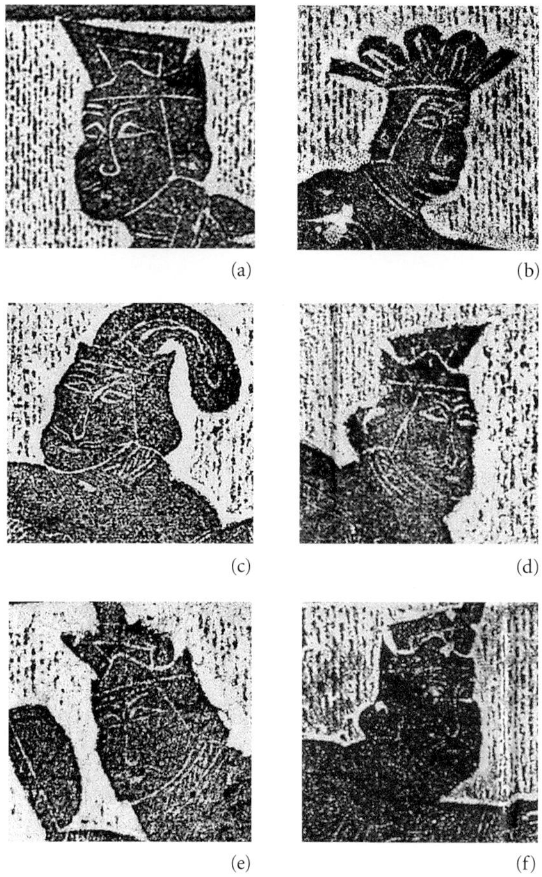

3.13 *Noses in three-quarter profile.* A comparison of facial details from Offering Halls 1–3, Wuzhaishan, Jiaxiang County, Shandong. Latter Han period, ca. second century CE. Ink-on-paper rubbings (details). Princeton University Art Museum. Far Eastern Seminar Collection. Photos by Bruce M. White.
Offering Hall 1 (nose as fishhook shape, hooking away from body)
(a) 2002-307.1
(b) 2002-307.2
Offering Hall 2 (nose as teardrop shape)
(c) 2002-307.18
(d) 2002-307.19
Offering Hall 3 (nose as fishhook shape, hooking toward the body)
(e) 2002-307.35
(f) 2002-307.36

tomb artisans. On those work crews in the Valley of the Kings, the preliminary draftsmen ranked somewhat higher than the sculptors or painters but below the crew foremen and scribes.[59] On Han work crews, precedence is harder to discern, yet since the master masons were listed before the draftsmen in one detailed roster inscription, this might indicate the master mason's overall control of the team and not just his temporal position in the production process. Under these master artisans, toiled several apprentices (*di*), who probably carried out the more repetitive or onerous tasks. Their numbers are included in the worker totals found in inscriptions, but their names are rarely given.[60] Such a division of labor into carvers/draftsmen and skilled/unskilled categories enabled the valuable labor of the most skilled masters to be efficiently employed, allowing greater profit.

Inscriptions reveal a few clues concerning the length of time required to complete a stone offering hall. Unfortunately, this evidence is often buried beneath litanies of expended labor, exaggerated for rhetorical effect. Xiang Tajun, the former official from Donge County, died in 150 CE at the age of ninety, and his wife died the following year at the age of eighty-six. Their children began to construct an offering hall in 152 CE, but it was reportedly not completed until two years later, on August 23, 154 CE

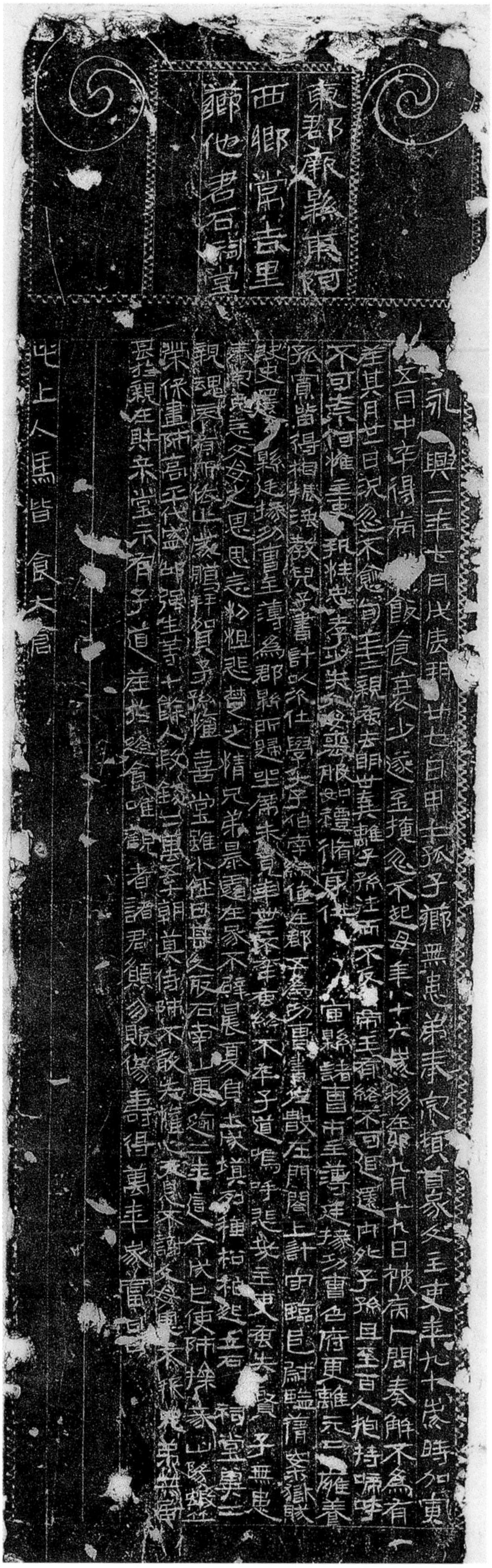

3.14 *Inscription on doorpost from offering hall of Xiang Tajun.* Latter Han period, dated August 23, 154 CE. Ink-on-paper rubbing. H. 120 cm. W. 18 cm. Palace Museum, Beijing. Photo courtesy of Palace Museum, Beijing.

(see figure 3.14).[61] The inscription on the offering hall of An Guo, a clerk from Xu County, extravagantly claims that his monument took "many months" and required "an incalculable amount of labor"[62] (see epigraph to this section). From the dates mentioned in the inscription, it appears the offering hall was actually completed about eleven months after An Guo's death.[63] An offering hall dedicated to a certain Huan Chan was completed a little over eight months after his death. It is unclear, however, how long after his decease that his two younger brothers commissioned the monument.[64] An offering hall found near Qufu, Shandong, took only a little over one month to complete.[65]

We also have incomplete information regarding the number of artisans typically summoned for a project. In the Xiang Tajun inscription, it appears that four master artisans are mentioned by name (two masons, one draftsman, and one other), but more than ten men were said to be involved. In the An Guo inscription, three artisans are clearly named (Wang Shu, Wang Jian, and Jiang Hu), with the possible inclusion of two others. For comparison, the stones for one Latter Han prince's tomb were quarried and dressed by over 120 masons.[66] Clearly, the division of labor suggested above allowed the most skilled masters to perform their work expeditiously, earn their commission, and move on to the next job. They likely were not present for the entire duration of the project.

Precision and Laborsaving Devices

Like their lacquering comrades, stone carvers and draftsmen in Han China developed a suite of tools and techniques to increase precision, economize materials and skilled labor, and maintain a baseline level of quality. First, it is apparent that the preliminary sketches for carriage wheels were laid out using a compass (*gui*) to ensure rapid, perfect circularity. The middle of the hub often reveals an indentation where the compass point was anchored. In addition, the diameters of all wheels on a single stone are identical, even on wheels "receded" farthest into the background. The use of the compass appears to have broadened over time, for on second-century carvings from central Shandong, even the rumps of horses and the outlines of people were rendered as perfect arcs with a compass.[67] Compasses were clearly used to execute the simple, repetitive hanging-curtain, jade-ring, and coin-filled border patterns that separate pictorial registers.[68] No actual Han compass has yet been unearthed, but the stone carvers themselves frequently illustrated the tool held in the hands of the creatrix Nüwa (see figure 3.11, right). Fuxi, Nüwa's consort, carries the carpenter's square, another tool vital to masons and draftsmen. While draftsmen could use a carpenter's square to lay down short segments, lines longer than a foot were apparently drawn using a tool similar to the *modou* of later Chinese craftsmen. This was basically an inked string, drawn taught and snapped down to produce a black line.[69]

Stencils carrying entire design units were apparently also used by stone carvers to construct the pictorial scenes on some monuments, especially those on *que* (pillar-gates) and tomb doors (see figure 3.12).[70] One can trace several lines of evidence pointing to stencil use. First, on the few stones where traces of preliminary sketches remain, the painted line is sometimes composed of distinct segments of unmodulated width, unlike the spontaneous line of an original brush painting. Occasionally, one even sees evidence that a brush has slipped suddenly out of the bounds of the stencil. Second, motifs produced multiple times from stencils measure precisely the same size.[71] Finally, stenciled motifs often overstep the bounds of scene registers, leaving a hoof or tail dangling in a border area. Some stencils apparently held entire compositions, while others just contained an individual motif. Based on analogy to contemporary practice, Chinese archaeologists speculate that stencils were likely made of coarse fabric or thin wooden sheets. Ultimately, the use of stencils in stone carving derives from the older tradition of stamping decoration on hollow tomb bricks. Judging by current evidence, the pervasive use of stencils appears to have been limited to carvers working in western Shanxi and northern Shaanxi. Stencils economize on the skilled labor of master draftsmen, ensuring exact replication and mirror-reversal at the cost of flexibility of composition and spontaneity of execution.

Far more common than the deployment of stencils was the use of patterns. Reliance on patterns can be inferred from the structure of the images themselves, even though no actual examples of patterns survive. The patterns probably consisted of line drawings of individual motifs or whole compositions brushed onto semitransparent silk or paper (fairly well available by the second century CE). The images appear to have served merely as guidelines to the draftsman and, unlike stencils, were not slavishly traced onto the stone. However, the draftsmen do appear to have often copied the image onto stone using the same scale as the pattern. One sometimes finds body parts extending beyond the register lines or necks ducking awkwardly to avoid an implied ceiling.[72] The semitransparent material of the pattern would have also made it possible to flip the pattern over and use a mirror-reversed image to better suit a particular composition.

To see how patterns might have been used to construct a scene, consider the two representations of wheelwrights' shops in figure 3.15. In figure 3.15b, we see at the left a wheelwright bent over a wheel segment, assisted by his wife, who stands behind him. To their right is a scene of brewing, in which an imbibing laborer, clad only in trousers, is supervised by an armed official. It is a symmetrical composition, centered on the wheel hub, with ample remaining open space. In the other version (figure 3.15a), the draftsman was allotted less space, and changes had to be made. He has moved the wheelwright to the middle and mirror-reversed and shifted his wife to a spot in front of him. The incomplete wheel has been lifted out of the way to a spot on the wall, with the unfinished portion rotated to face the wheelwright. The beer maker has also been mirror-reversed, and his supervisor has disappeared. Due to the tight quarters, the beer maker's table now overlaps the leg of the wheelwright. Clearly, these alterations allowed the same composition to be adapted to the narrower register of the second scene. Reconfigurable pattern modules made such accommodation easier.

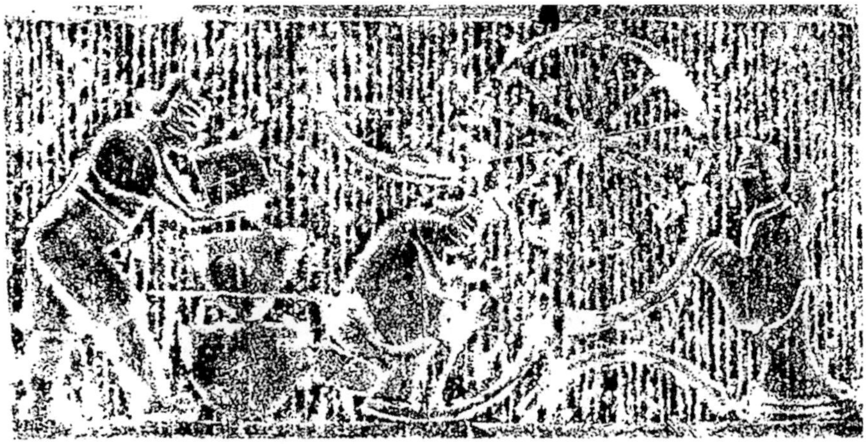

(a)

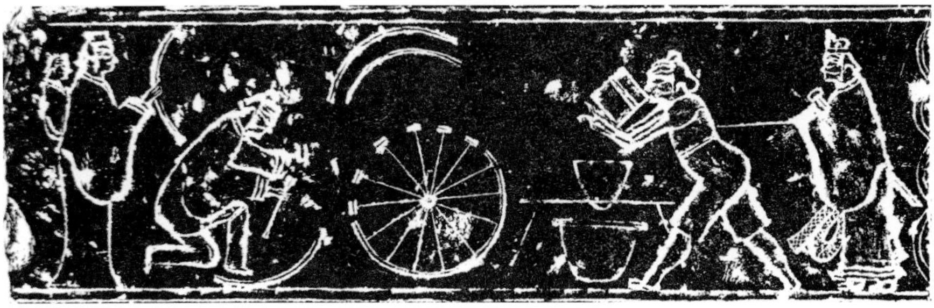

(b)

3.15 *Wheelwrights' shops*
(a) Latter Han period, ca. first century CE. Ink-on-paper rubbing. W. 43.5 cm. Shandong Provincial Museum. From Chavannes, *La sculpture sur pierre*, pl. 43. Stone found at Liu Village, Jiaxiang County, Shandong. (b) Latter Han period, ca. first century CE. Ink-on-paper rubbing. National Museum of Chinese History, Beijing. Photo courtesy of Shandong Fine Arts Publishing House. Stone found at Hongshan Village, Jiaxiang County, Shandong.

Notice, however, that the corresponding figures in the two scenes are in no way identical tracings, for one can detect many subtle differences between them. Both sets of images, however, derive ultimately from the same pattern sheets.

Pattern sheets were likely one of the means through which stone-carving traditions were perpetuated. The founding master of a particular tradition might have disseminated his style among his disciples by allowing them to copy his patterns. When an apprentice later founded his own workshop, he might take the patterns with him. Modifications to the transmitted designs or the addition of stock motifs purloined from other traditions would serve to differentiate this new master draftsman's style from that of his teacher.

Customizable Prefabrication

Imperial and royal tombs were unique, custom-designed creations, built for patrons with very deep pockets. Moderately wealthy families in the provinces endeavored to convey some of the appearance of lavish productions without expending the unattainable levels of cash. Stone carvers in North China accommodated these needs with a system of customizable prefabrication that allowed most elements of a monument to be constructed and decorated off-site using standardized modules. Within this system, the patron was given certain customizable options, much as we experience in a modern car showroom, to make his monument distinctive and give it the *appearance* of a unique artistic creation.

Standardized pictorial scenes, built up from stencils and pattern sheets, were usually confined to a single stone. Generic types included scenes of carriage and horse processions, the Queen Mother of the West (Xiwangmu), food preparation, entertainers and musical ensembles, stories of filial piety, and many more. These scenes were no more individual creations of an artist than are the parts of a Toyota Corolla. Few things demonstrate the modularity of the carved blocks better than the boundaries of decorative borders. A popular border in Shandong is a multilayered combination of wavelike curtains and diamond-shaped lozenges (see figure 3.16). To give the impression that the decoration was seamless from block to block, carvers usually tried to end the decorative band at the midsection of a lozenge and the exact crest or trough of a wave. Sometimes, however, a miscommunication could lead to the slight misregistrations one sees in figure 3.16.

Another example of customizable prefabrication can be seen in the so-called pavilion scene that adorns the rear walls of many stone offering halls from Shandong (see figure 3.17). This scene has been subjected to innumerable interpretations over the years, but the one that is most convincing reads it as an homage scene to the male deceased.[73] Younger male figures, interpreted as the deceased's sons or grandsons, kowtow in reverence before him, while sequestered women, interpreted as his mourning wife and concubines, are seated upstairs. It is striking to note that versions of this scene made in the same workshop, or at least within the same tradition, portray anywhere from one to six mourning females seated in the upper level.[74] This makes perfect sense, since men of different levels of wealth and social standing could take any number of concubines in addition to one primary wife.[75] I would argue that the stone carvers anticipated this variable situation and prefabricated at least six versions of the homage scene. When placing an order, the patron would specify the number of widows, and the appropriate, already-completed stone would be pulled from stock.

For another case of how prefabricated modules could be customized, consider the use of scene labels. Many carved pictorial scenes were supplied in the workshop with spaces for labels near major figures that might be identified as specific individuals from myth, history, or the deceased's social world. For example, the carriage and horse processions commonly seen along the lowest and highest registers of offering halls and on the lintels of tombs often reveal a small rectangular space near each vehicle or mounted rider. Later, these could be filled in with a generic title of a member in the funeral cortège or with a specific title that the deceased individual held

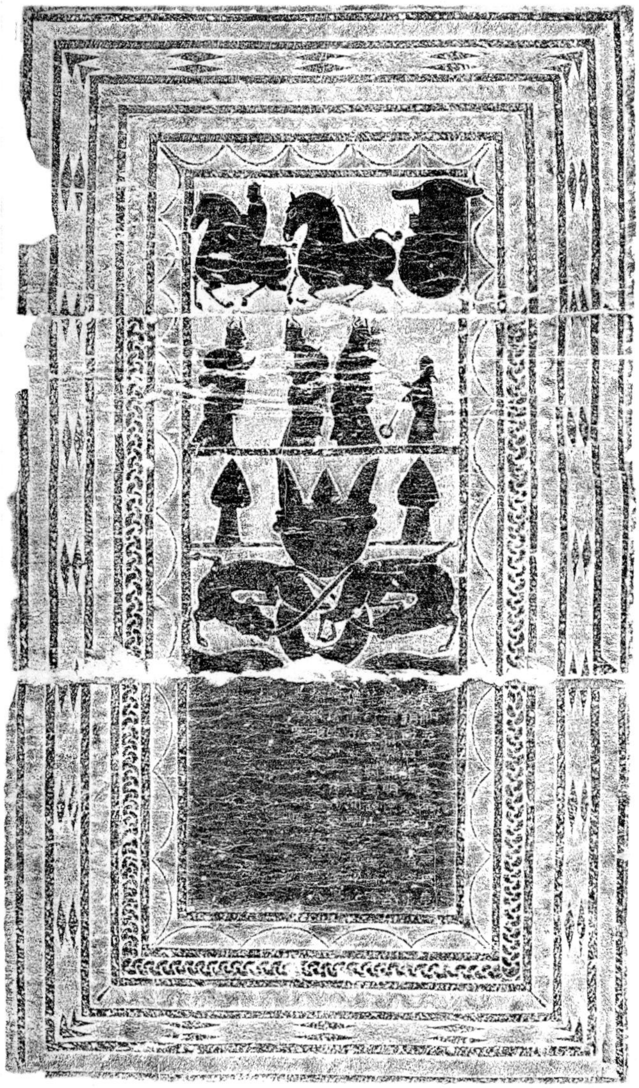

3.16 *Three stacked blocks.* Latter Han period, dated April 21, 147 CE. Ink-on-paper rubbings. From north face of western pillar-gate, Wuzhaishan, Jiaxiang County, Shandong. Photo courtesy of Shandong Fine Arts Publishing House.

during his career. Leaving the labels blank during preassembly enabled the artisans to make only one version of the procession scene. Later, probably at the cemetery site during final assembly, the patron could request that the labels be filled with specific textual content, customized to the situation of the deceased.

Though figures were often provided with such labeling space, many of these spaces were not permanently inscribed with text and appear blank to us today.[76] All the blank labels might be a by-product of the division of labor. According to the reconstruction of Lai Fei, to make an inscription, the text was first written in red ink and only later carved into the stone.[77] It is possible that the many "empty" Han labels may have undergone the first stage of painted calligraphy, yet only a few were selected to receive a permanent, final carving. It also appears that the artisans responsible for writing the captions were different from the draftsmen who laid out the scenes. In some

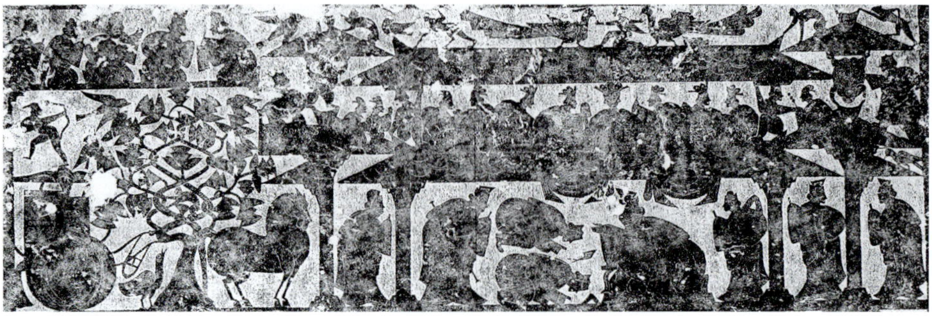

(a) ONE-WIDOW HOMAGE SCENE

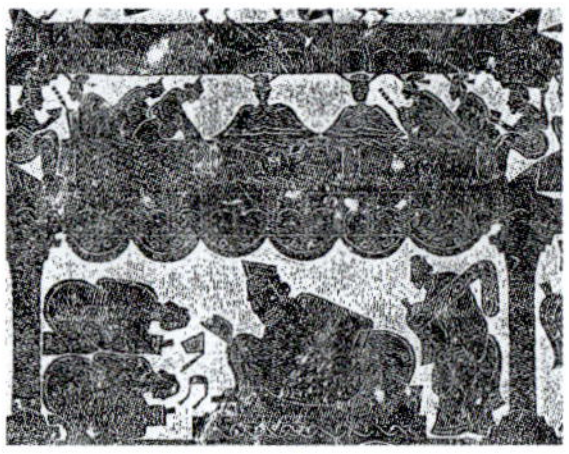

(b) TWO-WIDOW SCENE

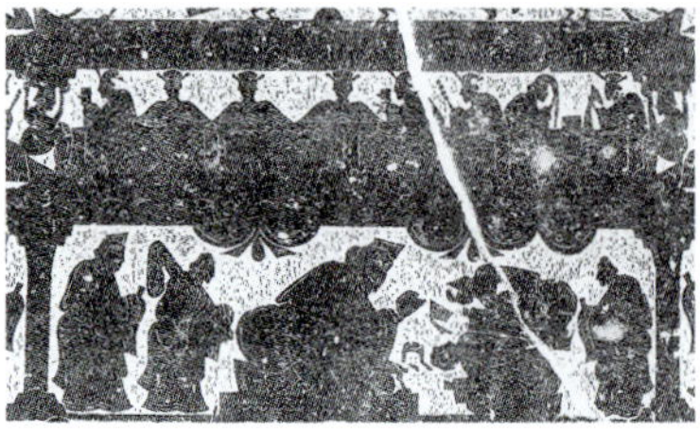

(c) THREE-WIDOW SCENE

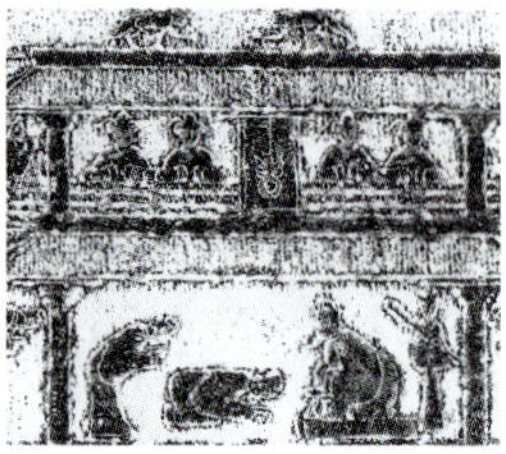

(d) FOUR-WIDOW SCENE

3.17 *Homage scenes from stone offering halls in Shandong.* Latter Han period, ca. second century CE. Ink-on-paper rubbings.
(a) Detail of Offering Hall 2 from Wuzhaishan, Jiaxiang County, Shandong. Princeton University Art Museum. Far Eastern Seminar Collection, 2002-307.24. Photo by Bruce M. White.
(b) Shandong Stone Carvings Art Museum. Stone excavated from Songshan, Jiaxiang County. From Zhu Xilu, *Jiaxiang,* pl. 62.
(c) Shandong Stone Carvings Art Museum. Stone excavated from Songshan, Jiaxiang County. From Zhu Xilu, *Jiaxiang,* pl. 64.
(d) Shandong Stone Carvings Art Museum. Stone excavated from Wulaowa, Jiaxiang County. From Zhu Xilu, *Jiaxiang,* pl. 90.

cases, a label writer misunderstood the story intended by the draftsman and labeled a scene incorrectly.[78]

For now, let us leave these clever and efficient stone masons and return to them in chapter 4, when we will look at their marketing techniques and geographic mobility.

THE WORKSHOP LABOR ENVIRONMENT

No special claim can be made that artisans in early imperial China toiled any harder than workers from the other three occupational classes. Elite authors sometimes describe for us the backbreaking toil of the peasant farmer or reveal at length the harried and sometimes hazardous careers of bureaucratic officials. Out of jealousy and political interest, they also claim that merchants expended little real effort but could reap huge profits. Few texts, however, tell us what it was like to work as an artisan in early imperial China.

The working hours of artisans would have been determined by their conditions of employment and the season of the year. Since artisans employed in imperial factories had to be supervised at all times by factory officials, one might presume that they worked the same hours as their supervisors. Like other bureaucrats during the Han, factory officials were probably given one day to rest out of each five-day period. This was called the day for "rest and washing one's hair" (*xiumu*) and was provided for by Han administrative law.[79] Since bureaucrats usually lived and slept in their offices (or in dormitories) during the week, this was the only opportunity to visit their families at home. Thus, we may infer that free and conscripted artisans at imperial factories might have also been allowed one day out of five to rest and might possibly have been allowed to return home to visit nearby family members.

Factory officials, and presumably state artisans as well, were also given certain festival holidays off each year, including the Winter Solstice, the Summer Solstice, the Day of Concealment (Fu), the Lunar New Year, and the La New Year.[80] By Tang times, the number of official festival holidays had increased to fifty-three days per year, though the "weekend" rest had been reduced to one day in ten.

The length of each workday for an artisan was often determined by the duration of daylight. The Qin statutes and the Tang statutes both recognized that the length of the workday, and thus the size of the work quota, for the winter months should be shorter than that for the summer months.[81] Artisans could, of course, have worked by lamplight, but the cost of the oil, the dangers of fire, and the diminishing returns from fatigued laborers argues against this as a widespread practice in imperial factories.

Private workshops presumably could maintain whatever working hours they desired. Some activities, however, were restricted by the time of day. For example, if artisans operated a stall in the official marketplace to sell their wares, they would have to wait until noon for the drum of the market tower to sound and the trading day to begin. The market remained open until just before sunset each day. We may assume that artisans occupied themselves with manufacturing and preparations before and after these times, but the sanctioned business hours were sharply restricted in imperial China until at least the ninth century.[82]

The products and conduct of artisans in imperial factories were required to be under constant inspection and scrutiny, and violations could result in significant fines or corporal punishment. For example, according to the Qin statutes, if the inspected products of an imperial workshop were judged poor (*dian*), all the officials and artisans at the factory were to be fined on a sliding scale according to their position in the factory hierarchy. The factory head would be fined the value of one suit of armor; his assistant and the foreman of the individual workshop unit would each be fined the lesser value of one shield; and the producing artisans would be fined only the value of twenty sets of armor-plate laces. If their goods failed inspection for three straight years, the fines were more than doubled.[83] Officials, along with free and conscripted artisans, were monetarily fined for shoddy work, since presumably they had the means to pay such fines. Convict laborers who worked alongside the free artisans, however, were given fifty to one hundred strokes of the bamboo pole if their work failed inspection.[84] This social distinction for corporal punishment was modified somewhat, however, when the violation went beyond shoddy work and crossed into the domain of wastage, embezzlement, or outright theft. If a free or conscripted state artisan stole raw materials or finished goods worth one copper coin or less, he or she was to be beaten. If the stolen goods were worth more than one coin, all the artisans in his or her work unit (*cao*) were apparently beaten as well, in accord with the Chinese legal concept of mutual responsibility.[85] Convict laborers convicted of stealing goods worth more than 110 coins were sentenced to death.[86]

We know from these Qin legal texts that the discipline of free and unfree artisans at state-run workshops was quite harsh, and we can probably assume that the situation was similar in private workshops. No texts survive to tell us the treatment of artisans in Qin and Han private workshops, but texts from the late imperial period confirm that the harsh discipline imposed on a workshop apprentice was often little different from that imposed on a domestic servant or slave.[87]

Granted that most physical labor taxes a worker's body, it is also clear that some of the artisan fields in early imperial China entailed additional physical dangers that jeopardized the health and safety of the worker to an even greater degree. Sometimes, the physical danger to artisans arose merely from serving a cruel and capricious ruler like the Second Emperor of Qin (Qin Ershi) (r. 209–207 BCE). The historian Sima Qian tells us that when the Second Emperor had finally completed his father's necropolis at Mount Li, he was warned by an adviser that the artisans who had fashioned the inner chambers knew too much about its entrances and its treasures. Thus, the Second Emperor had the tomb artisans sealed alive in his father's sepulcher for eternity.[88]

One can imagine the hazards faced by mural painters, who prepared toxic white-lead pigments, or by the jade carvers, who were subjected to the fine stone dust that can lead to the respiratory disease silicosis. But, rather than merely imagine the dangers faced by Han artisans, let us instead review the textual and archaeological evidence concerning workplace health hazards.

Of all the artisan fields practiced in early imperial China, metallurgy probably imperiled the laborer to the greatest extent. Even today, mining, smelting, and casting are still some of the most dangerous jobs, and tens of thousands of people die each year in mining and metals-industry accidents around the world.[89] At each stage in the process of creating metal objects, explosive, traumatic, and poisonous dangers threaten the worker. The beginning of the metal-winning process encompasses mining and ore processing. Chapter 6 will investigate the physical hazards facing workers during these preliminary stages. During the subsequent smelting stage, a crucial ingredient is large amounts of charcoal, which provides not only the melting heat but also the necessary carbon for the chemical reaction that frees the metal from the ore. The charcoal is obtained by felling trees and roasting the logs in a charcoal furnace.

Deforestation caused by indiscriminant harvesting of trees for charcoal production can lead to extensive erosion and even permanent changes in climate. In one tragic incident from the Han, it led to the death of over one hundred workers. The story is told from the perspective of a boy named Dou Guangguo, who was kidnapped from a poor family around 190 BCE, when he was four or five years old, and sold into slavery. After his slave contract was sold from one master to another, he eventually found himself making charcoal for a private iron industrialist in Yiyang, near Luoyang in present-day Henan. He and his fellow slaves had apparently denuded most of the hillside upon which they were working, for one night while they slept, the entire mountain gave way and buried more than one hundred men and boys alive. Only the slave boy Guangguo lived to tell his tale. The boy's tragic odyssey ended happily, however, for his elder sister, who had previously been sent to serve in the palace, would one day become empress of Han China, free her younger brother from servitude, and have him enfeoffed as a marquis.[90]

The smelting of iron ore in a blast furnace was clearly one of the most dangerous stages in the metallurgical process. The most catastrophic failure of a blast furnace is called a "furnace breakout," in which the walls of the furnace fail and molten metal explodes out the fissures. The *History of the Former Han* records that a potentially deadly furnace breakout occurred during the reign of Emperor Cheng, sometime during February or March of 27 BCE.[91] Thirteen artisans were working around a blast furnace at the Iron Monopoly Office of Pei Commandery (present-day Jiangsu). Most were probably engaged at the bellows providing the draft. When they opened the tap hole at the side of the furnace to bleed off the slag and let the iron run out, nothing poured forth. Suddenly, the furnace started to make strange noises. Some said it sounded like rolling thunder, making a "*long-long*" noise.[92] Others said it was more like the sound of drums. The workers panicked and fled from the scene. Soon after, the whole furnace was ripped apart by a tremendous explosion. When the workers returned to survey the damage, they found a huge crater in the ground. The furnace had been blasted into eleven pieces, and all the iron of the smelt lay around the site like "scattered shooting stars."

A material cause for the explosion at the Pei Commandery iron furnace was never sought, for the event was interpreted as a warning from Heaven. Since the element metal was not supposed to fly, the explosion at the furnace was interpreted to mean that the relationship between the five elements was out of balance. Heaven sent this message as an omen of the impending machinations of the emperor's consorts and maternal relations. Technically, according to the analysis of Donald Wagner, the breakout was almost certainly caused by what is "known as 'scaffolding': if the furnace burden adheres to the side of the furnace it can accumulate, forming a 'scaffold,' which prevents the charge from descending. When the scaffold suddenly falls, an explosion can occur."[93] Alternatively, the refractory clay lining of the furnace may have been degraded from prolonged use, allowing hot gas and metal to rip a large fissure in the two-meter-thick furnace walls.

In our modern industrial world, similar hot-metal breakouts still occur. A breakout at the number 5 blast furnace at the Corus Steelworks in Port Talbot, Wales, in 2001 resulted in the deaths of three workers and serious injury to more than a dozen others. Local residents also reported hearing something that sounded like rolling thunder just before the tremendous explosion lifted the 5,000-ton furnace eighteen inches off the ground, immersing the attending workers in molten iron to a depth of two feet. Apparently, in the case of the Corus furnace, water had seeped into the furnace chamber through leaks in a cooling jacket that surrounded the furnace. The water became superheated steam and blew apart the enormous structure.[94]

Beyond the explosive dangers of the smelting and casting operations, more subtle dangers lurked for the Han artisan who finished metal products. Bronze vessels made for wealthy Han patrons were often gilded or silvered after casting. This was accomplished by a process in which the precious metal was combined with liquid mercury to obtain a viscous amalgam. The amalgam was painted over the surface of the metal, and the object was then placed in an oven and roasted at a low temperature (250–350°C), evaporating the excess mercury and leaving behind a well-bonded coating of gold or silver.[95] The process probably originated in China, for the oldest objects showing evidence of amalgam gilding from China date to the fifth or fourth century BCE, at least two centuries older than the earliest datable mercury-gilded pieces from the West.[96] Mercury distillation was discovered by alchemists in early China, who sought it for their poisonous cocktails of immortality.[97] The Han Chinese referred to the gold amalgam used to cover vessels as *huangtu* (gold paint). Later in China, this process was called *liujin* (beautiful-metal gilding). The work was clearly hazardous. When the amalgam of precious metal and mercury was heated, it released toxic mercury vapor. If handling precautions and ventilation were not adequate, the artisans would eventually become "mad as hatters" from the effects of mercury poisoning (nervous system damage, kidney impairment, lung disease, etc.). Symptoms of mercury poisoning may not develop for decades, however, if the artisans had only low-level exposure to the toxin. It is known that a Han gilder named Gu held his post at an imperial lacquer factory for at least eight years.[98]

While the dangers of metal crafts were potentially lethal to the artisan, those associated with lacquerwork were just irritating, literally. The lacquer fluid is derived from the sap of the *Rhus verniciflua* tree, a relative of the poison oak plant.[99] Until fully set, the lacquer fluid and its vapors are toxic to humans and cause severe dermatitis (inflammation of the outer layer of skin) upon contact.[100] This toxicity was a serious occupational hazard for lacquer workers during the Qin and Han periods and remains so for lacquer workers today. In an early Han period medical text found in Mawangdui tomb 3, lacquer dermatitis is identified as the disease *xiu*. Several treatments are proposed, including an exorcism by proxy (see section below on the religious beliefs of artisans). One of the more pharmacologically based remedies was said to provide protection for life.[101] Later traditional Chinese medical texts insisted that the tissues of crabs and shellfish were also a good antidote to lacquer exposure and helped to actually remove the irritant from the skin.[102] Dermatitis is still prevalent among lacquer artisans in modern East Asia. Recent studies of Japanese craftsmen who were just beginning to learn the art of lacquerwork revealed that nearly all the subjects developed dermatitis within a month of beginning their instruction. The sensitivity disappeared in nearly all cases within nine to ten months of first exposure, but only if the craftsman were exposed to the lacquer fluid continuously, and for increasing durations, during the study. In the profession's jargon, they were said to have been "hardened" to the lacquer.[103] The medical term is *hyposensitized*. Popular tradition in Japan says that lacquer workers should chew raw lacquer to become hardened even faster. Such hardening explains why the above-mentioned Han treatments for lacquer dermatitis could be effective for life. Lacquer artisans also had to be careful not to inhale the fumes of raw lacquer, for lacquer dermatitis was not limited to skin contact. Severe respiratory problems could develop upon vapor inhalation. Recurrent sanding of the lacquer surface in preparation for the next layer also would have filled the air of the workshop with hazardous particulate matter.

Lacquer artisans during the Han may also have been required to work nearly naked under hot and humid conditions. The eighteenth-century Chinese lacquer artisans observed by the French Jesuit missionary Père d'Incarville were required to strip off nearly all their clothes to prevent dust and fibers from settling on the wet lacquer and ruining the coating.[104] Working nearly naked may have been a relief for the artisans, since lacquer workshops often maintained artificially elevated levels of heat and humidity. The chemical process of polymerization of the lacquer coating requires a constant temperature between 25 and 30°C and a relative humidity between 75 and 85 percent. In South China, these conditions prevailed naturally, but in North China they were created artificially by pouring water over hot rocks, much like a European sauna.[105]

RELIGIOUS BELIEFS OF ARTISANS

It is difficult to investigate the religious beliefs of the common people in early China, due to the biases of elite authors and compilers. Through received texts, we learn about popular religiosity only when it is being criticized by elites as being vulgar, wasteful, or politically dangerous. The present-day scholar Poo Mu-chou has characterized popular religion in early China as a set of beliefs and practices designed to seek "personal welfare."[106] By this, he means that the general population sought to attract good luck and to dispel misfortune in order to bring about a better life in this world. At festivals tied to the life cycle or to the agricultural cycle, people performed rituals to purge evil spirits and to nourish and protect themselves, their crops, and their ancestors. They also restricted their activities based upon "daybooks" (*rishu*), the mantic texts we encountered in the last chapter which indicated auspicious and inauspicious days on which to carry out dozens of mundane activities like procreation, traveling, eating, house construction, and even cutting fabric for clothes. The wearing of talismans, chanting of incantations, performance of exorcisms, and a whole series of other ritual activities were practiced to protect the person from harm and attract health, wealth, and progeny.

While in their residences, artisans undoubtedly participated in this shared foundation of beliefs. And since their craft was such an integral part of their lives and identity, we can hardly expect them to have kept their beliefs out of the workshop. Meager as the current evidence may appear, it does seem that craftsmen indeed solicited the help of benevolent deities in their work.

It appears that those crafts perceived as most susceptible to divine interference and in need of supernatural protection were metallurgy, ceramics, and lacquerwork. All of these crafts involved complex transformative processes whose technology was poorly understood by the artisan, except at the practical level. In many prescientific cultures, smelting and casting operations were often the focus of intense ritual activity. A successful outcome was never assured, and it was often impossible to determine any material cause for failure. Iron smelters observed in Africa during the nineteenth and twentieth centuries were not permitted near the furnace if their wives were menstruating or had recently miscarried. The men were also not allowed to engage in sexual intercourse for the entire duration of the smelt. The smelters believed that the belly of the furnace was a female womb designed to give birth to iron, and the intrusion of any extra, unpredictable female energy would almost guarantee a miscarriage of the iron.[107] In early China as well, the smelting operation was viewed as a mystical, unpredictable, and sometimes sexualized process.

In the *Annals of Wu and Yue* (Wu-Yue chunqiu), a collection of history and folk traditions from two ancient southern states compiled by Zhao Ye (fl. first century CE), the story is told of a master sword maker from Wu named Ganjiang and his wife, Moye.[108] Ganjiang was asked by King Helü of Wu (r. 514–496 BCE) to produce two magnificent swords. Though he had observed all the proper rituals and supplicated the appropriate deities, after three months of effort, Ganjiang could not make the metal "melt, sink, and flow" properly. His wife, Moye, told him that "the transformation of Spirit and Matter requires a person for its accomplishment," meaning that a person must be sacrificed to achieve metallurgical transformation. In the *Annals of Wu and Yue* version of the story, Ganjiang and Moye merely cut off their hair and fingernails and throw them into the furnace. In some later versions of the story, the wife sacrifices her whole body to the fiery furnace and joins with the Furnace God to make the smelt successful. With three hundred male and female servants working the bellows and charging the charcoal, the two swords were finally consummated. In this tale both male and female energies were needed to make a successful smelt, a process viewed as analogous to a sexual union resulting in birth.

Another story of furnace sacrifice, adapted to a new medium, was told among the porcelain workers at the great ceramic center of Jingdezhen during the eighteenth century.[109] In their variation, the emperor ordered the potters to produce an intricate pattern. They failed numerous times and told him it was impossible. Finally, after suffering the tortures of the overseers who demanded results, one potter threw himself into his kiln and was consumed by the flames. That batch of porcelain came out perfect, and the emperor was satisfied. In the story, the unfortunate potter was later elevated to be the patron god who watched over the workers at Jingdezhen. The mythological nature of these stories is very clear, and most likely actual self-immolations by artisans rarely, if ever, occurred. But the persistence of these tales points to an acknowledgment of the intense spiritual forces thought to determine the outcomes of transformative processes like ore smelting and porcelain firing.

In the legends of early China, it was not only living beings that were consigned to the fiery furnace. In some stories, objects imbued with numinous power could also help to complete the process of transformation. The *Record of Gleaned Remnants* (Shiyiji) by Wang Jia (d. ca. 390 CE) contains another incident of furnace sacrifice in the making of a magnificent sword. Like the story of New Feng translated in the last chapter, this tale involves the Honorary Grand Supreme Emperor of the Han (Taishanghuang), the father of the Han founder, Liu Bang.

> When the Honorary Grand Supreme Emperor of the Han was still of humble status, he used to carry a three-foot-long blade at his belt. On the blade was an inscription whose characters were difficult to recognize, though it was suspected that the weapon was made during the time when King Gaozong of the Yin [i.e., King Wuding of the Shang] attacked the Guifang barbarians [ca. 1200 BCE]. Once, when the Supreme Emperor was traveling through the hilly regions around Feng and Pei, he encountered in a desolate valley several men at work smelting and casting. The Supreme Emperor rested for a while near them and inquired, "What kind of object are you casting?"
>
> The artisans laughed and replied, "We are casting a sword for a Son of Heaven. Be careful not to leak word of this."
>
> The Supreme Emperor considered that they might be pulling his leg, yet he showed no signs of doubt on his face.
>
> One of the artisans then said, "The iron we are casting today is particularly hard and quite difficult to successfully grind [sharp]. Now, if we were to obtain the blade that you, sire, have hanging at your waist and could mix it in with the smelt, then we could make a truly godlike object (*shenqi*), one that could conquer all the lands under Heaven. The astrological configuration would help one [who uses this sword] to exterminate the many treacherous ones. Since the element of wood is currently waning, while the element of fire is ascendant,[110] this is particularly ominous."
>
> The Supreme Emperor said, "I call this object a dagger. In sharpness, it has no equal. In the realm of water, it can cleave hornless serpents and dragons, while on land it can smite tigers and rhinoceroses. Even among the goblins and demons, there are none that can overcome it. It can hew jade and engrave metal, and yet its cutting edge never curls."

One of the artisans said, "If we cannot obtain this 'dagger' and alloy it in our casting, then even if we had the concentrated brilliance of Master Ouye[111] and could use the whetstones of Yue to hone the cutting edge, in the end we would still make an inferior object."

The Supreme Emperor thereupon removed the dagger from his waist and tossed it into the furnace. Suddenly, smoke and fire covered the sky, obscuring the sun and transforming day into night. In a very short time, the sword was complete. They killed three sacrificial animals and anointed (*xin*) the sword with their blood. One of the casting artisans then asked the Supreme Emperor, "When did you obtain that dagger?"

The Supreme Emperor responded, "During the reign of King Zhaoxiang of Qin [306–251 BCE], I was traveling when I met with a rustic fellow standing on the ridges between the fields. He gave it to me and told me that it was a numinous object from the time of the Yin dynasty and had been handed down from generation to generation. On it were written ancient characters that recorded the year and month."

When the new sword was complete, the artisans inspected it and saw that the inscription [from the old blade] was still visible, and this allayed any of their formerly held doubts [about the ancient blade].

The artisans then took the newly made sword and gave it to the Supreme Emperor. He gave it to Gaozu [i.e., Liu Bang], who hung it at his waist and used it to exterminate his treacherous foes, until he settled all under Heaven.[112]

Just as in the Ganjiang and Moye story, this sword-making legend involves an auspicious sacrifice to the furnace to facilitate the smelting of an almost supernaturally powerful blade. The author (or at least transmitter) of the story, Wang Jia, was a reclusive Daoist alchemist and Master of Techniques (*fangshi*) who lived during the Former Qin dynasty (351–94 CE). He likely took such rituals as furnace sacrifice quite seriously in his line of work. The other ritual activity seen in the story is that of *xin* (anointing with blood). This was a fairly common ritual, attested in many pre-Qin and Han period texts. It was carried out to sanctify such newly created structures as ancestral temples or objects like ritual bells, drums, swords, or mirrors.

To observe material traces of another metalsmith's ritual, consider a bronze, bivalve coin mold dating to the Former Han period, housed in the American Numismatic Society collection in New York (see figure 3.18). At the top of the mold, near the pouring spout, the Han artisan cast two small symbols into the bronze. The one on the right, with its long sinewy form and characteristic stripes, clearly represents the White Tiger of the West (Baihu). The coiled form on the left is more difficult to discern but probably represents the Green Dragon of the East (Qinglong). Along with the Vermilion Bird of the South and the Dark Warrior of the North, these animals constituted the ruling spirits of the cardinal directions. They were not really gods in the proper sense, deserving of prayer and sacrifice, but they were quite important as symbols of

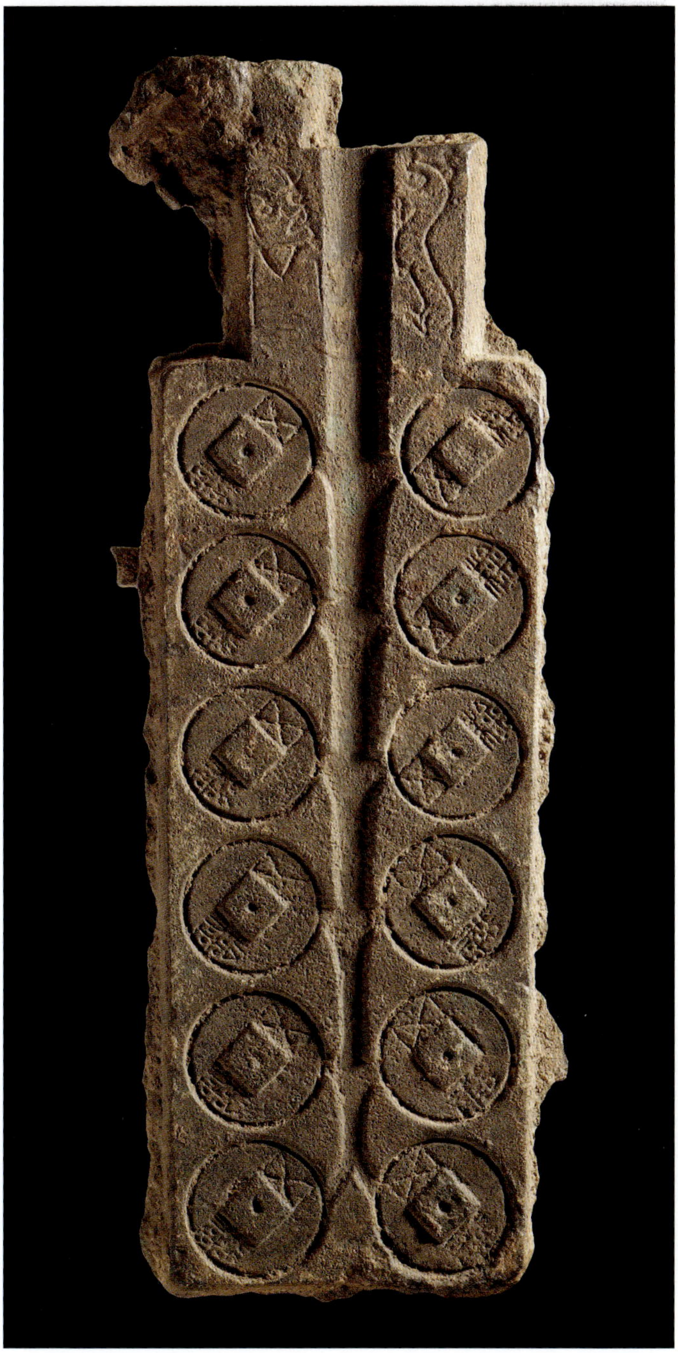

3.18 *Coin mold.* Former Han period, ca. 113 BCE–7 CE. Bronze, with cast decoration and securing clamps. L. 22.8 cm. W. 8.7 cm. American Numismatic Society, New York, 1918.71.2. Photo courtesy of American Numismatic Society.

cosmic power. They are commonly painted on tomb walls or cast onto bronze mirrors—sites and objects where proper orientation to the cosmos is viewed as important. To our modern minds, directional orientation appears to be unrelated to the successful outcome of a casting operation, but to the Han founder who cast this coin mold, nothing could be left so mercilessly to chance. It appears that our cautious caster might have used these dragon and tiger registration symbols to orient his casting mold to the east-west cardinal points before pouring in the bronze. By properly arranging his tools with respect to the cardinal directions, he hoped to remain in accord with the unfathomable cosmic forces that determined whether his coins would come out of the mold perfectly formed. A few other published coin molds from the Han period also have auspicious markings in the same location. On one comparable mold, this time carved from stone, the words *ji* (auspicious) and *ping* (peace) were carved on either side of the pouring spout.[113] Such marks give us insight into the thought processes of certain craftsmen who projected their religious beliefs into the workshop space.

We have just met one canonized craftsman who became the patron of a particular group of artisans, but our immolated potter from Jingdezhen does not stand alone. We know that during the Ming (1368–1644 CE) and Qing (1644–1911 CE) periods, almost every major craft guild had a designated patron saint or deity.[114] These were often chosen from the ranks of legendary craftsmen, historical and legendary rulers, famous philosophers, or deities of the popular pantheon. For example, all those who belonged to the Carpenter's Guild of Peking worshiped Gongshu Lu Ban (also known as Gongshu Ban), a semihistorical figure from the fifth century BCE who was said to be a contemporary of Confucius. Lu Ban, as he was popularly called, was reputed to be a brilliant carpenter who never wasted any wood, nor did he need guidelines for sawing. He invented ingenious counterweighted siege ladders and a wooden bird that supposedly flew for three days without coming down.[115] The carpenters of Peking feasted and kowtowed in worship to an idol of Lu Ban at every guild meeting to give thanks to him for handing down the techniques of carpentry. They often jockeyed for position in front of the idol at the banquet, hoping to receive some divine inspiration from the founding master of the craft. Scholars have noted a strong similarity between the modes of worship at these guild meetings and the traditional cult of the ancestors.

Thanks to the observation of Western scholars, we know quite a lot about the patron deities of craft guilds in China at the end of the imperial era. What few realize, however, is that this tradition goes back to at least the Qin and Han periods, if not earlier. For example, the families of ironworkers in southwest China during the early empires worshiped a figure they called the Iron Ancestor (Tiezu). According to the *Account of the States South of Mount Hua* (Huayang guozhi), compiled ca. 342–8 CE by Chang Qu (ca. 291–361 CE) and constituting the oldest surviving Chinese regional gazetteer, there was an ancestral shrine (*miao-ci*) dedicated to the Iron Ancestor atop a mountain in the area of Linqiong, at the southwest edge of the Chengdu Plain in present-day Sichuan.[116] This was an area rich in iron ore, and during the third century BCE, the Zhuo family set up large ironworks here after being exiled from their native state of Zhao by the First Emperor of Qin (see chapter 6). A century later, the Han Empire established government ironworks in the same area.[117] A later gazetteer also mentions a shrine to the Iron Ancestor in this area and comments that the families of ironworkers frequently sacrificed at the shrine.[118]

What is still unclear, however, is just who the Iron Ancestor represents. He might have been a legendary inventor of iron metallurgy, such as the great mythic character Chi You, who is credited with first using metal to cast weapons.[119] Or, possibly, he may have been an ancestor of the Zhuo family who had been smelters for generations and had brought ironworking to Linqiong. The name of this patron saint and the form of his worship clearly anticipate later Chinese practice in which the worship of craftsmen's patron saints paralleled ancestral rites.

During the Qin and early Han periods, some lacquer workers believed in a spirit called the Lacquer King (Qiwang). According to the liturgy of an exorcism for lacquer poisoning found in the medical text *Fifty-two Recipes to Cure Disease* (Wushier bingfang) (compiled ca. 200–168 BCE), the Lacquer King was sent down to earth by the Heavenly Thearch (Tiandi) to help artisans lacquer armor and weapons.[120] But on occasion he turned against the divine ruler's mandate and caused a horrible rash to appear on a craftsman's skin (the contact dermatitis described earlier). To heal this condition, the shaman/doctor had to smear pig, chicken, or rat feces on a physical representation of the Lacquer King (probably a proxy statue), hit it with his shoe, threaten to stab it, or have the victim spit on it seven times (fourteen times for women) to punish the god for his misdeeds and exorcise his influence from the skin of the worker.

The Lacquer King of the lacquer craftsmen differs in character from the Iron Ancestor of the metalworkers. Judging by his title and his role in the text, he was not viewed as a family ancestor or an originator of the craft like the Iron Ancestor or Lu Ban. Rather, he was considered to be an enfeoffed king (*wang*) in a celestial empire ruled by the Heavenly Thearch, the principal god of the popular pantheon and the ruler of the underworld.[121] Just as the terrestrial emperor of the early Former Han dynasty enfeoffed his sons and generals as kings (*wang*) to delegate his authority in the provinces, the Heavenly Thearch enfeoffed the Lacquer King with the task of effecting the difficult transformation of *Rhus verniciflua* tree sap into finished lacquer. It is clear that the Lacquer King was not slavishly worshiped by the craftsmen, however, since they could punish him in the name of the Heavenly Thearch for disobeying divine orders and causing disease.[122] It is also interesting to note that the context of the liturgy suggests that the Lacquer King was worshiped in the form of a physical idol. This occurs fully two centuries before the arrival of Buddhism (ca. 50–100 CE), which scholars had formerly assumed brought with it the earliest use of cult statues in China.

FEMALE ARTISANS

During the Qin and Han periods, women (and girls) were an indispensable segment of the artisan labor force. In some craft fields, they even seem to have constituted the overwhelming majority. The idealizing myth promulgated by elite authors and Confucian moralists was that men plowed while women reared children, prepared food, and, in their spare time, wove cloth.[123] In reality, peasant women often assisted their husbands in the fields; the majority of agricultural slaves appear to have been women;[124] and many married women and widows produced goods for the market on a regular basis. Abundant textual and inscriptional evidence also demonstrates that large numbers of female artisans were employed in both private workshops and government factories.

WOMEN IN PRIVATE WORKSHOPS

In privately owned workshops it seems that a woman could perform a broad range of roles, depending on her individual circumstance. Some women were newly widowed (or had absentee husbands) and became independent artisan/entrepreneurs to support the family.[125] The *History of the Former Han* tells the story of the mother of Zhai Fangjin (d. 7 BCE), who so wanted him to continue his Classical studies in the capital that she set up shop weaving sandals and sold them in the Chang'an markets to support him.[126] He later went on to become chancellor from 15 BCE until his death in 7 BCE. Her efforts are portrayed as pious self-sacrifice for the success of her son, but in reality, she was supporting herself by her sandal-making as well. We hear of Widow Zhai only because her son later became powerful, but desperate situations similar to hers must have arisen very frequently among the working classes. A truly exceptional case is that of a widow named Qing who lived in southwest China during the third century BCE. She took over her family's enormous cinnabar mining and processing business, presumably upon the death of her husband, and the business flourished under her control. Her dedication was recognized by the First Emperor of Qin, who built a memorial in her honor.[127]

In many cases, it seems that the wives of artisans assisted their husbands in a variety of professional and domestic support roles. A pictorial stone found in 1954 in Shandong depicts what is clearly a wheelwright's shop (see figure 3.15b).[128] As discussed above, the scene is not unique and was probably a local stock motif (see another example in figure 3.15a). In the version seen in figure 3.15b, the second person from the left is the male wheelwright. Possibly, he is meant to represent Wheelwright Pian, the character who takes part in a famous dialog with Duke Huan of Qi (r. 685–643 BCE) (translated in chapter 2).[129] The wheelwright is kneeling on the shop floor, securing a segment of the felloe with his right foot, while he prepares to chisel out a groove to fit the felloe to the incomplete wheel shown to his right. A woman stands behind him, and we may presume she is the artisan's wife. In her hand she holds another wheel segment, prepared to hand it to her husband when he requires it. She carries their infant child on her back. This rubbing is taken from one of the lower registers of a larger tableau representing a layered cosmos of gods, immortal spirits, and the realm of humans. The workshop scene clearly belongs to the mundane world. The stone carver who originally designed this stock motif would have been keenly aware of the appearance and organization of workshops. Perhaps, he even drew on the circumstances of actual families he knew in his artisan quarter. No finer pictorial example could be cited to demonstrate the cooperative nature of marriages among the working classes.

For a literary example, the reader will recall the story of the master sword maker of Wu named Ganjiang and his wife, Moye, referred to above. In this legend, which clearly belongs to the realm of myth, the male artisan was unable to accomplish his task of smelting the metal until he realized that it took the cooperation of male and female influences to achieve metallurgical union.

Another example, this one more historical, shows us a realistic, cooperative, entrepreneurial spirit between husband and wife. Sima Xiangru (ca. 179–117 BCE) was a young man from Chengdu of literary bent who once traveled to the imperial palace of Emperor Jing and then to the Liang Princedom in search of an official career. Disappointed by circumstances, he returned to his native Shu Commandery (present-day Sichuan) to settle down. At a party he fell madly in love with Miss Zhuo Wenjun, the newly widowed daughter of Zhuo Wangsun, one of the empire's richest iron industrialists and slave owners. The couple eloped, much to the consternation of Mr. Zhuo, who disowned his wayward daughter. Xiangru and Wenjun lived in abject poverty in Chengdu within "four walls, containing nothing," until she finally told him she could not live in penury anymore. Selling their meager capital, Xiangru and Wenjun bought a liquor shop in nearby Linqiong. In their division of labor, Xiangru made the product and performed other odd jobs for pay, while Wenjun personally operated the store, which we know from pictorial depictions consisted of a stall that was open to the street and in which large jugs of beer were embedded beneath the counter. Upon hearing of this situation, Wenjun's father was shamed even further, since he knew that no upper-class woman should be so visible and accessible to common men on the street. Even though Xiangru and Wenjun were not properly artisans, since they were producing and selling alcohol, the distinction is not very great in practical terms. Also, one could argue that the couple's tidy division of labor may have been a later literary embellishment by the historian Sima Qian, who may have wished to lift the stigma of "merchant" from Sima Xiangru, one of his heroes and a man who would later rise to high official position at the court of Emperor Wu. But Sima Qian admired merchants greatly and thus would have had no motivation to change the story to suit elite tastes. Xiangru and Wenjun's arrangement of husband-manufacturer and wife-proprietress may have been quite common among the merchant and artisan classes.

WOMEN IN STATE WORKSHOPS

The early Chinese imperial state had few qualms about employing female artisans in official workshops. In fact, according to the Han statutes, the state maintained a standing quota in which conscripted adult female (*ding nüzi*) artisans were preferred to male or child artisans in a ratio of 2 to 1.[130] An untold number of women were probably also hired by the state for cash wages. Most women artisans in government workshops appear to have been employed in textile production and lacquer painting.

The empire of the Former Han operated several large textile mills, both in the capital area and in the provinces. These outfitted the emperor and his harem with fine embroidered silk garments and provided various lesser-grade textiles to use as gifts for officials, commoners, and foreign dignitaries.[131] The largest textile production "complex" was located in Qi Commandery, in present-day Shandong.[132] Called the Three Offices for Garments in Qi (Qi San Fuguan), it consisted of three separate facilities that were said to have employed several thousand artisans each in the years just before 44 BCE.[133] Since the remains of these mills have not been located, it still cannot be determined whether production was centralized in large factory-like buildings, or whether the weaving and embroidery were farmed out to women working in their own homes. Regardless, the system was inordinately expensive for the state to maintain and was shut down to save costs on several occasions. When it was shut down for a second time, in 7 BCE, it was said that the continued production of brocades, embroidery, and other "difficult to produce" textiles was "harming women's work" (*hai nü gong*).[134] What this imperial edict implies is that the Qi factories employed so many women that the government felt that the traditional female production of clothing for the household was being jeopardized. The unnamed official who penned these words for the emperor was also insinuating that women's moral health, and that of the empire, was being endangered by women working for interests outside the home. Earlier, the Qin state had also employed female artisans in textile production, and we know from the Qin administrative regulations that the work output of women was highly respected in this field. The Qin "Work Norms for Artisans" clearly states that, "for women who use the needle to make embroidery and other things, [the work of] one woman is equivalent to [that of] one man."[135]

Because lacquer vessels made at the capital and in regional workshops were frequently inscribed with the names and native places of the artisans who made them, we actually know more about women in the lacquer industry than in any other craft field. Dozens of lacquer vessels excavated from the late Qin period and incipient Han period tombs in present-day Yunmeng County, Hubei, carry brands and inscriptions that tell us where they were made and who made them.[136] The phrase *ting* or *Xian ting* had been fire-branded on the cores of many of the Yunmeng pieces. These have been interpreted by most scholars to mean that the vessels (or at least the cores) were produced under the supervision of the market officials of Xianyang, the capital of the state and empire of Qin, near present-day Xi'an City (see figure 3.19c). In addition to the official marketplace brands, many pieces were also needle-incised with the names of the artisans who painted the final lacquer coatings and decorative patterns (see figure 3.19b).

The given names of the artisans incised into the finished lacquers are prefixed by the age category or rank of the artisan and sometimes by the names of their native villages. It is interesting to note that the vast majority of the artisans named on these pieces are either girls or women. According to Qin law, a minor female (*xiao nüzi*) was any girl under six *chi* and two *cun* (approx. 1.43 m) in height.[137] For minor girls, the laquer inscription usually says "minor girl" (*xiao nüzi*), with no given name appended. Clearly, these girls were apprenticed to some female or male full-fledged artisan and were not required or, possibly, allowed to write their names on the pieces. When girls' names do occur, they are found most frequently on the simple-to-execute eared cups and not on the more complex toiletry boxes or stacking-cup sets. The names of girls and boys (*xiao nanzi*) have occasionally been found on pieces that also carry the brands of marketplace officials on their wooden cores. This suggests that minors were employed in both private and government-run workshops.

The names of adult females (*da nüzi*) are far more common on the Yunmeng lacquers. In fact, three or four named women may have been responsible for making or decorating most of the lacquers imported into the Yunmeng area and later found in the Shuihudi and Dafentou tombs. Judging by the poorly formed characters in these rushed, needle-drawn inscriptions, it appears that the names were carved by the artisans themselves and not by a supervisory official or later owners of the pieces.[138]

One of these versatile and prolific lacquer painters was a woman we know only as Woman Ao (*da nüzi Ao*). Judging by the full form of her workshop signature, her residential registration was in Huan Village, a hamlet probably located somewhere near the Qin capital of Xianyang. Her given name, Ao, is not a common one among the known names for women in early imperial China and carries the connotations of "sturdy horse" or "stubborn and resolute." It was the given name of a famous Qin general and minister, Meng Ao (d. 240 BCE), who would have been a contemporary of Woman Ao's parents or grandparents.

Woman Ao was certainly resolute and versatile in her production. Among the eighty-one lacquers found in tomb 1 at Dafentou, she signed at least twenty-three of them, including five different types of vessel.[139] Some of her creations are shown in figure 3.19. The shallow bowl shown in figure 3.19a is decorated in all black on the exterior, but the interior is occupied with an array of geometric bands in the upper registers and a swirling constellation of dragon, bird, and cloud forms at the base. The design displays a liveliness and spontaneity that belies its programmed modularity. It is a skilled production, but certainly not a masterpiece. When designs similar to these were later borrowed by imperial factories to be mass-produced, all appearances of spontaneity would be removed from the pattern. The lacquered box in figure 3.19c is a beer-cup holder made or decorated by Woman Ao. She signed both the lid of the box and the individual cups. Though the box and cups were found separated at the time of excavation, it is clear that the box was meant to hold the six cups in an ingenious stacking scheme that required standardization of size and form to ensure proper fit.

Her artistry and technical skill are obvious, but it is much more difficult to discover the professional and social standing of Woman Ao. Some of the pieces she signed also carry official marketplace brands on their cores, suggesting that she made them under official supervision. Yet many of her other pieces carry only her signature. Satō Taketoshi has argued that such a configuration suggests that Woman Ao

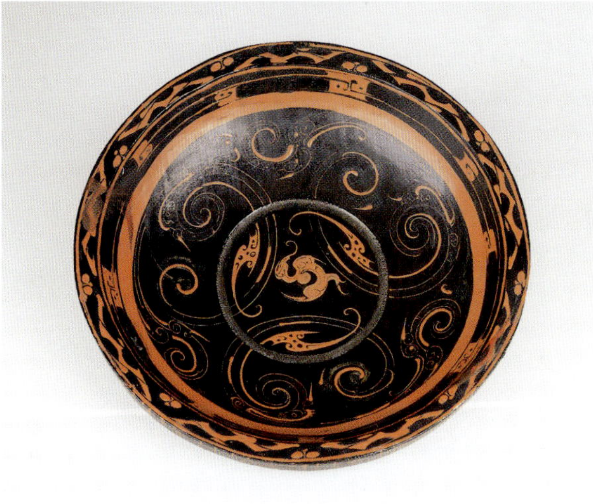

(a)

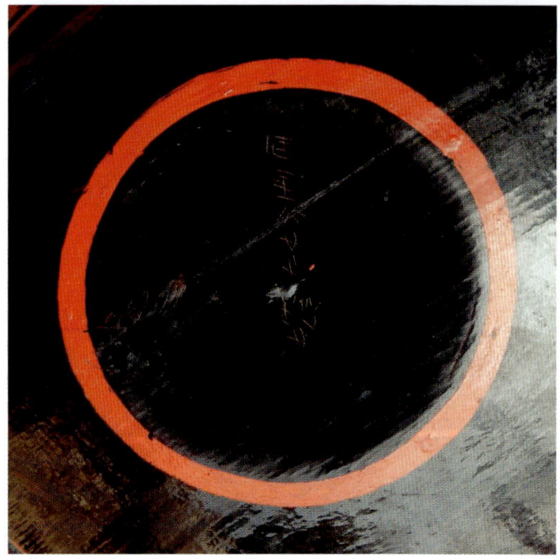

(b)

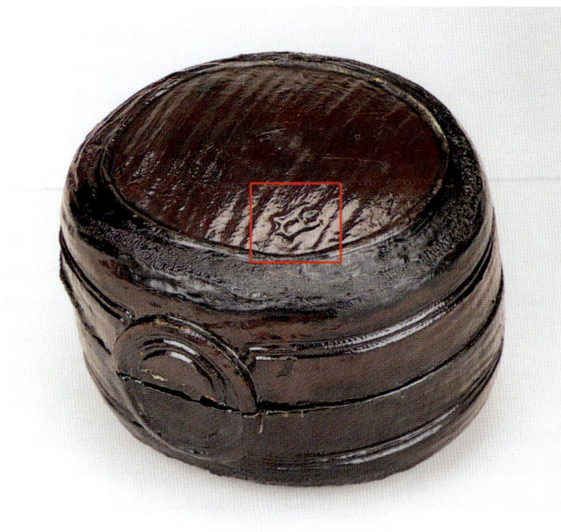

(c)

3.19 *Lacquerware made by Woman Ao*
(a) *Shallow bowl.* Qin period, ca. 221–207 BCE. Painted lacquer over wooden core. D. 18 cm. Hubei Provincial Museum. Photo courtesy of Hubei Provincial Museum.
(b) *Incised inscription on base of (a) reading "Woman Ao of Huan Village."*
(c) *Case for cups.* Highlighted area indicates branded word *ting*, "[market] pavilion," on the wooden core. Qin period, ca. 221–207 BCE. Painted lacquer over wooden core. L. 16.5 cm. H. 11.5 cm. Hubei Provincial Museum. Photo courtesy of Hubei Provincial Museum.
(d) *Interior of (c) with one beer cup in place.*

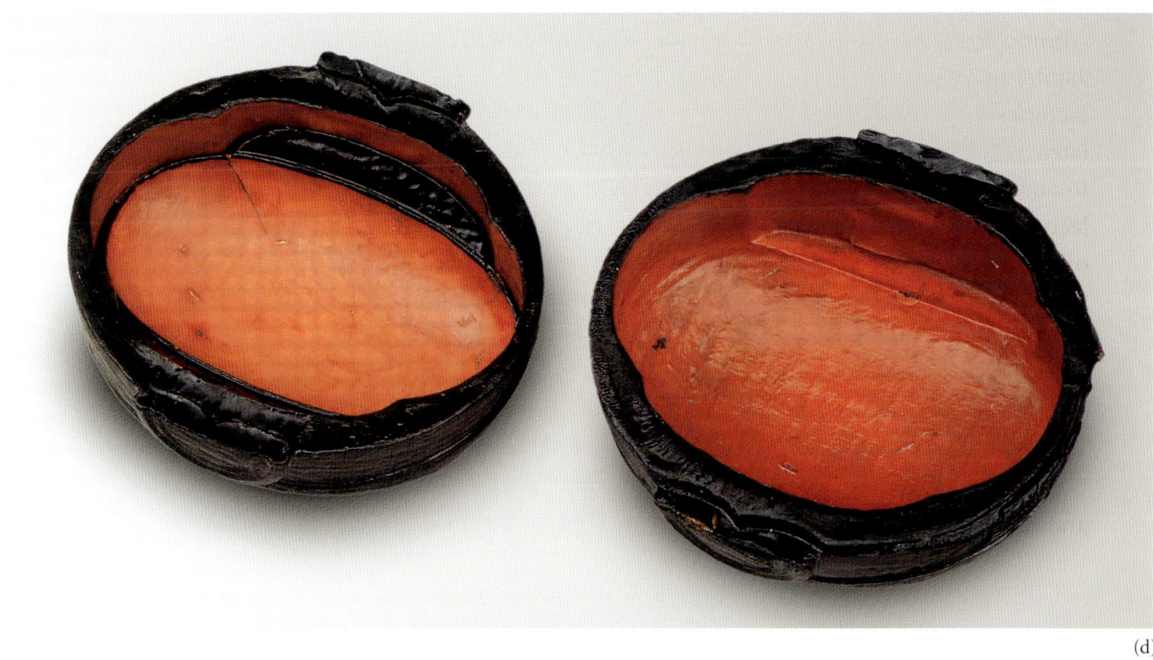

(d)

carried out her work in two different locations.[140] Her primary work location was probably in a private lacquer workshop in Huan Village, near Xianyang. Occasionally, though, she was conscripted along with other lacquer artisans to labor in the official workshops supervised by the Xianyang market officials. We cannot know for certain, but it is doubtful whether she was the chief proprietress of the Huan Village private workshop. She probably worked alongside others members of her family in a joint enterprise or alongside other hired women artisans under a master artisan or shop owner.

Judging by these Qin period inscriptions, women were substantially represented in the privately run and government-supervised lacquer workshops of the capital. Like embroidery, lacquer painting was an intricate, detail-oriented activity that may have favored a smaller, more agile hand. It is also possible that government officials and private patrons simply favored the style of designs produced by female artisans.

Han period quality-control inscriptions point to an even broader role for some women in imperial lacquer workshops, at least during the Former Han period. Like the Qin government-sponsored lacquers, Han imperial lacquers carry mandated inscriptions naming the artisans who made them. More elaborately, the Han pieces also name the officials and clerks at the factory who supervised production. Of the dozens of different artisan names found on extant imperial lacquers, many are androgynous and could be construed as belonging to either males or females.[141] Examples include Ping (Placid), Feng (Abundance), and Chang (Constancy). Some names, however, undoubtedly belonged to women artisans. A woman who went by the shop name of Mu Fang (Mother Fang) worked in the higher-status position of *huagong* (design painter) in the years around 85 BCE at the Western Workshop of Shu Commandery, the imperial luxury-goods factory in Chengdu. Alongside Mother Fang, on the same work crew, was an artisan named Mangliu (Rushes and Willows), likely another female. Mangliu served in the inferior-status position of base-coat lacquerer (*xiugong*) and may have been a junior apprentice.[142] A woman called Yi Wan (Auntie Wan) worked as a lacquer painter at the Tribute Workshop (Gonggong) at the capital in 28 BCE.[143] There were probably many other women working in these Han factories, but their gender disappears beneath the more rigid naming conventions of later decades, when only a single graph was used to identify each artisan. It is curious to note that women artisans were mentioned only in conjunction with painting in the lacquer workshops. No woman's name has ever been discerned among the core carvers or gilders. A similarly gendered division of labor in lacquer production is seen among the Nuosu people of contemporary Yunnan in southwest China, who still practice traditional techniques of lacquerwork. Among the Nuosu, core carving is men's work, while Nuosu women are primarily responsible for painting the lacquer designs.[144]

One further exceptional case demands attention, however. In 85 BCE, the Western Workshop of Shu Commandery employed a woman called Mother Yi (Mu Yi) as a Foreman Clerk (Lingshi).[145] This was not an artisan position at all but entailed scribal and accounting functions requiring a fairly high level of literacy. Some Foreman

Clerks in the civil bureaucracy had to pass an exam requiring knowledge of nine thousand different Chinese characters. The position of Foreman Clerk usually carried no official bureaucratic rank but did merit a regular salary of around 480 coins per month in the years around 85 BCE.[146] In addition, the Yi in Mother Yi's name is a common graph denoting non-Han ethnic groups to the northeast and southwest of Han China. Thus, it seems doubly remarkable that not only would a government factory employ a woman in a scribal position of great responsibility, but a non-ethnic-Han woman at that. My suggestion would be that Mother Yi had been an artisan at the factory for a number of years and was eventually promoted to the Foreman Clerk position because of her long experience. Women were not allowed to become officials in the civilian bureaucracy, so it would have been impossible for Mother Yi to pursue her bureaucratic career outside the insulated world of her factory in Chengdu. You could say that she had hit the "lacquer ceiling" in her occupation. In summary, it should be quite clear from the evidence adduced above that the idealized concept of the stay-at-home wife was a status symbol of the elites in Qin and Han society. As today, the families of the working classes could not afford this luxury and utilized whatever labor was at their disposal to earn a living.

The Qin and Han period workshop was a flexible concept, for a workshop existed wherever an artisan practiced his or her craft. Workshops could be inside or outside, mobile or permanent. They could employ as few as one master artisan or as many as several thousand artisans, as in the case of the Three Offices for Garments in Qi. The training of artisans in early China seems to have been similar to that seen in traditional cultures elsewhere: boys and girls served for a period of time as apprentices to a master artisan who taught them the craft in exchange for near-servile obedience.

Private workshops made products for the market, while state-run workshops produced for the ruler and the elites, but both types of production unit were pressed by competitive forces and/or increasing demands that encouraged labor- and material-saving techniques of mass production. These techniques were deployed, not on the unique masterpiece creations made for the emperor or his nobles, but rather on those mass-produced objects sold to those who sought some of the look and cachet of a customized piece. In state-run workshops, every stage of the process was regulated by quality-control procedures that sought to guarantee a baseline of quality and to deter shoddy work through a system of personal and group responsibility.

Working hours for artisans followed the rhythm of the seasons and the schedules of official markets and supervising bureaucrats. Private artisans could work as hard as they wished in search of profit, while in government factories, usually only convict laborers serving as artisans were worked beyond the limits of human endurance (see chapter 6). Certain artisan fields could seriously imperil the health of a worker. The most hazardous field was clearly metallurgy, where mortal dangers like cave-ins, landslides, explosions, burns, and toxic gases threatened the artisan at every stage.

Most other fields, like lacquerwork and textile processing, entailed only minor health hazards that were more annoying than life-threatening.

The risky nature of their occupation and the uncertain outcome of production processes encouraged Chinese artisans to extend the popular religion of personal welfare, with its compulsive concern with avoiding misfortune and seeking protection, into the workshop space. They worshiped patron deities and observed ritual precautions to confer some sense of control over what must have seemed divinely controlled processes enmeshed in a web of arbitrary and capricious forces.

We are conditioned by textual sources to expect early imperial Chinese workshops to have been male domains, but this view is only an idealizing smokescreen, obscuring a far more interesting social reality. Some workshops, such as those for building construction and metallurgy, do appear to have been mostly male enterprises, but others, such as lacquer and textile shops, appear to have been mixed-gender environments with a strong female component. If Qin and Han laws had not mandated that artisans like Woman Ao and Mother Fang affix their names to their products to assume final responsibility for their work, we may never have known this.

4

ARTISANS IN THE MARKETPLACE

They greatly expanded the Nine Markets [of Chang'an],
Joined by encircling walls, girdled by gates.
From the flag pavilions, five stories high,
Officials looked down to inspect the countless shop rows.
The Zhou institution [that supervised the market] was the Daxu;
Now, it is the Commandant.
Precious wares arriving from all quarters,
Gathered like birds, amassed like fish scales.
Sellers earned double profit, but buyers were never lacking.
And then:
The peddlers, shopkeepers, and common people,
Male and female vendors, selling cheap,
Sold good quality mixed with the shoddy,
Dazzling the eyes of the country bumpkins.
Why exert oneself in performing labor,
When devious earnings were so plentiful?

EXCERPT FROM ZHANG HENG (78–139 CE), "WESTERN METROPOLIS RHAPSODY"[1]

Unless artisans worked for the state or under the patronage of a noble lord, they needed to sell their products to someone else to make a living. This was commonly carried out in a *shi*, conventionally translated as "marketplace." This chapter surveys what we know about Qin and Han marketplaces, reviews theories concerning how they were integrated into larger exchange and distribution networks, and investigates some of the techniques used by artisans and merchants to sell their wares in a competitive environment.

As reviewed in chapter 1, scholars of the Primitivist camp like Moses Finley and Karl Polanyi strongly denied the existence of price-setting markets and other features of modern market capitalism in the ancient world. They claimed that Modernist scholars like Michael Rostovtzeff distorted the ancient evidence by projecting a capitalist worldview onto a past that was fundamentally different from the present. For Polanyi, reciprocity and redistribution were the predominant modes of exchange throughout most of human history. He claimed that true market exchanges did not become prominent until the nineteenth century in the West. Finley and Polanyi claimed that prices in early societies were established by tradition and law, not supply and demand. However, none of these scholars endeavored, nor was equipped, to address the Chinese evidence for price-making markets and competitive marketing practices. If they had, perhaps their positions would not have been so dogmatic.

In the previous chapter, we encountered the precocious methods of mass production deployed in Qin and Han workshops, similar to those first seen during the First Industrial Revolution in the West. In this chapter, I present a body of evidence demonstrating that competitive markets during the Han were also very well developed. I might have addressed Polanyi and his camp directly, by showing that commodity prices during the Han were indeed tied to supply and demand, no matter how unsuccessfully the state tried to buffer them or peg them to an official amount. Instead, I would like to focus (in the latter half of this chapter) on product advertising and other marketing techniques used by artisans to outsell their competition. These appear surprisingly modern in many ways and help to demonstrate that features of the ancient economy were different from those of the present age only in their particulars and in degrees of development but were not so different in their basic nature. To begin, let us first travel back a little earlier than the Han to see the origins of competitive markets in China.

The Warring States period (ca. 453–222 BCE) is properly viewed by many as the true axial age in ancient China, when the archaic past was cast off and the true potential of the people and the land was unleashed, leading to the first great explosion of economic growth in East Asia. Briefly sketched, the decline of Zhou royal authority and the near-complete autonomy of the regional states eventually led to powerful interstate competition. Petty wars over precedence and pride, basically family squabbles, gave way to wars of annexation and annihilation between hostile states. To survive in this competitive environment, the rulers of states, in conjunction with their chief ministers and men of the rising class of *shi* (technocrats), began to devise programs of state self-strengthening. Their reforms and initiatives sought to enrich the state by increasing agricultural production, spurring population growth, and encouraging more efficient weapons production. The introduction of iron agricultural tools capable of tilling harder soil, the use of human and animal fertilizer, and the digging of large-scale, state-sponsored irrigation works led to an agricultural boom and a subsequent doubling (or by some estimates tripling) of the population over the course of the period. Feudal regimes with agricultural serfs gave way to centralized states with free, tax-paying peasant populations. Frequent interstate contacts for both peaceful and belligerent reasons led to improved road infrastructure. Further, increases in the size of state territory in which merchants could safely operate, increases in social and geographic mobility, and a growing trend toward regional specialization led to increased intrastate and interstate commerce.

During this period, as in late medieval Europe, towns arose at the foot of castle keeps as centers of economic activity and to house those who served the sovereign. The Chinese towns (*guo*) sometimes housed bustling marketplaces, where rural commodities, luxury goods, and the specialized products of many regions were sold side by side. Of course, such markets were established and taxed by the lord who lived in the neighboring walled palace-city. To facilitate commerce, rulers cast the first bronze coinage, much of it in the shape of tools such as spades or knives. No longer attached to the land, enterprising commoners during this time were capable of supporting themselves, or even becoming rich, without ever touching the soil. People flocked to the towns, which eventually grew into true cities with urban populations surpassing fifty thousand people. The massive wealth creation in society eventually trickled down to create several classes of nouveaux riches. Ministerial families, high-level bureaucrats, merchants, as well as salt and iron industrialists, began to compete with each other in conspicuous consumption and ostentatious display. In most cases these groups lacked access to the state-owned luxury workshops; thus, the demand from these groups was satisfied by an emerging corps of private luxury workshops in the cities or in private employ. Writers of the day remarked that the highest profit margins, sometimes as high as 10,000 percent, could be obtained in the city markets by trade in exotics like jade, pearls, and kingfisher feathers.[2]

The same types of cities and markets could be found in several of the regional states. When the Qin annexed the last of the contending states in 221 BCE, they merely codified the particular Qin version of market facilitation and regulation. It was this system that was inherited by the Han.

MARKETS DURING THE QIN AND HAN PERIODS

Just as G. William Skinner divided late imperial China into nine "physiographic" units of economic analysis he called macroregions, so we too can divide the Han Empire into at least six different economic macroregions based upon geographic features such as watersheds, specialized natural resources, and traditional trading pat-

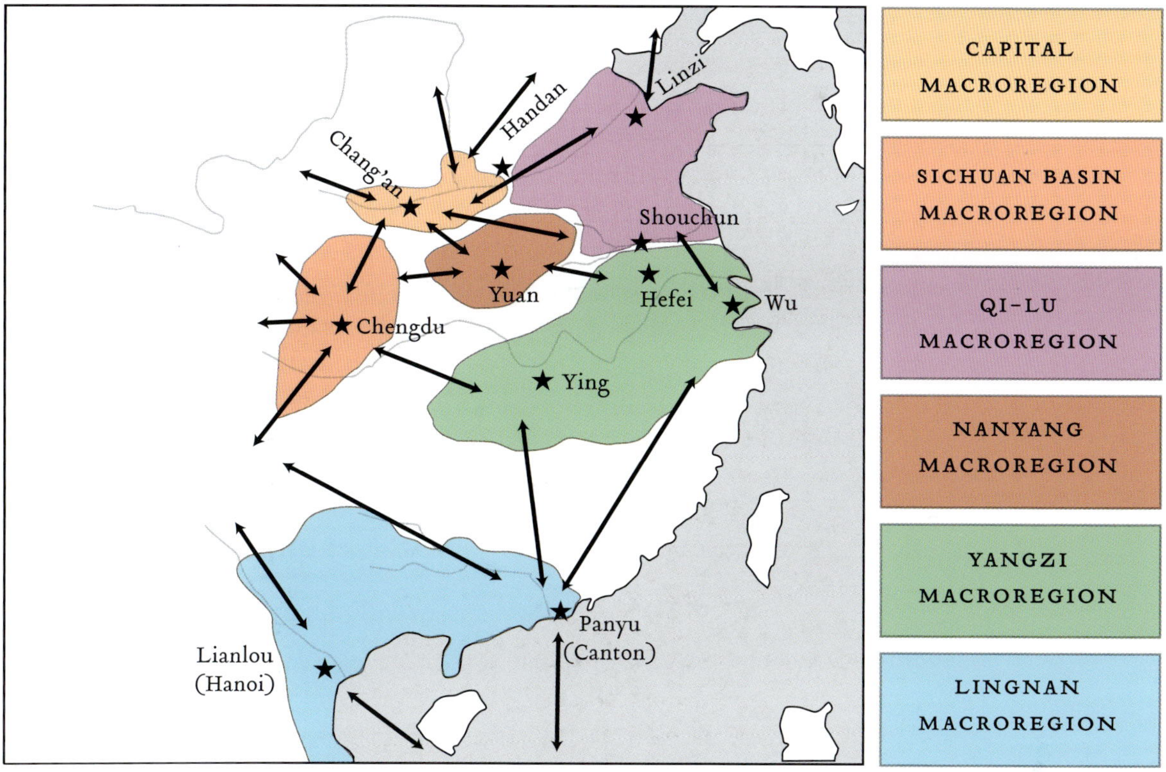

Map 4.1 *Key Former Han economic macroregions (ca. 100 BCE)*

terns.[3] Fortunately, the great Han historian Sima Qian has already performed much of this analysis for us. In chapter 129 of the *Historical Records,* "The Biographies of the Capital Accumulators" (Huozhi liezhuan), he includes a detailed description of the various regions of the empire.[4] His scheme is partly based on old Warring States period political boundaries, but his division also draws heavily on natural barriers and characteristic local resources.[5] Map 4.1 displays a simplified sketch of the major economic macroregions of the Former Han and their interactions around 100 BCE. Note that, just as Skinner concluded for the late imperial period, the macroregions often overstep political/provincial boundaries, for they obey their own geographic and economic determinants.

According to Sima Qian, each of the great economic macroregions of the Han was centered on one or more *duhui* (metropolitan nexus). The *duhui* were large urban centers like Chang'an, Linzi, and Chengdu that served as marketing and distribution centers for goods from their own hinterlands and for trade products from other macroregions. In many cases, they also served as provincial capitals.[6]

The capital macroregion, centered on the imperial city of Chang'an, possessed the most fertile fields and one of the greatest concentrations of population and wealth in the empire. The city itself housed 246,200 residents in 2 CE, but nearly two million people lived in the greater metropolitan area.[7] It was also figuratively the hub of Far Eastern trade, prompting Sima Qian to remark that people and goods converged on the capital area like "spokes of a wheel." In fact, the Qin state may well have chosen the area as its ultimate capital because of its ideal location straddling multiple trade routes and not merely because of its vaunted natural defenses.

To the west, the capital macroregion monopolized access to the Gansu Corridor, the narrow route leading to the products of Central Asia (horses, furs, felt, jade). To the east, it traded with the dense population centers along the middle course of the Yellow River. To the south, the capital macroregion communicated with the Sichuan basin macroregion, which comprised much of present-day Sichuan and was centered on the metropolis of Chengdu (population in 2 CE: 76,256 households, approximately 230,000 people). A rich agricultural breadbasket, the Sichuan macroregion also possessed valuable natural resources like cinnabar, gold, iron, and timber. It was well connected to the capital area by mountain roads and also trafficked in young slaves from Yunnan to the south and horses from the Tibetan Plateau to the west. It was even possible to communicate through river networks from the Red Basin of Sichuan all the way to the sea at Canton or Hanoi.

The Qi-Lu macroregion included the Shandong Peninsula and most of the lower Yellow River floodplain. It was a densely populated area, known for its fishing resources and salt and silk production. Its marketing nexus, located between Mount Tai and the sea, was the city of Linzi. In addition to its trade connections with the major macroregions to the west and south, the Qi-Lu region also traded to the north with the Yan region (present-day Beijing), providing access to the Bohai Sea area, including the Korean Peninsula.

The Nanyang macroregion was centered on the great industrial city of Yuan (47,547 households, approximately 144,000 people) and comprised much of present-day Henan. It produced large quantities of iron and helped to bridge the trading distance between the capital area and the valleys of the Yangzi and Huai rivers.

The Yangzi macroregion was not as densely populated during Han times as it would become in later centuries, but it was still an important economic zone for the Han Empire, providing minerals and other natural resources.[8] Sima Qian divided it into three different areas (West Chu, East Chu, South Chu), each with its own marketing center (Ying-Jiangling, Wu, Shouchun), but for simplicity's sake, we will view it as one region. The middle and lower Yangzi drainage was rich in tin, copper ore, fish, and timber products. Within this zone of multiple marketing centers, the district of Hefei (in present-day Anhui) was singled out by Sima Qian as a special type of marketing nexus he called a *shuhui* (transshipment center). Hefei was located precisely between the Yangzi and Huai rivers and was connected to both of them by canals and tributaries. Thus, it was uniquely situated to integrate trade between the two great waterborne networks of the empire.

The most southern region in the empire, the Lingnan macroregion, was formerly occupied by the independent kingdom of Nanyue, which was conquered in 111 BCE and assimilated into the Han Empire. The moderately populated area traded its rare products—pearls, tortoiseshell, feathers, tropical fruits, and fragrant woods—to the

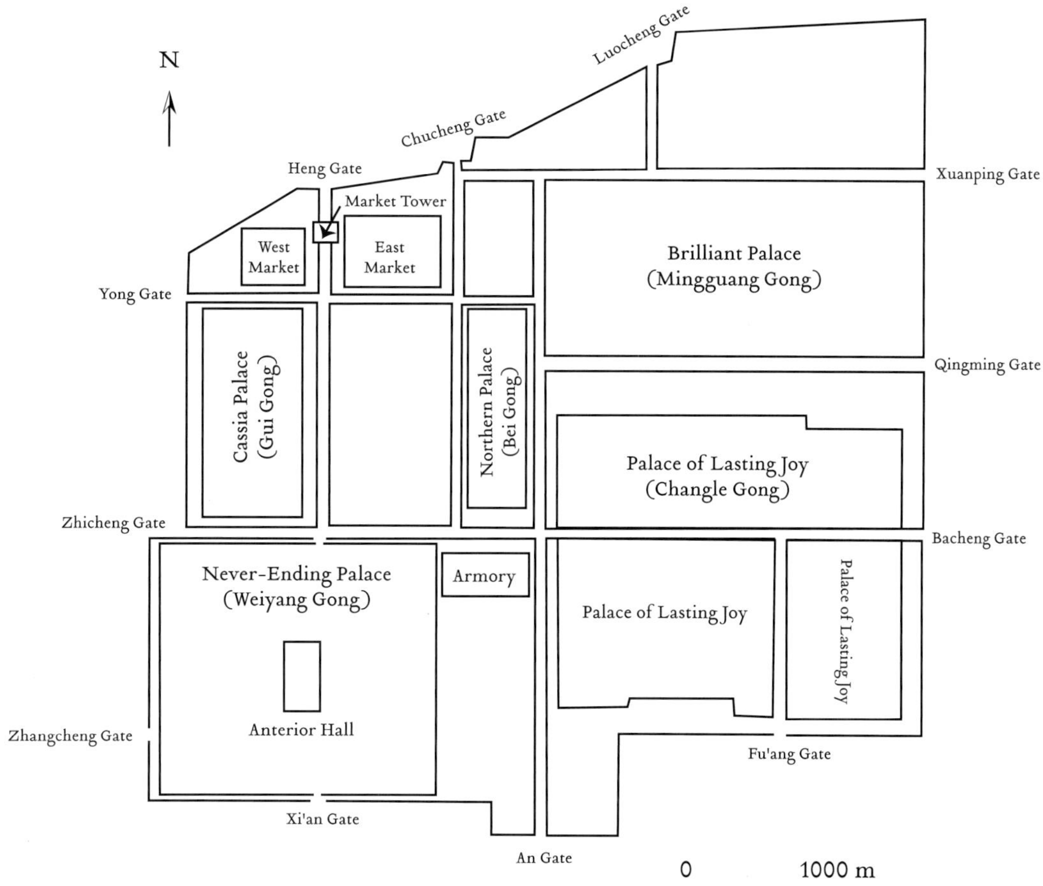

4.1 *Former Han capital of Chang'an.* Shape of walls, after 190 BCE; layout of palaces, after 101 BCE. Drawn by Anthony Barbieri-Low, based on *Kaogu* (1996.10): p. 2, fig. 1.

north for necessities like iron and silk. Even more important, through its key ocean ports of Panyu (Canton) and Lianlou (Hanoi) it provided crucial access to the products of the Southeast Asian and Indian Ocean trade.

The key trading venue in a *duhui* metropolitan nexus was the official marketplace. These were bustling quarters of commercial activity, where Han poets have said that conditions were so crowded that a visitor could barely turn his head around.[9] Regrettably, few, if any, traces of these once-thriving market areas survive aboveground. But, drawing on textual, pictorial, and archaeological evidence, it is possible to reconstruct a fairly clear picture of what the official markets in the capital of Chang'an and in the regional center of Chengdu looked like and how they operated.[10] Much of the same description would probably apply to official marketplaces in the other *duhui*.

The official marketplace of Chang'an was located in a rectangular section of the northwest quadrant of the city (see figure 4.1).[11] To get to the market area of Chang'an, one usually first approached the capital from the north, crossing over the Wei River Bridge (Wei Qiao) and traveling the final 1,200 meters to the city wall.[12] One could then pass into the city through one of three gates, either the Yong Gate in the western wall of the city or the Chucheng or Heng Gates in the northern wall.[13] Passing through the Heng Gate was the most direct approach. These three entrances constituted the main public-access gates into Chang'an, since most of the remaining nine gates opened directly onto interior palace gates. By restricting merchant entry to these remote portals, the government hoped to keep traders and other assorted riffraff well away from the imperial palaces that filled up most of the remainder of Chang'an. Every gate into the city had three lanes, each wide enough to accommodate up to four carts running abreast (6–8 m). The center lane was reserved for the use of the emperor, his emissaries, and certain honored senior citizens.[14]

The market area of Chang'an was bisected into two zones by the north-south street leading out of the Heng Gate, apparently called by some Huayang Avenue.[15] The Eastern Market (Dongshi) was established by the founder of the Han in 201 BCE, the same year he changed the name of the old Qin capital area of Xianyang to Chang'an and long before any city wall was erected. At that time it was called the Great Market (Dashi).[16] The Eastern Market appears to have been where most of the general merchandise marts were located. The Eastern Market covered an incredible 500,000 square meters. That is 25 percent larger than the total enclosed space of the Mall of America in Bloomington, Minnesota, the largest shopping mall in the United States today.[17] The Eastern Market area also served as a public stage for the execution of criminals, whose bodies were cast away to the ravages of dogs and scavengers. It was here, early on a March morning in 154 BCE, that Chao Cuo, the Censor in Chief to Emperor Jing, was dragged from his carriage, summarily charged with treason, and cut in two at the waist, all in a futile attempt to avert the Rebellion of the Seven Kingdoms.[18]

The Western Market (Xishi), covering approximately 250,000 square meters, was officially founded in July 189 BCE, eight months after the completion of the city wall.[19] It may have housed general merchandise stalls as well, but it appears mainly to have served as a major manufacturing center, filled with state-run and private workshops that ranged in size from small workshops to enormous factories. Recent archaeology in the Western Market area has revealed an enormous kiln site for mass-producing tens of thousands of terracotta human figurines for royal burials;[20] an official mint dating to the middle of the Former Han;[21] an iron-casting site for making carriage fittings, belt hooks, and other items;[22] and a privately run workshop for making simple terracotta funerary figurines of people, horses, and birds.[23]

Textual and archaeological information concerning the appearance of official markets can be confirmed and supplemented by depictions impressed on tomb bricks found in Sichuan. Figure 4.2 depicts a bird's-eye view of an official market, illustrating many of the features described in texts and uncovered during archaeological surveys. It is probably a schematic depiction of the Blue Ram Market (Qingyangsi) of

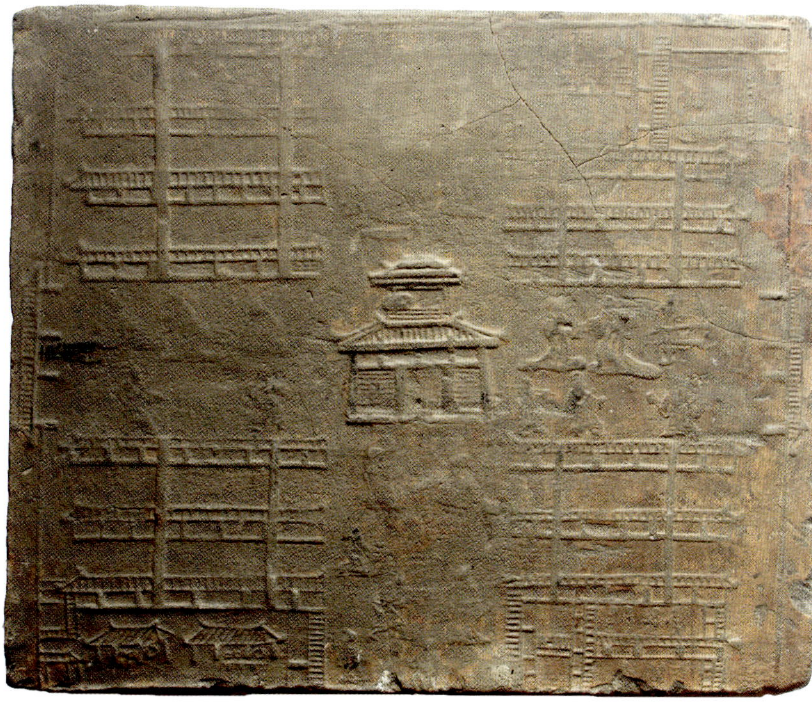

4.2 *An official marketplace.* Latter Han period (25–220 CE). Ceramic brick. H. 40.5 cm. W. 47.5 cm. Sichuan Provincial Museum. Photo courtesy of Sichuan Provincial Museum. Collected in 1965 from Xinfan County, near Chengdu, Sichuan.

Chengdu, a marketplace frequented by Han Chinese and non-ethnic-Han customers.[24] We know each official market area was girded round by a high market wall (*huan*) made of rammed earth and penetrated by a limited number of market gates (*hui*).[25] The market in figure 4.2 appears to have only three entrances (lacking a fourth at the bottom), each with three lanes.[26] Surveys have revealed that the Western and Eastern Markets of Chang'an were each surrounded by a wall five to six meters thick. Each side of the walls had two entrance gates, making for eight gates into each market.[27] Market gates were guarded at all times by officers who barred access to the area outside official market hours and who checked the credentials and intentions of all those entering.

Within the walls, the official market sector was divided into smaller quarters by a series of wide N-S/E-W avenues (*sui*), running between the main gates. The official market depicted in figure 4.2 has only two *sui*, but archaeology has revealed that the Western and Eastern Markets of Chang'an each had four *sui*, dividing those markets into nine sectors.[28] Each sector was further subdivided into lanes (*shilie*; *shisi*) of market stalls, grouped according to the type of merchandise.[29] Thus, all the silk peddlers conducted business on one lane (or on several adjacent lanes), while all the mutton sellers operated on a different lane. We know from a colorful story recorded in the *Historical Records* that diviners cracked shells and tossed milfoil stalks on their own lane in the Eastern Market of Chang'an called Diviner's Lane (Busi).[30] One can clearly see the orderly arrangement of an official market into quarters with lanes of stalls in figure 4.2. The stalls appear to have been striplike structures (narrow but deep), much like one finds in crowded Chinese markets today. The width of stalls allotted to merchants may have varied depending upon the type of merchandise sold. According to an excavated late Warring States text on market regulations, authorities should ideally strive to give the widest stalls (not exceeding 2.31 meters) to those selling bulky, low-value commodities like grain, while those selling more valuable and compact merchandise like gemstones should be given narrower stalls.[31]

In the center of any official market stood a multistoried tower where government officials observed and regulated market activity (see center of figure 4.2). The building was called by various names, including "flag pavilion" (*qiting*) and "market tower" (*shilou*).[32] The market tower of the Chang'an marketplace, whose foundations measure a colossal 147 meters (E-W) by 56 meters (N-S), was part of an even larger administrative complex located precisely between the Eastern and Western Markets.[33] Adorned with a bright flag, the top floor of the market tower also housed a large drum. Based on an analogy to later market practice during the Six Dynasties (222–589 CE) and Tang (618–907 CE) periods, the drum was probably struck hundreds of times to sound the opening and closing of the market.[34] Anyone who has seen footage of the bell sounding the end of the trading day on the floor of the New York Stock Exchange will realize that traders will not stop haggling unless repeatedly reminded by a loud percussion device.

Even though it appears unlikely that artisans and merchants were allowed to live permanently within the walls of the official marketplace of Chang'an, they were allowed to warehouse their goods in permanent storage facilities (*shichan*) abutting the interior faces of the walls.[35] These may be some of the buildings depicted at the bottom left and upper right of the scene in figure 4.2. It may be that the residential restriction was not as severe in the provincial official markets, for there is some literary evidence that artisans did live and work in homes located near their stalls in the official Chengdu marketplace.[36]

If a resident of suburban Chang'an found it inconvenient to travel all the way into the capital to buy things, he or she had other options. Scattered textual references mention additional markets established around the capital like a constellation of stars.[37] Some were established near major construction projects like imperial tombs, near government granaries, or near concentrations of bureaucrats and potential consumers. Others arose spontaneously near key bridge crossings or on roads connecting major towns. One market was founded near the Imperial Academy (Tai Xue), so that the students enrolled there could have a convenient place to buy books and supplies.

The marketing needs of the more than fifty million registered Han population could hardly be met by just a handful of urban *duhui*-megamarts like those of Chang'an and Chengdu. The vast majority of the Han population lived in rural areas, far away from the metropolitan markets, yet every peasant needed to earn some cash from his agricultural products to remit certain taxes that were payable only in coins. That cash could be gained only by selling his products in a market somewhere.[38]

Han textual sources point to the presence of numerous periodic fairs and regular local markets that integrated cities and towns with the rural hinterland.[39] Though

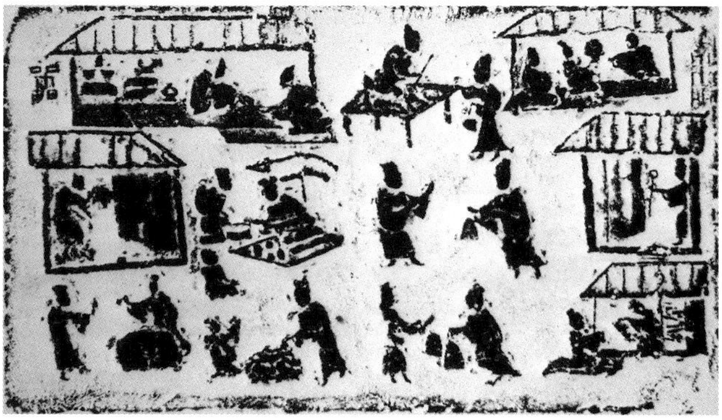

4.3 *Bustling marketplace.* Latter Han period (25–220 CE). Ink-on-paper rubbing from ceramic brick. H. 28 cm. W. 49 cm. Xindu County Cultural Bureau. From Lim, pl. 16.

later legends claimed that these local markets were established on sites where some great personage once stopped to rest, they also just happen to be ideally sited geographically on the periphery of major urban centers. Some of these local markets appear to have specialized in just one commodity, like rush mats or tea, while others had a broader merchandise base. The local markets and periodic fairs were not as heavily policed as the official urban markets. Nor does it appear that merchants were confined to permanently leased stalls. Figure 4.3 is a rubbing of another ceramic brick, this one found near Chengdu. It may represent activity at a smaller, local market in contrast to the large, official market shown in figure 4.2. Judging by this image and other literary references, it appears that some artisan-merchants in local markets set up makeshift kiosks while others merely spread a blanket on the ground and began to sell their wares (see middle left of figure 4.3).

The research of Utsunomiya Kiyoyoshi (b. 1905) and Sahara Yasuo (b. 1958) has demonstrated how the Han official urban markets and the numerous local markets operated in an integrated system.[40] City-made products like women's cosmetics or fine lacquerware were sold first in the urban markets to traders, who later transported them to the local markets for sale. Local products like mats, tea, or foodstuffs were first sold in rural markets to city traders, who then transported and sold them to urban residents in the larger emporia. Large military encampments had their own official markets,[41] and even the enemy nomads were integrated into the market structure. Markets established along the frontier to the north and northwest provided an opportunity for the Xiongnu and other nomadic pastoralists to trade their desirable produce of hides and wool for luxuries like silk and lacquer and commodities like grain and liquor.[42] There also seems to have been a thriving market in contraband goods across the borders, and officials even suspected that people were smuggling goods inside the coffins of deceased soldiers and officials whose bodies were being returned to China![43]

An artisan who chose to sell his or her own products in one of the official urban marketplaces entertained the prospect of making a tremendous profit. That opportunity, however, carried with it substantial social, financial, and legal burdens that made being an artisan-merchant a very risky business indeed.

As discussed in chapter 2, before the Warring States period artisans (*gong*) and merchants (*shang*) were truly distinct occupational castes. The majority of artisans made objects for the feudal lords or for noble families and did not market their products directly.[44] Merchants traded goods between states, sometimes under the sponsorship of nobles and sometimes using their own capital.[45] After the explosive growth of the private-sector market economy during the middle Warring States period, the line between artisan and merchant began to blur. During that time, many artisans operated their own independent workshops and needed to sell their products to someone to earn a living. In practical terms, this made them merchants, yet artisans continued to be treated as a separate social class from merchants for centuries to come. Even though Han laws imposing new taxes on merchants (ca. 120 BCE) recognized that many artisans also performed the functions of merchants, it was not until 596 CE, during the Sui dynasty, that an imperial edict finally lumped artisans and merchants into the same category, barring them both from official service.[46]

During pre-Qin times, there is no evidence that being a merchant carried any social stigma or political restriction.[47] Some of the most powerful men in the contending states, like the kingmaker Lü Buwei, were unabashed merchants and traders. Even the First Emperor of Qin consorted with and respected rich merchants. This reality does not quite square with the Legalist doctrine promoted by Shang Yang (d. 338 BCE) in the state of Qin, which sought to suppress merchant activity in favor of agriculture as a means of enriching the state.[48] It is only toward the end of the reign of the First Emperor of Qin that we see the first edicts that grouped merchants together with dishonored groups to mobilize them for dangerous and onerous tasks.[49]

Social restrictions on merchants would become much more stringent under the succeeding Han dynasty. Under the restrictions put in place by the founder of the Han, which were designed to encourage a return to agriculture in a war-ravaged land, merchants were no longer allowed to wear fine silks, carry weapons, ride on saddled horses, sit in ostentatious carriages, or become government officials. The founder also greatly increased their burden of taxes and required fees.[50] Despite some notable slackening of these rules during the following reigns, especially during that of Emperor Wu (r. 141–87 BCE), some form of sumptuary restriction and political prohibition against merchants remained in the legal statutes throughout the Han period.

During the Qin and Han periods, it appears that resident merchants who operated stalls in the official marketplace were called *gu*, while mobile traders and speculators were called *shang*. Only *gu* merchants universally had to enter their names into a market register (*shiji*), which was the equivalent of the household register for peasants.[51] The market register clarified the blurring social distinctions and made one's status quite unambiguous; if you were on the register, you were a merchant and were then subject to the laws and sumptuary rules attendant upon that status. When the government went looking for groups of despised peoples to settle on newly conquered land or to conscript for unpopular military endeavors, they often turned first to the market registers for recruits.[52] The merchant stigma was hard to escape, for even though a man might give up the marketplace to become a peasant, if either his parents or grandparents had been formally registered as merchants, he was still considered a merchant for recruiting purposes.

Beyond the social stigma of being labeled a despised merchant, artisans who sold their products in the official marketplace were also subject to several fees and taxes payable to the state. If one was registered in the market and wanted to operate a permanent stall, one had to pay a yearly market tax (*shizu*) on one's place of business to the officials in the marketplace.[53] If one did not pay the fee, the penalties could be severe.[54] For much of the Han period, those over seventy years of age who had received a "dove-finial staff" from the government and all those over sixty years of age without male offspring to support them were given a permanent waiver of the market tax.[55] Occasionally, refugees were given a temporary remission of the market tax to help them get back on their feet. During the Former Han, most of the money from the market tax went directly into the Privy Treasury of the emperor (Shaofu) and was used for the upkeep of the court.[56] The amount gained from the market tax could be enormous. Though we do not know the amount each individual artisan-merchant paid for his or her stall, or whether some merchants paid more than others, we do learn from one account that the estimated (and probably exaggerated) market tax from the metropolitan market of Linzi in the Qi-Lu macroregion was said to bring around ten million coins per year into the emperor's Privy Treasury.[57]

Apparently, although artisan-merchants had to pay a fee to rent space in the market, they did not have to pay taxes directly on the amount of goods sold. There is some suggestion, however, that the volume of transactions might have been indirectly taxed through a fee on each notarized contract. Though they were not directly liable for the tax on farm fields (*tianzu*) paid by peasants, artisans and merchants were responsible for paying the other capitation, property, and labor taxes levied against the general population. First, like all other members of the population, in the eighth month they had to pay a once-yearly poll tax (*suanfu*) on each adult member of the household. For the regular population, this liability usually amounted to 120 coins per year for each adult member of the household (fifteen to fifty-six years). For artisans and merchants registered in the marketplace, however, the amount was doubled to 240 coins per person.[58] Since, during much of the Han, artisans and merchants also had to pay a double poll tax each year (240 coins) for each slave owned and 20 coins for each minor child (initially three to fourteen years, later seven to fourteen years), this tax could amount to a great drain on resources.[59]

The property and capital tax (*suanzi*; *suan minqian*) was even more onerous and was weighted selectively against artisans and merchants. It was basically an annual tax on all cash reserves and physical assets. Though there is evidence that the tax had existed before his reign, in 119 BCE Emperor Wu increased the rate and scope of the tax, raising it to as high as 9.5 percent on the assets of unregistered merchants and traders and 4.75 percent on the assets of artisans (including founders) recorded on the market registers.[60] The rate for the general population may have remained as low as

TABLE 4.1. RATES OF TAXATION ON PRODUCTS MINED FROM IMPERIAL LAND (CA. 186 BCE)

Product	*Rate of Taxation by Government*
Salt	16.67% of product, in kind
Sale (long-term lease?) of silver mines	10% of cash receipts
Iron ore	20% of product
Finished iron goods	20% of product (on top of the ore tax)
Lead	10% of product
Gold	13.33% of product, assessed daily
Cinnabar	9.38% of product, assessed monthly; the statute assumes that male miners' yield is 50% greater than female miners' yield[1]

Source: ZJS, 192 ("Ernian lüling," slips 436–8). This is part of the "Statute on Currency" (Jinbu lü).

Note: The part of the statute dealing with taxation of silver production is too fragmentary to interpret properly and has not been included here.

[1] In the section on cinnabar it is unclear if the amounts provided are absolute numbers or ratios. Based on the suggestion of Hsu Cho-yun, I have read them as ratios.

1.2–1.9 percent. Merchants now also had to pay 380 coins per year for each vehicle they owned and 190 coins for each boat over five *zhang* (approx. 11.5 meters) in length. Each head of household was allowed to calculate his own tax liability, but if he concealed his wealth and was denounced by his neighbors, he would be banished and all his property confiscated by the government. Half of the confiscated property would later be given to the informant.[61]

Industrialists engaged in certain enterprises had to pay excise taxes to the government. Before the Han government set up the monopoly on salt and iron sometime shortly after 119 BCE, private entrepreneurs were allowed to go into the hills and extract metal ores or process salt for personal profit. Since all the mountains and streams legally belonged to the emperor, industrialists were charged an excise tax on their mining operations that went to the Privy Treasury, just like the market tax. A fascinating statute preserved in the Han legal texts from Zhangjiashan records the rate of taxation for various products taken from imperial land (see table 4.1).[62] Note that in iron production, the government managed to tax both the ore and the finished products. Apparently, even before the monopoly, iron production was still a very profitable sector for the government. In sum, the taxes and fees imposed on merchants and artisans were quite heavy and at times punitive. This was an intentional move on the part of the government to discourage commerce and to stimulate agriculture. With so much overhead, an artisan-merchant who was not skilled at tax evasion or who could not clear at least 100 percent profit per year would probably end up in the red.

A tight web of laws and supervision regulated the official marketplace. Each lane of stalls in the official marketplace was under the supervision of a senior merchant, probably selected from among his peers, known as the *liezhang* (row head). It was his responsibility to vouch for the honesty and integrity of all the merchants on his row. The merchants on his row were further divided into mutual-responsibility groups of five persons each. If any of the five merchants violated the law or otherwise engaged in shady practices, it was the duty of the other four members in his group to denounce him to the row head and the market officials. If they did not, they would all be severely fined and could lose their stalls permanently. One finds concrete evidence of this system in both the Qin and Han legal statutes. For example, the "Statute on [Passes] and Markets" from Zhangjiashan states in part:

> Those who sell goods in the marketplace yet do not self-report, but rather conceal, their liability for [market] tax will be implicated as having stolen the amount they concealed. All their merchandise and cash receipts will be confiscated by the government. Their stall in the marketplace will be taken away. Their row head (*liezhang*) and those among their five-person mutual-responsibility group who did not denounce them [before the arrest] will all be fined one *jin* (10,000 coins) each.[63]

The mutual-responsibility marketplace system must surely date from the middle Warring States period, for a post similar to the row head is mentioned in the *Ritual System of the Zhou* (Zhouli) and in the text on market regulations from the tomb at Yinqueshan.[64] Systems of mutual responsibility among proprietors of market stalls continued well after the Qin and Han periods. In later periods, the word *hang* (row) gradually replaced *lie* as the standard word for a row of market stalls. When artisans and merchants later banded together for collective protection of their profit and profession, the word *hang* became close in meaning to the English word "guild."

According to a Qin statute, objects for sale in the official marketplace were to have price tags hung from them that stated the exact cost in coins. If the object cost less than one coin of *banliang* denomination, it did not need to carry a tag.[65] Presumably, this regulation was intended to reduce arguments and lawsuits over price-switching scams. The recovered digests of the Qin and Han legal statutes both state that cash money earned by state-run and private enterprises in the marketplace must be placed within a ceramic or bamboo money-box (*qianxiang*). Apparently, this till had a small opening through which it was easy to deposit funds (and contracts or other documents) but difficult to withdraw them. The funds were to remain in the till until government officials could inspect the written sales contracts and confirm that the appropriate government funds or taxes were retained.[66] Those not following the cashbox regulation were fined the value of one suit of armor during the Qin. The Qin regulations also state that artisan-merchants were prohibited from selectively circulating coins by retaining heavy or high-quality coins and pawning off light or defective coins on employees or customers. They were to accept all obviously legal coins and leave the determination of counterfeiting to the state.[67]

Purchases in the official marketplaces were recorded on contracts (*quanshu*; *quanyue*). These consisted of bamboo or wooden documents in two or more parts, each carrying an identical copy of the contract text. After the two parties and any witnesses were read the contents of the texts, the contract was divided between the parties to serve as independent proof of the terms of the transaction. Market officials may have also charged fees for notarizing certain contracts. It appears from Zheng Xuan's (127–200 CE) commentary on the *Ritual System of the Zhou* that during the Han there was a type of long contract for items like horses, cattle, or slaves and a shorter type for less-expensive items like weapons, vessels, and foodstuffs. It is unclear at which price threshold a contract was legally required.[68]

Han contracts were very specific. We know that the contract for a slave could state the date of the transaction, the name, gender, and age of the slave, the price in cash, and all the duties the slave would be required to perform for his or her new master.[69] The contract system allowed both parties in a transaction legal recourse after a breach in terms. The "Statute on Malicious Harm" (Zeilü) stated that if either party to a contract added or subtracted terms at a later date to benefit themselves unilaterally, the ill-gotten profit would be considered stolen property and would be prosecuted under the severe terms of the "Statute on Robbery" (Daolü) (see table 6.2).[70] Only a few market contracts, all of them from the sale of textiles on credit, have been recovered by archaeologists, but numerous "[tomb] land purchase contracts" (*maidi quan*) have been found in Han tombs.[71] Some of these texts appear to be actual contracts, complete with dates, land surveys, prices, and witnesses, whereas others seem to be ritual texts in which the tomb owner asserts his legal right to the land of his burial before all terrestrial and supernatural parties. Testamentary documents during the Han were also a type of contract, called a *xianling quanshu* (contract of directives issued prior to decease). According to a Han statute, the only legally binding will was a fully witnessed, notarized, and copied-in-triplicate *xianling quanshu* filed with the local authorities.[72] During the 1980s, archaeologists uncovered a complete will (dated 5 CE) from a tomb in Jiangsu which detailed a complex estate settlement of a very nontraditional family.[73]

A complex hierarchy of bureaucrats was specifically appointed to collect the taxes and enforce the laws of the marketplaces. Their posts were fully integrated into the Han system of ranks and promotions, so that one could move from serving in a market post to a parallel position in the regional administration or imperial factory bureaucracies.[74] The Eastern and Western Markets of Chang'an were each supervised by a Market Magistrate (Dongshi Ling, Xishi Ling), ranked at 600 *shi*, the same rank and salary held by County Magistrates serving in moderately populous districts.[75] They were under the direct authority of the Metropolitan Governor (Jingzhao Yin).[76] For the Former Han period, we do not know the exact size of the Chang'an Market Magistrates' subordinate staff, but during the Latter Han period, the official markets of the capital of Luoyang were overseen by a Market Magistrate with a subordinate staff of forty-four men.[77] During the Former Han, the smaller suburban markets in the greater metropolitan Chang'an area and the other official metropolitan *duhui* markets like Chengdu, Linzi, Handan, and Yuan were run by a slightly lower ranked Market Head (Shizhang), parallel to the position of County Magistrates serving in less-populous districts.[78] Regional markets at the county (*xian*) level were under the supervision of a Market Bureau Head (Shiyuan) in the county office.[79] At the township (*xiang*) level, it appears that the small local markets were under the authority of a Market Overseer (Shisefu).[80] These market officials worked within the market tower building and were responsible for collecting the market tax, maintaining public safety, approving and taxing contracts, enforcing the laws on product standards and integrity, and, in the case of the capital markets, establishing official prices for some commodities. To incarcerate those who violated the market laws, both the Eastern and Western Markets of Chang'an also operated their own jails.[81]

MARKETING TERRITORIES

Over how wide an area did artisans *personally* market their skills and products? Did they concentrate their efforts in one macroregion or did they travel the empire widely, looking for promising commissions and profitable markets? Let us first investigate the problem of marketing area by revisiting the stone carvers we met in the last chapter. We will examine the evidence from private commissions, in which artisans are paid cash in a coercion-free market transaction, and from royal commissions, in which stone carvers might be conscripted from a wide geographic area and compelled to work on a project.

Let us first consider the case of the private commission. As you may recall, the children of a man named Xiang Tajun hired more than ten artisans to build a stone offering hall in 152 CE (see figure 3.14). Though the structure was built just southwest of Donge County (see map 4.2, marker 2), at least one of the named masons who carved the stones came from Xiaqiu County in Shanyang Commandery, 105 kilometers from the tomb site. The draftsman Dai Sheng came from even farther away, from Gaoping Town, a marquisate embedded in Shanyang Commandery, 130 kilometers from the construction site and 40 kilometers from the home base of the Xiaqiu masons.

This seems relatively far to travel for a moderately well paying commission. The pictorial carvings on the doorpost of Xiang Tajun's offering hall are in a style familiar from the so-called Wu Liang Shrine and other monuments from central Shandong. In fact, the Xiang Tajun monument marks the northernmost extent of that drawing style. In Latter Han times, there were several tributary rivers and broad marshes leading northwest from Shanyang into Dong Commandery that could have facilitated transportation of the work crews, yet it is interesting to note that the masons came from one location and the draftsman came from another to work on the same job. We

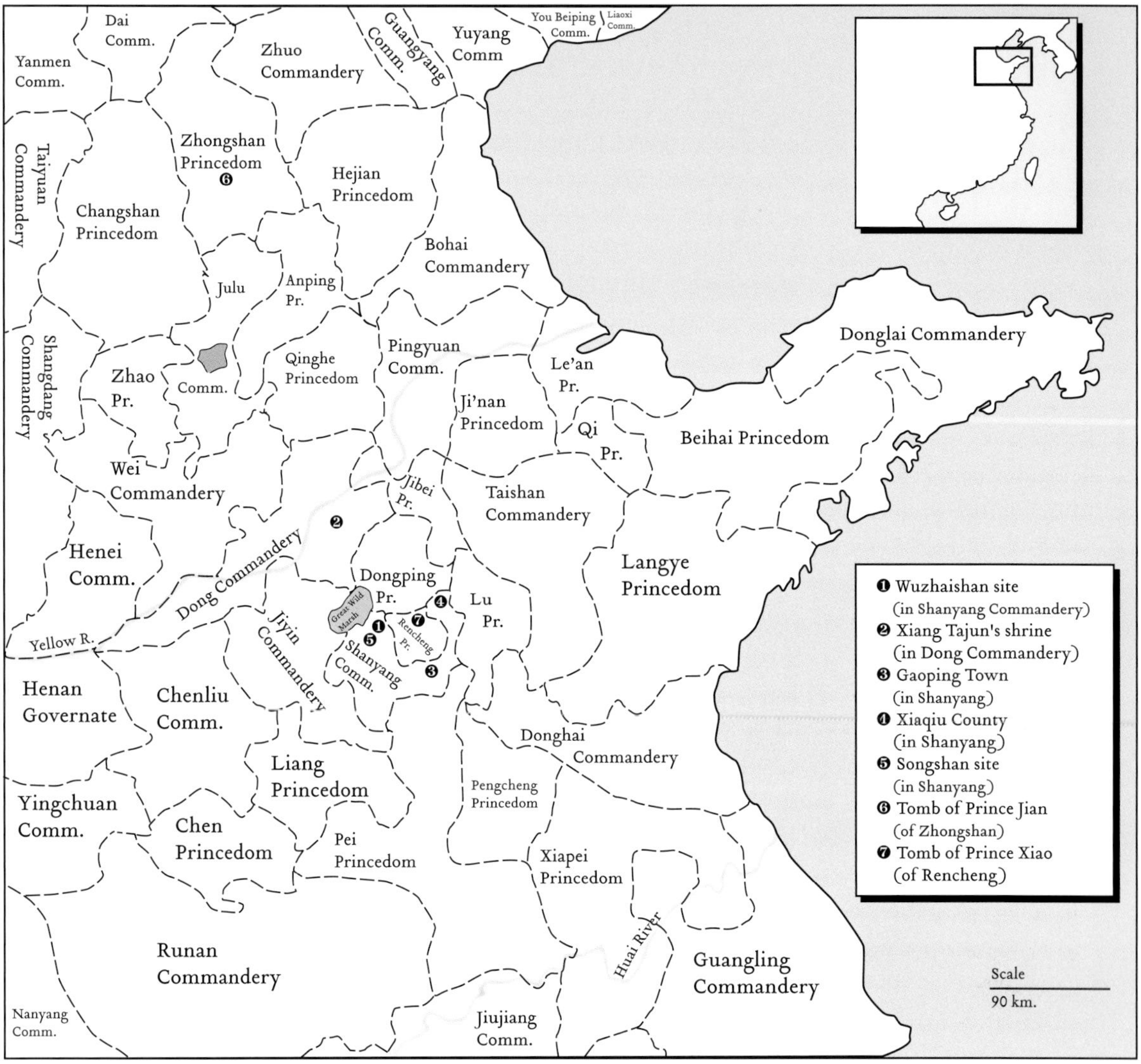

Map 4.2 *Northeast China during the Latter Han period, ca. 140* CE. Map drawn by Anthony Barbieri-Low, based on Tan, vol. 2, maps 44–5, 47–8.

cannot know if these two teams always worked together or if they were subcontracted independently by the master builder on the project, a man of unknown origin named Cao Yi. It may also be incorrect to assume that these men traveled to the worksite in Donge with only their persons and their metal tools, using local stone materials. The men say they took their stones from the "southern mountains," and in this case that figurative location might be taken literally. The workers came from the south, and their home locations in hilly Shanyang certainly possessed more quarries than the Yellow River floodplain around Donge. It may be that certain crews had access to only one particular quarry, which effectively anchored their home base and restricted their mobility to the maximum efficient transport distance over waterborne networks. At some distance from a potential private commission, either the cost of transport outstripped the compensation or word of the potential job did not reach.

In qualification of that conclusion, we then meet a master mason from Lu Princedom named Shi Juyi, who apparently ventured considerably farther from home to complete stone pillar-gates and spirit-path columns (dated 105 CE) for a deceased clerk surnamed Qin, buried near present-day Beijing.[82] This was a full five hundred kilometers from Shi Juyi's native place in Lu. Given the number and complexity of the monuments he carved, perhaps the commission was worth the long trip. Alternately, Shi Juyi may have immigrated to the area from Lu years before. Despite the distance between them, the Lu and Beijing areas are still both located on the vast northeast China plain and could be considered part of the same geographic macroregion.

Now, let us consider how far a mason might be required to travel for a royal tomb project. Throughout the Han, the emperor enfeoffed some of his sons in large, incoming-producing territories relatively distant from the capital. These feudal princes (*zhuhou wang*) had no real power after about 145 BCE but still enjoyed quite lavish lifestyles and burials. Many of their tombs have been excavated in recent decades, and two in particular from the northeast provide compelling data to address the issue of stone carver mobility.

In 1959 Chinese archaeologists excavated a large tomb in Ding County, Hebei, that likely belonged to Liu Yan, Prince Jian of Zhongshan (r. 54–90 CE), a junior son of the founder of the Latter Han dynasty.[83] The tomb mound was still more than twenty meters high when excavated, and the central brick chamber was reinforced by a retaining wall comprising four thousand sandstone blocks, each weighing over three hundred kilograms. More than 174 of those blocks were inscribed by functionally literate masons with their full names, native places, and the source of the stone (figure 4.4d–e).[84]

The sandstone blocks themselves came almost exclusively from two counties within Zhongshan, just to the north of the tomb site (30–70 km away). However, the majority of the 120 named men who carved the blocks came from much farther away. Though nearly 40 percent of the masons came from within Zhongshan itself, most of the remaining 60 percent came from three princedoms far to the southeast: Lu Princedom (360–430 km distant), Liang Princedom (400–60 km), and Dongping Princedom (300 km) (see map 4.2).

We are very fortunate to possess a historical account of this grand tomb-building enterprise that helps explain why the masons ventured so far to work on this project. In Liu Yan's biography in the *History of the Latter Han*, we are told that the mighty Empress Dowager Dou (Dou Taihou) and her eldest brother, Dou Xian, who held regency power from 89 to 92 CE, jointly ordered the princedoms and commanderies surrounding Zhongshan to contribute men and materials for Liu Yan's tomb.[85] It is said that more than ten thousand artisans and convict laborers from more than eighteen commanderies were sent to work on the tomb, including, apparently, the stone carvers who recorded their names on the blocks. The historical account makes clear

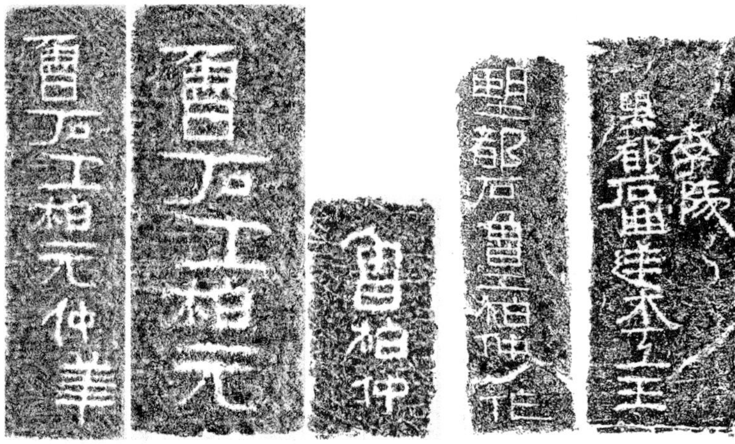

(a) (b) (c) (d) (e)

4.4 *Mason signatures.* Later Han period, ca. 84–93 CE. Ink-on-paper rubbings. Sizes vary, not reproduced to comparable scale.
(a) "Lu Masons Bai Yuan, [Bai] Zhong, [Bai] Hua." From Shandong Sheng Jining Shi Wenwuju, p. 118 (right).
(b) "Lu Mason Bai Yuan." From Shandong Sheng Jining Shi Wenwuju, p. 118 (left).
(c) "Lu [Mason] Bai Zhong." From Shandong Sheng Jining Shi Weuwuju, p. 120 (upper left).
(d) "Stones from Wangdu. Made by artisan Bai Zhong from Lu." From Hebei Sheng Wenhuaju Wenwu Gongzuodui, p. 188, rubbing 19.
(e) "Stones from Wangdu. Carpenter Wang Jiling from Quni County." Hebei Sheng Wenhuaju Wenwu Gongzuodui, p. 189, rubbing 155.

that the artisans were conscripted for this job and that their labor was considered tax tribute (*diao*). Thus, although they were not paid cash, their work should still be considered as compensated, since it commuted taxes that might have been paid in cash.

The princes of Lu, Liang, and Dongping were closely related to Liu Yan, so they may have felt more obligated than the governors of nearby commanderies to contribute labor and materials to the project.[86] As a sidelight, it is interesting to note that one of the men sent to work on the prince's tomb, a certain Wang Jiling, recorded his profession on at least one stone as *mugong* (carpenter) (see figure 4.4e).[87] Apparently, it did not matter on this job that in his ordinary line of work he was more accustomed to hewing timber than stone.

Many of the conclusions reached from Liu Yan's tomb at Zhongshan are confirmed by the more recent excavation of a tomb likely belonging to Liu Shang (r. 84–101 CE), Prince Xiao of Rencheng, almost 350 kilometers away in central Shandong (map 4.2).[88] Liu Shang was a nephew of Liu Yan and a grandson of the dynasty founder. His tomb also contained a retaining wall whose stones were inscribed with masons' names (see figure 4.4a–c). Judging by place-names mentioned in the inscriptions, his tomb was probably built sometime between 84 and 93 CE, around the same time as Liu Yan's tomb.

To work on Liu Shang's tomb, masons also came from a variety of places. His elder brother's princedom of Dongping (40–70 km distant) contributed 31 percent of the named masons. The princedom of Lu (40–85 km) and his cousin's princedom of Liang (120–60 km) supplied nearly 45 percent of the men. Liu Shang's own small fief of Rencheng contributed only 6 percent of the carvers. A few random men came from commanderies as far as 360 kilometers distant.

It is apparent from reading through the masons' names on these blocks that the stone-carving profession often ran in families. Three men with the Bai surname from Lu, probably brothers, worked on the Prince of Rencheng's tomb. On two stones found at the site they recorded their names together, probably in birth order, as "Bai-Yuan-Zhong-Hua," in other words, "Bai Yuan, [Bai] Zhong, and [Bai] Hua" (see figure 4.4a).[89] On two other stones, Bai Yuan and Bai Zhong recorded their names separately (see figures 4.4b–c).[90] The Bai family came from the seat of the Lu Princedom, only about forty kilometers from the tomb site. Shortly before or after his work on the Rencheng tomb, however, Bai Zhong, the presumed second-eldest son, volunteered or was conscripted to work on Liu Yan's tomb in Zhongshan as well. His name shows up quite clearly, in roughly the same hand, on blocks from that site (see figure 4.4d).[91] For the Zhongshan job, he traveled more than 360 kilometers, in the company of twenty other masons from Lu.

To summarize, it appears from inscriptional evidence that stone carvers were rarely enticed or compelled to travel more than five hundred kilometers from their home base to work on a project, regardless of whether it was a private commission or a royal conscription. The normal operating radius seems to have been even smaller. In effect, carvers operated within one macroregional area, defined by drainage basins or contiguous geographic features. This might help explain the rather clear boundaries between regional styles of stone carving on Han pictorial stones. There is no evidence that stone carvers from Shandong were ever invited or enticed to travel to Sichuan or Nanyang for jobs, or vice versa. If such interregional movement had been a regular occurrence, we might see more Shandong-style carving and motifs in those regions. That is not to say that people and motifs did not travel the empire at all, just that regular cross-pollination does not seem to have been a common occurrence.

Literary evidence also supports the idea of a limited direct-marketing territory for artisans. In the famous story (translated in chapter 2) of the virtuous court lady Wang Zhaojun, who refused to bribe the court portrait artists to paint her favorably, we are told that after all the artists were executed in the marketplace for their deceit (ca. 33 BCE), their families were investigated, and all their wealth confiscated. Following this mention, there is a list of the artists implicated in the scandal, prefixed by the names of their native places, possibly copied from some original court document.[92] Mao Yanshou, said to be the greatest portrait painter of the age, was a native of Duling, the tomb town established near the mausoleum of Emperor Xuan, twenty kilometers to the southeast of the palace center. The painter Chen Chang was a native of Anling, the town raised near the necropolis of Emperor Hui, only fourteen kilometers northwest from the Chang'an city center. Liu Bo and Gong Kuan were said to come from New Feng, the re-created village made for Liu Bang's father, located only thirty-three kilometers to the northeast of Chang'an. Yang Wang is mentioned as a native of Xiadu, a mere fifteen kilometers southeast of the palace center. Therefore, if we can rely on any of the details recounted in the *Miscellaneous Notes on the Western Capital* account, it seems that the palace drew its master portrait painters only from the immediate vicinity of the capital. None of these men came from more than one day's journey away. Their services were apparently not in constant demand by the emperor, so it seems unlikely that they were allowed to live in the palace full-time. They probably commuted from their home workshops when summoned. The capital macroregion was densely populated, so the court was probably never in want of suitable talent. In fact, great artisan families may have intentionally migrated toward the epicenter of wealth and patronage over the course of the dynasty. What nineteenth-century painter would not want to work in Paris?

Thus, judging by epigraphic and literary sources, it seems that Qin and Han artisans were not very geographically mobile. It appears that stone carvers and master painters sought commissions only in one economic macroregion and endeavored to establish a strong local workshop tradition in the core area. This partially explains why the regional stone-carving traditions during the Han were so characteristic and distinct. Transportation costs might also have been a factor limiting the direct-marketing area of some artisans. Stone carvers probably needed to transport tons of materials to a job site, for there was no guarantee that they could obtain access to quarries in the local area. Despite the economies of river transportation over road travel, the distance for economically rational material transportation tapers off quickly from the quarry area. Even the court seems to have drawn its master artisans only from the area immediately around the capital. There are no records which indicate an empirewide search for the greatest artisans to serve the palace, unlike analogous searches conducted to find great scholars for the bureaucracy or dazzling beauties for the harem.

That is not to say that the products made by a Qin or Han artisan might not find themselves much farther afield through down-the-line trade or other distribution mechanisms. Some Chinese artisans even appear to have made products specifically targeted to the needs of non-ethnic-Han customers beyond the frontiers. In 1999, archaeologists uncovered a medium-sized grave in the northern suburbs of Xi'an City belonging to the Qin state and dated to the late Warring States period (ca. 250–222 BCE).[93] The lone tomb occupant was a man, probably named Cang, who appears to have been a bronze caster by trade, for he was buried with a representative set of his tools, including clay models for producing casting molds, a whetstone, and various iron finishing tools. The twenty-five casting models found in Bronze Caster Cang's tomb represent a fascinating repertoire of work. Slightly more than half consist of models for making bronze plaques, bosses, and saddle ornaments of the "Ordos type," used by northern nomadic pastoralists like the Xiongnu and other related cultures. The remainder of the models were used to produce traditional Chinese ritual vessels, weapons, lamps, and carriage parts. The form of his burial and its attendant grave goods strongly suggest that Cang himself was an ethnic-Han Chinese craftsman. Thus, it appears that Bronze Caster Cang, working just south of the metropolitan Qin state capital of Xianyang, was adept at making bronze products for two entirely different markets. His divergent styles show a sensitivity to the tastes of a metropolitan Chinese clientele and to those of the nomadic horsemen who lived north and west of the capital, beyond the early Qin version of the Great Wall. Bronze Caster Cang may never have personally conducted business with a Xiongnu client. I would hypothesize that his Ordos-style bronze plaques were sold in the capital market of Xianyang to traders who brought them up to the frontier markets beyond the customs barriers.

Now, let us look even further beyond the heartland of China and see where marketing and trading systems could carry the products of the Qin and Han artisans. During the 1920s, imperial Japanese archaeologists excavated dozens of lacquer vessels from Han tombs in North Korea. Many of these lacquers had originally been made in imperial and private workshops in the city of Chengdu, two thousand kilometers away. The pieces made in imperial workshops for use by the emperor and his court were probably acquired as gifts from the sovereign. The privately manufactured pieces were probably first sold in the Chengdu market to traders, who then transported them to the capital market of Chang'an. There they were probably resold at a higher price to junior officials, who later brought them in their baggage to their new posts in Lelang Commandery (North Korea). Lacquer vessels decorated in a similar style, and probably also produced near Chengdu, were found in the famous hoard from Begram in Afghanistan.[94] Those pieces probably followed a tortuous multistage route of gifting and trading from Chengdu, up through the Gansu Corridor northwest of the capital, hopscotching across the oasis towns of the Tarim Basin, and finally up over the Pamirs to Afghanistan. Thus, the ultimate trading network for Chengdu-style lacquer vessels spanned nearly five thousand kilometers in the first to second centuries CE.

Han silk textiles, many sporting figural designs and auspicious phrases written in Chinese, have been found as far away as Palmyra in Syria.[95] The trade mechanisms that brought these precious fabrics so far from their point of origin are still a matter of controversy.[96] There is no concrete evidence that they were produced for export by any privately run workshop, nor is there any evidence during the Han for the type of long-distance trading caravans and regular Indian Ocean traffic that are known from later centuries. From around 125–115 BCE onward, Chinese official envoys bearing silks had traveled westward as far as Parthian Iran, seeking military allies and diplomatic contact (and personal profit). Chinese sovereigns also regularly gave large gifts of silk to nomadic chieftains as part of the tributary system of foreign relations. It may be that these were the textiles, produced by artisans in imperial factories, that eventually made their way to sites like Palmyra.

It was not only luxury items like lacquer or silks that were traded over such distances. When the great Han explorer and diplomat Zhang Qian (d. 113 BCE) was in Daxia (the Bactria area of northern Afghanistan) around 128 BCE, he saw bamboo staves and hemp cloth that he knew came from the area of present-day Sichuan. When he asked the people of Daxia where they had acquired the articles, they said that their traders had acquired them in the markets of the Gangetic kingdoms of India to the southeast.[97] The most logical solution is that the cane and cloth had been traded from Sichuan, southwest through Yunnan and Burma, into India (a traditional route in later times), upstream on the Ganges, then across the Hindu Kush into northern Afghanistan. Numerous intermediate merchants probably participated in this down-the-line trade, for rarely is the direct, long-distance transportation of heavy commodities like bamboo economical for the trader. However, this casual observation of Zhang Qian's provides some of the most valuable textual evidence in the ancient world for the movement of nonluxury items several thousands of kilometers from their place of manufacture.

MARKETING TECHNIQUES

An investigation of the marketing techniques used by artisans and merchants provides the strongest body of evidence supporting the existence of competitive-market elements in the Han economy. Numerous pieces of evidence suggest that Han artisans cut corners on quality, recycled materials, created knockoffs of high-status designs, borrowed imperial factory marks, composed rhyming advertising jingles, and engaged in blatant self-promotion, all to increase their profit and market share. Artisan-merchants during the Han seem to have been well aware of their competition and were quite determined to outsmart them in the marketplace.

SKIMPING AND RECYCLING

One of the ways to increase profit is, of course, to cut costs. Han artisans were constantly tempted to cut costs by skimping on materials, adulterating substances, and otherwise passing off shoddy goods as high-quality products. The Han laws contained market statutes specifically punishing offenses related to shoddy goods, undersize textiles, and skewed market scales (see translations in chapter 2). The fact that such laws as these were penned at all suggests that shady practices must have been quite common. Sometimes, as we saw in the quotation from Cui Shi translated earlier, the deceitful manufacturers directly imperiled the well-being of the state through such tricks.

A different, and sometimes equally immoral and illegal way of cutting material costs, was to recycle existing materials. Repeatedly in the last two chapters, we have visited the world of the Shandong masons and stone carvers who fashioned funerary monuments for the wealthy and moderately wealthy. During the heyday of the stone-monument craze in the mid–second century, it probably seemed like the funerary business would grow perpetually, as upstart families competed to outspend each other on final expenses. Starting around 184 CE, however, there were tremendous economic and social upheavals in the Shandong area that decimated the population and collapsed the high-end funeral business.[98] After those disruptions, dated monuments are few and far between, and one cannot escape the impression that the bubble had burst.

The desperate times accelerated a trend that had already begun a few decades earlier. Namely, during the late second century and continuing through the fifth century, funerary artisans often found it more convenient and economical to plunder stones from the aboveground monuments and belowground tombs of their neighbors' ancestors rather than quarry, dress, and decorate new building materials. Using a more delicate turn of phrase, one could say they were engaged in *recycling* abandoned stone monuments. Archaeologists have excavated numerous tombs in North China dating from the third to fifth centuries that were made from reused stones originally part of first- and second-century monuments.[99]

Even during the height of the building boom, vandalism and looting were already a pressing concern for tomb builders and mourning families alike. One passage near the end of the inscription on An Guo's monument (February 2, 158 CE) warned:

> To all you young men who herd horses, cows, and sheep! Be like the children of good families. If you enter into this hall, please just look around. Do not efface the images or carve graffiti. If you do not, then you will be granted long life. Do not maliciously cause damage! Otherwise, may misfortune rain down on you and your descendants.[100]

Needless to say, this warning went unheeded, for a few decades after the monument was dedicated, its parts were dismantled and reused in another tomb.[101] That tomb was excavated along with three others between 1978 and 1981 at the sites of Songshan and Wulaowa in Jiaxiang County, Shandong.[102] All four tombs tell a similar story. The crypts are moderate in size and many of the stones of their walls, ceilings, and floors were clearly looted from earlier aboveground offering halls and belowground tombs dating from about 67 to 158 CE. Some stones had been cropped, and all were haphazardly placed in the new tombs and coated with plaster.

It is quite telling that all the pictorial stones from these graves had been coated with an obscuring layer of lime plaster, up to one centimeter thick, which completely concealed the pictorial scenes. It would be a mistake to interpret this effacement as revealing the tomb masons' desire to hide their culpability in grave robbing. Rather, we should see this as a ritual de-sanctification of the earlier images, rechristening the stones for a new purpose. Images have power, and which images are placed in one's tomb can be a sensitive subject. It appears that by the time of the Songshan and Wulaowa tombs (third to fourth centuries) Han conventions of homage scenes, filial paragons, winged deities, and chariot processions had lost much of their significance.[103] One might even suggest that they had been discredited with the fall of the Han and their ruling ideology—best to whitewash away such inauspicious images and remove any malicious influence that might still be attached to them from their earlier association with death and the extinguished family lineage that allowed them to be ravaged by looters.

The situation calls to mind the similar fate of Pharaoh Akhenaten's (r. ca. 1379–1362 BCE) monuments in Egypt.[104] After the death of the heretic pharaoh and the discrediting of his ideology, his successors, such as Rameses II (r. ca. 1304–1237), reused thousands of stone blocks from his buildings at El-Amarna and Thebes. Yet, since the blocks displayed heretical scenes of the repudiated ruler and his ideology, the stones were used only as filler *inside* temple pylons and wall foundations, which preserved their material value as stones while ritually killing and burying their iconic power.

Another series of tombs in the Shandong and Nanyang areas sought even greater economy than that seen at Songshan. In these post-Han tombs, the walls and floors were made of less-expensive ceramic bricks (often recycled), while the flat roofs were planked over with stone slabs about 1.1–1.4 meters in width.[105] The roof slabs were salvaged from a variety of Latter Han funerary monuments and cropped to a uniform length. On one slab you might see the carved handle of a tomb door, another might have been an offering table, while another was likely the back wall of a small offering hall. The content and location of the images on the roof slabs seem to have been immaterial to the new tomb builders. In these bargain creations, no decorative program was intended, for all that mattered was the cost savings from recycled materials. It was more economical to just lay six or seven recycled stone planks over the crypt and have done with it, rather than properly roof over the tomb with a genuine brick vault, a design that would have required the tomb to have been dug deeper.

Lavish tombs are fueled by demand from wealthy customers. When the bottom dropped out of the market, the healthy commissions were no longer forthcoming for the stone carvers. To stay in business, they downsized their plans and cut material costs wherever they could. That meant no longer using new stone materials and no longer carving original decoration.

A final brief example of this sordid business will add a human perspective to the stone-monument reuse market. In 1973 archaeologists excavated a small shaft tomb near present-day Nanyang, Henan.[106] It was similar to the type just described, with brick walls and a stone-slab ceiling made from recycled materials. The presence of certain coins and ceramics dates the tomb to the mid–third century. Three of the five ceiling slabs used to cover the crypt still carried cropped decorative scenes. On one of these three stones was depicted a scene of entertainers at a banquet, of the type commonly seen on the walls of Nanyang tombs from the Latter Han period (see figure 4.5). The leftmost portion of the banquet scene appears to have been intentionally effaced to clear the ground for an inscription. The 136-character text is an epitaph, lamenting the untimely death of a five-year-old boy named Aqu of the Xu family who

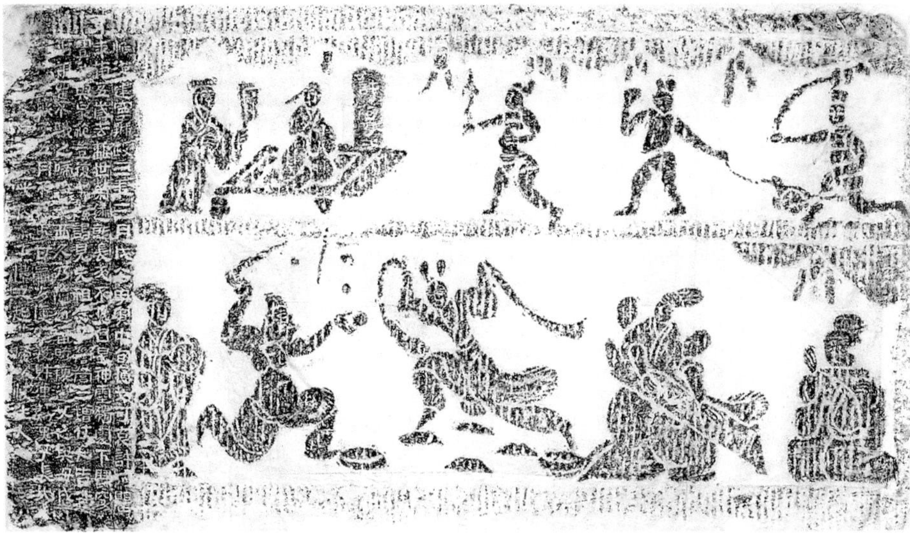

4.5 *Epitaph of Xu Aqu.* Latter Han period, dated April 25, 170 CE. Ink-on-paper rubbing. H. 69 cm. W. 109 cm. Han Pictorial Gallery, Nanyang, Henan. Zhongguo Huaxiangshi Quanji Bianji Weiyuanhui, vol. 6, pl. 202.

died on April 25, 170 CE. It reads in part: "Oh the pain, pitiful little Xu Aqu. . . . He was barely five years old when he left this world and departed for the long night, never again to see the sun and stars. His spirit dwells alone and descends into the dark realm, forever to be cut off from his family. How can they again see his face?" Though poignant and dramatic, the epitaph is rather inelegantly written in rhyming four-character phrases, consisting mostly of boilerplate clichés about death and mourning. Little Aqu's name was also added as a caption to the young male figure seated on the dais to the left of the entertainers.

Reconstructing from these clues, it seems that this durable slab saw use in three separate funerary structures over a period of at least a century. It began its life as a wall slab in a wealthy Nanyang tomb built during the early second century. In 170 CE, the stone, which had been looted from the original tomb, was reused in a makeshift monument for a five-year-old named Xu Aqu. Space was cleared for an epitaph by grinding down the original bas-relief, and the figure of the rich adolescent who was enjoying the banquet in the original scene was recaptioned to indicate the deceased Aqu. Finally, Aqu's monument was itself plundered sometime in the early third century, and the banquet slab was trimmed for use as a roof slab in the tomb of an unnamed occupant. Just as today, when the clothes and cars of the rich eventually trickle down in secondhand markets to become the shabby possessions of the poor, so expensive pictorial stones of the Latter Han period could find themselves reused in a cascading series of cheaper and cheaper contexts.

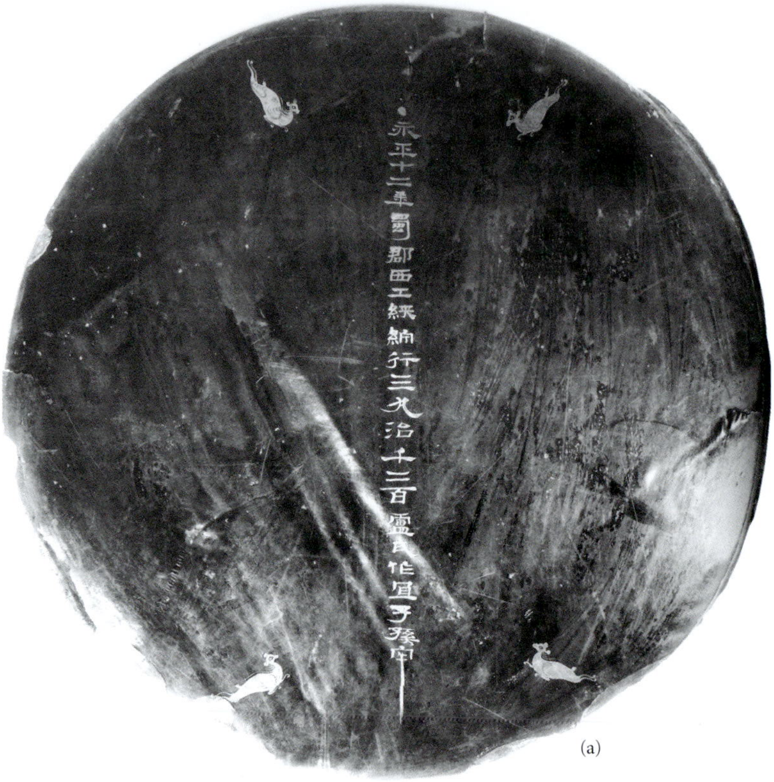

(a)

4.6 *Lacquer tray.*
(a) Underside with inscription.
(b) Interior, detail. Latter Han period, dated 69 CE. Lacquer over fabric-reinforced wooden core. D. 54 cm. From Harada and Tazawa, pls. 56, 58.

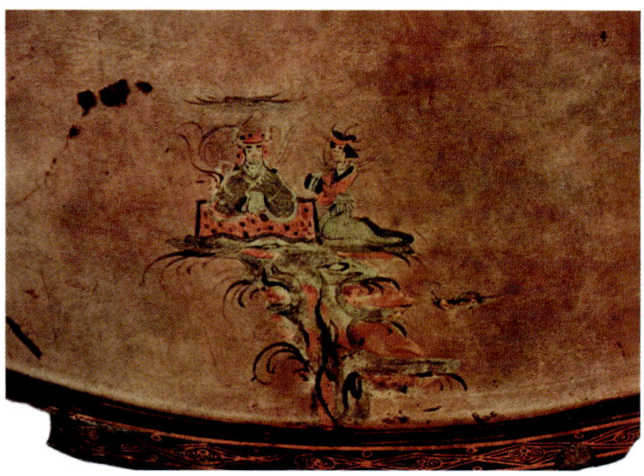

(b)

KNOCKOFFS AND JINGLES

By passing off shoddy goods or recycling materials, Han artisans could increase their profits by cutting costs, yet it is in the realm of brand identification and advertising that we really see the creative side of early Chinese marketing. In 1925 Japanese archaeologists excavated two large lacquer trays from the tomb of Wang Xu, a provincial official who served in the Han commandery of Lelang, located near present-day P'yôngyang, North Korea.[107] One of these trays is displayed in figure 4.6.

The platter measures about fifty-four centimeters in diameter and is constructed by the repeated application of lacquer fluid over a fabric-reinforced, wood core. The background of the interior was painted red, while the ground of the underside was painted black, all in accord with Chinese lacquer-painting traditions. The interior of the platter (figure 4.6b) displays a marvelous polychrome miniature portrait of a deity seated on a raised platform, sheltered by a canopy, and supplicated by a kneeling male. The iconography of the image clearly identifies the central figure as the Queen Mother of the West (Xiwangmu), the popular deity of the Han immortality cult. The interior also sports tiny images of dragon and tiger directional animals, important symbols of geomantic power for the proper placement of tombs and offerings. The presence of the Queen Mother of the West and the directional animals suggests that this platter may have been purchased specifically for burial.

On the underside of the platter (figure 4.6a) the lacquer artisans emblazoned their creation with a large inscription and surrounded it with leaping deerlike animals:

永平十二年, 蜀郡西工, 夾紵行三丸 (垸), 治 (值)千二百, 盧氏作, 宜子孫, 牢.
The twelfth year of the Yongping era [69 CE].
The Western Workshop of Shu Commandery.
Ramie cored and coated with several layers of mixed lacquer and ash
[for strength]. It is worth twelve hundred coins.[108]
Made by the Lu family.
May it bring you sons and grandsons.
Very sturdy.

After the date notation, the inscription claims that the platter was made at the Western Workshop of Shu Commandery (Shu Jun Xigong), the illustrious state-run factory in Chengdu which operated more or less continuously for three hundred years, supplying the Qin and Han emperors with weapons, gilded bronzes, decorative knives, and lacquer tableware. This claim is followed by some slightly exaggerated descriptions of the object's construction and monetary value. Then, there is the peculiar mention of a Lu family as the manufacturers, followed by the auspicious slogan *yi zisun* (may it bring you sons and grandsons) and the word *lao,* which in this Han context probably means "very sturdy."[109]

The style of decoration reveals clearly that this platter *was not made* at the Western Workshop of Shu. Its appearance is very distinctive, and it does not resemble any other piece known to have been made at the Western Workshop. Surviving, genuine imperial pieces made at the Western Workshop during this time (ca. 69 CE) are largely undecorated, following the Confucian-inspired suppression of ornament at court. Nor does the decoration on this flashy piece correspond to the earlier heraldic style that was characteristic of the Western Workshop between about 30 BCE and 14 CE (see figure 3.6a–c).[110]

The phrasing and placement of the inscription also preclude the possibility that this piece was really made at the Western Workshop. As mentioned earlier, inscriptions were legislated for objects made in state-run factories since at least the late fourth century BCE. A legitimate Western Workshop inscription would have mentioned not only the year and place of manufacture but detailed product specifications and the names of the artisans and supervisors responsible for the object's production, listed in order of precedence. This dry, detailed document would have been engraved in an unobtrusive location on the lacquer with a sharp stylus, using minute graphs. Figure 3.6c shows a typical Western Workshop inscription, in this case from an eared cup used for drinking beer, dated 4 CE. A detailed analysis of that inscription (and many similar examples) reveals the fine division of labor and the complexity of management at Han state-run workshops (see chart 3.1).

It appears that a private lacquer workshop in Chengdu, operated by the Lu family, borrowed from the tradition of quality-control inscriptions and modified it to suit more commercial purposes. Though the Lus began their inscription conservatively enough with the year of manufacture and the factory name, they then proceeded to express crass notions of monetary value and rattle off auspicious slogans concerning fertility. The phrases are broken up into three- and four-character units, following the traditions of popular verse and incantations meant to ward off evil. Such phrases never appear within the quality-control inscriptions on genuine imperial products. They often appear, however, on privately produced pieces with no explicit claim to imperial provenance.

As for the placement of inscriptions, private workshops would often write their enlarged inscriptions in a central location. The inscription on this platter was painted in brilliant vermilion lacquer. It was executed in a decorative clerical script, displaying dramatic thickening and thinning of line and a dashing, trailing flourish at the end of the final graph. The four leaping deer which seem to vault toward the inscription further highlight the text. The same four deer appear on the other Lu family–manufactured platter from Wang Xu's tomb and may have been their trademark.[111]

What was the Lu family trying to accomplish here? Were they trying to make a high-quality counterfeit of an imperial lacquer platter? Were they trying to deceive their customers into thinking that their products were made at the Western Workshop of Shu Commandery? I do not think so. The upper levels of official society were well aware of the Western Workshop and its lacquerware, for many officials owned one or more examples of its products. In order to demonstrate his munificence, the emperor would often award presents of lacquer tableware to officials serving in the capital and provinces. In fact, in the very same tomb that yielded these two platters, there were two genuine imperial lacquer cups, one made at the Western Workshop of Shu Commandery and one at its sister factory in Guanghan Commandery, gifts from the emperor or some other high official for meritorious service.[112] Thus, the Lu family workshop's motivation for borrowing the name of the imperial lacquer factory to label their products was probably not deception. Most well-placed and knowledgeable people who might come across this piece in the marketplace would not be fooled into believing it was a genuine imperial piece. Nor was the Lu family platter intended to be a cheap (meaning poor-quality) knockoff. It is very well made, and the list price was almost two weeks' salary for a county magistrate during the Latter Han.

It appears that the Lu family workshop borrowed the name of the Western Workshop to *lend cachet* to their products in a manner similar to the practice of some American teenagers during the 1980s–90s in which a young man would tear the hood ornament off a Mercedes luxury sedan and mount it on the hood of his Chevy. No one is fooled into thinking that his Chevy is really a Mercedes, but somehow he hopes to associate his car, and his personal image, with a high-status object like the Mercedes luxury car. According to literary descriptions, the Chengdu marketplace where this platter was probably made was filled with lacquer workshops, and competition was apparently fierce for market share. Industrious proprietors, the Lu family sought to invest their lacquer platter with every conceivable selling point. Namely:

1 *It is well constructed,* as fine as any piece made by the Western Workshop of Shu Commandery.
2 *It is fashionable and beautiful.* It is painted with decorative red calligraphy, which would appeal to scholar-officials who had begun to appreciate the burgeoning art of calligraphy, and it is painted with the image of a popular deity.
3 *It is valuable.* (Of course, even though the declared value is 1,200 cash, if you went around to the back of the shop, Mr. Lu could probably have given you a discount.)
4 *It will bring good luck and male offspring.* The painted images promise to give you fortune in this life and the next. The leaping deer were a pun on the word "deer" (*lu*), which was a homophone with another word that meant "income."[113] The auspicious directional animals could direct you to paradise, and the Queen Mother of the West could confer immortality on your soul when you got there.

The same aggressive advertising techniques can be seen in the market for bronze mirrors during the latter half of the Han dynasty.[114] Many bronze mirrors from the Wang Mang (9–23 CE) and Latter Han periods (25–220 CE) claim to have been made at the Shangfang (Directorate for Imperial Manufactories). The Shangfang was a large, multipurpose imperial workshop located within the walls of the principal Han palace and was responsible for making limited production runs of fine articles like bronzes, lamps, and weapons for the emperor's personal use. As we shall see in the next chapter, it also kept on staff a number of court painters skilled in portraiture and narrative painting.[115]

None of the hundreds of extant mirrors whose inscriptions claim they were made by the Shangfang can be convincingly declared genuine. It has been suggested by one scholar that most of these mirrors were indeed made by the Shangfang, but that they were produced for the market by the government or constituted surplus production dumped on the market.[116] This theory is undermined by the fact that some Han mirrors claim to have been made *simultaneously* at the Shangfang and at other

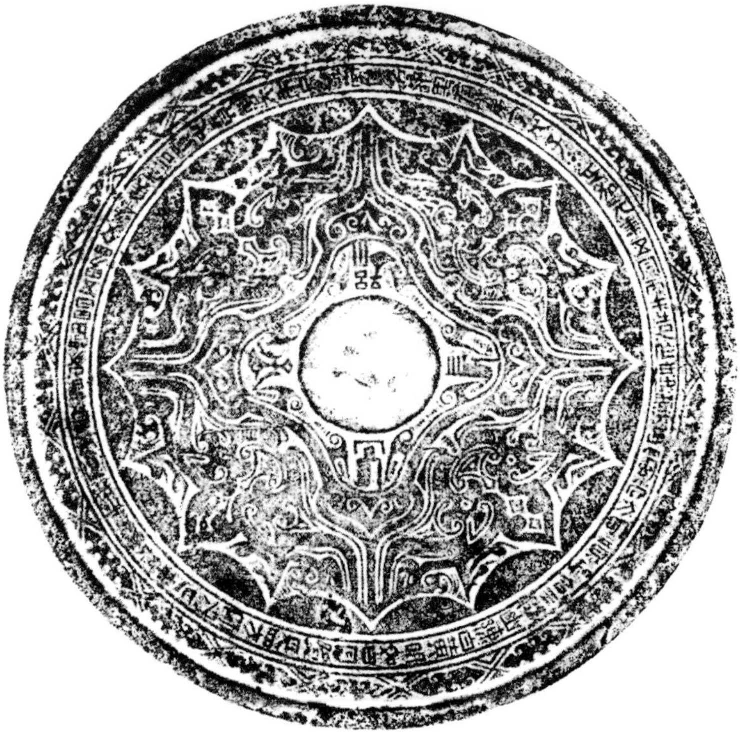

4.7 *Mirror* (backside). Latter Han period, dated June 23, 145 CE. Ink-on-paper rubbing of bronze mirror. From Umehara, *Kan Sangoku*, pl. 6.

illustrious imperial factories. For example, figure 4.7 depicts a bronze mirror "dated" June 23, 145 CE.[117] The inscription reads:

□加（嘉）元年五月丙午。
造作廣漢、西蜀、尚方、明竟（鏡）。
和合三陽（祥），幽練白黃。
明如日月，照見四方。
師□延年，長樂未央。
買此竟（鏡）者，家富昌。
五男四女，為侯王。
后買此竟（鏡），居大市。
家□掌佳名□里有八弟□戊（武）子。

In the fifth month of the first year of the [Yong]jia era, on the *bingwu* day [June 23, 145 CE], made a Guanghan [Commandery, Office of Workmen], Western Shu [*sic*], Shangfang brilliant mirror.

I have harmoniously combined the three auspicious metals,[118]
and refined the white [tin] and the yellow [copper] by a secret formula.

As brilliant as the sun or the moon, its reflection enables one to see to the ends of the earth.
It will enable one to extend his life and have eternal happiness without end.
For one who buys this mirror, may his family become rich and prosperous.
May he have five sons and four daughters, and may they all become [or marry] marquises and princes.
For one who buys this mirror secondhand, may he occupy a prominent place in a large market.
May his family acquire a good name, . . . [fragmentary, unclear passage].[119]

Focusing for now just on the header of the inscription, this mirror not only claims to have been made at the Guanghan imperial factory, the Western Workshop of Shu Commandery, and the Shangfang, but the names of the factories have been jumbled together and some have been written incorrectly. It would be like having a used-car salesman claim his vehicle was a Mersaydeez-BWM-Poorsha. Interestingly, the first two Han factories mentioned in the inscription were actually no longer in operation when the mirror was made. Clearly, the factory names had fallen into the public domain and had become merely illustrious words, conjuring up glorious treasures of past emperors. They had become slogans, catchphrases with which to imbue a product with greater snob appeal, greater quasi-magical power, and greater marketability.

Remaining in the genre of bronze mirrors for a while will enable us to look at another fascinating marketing technique: the magico-auspicious, rhyming jingle. Figure 4.8 depicts a Han bronze mirror of the late second or earlier third century CE that also claims to have been made by the Shangfang.[120] The inscription cast around the outer rim reads:

尚方作鏡，真大好。
上有仙人，不知老。
渴飲玉泉；飢食棗。
俳佪神山，采芝草。
壽敝金石，西王母。

Mirrors made by Shangfang are really all the rage.
On them are immortals who know nothing of old age.
If parched, they drink of jade; when hungry, sup on dates.
They rove about on the hills of the gods, plucking fungus and herbs that are blessed.
Long life to you, longer than metal or stone or even the Queen of the West.[121]

The inscriptions on mirrors like this one and the previous example were written in rhyming doggerel verse, in lines of three to eight characters each. Seven characters is the most common format, and some mirrors even make the claim that the literary

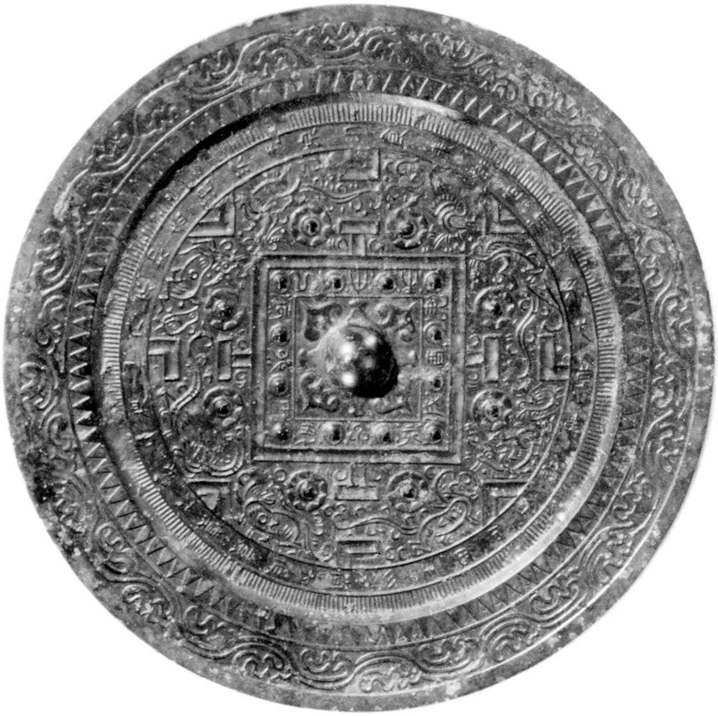

4.8 *Mirror* (backside). Latter Han period, ca. late second or early third century CE. Bronze. D. 20.9 cm. Weight 1,239 g. Moriya Collection, Kyoto National Museum. Photo courtesy of Kyoto National Museum.

form of the seven-character verse (with 4-3 syllable division) was actually first used on mirror inscriptions.[122] Usually the same rhyme is held throughout the verse. In the case of the mirror in figure 4.8, the final syllables of *hao, lao, zao, cao,* and *mu* no longer exactly rhyme in modern Mandarin, but they do rhyme perfectly in modern Cantonese (*hou, lou, jou, chou, mou*) and certainly seem to have rhymed during the Han.[123] Sometimes, if a line fell short by one graph, the filler character *xi* 兮 was used as a verbal pause, just as in classical poetry. Other mirrors from this time period carry slightly different verses, though the same phrases or subphrases often seem to have been shuffled around to produce only a limited variation.

The phrases in the inscriptions are similar in form to popular rhymes and magical incantations, and this fact gives us some hint as to the dual purpose of the verses. We would be grossly biased by our modern worldview if we interpreted these jingles as pure advertising slogans, with catchy rhymes to delight the purchaser. We would also be nearsighted if we considered them only as ritual texts or even superstitious gibberish, with no power to push the product out the shop door. Clearly, they were intended to serve *both purposes.*

Often, mirrors refer to the quality of the product specifically, making claims like "brighter than the sun or the moon; brighter than any mirror the world has ever seen!"[124] Some Latter Han mirrors claim to bring the purchaser many advantages, and surprisingly the purchaser (*maizhe*) or "one who buys this mirror" (*mai ci jingzhe*) is mentioned specifically, as on the mirror seen in figure 4.7. The advantages are categorized for each potential customer, lest someone be left out. Some inscriptions claim that if you purchase the mirror, it will ward off bad luck and attract good luck, give you sons and grandsons, or grant you a long, happy life (sometimes just by gazing into it). If you are an official, the mirror promises that you will achieve high office or even be ennobled.[125] For men, some mirrors promise a beautiful wife; for women, a good, or at least successful, husband and a happy marriage.[126] If you are a merchant, one mirror promises that you will make one-hundred-fold profit.[127] For pastoral families, some mirrors promise "five horses and a thousand head of sheep."[128] Other mirrors, such as that shown in figure 4.7, even mention benefits accruing to secondhand purchasers (*hou mai ci jing*), who can still obtain powerful advantages.[129]

Latter Han mirrors also stressed family brand identification. Extant examples are attributed to dozens of different workshops: those of the Cai, Zhang, Zhi, Long, Li, and Lu families. The list is quite long, for mirror casting was a bustling business during the Latter Han. Even some mirrors that purloined the names of the Shangfang or the Western Workshop of Shu paradoxically boasted that they were also made in a particular family workshop.[130] Family brand identity was clearly as important, or possibly more important, than pushing the fictitious connection to an illustrious imperial factory.

In sum, inscriptions on lacquer vessels and bronze mirrors that borrowed the name of one or more imperial factories were part of a whole marketing package that included the decoration on the object, the family brand name, the general quality of the product, and the auspicious symbols and words that permeated all visual realms of material culture. All of these contributed to the efficacy of the product, both mundane and magical.

Surprisingly, rhyming jingles were not limited to the auspicious quasi-magical phrases on expensive bronze mirrors. Some are also found on objects as mundane as the iron axle bushings for carriages. In 1975, archaeologists recovered a hoard of Latter Han iron parts and tools along with the molds for making them at a site near Zhenping in present-day Henan.[131] The items were all stuffed into a large ceramic jar, probably stowed for safekeeping during some emergency. The site itself does not appear to be part of a workshop but rather appears to have been the remains of a habitation area for ironworkers. Among the iron objects in the hoard were a group of hexagonal axle bushings (*gang*), used to reinforce the hubs of carriages and carts and to provide a smooth turning surface for the axle tree. Two of the bushings from the hoard were inscribed with the following rhyming couplet (note that the end rhyme was closer in antiquity than it sounds today in Mandarin Chinese)[132] (see figure 4.9):

王氏大牢工（釭）
Wang shi da lao gang
作真倱（輥）中。
zuo zhen gun zhong

Made by the Wangs—a bushing big and strong.
Bored straight and true—all the way through.

Like the mirror jingles, these advertisements were clumsily rhymed in doggerel verse and contain several phonetic loans for other, more difficult graphs (including the word for "bushing"!). They were designed to hype the quality of the product. In this case, the Wang family artisans claimed that their large bushings were sturdy and that the interior surfaces were perfectly straight and smooth, preventing undue wear on the axle. Ironically, all the Wang family–made bushings from the Zhenping hoard exhibit casting flaws and other defects. The inside sleeves of the bushings are riddled with air-bubble pockmarks and would have made terrible bushings for carriage hubs. Perhaps, we should give the Wang family the benefit of the doubt and assume that these bushings were rejects, destined to be melted down and recast. Otherwise, we have a perfect example of an advertising claim not matching up to product performance.

These examples reveal a precocious sense of self-awareness on the part of the artisan-merchants that we might call "market consciousness." They were aware of the cachet of famous names and the value of family brands, and they were not shy about using these for promotion in a competitive-market environment. Similar to the Wang family iron casters, stone carvers from Shandong did not hesitate to directly promote themselves and their products. Epitaphs on certain stone monuments claim that the monuments were made by *minggong* (famous artisans) or *qiaogong* (skillful artisans) who only used *mingshi* (famous stone).[133] Yet, as we saw in chapter 2, these epitaphs were probably not composed by the patrons who commissioned the monuments but rather were written by the stone carvers themselves. Such a conclusion puts a very

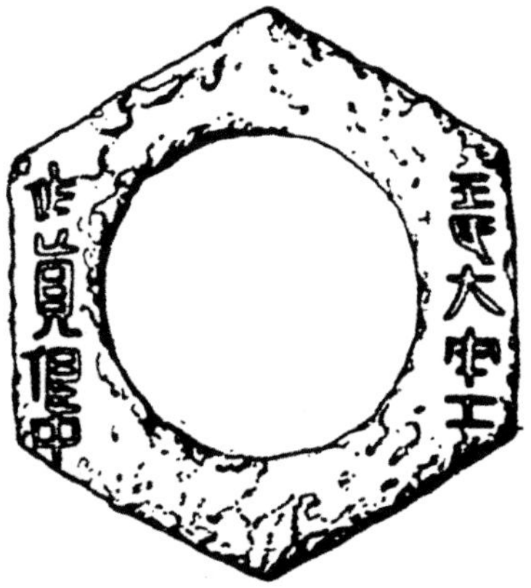

4.9 *Axle bushing.* Latter Han period (25–220 CE). Iron. Outer diameter 7.9 cm. Inner diameter 5.0 cm. From Henan Sheng Wenwu Yanjiusuo and Zhenping Xian Wenhuaguan, p. 248, fig. 6.

different rhetorical spin on the meticulous naming of so-called famous artisans in the inscriptions, which then amounts to nothing more than self-aggrandizement and unabashed advertising. In the short epitaph on the monument commissioned by one Zhang Wensi for his father (September 83 CE), the stone carver who wrote the inscription, a man named Wang Ci, had the audacity to promote his products on the solemn monument, making a claim of magical efficacy for his handiwork. He claims, "Because Wang Ci made this, your family will flourish."[134]

The recently discovered Latter Han painted tomb of Prince Bin in Xunyi County, Shaanxi, provides a final example of artisan self-promotion that is almost too audacious to be believed.[135] The tomb, which was discovered on the grounds of a brick factory in October 2000, belonged to a man who called himself Prince Bin (Bin Wang), who died toward the end of the second century, amid the chaos of the fall of the Han. Prince Bin is unknown from any historical text and appears to have been some sort of upstart aristocrat or military figure who was claiming to be a legitimate ruler, with civil and military power. The coffins of Prince Bin and his consort, in the rear chamber of the tomb, were flanked by two wall murals. The one on the left wall depicted an audience scene in which the deceased Prince Bin was seated holding court with a general surnamed Guo and receiving the homage of various other civil and military officials.[136] Near the end of the row of portraits is that of a master painter (*huashi gong*). Across the chamber from this mural is a complementary mural depicting the spouses of each of the men portrayed on the left-wall mural, including the wife of the painter (*shi furen*).[137] Scholars agree that the master painter portrayed is none other than the man who painted the murals in the tomb. He does not provide his full name, only the title of master painter.

The audience scene in the coffin chamber of Prince Bin's tomb seems to tell a story of overlapping, mutually reinforcing interests on the part of the master painter and the upstart Prince Bin. The painter seems to have wanted to promote the quality of his work and his close association with Prince Bin, which he accomplished by brazenly painting his own portrait in the most solemn, most central image in the entire tomb. As the inscription near the entrance of the tomb suggests, the tomb was meant to be viewed by numerous visitors before it was sealed, and they were accordingly asked to please remove their shoes before entering. Thus, the master painter could expect a host of potential future customers to file past his portrait. This was an opportunity to proclaim his intimate favor with the deceased prince and display his artistic prowess at the same time. On the other side of the equation, the prince would have wanted to portray himself as a legitimate ruler, complete with a suitable entourage of military and civil officials (and their wives). A legitimate royal court should almost certainly employ a master figure painter, so the presence of the painter among the other officials served to bolster Prince Bin's claim to legitimacy as well.

The facial features of the master painter are quite generic and cannot be considered a true self-portrait of the artist, even in the limited sense of Raphael's stealthily hidden self-portrait in the *School of Athens* or Michelangelo's morbid self-portrait in the *Last Judgment*. For the master painter of Prince Bin's tomb, his self-proclaimed title in the brush-written inscription next to his visual self-representation was his *real* self-portrait. In this time before the deep penetration of Buddhism into Chinese society, the written word was still the ultimate icon and the best medium for self-promotion. The image itself was still secondary.

It appears, based on current evidence, that the aggressive marketing techniques described in this section, such as the borrowing of imperial factory marks or the use of rhyming jingles and family brands, first emerged only during the early first century CE and reached their peak during the final decades of the Latter Han. There is almost no evidence for such blatant commercial promotion during the Qin or Former Han periods, when, not coincidentally, state control of the economy was at its peak and legal statutes and sumptuary regulations were more effectively enforced. Thus, it appears that the early development of commercial advertising of the type seen during the Latter Han was facilitated by a retreat of stringent state controls over production, distribution, marketing, and consumption. As the state fell apart, the market flourished.

5

ARTISANS AT COURT

"The Emperor's Writing Brush"

The shaft of the imperial brush was inlaid with precious materials and the hair of the brush was all the finest fur of the autumn rabbit. Lu Hu, the Capital Master Artisan, made it. He used other various precious materials to make the case for the brush. Into the wood of the case, he inlaid jade disks and kingfisher feathers. All told, the brush and its case were worth a hundred jin of gold.

—MISCELLANEOUS NOTES ON THE WESTERN CAPITAL[1]

Some artisans were insulated from the din of the marketplace by the high walls of the palace. Using only the finest materials, these court artisans worked for patrons who had very deep pockets and the highest expectations for the final product. The term "court artisans" actually encompasses men and women of widely varying roles and statuses. Some were famous master artisans working in small palace workshops, while others were anonymous, semiskilled laborers toiling on production lines in

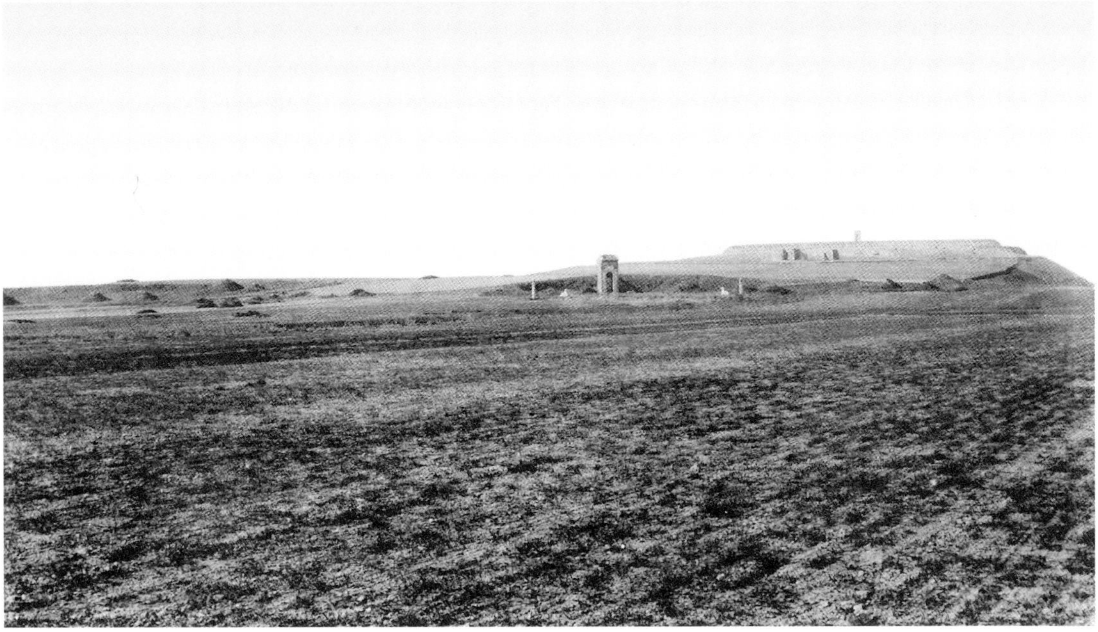

5.1 *Remains of the Han Weiyang Palace looking from the southeast to the northwest.* From Adachi, pl. 40 (photo ca. 1906–10).

larger factory-like settings. The hundreds of artisans who worked within the Qin and Han palaces helped to build and decorate the gilded world of illusion in which the Son of Heaven and his court resided. Without their lavish productions in silk, bronze, jade, lacquer, and paint, the imperial seat would have been no more than a shabby fortress along the Wei River. As Counselor in Chief Xiao He, the man responsible for the awe-inspiring design of the Han's main palace, the Weiyang Palace, once argued, "if the Son of Heaven does not dwell in magnificence and beauty, he will have no way to manifest his authority."[2]

All of that magnificence and beauty is now irretrievably lost. Where once the palaces and towers stood, nothing more than low mounds and farm fields remain (see figure 5.1). The Qin palaces at Xianyang and their Han successors across the river at Chang'an were not stone castles perched atop acropolises, but timber-framed buildings protected by walls of rammed earth. Almost nothing survives, save for their buried foundations and a few scattered relics. The only vestiges of once-dazzling palace murals are a few palm-sized fragments recovered by archaeologists during recent excavations. Of the glittering gold, lacquer, and jade furnishings that once filled the palace chambers, only a few outstanding examples like the Changxin Palace lamp survive, buried in distant tombs and tarnished by the passage of time. These can only hint at the magnificence of this lost splendor.

One category of sources we do possess that helps us reconstruct this lost visual world is contemporary or near-contemporary textual descriptions. Poets rhapsodized on the majesty of the imperial palaces, and historians described their treasures, both often as a means to criticize such frivolous display. Their accounts are often filled with exaggeration for rhetorical purpose, so one must be careful using this material. Scattered anecdotes in other written sources also help to fill in some of the missing pieces concerning famous paintings or ingenious contraptions made by court artisans.

Those studying the masterworks of Greek bronze statuary are fortunate to possess not only eyewitness textual accounts from classical authors but also second- or third-generation Roman copies in marble that can give them some indication of the masters' original vision. For early imperial China, only in rare instances do we have that luxury. Except for one possible case discussed below, no later copies of famous Qin or Han works survive to reveal even a glimpse of the brilliance of the original work. All we have are the images on carved stones and the painted murals found in tombs, which might be distantly related copies of palace murals and scrolls filtered through the medium of pattern sheets.

This distressing situation leads to a fundamental difficulty when discussing artisans and their works made for the court. We know the names and minimal biographical details of some famous painters and craftsmen who worked at the court, and in some cases we have textual descriptions of their paintings or objects, but we do not possess the original objects (or even secondhand copies) to compare with these accounts. On the other hand, archaeologists have retrieved for us dozens of objects and a few magnificent paintings made for royal or imperial courts, yet in nearly all cases, we have no names to attach to these splendid works. This state of affairs creates a chasm of understanding between the artisan and the object that is difficult to bridge.

With these considerations in mind, I have structured this chapter in a rather unorthodox and lopsided fashion. In the first part of the chapter, I present an extensive investigation into the types of visual and material culture ("art") in use at court and the purposes for which these items were created. This will enable the reader to better understand the role of art at court and the types of objects that might be found there. In the second part of the chapter, I look at some of the men and women who made objects and images for the court, focusing both on the professional artisans employed by the court and on the amateur scholar-official artisans who worked in the emperor's service.

THE NATURE OF VISUAL AND MATERIAL CULTURE AT THE EARLY IMPERIAL COURT

The visual world of the Qin and Han courts was suffused with all manner of images and objects. Presented in a variety of formats, they were made for different purposes and targeted at specific audiences. The aim of this section is to provide a representative cross section of the visual world of the court, to give the reader some impression of the types of objects and images that could be found there and of the purposes for which they were created. We will investigate murals, screens, and hand scrolls of exemplars; paintings with hidden political messages; ritual images of deities; illustrated maps and battle accounts; decorative murals; equine statuary; even tableware and other room furnishings. I have also included a brief section on theatrical spectacles held at court, since these too were meant to dazzle the eyes.

PAINTINGS OF EXEMPLARS

And here [in the Lingguang Palace of Lu] all Heaven and Earth is painted . . .
The Yellow Emperor, Tang the Victorious, and the Great Yu,
Each crowned as he was crowned and robed as he was clad.
The Three Kings were there, many riotous damsels and turbulent lords,
Loyal knights, dutiful sons, mighty scholars, faithful wives,
Victors and vanquished, wise men and fools,
None was missing from his place.
The evil were depicted to admonish the current age,
While the good were portrayed to uphold to later generations.

WANG YANSHOU (CA. 124–48 CE),
"RHAPSODY ON THE HALL OF SPIRITUAL LIGHT"[3]

Most official paintings used at court were political and didactic in their intent, regardless of whether they were publicly displayed or privately viewed. Palace murals depicting the great ministers and generals of the preceding generation were commissioned at least as early as the reign of Emperor Xuan (r. 74–49 BCE), and there are some suggestions that the practice may have begun as early as the reign of Emperor Wu (r. 141–87 BCE) or even Emperor Gaozu (r. 202–195 BCE).

In the third year of the Ganlu era (51 BCE), Emperor Xuan, who had helped to restore stability and prosperity to the realm, wanted to make a statement about his place in the history of the Han dynasty. He commissioned palace artisans to paint a mural in the Unicorn Hall (Qilin Ge) depicting eleven great generals and ministers who had served as the "arms and legs" of the sovereign during his reign.[4] The Unicorn Hall was a building within the Weiyang Palace complex at Chang'an, possibly just to the east of the principal imperial audience hall (see figure 4.1). During the reign of Emperor Wu, a *qilin* beast (unicorn) had been captured in the imperial park and its image was painted on the walls of this hall.[5]

The structure of the *History of the Former Han* description of Emperor Xuan's mural clearly suggests that the generals and ministers were painted in a predetermined sequence, probably from right to left, ranked according to the merit of their contribution to the state. Each portrait was captioned with the man's name, his noble title (if he held one), and the title of the highest official position he had occupied at court or in the military. From later accounts, we know that the portraits were probably executed on a ground of light-red plaster, separated by colored frames, and accompanied by titles and eulogies written next to the images.[6] The men depicted on the Unicorn Hall mural were as follows:

1 Chariot and Horse General Serving as Commander in Chief, Marquis of Bolu, family name Huo (viz., Huo Guang) (died in office, 68 BCE).
2 General of the Guards, Marquis of Fuping, Zhang Anshi (died in office, 62 BCE).
3 Chariot and Horse General, Marquis of Longe, Han Zeng (died in office, 56 BCE).
4 General of the Rear, Marquis of Yingping, Zhao Chongguo (died in retirement, 51 BCE).
5 Counselor in Chief, Marquis of Gaoping, Wei Xiang (died in office, 59 BCE).
6 Counselor in Chief, Marquis of Boyang, Bing Ji (died in office, 55 BCE).
7 Censor in Chief, Marquis of Jianping, Du Yannian (died in retirement, 52 BCE).
8 Chamberlain for the Imperial Clan, Marquis of Yangcheng, Liu De (died of old age, 56 BCE).
9 Privy Treasurer, Liangqiu He (died of old age, 50 or 49 BCE).
10 Grand Mentor of the Heir Apparent, Xiao Wangzhi (died of suicide, 47 BCE).
11 Supervisor of Dependent Countries, Su Wu (died of old age, 60 BCE).

The completion of the mural was apparently timed to coincide with the first visit of a Xiongnu leader (titled the *shanyu*) to the Han court.[7] It was probably designed, in part, to impress the *shanyu* with the quality of Han generals and officials. The Xiongnu leader, whose full name and title was Huhanye Shanyu, came to Chang'an in the first month of 51 BCE and was treated with respect as a "guest ruler," ranked above the enfeoffed princes of the Han Empire. During his visit, he was said to have been shown the *zhenbao* (treasures of the realm), which may have included a visit to the Unicorn Hall, where some important state documents and objects were housed along with the mural of worthies. Huhanye Shanyu would have been intrigued to see on the wall the likeness of Su Wu (no. 11), a man who had been virtually imprisoned in Xiongnu territory for nearly twenty years but had steadfastly maintained his loyalty to the Han. His appearance on the mural was probably not an accident. It was just one political statement among many on this very important state "document."

Let us analyze the political content of this mural a bit further. First, you will notice that the first eight men all ranked as full marquises. By standard order of precedence, they had to be listed first. Second, the historian Ban Gu remarked that all of the men on this roster were men who had *shanzhong* (died well). In fact, not all of the men on the mural were deceased at the time of its completion. Those who had already died had either expired of old age while in office or had passed away at home in peaceful retirement. A high official in the Han who could die so peacefully was truly fortunate. Those who were still alive, like Zhao Chongguo (4), Liangqiu He (9), and Xiao Wangzhi (10), were either in high imperial favor or had recently been rehabilitated at the time of the commission. Of course, there is always a risk when you make a commemorative image of a living person that they will later suffer disgrace. In this case, Xiao Wangzhi ran afoul of powerful eunuchs at court and committed suicide in 47 BCE rather than face legal proceedings.

Those men at the top of the list, especially the first six, had all been instrumental in placing Emperor Xuan on the throne in 74 BCE, during a turbulent succession crisis that saw the previous emperor (Liu He) in power for only twenty-seven days. Many of the men on the list had also aided Emperor Xuan personally or had supported the imperial house at crucial moments. Bing Ji (6) had protected the infant Liu Bingyi (Emperor Xuan) when his father and grandfather had been driven to suicide in 91 BCE. Zhang Anshi (2) was a close personal friend of the emperor and had foiled a plot to kill the previous legitimate emperor. Wei Xiang (5) had helped to uncover and suppress the treasonous plot of the Huo family, and Liangqiu He (9) had foreseen a plot on Emperor Xuan's life.

Of all the men on the list, only Huo Guang (1) did not have his personal name recorded on the mural. This was a special privilege, for the avoidance of personal names was usually reserved for emperors or enfeoffed princes. Huo Guang had helped to save the empire after the ruinous exploits of Emperor Wu and had controlled the realm as a virtual regent from the death of Emperor Wu in 87 BCE until his own death in 68 BCE. He was buried with a jade suit, a special tomb of cypress timbers, and other status markers usually reserved for the tombs of emperors. Shortly after Huo Guang's burial, it was revealed that his wife had previously poisoned Emperor Xuan's Empress Xu after childbirth (in 71 BCE). Huo Guang's widow and her sons then plotted rebellion and were all executed or forced to commit suicide in 66 BCE. It is quite remarkable that Emperor Xuan did not hold any personal ill will toward Huo Guang and included him on the mural in such a place of distinction.

Some very notable men of the age of Emperor Xuan did not make the exclusive list, and I would again argue that the reasons for their exclusion were highly political. Huang Ba was the current Counselor in Chief (Chengxiang) at the time of Huhanye Shanyu's visit, but he had recently fallen out of favor with Emperor Xuan because of some missteps. Yu Dingguo, who was acting as Censor in Chief (Yushi Daifu) in early 51 BCE, may have been excluded because of animosities he engendered in his earlier post as Chamberlain for Law Enforcement (Tingwei). Of more immediate political impact, the proposal of Huang Ba and Yu Dingguo to treat the visiting *shanyu* as a submissive vassal had just been rejected in favor of Xiao Wangzhi's (no. 10 on the list) proposal to treat him more respectfully, as a guest ruler. Zhang Chang was another man who had aided in Emperor Xuan's succession, but his subsequent political career had been tainted by a few setbacks. Xiahou Sheng was a great scholar of the age and had held many high positions, but he had once been jailed along with Huang Ba for disrespect. Being excluded from the mural of great ministers must have been a great blow to these men and to their descendants. As the Latter Han scholar Wang Chong (27–100 CE) relates in his *Discourses Weighed* (Lunheng), "During the time of Emperor Xuan, captioned portraits of the distinguished officials of the Han were painted. The sons and grandsons of men who were not among those represented in the paintings were ashamed. Why is this? Their fathers and grandfathers were not worthy, so no portraits were made of them."[8]

Beyond the political agenda, the portraits in the Unicorn Hall were also meant to be both commemorative and didactic. The *History of the Former Han* clearly states that all the men on the mural "were men of merit and virtue whose names were known to the world of their time, and in this way they were held up as examples and given further recognition, making clear that they had assisted the ruler in bringing about a renaissance of the state."[9] The verb used to describe the execution of their portraits was *fa* (to make a model of). In other words, not only were the physical appearance and carriage of these great men supposed to serve as a model for men of later ages, but by extension, so too were their actions of loyalty and bravery.

After the mural in the Unicorn Hall was unveiled, probably during the first lunar month of 51 BCE, the painting was likely copied at least once onto a silk hand scroll. We can infer this from the way that Ban Gu describes the mural, for it seems that he was actually reading from a portable copy of the original mural, probably preserved in the same palace archives that he so often consulted in compiling his *History of the Former Han*. Furthermore, among the famous ancient paintings known to Zhang Yanyuan (ca. 810–80 CE) and recorded in his *Record of the Famous Painters of Successive Dynasties* (Lidai minghua ji) (ca. 847 CE) is a scroll painting called *Captioned Portraits from the Han Unicorn Hall* (Han lin'ge tu), which probably was a later copy of the wall mural images from the Unicorn Hall.[10]

The mural itself was not left entirely unaltered by subsequent emperors. It continued to be part of the ongoing political discourse at court. Sometime in 9 or 8 BCE, when the non-Han border people known as the Qiang were causing problems, Emperor Cheng (r. 33–7 BCE), the grandson of Emperor Xuan, wanted to exhort the current generation of ministers to follow the example of men like Zhao Chongguo (no. 4), who had helped Emperor Xuan to control the border peoples with great skill and ingenuity. Emperor Cheng summoned one of the court poets, none other than the great rhapsodist Yang Xiong (53 BCE–18 CE), to compose a eulogy honoring Zhao Chongguo and ordered Yang to copy it onto the Unicorn Hall mural next to Zhao's image.[11]

I would draw an analogy between the Unicorn Hall mural and the most famous painting from the early People's Republic of China, Dong Xiwen's (1914–73) *Founding of the Nation* (Kaiguo dadian). Dong's enormous oil painting (230 by 400 cm) was painted in 1952 to adorn the new Museum of Revolutionary History in Beijing. It portrayed Chairman Mao atop Tiananmen, proclaiming the founding of the PRC and accompanied by the great leaders of the revolution, ordered by rank, including General Zhu De, Liu Shaoqi, Madame Song Qingling, Zhou Enlai, Guo Moruo, and General Gao Gang. Unlike the denizens of the Unicorn Hall mural, the persons portrayed in *Founding of the Nation* were all still alive when it was painted. As members of the new government were disgraced, purged, or rehabilitated, the painting was altered to reflect the new political reality, effectively rewriting history. As one example, the man standing next to the balustrade in the original painting, General Gao Gang, was purged in 1954 and committed suicide the following year. When the painting was once again exhibited in 1955, Gao had been replaced by a potted plant. Subsequent changes to the painting, to erase and replace figures, have rendered the original almost unrecoverable.[12]

The original Unicorn Hall mural was surely destroyed in the civil war at the end of the Wang Mang period when all the palaces burned down, but it lived on in portable copies, such as the one Ban Gu seems to have consulted when writing his account of the painting in the *History of the Former Han*. The Unicorn Hall mural also lived on in the minds of men at court. It became the inspiration for a similar mural painted in a building on the Cloud Terrace (Yun Tai) in the Southern Palace of the Latter Han capital of Luoyang.[13] The Cloud Terrace mural was commissioned by Emperor Ming (r. 57–75 CE) around 60 CE and portrayed the twenty-eight generals and statesmen who had helped Emperor Guangwu (r. 25–57 CE) ascend the throne and restore the Liu family to power. Later, the portraits of four others were appended.[14] Like the Unicorn Hall mural, it was a conscious propaganda gesture, proclaiming the renaissance of the Han house, and once again the inclusion or exclusion of certain individuals was highly political. The famous conquering general Ma Yuan (14 BCE–49 CE) was conspicuously absent, even though his daughter had become empress on April 8, 60 CE. His posthumous disgrace in 49 CE probably excluded him from depiction on the mural.[15] The *Record of the Famous Painters of Successive Dynasties* mentions the two murals in the same breath, saying, "Loyalty and filiality were exhausted by the figures in the Cloud Terrace; ardent and virtuous were all those in the Unicorn Hall."[16] In 177 CE, Emperor Ling (r. 168–89 CE) ordered another mural of two recently deceased ministers painted on the walls of one of the main palace halls, with eulogies written by the scholar-artist Cai Yong (see below).[17]

The murals of the great generals and ministers of the past which adorned the memorial halls and audience chambers of Han palaces were certainly designed to fulfill several functions. They were painted to honor the memory of past worthies, to reward their descendants by association, and to encourage the men of the present generation to follow their examples in supporting the state. The mural projects were certainly political in their intent, since they honored only a select group of men who were perceived by the current generation as having upheld certain principles and actions. Other men were excluded from the presentation for entirely political reasons. By commissioning such murals of exemplary officials, the current emperor also hoped to associate himself with the great Han emperors of earlier generations, who had proudly proclaimed the accomplishments of their age. As a lasting document, these murals were meant to be didactic, in that they displayed behavioral models for emulation.

Another distinct group of palace images were designed to be even more overtly didactic. These consisted of cycles of narrative illustrations portraying culture-hero gods, sage-kings of the past, evil last rulers of dynasties, filial sons, virtuous women, and evil queens (see epigraph to this section). The pictures were often accompanied by short eulogy texts (*zan*) that explained the characters' exemplary virtues or personality flaws. The great poet of the Wei ruling family, Cao Zhi (192–232 CE), once composed a cycle of eulogies for a series of murals that were painted around 214 CE in a room at the new Jian'an period palace complex at Ye. Nearly two dozen of these eulogies survive and are prefaced by an introduction by the poet, explaining the didactic, moral purpose of exemplary portraits:

> Of those who look at illustrations, there is not one who, beholding the Three August Ones or the five Emperors, would not look up in reverence, nor any who, before a painting of the cruel rulers of the three decadent ages, would not be moved to sadness. There is no one who, seeing a picture of usurping ministers stealing a throne, would not grind his teeth; nor any who, contemplating a fine scholar of high principles, would not forget to eat; who, at the sight of loyal vassals dying for their principles, would not harden his own resolve; and who would not sigh at beholding banished ministers and persecuted sons. There is no one who would not avert his eyes from the spectacle of a licentious husband or a jealous wife; and there is no one who, seeing a virtuous consort or an obedient queen, would not praise and value them. From this we may know that paintings are the means by which events are preserved so as to serve as a mirror [for reflection on one's behavior].[18]

The cycles of exemplars were painted not only on the walls of palace halls but also on hand scrolls for personal use and on the wooden screens (*pingfeng*) that surrounded the platform used for sitting during the day and sleeping at night. The audience for these images included high officials, the women of the imperial harem, and even the emperor himself. Most were probably commissioned directly by the emperor, but others seem to have been voluntarily submitted by ministers and scholars who wanted to communicate certain moral and political points to the sovereign.

In the most vivid demonstration of how a didactic screen would ideally affect the sovereign, Ban Gu's *History of the Former Han* records the story of an encounter (ca. 17 BCE) between Ban Gu's great-uncle Ban Bo (ca. 47–9 BCE) and Emperor Cheng:

> One day, the emperor was seated in a tented pavilion and had unfolded a painted screen depicting Zhou [the last king of the Shang] leaning on his consort Da Ji, engaged in a long night of drunken debauchery. Because Ban Bo had only recently recovered from his long illness, the emperor paid him special attention. Thereupon, the emperor turned and pointed to the images and asked Ban Bo, "Was Zhou really immoral to this extent?" Ban Bo replied, "The *Book of Documents* says that he relied on the words of a woman. But why then was he so dissolute in court? This is really a case of [what the *Analects* talks about

when it says,] 'All the filth flows downstream.' [Zhou]was not so [wicked] as all that."[19] The emperor said, "If this is not the case, then what is this painting admonishing [me] about?" Ban Bo said, "Drunkenness is what Weizi warned about and why he left.[20] Bellowing drunk and crying out, that is why the poet of the *Ode* is endlessly crying. All of the admonishments about immorality and disorder in the *Book of Songs* and the *Book of Documents* are rooted in alcohol." The emperor loudly sighed and said, "It has been a long time since I have seen Mr. Ban. Today, I once again heard his conscientious words."[21]

The incident and the dialogue recorded in this story may have transpired nearly as told by the author, Ban Gu, for he certainly could have heard this family story on his father's knee. In the story, the sickly but loyal minister Ban Bo is warning Emperor Cheng about his heavy drinking bouts and improper behavior with his consort (and soon-to-be empress) Zhao Feiyan and with cronies like Zhang Fang and Chunyu Zhang. Ban Bo was currently serving as Grand Master for Splendid Happiness (Guanglu Daifu), an imperial advisory post that entailed remonstrating with the emperor in this way. Ban Bo wanted the emperor to resume his scholarly activities, and the instigation for his admonitions may have originally come from Emperor Cheng's mother. Through the medium of the painted screen, Ban Bo was warning Emperor Cheng that he would suffer the same fate as King Zhou of the Shang, the loss of his life and his empire, if he did not mend his ways. It is interesting that Ban Bo steered the criticism suggested by the painting away from the influence of evil women and instead toward the evils of drinking, which was probably a safer political topic than confronting the powerful Zhao Feiyan.

Didactic scenes of exemplars did not always achieve such a rapid admonitory effect on the sovereign. Sometimes their use tragically backfired on the ministers who failed to use them skillfully to remonstrate with the emperor. Yang Yun, a grandson of the historian Sima Qian, served under Emperor Xuan in the high post of Chamberlain for Attendants (Guangluxun). Once, probably in 58 or 57 BCE, it was reported that Yang Yun was walking through the Western Pavilion at the palace and remarked on the murals of exemplary rulers on the walls. He pointed specifically at the images of the evil rulers Jie (the last Xia king) and Zhou (the last Shang king) and sarcastically remarked to another official, "When the emperor passed through here, he asked to hear about their sins in great detail so that he could learn to emulate them!" The portraits in the Western Pavilion also included those of the sage-kings Yao, Shun, Yu the Great, and Tang the Victorious, but Yang Yun did not compare Emperor Xuan to them.[22] These offhand remarks were later used by Yang Yun's political enemies at court to have him charged with *dani budao* (gross immoral conduct), a blanket charge for those who openly criticized the emperor. He was saved from execution by Emperor Xuan, who dismissed him from his position and stripped him of his marquisate. He was later executed after a follow-up investigation found him to be without remorse.

Liu Xiang (79–8 BCE) was another official who served at the court of Emperor

Xuan, as well as under his successors Emperor Yuan and Emperor Cheng. Around 17–15 BCE, he became dismayed at Emperor Cheng's improper behavior and his servile attachment to Zhao Feiyan and her younger sister Zhao Zhaoyi. Probably as a way to express his disapproval of the behavior of these women, he compiled a collection of biographies of virtuous and evil women throughout history called the *Arrayed Biographies of Women* (Lienü zhuan). It seems that, from the very beginning, this text was accompanied by a set of illustrations portraying each of the women's stories. Based on his own bibliographic notes, abstracted in chapter 30 of the *History of the Former Han*, we know that the full title of the book was actually *Illustrated Arrayed Biographies of Women with Encomiums* (Lienü zhuan songtu).[23] It was designed to be what Wu Hung has called a "moral handbook" for those at court.[24] Liu Xiang's own bibliographic notes explain his reasons for composing the book and inform us that it was quickly adapted to another visual format. He writes, "I, along with my son, the Gentleman Attendant at the Palace Gate, Liu Xin, compiled the *Arrayed Biographies of Women* and divided them into seven book sections according to categories. The purpose of this work is to make evident behavioral models for the poor and for the rich, for the glorious and for the lowly, and to make distinctions between right and wrong, success and failure. It was painted on the four panels of a *pingfeng* (room screen)."[25] Since this illustrated screen was probably created around 17 BCE, it may have been the same screen (with an illustration of the evil consort Da Ji) used by Ban Bo to remonstrate with Emperor Cheng.

At just about this time (ca. 16–15 BCE), Ban Bo's sister Ban Jieyu, who had been one of Emperor Cheng's consorts, was slandered by Empress Zhao (Feiyan). She saved her life by her quick wits and chose to serve Emperor Cheng's mother in the relative safety of the Palace of Lasting Trust. In her isolation, she wrote a poem of lament, which demonstrates how she used the paintings of exemplary women as a model for her upright behavior: "I spread out my paintings of women, and made them my mirror. Looked to my instructress, queried her on the *Book of Songs*; I was moved by the warning of the woman who crows, pained at the sins of lovely Baosi; I praised Huang and Ying, wives to the Lord of Yu; Admired Ren and Si, mothers of Zhou."[26] On an earlier occasion, when she was still in favor, Ban Jieyu had refused to ride in the emperor's palanquin by referring to portraits of past sage-rulers who only rode with high ministers.[27] After her death, she became one of the exemplary women in an expanded version of the *Arrayed Biographies of Women*.[28]

Figure 5.2 illustrates the surviving panels and borders of a lacquered screen found in the tomb of Sima Jinlong, a Northern Wei general who died in 484 CE.[29] Based on its position in the disturbed tomb, the screen may have once surrounded the stone funerary couch that held his coffin. Some think it may have once belonged to Sima Jinlong's highborn wife (d. 474 CE), who was also buried in the tomb. It portrays several stories found in the *Arrayed Biographies of Women* and was probably similar in layout to the original screen and scrolls designed by Liu Xiang and his son. The panels were painted on both sides and divided into four registers. The painted stories,

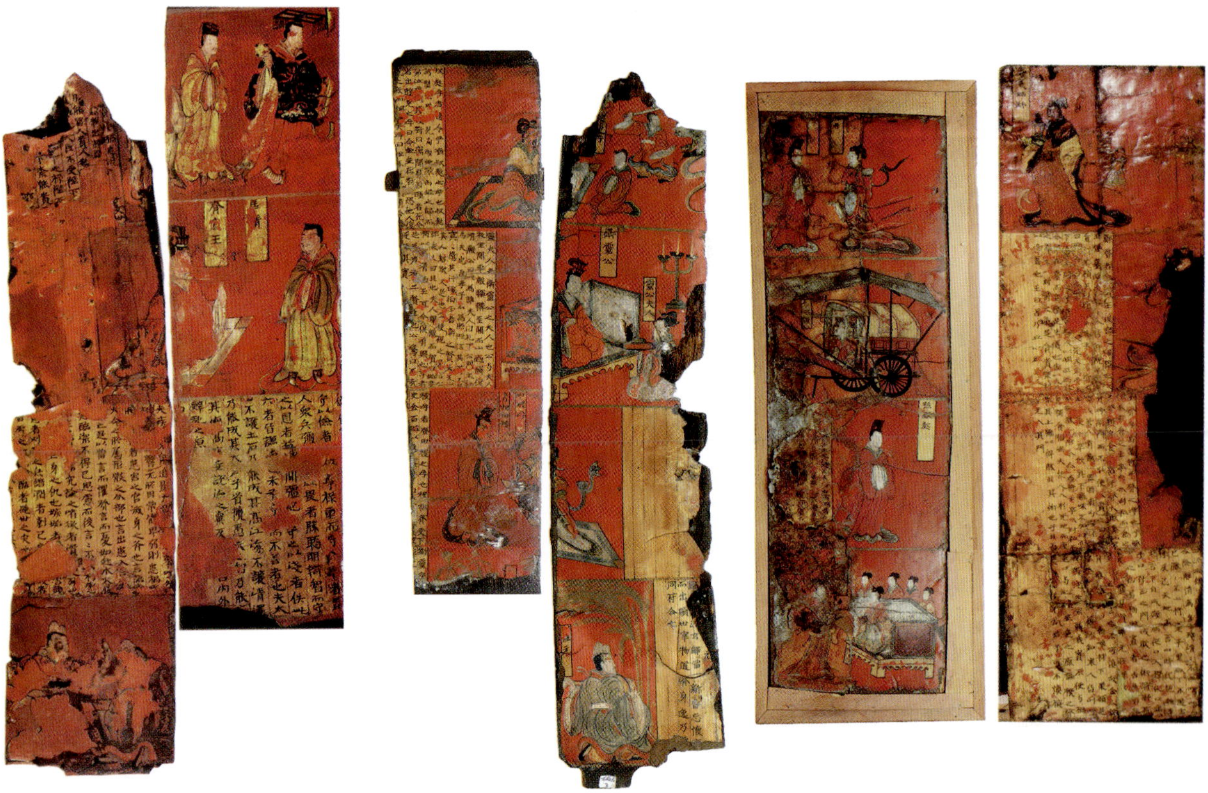

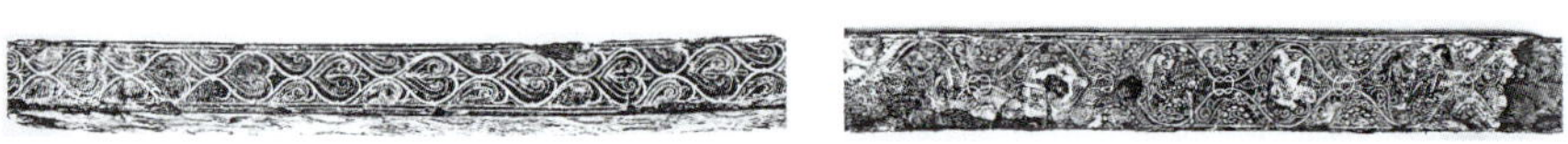

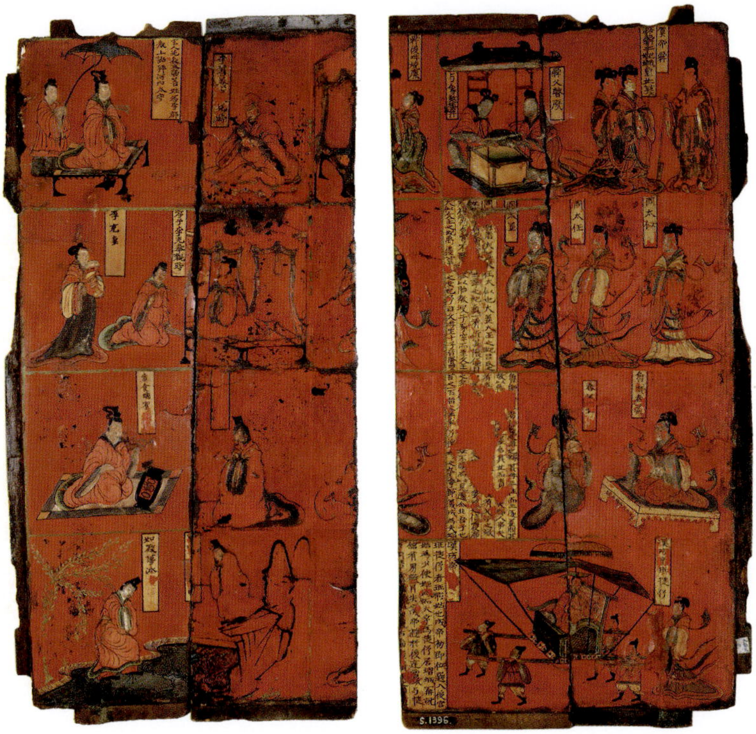

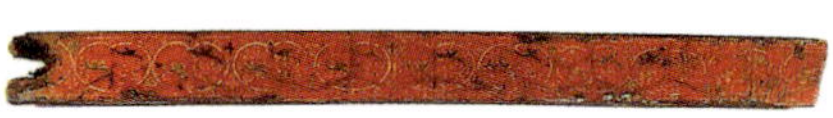

5.2 *Paintings of exemplars.* Northern Wei, mid–fifth century CE, before 484 CE. Lacquered wooden panels from screen. H. 80 cm. W. 20 cm. Shanxi Provincial Museum, Datong Municipal Museum. Photos courtesy of Cultural Relics Publishing House.

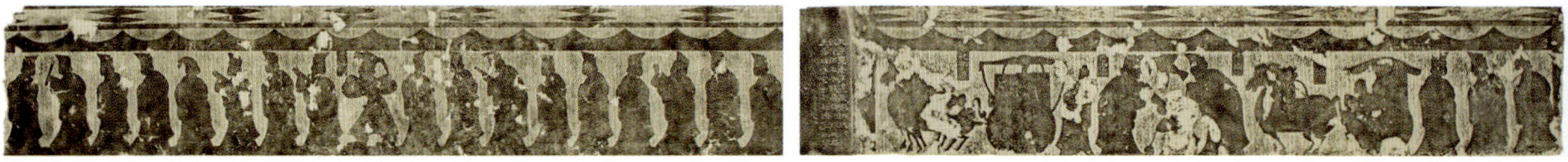

5.3 *Confucius and his many disciples.* Latter Han period, second century CE. Ink-on-paper rubbings. Princeton University Art Museum. Far Eastern Seminar Collection, 2002-307.1, 2002-307.3, 2002-307.KL, 2002.307.10. Photos by Bruce M. White. From Offering Hall 1, Wuzhaishan, Jiaxiang County, Shandong.

which are accompanied by a brief text of the plot and moral, are often divided into several scenes, with added captions for the major figures. The scene at the bottom of the rightmost panel (in figure 5.2) depicts the story of Ban Jieyu refusing the inappropriate invitation to ride in the imperial palanquin with Emperor Cheng.

During the Latter Han, the students in the palace academy known as the Vast Capital Gate Academy (Hongdumen Xue) were also exhorted with murals of exemplars painted on the walls of their school. The Vast Capital Gate Academy had been founded by Emperor Ling on March 15, 178 CE, within the grounds of the Southern Palace to counterbalance the influence of the regular Imperial Academy (Tai Xue), which was filled with Classicist scholars.[30] The move was part of the ongoing conflict between the eunuchs at court (who had suggested the new school) and the Classicist scholars. The students in the new academy were trained to write government documents, compose poetry, and learn "bird script" calligraphy.[31] Immediately, there was a significant battle at court over which images were most appropriate to serve as models for the students in the new school. This was over and above the heated debate over whether the new school should have been established at all. It appears that some of the murals in the new school's halls portrayed images of and eulogies to thirty-two of the school's brightest lights, including its chief proponents Yue Song and Jiang Lan. The Director of the Imperial Secretariat (Shangshu Ling), Yang Qiu, complained that such a practice was not in line with classical or imperial precedents. He argued in a memorial to the throne that men like Yue Song and Jiang Lan were less than nobodies; they were hangers-on who had achieved nothing and written nothing of lasting moral value.[32] They had merely submitted a poem or two or had written some pretty calligraphy. To put up murals with eulogies featuring such upstarts was tantamount to heresy. Cai Yong was another official who objected to the whole concept of the Vast Capital Gate Academy, arguing that the students in residence were mere performers and craftsmen.[33] In the end, it seems that Cai Yong and Yang Qiu may have partially won their argument. Even though the Vast Capital Gate Academy was not shut down, sometime in 178 CE Emperor Ling ordered the palace painters to paint portraits of Confucius and his seventy-two disciples on the walls of the school to exhort the students. Confucius and his students were the heroes of Classicists like Cai Yong, and such a mural was more in line with what he and Yang Qiu thought should be por-

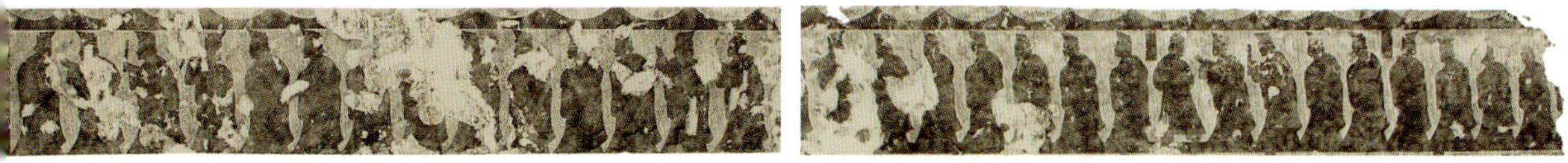

trayed on walls in the capital.[34] This gesture may have come too late for Cai Yong to enjoy, for he was arrested during the eighth month of 178 CE and later exiled.[35] It is ironic but fitting that when Cai Yong died during his second prison stay in 192 CE, people from his home province made exemplary portraits of him to honor his memory.[36]

Like many palace murals, the original Vast Capital Gate Academy mural of Confucius and his disciples was copied onto silk. Copies of this painting survived until Tang times, but none are presently extant.[37] Figure 5.3 is a rubbing from a stone tomb shrine (ca. 150 CE) that displays a portion of the "Confucius and his disciples" genre scene, common to offering shrines in the Shandong area. Few of the individual disciples of Confucius are captioned or identifiable, save for Zi Lu, who is shown wearing his distinctive rooster hat.

IMPERIALLY BESTOWED PAINTINGS

A bestowal of a painting from the emperor could convey a thinly veiled political message to the recipient. When the aging Emperor Wu was near death, he decided to choose one of his youngest sons, Liu Fuling, a boy of only eight years, as his successor. When Emperor Wu considered which of his ministers was capable of safeguarding the empire until the boy reached his majority, he settled on Huo Guang (ca. 131–68 BCE), the very circumspect and upright younger half brother of the famous late general Huo Qubing. To signal his intent, Emperor Wu had painters from the office of the Yellow Gate (Huangmen) paint a picture of the Duke of Zhou assisting the infant King Cheng, supporting him on his back, while receiving the feudal lords in audience. King Cheng was the son of King Wu (Wu Wang), the man who conquered the Shang dynasty, ca. 1045 BCE. Shortly after the conquest, King Wu died, passing the throne to his infant son. For the next seven years King Wu's younger brother Dan (the Duke of Zhou) acted as regent for King Cheng and was instrumental in consolidating the new Zhou dynasty.

The *History of the Former Han* account records that, a short while after receiving the painting and as Emperor Wu neared his end, "Huo Guang, in tears, said, 'If that which I dare not speak about should occur, who ought to be appointed as successor?' The Emperor replied, 'Have you yet not perceived the meaning of the picture I gave you? I want my youngest son set up, with you to act the part of the Duke of Zhou.'"[38] For most of the next twenty years, Huo Guang acted as a virtual regent over two young emperors and was the most powerful man in the empire, though he remained only a minister and general in title.

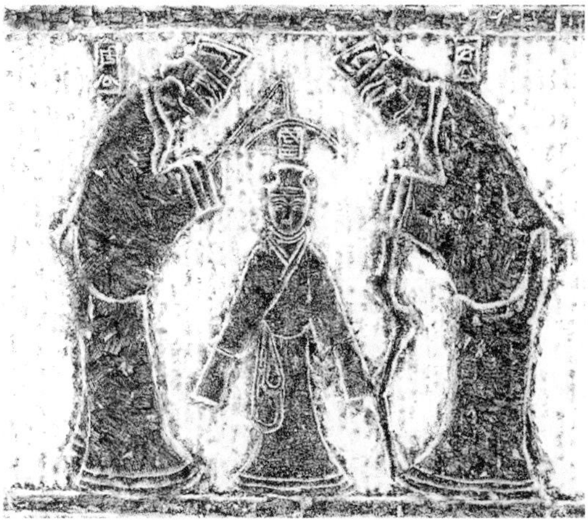

(a)

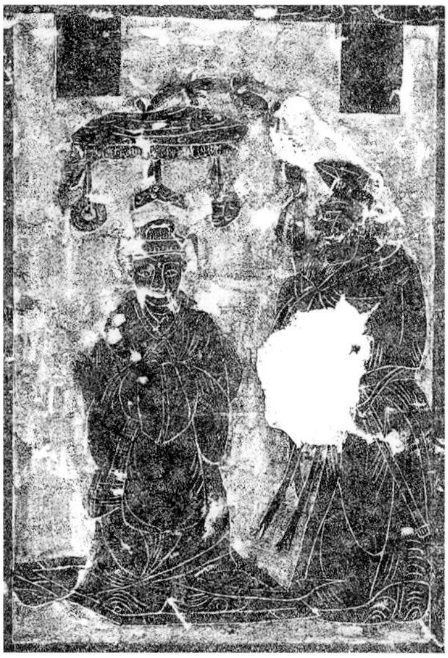

(b)

5.4 *The Duke of Zhou assisting the young King Cheng*
(a) (Left to right) "Duke of Zhou," "King Cheng," "Duke of Shao." Latter Han period, ca. 25–88 CE. Ink-on-paper rubbing (detail). W. 48 cm. Wu Family Shrines Cultural Relics Preservation Department. From Jinglaoyuan, Jiaxiang County, Shandong. Photo courtesy of Shandong Fine Arts Publishing House.
(b) From north wall of central chamber of tomb at Yi'nan, Shandong. Latter Han period, ca. 170–80 CE. Ink-on-paper rubbing (detail). Photo courtesy of Shandong Fine Arts Publishing House.

Based on the context of the story, it seems that the painting commissioned by the emperor was in a portable format, probably a hand scroll on silk. The passage states that the painting was *ci* (bestowed) on Huo Guang by the emperor. One would not use this particular verb if the picture had been painted as a mural in a public palace space. We can obtain some impression of the original appearance of this composition by looking at carved images from tombs and shrines of the Latter Han from Shandong. Figure 5.4 shows two examples of the typical Shandong composition of the Duke of Zhou assisting the young King Cheng at a court audience. The Duke of Zhou is usually shown holding a canopy over the young sovereign's head and not carrying him on his back as suggested by one interpretation of the *History of the Former Han* passage. The composition, which is very common in Shandong stone carvings, may in fact be distantly related to palace images on murals and scrolls of the same scene.

Sometime before this gift to Huo Guang, Emperor Wu made another bestowal of a painted image, this time to Jin Midi (134–86 BCE). Jin Midi was an ethnic Xiongnu who had once been the heir apparent of the Xiuchu King of the Xiongnu, a regional vassal who served under the supreme *shanyu*. When Han armies defeated the Xiuchu King's forces, he planned to surrender to the Han to escape the wrath of his lord, then changed his mind. He was later killed by his Xiongnu allies. His wife, his elder son Jin Midi, and a younger son were taken prisoner by the Han army and made government slaves. Midi later caught the attention of Emperor Wu and quickly rose to very high positions of favor. The *History of the Former Han* records the following story in Jin Midi's biography:

> Jin Midi's mother had trained her two sons very carefully so that their behavior was without reproach. When the emperor was told of this, he expressed his admiration for her, and after she died of illness, he commanded that a portrait of her be painted in the Palace of Sweet Springs with the label "Consort of the Xiuchu King." Whenever Jin Midi came into the presence of the portrait, he would always bow, face the portrait, and shed tears before proceeding on his way.[39]

The Palace of Sweet Springs (Ganquan Gong) often served as Emperor Wu's place of residence and was where he conducted official business. From the text, it is clear that the painting was a wall mural in the palace and not a portable scroll like that given to Huo Guang. Furthermore, the portrait is called a *tuhua,* which in this context means "an illustration with textual caption."[40] It is not clearly stated whether the portrait was part of a larger program of vassal kings and chieftains or whether it exclusively filled one wall. The account's mention of the physical motions of Jin Midi before the image is interesting. Obviously, the portrait of Jin Midi's mother served as a ritual focus for the son. Every time he passed the picture in the palace, he would perform the same ritual observance, making the image a very public type of ancestor portrait. We possess no concrete information proving that ancestor portraits were already part of the imperial cult during the Han, but the story of Jin Midi suggests that image worship of ancestors at court may have already begun at this early date.

Emperor Wu chose to make this painting as a public presentation because he wanted to send two different messages. Privately, he wanted to express his sympathy and support for Jin Midi on the loss of his beloved mother. Publicly, he wanted to signal his political support for Jin Midi at court, in the face of opposition from those who resented the high position given to a foreigner and former enemy. No copies of the original portrait of Jin Midi's mother survive, but the tale of his worship of her image appears to be illustrated on the back wall of the famous Wu Liang Shrine in Shandong (see figure 5.5).[41] In the carving, Jin Midi is shown bowing in a palace-style structure before what looks like a statue of his mother, rather than a painting on the wall.

RITUAL PAINTINGS OF DEITIES

Though much of the painted visual culture at court consisted of didactic murals, screens, and scrolls of exemplars, a few scattered anecdotes in Han and post-Han

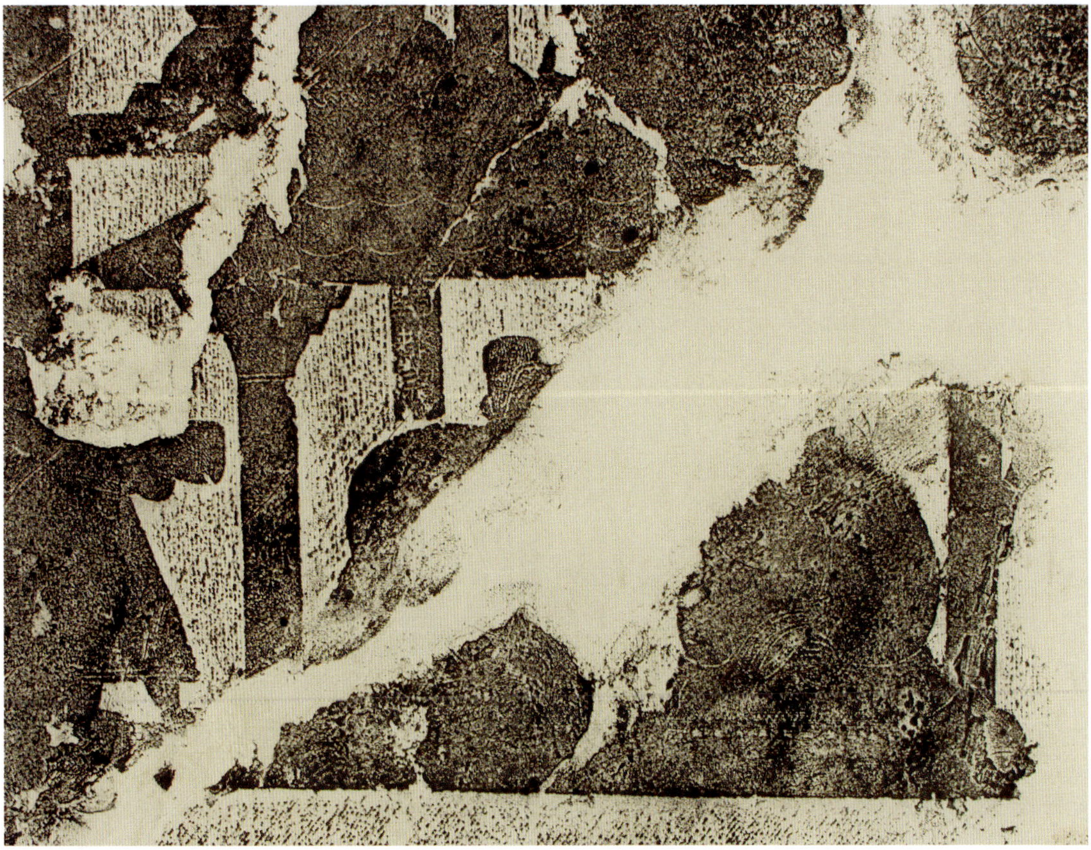

5.5 *Jin Midi worshiping the image of (probably) his mother.* Surviving caption at left reads *ji duwei*, "Commandant of Cavalry." Latter Han period, ca. 150 CE. Ink-on-paper rubbing. Princeton University Art Museum. Far Eastern Seminar Collection, 2002-307.35. Photo: Bruce M. White.

sources suggest that court paintings could serve other ritual or military functions as well.

On a day in 51 BCE, Wang Zhengjun (71 BCE–13 CE), one of the longest-lived and most powerful women of the Former Han and Xin dynasties, gave birth to an infant boy named Liu Ao, who would later reign as Emperor Cheng (r. 33–7 BCE). At the time, Zhengjun was a consort of the heir apparent, Liu Shi, who would later reign as Emperor Yuan (r. 48–33 BCE). They were living in the Heir Apparent's Palace within the Weiyang Palace complex in the capital of Chang'an. The *History of the Former Han* records that she labored and gave birth to the boy in a room called the Painted Hall of the First Lodge (Jiaguan Huatang).[42] Ying Shao (ca. 140 CE to before 204 CE), an early commentator on the *History of the Former Han*, appended a note to this passage, explaining that the Painted Hall was referred to as such because it contained a mural of a figure called Jiuzimu (Nine-Son Mother).

Who was this Jiuzimu and why would her picture adorn a birthing room in the palace? That story is a very tangled skein whose threads are difficult to unravel. The name Jiuzimu could refer to one of two female figures in ancient China. It might have referred to a widow of the State of Lu who lived in the fifth century BCE and whose life was chronicled in the *Arrayed Biographies of Women* by Liu Xiang, the work discussed above.[43] This widow had nine sons, whom she taught well, and she was duly honored by the Duke of Lu with the title Mother Teacher. She is referred to in the text as *jiuzi zhi mu* (the mother of nine sons). Even though the Widow of Lu was a fine paragon for rhetorical use in other didactic contexts, her presence in a birthing chamber would be highly inauspicious. She was a widow whose husband died young, and this would not be the proper image to adorn a room where wives of princes and emperors gave birth.

More convincing is the theory that the Jiuzimu mentioned by Ying Shao refers to a goddess in the popular pantheon of early China.[44] The "Heavenly Questions" (Tianwen), a literary piece contained in the *Elegies of Chu* (Chuci) and likely adapted by the hand of Qu Yuan (ca. 300 BCE) himself, mentions a figure called Nüqi, who had nine sons without the aid of a male partner.[45] Based on other references to her in pre-Han texts, she seems to have been a goddess of fertility, creation, and destruction, akin to the even more powerful Nüwa. It is probable that she was the goddess depicted on the walls of the Painted Hall of the First Lodge. If we assume this to be the case, then we must conclude that her image was painted there more for magical efficacy than for didactic purposes. Consorts to emperors and heirs apparent wanted to bear sons for their husbands because only that way could they gain power and favors and then pass the bounty on to their extended families. During confinement and labor, palace women could gaze upon the goddess who granted sons and pray for her divine intervention.

What would an image of Jiuzimu/Nüqi look like? With the introduction of Buddhism into China beginning in the Latter Han, the native goddess Nüqi became confused and conflated with the Buddhist deity Hāritī.[46] This confusion may have already begun by the time Ying Shao wrote his notes on the *History of the Former Han*. Hāritī was originally a smallpox-inducing ogress in Indo-Iranian myth who had hundreds of offspring and liked to devour the children of mortals. She was later incorporated into the Mahayana pantheon, according to a story in which the Buddha took away one of her beloved boys to teach her a lesson. From that day forward, she became a protector of children and a Buddhist deity to whom people prayed for male offspring. She was frequently depicted in the Gandharan region of northern Pakistan and eastern Afghanistan, from where her imagery likely entered China around 200 CE.

According to the book on southern Chinese social customs, *Record of the Seasonal Observances of the Jing-Chu Region* (Jing Chu suishi ji) by Zong Lin (ca. 500–63 CE), women in the Changsha area of southern China who were without sons prayed to Jiuzimu to bring them male offspring.[47] On the eighth day of the fourth month, infertile people would gather in the market and supplicate a statue of Jiuzimu with unleavened cakes to beg for sons. Paintings and sculptures of Jiuzimu/Hāritī were quite

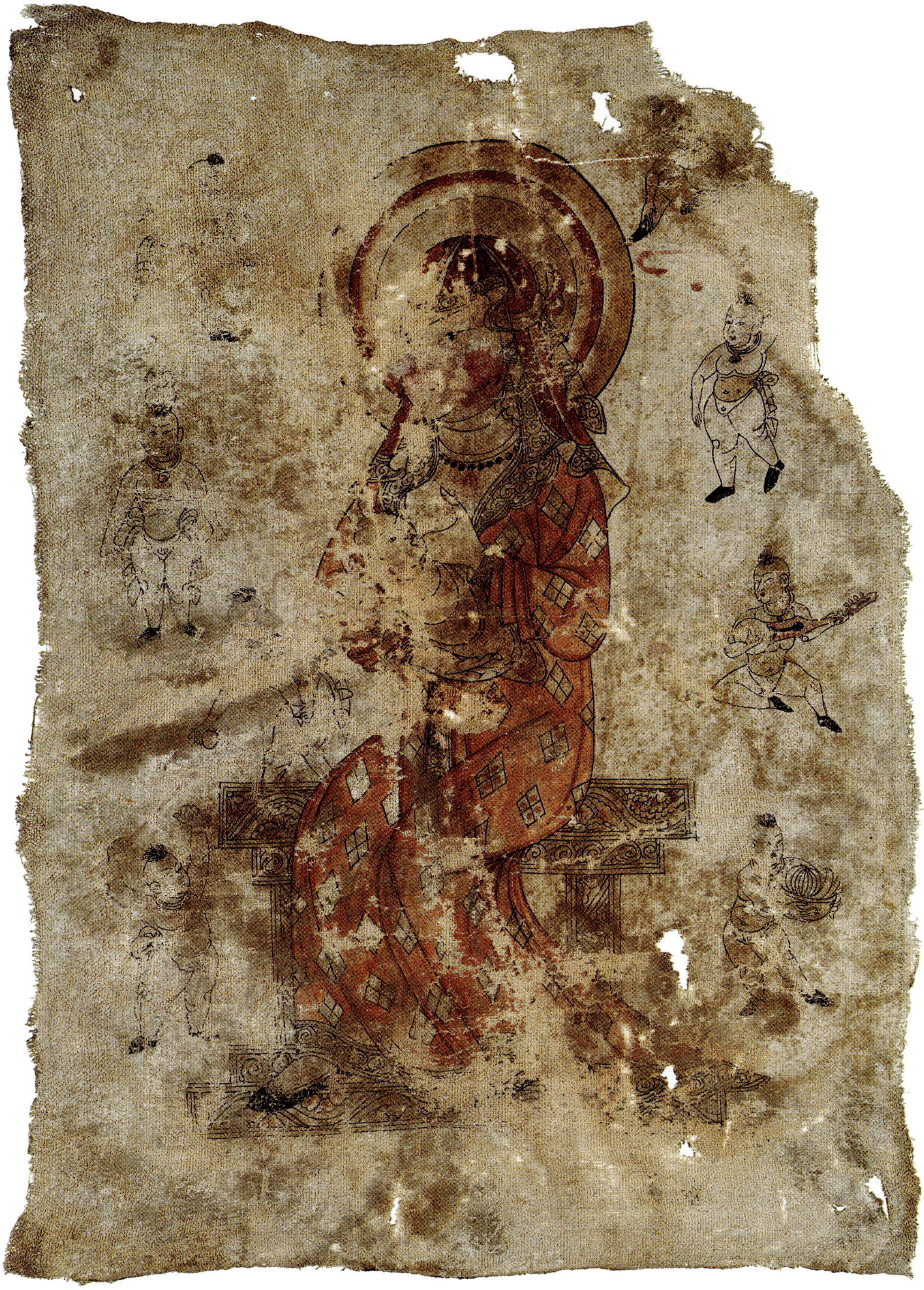

5.6 *Jiuzimu (Hāritī) and her nine sons.* Ninth to tenth centuries CE. Colored pigments on ramie. H. 51 cm. W. 37 cm. Museum für Indische Kunst, Berlin, MIK III 6302. Bildarchiv Preussischer Kulturbesitz/Art Resource, New York. Photo by Jürgen Liepe. Found in 1905 at the Jiaohe Gucheng (Yarkhoto) site near Turfan, Xinjiang.

common in Buddhist temples in medieval China, with famous examples by named artists.[48] A ninth-century polychrome painting on ramie of Jiuzimu was recovered by Albert von Le Coq (1860–1930) near Turfan in 1905 (see figure 5.6). It depicts a seated Jiuzimu nursing her youngest child while eight other children sport around her. The composition and the clothing of the central figure owe much to Indian and Gandharan depictions of Hārītī, but the treatment of the male children appears to show some affinity with Chinese painting traditions. Perhaps, this painting retains some vestigial traces of the native Chinese depictions of Jiuzimu/Nüqi. As such, it is our only clue to what the mural of Jiuzimu on the walls of the Painted Hall of the First Lodge may have looked like.

ILLUSTRATED BATTLE ACCOUNTS

Judging by textual and archaeological sources, it appears that Qin and Han generals and tacticians made extensive use of maps, charts, and diagrams to wage war. We know from excavated examples that maps drawn up for military use could be quite accurately scaled and contain numerous captions. The oldest surviving detailed maps from China were those drawn on wooden boards and found at the Qin period site of Fangmatan in Gansu, dated to around 300 BCE.[49] Moving forward a bit in time and sophistication, figure 5.7 depicts a topographic map painted on silk found in tomb 3 at Mawangdui (ca. 168 BCE). It appears to show the territory ranging from the Changsha Princedom of the Han (present-day Hunan) to the independent, and occasionally hostile, Kingdom of Nanyue (comprising much of present-day Guangdong and based near Canton). The map was probably drawn up in preparation for a military confrontation between the two powers around 183–180 BCE. Later, it was buried in the tomb of the son of Changsha's former prime minister, a man who may have held his father's former post and who was probably involved in some way in the frontier defense.[50] The rivers are scaled and accurately placed, and cities and towns are faithfully captioned, but the depiction of mountains and hills on the map is highly schematic.

Military commanders, like the famous Han general Li Ling, also brought mapmakers with them on campaigns deep into enemy territory to map the surrounding terrain for immediate tactical advantage and for future planning.[51] Books on the military arts (*bingshu*) from the Han period, like their counterparts in later ages, probably contained numerous illustrations, including pictures of battle formations, territorial maps, and types of weapons or siege engines. We can infer this from the bibliographic treatise of the *History of the Former Han* (chapter 30), which records military manuals by fifty-three different authors, some of them appended with several scrolls of captioned illustrations.[52]

An intriguing passage in the *History of the Former Han* suggests that the emperor (or victorious generals) may have also commissioned illustrated battle accounts for use at court. These appear to have been used for political purposes, for casual entertainment, and possibly as part of ancestral rituals. In an insightful work of

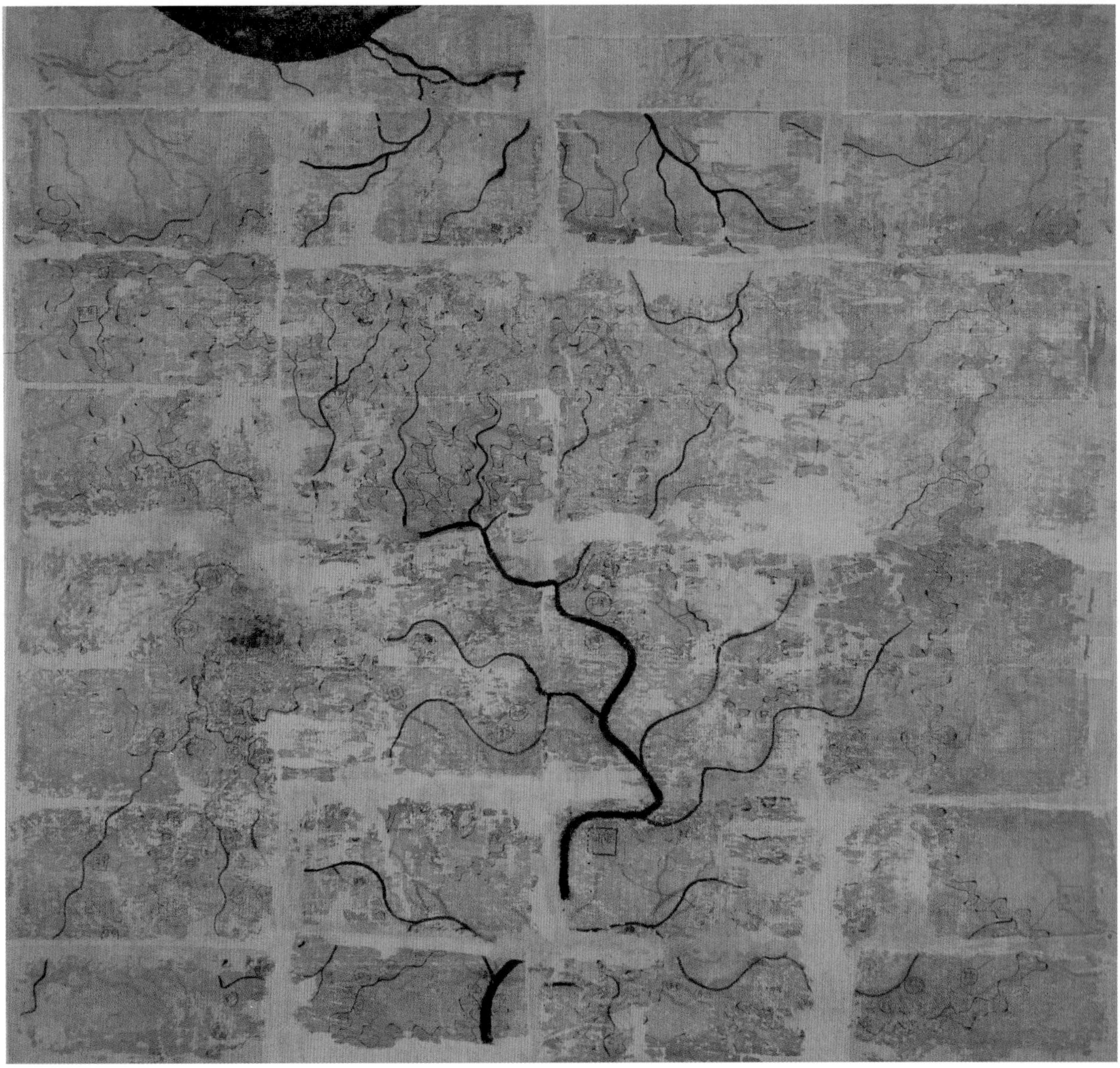

5.7 *Topographic map (south at top) from Mawangdui tomb 3.* Former Han period, ca. 183–168 BCE. Ink on silk. L. 96 cm. W. 96 cm. Hunan Provincial Museum, Changsha. Photo courtesy of Cultural Relics Publishing House.

textual criticism, the great Sinologist J. J. L. Duyvendak (1889–1954) demonstrated that Ban Gu's description of a Chinese victory over a Xiongnu fortress deep in Sogdiana (in chapter 70 of the *History of the Former Han*) was not copied from the general's archived report of the battle, as was the historian's usual practice. It was actually, Duyvendak argued, a description of a painting of the battle, incorporating the textual captions directly from the illustrations.[53]

Briefly sketched, the enemy in this encounter was Zhizhi Shanyu, elder brother of Huhanye Shanyu and a rival claimant to the Xiongnu throne, who had fled west across the Pamirs and into Sogdiana, establishing his own fortified city. In 44 BCE, he killed a Han envoy sent to negotiate with him. Sensing the danger posed by Zhizhi, a young Chinese officer named Chen Tang forged an imperial order calling up 40,000 local troops and launched a preemptive, long-distance campaign to bring Zhizhi Shanyu to justice. In late 36 BCE, Chen Tang and his nominal superior Gan Yanshou converged on Zhizhi's capital from two directions, surrounded his fortifications, and stormed the citadel, killing Zhizhi and more than a thousand of his followers.[54]

The account of the battle is told in picturesque and colorful detail. We are told of the rainbow-colored banners flying from Zhizhi Shanyu's walls, the "fish-scale" shield formation of his foot soldiers, and the taunting shouts of *dou-lai* (come and fight me!) from his men on the wall. What Duyvendak noticed, apart from the account's unusual vividness, was that the battle was described, not from a general's point of view, but from an eyewitness perspective that roamed the battle scene and described the action from various vantage points. The whole story was divided into a series of discrete "scenes," which suggests how the continuous narrative could have been divided on either a panel or a scroll into nine consecutive illustrations.[55] The use of certain repetitive phrases throughout the *History of the Former Han* account also suggested to Duyvendak that these were the captions to the pictures that were copied by Ban Gu directly from the original illustrations in the imperial archive.[56]

The illustrated, written report of the victory over Zhizhi Shanyu was used for several purposes at court when Chen Tang returned with it to Chang'an in the late winter of 35 BCE. It appears from an entry in the "Annals of Emperor Yuan" in the *History of the Former Han* that the illustrated battle account was first presented to the High Gods in the Suburban Sacrifice and then to the ancestors in the Imperial Shrine, reporting to them the great victory for the Han house.[57] A banquet was then held where the illustrated account was the center of attention. It was even "shown to the honored ladies in the imperial harem."[58] The scene that might have delighted the court ladies the most was the one that would have shown Zhizhi Shanyu's consorts fighting and dying alongside him on the fortress tower. Duyvendak argues that the fuss made over this painting at court was part of a campaign of political propaganda generated by Chen Tang and his supporters. If Chen Tang could sway the emperor and his wives to his side by dazzling them with an illustrated account of his exploits, then maybe he could extricate himself from a certain death sentence for having forged an imperial edict.[59]

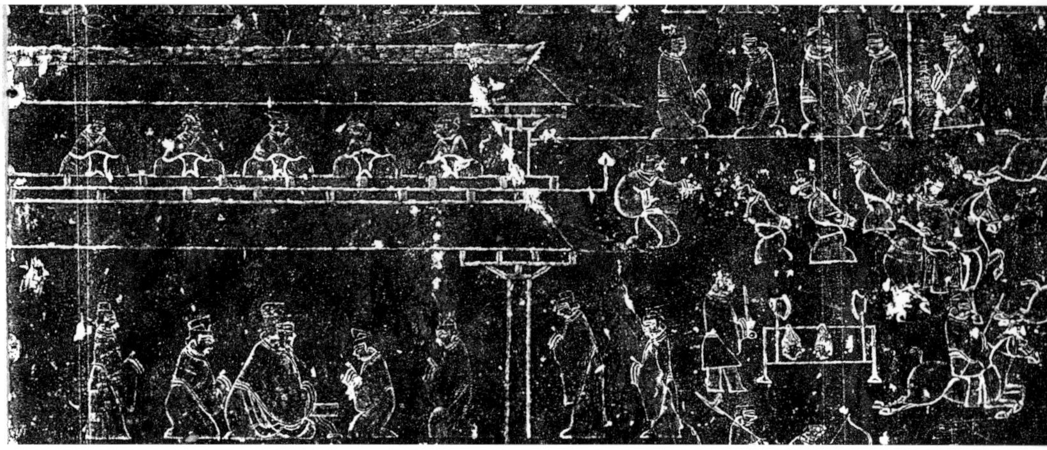

5.8 *The battle between Han forces and those of the king of the Hu barbarians.* Latter Han period, ca. 76–88 CE. Ink-on-paper rubbing (detail). W. 220 cm. West wall of shrine at Xiaotangshan, Changqing County, Shandong. Photo courtesy of Shandong Fine Arts Publishing House.

Unfortunately, no painted copy of an illustrated battle account like that of the defeat of Zhizhi survives from early China, but many stone funerary monuments from Shandong portray a scene that may be an indirect descendant of just such a painting. The scenes clearly depict a battle between the Han armies and the Hu barbarians, a blanket ethnonym which includes the Xiongnu and other groups to the north and west of the Great Wall. The several known Shandong compositions are all based on a limited set of stock motifs drawn from pattern sheets (see chapter 3). The most elaborate (and partially captioned) version of this scene is displayed on the middle of the western wall of the shrine at Xiaotangshan, which was built about one hundred years after Chen Tang's epic battle (see figure 5.8).[60] If we assume that this scene was based on a hand scroll, then we must begin viewing the scene at the rightmost portion. A large figure is seated at the lower right, leaning on an armrest and addressing a kneeling commander before him. A Han period caption behind the large figure identifies him as the king of the Hu barbarians (Hu Wang). Two men are seated at a nearby table, eating skewers of meat. Here, we are clearly in the Hu camp. To the far right, we see a large force of mounted Hu archers charging out of the hills. All of the Hu warriors wear a characteristic peaked felt cap. Just as in the Chen Tang painting, the barbarians are branded as the instigators of the conflict. The battle is joined in the middle of the composition (reading to the left). The vanguard of the Hu army has clashed with the Han forces, represented by twelve mounted warriors carrying halberds, swords, and bows. One Hu warrior had been decapitated and is seen flying from his horse, while another is hooked from his mount by a Chinese halberd. Other Hu soldiers lie dead on the ground. The dignified Chinese rider on the robust prancing horse farthest to the left probably represents the Chinese general. Moving farther

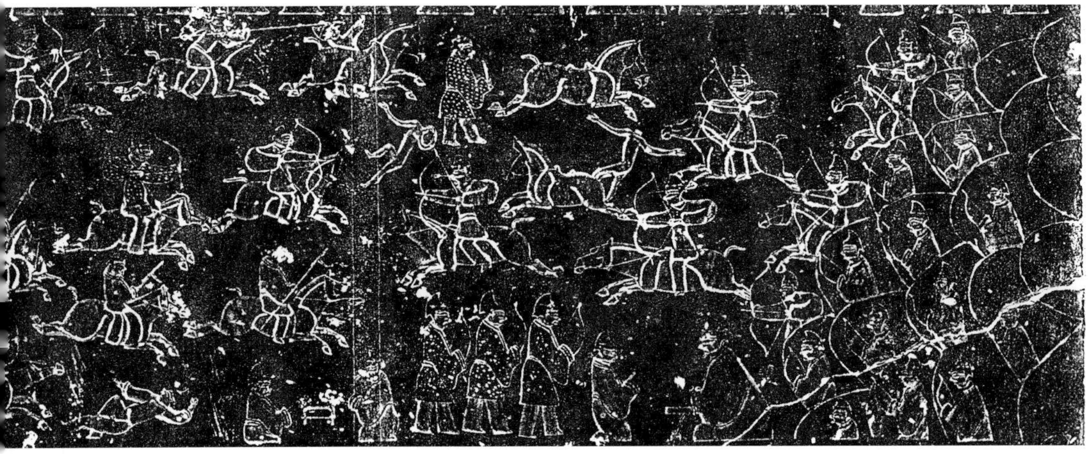

left to the third scene, we enter the Han camp and witness the aftermath of the victory. Three captured Hu are seen kneeling before a Chinese officer, their hands tied behind their backs. Below them is a rack holding two executioner's axes and two severed heads suspended by the hair. (We are told that Chen Tang captured 1,518 heads in his engagement.) In the fourth scene, at the far left of the composition, a large figure is seated in a pavilion. This is probably the leader of the Chinese forces, or possibly the emperor being informed of the victory.

It is unclear exactly which battle this four-part illustrated narrative was meant to recount. It may just be a generic scene referring to great victories over the Xiongnu, proclaiming the superior might of the civilized Chinese, but I would still argue that the images themselves are probably descended from painted scrolls depicting actual historic battles, perhaps even the one fought in the winter of 36 BCE by Chen Tang and Zhizhi Shanyu thousands of miles from the Han capital.

PALACE DECORATION AND FURNISHINGS

While it is true that most palace paintings were designed to instruct, to inform, to proclaim, or to entertain, other forms of visual display at court were simply meant to dazzle the eye, proclaiming unimaginable levels of wealth and unlimited access to artisan labor.[61] Textual descriptions and surviving objects show a marked preference for gilding, silvering, lacquering, inlay with precious stones, and embellishment with imported feathers, jade, and other rare materials. It seems that such ostentatious display is common to nearly all palace cultures.

The Qin and Han palace compounds encompassed hundreds of individual buildings, but only a few of these held portrait murals or historical-narrative screens like those described in the previous sections. The walls of many Qin and Han palace buildings appear to have been plastered and painted with decorative murals consisting of broad bands of color, cloud or vine scrolls, simple repeated geometric patterns, auspicious imagery, or generic scenes of entertainers, hunts, and processions.

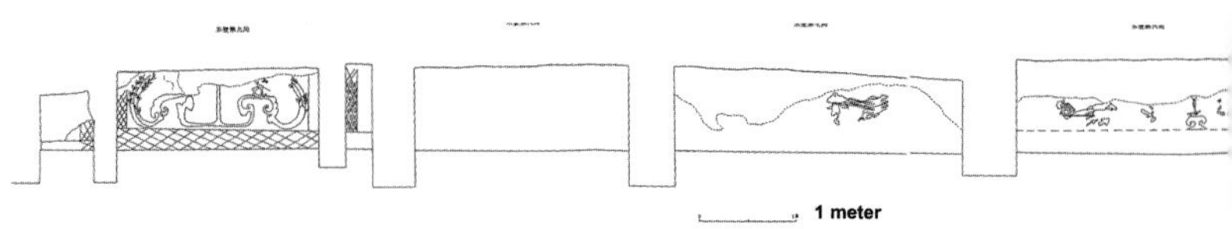

Excavations began in 1973 among the foundations of the Qin palaces on the north bank of the Wei River, northwest of present-day Xi'an City. This is where the Qin capital of Xianyang was located from about 350 BCE until its destruction in 206 BCE.[62] At least seven principal palace buildings were located within a rectangular, moated wall. They appear to have been built late in the Warring States period, before the unification in 221 BCE. A portion of Palace Building 3 (as numbered by the archaeologists) appears to have served as the royal stables. Like most of the palace buildings, Building 3 was girded by an open, colonnaded porch and connected to other structures by means of walled corridors, such as the type described in the *Historical Records,* through which the First Emperor of Qin traveled to conceal his whereabouts. Numerous painted fragments surrounding the building suggest that the colonnaded porch was decorated with colorful murals. Likewise, on both walls of a nine-bay-long walled corridor (32.4 m long by 5 m wide) connecting Building 3 with another structure, Qin artisans painted a series of murals, fortunately preserved in some sections along the east wall to a height of 20–108 centimeters. Figure 5.9 is a drawing of the overall plan of the east wall mural of this corridor.

Figure 5.10 shows a four-horse team harnessed to pull an enclosed royal carriage (now barely discernible). It is a detail of the northward-leading procession scene painted on the east wall of bay 4 (see figure 5.9) of the painted corridor. The horses were painted in a claret-colored pigment on a white plaster background. The four horses are drawn in stacked recession with no diminution in size. Interspersed between the carriage teams on this wall, one can still make out traces of at least three groups of pine trees which line the path of the vehicles. The scene might represent a procession along the Qin Royal Highway (*chidao*), which was a wide road lined with pine trees on both sides. This mural fragment, recovered from an insignificant hallway leading from the royal stables, gives us a tantalizing glimpse at what a central palace mural might have looked like during the Qin.

In late 2003, archaeologists announced the first discovery of palace murals from the Han palaces at Chang'an.[63] In the ruins of the Palace of Lasting Joy (Changle Gong), which served as the residence of the empress dowager during most of the Former Han, archaeologists found a large basement belonging to a palace building. Connected to the basement by a fifteen-meter-long tunnel-corridor was a smaller semisubterranean room. This room contained numerous small mural fragments, which may have fallen from their original placement on the ceiling. At the time of this writing, none of the mural fragments have been published. Descriptions in news reports indicate that the decoration consists of scrolls, lines, lozenges, and other geometric forms in red, cyan, purple, yellow, and white. The floor and steps of the semi-

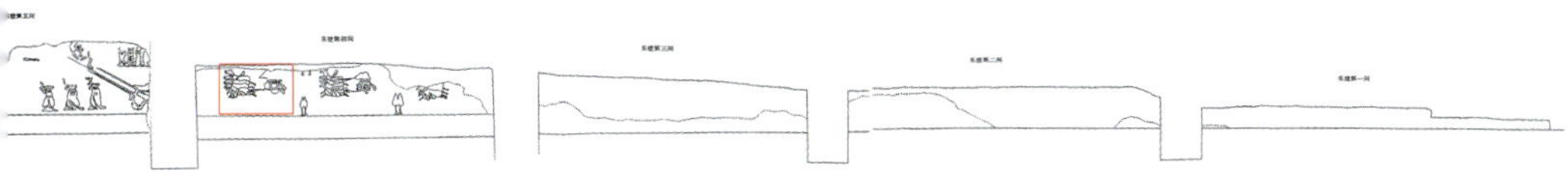

5.9 *Procession scene.* Late Warring States period, ca. 250 BCE. Xianyang Qin Palace site, Shaanxi. From Shaanxi Sheng Kaogu Yanjiusuo, *Qindu Xianyang*, fig. 441.

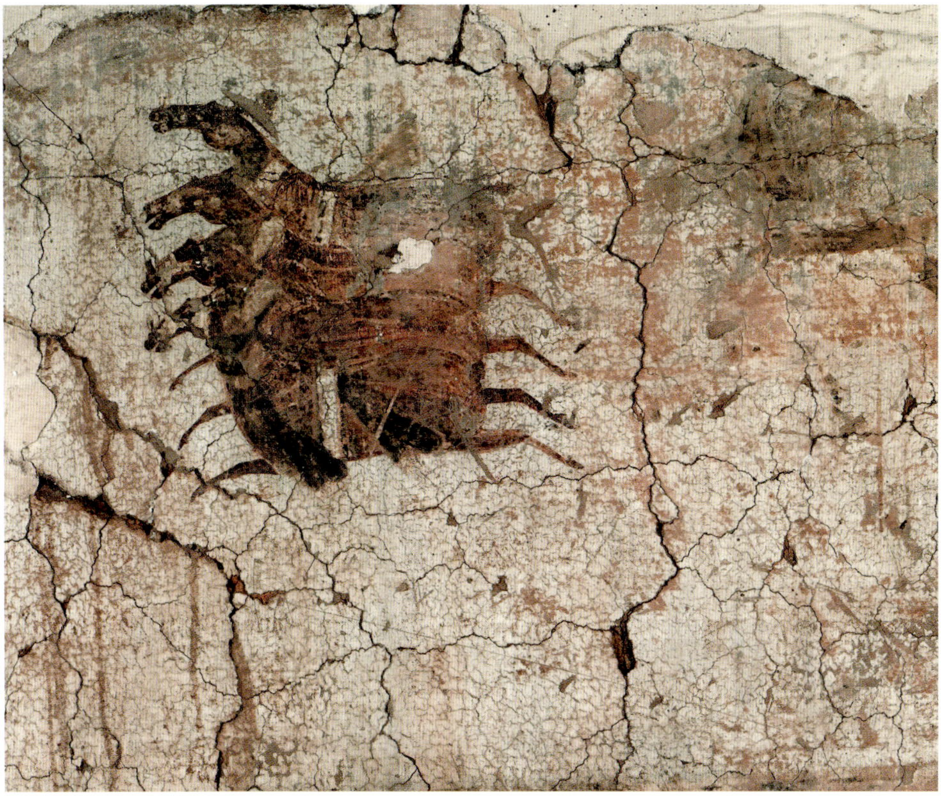

5.10 *Four-horse carriage.* Detail from bay 4 (counting from right) leftmost horse team of three. Late Warring States period, ca. 250 BCE. Paint on dry plaster. H. 86.7 cm. W. 106 cm. Cultural Relics Conservation Center of Xianyang City, Shaanxi. Photo courtesy of Xianyang Cultural Relics Bureau.

subterranean room were painted vermilion, which, according to Han texts, was a practice reserved for rooms of imperial residence.[64]

Texts that describe plastered and painted walls during the Han refer to the technique as *hu-fen* 胡粉.[65] It is not clear if the word *fen* 粉 (powder) refers here to powdered mineral pigments, such as powdered white lead, or to the powdered limestone used to make the base plaster.[66] Words prefixed by the character *hu* 胡 (northern barbarian) usually indicate a non-Chinese product imported from the west or northwest, raising the possibility that the technique of painting on wall plaster might have been imported into Qin and Han China from along the Silk Road.[67] More likely in this case, the character *hu* 胡 is a loan for *hu* 糊 (thick rice gruel, paste), referring to the sticky, gluelike nature of the plaster coating.

Archaeologists have reconstructed the technique by which the Qin murals were fashioned.[68] First the wall was prepared with a 5-centimeter-thick layer of mixed mud and straw. This was covered by a 0.8- to 1.0-centimeter-thick layer of fine clay, mixed with grain chaff. Then, the white lime plaster was applied to a thickness of 3–5 millimeters. Finally, the colored pigments were brushed onto the white ground. It appears that the painted palace murals from Xianyang and Chang'an were not made by the true fresco technique of applying pigments on wet plaster but were instead painted atop dry plaster. The pigments used in the Qin murals were almost all mineral pigments, and the colors are still vibrant today. Some textual accounts mention that the paint for certain rooms was mixed with ground pepper so that, when warmed, the walls would emit their own incense to mask noxious summer odors.[69]

To give the reader a comprehensive visual tour of all the Han palaces is impossible here. Instead, I would like to begin with a description of one of the most lavishly decorated of all the palace buildings of the Former Han period, the Hall of Brilliant Sunlight (Zhaoyang Dian). It was built during the reign of Emperor Wu and served as a sort of Petit Trianon to lodge the highest-ranking women in the imperial harem.[70] During the reign of Emperor Cheng, the highly favored Zhao Zhaoyi resided there. The fullest description of the building is found in the current text of the *Miscellaneous Notes on the Western Capital.* The first few lines of the *Miscellaneous Notes* account are almost identical to the text of the slightly less elaborate version found in chapter 97 of the *History of the Former Han.*[71]

> The Hall of Brilliant Sunlight
>
> The younger sister of Zhao Feiyan [viz., Zhao Zhaoyi] lived in the Hall of Brilliant Sunlight. The courtyard was all vermilion red in color, while the hall itself was lacquered in cinnabar red.[72] The threshold sills were all covered in gilded-bronze panels. The stairs were all of white jade. Where the laths of the wall were exposed to view, they were everywhere capped with gold collars and embedded with jade disks from Lantian, bright pearls, and kingfisher feathers. On top of the building, there were nine gold dragons, each holding nine gold jingle bells in its mouth and dangling five-colored feather tassels. These were attached with purple-silk cords with green decoration and gold and silver floral bangles. Each day that there was a pleasant wind, the pennants reflected the sunlight and flashed brilliant light upon the hall. The sound of the bells and the bangles startled and quickened everyone around. In the midst of the hall, there was a painted, wooden screen. The design on the screen was so fine, it looked like it was made with a spider's silk threads. There were jade armrests and jade couches, and mats of ivory. There was a carpet of black-bear pelts, the hair of which was longer than two *chi* (45 cm). When one slept on it, he could take the

hair and cover himself like a blanket. Though one might look for him, one would never find him. When one sat on it, his knees would disappear in its depth. Scattered all about were various braziers and incense burners. One was placed on this carpet. Even after more than one hundred days its supply of incense was not exhausted. The carpet was anchored by four jade weights that were flawless and dazzled with light. The windows were all made of green glass that transmitted the sunlight. Not even a single hair could hide on one of them. The rafters were all carved into the shapes of dragons and snakes that writhed around each other. You could clearly see their scales. Of all who saw this hall, there were none who were not struck with surprise and awe. The craftsmen who built it, Ding Huan and Li Ju, were the most skillful (*qiao*) artisans in the entire world. When the building was complete, he [Ding Huan?] told all of this to Fan Yannian, the son of his elder sister. Very few outsiders knew of it, and there was no one to transmit this information.[73]

The above description is remarkably picturesque and is convenient for our purposes because it lists most of the major types of palace furniture and decorative objects, including room screens, armrests and sitting tables, mats, carpets, decorative mat and carpet weights, and incense burners. A letter reportedly written by Zhao Zhaoyi, the most famous denizen of the Hall of Brilliant Sunlight, to her sister Zhao Feiyan is also recorded in the *Miscellaneous Notes on the Western Capital*.[74] It inventories thirty-five luxury gifts that she has given to Zhao Feiyan as a sort of trousseau to congratulate her upon her accession as empress in 16 BCE, and as such, many of the gifts are imbued with connotations of conjugal harmony. The nonlyrical, bureaucratic nature of the list, however, suggests that the text was originally some sort of palace inventory, which was later used to compose this apocryphal letter. A quick perusal of the list (table 5.1) enhances our impression of the level of conspicuous display in palace furnishings, clothing, and adornment.

Let us look in depth at a few of these types of objects, especially those for which we have actual surviving examples from the Han palaces. Bronze incense burners (*xunlu*, *xianglu*) were an important category of palace furnishing that served both practical and decorative functions. They could fill the room with fragrant incense or be used as portable braziers to warm the hands. They were often plated or inlaid with gold and silver and were intricately cast with openwork decoration to allow smoke to rise through the lid. As we just read in the description of the Hall of Brilliant Sunlight, one palace hall might be outfitted with several of them. Some were placed on the floor, while others might have been placed on tables or low platforms.[75]

In 1981 archaeologists discovered a burial pit near a large satellite tomb that was just east of Emperor Wu's mausoleum at Maoling, Shaanxi.[76] The most spectacular find from the pit was a gilded- and silvered-bronze censer (see figure 5.11). The censer bowl takes the shape of a mountainous isle floating amid the waves, supported by three arched dragons. These beasts perch on a pedestal in the form of a bamboo stalk,

TABLE 5.1. GIFTS GIVEN BY ZHAO ZHAOYI TO HER SISTER, EMPRESS ZHAO

1. A purple, round-brimmed hat, decorated with gold floral bangles
2. A veil of purple silk gauze, decorated with gold floral bangles
3. A short jacket woven of gold thread and polychrome silk brocade
4. A [matching] skirt woven of gold thread and polychrome silk brocade
5. A polychrome silk belt
6. A short jacket embroidered with a design of mandarin ducks[1]
7. A bed coverlet embroidered with a design of mandarin ducks
8. A bed mattress embroidered with a design of mandarin ducks
9. An embroidered waistcoat with inlaid gold thread
10. A pair of sandals inlaid with the seven precious materials
11. A carved jade bracelet with polychrome designs
12. Hairpins inlaid with semiprecious stones and decorated with the *tongxin* (identical heart) motif[2]
13. A golden headdress with suspended jewels that jingle
14. Ear-spools with the *hehuan* (harmonious joy) motif
15. A *zhen* (rigid pillow) made completely of amber
16. A rigid pillow with tortoiseshell decoration
17. A semicircular bracelet made of coral
18. A finger ring made of carnelian
19. A hand fan made of translucent talc
20. A hand fan made of peacock feathers
21. A hand fan made of kingfisher feathers
22. A "nine-florescence" hand fan of woven bamboo
23. A "five-brightness" hand fan[3]
24. A room screen of translucent talc panels
25. A room screen of colored glass
26. A golden, five-level, mountain-shaped incense burner (*boshanlu*)
27. A revolving room fan
28. A mat of woven coconut leaves
29. *Tongxin* plums, possibly with doubled pits(?)
30. *Hanzhi* plums
31. *Qingmu* (*Aristolochia debilis*) incense
32. Lignaloes incense
33. A drinking goblet made from a conch shell
34. Musk deer incense from Vietnam
35. A tree-shaped lamp with seven branches

1. The mandarin ducks were a symbol of conjugal fidelity and marital sexual relations.

2. Symbolic of conjugal harmony and love, apparently a floral scroll motif with intertwining leaves.

3. A special type of fan, reserved for the nobility during the Qin and Han and exclusively for the emperor in the Jin and later periods. It was ritually symbolic of the ceding of the throne from Yao to Shun.

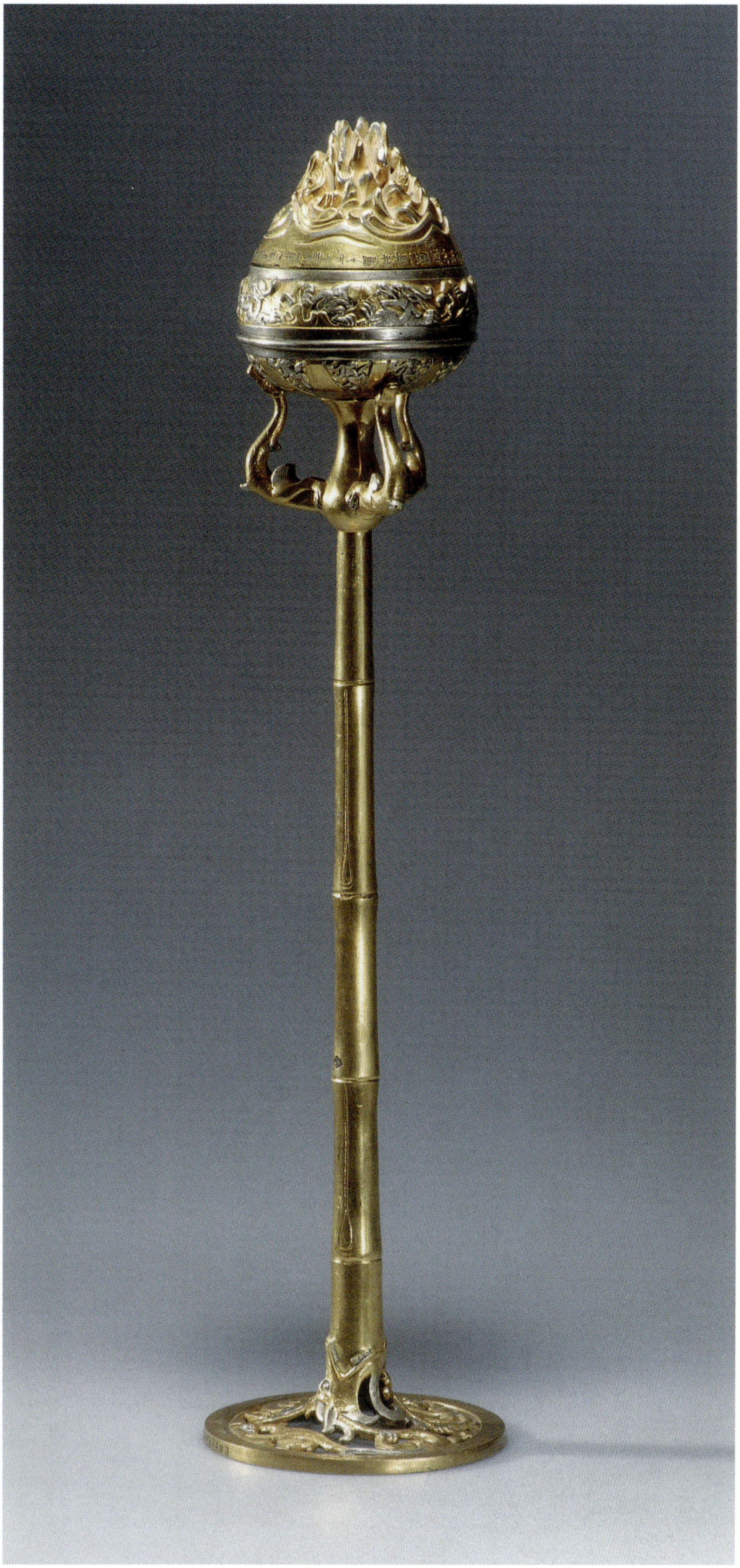

5.11 *Censer.* Former Han period, dated 137 BCE. Gilded and silvered bronze. H. 58 cm. Maoling Museum, Shaanxi. Photo courtesy of Cultural Relics Publishing House.

accurately modeled with bulging nodes. The bamboo stalk sits in the gaping mouth of two coiled dragons that inhabit the openwork, circular base of the piece. When incense was burned in the bowl, the smoke would have billowed out of perforations in the mountain-shaped lid, creating the impression of a mysterious island enveloped in fog.

Just like the Changxin Palace lamp that was discussed in chapter 1, this sumptuous piece was inscribed on each separate subassembly with quality-control and accounting inscriptions that give the physical measurements, manufacturing dates, and ownership history of the object. The inscriptions were engraved into the surface after delivery of the object and marred the finish greatly. The lid inscription runs for thirty-five characters and reads:

> For the Master of the Imperial Bedchamber of the Weiyang Palace, under the control of the Palace Servant Bureau;[77] one gilded incense burner (*xunlu*) set, with bamboo-jointed [stand]; combined weight of 10 *jin* and 12 *liang* (2.67 kg); fabricated in the fourth year [of Emperor Wu, 137 BCE] by the Palace Managers;[78] delivered in the tenth month of the fifth year [136 BCE]; item 3 of the *chu* production run.[79]

The base of the censer was inscribed along the outer rim with a similar text, though the details are given somewhat differently. The base inscription lists the combined weight of the censer and stand as exactly 11 *jin* (2.73 kg) and records the manufacturing workshop as the Attendant Workshop (Sigong) rather than the Palace Managers (Neiguan).[80] The serial number on the base is given as "item 4 of the *chu* production run," the number just after the one given on the lid.

Judging by the inscriptions, it seems that this magnificent piece may have once adorned the imperial bedchambers of the main Weiyang Palace in Chang'an. Perhaps, it once stood in the bedroom of Emperor Wu himself. It is a rare survival, an actual piece of palace decoration from the height of the Former Han's gilded age. Sometime after its fabrication, Emperor Wu, or possibly his grandmother Empress Dowager Dou (d. 135 BCE), probably gave the censer as a gift to his older sister, the Elder Yangxin Princess, the same woman who once owned the Changxin Palace lamp. When the princess died around 110 BCE, it was buried along with many of her prized palace furnishings in pits surrounding her tomb, which lay in the shadow of her brother's massive tumulus.[81]

Though the Weiyang Palace censer was certainly a spectacular decorative and functional piece of furniture, it was also imbued with ideological connotations. Many scholars argue that the rocky island on the censer lid was supposed to represent Penglai, one of the Islands of the Immortals, said to float somewhere in the Eastern Sea.[82] Both the First Emperor of Qin and Emperor Wu of the Han were obsessed with communicating with the denizens of these islands, immortals who might confer the secret of everlasting life. During his reign, the hopelessly gullible Emperor Wu fell victim to

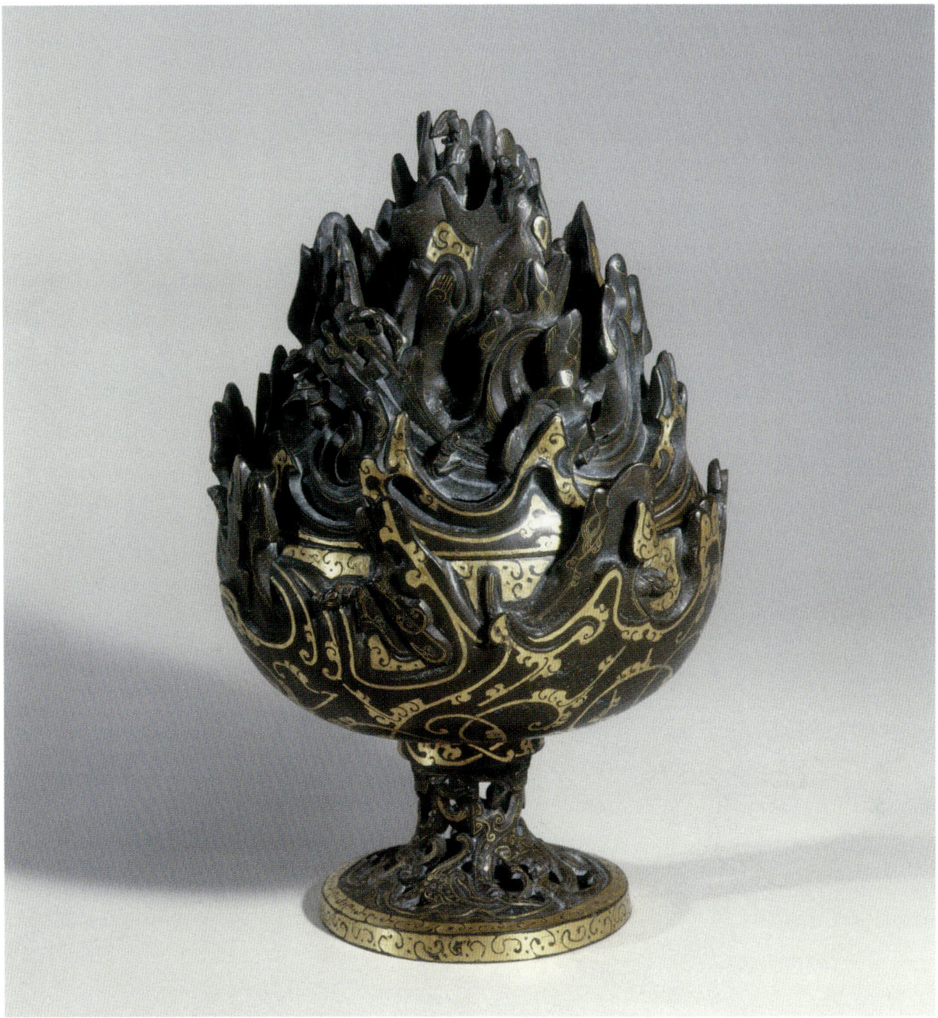

5.12 *Censer.* Former Han period, ca. 135–113 BCE. Bronze with gold and silver inlay. H. 26 cm. Weight 3.4 kg. Hebei Provincial Museum. Photo courtesy of Cultural Relics Publishing House.

numerous charlatans who claimed that they had visited this island or knew how to reach it.[83] Many of the so-called wizards claimed that immortals could be lured to the court itself if the emperor decorated its rooms and parks with sympathetic imagery that would make the immortals feel at home. Thus, the Weiyang Palace censer may have also served as a ritual object, summoning the immortals' spirits to the emperor's bedchamber. On a different level, it functioned as yet another piece of visual propaganda, supporting the emperor's controversial religious ideology and practices.

A shorter version of this same design, nearly contemporary in date to the Weiyang Palace censer, was found in the tomb of the Elder Yangxin Princess's younger half brother, Liu Sheng (d. 113 BCE), located at present-day Mancheng, Hebei (see figure 5.12).[84] On Liu Sheng's censer, we can really appreciate the details of the Island of the

Immortals. Dragons swim in the surrounding surf, while tigers and bears cavort among the peaks. Six vaguely humanoid figures dwell on its hills and in its valleys. Liu Sheng's censer is not inscribed, so we cannot determine in which workshop it was cast. Though it may never have been used at the imperial court in Chang'an, it was certainly used at a royal court, since Liu Sheng was Prince of Zhongshan and a brother of Emperor Wu.

The Han palaces were also provided with a multitude of vessels for serving food and drink. A single palace banquet might require thousands of place settings. Fashioned in both bronze and lacquer, most of these dining vessels were mass-produced using production-line techniques in imperial workshops in Shu and Guanghan Commanderies (present-day Sichuan).[85] Figure 5.13 is remarkable *zun*-type vessel used in the Latter Han palace in Luoyang for serving a high-alcohol grain beverage called *yunjiu*.[86] It seems to have later been given as a gift to some high official who buried it in his tomb. It was found somewhere in Shaanxi before World War II and later was confiscated by the government and placed into the collection of the Palace Museum, Beijing. It consists of a lidded cylindrical container with ring-handles and a broad, platter-like tray. Both the container itself and the circular support have undergone amalgam gilding. Each is supported by three delightful squatting bears, embellished with cast and incised decoration and inlaid with turquoise and other semiprecious stones. The circular stand was inscribed at the factory with a quality-control and accounting inscription which reads:

> Made in the twenty-first year of the Jianwu era [45 CE] at the Western Workshop of Shu Commandery. An imperial-use carafe [in the shape of a standard grain measure] with stand, on feet of carved, squatting bears, decorated with bluish-green jewels [turquoise]. Diameter of the bronze stand, two *chi* and two *cun* (52.25 cm). Made by gilder Chong, mold (or model?) carver Ye, metalsmith Kang, and master artisan Ye. Managed by Commandery Clerk for Workshop Inspection Yun, Factory Chief Fan, Assistant Factory Chief Meng, Bronze Bureau Head Xun, and Foreman Clerk Yun.

We know that this piece was reserved for use in the palace because the inventory label calls it a *shengyu* ([he who] rides in the carriage) piece, a euphemism for items used only by the emperor and his court.[87] The inscription records the names of four artisans who worked on the piece and five bureaucrats who supervised their work. A carafe like this would have been placed on a low lacquer table, and the *yunjiu* would have been scooped out with a ladle.

Sometime during World War II, villagers near the city of P'yôngyang in Korea looted a tomb dating from the Wang Mang or Latter Han period. One of the objects from the tomb was a lacquer platter with a gilded-bronze mount. The platter was decorated with cloud scrolls and animal designs in red lacquer on a black-lacquer ground, identical to the palace platter seen in figure 3.6a. Two incised inscriptions

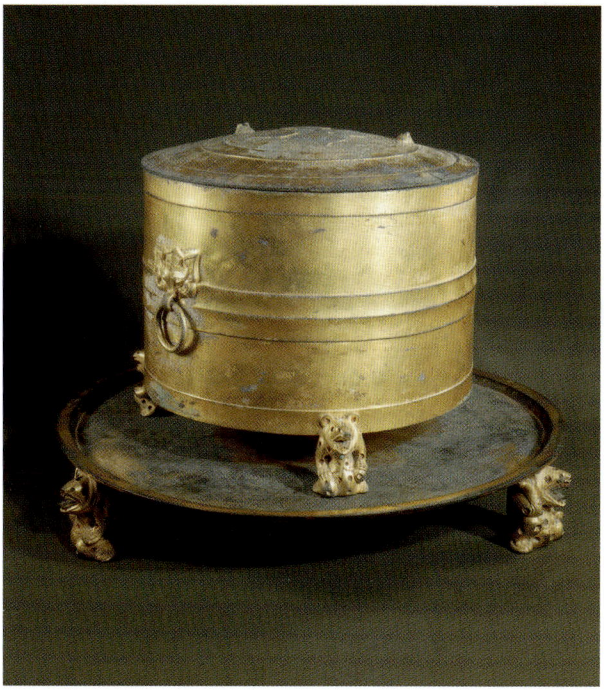

5.13 *Zun-type vessel with stand.* Latter Han period, dated 45 CE. Gilded bronze with semiprecious-stone inlay. Vessel: H. 28.5 cm. D. 30.3 cm. Base: H. 9.5 cm. D. 55.8 cm. Palace Museum, Beijing. Photo courtesy of Cultural Relics Publishing House.

also adorn the platter, one under the rim and one on the bottom. Under the rim was a factory inscription recording the artisans and supervisors who produced this piece late in 8 CE at the imperially run Western Workshop of Shu, the same factory that made the gilded carafe just discussed. The inscription under the rim reads:

> Made in the third year of the Jushe era [8 CE] by the Western Workshop of Shu Commandery. A food platter with a ramie core and . . . painted with designs and lacquered in black and red, fit for use by the emperor. . . . Made by lacquerer [name character unreadable], topcoat-lacquerer Bing, gilder Dang, design-painter Gong, red-lacquerer [name character unreadable], touch-up artisan Ping, and master artisan Yi. Managed by Probationary Commandery Clerk for Workshop Inspection Yan, Factory Chief Liang, Probationary Assistant Factory Chief Qin, Lacquer Bureau Head He, and Foreman Clerk Xu.[88]

Once the platter was delivered to the palace a few months later, it was given a second inscription recording the date of inventory, the palace office where it was to reside, and a serial number within the entire received order of place settings. That text was inscribed in a prominent location on the bottom of the piece in a more decorative, archaizing script:

> The Provisioner of the Chamber of Eternal Joy (Changle [Shi]); in the first month of the first year of the Shijianguo era [January 15–February 13, 9 CE]; received number 2,173 of 3,000.

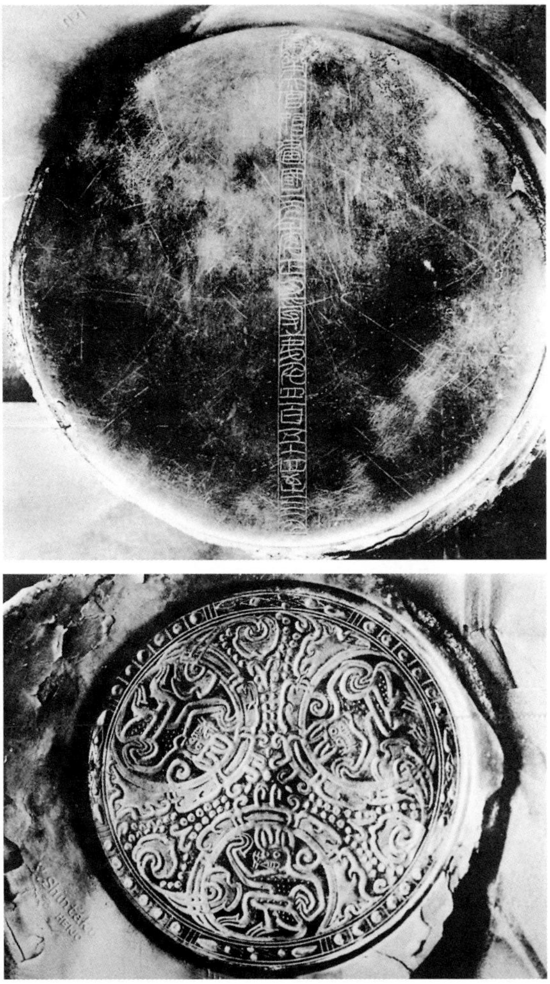

5.14 *Fragment of imperial lacquer food platter.* Late Former Han period to incipient Wang Mang period, dated 8 CE. Lacquer over fabric core. From Umehara, *Shina Kandai,* pl. 35. Looted in 1923–4 from the Lelang Han Cemetery, P'yôngyang, North Korea. Current whereabouts unknown.

The palace inscription tells us that this piece was to be used in the Chamber of Eternal Joy (Changle Shi), which was the new name Wang Mang gave to the Palace of Lasting Joy (Changle Gong), the residence occupied by the empress dowager and grand empress dowager during the Former Han. The office of Provisioner (Taiguan) was responsible for the imperial kitchens and the preparation and serving of all banquets. Another piece from this same large dinner service order was also unearthed at Lelang, and this is the only piece for which we have a photographic record (see figure 5.14).[89] The rim of this vessel was completely destroyed, so only the second, palace-written inscription is preserved (upper portion of figure 5.14). It was recorded with serial number 1,454 in the same shipment of 3,000 pieces.

Let us now look at one final object that very likely decorated one of the Former Han palaces at Chang'an (see figure 5.15). This magnificent bronze horse stands 62 centimeters tall, about one-third life size. It was gilded over its entire surface using the mercury-amalgam gilding technique described earlier. It was sensitively modeled in the round, with its ears pricked up and eyes wide open. The mouth, mane, and tail are given extra details, and the genitals, which were soldered in place, are realistically

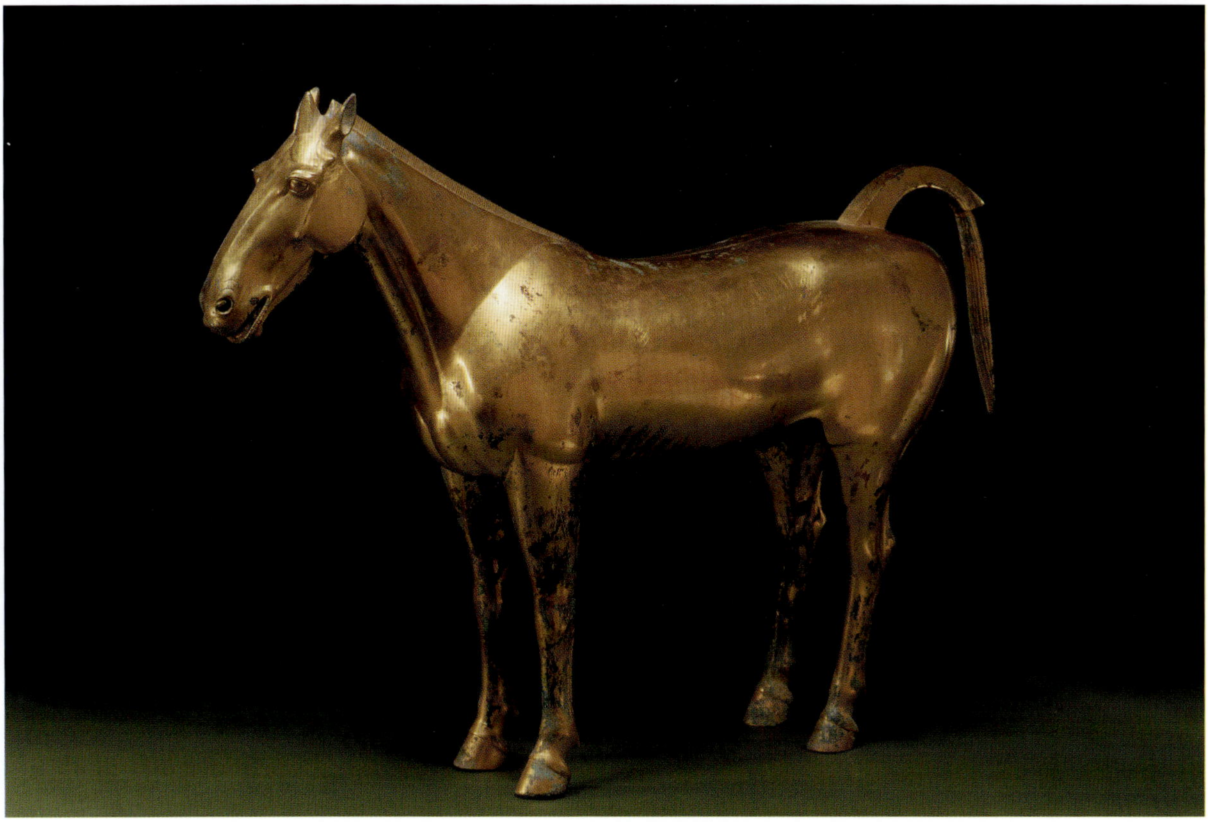

5.15 *Model horse.* Former Han period, ca. 130–110 BCE. Gilded bronze. L. 76 cm. H. 62 cm. Weight 25 kg. Maoling Museum, Shaanxi. Photo courtesy of Cultural Relics Publishing House.

rendered. The ingenious caster even made a hole for the horse's anus to serve as a vent for the casting gases! Traces of rust around the mouth suggest that it once wore a complete bridle.

The horse was found in the same burial pit with the Weiyang Palace censer described above and, like many of the bronzes in that pit, probably once belonged to the Elder Yangxin Princess, sister to Emperor Wu. Other writers who have commented on this piece might be correct in saying that it represents one of the *tianma* (heavenly horses) of the Ferghana Valley that Emperor Wu wanted to import into China.[90] But the symmetrical "horse show" stance and the anatomical details of this piece lead me to believe that there is something more to this horse than meets the eye.

I would argue that this horse was a contemporary copy of a very famous gilded horse statue presented to Emperor Wu by a man named Dongmen Jing, a great expert in judging horses. Dongmen Jing intended his statue to serve as a model (*fa*) of perfect horse physiology, based on the physique of the superior Dayuan (Ferghana) horses. It was set up outside the Lu Ban Palace Gate of the Weiyang Palace, the name of which was then changed to the Golden Horse Gate (Jinma Men).[91] The statue was a famous fixture in the capital for nearly two hundred years. Since the gilded horse shown in figure 5.15 was made at this same time and appears as a model horse would look, I suggest that it might be a contemporary copy made after Dongmen Jing's famous piece and given to the emperor's sister as a gift.

The story of Dongmen Jing's horse statue does not end there. It stood in Chang'an until after the end of the Former Han, surviving the predations of Wang Mang and the burning of the palaces by the Red Eyebrow rebels in 25–6 CE. In 62 CE, Emperor Ming of the Latter Han brought the gilded horse to the new capital of Luoyang, along with another famous statue made under Emperor Wu of a Feilian Beast, and set them both up outside the gates of the Lodge of Tranquil Joy (Pingle Guan), an outlying palace just outside the northwest city gates of Luoyang. The statues stood there until 190 CE, when the tyrant Dong Zhuo melted them both down to cast bronze coinage.[92]

Dongmen Jing's horse also served as the inspiration for a similar statue cast in 44 CE by the great Latter Han general Ma Yuan.[93] General Ma Yuan was a renowned expert in horse physiology and had studied under a famous lineage of northwestern horse masters. After Ma Yuan had defeated the Vietnamese chiefs led by the rebel Tr'ung sisters (43 CE), he melted down their bronze Dongson-style drums and cast a *mashi* (model horse) to present to the emperor. The horse was later set up below the Hall of All-Embracing Virtue (Xuande Dian). Ma Yuan commented in a memorial to the throne that his model was a physical manifestation of all he had learned of horse physiognomy theory and could be used as a guide to select the best horses for the empire.

Ma Yuan was also the author of a treatise called the *Method of Evaluation through the Bronze Horse* (Tongma xiangfa), in which he stated the ideal horse's features:

> The two nostrils should be clearly separated. The upper lip should be taut and straight, and the inside of the mouth red and shiny. This horse could run a thousand *li*. There should be a depression below the jaw. The lower lip should be relaxed and extended. The incisors should incline forward. If the upper incisors are one *cun* distant from the molars, then this horse can run only four hundred *li*. If the incisors are like sword tips, then this is a thousand-*li* horse. The eyes should be large and glistening. The belly should be full and the flanks narrow. The last rib should be long. The cannons of the legs should be thick, and [the fetlock joint] flexible. The ribcage should be level and full, and the perspiration furrows deep and long. The kneecaps should stick out, the forearms should not bow inward, and the knees should be square. The hoofs should be three *cun* thick and hard as stone. The mane should stand up like a crown on the spinal column, and the withers should rise up by three *cun*. The jawbone should be wide, and the chest area at the base of the neck should be at least one *chi* in breadth. This horse can run for a very long distance. The cheek area (for haltering) should be squarish, and the breast straight and prominent. The muscles on either side of the breast should appear parted, so that when you gaze at them from afar, they look like a pair of ducks.[94]

Ma Yuan's memorial and essay make it clear that bronze horses such as the one in figure 5.15 were used by experts to judge the quality of living horses. There were apparently many traditions of horse physiognomy, and Ma Yuan states that he consciously combined several of these theories into his model. It is up to the reader to decide how closely Ma Yuan's ideal horse matches the excavated model from Maoling. Han horse models were not necessarily cast to life size. Ma Yuan's 44 CE statue was only 80.9 centimeters tall at the head. The Maoling horse is only 62 centimeters high, so Dongmen Jing's original sculpture may not have been life size either. Chinese casters were certainly capable of making life-size or even monumental bronze statuary when required.[95] How the Elder Yangxin Princess might have used her gilded horse is unknown. For her, it may have only been a piece for sumptuous display.

VISUAL SPECTACLES

Any imperial court worth its salt is wont to put on a flashy show now and then. Some of the visual spectacles arranged for the Han court were so dazzling that even Louis XIV might have been envious. One rollicking spectacle performed at the Qin and Han courts from at least 208 BCE onward was called the Horn-Butting Games (*juedi*).[96] These competitive games seem to have included archery contests, chariot racing, acrobatic entertainments, music, and possibly gladiatorial fights between men and animals. By most interpretations, one event included men dressed in costumes and wearing horns, literally butting into one another like bulls! On several occasions, the games were performed before foreign ambassadors. The people of the Han were said to come from almost one hundred miles away from Chang'an to view the games. During the reign of Emperor Wu, the games were held on at least two occasions, during 108 and 105 BCE. On the first occasion, the Horn-Butting Games may have been staged in the large courtyard area of the Weiyang Palace itself.[97]

The lengthiest and most vivid description of the Horn-Butting Games is found in the "Western Capital Rhapsody" (Xijing fu) by Zhang Heng. Zhang Heng was supposedly describing the games as staged under Emperor Wu of the Former Han, but since Zhang lived two centuries after that time, his account probably more accurately describes visual spectacles at the Latter Han court, mixed with textual information he was able to obtain about the Former Han games. His description of acrobatics matches quite closely with visual depictions on Latter Han pictorial stones, especially those from the tomb at Yi'nan, Shandong. The whole text is too long to include in this section, but here is a representative excerpt from the rhapsody:

> Looking down upon the broad arena, we view the wondrous feats of the Horn-Butting Games. . . .
>
> They juggle balls and swords up and down and walk tightropes, meeting halfway across. On a re-creation of Mount Hua, tall and towering, with its knolls and ridges jaggedly jutting, sacred trees, magic plants, and vermilion

fruits thickly spread, they assemble a troupe of sylphlike performers. They frolic with panthers and dance with bears. A white tiger plucks a zither. An azure dragon plays a flute. . . . Before the tune has ended, clouds rise and snow falls. At first it seems to flurry lightly, then it begins to fall thick and fast. From the covered walkways and storied passageways, they roll stones to create the sound of thunder. Thunderbolts crash and echo repeatedly. Their rumbling roar is like heaven's wrath. . . . Conjurers, quicker than the eye, change form, sunder bodies, swallow knives, exhale fire, and darken the arena with clouds and mist. [Artisans] draw on the ground and create rivers, making the Wei River flow into the Jing River. . . . Then they erect a show wagon and hoist a tall banner on a pole. Young lads display their skill, flipping and gliding from the pole. Suddenly, they throw themselves upside down, catching themselves with their heels.[98]

Zhang Heng's account probably served as one of the sources for a similar description of the competitive games in the *Happenings from the Reign of Han Emperor Wu* (Han Wu gushi).[99] In that version, we are told specifically that court artisans provided the naturalistic stage design for the games within the Weiyang Palace courtyard. They simulated "clouds, rain, thunder, and lightning that were no different than the real thing. They painted the ground to simulate rivers and heaped up stones to construct mountains."[100] It must have been quite a show.

During the Han period, the first day of the lunar New Year, which fell between January 21 and February 20, was regularly celebrated with a massive ceremony at court, attended by thousands of invited nobles, regional officials, and foreign ambassadors.[101] After the emperor was presented with the accounts of the empire and the tribute and praise of his invited guests, a feast was served, followed by rousing entertainments. According to the account in the *Administrative Observances of the Official System Selected for Use* (Hanguan dianzhi yishi xuanyong), written by the Latter Han writer Cai Zhi (d. 178 CE),[102] the ceremony ended with a spectacle filled with music, magic, and visual delights, similar to the performances displayed at the Horn-Butting Games:

When all were seated, the banquet was served. Then, music and entertainments were performed for the hierarchy of guests. The Sheli Beast[103] entered from the west and pranced around the ridgepoles of the courtyard. When it was finished, it dove into the coursing water at the front of the hall and transformed into a giant flounder. It danced around in the water and coughed out a mist which obscured the sun. That act completed, it transformed into a yellow dragon, eight *zhang* (ca.19 m) long, which banished the mist and pranced in the courtyard, bright and splendid in the sunlight. The performers then took two big silk ropes and tied them between two columns several *zhang* apart. Two singing girls walked along the tightrope, dancing facing toward each other. When they

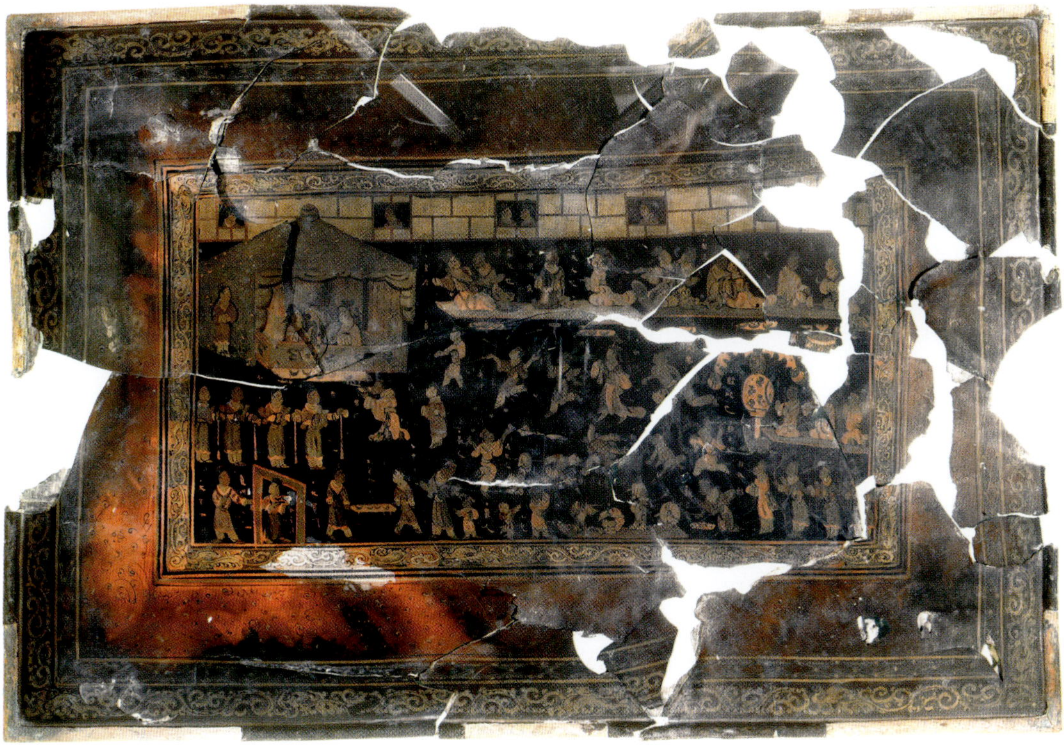

5.16 *Banquet and entertainment in the imperial palace.* Latter Han or early Three Kingdoms period, ca. 200–49 CE. Lacquer on fabric-reinforced wooden core with gilded-bronze mounts. L. 82 cm. W. 56.5 cm. Ma'anshan Municipal Museum. Excavated from the tomb of Zhu Ran (d. 249 CE), Ma'anshan City, Anhui. Photo courtesy of Cultural Relics Publishing House.

> met in the middle they brushed shoulders, without falling off. Then they curled up into a ball and hid their entire bodies in a two-liter container. Bell and chimestone music was also played, and when the singing girls and dancers were done, they made a fish and dragon procession. The eunuch Palace Attendants sounded the three calls, and the Receptionists beckoned the high officials and ministers to bow twice and withdraw in procession. The ceremony was over.[104]

Figure 5.16 is a lacquer tray-table depicting a similar type of grand banquet in an imperial palace. The tray, which was constructed of lacquer on a fabric-reinforced wooden core and fitted with a gilded-bronze rim, was discovered in the tomb of Zhu Ran (182–249 CE), a famous Three Kingdoms period general. The single character *guan* (official) painted on the back indicates that it was a palace piece used in a royal court.[105] Despite the dark and ruined condition of the platter, one can still make out an emperor seated in the tented pavilion on the upper left, leering provocatively at his concubines.[106] The empress (captioned Huanghou) is seated to the right of the tent, on a raised dais that also supports other honored guests, many accompanied by captions. She appears a tad jealous of her consort's amorous activities. Armed guards stand in front of the pavilion. In front of them, at the lower left, we see palace servants carrying food to the banquet through a doorway. The entire right-hand portion of the tray-table is taken up with a scene of entertainments, including jugglers, contortionists, acrobats, and musicians. It is a very busy scene, with over fifty human figures, skillfully executed in the limited color palette of lacquer paint by artists working in Chengdu in the early third century.

Such was the visual world of the Han court, as best as we can reconstruct it today from scattered texts and buried relics. But now we must ask the crucial question: Who painted all these murals and screens, cast and gilded these bronzes, wove and embroidered the silks, and ground the jades?

ARTISANS IN THE PALACE

The information concerning court artisans is very sketchy, and detailed biographies are not to be expected. From the limited information, it appears that artisans in the palace cluster into two major groupings. The first and by far the largest group were rank-and-file artisans who were hired or summoned to make objects for the palace. With them, I would also group the unfree workers like conscripts, convicts, and slaves, discussed in detail in the next chapter. The second type of artisan working in the palace was a small group of men who combined the roles of scholar-official and artisan. These men were much higher in status than the professional artisans, and their lives are much better documented. Clearly, there was a systemic bias against the professional artisans. On projects in which the two types of artisans worked collaboratively, the lion's share of the credit usually went to the high-ranking amateur who initiated the work or penned the captions, and not to the lowly craftsmen who performed the majority of the commission. The remainder of this chapter will concern these two groups of individuals who fashioned the visual world of the palace.

THE PROFESSIONAL COURT ARTISAN

During the Qin and Han periods, the palace operated many different workshops and factories that made articles to be used by the court and the harem and for placement in imperial tombs. These were staffed by all manner of state artisans, including hired masters, conscripted artisans, convicts, and government slaves. Often these bureaus had overlapping responsibilities. For example, we know that at least three different textile workshops operated within the grounds of the Weiyang Palace, all making clothing for the emperor and his ladies. A few workshops were located within the walls of the palace itself, while others were situated elsewhere in the capital area, such as in the Western Market of Chang'an or in Shanglin Park. Summarizing the complex organizational history of all these production units is not possible here. For a detailed account, the interested reader may consult my earlier work on that subject.[107] At this point, I would like to focus on two important palace workshops that made the types of luxury objects and painted images discussed in the previous section: the Yellow Gate and the Shangfang. This will be followed by a discussion of the careers of the few professional court artisans recorded in our sources.

The Yellow Gate (Huangmen)

Many of the talented painters of the two Han dynasties were kept on call in a special unit referred to as the Yellow Gate (Huangmen).[108] The name originally referred to the door to the private quarters of the emperor and his harem. It was a eunuch-run office, employing persons of special talent. It employed jugglers, dwarves, diviners, musicians, actors, physiognomists, poets, painters, and anyone else the emperor wished to have near his person. This unit apparently also staged the Horn-Butting Game spectacles for Emperor Wu.[109] Sorcerers and diviners were probably higher in status and allowed closer to the emperor than the actors or painters, but all were on call. During the Latter Han, the Yellow Gate even operated a fife and drum corps of 145 men.[110] The office was controlled and financed by the Privy Treasury (Shaofu), the financial division of the treasury that supported the emperor's activities. The Yellow Gate was controlled by a eunuch, the Director of Eunuch Attendants (Huangmen Ling), ranked at 600 *shi* during the Latter Han. He controlled several subordinate eunuch-run offices, in charge of different services for the emperor.[111]

According to the *History of the Latter Han* and one other Latter Han text, one of the offices controlled by the Yellow Gate was a Room Painting Bureau (Huashi Shu). This may have been the unit that employed both the talented mural painters who made the figural and decorative frescoes and the lowly whitewashers who applied plaster and monochrome pigments.[112] It was anonymous painters from the Yellow Gate who executed the painting with the political message given by Emperor Wu to Huo Guang, the one that showed the Duke of Zhou supporting the infant King Cheng.[113] Unfortunately, we do not know the name of any painter who worked for the Yellow Gate during the Han. Some were probably eunuchs, though it is doubtful that all of them were. If I had to speculate, I would surmise that Mao Yanshou, Chen Chang, Liu Bo, and the other painters mentioned in the *Miscellaneous Notes* story concerning Wang Zhaojun (see chapter 2) were all painters under the supervision of the Yellow Gate. Mao Yanshou, if such a man ever existed, must have been a eunuch, for he was allowed to paint portraits of the women in the emperor's harem.

The Directorate for Imperial Manufactories (Shangfang)

The largest imperial workshop within the walls of the Weiyang Palace was the versatile Shangfang (Directorate for Imperial Manufactories). It was originally a Qin institution. According to the research of Yonezawa Yoshio, the Shangfang was at first a palace department which managed the many masters of techniques (*fangshi*). This group included physicians, wizards, alchemists, and other specialists who claimed to have exclusive knowledge or fantastic powers. Some of the alchemists used smelting furnaces in their attempts to make gold from base metals. Probably as part of this activity, the bureau began to cast fine luxury objects for the sovereign. The two functions of wizardry and manufacturing operated in parallel for some time. Then, during the reign of Emperor Wu, many of the masters of techniques were discredited and executed. Apparently, the manufacturing function that had accrued to the office continued.[114]

The offices and workshops of the Shangfang were located in the northwest quadrant of the Weiyang Palace complex, in the shadow of the Workshop Gate (Zuoshimen).[115] This is the gate where artisans entered the palace precincts and where raw materials were delivered. The Weiyang Palace was outfitted with four main gates which all converged on the Anterior Hall (Qian Dian). The principal ceremonial gate of the Weiyang Palace was apparently on the eastern side of the compound. The Workshop Gate was not a main gate, for it was situated well off to the side of the northern palace gate and did not connect directly with any of the roads to the Anterior Hall. Thus, the artisans were literally arriving at the "side door" of the palace.

During the Former Han, the Shangfang was financed and controlled by the Privy Treasury. The bureau was headed by a director (*ling*) and an assistant director (*cheng*).[116] Because these posts are listed in the *History of the Former Han* with other traditionally eunuch-run offices, Hans Bielenstein argues that the top officials of the Shangfang during the Former Han were eunuchs.[117] At least by the reign of Emperor Wu, the Shangfang had been divided into left, right, and central divisions, each of which reportedly specialized in one category of object. During the Latter Han, the Shangfang remained under the Privy Treasury. In addition to its director and assistant director, it acquired another layer of eunuch control in the person of a supervisor (*jian*). During the Latter Han, the office was staffed by nineteen minor officials and clerks.[118]

Judging from received texts and inscriptions on surviving objects, the Shangfang made luxury bronzes, high-quality weapons, mirrors, and other *haowu* (fine things) for the emperor's use.[119] As we saw in chapter 4, bronze mirrors made by the Shangfang were so famous that unscrupulous forgeries claiming to have been cast at the Shangfang permeated the marketplace. Whenever there was a call for austerity from ministers at court, the expensive Shangfang was always a target.

The Shangfang also kept on staff or on call a number of painters who were skilled in portraiture and narrative painting. Whereas, during the Former Han, imperial painting commissions seem to have been given more often to the Yellow Gate, during the Latter Han, the Shangfang seems to have been called upon more frequently to create palace murals. According to the fragmentary text of a eulogy on Han painting, Emperor Ming of the Latter Han once ordered the illustrious scholars Ban Gu (32–92 CE) and Jia Kui (30–101 CE) to abstract edifying stories from the Classics and the histories. The emperor then had professional painters (*huagong*) from the Shangfang paint the stories on the walls of the palace. In all, there seem to have been fifty panels, beginning at the dawn of creation with the god Fuxi.[120] The division of labor on this project points to the different roles and statuses of the court scholars and the professional painters. Ban Gu was an intellectual from a family of career officials and was employed to collate texts in the history office of the Eastern Library. His most famous work is the invaluable *History of the Former Han*. Jia Kui was a Classical scholar of great renown from a lineage of famous officials and was jointly appointed with Ban Gu as imperial historiographer. Only men of their class were deemed appropriate for selecting and writing the stories for the mural project. The professionals from the Shangfang were then brought in to execute the actual paintings, which was viewed as a less exalted activity.

The *Record of the Famous Painters of Successive Dynasties* records the names of two painters, Liu Dan and Yang Lu, who were classed as *daizhao* (awaiting the imperial summons) at the Shangfang.[121] They were said to perform most of their actual commissions during the Guanghe era (178–83 CE) in the Vast Capital Gate Academy (Hongdumen Xue), the rival imperial academy for men of creative talent founded by Emperor Ling. Nothing more is known of these two men than this, and we would not even have their names were it not for Zhang Yanyuan's quotation from the now-fragmentary *History of the Latter Han* (Hou Hanshu) of Xie Cheng (ca. 223 CE). The "Biography of Yang Qiu" in Fan Ye's *History of the Latter Han* states that the mural of Yue Song and the other students of the academy (see above) was painted by artists from the Central Office of the Shangfang (Zhong Shangfang).[122] It is not stated who painted the great mural of Confucius and his disciples that adorned the walls of the same building. Perhaps, since Liu Dan and Yang Lu were said to have worked for the Shangfang and had painted commissions in the Hongdumen Xue, they were involved in both projects.

The Famous Professional Artisan: Ding Huan

Ding Huan was a famous artisan, some might say a "legendary" artisan and inventor, who made lavish objects and ingenious devices for the Han court. We met him briefly above as one of the co-designers, along with Li Ju, of the Hall of Brilliant Sunlight. In that story, the two men were called the "most skillful (*qiao*) artisans in the entire world." Ding Huan is not mentioned in any of the official Han histories; he first appears in the *Miscellaneous Notes on the Western Capital*, a work brought into its present form in the fourth to sixth centuries. This fact has led many historians to suppose that Ding Huan was merely a literary creation of later authors and not a historical personality. The avoidance of some tabooed written characters in his story suggests to me that Ding Huan's tale may have first been written during the Latter Han period.[123]

We cannot even be certain of the transcription and pronunciation of his name. The current text of the *Miscellaneous Notes* writes his name as Ding Huan 丁緩, while Yin Yun's (471–529 CE) *Minor Tales* (Xiaoshuo) writes Ding Shou 丁綬, probably a scribal error for the previous form. The *Imperial Overview of the Taiping Era* (Taiping yulan) and the *Record of Elementary Learning* (Chuxueji) encyclopedias give his name in a multitude of forms, including Ding Shuan 丁諼 and Ding Hu 丁護, while the *Broad Notes from the Taiping Era* (Taiping guangji) writes Ding Yuan 丁媛; these variants probably owe as much to oral transmission as to copyists' errors.

The *Miscellaneous Notes* story does not mention under which emperor Ding Huan served. For reasons I cannot determine, Joseph Needham estimated that Ding Huan was active around 180 CE, during the Latter Han period.[124] Several clues, however, point to his service under Emperor Wu (r. 141–87 BCE) of the Former Han. First, the version of Ding Huan's story in Yin Yun's *Minor Tales* is prefaced by the phrase "in the time of Emperor Wu."[125] (This chronological marker is missing from the current text of the *Miscellaneous Notes* account, which most scholars believe was the source of Yin Yun's *Minor Tales* version.) Second, Ding Huan was credited with building the Hall of Brilliant Sunlight, which, according to the *Yellow Plan of the Three Capital Districts* (Sanfu huangtu), was built no later than the time of Emperor Wu. Third, the types of objects Ding Huan was credited with making, such as *boshanlu* incense burners, were quite popular at the court of Emperor Wu. Finally, it should be mentioned that numerous courtiers of Emperor Wu's Camelot-like era became larger-than-life figures in later literary accounts, including such men as Dongfang Shuo and Li Yannian.

In the story of the Hall of Brilliant Sunlight, it seems that Ding Huan had neither apprentices nor heirs and told the story of his greatest creation only to his elder sister's son, Fan Yannian. Might we suppose that Ding Huan had no children because he was a castrated palace artisan? It is an intriguing possibility. He certainly had privileged access to the quarters of the emperor and his harem. If I had to speculate which palace bureau Ding Huan worked for, I would have to guess that he worked for the Shangfang. The Shangfang seems to have made a much broader range of objects than the Yellow Gate and was equipped with the casting facilities needed to fashion Ding Huan's metal wonders.

Let us look at some of the objects Ding Huan was credited with making for the court. The longest account of Ding Huan in the *Miscellaneous Notes* begins: "The clever and skillful Chang'an artisan named Ding Huan made an ever-full lamp (*changman deng*). It had very extraordinary decoration, sporting seven dragons and five phoenixes which were supported by lotus-shaped platforms resting on stalks."[126] This lamp seems to have been a long-burning oil lamp, probably with multiple arms and lamp pans. Recall that Zhao Feiyan's trousseau (see table 5.1) contained a type of multi-armed lamp as well. Needham supposed that "ever-full" referred to a system to replenish the fuel oil from an outside reservoir whenever the level dropped to a certain point, obviating the frequent need to refill the lamp.[127] No archaeological examples of this type of lamp have yet been found from the Han period, but similar devices existed in the Near East and India in slightly later times.

The *Miscellaneous Notes* also states that Ding Huan designed "a nine-level, hill-shaped incense burner (*boshanlu*). It was carved in openwork with strange birds and fantastic beasts and exhausted the possibilities of strange spirits and wonders. All of these moved about naturally."[128] Needham speculated that the moving animals and spirits on the censer were animated by the force of rising currents of hot air traveling through the apertures of the censer lid.[129] With this masterful contraption, Ding Huan seems to have surpassed even the lavish design of the Weiyang Palace censer illustrated above, which now seems quite modest and static in comparison. Zhao Zhaoyi's gift to her sister included a five-level *boshanlu*, but it is not mentioned whether it had moving figures. Though many *boshanlu* censers have been found that were decorated with cast figures of spirits and animals, no example with moving parts has ever been found from the Han period.

Ding Huan is also credited with inventing a human-powered air-conditioning device for the Han palace. The *Miscellaneous Notes* states: "Ding Huan also made a fan consisting of seven wheels, each ten *chi* (2.3 m) in diameter. They were all connected [by gears] with one another and set in motion by [the power of] one man. The whole hall became so cool that people would even begin to shiver."[130] Needham speculated that Ding Huan's seven-wheeled fan may have been powered by a hand crank mechanism, though he thought that a pedal or treadle drive was also probable.[131] The use of similar devices in eighth-century Tang palaces is documented.

Ding Huan's most ingenious invention, or *reinvention* in this case, was called the censer amid the covers (*beizhong xianglu*). It is also the contraption for which we have the most concrete archaeological evidence. The *Miscellaneous Notes* and the *Minor Tales* describe it in great detail:

> [Ding Huan] also created an incense burner which lay on the bedclothes. It was also called the "censer amid the covers." Originally, it was invented by an artisan named Fang Feng, but later the transmission of his technique among his disciples was cut off. It was not until Ding Huan that it began to be made again. To make it, he fashioned [a series of] mechanically connected rings. The censer could roll in any direction, and yet the central incense-burning chamber would remain level. Thus, one could position it on the bed covers. This is how it acquired its name.[132]

The description makes clear that the incense-burning chamber rested inside a series of pivoted gimbals, concentric rings positioned at right angles to one another, ensuring that no matter which way the censer rolled, the weighted burning chamber would remain in horizontal equilibrium and the contents would not spill out. The mechanism is none other than the Cardan suspension, named after the Italian Renaissance author Jerome Cardan (Girolamo Cardano) (1501–76 CE) who described it. Soon after his time it was used to suspend ship's compasses and other instruments, but earlier textual references make clear that it was known in the West as early as the ninth century CE and was often used to suspend oil lamps. The *Miscellaneous Notes* account says that the inventor Fang Feng first made this device, but his tradition was cut off.

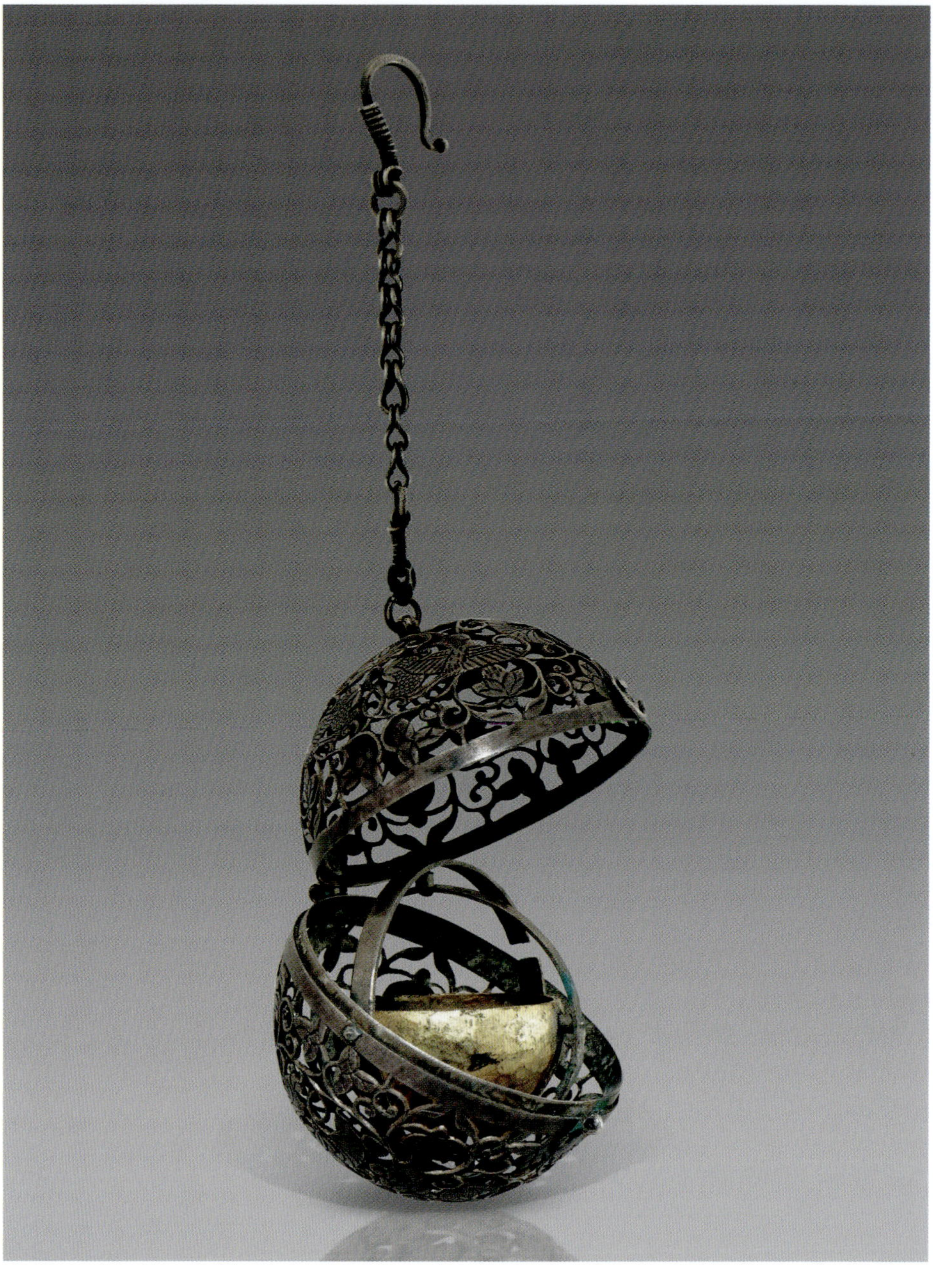

5.17 *Censer with leveling mechanism*. Tang period, ca. eighth century CE. Silver, with gilded-silver incense bowl. D. 4.5 cm. Weight 35 g. Shaanxi History Museum, Xi'an. Photo courtesy of Shaanxi History Museum.

Ding Huan merely reinvented or perfected it. A passage in the "Rhapsody on the Beautiful Person" (Meiren fu), attributed to Sima Xiangru (d. 117 BCE), suggests that the Cardan suspension was already present during the time of Emperor Wu.[133] The oldest (and finest) incense burner based on the Cardan suspension found in China thus far is an eighth-century silver example from the famous Hejiacun hoard in Xi'an (see figure 5.17).[134] Though this example is quite small and meant for hanging, not rolling about on the bed, one can clearly see how Ding Huan's device operated by looking at its interior mechanism.

It is clear from the fragmentary accounts of Ding Huan that he was considered nothing greater than a brilliant professional craftsman. He is usually just called a *gong* (artisan) or a *jiang* (architect), and apparently he never held any official position or rank. Though he walked through palace halls, was probably well compensated for his work, and may have personally addressed the emperor on occasion, his social standing was probably no higher than that of the lowly wall painters or weavers employed in the palace workshops.

THE SCHOLAR-OFFICIAL ARTISAN IN THE LATTER HAN

During the Latter Han period, a new type of artisan became prominent at court whose status was fundamentally different from that of professional craftsmen like Ding Huan, Mao Yanshou, or Liu Dan. They were primarily scholars and officials, but they also had amateur vocations as painters or skilled inventors. Because they were imperial officials, we know much more about these men than we can ever know about shadowy figures like Mao Yanshou or Ding Huan. Many have biographical notices or complete biographies in the official histories. They were recommended to office for their literary talent or for their general reputation, but they happened to have artistic skill as well. There is no record of a scholar-official artisan who was recommended for office solely because he was a masterful painter. Two men in particular, Zhang Heng and Cai Yong, were polymaths of amazing ability who seem to have been skilled at everything. They will be discussed at length below.

Scholar-official artisans operated in a gray area of the social landscape during the Han. They were members of the lofty class of scholars who "labored with their minds" and, thus, according to Mencius, deserved to rule over others. Yet they were also drawn by their abilities and their inclinations to engage in what had normally been considered artisan activities, reserved for those who "labored with their brawn." When these officials chose to focus on craftsman-like activities rather than concentrate on securing promotions like everyone else, they had to endure the censure of their more traditionalist colleagues. Ma Jun, the great third-century CE inventor and minor court official, was ridiculed on several occasions by court scholars because "his powers of exposition fell far behind his mechanical ingenuity." Since he could not express in lofty words the importance of his technical inventions, such as the chain-driven water pump, his devices were not put into widespread use.[135] Let us look now at the lives of some of these scholar-official artisans.

Liu Bao was a career official who served during the Latter Han. He eventually reached the important post of governor of Shu Commandery (present-day Sichuan). According to a now-lost work on painting by Sun Changzhi (fl. ca. 502–20 CE) called

Notes in Exposition of Painting (Shuhua ji), as quoted in the *Imperial Overview of the Taiping Era,* Liu Bao was active during the reign of Emperor Ling (169–89 CE).[136] The *Record of the Famous Painters of Successive Dynasties* cites the same source but records that Liu Bao was active under the preceding reign, that of Emperor Huan (147–68 CE). Both texts record that "Liu Bao once painted a picture of the poem 'Milky Way' that made those who saw it feel hot. Likewise, he painted a picture illustrating the poem 'North Wind,' and those who had felt hot suddenly felt cold when they saw it."[137] It is unclear from this anecdote if these two paintings were wall murals or portable scrolls. There is no mention of Liu Bao working on commissions for the emperor or any other government bureau. He appears to have been an official who painted for enjoyment and who seems to have been quite a skilled amateur.

Zhao Qi (ca. 110–201 CE) was another Latter Han scholar and official, in this case of quite high rank, who seems to have been an amateur painter.[138] He lived through almost the entire second century CE, personally experienced the worst episodes of the harrowing collapse of the Han dynasty, and still managed to die a natural death. He was born in the Chang'an area and showed remarkable ability in learning the Classics and the traditional arts of the gentleman. He took on many low-level official posts as a young man, then was stricken with a serious illness in his thirties and remained bedridden for seven years. Running afoul of powerful eunuchs around 158 CE, he changed his name and fled into exile, at one point selling pancakes in the market of Beihai. He was rehabilitated for a while, then barred from holding office for ten more years. He served in various high positions in the twilight days of the Han, reaching as high as Chamberlain for Ceremonials (Taichang). He was the author of the earliest commentary on the *Master Meng* (Mengzi) text to come down to us and of another important text describing the Former Han capital of Chang'an. His biography in the *History of the Latter Han* records: "He had a tomb made for himself in advance [of his death]. He depicted the four figures of Ji Zha, Zichan, Yan Ying, and Shu Xiang occupying the places of guests, while he painted a portrait of himself occupying the position of the host. For each of these likenesses, he composed a eulogy."[139]

Zhao Qi was nearly ninety years of age when he painted the walls of his tomb.[140] The figures he chose to depict were all great nobles and ministers of the Spring and Autumn period (722–481 BCE) who were known for wisdom, loyalty, or propriety. By placing himself among their company, in the position of host, Zhao Qi was clearly making a political statement about the moral destitution of the ruined age in which he lived. A description of Zhao Qi's tomb paintings is recorded in Li Daoyuan's sixth-century work *Commentary on the Classic of Waterways* (Shuijingzhu), suggesting that the tomb was known (and visited) in later centuries. It was said to have been built in the midst of the old Chu capital of Ying (present-day Jiangling, Hubei).[141] His crypt has not been found by archaeologists, and no other paintings by Zhao Qi were known to authors of later periods. It does not seem that he ever painted for royal commissions or for private patrons.

The Famous Scholar-Official Craftsman: Zhang Heng

Zhang Heng was born in 78 CE in Nanyang Commandery (present-day Henan).[142] His family was said to have maintained an illustrious reputation for generations, and we know that his grandfather Zhang Kan had been governor of Shu Commandery. Zhang Heng excelled at literary pursuits and studied the Classics at the Imperial Academy. As his reputation grew, he was recommended for office numerous times, refusing all offers until Emperor An personally summoned him to be a Gentleman of the Interior (Langzhong), from whence he was quickly promoted to Grand Astrologer (Taishi Ling), the post responsible for observing celestial phenomena and preparing the official calendar. Though he was occasionally rotated to other posts, once even serving as the Administrator (Xiang) of the Hejian Princedom (136 CE), Zhang returned to his beloved position as Grand Astrologer on and off until his death at the age of sixty-two in 139 CE. During his career, his contemporaries criticized him for his lack of ambition, to which Zhang responded with a long essay defending his pursuit of theoretical and experimental knowledge.

During his life, Zhang Heng's talents manifested themselves in an astonishing number of fields. As a poet, Zhang composed the "Rhapsodies on the Two Capitals" (Erjing fu) in emulation of and counterpoint to the rhapsody on a similar theme by Ban Gu.[143] As a cartographer, he may have been the first man in the Far East to introduce a grid system for maps.[144] As a mathematician, he improved on earlier estimations of the value of pi.[145] During his tenure as Grand Astrologer, he built an improved armillary sphere which added horizon and meridian rings to the device, supplementing the standard equatorial and ecliptic rings.[146] He also constructed a water-powered orrery that could predict the movement of the planets and stars.[147] He even found time to compose erotic verse in the female voice.[148]

One of Zhang Heng's most ingenious inventions was a seismograph that he constructed in 132 CE and that was installed in the Bureau of Astronomy and the Calendar at the capital.[149] He called the device a *houfeng didong yi* (earthquake weathercock), for it was able to determine the direction an earthquake came from, just as a weathercock can for the winds. A modern reconstruction of Zhang Heng's device can be seen in figure 5.18. According to descriptions in the *Continuation of the Han History* (Xu Hanshu) and *History of the Latter Han,* the device consisted of a large bronze jar, nearly six feet across, with a domed lid. Around the outside of the vessel were eight dragon heads, each of which held a bronze ball in its mouth. When an earthquake occurred somewhere in the empire, it induced a centrally placed, inverted pendulum within the vessel to trigger just one of the dragons to drop its ball into the mouth of one of the bronze toads arrayed around the base of the device.[150] This would indicate the direction of the tremor's epicenter. Once, probably in 138 CE, the device was triggered, but no one at court felt any earthquake. Doubts began to arise concerning Zhang Heng's invention until notice arrived at the capital several days later that an

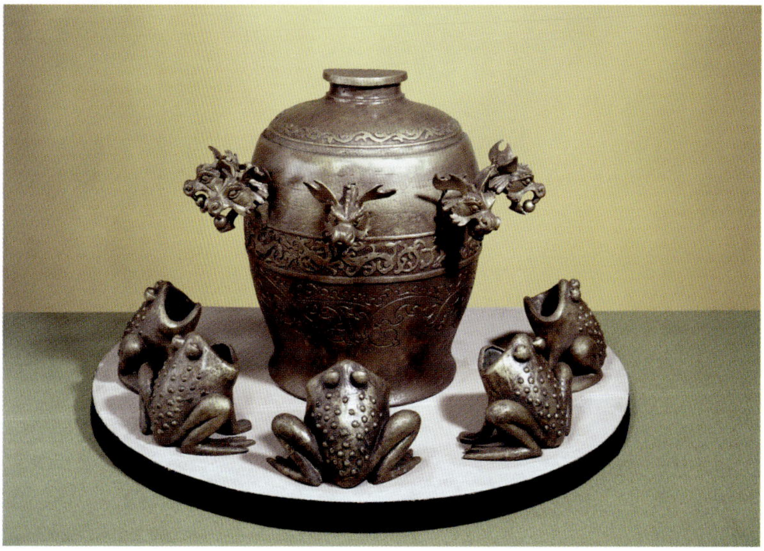

5.18 *Modern reconstruction of Zhang Heng's seismograph.* Bronze model. Science Museum, London. Photo courtesy of Science Museum/ Science and Society Picture Library.

earthquake had occurred in the Longxi area, about four hundred miles from the capital.

Zhang Heng's biography in the *History of the Latter Han* states that "he excelled at ingenious mechanical devices," and from his celestial instruments and remarkable seismograph we can certainly see that this was true.[151] He once stated that he had carved a wooden contraption that could fly on its own power.[152] But a question we must ask is whether Zhang himself made these devices with his own hands, or whether he merely designed them, leaving the physical construction to artisans working in one of the government shops. The texts say that he *zao* (created) or *zuo* (made) the seismograph of 132 CE, but are we then to assume that he cast the great vessel, carved the molds for the dragons and toads, tooled the mechanism, and so on? This is hardly reasonable. Unlike Ding Huan, Zhang Heng was an official of moderately high rank and could not be seen sweating in the foundries with the *gong* artisans and the government slaves. Most likely, he worked collaboratively with the professional casters and mold makers in the imperial workshops. He probably made and tested prototypes of the central mechanism himself and then later commissioned the metalsmiths to make the entire device in bronze. Most likely, it took several experimental attempts to arrive at a successful working model.

The official biography and extant writings of Zhang Heng attest to his importance as a writer and protoscientist, but later legends also proclaim him as a painter of almost supernatural prowess. In the *Record of the Famous Painters of Successive Dynasties,* Zhang Yanyuan repeats a popular tale with Zhang Heng as the protagonist:

> Once upon a time in the mountains near Pucheng County in Jianzhou there was a beast called the *haishen* which had the body of a pig and the head of a man. It was so ugly that all the demons hated it. It was fond of coming out of the water onto rocks by the shore, where Zhang Heng went to sketch it. The beast

> plunged into the pool and would not come up. Someone said, "The animal is afraid of anyone making a picture of him. That is why he won't come out. You had better put aside your paper and brush." He complied and the beast in fact appeared. Zhang Heng sat with folded arms without moving and stealthily sketched the animal using his toes [to hold the brush].[153]

This story is very charming but has no basis in historical reality. It is clearly a piece of later hagiography, conflated with popular legend. Nearly the same tale is found in other collections, with the great architect Gongshu Ban (Lu Ban) or an anonymous painter at the court of the First Emperor of Qin as the cunning artist.[154] Even though there is no evidence that Zhang Heng painted portraits or any other genre subject, his skill as a cartographer extraordinaire might still merit his classification as a painter.

The Famous Scholar-Official Artist: Cai Yong

According to a later fanciful legend, when Zhang Heng died in 139 CE, his spirit passed into the body of a married woman of the Cai family, who conceived by this spirit and later gave birth to a boy named Yong.[155] By the end of his turbulent life, Cai Yong was to become one of the most famous scholars in the dying empire of the Han and a prototype for the kind of scholar-artist one is familiar with from later periods of Chinese history.

Cai Yong was actually born in either 132 or 133 CE in Chenliu Commandery (present-day Henan).[156] Both his mother and his father came from influential families. His grandfather had been a minor official, though his father had been frustrated in his attempts at an official career. His father died when Yong was in early adulthood, and shortly thereafter, his mother contracted a chronic illness and died after three years. Yong's filial behavior in support of his ill mother and his steadfast mourning at her tomb earned him a great reputation for filial piety. His classical education was supervised by the great scholar-official Hu Guang (91–172 CE). In 159 CE, when he was living with his uncle, Cai Yong was summoned to court because of his virtuosity at playing the *qin* (zither). This was just after the eunuch-inspired coup that deposed the dictator-regent Liang Ji. Cai Yong set out for the capital of Luoyang but never reached the city, feigning illness. He did not desire to be associated with the eunuchs or to be appreciated by the emperor only as a talented musical performer. He spent the next decade or so avoiding the poisonous politics at court, studying ancient literature, and composing the eulogy texts for funerary stelae for famous scholars and officials.

In 170 CE, he was finally coaxed to serve at court and was quickly promoted to the post of Court Gentleman for Consultation (Yilang), an advisory post to the emperor. He was sent to the Eastern Library (Dong Guan) to help collate texts for the official Han history, and he assisted in establishing the standardized text for the Confucian Classics. In the late summer of 178 CE, after a secret memorial he wrote at the request of the emperor leaked out, Cai Yong was slandered at court by enemy factions, charged with a serious crime, and sentenced to death. His punishment was later commuted to hard labor, under which he (and his family members) were locked in iron collars and fetters and sent into exile on the northern frontier (present-day Inner Mongolia). After nine months, he was released during an amnesty but spent the next decade roaming the southern parts of the empire. In late 189 CE he was forced to return to court to serve the maniacal tyrant Dong Zhuo. He quickly rose in power under the corrupt regime, but his days were numbered. When Dong Zhuo was assassinated in May 192 CE, Cai Yong was charged with treason and died in prison shortly thereafter.

Cai Yong was clearly a man of many talents, but his greatest fame came from his literary accomplishments, one of which was his innovative use of the *fu* (rhapsody) genre for personal expression. We are told that he was also skilled at numerical calculation, astronomy, and musical theory.[157] But Cai Yong was also recognized by later generations for his talents in portrait painting and calligraphy, activities that we would be inclined to classify as artistic endeavors and that in Latter Han society were probably still considered by most as artisanal activities unworthy of a lofty scholar. All that Cai Yong would admit to in his own writings was that he would occasionally "apply names to likenesses" (*xingming maozhuang*), alluding to the honorable tradition of literary scholars (like Yang Xiong) adding the captioned encomia to palace murals of exemplars.[158] Perhaps this phrase was actually a euphemism for the production of the painted portraits as well. In 177 CE, at the behest of Emperor Ling, Cai Yong composed just such a eulogy to place next to a palace mural of his beloved teacher Hu Guang, who had died five years previously.[159] In any case, we should be suspicious when we discover that all the texts that describe Cai Yong as an illustrious painter and master calligrapher were written centuries after his death. Nevertheless, let us look at some of the artistic productions attributed to him.

Zhang Yanyuan's *Record of the Famous Painters of Successive Dynasties* records an illustrated scroll of the *Arrayed Biographies of Women* (Lienü zhuan) by Cai Yong and another painted work attributed to him called *Picture of Lecturing and Learning* (Jiangxue tu). These were supposedly still extant in Zhang's day (ninth century CE).[160] We have no way of knowing what these pictures looked like, but the subject of female virtues was something upon which Cai Yong had written a separate tract called "Admonitions for Women" (Nüjie), in which he urged women to spend as much time cultivating their minds as making up their faces.[161]

The *Notes in Exposition of Painting* of Sun Changzhi records a very significant imperial commission ordered by Emperor Ling from the hand of Cai Yong: "Emperor Ling commissioned Cai to paint portraits of Yang Xi and five generations of generals and ministers of the family of the Marquis of Chiquan in a department building. He then commanded Cai to compose eulogies and write them out in his own hand. Cai's calligraphy, the paintings, and the eulogies all commanded fame in the world and at the time were known as 'The Three Beautiful Things.'"[162] The text clearly indicates that Cai Yong painted the images himself, composed the eulogies, and wrote them next to the paintings. This seems to be the first recorded instance where there was no division of labor between the scholar who wrote the text and the painter of the portraits. Though the text says that the three creations were viewed as one artistic program, Gong Kechang suggests that the paintings were executed before Cai Yong's arrest in 178 CE but that the encomium was written after 189 CE when Cai was serving under Dong Zhuo.[163]

The five generations of the Yang family portrayed in the mural included two men, Yang Ci (d. 185 CE) and his son Yang Biao (142–225 CE), whom Cai Yong knew well. When the mural was painted, Yang Ci and Yang Biao were still alive.[164] One wonders if the portraits were made from life, for there is evidence of such a practice during the Latter Han.[165] One also wonders if Cai felt honored to have been asked to paint a portrait of Yang Ci, a man he greatly admired. Then again, how would Cai have felt painting a picture of Yang Biao, who held the same official post as Cai but who was ten years his junior? Did Cai feel humiliated, as the high Tang official and master painter Yan Liben had felt, because the emperor had assigned him the tasks of a mere craftsman? Was this commission painfully reminiscent of his initial summons to court in 159 CE solely for a zither recital?

The artistic project that Cai Yong is most closely associated with is the Stone Classics of the Xiping era (see figure 5.19), an enormous undertaking to collate and inscribe onto stone more than 200,000 characters of canonical literary texts.[166] The account in the *History of the Latter Han* reads as follows:

> Cai Yong recognized that the current text of the Classics was far removed from the sages, and that the written texts had many errors. Vulgar scholars had made strained interpretations, causing doubt and misapprehension for later students. In the fourth year of the Xiping era (175 CE), Cai Yong, along with the Leader of the Gentlemen of the Interior for Miscellaneous Uses, Tangxi Dian, Grand Master for Splendid Happiness Yang Ci, Grand Master of Remonstrance Ma Midi, Court Gentlemen for Consultation Zhang Xun and Han Yue, Grand Astrologer Shan Yang, and others, joined in a memorial to ask the emperor to collate and standardize the texts of the "Six Classics."[167] Emperor Ling approved this.
>
> Thereupon, Cai Yong himself wrote them out in vermilion ink on stone tablets and commissioned artisans (*gong*) to engrave them and place them outside the gates of the Imperial Academy. Thereafter, later scholars and students of subsequent generations all used them for correction. When the tablets were first erected, those who came to inspect them and make tracings from them numbered about a thousand carriages a day, filling up the streets and pathways.[168]

As the account says, the project was initiated in 175 CE, but according to a reliable later source it was not completed until 183 CE.[169] At that time, more than forty completed stelae were set up in a U-shaped formation just east of the lecture hall of the Imperial Academy (Tai Xue), which was located one kilometer south of the capital of

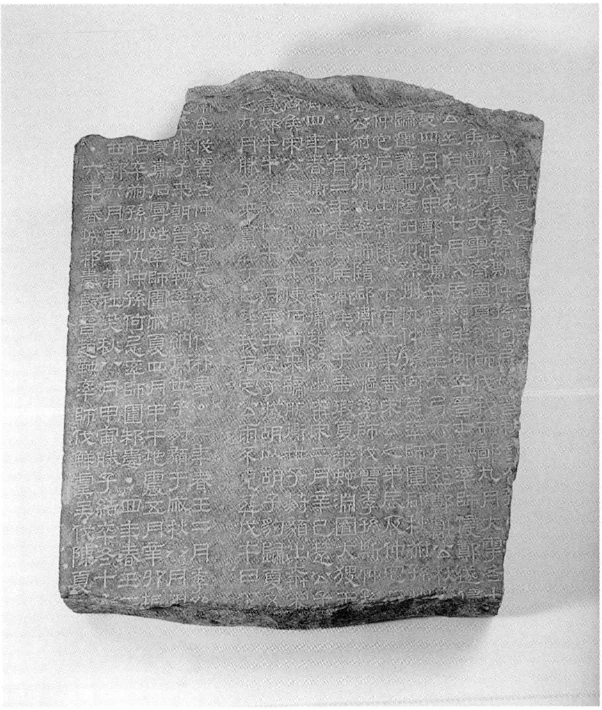

(a)

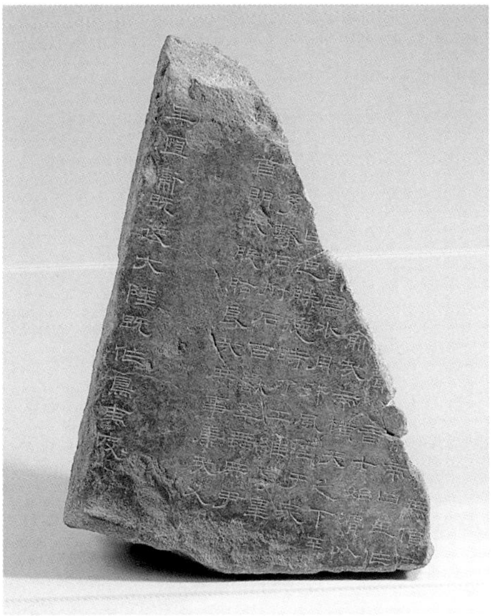

(b)

5.19 *Stone Classics of the Xiping era.* Latter Han period, 175–83 CE. Stone. (a) Portion of *Spring and Autumn Annals* (Chunqiu), starting with fifth year of Duke Ding (505 BCE) and ending with sixth year of Duke Ai (489 BCE). L. 55.5 cm. W. 49.5 cm. D. 15.5 cm. (b) Portion of *Book of Documents* (Shangshu), "Yi Ji" chapter. L. 42 cm. W. 29 cm. D. 16.5 cm. Institute of Archaeology, Chinese Academy of Social Sciences. From Ōsaka Shiritsu Bijutsukan and Yomiuri Shinbun Ōsaka Honsha, pl. 12. Excavated in 1980 from the site of the Imperial Academy (Taixue), Luoyang, Henan.

Luoyang. Each stele measured about 2.4 meters high by 0.96 meters wide and was carved on the front and the back, so that one could read the text across all the faces first, then continue onto the backs. The installation was later covered with a roof, protected by railings, and patrolled by armed guards.[170] The tablets were damaged during the tyranny of Dong Zhuo in 190 CE and later moved from place to place, suffering further attrition. By the seventh century, only about 10 percent was preserved. Today hundreds of rubbings and stone fragments survive from the Stone Classics, constituting less than 4 percent of the original.[171] Some stone pieces were even reused in bridges and other constructions.[172] The large fragments seen in figure 5.19 were excavated in the 1980s from the original site of the Imperial Academy at Luoyang.

If we are to believe the account of Fan Ye (398–446 CE), the author of the *History of the Latter Han,* Cai Yong alone was responsible for writing out the complete texts of the Classics in his own hand, using vermilion ink.[173] The calligraphy of the Stone Classics is written in the upright and staid clerical script (*lishu*). Cai Yong considered that only clerical script and seal script (*zhuanshu*) were suitable for conveying the words of the sages.[174] As you will recall, he roundly criticized Emperor Ling's founding of the Hongdumen Xue, which trained young men to write in decadent, decorative script forms like bird script (*niaozhuan*).[175]

It is important to note the division of labor indicated for the project. Cai Yong, the lofty scholar and consultant to the emperor, was said to have used only his brush to write the characters onto the stones. The laborious task of carving these traces deeply into the stone was carried out by an unknown number of professional stone carvers commissioned by the court. These artisans recorded their names on the Stone Classics as well, and by pure accident, we are fortunate to possess the name of one of these men. His name was Chen Xing, and he carved his name at the end of the text of the Confucian *Analects*.[176] Several surviving fragments also demonstrate that Chen Xing and his fellow stone carvers engraved practice inscriptions along the sides and bases of the stelae, in places where the marks would not show in the final presentation.[177] Though the burden of carving the final version of the *Analects* and the other texts belonged to Chen Xing and his fellow carvers, Cai Yong is given the lion's share of the credit, since the calligraphy and the intellect behind the edited words of the sages *supposedly* belonged to him.

Fan Ye's famous account of the Xiping era Stone Classics in the *History of the Latter Han* has had so much influence on Cai Yong's later reputation as a master calligrapher that its claims should be further investigated. Already in the Northern Song, the antiquarian-epigrapher Hong Gua had strong reasons to doubt that Cai Yong was the lone calligrapher on the project.[178] First, it is unlikely that Cai Yong would have been allowed to brush all of the calligraphy of the Stone Classics himself. He was one of more than twenty-five compilers and editors mentioned in conjunction with the project, some of whom outranked him greatly at court.[179] Ma Heng (1881–1955), a specialist in the study of the Stone Classics, has also questioned whether it would have been physically practical for one man to write over 200,000 characters.[180] The most damaging evidence against the theory that Cai Yong wrote the entire text of the Stone Classics comes from looking at the dates of the project and the style of the calligraphy itself. The memorial suggesting the project to the emperor was submitted only in 175 CE. The project was completed eight years later in 183 CE. As you will recall from his biographical sketch above, Cai Yong was arrested and sent into exile at the close of 178 CE, only three or four years into the project. It is unlikely that he could have completed the calligraphy for the whole project before his imprisonment. Though the calligraphy in the two fragments presented in figure 5.19 could conceivably have been brushed by the same hand, other scholars have noted that several different writing styles are clearly present among the entire corpus of recovered fragments.[181] At any rate, I do think it likely that Cai Yong did contribute some of the calligraphy seen on the Stone Classics, at least for the stelae of the *Book of Etiquette and Ceremonial* (Yili), which the *Record of Luoyang* (Luoyang ji) of Lu Ji (261–303 CE) says recorded the names of Cai Yong and Ma Midi above the text.[182] It is only because of Cai Yong's later fame as a great literary figure and calligrapher that the historian Fan Ye saw fit to inflate the importance of his contribution to this project.

The received textual tradition handed down from early imperial China portrays the visual world of the Qin and Han courts as an awe-inspiring feast for the eyes, filled with jades, lacquered and gilded vessels, painted screens, and sumptuous silks, all surrounded by lacquered and painted walls. Excavated objects and the material remains of the palaces themselves only serve to confirm and reinforce the picture gained from reading texts. If anything, we still underestimate the magnificence of this lost and sheltered world.

The opulence of the early imperial court was sustained on the backs of the common people. The emperor maintained his lavish lifestyle with his own privy purse, known as the Privy Treasury (Shaofu), which collected a head tax on children, a yearly tribute in gold from nobles, a rent on market stalls, and excise taxes on the use of imperial land for forestry, mining, and fishing. During the Former Han period, this treasury was kept separate from the state treasury that funded the army and the bureaucracy. The money collected by the Shaofu was used to furnish the palace, clothe and outfit the emperor and the palace ladies, support the myriad staff, stock the massive kitchens, and stage the great spectacles. Palace expenses tended to grow inexorably over time, straining the finances of the empire and increasing the burden on the common people. Despite frequent calls for austerity from ministers at court, and occasional reductions in actual spending, the emperors' spiral of tax-and-spend continued more or less unabated.

With money coming from the Privy Treasury, the court operated several different workshops and factories in the capital area. These bureaus likely employed thousands of male and female free artisans, conscripted artisans, and government slaves to build, decorate, and maintain the palaces for the living emperor and the palace of the deceased emperor in his tomb. In this chapter, we encountered only the offices of the Yellow Gate and the Shangfang, but these were just two locations of artistic production among many at court. There were also the Eastern and Western Weaving Shops (Dong Zhishi, Xi Zhishi), which wove and embroidered the silk vestments worn by the emperor and his ladies; the workshop of the Carpenter of the Eastern Park (Dongyuan Jiang), which made the coffins, jade suits, and portable funerary articles for the imperial tombs; and the Imperial Workshop (Kaogong), which produced large quantities of weapons, bronze vessels, and lacquers. We will never know the names of most of the men and women who worked in these factories and workshops, but the names of a surprisingly large number are preserved for us in the inscriptions etched by workshop scribes onto lacquer vessels and bronzes made for imperial use.

We know almost nothing about how these common professional court artisans were compensated for their work. Were they paid in cash or merely fed, clothed, and housed by the state? The nature and amount of their compensation probably depended on whether they were summoned, hired, or conscripted for the job. We do know that master court artisans could be very well compensated for their work, either with monetary rewards or with promotions of rank and title. You will recall from the story told in chapter 2 that Gaozu's chief architect Hu Kuan was given great gifts of gold by those who were happy with the accuracy of his reconstruction of New Feng. In the next chapter, we will briefly meet Qiu Yan, the chief architect employed by Wang Mang to construct a new shrine complex. He was made a minor noble for his efforts. Of course, the unscrupulous portrait painters in the *Miscellaneous Notes* story of Wang Zhaojun managed to make great fortunes through bribes and extortion. One can also imagine that independent artisans who completed a commission for the court would probably do so quite willingly without pay, just as men like Josiah Wedgwood did during the late eighteenth century in England. Their outside business would probably pick up quite briskly when they could claim to be "artisan to the crown."

Finally, the emergence of scholar-official artisans seems to have been a new development during the Latter Han. However, their role in creating the visual and material splendor at court was still very minor during the early empires, and later authors tended to inflate the actual artistic contributions of men like Zhang Heng and Cai Yong to fit their own interpretations of the past. By such means, the poet and mathematician-astronomer Zhang Heng was transformed into a great painter, and Cai Yong was nearly apotheosized into the founder of the art of calligraphy. Men of the scholar-official artist type would become more and more common in later centuries, until the group finally realized class consciousness during the Northern Song under the leadership of Su Shi (1037–1101 CE) and his circle. By the Yuan and Ming periods, the scholar-official artists would stake their claim to a definitive style of art as well, the so-called *wenren hua,* or "literati painting," style.

6

ARTISANS IN IRONS

In the previous chapter, we met some of the illustrious professional artisans and amateur scholar-official artisans of early imperial China, men patronized by the emperor and the elites of society to fashion their gilded world. During their lives, these men often garnered great fortunes of money or reputation and lived in fairly comfortable conditions at court. In this chapter, we examine their polar opposite: the often-anonymous men and women who fashioned objects under the burden of the collar and the threat of the cane. We will look at the three most important categories of unfree artisans. Toiling together in great numbers and accomplishing great things, they were the coerced, the convicted, and the enslaved.

Economists and labor historians have long recognized that the arbitrary division of labor pools into free and unfree categories is too simplified and not very useful. Rather, it is better to see the conditions of labor as a continuum of coercion, gauged upon criteria such as degree of control over work, restriction of movement, restriction of life choices, or quality of living conditions.[1] Choosing different variables might result in a slightly different scale, but here, for our purposes, is a continuum of artisan labor from most free to most unfree based upon the first three criteria listed above.

1 Self-employed artisan
2 Wage labor artisan
3 Indentured artisan
4 Apprenticed artisan
5 Conscripted artisan
6 Convicted-criminal artisan
7 Slave artisan

We met men and women of the first four categories in previous chapters, so we may pass over them quickly here. It suffices to say that among this group, only numbers 3 and 4 could be considered unfree to any great extent. An indentured artisan voluntarily gives up his labor freedom to work for a specified period of time, for a specified reward. In fact, the only factors that often distinguish an indentured laborer from a wage laborer are the length and enforceability of his contract. The apprentice in an artisan's workshop begins to slide into the real domain of unfree labor. Though voluntarily in the service of a master to learn a valuable trade, his restricted freedom can be as severe as that of a personal slave, but the outcome is far more hopeful. He (or his parent) is essentially trading his freedom during a period of his life for the prospect of a future career as a master artisan. That being said, the focus of this final chapter will remain on the last three categories on our list: the conscripted artisan (*zu*), the convicted-criminal artisan (*tu*), and the slave artisan (*nu-bei*).

Monumental public works in China, such as palaces, temples, and tombs, were complex undertakings requiring the labor of thousands, or sometimes hundreds of thousands, of men and women of varying levels of skill. Unskilled labor played a crucial role in laying foundations and moving mountains, but medium-skilled and highly skilled artisans were also needed to design, decorate, and furnish these complex creations. Each monumental public project presented the master builder with a unique combination of problems, involving issues of timing, political impact, resource procurement, and labor hazards. The state had at its beck and call at least seven different artisan groups to assist in its projects: (1) lead architects, (2) master artisans, (3) hired craftsmen working for money, (4) skilled artisans conscripted by the state, (5) unskilled peasants conscripted by the state, (6) criminals sentenced to hard labor, and (7) government-owned slaves. I argue that the state used an economic decision-making process when selecting which of these groups to employ, in what combination, for how long, and in what capacity. It was a cost-benefit analysis based upon the skill level required for different tasks, the physical dangers incurred by the workers, and the direct or indirect costs to the peasant-based economy.

THE CONSCRIPTED ARTISAN

The Master said, "A country of a thousand war-chariots cannot be administered unless the ruler attends strictly to business, punctually observes his promises, is economical in expen-

diture, shows affection towards his subjects in general, and uses the labor of the peasantry only at the proper times of the year."

CONFUCIUS, THE ANALECTS[2]

It has often been noted by scholars of traditional China that the common people owed two forms of "taxes" to the state: (1) land and capitation taxes paid in grain or coin and (2) civilian and military labor services.[3] These labor service taxes have a very deep history in China, evolving out of the services rendered to clan elders, kings, and aristocratic lords in Shang and Zhou times.[4] With every able-bodied commoner technically required to render labor service for some portion of each year, the state was provided with a plentiful source of coerced labor to use in public-works projects. It has been argued that this pool of laborers, working temporarily but regularly for the state, helped to suppress the kind of widespread slavery seen in the Roman Empire.[5] If properly managed by the state, this corvée[6] system could provide the needed functions of tax-grain transport, infrastructure repair, and hydraulic engineering. If, however, the state abused this resource, such as by calling up farmers for labor service during the planting or harvest seasons, disaster could ensue. Thus, the state needed to make balanced economic decisions in its use of the three classes of coerced labor treated in this chapter (conscript, convict, and slave).

During the Qin and Han periods, both military and civilian labor conscripts were referred to as *zu*. The details of military conscription have been treated thoroughly by Michael Loewe and are not directly relevant to this chapter.[7] On the civilian side, all men were required to register for statute labor service (*yao yi*). Scholars used to believe that, during the Han, initial registration (*fu*) of males for labor service was required at twenty or twenty-three years of age.[8] Now, after archaeologists have discovered portions of Qin and Han laws that specifically address registration for statute labor, these views must be altered. What these unearthed texts reveal is that under the Qin and the first reign of the Former Han, a man registered as young as fifteen to seventeen years of age.[9] In addition to absolute calendar age,[10] which could be obfuscated, a man's height also determined when he was required to register and what tasks he might perform. It appears from the statutes that if a male was 6 *chi* and 5 *cun* (approximately 150 cm) tall, he was considered an adult and ready to do a man's work. If he was of age but a bit under 150 centimeters, he might be registered as "small" and be given minor duties.[11] If he was shorter than 6 *chi* and 2 *cun* (approximately 143 cm), even though of registration age, he was considered handicapped and was excused from service.[12] In the first five years of registration, between fifteen and twenty, young men seem to have been liable only for minor corvée duties.[13]

By 186 BCE, during the reign of Empress Lü, we see a much more complex registration system in place, with fine distinctions based on the rank of the registering man or his father within the Han system of meritocratic ranks (see table 6.1).[14] The rank system was originally instituted by the Qin as a means to reward military accomplishments and to limit the social and political power of aristocratic lineages. During the Han, ranks were given out by the emperor on special occasions such as the birth of an heir or for special service to the state. There were twenty (or twenty-one) steps on the rank scale, but commoners (nonofficials, nonnobles) could hold only the first eight. Ranks could be surrendered during trials to reduce the severity of punishments.[15]

By 186 BCE men had to be registered at twenty, twenty-two, or twenty-four under this system, although fifteen- to nineteen-year-old unregistered youths could still be used for minor conscript duties like grain transport.[16] When it is reported in the *History of the Former Han* that Emperor Jing (r. 157–141 BCE) changed the registration age to twenty in 155 BCE, he seems to have merely reissued the law promulgated in Empress Lü's time.[17] There is some evidence that around 86–81 BCE, Emperor Zhao (r. 87–74 BCE) further raised the initial registration age to twenty-three years.[18]

According to the Han statutes found at Zhangjiashan, dated 186 BCE, a man was exempted from conscription due to age (*mianlao*) sometime between fifty-eight and sixty-six years of age, again depending on rank (see table 6.1).[19] The retirement age listed in *Old Observances of the Han* (Han jiuyi) of Wei Hong (fl. 25–57 CE) represents a further relaxation of this early Former Han system, with ranked men retiring at fifty-six and unranked men retiring at sixty.[20] An interesting feature revealed by the Han statutes from Zhangjiashan is the status of "dim-sighted elderly" (*huanlao*).[21] When a man reached between fifty-eight and sixty-two years of age and was given this status, he was assigned only fifteen days of conscript duty (50 percent time) and allowed to serve within his local area only, rather than have to journey far away.[22] He was also not required to serve as a military conscript if he had been ill for a full year. This was a kind of half-retirement status that lasted for four years, until a man qualified for full retirement from the labor service.

It is clear from these numbers that there was a trend after the fall of the Qin and throughout the Han period of increasing the age of initial registration of unranked men (from fifteen to twenty to twenty-three), reducing their retirement age (from sixty-six to sixty), and introducing the semiretired status. What was the government's reason for this shift? One could argue that with the increasing population, there was a greater pool of men to serve in the conscript labor force, and thus the age limits could be relaxed. It seems, however, that the Han government explicitly wanted to reduce the labor demands on the peasant population to an acceptable burden and thus avoid the accusation laid on the short-lived Qin of having exhausted the people and losing the mandate to rule.[23]

During the years of his active registration, a man was liable to be called up for one month of labor service per year, on whatever task the government saw fit.[24] The government official responsible for raising a levy of men and sending them to the work site was apparently the Township Overseer (Xiang Sefu), the lead official in the bureaucracy below the county level and the man nominally in charge of all tax collection.[25] The Township Overseer would receive a conscription levy from the

TABLE 6.1. AGES FOR REGISTRATION, SEMIRETIREMENT, AND RETIREMENT (CA. 186 BCE)

Rank of Father of Person to Be Registered (0 is lowest; 20 is highest)	*Rank of Minor (xiao jue)*[1] *(i.e., the person to be registered)*	*Age of Initial Registration (fu)*
Rank 4 or lower[2]		20
Rank 5 to rank 9	Rank 2 to rank 4	22
Rank 10 or higher[3]	Rank 5 or higher	24

Rank of Man	*Beginning Age for "Dim-Sighted Elderly" (huanlao)*
Rank 4	58
Rank 3	59
Rank 2	60
Rank 1	61
Rank 0.5 and commoner[4]	62

Rank of Man	*Age for Elderly Exemption (mianlao)*
Rank 5 and higher	58
Rank 4	62
Rank 3	63
Rank 2	64
Rank 1	65
Rank 0.5 and commoner	66

1. The term *xiao jue* (rank of minor) is not attested elsewhere but seems from the context to connote ranks held by minors in their own names. Loewe, *Records of Han Administration,* 2:367–71, records a man who was given at least seven orders of rank while still a minor (*xiao nan*).

2. The range "rank 4 or lower" could indicate a lower rank limit of Gongshi (rank 1), Gongzu (rank 0.5), or all the way down to commoner (*shiwu*) status.

3. The rank of Qing found in the Zhangjiashan slips is not known in the extant Han lists, but under the Qin system, rank 10 was known as Keqing. It is clear from the context of this passage that rank 10 or higher is indicated. See Loewe, "Aristocratic Rank," 103.

4. The lowest rank above commoner (*shiwu*) listed in the Zhangjiashan slips is Gongzu. This rank is unknown from other received sources, but since it is lower than the rank of Gongshi, which is referred to in most works as rank 1, but still above the status of commoner, I have listed it as rank 0.5.

County Magistrate (Xian ling) or from some central government authority. The levy would have been calculated in person-months, following construction calculations of the type described in chapter 3. The officials were held accountable for these labor estimates and were fined or punished if the job required the conscripts to be held for additional time.[26] These numbers were also levied proportionately, so that locations farther from the worksite, and thus requiring more transportation, would need to contribute fewer men. It appears that the government never sought to conscript 100 percent of registered males for labor service each year, though it does appear that the percentage called to civilian labor service was higher than that called to military duty.[27] Based on the practical problems in the Han mathematical primer, *Nine Chapters on the Mathematical Arts*, it seems that from 13 to 33 percent of households might have to contribute one laborer each solely for the transport of tax grain each year.[28] Assuming that civilian labor conscription was restricted in the same way as military conscription, it would have been illegal for the Township Overseer to conscript more than one registered adult from the same household at the same time. If he did so, he would be fined a significant sum of money.[29] Evidently, such a practice would have left a farm household short-handed and endanger the crops. It was expressly stated in the Han legal statutes that the officials responsible for calling up conscripts were to do so only according to the "proper time (*shi*) and the proper circumstance (*an*)."[30] If public officials called up men or women outside these stipulations, they could be fined.

Clearly, the intent of these legal regulations was to protect the peasantry from unwarranted labor conscription, especially during key agricultural periods. But how do we know that these beneficent rules were ever carried out? Was not the Qin dynasty infamous for overburdening the people with labor duties?

A recent spectacular archaeological discovery is starting to provide an answer to these questions. In 2002, archaeologists at the site of Liye in Hunan discovered administrative documents from the Qin period on more than 36,000 wooden boards that had been dumped down a well during the chaos at the end of the dynasty. These documents promise to reveal how the Qin administration actually did function, not just how it was supposed to function.

In one of the few dozen documents published so far, a communication dated March 30, 220 BCE, the governor of Dongting Commandery sent a stern reminder to his subordinate officials to properly conserve the labor of the peasantry.[31] After quoting the appropriate Qin ordinance regarding this issue, the governor further adds, "Agriculture is about proper timing. It is not desirable to mobilize the common people." Local officials were told explicitly in this letter to exhaust all other sources of labor (especially convicts) for tasks such as transport duty before mobilizing any peasants. Those lower officials found to be in violation of these regulations were to be prosecuted. The letter was sent during the second month of the lunar year, right in the middle of the planting season. What the Liye documents published thus far reveal is that, at least during the early years of the Qin Empire, government officials did strive to protect the common people from unnecessary labor conscription, especially during key times of the year like the planting season.

There were apparently several legal ways to gain exemption from statute labor duty. First, those holding rank 9 and above, meaning officials and aristocrats, were usually exempt from labor service.[32] There is also substantial testimony that one could buy a personal one-year exemption from labor service for two thousand coins. This money theoretically went to pay for the hiring of a substitute laborer, a practice which was apparently known as *jian geng*. The salary paid to the replacement was sometimes referred to as the *pingjia* (fair price). Exemption from military garrison duty could apparently be obtained for three hundred coins.[33] During the Latter Han, the practice of mercenary exemption seems to have become even more common. Thus, with the officials, nobles, and the wealthy flush with exemptions, only the poor peasants were left to fill the ranks of the labor service. For extra money, they might even be tempted to serve on a mercenary labor gang for a longer stint.

The emperor could also grant labor service exemptions (*fuchu*) under special circumstances. These could be for one year or for life and were highly prized. On several occasions during the Han period, the emperor exempted whole areas of the empire afflicted by bad harvests. More than once, the founder of the Han exempted for life the citizens of whole regions (including his hometown) to reward them for their loyalty. On occasions when the government was short on cash, rich families could buy a lifetime exemption for one family member by contributing grain or slaves to the state.[34]

If a man attempted to avoid initial registration or ignored a conscription notice, the penalties could be rather severe. If he never showed up at all when the other men were convening in the village to depart, this was considered *bushi* (evading labor service) and was punishable by fifty or more strokes of the bamboo pole.[35] If he answered the conscription order but later left the job site prematurely, this was considered the crime of *fayao* (failing in statute labor).

As mentioned previously, each man of registration age was technically liable for one month of conscript labor each year. This might be performed in his local area, known as *yizhong* (within the town) labor, or many kilometers away on a provincial or capital project. As for local work, much of this involved the movement of earth. The Han statutes mention conscripted tasks such as cleaning and repairing roads and bridges, excavating into hills or ponds, digging or dredging canals and trenches, and clearing out stagnant water from moats and ponds.[36] The Qin statutes further mention erecting or repairing walls for local government buildings. Such work had to be guaranteed by the conscripts, for if it proved shoddy, they would have to repair it and not count the time as conscript labor.[37] Persistent rain automatically canceled a summer levy, and work on earthen walls then had to be postponed until late autumn, after the harvest.

We do not know precisely how well conscripts were treated on the jobsite, but we do know that officials were concerned that they did not work too hard and that they were clearly differentiated from convicts laboring on the same site. The government set quotas for how much earth was to be moved by each man over the course of his one-month stint, but these quotas do not seem too onerous and were adjusted according to the season and the hardness of the ground.[38] It seems from the sources that conscripts provided their own clothes, and if they were working locally, their own families provided them with food. If they were away at the capital, the state probably gave them grain rations, since they at least provided that for convict laborers.[39] Their tools were borrowed from the state and had to be returned in good condition to avoid fines.[40] Sometimes, the sources give us a glimpse of rough conditions. For example, the Qin legal texts mention workers of two different conscript labor road crews brawling on the job.[41] Overall, one gets the impression that local conscript duties primarily benefited the peasant and merchant laborers themselves. Better dams and canals helped the peasant farmer to increase productivity and avoid disaster, and improved roads and bridges helped the peasant and the merchant to transport their products. Yang Liansheng argues that the Chinese state based its conscription policy on the economic concept of *jun* (equalization), which seeks to distribute burdens and benefits fairly among the population.[42]

Though corvée labor was normally performed locally, and usually benefited the worker directly or indirectly, large numbers of conscripts were occasionally called to work on projects for the central government, some of limited practical value. On at least two occasions, conscripts were called up to heap earth upon large tomb mounds for an emperor's mother. In 86 BCE, Emperor Zhao summoned twenty thousand conscripts to rebury his mother in regal style in her own funerary park near the capital of Chang'an,[43] and in 5 BCE, Emperor Ai (r. 7–1 BCE) called up fifty thousand conscripts from several provinces to construct the tomb of his mother.[44] As will be seen shortly below, tombs of emperors were usually built over a period of many years by convict laborers, who died in great numbers on the job. The tombs just mentioned were built for emperors' mothers, however, and were probably completed quite quickly, possibly within the one month normally allotted for statute labor.

We also find frequent mentions of statute labor used to transport tax grain on a regular basis. Often these were quick overland trips from the local county to the commandery seat on government-provided carts.[45] But conscripts were also used further up the supply chain to transport 4 million *hu* (80 million liters) of tax grain each year by river from the breadbasket areas of the empire to the capital for consumption by the bureaucrats and idle elites. It was said by Geng Shouchang, a high-level official and reportedly a brilliant mathematician, that this inefficient delivery system employed sixty thousand conscript laborers per year in the years before 57 BCE. He said he could reduce that figure by more than 50 percent by buying the grain from localities near the capital instead.[46]

Squandering the peasant's valuable time on government labor projects was always a dangerous trade-off. If too many men (or women) were not at home on the farm during crucial periods such as the planting or the harvest, crops might fail and mass famine and unrest would result. This was the reasoning behind the prohibition against two males of the same household serving simultaneously. Gong Yu, a high minister during the reign of Emperor Yuan (r. 48–33 BCE), brought home this point in vivid fashion when he described the effect of the state employing more than one hundred thousand convicts, conscripts, and officials (working together in unknown proportions) for mining and smelting iron (for tools) and copper (for coinage). He claimed that since an average farmer can feed seven people with his labor, then if more than one hundred thousand men were working for the state instead, somewhere more than seven hundred thousand people must be starving![47]

Sometimes, however, calling up men and women for state labor projects was a matter of life and death for millions of commoners, and not just wasted labor for inefficient fiscal schemes or lavish burials for elites. In the early autumn of 29 BCE, the powerful and fickle Yellow River, the lifeblood and sorrow of North China, broke through its banks at two locations. According to damage assessments compiled at the time, it quickly inundated thirty-two counties and more than 150,000 *qing* (approximately 691,000 hectares) of prime farmland under nearly three *zhang* (6.93 m) of water and destroyed forty thousand private and government buildings. As government officials argued blame (and one committed suicide), 97,000 men, women, and children took refuge on the highest hills they could find to await rescue. The government soon sent out a fleet of five hundred ships to feed and rescue the refugees and then set about repairing the dikes. Wang Yanshi was given a special commission to repair the damage. During the early winter (safely after the harvest) he levied an untold number of conscripts to fill enormous bamboo containers with gravel, each one 9.24 meters long and 5.3 meters in diameter; each container was loaded onto two boats, maneuvered into position, and then sunk in the breach to stem the flood. It took thirty-six days to repair the dikes, a remarkably short time. We are told that Wang Yanshi was generously rewarded with titles and gold, and that "those conscripts who worked to quell the Yellow River were to have recorded that they served the equivalent of six months of frontier conscript duty," a generous reward for valorous service to the empire. Two years later, when the Yellow River broke out at a different place, Wang Yanshi was called back into action (accompanied by other officials jealous of his previous rewards). This time it took him six full months to close the gap, yet those conscripts who stayed for the entire task were still only given the same six months' credit against frontier conscription duty. Those who worked as mercenary replacements for two thousand coins were given no duty credits at all.[48]

Before turning to the question of artisan-specific conscription, I would like to look at one more great state labor project, which is remarkable not only for its sheer scale but also for what it reveals about the economic decisions made by the state in the use of conscript labor as opposed to convict labor.

When Liu Bang, the first emperor of the Han dynasty (r. 202–195 BCE), decided early in 202 BCE to move his capital from Luoyang in the east to the location of the old Qin dynasty capital in the west, he was faced with only the smoldering ruins of once-magnificent palace structures, thoroughly looted and torched by his rival Xiang Yu.[49] But this area "within the passes" (*guanzhong*) was ideally situated to defend the precarious new empire, so Liu Bang chose to reside there anyway.[50] Fortunately, just across the Wei River, an outlying Qin palace called the Palace of Prosperity and Joy (Xingle Gong) had survived the devastation.[51] Liu Ji changed its name to the Palace of Lasting Joy (Changle Gong) and made it his official throne hall.[52] Then, while he remained absent from his new capital, off suppressing the numerous rebellions of his former generals, his Counselor in Chief, Xiao He, and his army engineer and lead architect, Yangcheng Yan, built (from 200 to 198 BCE) the much more impressive Weiyang Palace, to ensure proper dignity and magnificence for the new empire.[53] The two palaces had their own gates and outer walls, but what this expanding "city" of palaces, markets, armories, and granaries lacked was a true outer perimeter wall. In fact, most major cities in 202 BCE lacked walls, since the First Emperor of Qin reportedly had them all torn down shortly after 221 BCE as part of his plan of universal disarmament following centuries of civil war.[54] In one of his earliest edicts (November/December 202 BCE), Emperor Gaozu (Liu Bang) ordered that the cities of the empire begin to rebuild their perimeter walls,[55] but the capital itself was "defenseless" until the reign of his son and successor, Emperor Hui (r. 195–188 BCE).

The construction of the city wall of Han Chang'an was a monumental undertaking. Archaeological surveys have revealed that the walls, which form somewhat of a trapezoid, travel a perimeter of 25,700 meters, enclosing an area of thirty-six square kilometers. The longest single segment (the south wall) ran for 7,600 meters. It appears that the original height of the wall, built of rammed earth, was over 12 meters and the base was 16 meters thick.[56] The wall was surrounded by a defensive moat, 8 meters wide and 3 meters deep. The project would have required moving more than 5.76 million cubic meters of soil from the area of the moat and beyond to build up the earthen wall.[57] Today, the wall survives in only a few scattered, heavily eroded segments.[58]

The first mention of the wall construction comes in February 194 BCE, but the brief passage in the "Imperial Annals of Emperor Hui" contained in the *History of the Former Han* does not mention how much of the wall was completed at that time nor who performed the work. Perhaps, all that occurred at this time was the planning, surveying, and ritual inauguration of the wall. Later texts suggest that construction began with the northwest corner of the wall.[59] Two years later, shortly after the death of Counselor in Chief Xiao He, lead architect Yangcheng Yan greatly accelerated the construction with one of the single largest conscriptions of the entire Han period.[60] In the spring of 192 (February 5 to March 6)[61] the emperor[62] ordered that 146,000 able-bodied men and women from an area within a radius of 600 *li* (249 km) of the capital of Chang'an be conscripted to work on the wall. It is reported that they worked for only thirty days and were then sent home. An early-fourth-century CE commentary on this passage reports that the conscripts finished just one side of the wall (probably the west wall) before departing.[63] Even in the modern world, the logistics of transporting, organizing, and feeding that many people on a work site would be mind-boggling. About five months later, in July 192 BCE, the construction was resumed, but this time the emperor brought in twenty thousand hard-labor convicts (*tuli*) drawn from the jails of the enfeoffed princes and marquises.[64] A year later, the wall was said to be half done.[65] Then, during the first month of spring of 190 BCE (February 13 to March 14), another large call-up was issued, this time for 145,000 conscripts from within the same 600-*li* radius. Again, they worked for only one month and went home.[66] Following a terrible drought that summer, the wall was finally completed, presumably by the aforementioned convicts, by October/November of 190 BCE.[67] To celebrate, the emperor granted an increase in rank to all heads of households in the empire.

I would argue that there was an economic logic behind the timing of these building phases and the type and number of laborers used. First, you will notice that the building phases which specifically mention regular conscripts took place in the first month of the lunar calendar, most of which usually falls in February. According to the agricultural instruction contained in the Latter Han almanac *Monthly Ordinances for the Four Peoples* (Simin yueling) (ca. 150 CE) of Cui Shi, no major planting or sericulture activities have begun by the first month.[68] It was acceptable at this time to send male children off to school and to prepare medications, repair items, etc. This would have been the ideal time to call up farmers or their wives to work for one month on a project of great importance. If the peasants were called away later in the spring, such as during April or May, this would have endangered the main planting season for millet, beans, and rice. If conscripted during midsummer, the weather would have been dangerously hot and torrentially rainy, and no one would have been at home to control the weeds among the important crops. "Do not miss this time [for weeding]," the same almanac urges. If peasants were conscripted in the fall, the all-important harvest season might be jeopardized. Thus, the state realized that the labor of peasant conscripts could be called upon only during the agricultural slack season, lest the economic basis of the empire's wealth be imperiled.

The convicts, on the other hand, had no seasonal restrictions and could be worked at any time, regardless of the weather. You will recall that they were brought in on the job during July 192 BCE, right in the middle of the blazing North China summer and shortly before the harvest months, a time when no normal labor conscription should ever take place. The convicts probably worked continually, year-round.[69] This can be inferred from the fact that even though the second group of conscript laborers was released on March 15, 190 BCE, the wall itself was completed by other hands in October/November of the same year.[70] The labor output of malnourished convicts was apparently equivalent to that of healthy conscripts, since the labor of 20,000 convicts working for seven months was equated with the labor of 146,000 conscripts working for one month.

The 600-*li* (249 km) radius of the conscription order is also significant. Such a broad net would have covered many of the most populous provinces and cities of the empire and could probably have netted at least one million eligible laborers.[71] But since the purpose of conscription was to provide the state with a reasonable amount of coerced labor without stressing the agricultural or domestic foundations of the empire, only about 15–20 percent of the eligible laborers were called up, and never more than one from the same family. Casting such a broad net actually made the impact of the conscription order less severe.

The final point to mention is the inclusion of women in the conscription. During pre-Han times, and most notably during the Qin, it was not unusual for women to be required to perform labor services for the state. Under Han law it was technically illegal to conscript women, minors, or the elderly for statute labor.[72] The Han government made exceptions, however, to this rule. Later dynasties also struggled with this issue, outlawing labor service for women, only to conscript them anyway for important capital and local projects. Eventually, female conscript labor was entirely phased out, for it appears no women performed labor service after the Tang period.[73]

We are clearly told that women "worked" on the Chang'an walls project, but it remains unclear what activities they performed. Did they shoulder baskets of earth with the men, carry them up ladders to the top of the wall, pour them into wooden forms, and then ram the dirt with wooden tampers? Or, possibly, did they serve only in a domestic-support function in the camp, providing the cooking and cleaning for the male members of the workforce? Perhaps we can find a clue by using the practical construction calculations of the *Nine Chapters on the Mathematical Arts* primer. We see that the 4,900-meter-long west wall of Chang'an contained approximately 823,200 cubic meters of rammed earth. This was derived from 1,097,600 cubic meters of excavated soil.[74] The normative quota of soil to be excavated, transported, and pounded by a Han conscript worker in one month during the spring was 7.55 cubic meters.[75] Thus, to build the west wall of Chang'an would have required approximately 145,377 person-months of labor. This estimate fits remarkably well with the actual conscription totals for men *and* women listed in the *History of the Former Han* (146,000), and thus, it appears that the women on this project may have shouldered physical labor along with the men.

Even though every able-bodied man during the Qin and Han periods had to register with the government for regular statute labor service, it appears that specialized artisans had to undergo a separate registration, to be listed and called up according to their skills. In fact, Yang Liansheng argues that this was a continuous feature of labor service throughout imperial Chinese history.[76] To cite one of his examples, during the Ming period, government work projects were required to conscript one skilled artisan for every five unskilled laborers. It seems to have been an economic concern of the state that specialized labor not be wasted on unskilled tasks, and that each labor pool be exploited to maximum advantage without stressing any source, or the entire system, to the breaking point.

The evidence for separate artisan conscription during the Qin and Han periods was not, until recently, as detailed as that for later dynasties. Among the titles mentioned in Qin weapons inscriptions, we find *gonggeng zhang*, which could be translated as "foreman of the conscripted artisans."[77] There is also mention in the Qin legal texts of the practice of "artisan tribute" (*gongxian*), which might be interpreted to mean that artisans could submit a portion of their manufactured objects to the state as tribute rather than labor in a state enterprise.[78]

The most explicit proof comes from the recently published Han legal texts found in tomb 247 at Zhangjiashan. Among the twenty-eight quoted statutes and ordinances is one entitled "Statute on Exemption from Corvée" (Fulü):

> [For those who are recruited for] artisan labor service in offices set up in the counties [but under the direction of the central government], exempt their entire household from regular labor service and separate out the artisans. Proportionately, take the three most skilled artisans of any group of ten and make them [the group qualified for] exemption. [Of these three], two should be adult females and one can be another type [i.e., male or child]. Do not levy a poll tax or a statute labor tax [on their households]. If their family is not required to perform statute labor, then some other household in the county is entitled to the exemption. If the entire county has already been exempted from labor service and there is no one else to give exemption to, then grant the exemption to persons in the county in which the government bureau [performing the work] is actually located. When the novice artisan has apprenticed for one year, then [his/her household] obtains the exemption. In each case, rank them by their level of ability. For those who after two years have still not mastered the required skill, do not make them [a state artisan whose family gains] exemption.[79]

What this passage from the Han statutes makes clear is that artisans were separately identified by the state for special corvée labor to be performed in government offices and factories. It does not mention how long they had to work for the state, but it is made clear that their entire households (*hu*) would be exempt from regular conscript duties because of their contribution. I would assume that the service was year-round. It may have been similar to the Tang system under which the state artisan served nearly a month of the year without pay but was paid for the remainder of the year. What is also interesting to note is that the state selected only the cream of the crop (top 30 percent) for what amounted to a privileged distinction for the family, basically a tax break. Among this group, the quota for women over men was two to one. This was probably due to the great demand for female specialties such as weaving and silk embroidery. The final exemption for the family, however, was granted only after a probationary period. As you can see, if after two years their skills did not achieve perfection, they would be released from artisan corvée and probably returned to the regular conscript rolls.

We can get an impression of the kind of work performed by conscripted artisans by looking once again at the Western Workshop of Shu Commandery, the government luxury-goods factory located in Chengdu. As was explained in chapter 3, the lacquer production process at the Western Workshop was finely divided along a kind of premodern assembly line. Each worker performed just one stage of a process on a large number of pieces and then passed the batch along. When making a lacquer cup, the task that required the most time but comparatively the least skill was the application of the base coats of mixed lacquer and ash to the carved wooden base. This task was called *xiu* (basecoat lacquering) at the Western Workshop, and the person who performed it was called a *xiugong* (basecoat-lacquer artisan). This was a simple task, but it required a comparatively large group of artisans who not only were familiar with the properties of lacquer paint but also had already been hyposensitized to the toxic effects of the fluid. This work was probably best performed by lacquer artisans conscripted from one of the many private lacquer workshops in the Chengdu area. The conscripted artisans would not need to learn the imperial patterns that the lead painters had to master or the exacting proportions that the wood carvers had to know. When one looks at the roster of names of the artisans who worked on lacquer cups and plates at the Western Workshop, it is striking that the names of the *xiugong* show the most variety within any year and the most turnover from year to year.[80] These men (and women) were most likely conscripted lacquer artisans performing their "rotation of labor" (*geng*). As we saw from the Han statutes, this was actually a privilege and gave their families a break from other labor service.

In addition to the legal stipulations concerning artisan corvée and the few scattered clues to how it was applied in practice, there is also unmistakable anecdotal evidence from a very famous building project that artisans were conscripted separately from other nonagricultural labor to work for the state. As mentioned above, constructing enormous palaces and temples required not only mass gangs of unskilled labor to build the foundations and walls (provided by conscripts and convicts) but also the finely tuned skills of hundreds of master craftsmen to design, finish, and decorate the work: architects, founders, gilders, wood-carvers, painters, etc. The Qin and Han historical records are mostly silent about the source of the craftsmen needed to put the finishing touches on great building projects, but in one instance we have explicit and lurid detail. In 20 CE, twelve years after Wang Mang (46 BCE–23 CE) declared the Han dynasty defunct and proclaimed his Xin dynasty (9–23 CE), he felt the need to erect nine enormous shrines to legitimize his fictive ancestral ties to the sage rulers of antiquity and to distract the people from the true causes of the current economic distress. Originally, he had continued ancestral services to the deposed Liu family line, probably out of deference to his powerful aunt who had been the empress of the Han emperor Yuan. Later, he would desecrate many of these shrines, intent on replacing them with ancestral shrines to his own family.[81] In July/August of 20 CE, he divined by cracking turtle shell[82] that the best location for the new buildings would be on prime land just south of the Chang'an city walls, and on September 25, 20 CE, he personally inaugurated the foundation work with three ceremonial tampings. He then issued a wide summons for artisans from all over the empire to come to Chang'an to work on his shrines.[83] His edict does not say whether these were summoned as paid workers or conscripted without pay. The verb used in the text, *zheng* (to muster), is often seen in military and civilian labor contexts and strongly suggests that the artisans had no choice in the matter. Later in the account, it is revealed that many were in fact conscripted men (*zu*).

Like other vain rulers throughout history, Wang Mang's desire to aggrandize his accomplishments through monumental architecture was greater than the ability of his treasury to cover the costs. So, just as the "great builder" Rameses II (r. ca. 1304–1237 BCE) of Egypt's New Kingdom tore down the temples and palaces of pharaohs of the Eighteenth Dynasty (especially those of the heretic pharaoh Akhenaten) to build some of his monuments at Thebes, Wang Mang had his workers cannibalize ten Former Han palaces and lodges west of Chang'an to obtain the timbers and roof tiles necessary to complete his ambitious Nine Ancestral Shrines project.[84] The new buildings were immense and designed to inspire awe. The Shrine of the Original Ancestor (Huangdi Taichuzu Miao), built to honor the Yellow Emperor, whom Wang Mang claimed as his ancestor, was said to be forty *zhang* (approximately 92.4 m) in length and breadth and nearly seventeen *zhang* (approximately 40 m) high at the roof ridge, consisting of several levels. The artisans were told to decorate the buildings more lavishly than any previous structure. The crossbeams were supported by bronze brackets, and the buildings' woodwork was further embellished with silver and gold openwork. The decoration was said to have "exhausted the limits of the workmen's skill (*qiao*)."[85] All of this came at great cost, both material and human. The work, which was completed in about eighteen months (by January/February 22 CE), was said by Ban Gu to have cost several tens of millions of coins, and the conscript and convict laborers who died on the project were said to have numbered in the tens of thousands.[86] The implied rebuke in this complaint is that only convicts were supposed to die during such construction projects, not innocent conscripts. One professional artisan engaged by Wang Mang fared much better. This was Qiu Yan, who served as Capital Architect (Dujiang). He was probably the only supervisor on the project who had any real construction skills. He was granted a flowery, landless aristocratic title: Noble of the Interior of Handan Hamlet.[87] Qiu Yan's work would not stand for long, however. One and a half years later, Wang Mang's severed head would be swinging in the marketplace at Yuan, and his Nine Ancestral Shrines, designed to endure for "ten thousand generations," would go up in flames under the rebel torch.[88] Archaeologists rediscovered the remains of their foundations during the 1950s.[89]

Though conscription of artisans and nonartisans was a fixture throughout traditional Chinese history, certain developmental trends can be seen in this institution. Yang Liansheng notes that from the fall of the Han until Tang (618–907 CE) and Song (960–1279 CE) times, local governments lost much of their control over their finances to central authorities. From Song times onward, local authorities did not even have the money necessary to carry out important infrastructure repairs, and thus they began to rely more heavily on local gentry to provide the funds necessary to maintain roads and bridges. Yang also argues that the trend seen already during the Han of peasants paying a fee to hire replacements increased in later dynasties, with more and more labor performed by hired replacements. Finally, he notes that military labor (a source not really discussed in this book) on major construction projects became far more important in later dynasties, especially under the Song and Ming (1368–1644 CE), when military labor made up more than 30 percent of the labor force.[90]

THE CONVICT ARTISAN

On a cold winter day in North China (Sunday, February 2, 13 BCE), Su Ling, a convict laborer sentenced to work in a government iron foundry in Shanyang Commandery, led 228 of his fellow convicts in a revolt against the state. The revolt started small, as Su Ling and his men murdered the commandant of the foundry and the other government officials who had been their immediate tormentors. The rebels then proceeded to steal government weapons from the local arsenal, emboldening Su Ling to name himself general of a rebel army. They ravaged the countryside and gathered hundreds of additional supporters, by force of charisma or threat of the sword. The imperial government was slow to act in suppressing the rebellion and it quickly raged out of control, engulfing nineteen of the most populous commanderies and princedoms of the empire. One contemporary critic remarked that "they trampled underfoot the famous metropolitan centers and the great commanderies, gathering followers and seeking treasure, and they did not even feel the need to conceal their actions."[91]

The rebellion of the convict Su Ling was not an isolated incident. Two other armed insurrections of convict laborers had broken out in the previous ten years. Su Ling's rebellion was one of the largest armed challenges to the state in the first century BCE and was symptom and cause of the accelerating decline of the Former Han Empire. Reviewing this pivotal rebellion also provides an opportunity to describe the Han convict labor system that helped to instigate it.

Su Ling and his cohort were *tu* (criminal laborers), convicted under the complex and merciless Han legal system that ensnared a multitude of people, both guilty and innocent. The Han legal code (an evolving collection of statutes, ordinances, precedents, and case law) was a massive body of documents, by one estimate over seven million words in length, stipulating penalties for a myriad of infractions. There were 409 different provisions in the code calling for execution, with over 1,880 established incidents falling under those provisions![92] The most common penalty, however, was hard labor. Table 6.2 lays out the different hard-labor penalties in use during the early Former Han and some of the crimes for which they were warranted.[93] In general, assault, robbery, and willful destruction of property were the most common crimes leading to a sentence of hard labor. Despite the presence of one- and two-year penalties, most criminals were sentenced to four-, five-, or six-year terms, which might be reduced as their sentences matured or after official amnesties.[94]

TABLE 6.2. HARD-LABOR CRIMES AND SENTENCES DURING THE EARLY FORMER HAN PERIOD (CA. 186 BCE)

Hard-Labor Penalty for Men	*Corresponding Labor Penalty for Women*	*Length of Term*	*Crimes for Which It Was Warranted*
Tattooed wall-dawn (*qing chengdan*) (tattooing replaced after 167 BCE with shaved head and iron collar)	Grain pounder (*qing chong*)	5–6 years	a) Stealing goods worth more than 660 coins b) Conspiracy to commit murder or assault c) Malicious assault d) Selling or buying a free person e) Unfiliality to parents f) Malicious arson g) Forging documents h) Absconding to avoid taxation i) Making false statements in a capital trial j) Conspiring to counterfeit coins k) Forcing a woman to marry oneself (male) l) Fornication with brother's wife or slave (male)
Intact wall-dawn (*wan chengdan*)	Intact grain pounder (*wan chong*)	4 years	a) Forging seal of minor official b) Making intentionally false statements in official documents c) Injury to a person during fight with a weapon d) Stealing goods worth 220–660 coins e) Trying to avoid military conscription f) A person under ten committing murder g) Adultery with a stranger's wife (male)
Gatherer of firewood for the spirits (*guixin*)	Sifter of white grain (*bocan*)	3 years	No specific crimes warranting this three-year punishment are mentioned in the Zhangjiashan slips, though the category is explicitly enumerated in lists of punishments.
Shaved bondman (*nai li chen*)	Shaved bondwoman (*nai li qie*)	3 years	a) Tampering with official seals on documents b) Wife striking husband

			c) Striking older brother or sister d) Stealing goods worth 110–220 coins This penalty seems to disappear after 118 BCE and is collapsed into the *guixin-bocan* status. Originally, it seems to have been a kind of penal servitude for crimes of passion and petty theft.
Shaved robber-guard (*nai sikou*)	Work like that of a robber -guard (*zuo ru sikou*)	2 years	No specific crimes warranting this two-year punishment are mentioned in the Zhangjiashan slips, though the category is explicitly enumerated. On the bamboo slips from the Gansu Xuanquan site, the "Statute on Malicious Harm" (Zeilü) states that a child striking his aunt or uncle is condemned to this penalty. Earlier in the Han this same crime carried a three-year sentence.
Forced labor (*fu zuo*)	Forced labor (*fu zuo*)	3 months to 1 year	This sentence does not appear in the Zhangjiashan slips but is testified by wooden-slip documents and in *Han jiuyi,* 85. It might represent a commutation of harsher sentences or a penalty for misdemeanors.
Frontier labor fine (*shu fazuo, zishu*)		1 month to 1 year	This sentence does not appear in the Zhangjiashan slips but is testified by the Shuihudi Qin documents and in *Han jiuyi,* 85. It seems to be a penalty for certain crimes of negligence by officials or military officers.

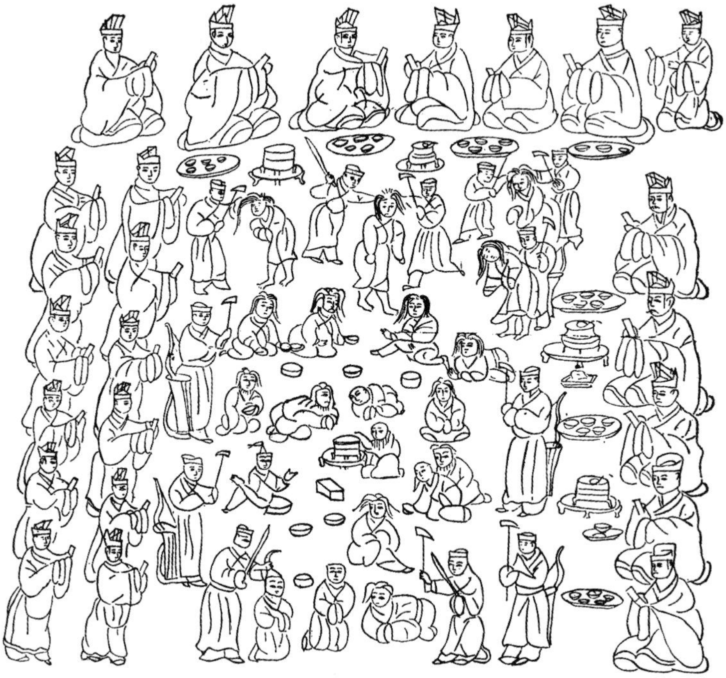

6.1 *Criminals beaten and shaved.* Latter Han period, ca. 126–67 CE. Line drawing of incised stone carving. W. 76 cm. Zhucheng Municipal Museum. From Zhucheng Xian Bowuguan, p. 18, fig. 6. Original stone excavated from Han tomb at Qianliangtai, Shandong.

The legal process that culminated in these sentences was reconstructed by the preeminent Western expert on Qin and Han law, A. F. P. Hulsewé, in his 1955 book *Remnants of Han Law.*[95] Though much of his description is still valid, Hulsewé's account can now be supplemented by information from two "casebooks" recently excavated from separate tombs in South China.[96]

Once a crime had been reported to local authorities, the County Magistrate and his assistant directed the criminal investigation. They instructed clerks to seal the crime scene, impound property, detain witnesses, and perform an autopsy, if necessary. After low-level county clerks had deposed the witnesses, compared their accounts, and received further expert testimony, suspects were formally charged, arrested, and placed in manacles in the county jail. A list of charges was drawn up, further material proof was brought forward, and the suspects were confronted with the written accusations and the statements of others. The suspect was encouraged to confess to the charges, and if he refused or frequently changed his story, the interrogation was aided by beatings on the thighs and buttocks with a one-inch-thick bamboo pole. Many less-hardy men died at this point from their interrogation injuries. Once the inevitable confession of the accused was read back to him and approved, all the documents were forwarded to the magistrate for sentencing. Some stages may have been conducted in open court (as in later imperial China), but no formal defense was allowed for the accused, either by himself or by his representatives. Family members (or the accused in noncapital cases) could appeal the sentence, but this meant another round of investigations and interrogation. If the appeal was baseless, the penalty was increased one degree in severity.[97] It truly seems that once one was accused in this system, there was little hope of exoneration.[98] Universal balance and public order demanded that *someone* pay for the crimes committed. Hopefully, that person was guilty, but that was not the most important concern. Legal debate centered more on whether the punishments were appropriate for the crimes, and less on whether innocent people were occasionally condemned. The key to not being declared guilty in this system was not to be charged in the first place.

After an accused criminal received his judgment, he or she was quickly shipped out to a labor unit to complete the sentence. Han prisons were not meant to be a final punishment, and few besides political prisoners spent much time in jail. Before being shipped out, most convicts received adjunct punishments, some of which could prove fatal.[99] Men and women condemned to the harshest labor penalty (five to six years) usually had their head hair and/or whiskers shaved (or hacked off) (see figure 6.1), their faces or shoulders tattooed, and their necks fitted with an iron collar. The iron collar was called the *qian* 鉗, a word which originally designated a tool like pincers or tongs. One can still make out the general shape of this tool in the right portion of the graph. Figure 6.2c shows one of these iron collars. It consisted of a horseshoe-shaped piece of iron with rings at either end. After this was placed around the convict's neck, a straight iron bar was slipped through the openings and then bent sharply to lock the collar in place. As this had to be performed once the collar was already on the person, it would have placed tremendous pressure on the neck and trachea. The convict may actually have had to lie on an anvil while the collar-lock was hammered into place. Manacles and fetters were also used to restrain convicts. Excavated examples of these are depicted in figures 6.2a and 6.2d. Figure 6.3 shows a contemporary Han depiction of fetters and manacles being used to restrain prisoners. It appears from the illustration that dogs and armed guards were also used to control convicts.

Special circumstances in his or her crime might also warrant amputation of the convict's nose, left foot, or both feet. In 167 BCE, Emperor Wen (r. 180–157 BCE) replaced these physical mutilations (*rouxing*) with severe additional beatings and the expanded use of fetters.[100] If we believe the historian Ban Gu, Emperor Wen was appalled that the mutilations and tattooing stigmatized a person forever, ruining a convict's chances of ever reforming his or her life. Emperor Wen's reforms had the unintended effect of leading to more convict deaths, since the maximum prescribed five hundred strokes of the bamboo pole (to replace left-foot amputation) usually killed even the healthiest man. The number was reduced to three hundred strokes in 156 BCE and to two hundred strokes in 144 BCE. Furthermore, the size of the stick was regulated and the beater was not to be relieved by a fresh man during the punishment. It seems clear that if too many convicts died, it would dry up one of the government's chief sources of brute labor for dangerous jobs. Humane mercy may have been one motivation for these reductions in beatings and mutilations, but economic reality was probably an important factor as well.

Convict laborers, especially shaved, iron-collared men with five- or six-year sentences, were sent to perform the dirtiest, most arduous, and most dangerous jobs for the state. Many were unable to outlive their term of labor. Though their penal

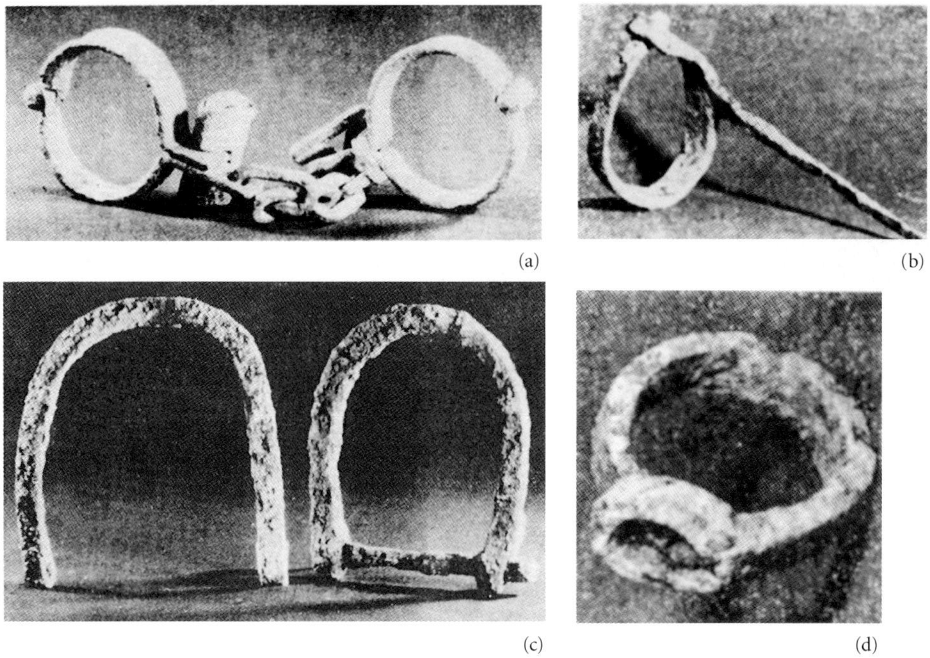

6.2 *Convict-laborer restraints*

(a) *Manacles with lock.* Qin period, ca. 221–210 BCE. Iron. L. 38 cm. From Qin Yong Keng Kaogudui, pl. 12.3. Excavated from the mausoleum of the First Emperor of Qin, Lintong, Shaanxi.

(b) *Collar with "fin."* Former Han period, ca. 152–146 BCE. Iron. L. 29.5–34 cm. From Qin Zhonghang, fig. 7. Excavated from the convict laborer cemetery near Emperor Jing's tomb.

(c) *Collars.* Qin period, ca. 221–210 BCE. Iron. L. 18 cm. From Qin Yong Keng Kaogudui, pl. 12.4. Excavated from the mausoleum of the First Emperor of Qin, Lintong, Shaanxi.

(d) *Fetter.* Former Han period, ca. 152–146 BCE. Iron. D. 9.5 cm. From Qin Zhonghang, fig. 11. Excavated from the convict laborer cemetery near Emperor Jing's tomb.

titles (see table 6.2) contained such descriptive phrases as *chengdan* ("wall-dawn," i.e., building walls from sunrise) or *guixin* (gathering firewood for the imperial spirits), these designations had already become empty titles by the Qin period. In fact, convicts of all grades often worked together in state-run factories and on public-works projects for the state. From textual and archaeological sources we know that they built palaces, dug tombs, shored up dikes, built roads and bridges, cut fodder for horses, harvested timber, transported tax grain, mined copper and iron ore, cast iron tools, minted coins, boiled brine into salt, and dyed fabric.[101] They were collected together from widely scattered parts of the empire to work on major projects and might toil hundreds of miles from their home districts.[102] They were often transferred in large blocks to work under the Chamberlain for the Palace Buildings (Jiangzuo Dajiang), the minister responsible for constructing palaces and digging imperial tombs at the capital. On many projects, they worked alongside regular conscripts from the local area who were performing their one month of labor service. It appears that female convicts were rarely given outdoor duties and were mostly employed in traditional female

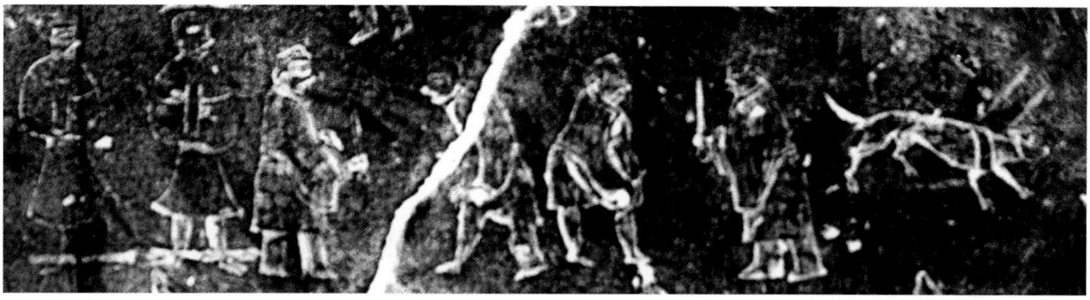

6.3 *Convicts wearing wooden fetters and iron manacles.* Detail of east wall of shrine at Xiaotangshan, Changqing County, Shandong. Latter Han period, ca. 76–88 CE. Ink-on-paper rubbing. Royal Ontario Museum, 2000.52.3.2. Photo courtesy of Klaas Ruitenbeek.

pursuits of grain processing or textile production. Some female convicts were apparently ordered to collect firewood in the hills but during certain amnesties were allowed to return home and hire substitute laborers by paying three hundred coins per month.[103]

Some of these tasks did not require skilled labor and could hardly be considered artisan activities except under the broad definition of "nonagricultural laborer." However, many convicts were employed in the stricter sense of the word "artisan" (making and decorating things) in government factories and on construction sites. Under the Qin, hundreds of thousands of convicts toiled together with the children born of government slaves to construct the First Emperor of Qin's opulent A-fang Palace and his mausoleum at Mount Li.[104] We also know from inscriptions that the Qin employed convict laborers of all grades in their weapons factories.[105] The given names of artisans were recorded on the weapons for purposes of quality control. When a convict artisan's name was recorded, it was prefaced by his penal title, such as "spiritual firewood artisan X" (工鬼薪 X), and followed by the names of the free artisans who worked on the piece. The Qin statutes stipulated that newly enlisted male convict laborers were forbidden to conceal the fact that they had artisan skills.[106] The state wanted to exploit their talents and did not want them wasting their energy in animal husbandry or domestic service. Women convict laborers in the Qin who were skilled in embroidery were not allowed to have their sentences redeemed by having a family member substitute for them.[107] When Qin convicts worked at a skilled task alongside free artisans, they were not expected to complete the same amount of work. Depending on the age and gender of the worker and the task involved, convicts were expected to fulfill one-fifth to two-thirds of the quota expected of a skilled free artisan.[108] The Han continued the practice of employing convicts in state-run factories but modified the practice somewhat, employing mostly wage-labor artisans and conscripted artisans at weapons and luxury-goods factories, while employing almost exclusively unfree labor (convicts, conscripts, and slaves) at state iron and copper mines and casting facilities.

Our rebel Su Ling and his fellow convicts were sentenced to work at one of the facilities run by the Iron Monopoly Office (Tieguan) of Shanyang Commandery.[109] These iron-processing facilities were part of the largest regional factory system operated by the Former Han government.[110] Early in the reign of Emperor Wu of the Former Han (r. 141–87 BCE), the Chinese launched a series of attacks against the nomadic pastoralists on the northern and western frontiers of the empire (the Xiongnu) that exhausted the funds in the state treasury. In order to replenish the treasury, the government placed a production and marketing monopoly on salt and iron starting around 120–117 BCE.[111] Henceforth, all iron agricultural tools, artisan tools, vessels, and weapons were to be made and sold by the state. The high officials who were put in charge of the state iron industry were actually former iron industrialists themselves.

According to the "Treatise on Administrative Geography" (Dili zhi), chapter 28 of the *History of the Former Han*, Iron Monopoly Offices were established in forty-eight locations within forty different commanderies and princedoms. Yang Yuan (1933–89) consulted additional sources and corrected those figures to fifty-three locations in forty-two commanderies and princedoms.[112] Thus, 40 percent of Han regional units had at least one Iron Monopoly Office. The offices were concentrated in the middle and lower reaches of the Yellow River, with present-day Shandong (twelve locations) and Henan (seven locations) leading the list. According to Han sources, Iron Monopoly Offices were located near iron-ore deposits. Those located in iron-poor areas are thought to have been involved in scrap-iron recycling or the casting of tools and weapons from ingots smelted elsewhere. The areas of highest concentration of Iron Monopoly Offices also coincide with the areas of highest concentration of population during the Former Han. Many Iron and Salt Monopoly Offices (including Shanyang's) had several branch locations called *biezhi* or *biezuo*, which were under the control of the main office. So the number of actual iron facilities in the empire was probably well over one hundred.

It is not certain how many convict laborers were employed by the Iron Monopoly Offices, but as you will recall, Gong Yu estimated the total number of convicts and conscripts employed for mining iron *and* copper around 44 BCE at one hundred thousand.[113] Estimates based on further textual references and archaeological remains suggest a figure somewhere between 10,000 and 50,000 convict laborers working in iron-processing facilities for the Former Han government.[114]

We can get some idea of the activities performed by convicts like Su Ling at an Iron Monopoly Office by looking at three of the large Han state-run iron facilities which have been excavated by archaeologists over the last fifty years. The site of Tieshenggou was a large (estimated total area, 2.16 hectares), vertically integrated facility located in the midst of iron-ore rich foothills in present-day Henan. It incorporated every stage of the iron production process, from mining to smelting to final casting.[115] It even included its own cemetery to dispose of dead laborers! During the Han it was referred to in inscriptions as Facility 3 of the Henan Iron Monopoly Office (*he-san*). The site of Guxingzhen, which was located just outside the walls of the Han period city of

Xingyang (10 km from present-day Zhengzhou), covered an incredible 12 hectares and primarily engaged in smelting and casting. It was designated Facility 1 of the same Henan Iron Monopoly Office (*he-yi*).[116] The site of Wafangzhuang was designated Facility 1 of the Nanyang Iron Monopoly Office (*yang-yi*) during the Former Han. The total site covers 2.8 hectares and was located within the walls of the lower town of the provincial capital of Yuan. It almost exclusively cast tools from ingots smelted elsewhere.[117] All three sites were located close to iron deposits and convenient river transport, and surprisingly close to large population centers. What follows is a composite picture of iron and steel production activities drawn from these three sites and from the copper-mining site of Tonglüshan in Hubei.[118]

The first stage in the production process was mining the iron ore. Depending on the configuration of the iron-ore deposits, Han iron mines could be strip mines, slanting shafts, or deep vertical pits with horizontal galleries. The Han period iron mine at Tieshanmiao and the copper mines at Tonglüshan have been probed to a depth of one hundred meters.[119] Individual shafts or galleries (sometimes as narrow as one meter) were probably worked by teams of two men, one wielding a six-kilogram iron hammer and the other an iron pickax. Replacement shifts of miners might huddle in a cave dwelling bored out of the hillside near the mineshaft, awaiting their turn in the pit. Ventilation of the shaft was provided by bamboo tubes, and the walls were reinforced with tightly fitted wooden beams. Once the ore was freed from the seam, it was lifted to the surface in buckets by a pulley system.

Since transporting iron ore is less efficient than transporting finished ingots, ore was usually smelted at sites fairly close to the mines. Convicts working at the smelting sites would crush the ore with iron hammers (or stone rammers) on stone anvils, until the fragments reached an optimal size, around three to six centimeters in diameter. Baskets of processed ore would then be transported to charge-mixing pits located just next to the smelting furnaces. Here, the ore would be mixed with crushed limestone (which served as a flux) and charcoal, much of it roasted from chestnut trees taken from local forests.

Han smelting furnaces came in several varieties. The largest and most productive was the continuous-smelting blast furnace, which could produce as much as one metric ton of cast iron per day from a fifty-cubic-meter hearth.[120] These furnaces required constant, laborious tending. Convict laborers would fill baskets of furnace charge (mixed ore, flux, and charcoal), climb onto the roof of the furnace, and pour the charge into the blazing aperture (1000°C–1,100°C). Meanwhile, other men labored at the bellows located to either side of the elliptical furnace. Judging by the depiction on the carved stone from Hongdaoyuan, Shandong, these bellows consisted of large airbags, suspended from above and compressed by several men working simultaneously, including one lying on the ground (see figure 3.3).[121] As many as thirteen to sixteen men might work around one large furnace.[122] Bellows work was exhausting and had to be continued as long as the furnace was operational.

When the cast iron was ready to pour, workers tapped the hole on the front of the furnace, poured off the slag, and then ran the molten iron into trenches along the ground to cast large pigs of iron. Once they had cooled, the convicts would need to transport these massive planks to storage pits and later to other furnaces for decarburizing into steel or final casting into tools and vessels. Moving these hulks would have been difficult indeed. The iron pigs found in a storage pit at the site of Tieshenggou weighed 500–1,000 kilograms each. Sometimes, a furnace would "blow out" and someone would have to remove the sintered iron bear from inside the compromised furnace. Several of these bears found at the Guxingzhen site weighed up to twenty metric tons! Recall that all of these onerous tasks were performed by men who were malnourished and often collared and fettered.

Some of the tasks around the Iron Monopoly Office were probably not performed by unskilled convict labor. These included supervising the smelt, designing intricate casting molds, and overseeing construction of new furnaces. Some of these tasks were performed by skilled government slaves, others by wage laborers. A typical Iron Monopoly Office branch factory also employed at least twenty officials on government salary and an unknown number of other clerks and subfunctionaries.[123]

The scale of iron production at these sites is difficult to estimate, but in the case of Tieshenggou, one can estimate, based on the size of the remaining slag heap, that the facility produced at least 5.26 *million* kilograms of iron in its estimated one century of operation, or about 52,600 kilograms per year. The enormous furnace 1 at Guxingzhen may have produced as much as 365,000 kilograms per year.[124] This may not seem like much by modern standards, but one must remember that this is 100 BCE, and these sites were only two of the more than one hundred state-run iron facilities during the Former Han. Donald Wagner conservatively estimated that each Iron Monopoly Office might have averaged 100,000 kilograms per year, for an empirewide annual total of about 5 million kilograms.[125] For comparison, an average blast furnace facility in pre–Industrial Revolution England (ca. 1715–20) produced about 304,000 kilograms of pig iron per year, out of a national output of 23 million kilograms.[126] The harsh treatment of workers in the early English steel mills is well known, but let us see how it compares to the treatment of convict laborers in the Han system.

The treatment of convict laborers at these facilities was callous at best. The government did not want them all to die, but they took no extraordinary measures to protect them from abuse. When a convict laborer first arrived at a site, he was given red hempen clothes and a red felt cap to distinguish him from conscripts or free laborers with whom he might work in the same area.[127] Different sets of clothes were issued for the deep of winter, and the weight of hemp padding to be used was standardized by law. The value of his clothes was also standardized, and it appears that a convict had to labor additional days to pay for his clothing rations if he could not provide his own.[128] His food was provided for by the state, and the amount of the ration was strictly regulated by law. Adult males were supposed to receive a maximum of 2/3 *dou* (1.33 liters) of millet per day (approximately 3,400 calories), a bit more if they were engaged in heavy labor. Women and children received proportionately less. If they misbehaved, the rations were cut in half to "starving" rations. There is no indication that they received any meat or vegetables.[129] A convict could be beaten by supervising officials for even the smallest infractions, but if the convict died as a result of the beating (within twenty days) officials had to pay a very large fine of 2 *jin* and 8 *liang* (approximately 620 g) of gold.[130] Since he was already a convict, any further infractions of the legal statutes, such as stealing, trying to escape, or striking a free man, warranted the death penalty.[131]

The wish of every convict laborer was for the emperor to proclaim a general amnesty. This occurred with surprising frequency during the Han period, usually when a new emperor ascended the throne or appointed his heir apparent but also after disastrous occasions like droughts or famine.[132] They were promulgated to proclaim not only the humaneness of the emperor but also his willingness to listen to the admonition of Heaven to lighten the burdens on the people, allowing them to "begin anew." It appears in the light of recently excavated texts that not all amnesties were created alike. A few released nearly all hard-labor convicts from the whole length of their sentences. Some only freed prisoners in a certain geographic area or working on a certain project.[133] Many were restricted to certain classes of convicts, and death-penalty cases were rarely included. Others appear to have only reduced the labor sentence by one or two degrees (e.g., five years to three, three years to one).[134] Even when a convict laborer's sentence was entirely commuted, he was not free to do as he pleased. He was allowed to take off his iron collar, fetters, and red clothes, but he was still required to finish out his sentence working for the state, often as a soldier in a frontier garrison.[135] His living conditions improved, and he was given the legal status of a commoner, but the mercy of an amnesty could not risk depriving the state of needed manpower. It appears that some convicts at Facility 3 of the Henan Iron Monopoly Office (the site of Tieshenggou) dreamed of amnesties. A number of pieces of pottery excavated from the site carry inscriptions hastily scratched into the fired clay. In many cases, these may have been the names of the owners of the pots. Some pieces were inscribed with auspicious slogans—magical incantations to bring about a better future. On one particularly poignant example, a man scrawled the words "*da-she*" on the rim of a vessel, which may have been a food container or chamber pot. His dream for the future is translated as "general amnesty."

Many convict laborers, however, would never live to see that dream realized. Death was more likely to signal their release from bondage. Malnutrition, infection from amputations, work accidents, and summary executions seem to have been common. Three graveyards of convict laborers dating to the Qin and Han periods were unearthed by archaeologists during the twentieth century. Their sheer size is staggering, and the casual, orderly, bureaucratic disposal of the bodies is chilling. The earliest of these convict graveyards was found about one and a half kilometers southwest of the tumulus of the First Emperor of Qin, famous for its magic army of terracotta figurines.[136] According to historical texts, a labor force of 700,000 convicts and slaves toiled to build the necropolis and nearby A-fang Palace of the First Emperor from

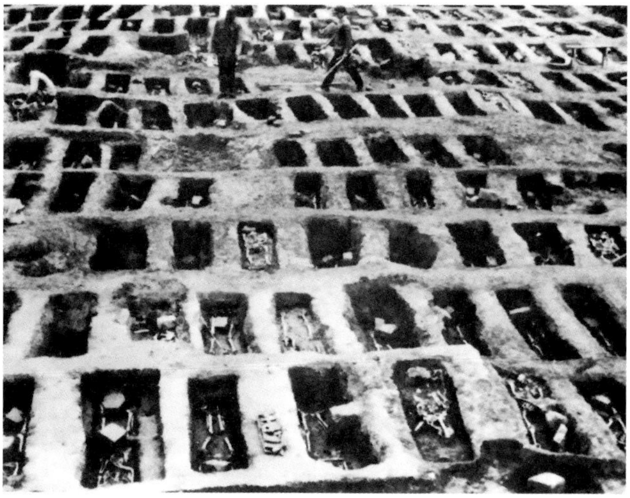

6.4 *Convict laborer graves near Luoyang, Henan.* Latter Han period, ca. 86–170 CE. From Zhongguo Kexueyuan Kaogu Yanjiusuo Luoyang Gongzuodui, pl. 4.

around 221 BCE until they were amnestied in 209 BCE to form an emergency army to defend the Qin from rebel assault.[137] Another large cemetery was found next to the necropolis of Yangling, which belonged to Emperor Jing (r. 156–141 BCE) of the Han dynasty.[138] He was buried with an estimated 100,000 smaller terracotta figures, under a tomb mound that would have taken an estimated 300,000 man-days to heap up. The third graveyard was discovered two kilometers southwest of the Latter Han capital city of Luoyang and was in use from around 86 to 170 CE (see figure 6.4).[139] These cemeteries point to strong continuities in the brutal treatment of convict laborers over a period of more than four hundred years.

Each of the three cemetery sites was enormous and was probably used for several decades. Tomb construction usually began when an emperor ascended the throne and was often completed only after his death. The Qin cemetery is estimated to have originally covered nine hectares; the Yangling cemetery, eight hectares, with 10,000 bodies; and the Luoyang cemetery, five hectares, with 13,000 bodies tightly packed. Except in the case of the Yangling cemetery, the graves were usually dug in orderly rows, very close together. Individual graves were the most common, but sometimes anywhere from three to ten people were heaped into one pit. The bodies were usually not accompanied by any grave goods, and only in the Luoyang cemetery is there any indication of the use of wooden coffins.

The overwhelming majority of the skeletons in these cemeteries belong to adult males between twenty and forty years of age (98.2 percent for the Latter Han Luoyang cemetery, 95 percent for the Qin cemetery).[140] The remaining number belong to young women, adolescents, or, in rare cases, children and infants. This supports the view that female convicts must have labored mostly at less-lethal, indoor tasks like grain processing and textile production and not on these outdoor construction sites. The male skeletons sometimes show signs of wear on the thoracic vertebrae and some have healed bone fractures in the legs. It is unclear, however, if these injuries were from their time of incarceration or from their normal backbreaking work as peasants and artisans.

A detailed study of the skeletons from the Luoyang cemetery has revealed that at least 7 percent of the adult males died from sudden, sharp-force or blunt-force trauma, almost always to the skull.[141] These injuries could have come from workplace accidents, fighting, or riot suppression. Since only those injuries which affected the bones are evident to us today, it is unclear how many men died of soft-tissue trauma (stabbing, throat cutting, etc.). A certain number of the laborers appear to have been summarily executed for postincarceration infractions: sometimes a skull is found a few feet from the body, and in other cases, a body appears to have been cut in two or to have been quartered by chariots.

Disease was probably the most common cause of death, for we hear complaints of inordinate numbers of convicts dying from disease during the Latter Han, leading Emperor Huan (r. 146–68 CE) to issue an edict in 149 CE allowing convicts some medical attention while in the camps and a proper burial after death (meaning they were given a coffin).[142] The jawbones and teeth of the skeletons from the Luoyang cemetery show a high frequency of advanced periodontal disease, deep cavities, and dental abscesses, probably brought on by malnutrition and physical stress.[143]

How do we know these bodies represent convicts and not just poor peasants or slaves? Confirmation of their convict status comes from two sources. First, many of the skeletons, especially from the Yangling site, still wear the iron collars and leg fetters stipulated in their punishment. The Yangling iron collars were particularly brutal. They weighed between 1,150 and 1,600 grams and had a sharp extension, the legal term for which was *chi* (fin), that projected downward 30 centimeters and would have made it impossible for the convict to lean over without impaling himself (see figure 6.2b). Other skeletons are missing the lower portion of a leg, indicating the punishment of foot amputation.

The second piece of evidence is even more explicit and in some ways more chilling. Many of the Qin skeletons were accompanied by a bureaucratically composed epitaph, which was scratched onto one or two broken pieces of brick and tossed on top of the corpse (see table 6.3). The Luoyang graves often included two epitaphs. One was originally placed inside the coffin on top of the deceased, while the other may have lain in the empty grave to reserve his place. These texts usually mentioned the name and native place of the deceased but in their fullest form might also mention his former work unit, his punishment, the jail he was transferred from, whether or not he had any rank or a guarantor for his conduct, and his date of death (see table 6.3). In the case of the Luoyang cemetery epitaphs, all this was capped by the sentence "[His] corpse is buried just under this" (*shi zai ci xia*).

Sun Ji draws on this disturbing phrase and other evidence to argue that these graves were intended only as temporary resting places.[144] He theorizes, based on the fact that some graves were later emptied and reused, that the government placed the markers in the graves and recorded the location so that family members could be

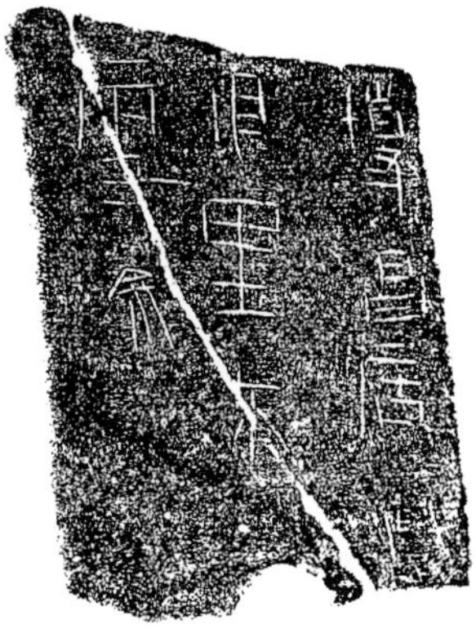

(a)

(a) Qin period, ca. 210 BCE.
Ink-on-paper rubbing of ceramic brick.
Museum of the Qin Emperor's Terracotta Warriors and Horses, Lintong County, Shaanxi.
From Shihuangling Qin Yongkeng Kaogu Fajuedui, ed., "Qin Shihuang ling xice Zhaobeihu cun Qin xingtu mu," *Wenwu* (1982.3): p. 8, fig. 34.
Excavated from the Qin cemetery at Zhaobeihucun, Shaanxi.

Transcription and translation:
博昌，居此（貲），用里，不更，余。
[Forced-laborer named] Yu, ranked Bugeng, from Yong Village, Bochang County [present-day Shandong], working off his unpaid fines

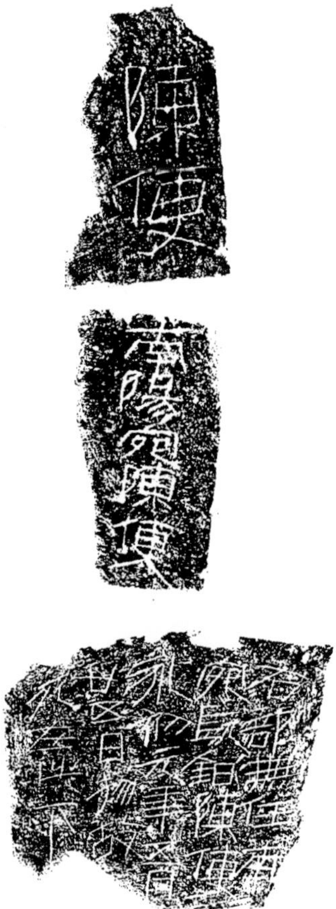

(b)

(b) Latter Han period, dated July 3, 107 CE.
Ink-on-paper rubbing of ceramic brick.
From Zhongguo Kexueyuan Kaogu Yanjiusuo Luoyang Gongzuodui, ed., "Dong-Han Luoyang cheng nanjiao de xingtu mudi," *Kaogu* (1972.4):
p. 6, figs. 5.1–3.
Excavated from the Latter Han cemetery at Xidajiaocun, Henan (grave T2M28).

Transcription and translation:
(Marker 1)
陳便 (on reverse)
Chen Bian
南陽，宛，陳便 (on obverse)
Chen Bian of Yuan County, Nanyang Commandery
(Marker 2)
右部，無任，南，宛，髡鉗，陳便，永初元年五月廿五日物故，死在此下。
Shaved and collared [five-year wall-dawn laborer] Chen Bian, from Yuan County of Nanyang Commandery, a worker without guarantor of the Right Work Section, died on the twenty-fifth day of the fifth month of the first year of the Yongchu era [July 3, 107 CE]. His corpse is located below this [marker].

notified and could retrieve the remains of their kin for proper reburial in their native place. One is reminded of the fields of mass graves found in Iraq in 2003, tagged with numbers and cross-referenced in some gruesome bureaucratic document of human disposal.

Judging by the names of the native counties inscribed in their epitaphs, it appears that the Qin and Han convicts were transported from the farthest reaches of the empire to work on the metropolitan palaces and tomb complexes. Most of the Qin workers came from the former kingdoms designated "East of the Pass," located in present-day Hebei, Henan, Shandong, and Jiangsu. The epitaphs from Luoyang point to an even wider geographic range for convict labor exploitation during the Latter Han. Though many of the laborers (37 percent) came from the commanderies of Yingchuan, Nanyang, and Runan, which were relatively close to Luoyang, the majority were drawn from thirty-six other commanderies, with one worker coming from as far away as present-day Vietnam. The majority of the deceased (56 percent) appear to have been five-year, collared, wall-dawn men (*chengdan*), who died during their first year of incarceration.[145]

What was the mortality rate in these labor camps? Apparently, it was quite high during the Latter Han. The scholar-official artist (and two-time convicted criminal) Cai Yong, whom we met in the previous chapter, claimed that when the court was building a pleasure garden west of Luoyang during 159 CE, "the convict laborers were freezing and starving. The number of those who did not survive to live out their fated years was very great."[146] Kong Rong (153–208 CE), another high official at the end of the Latter Han, claimed that in Luoyang, "among the convict laborers who built roads and bridges or who labored at miscellaneous tasks while incarcerated, ten died for each one that lived."[147] Although Kong's numbers were obviously exaggerated for rhetorical effect, they might have actually been quite close to the mark for such activities as deep-shaft mining.[148] However, we can actually arrive at a fairly close estimate of how many convict laborers died each day in Luoyang, since the bureaucrats at the capital labor camp buried the deceased in neat rows, interring bunches of corpses in chronological order every one to three days.

Thus, by sampling a few rows and dividing the number of graves by the span of days between the youngest and the oldest, we see that it appears that convict laborers died or were killed at a rate of approximately one to six people per day at a major imperial construction site (see table 6.4). This is corroborated by an extrapolation of the Yangling cemetery data in which an estimated ten thousand men died in the seven years (152–146 BCE) of Emperor Jing's tomb project (3.91 per day).[149] Apparently, since the pool of convict labor was constantly refilled, this was an acceptable mortality rate. Only once do we hear of an emperor bemoaning the fact that too many men were dying in the course of building his tomb.[150]

After that tour through the horrors of the Han penal labor system, we return now to the rebellion of Su Ling and his fellow convicts to search for three types of causes: proximate, regional, and systemic. For proximate causes, one need look no further

TABLE 6.4. RATE OF CONVICT LABORER DEATH IN LUOYANG CAMP

Location in Luoyang, Xidajiaocun Convict Cemetery	*Number of Excavated Graves in Row*	*Earliest and Latest Dated Grave (Not All Are Dated)*	*Number of Days in Interval*	*Average Number of Burials of Convicts per Day*
Long trench 2	78	永初元年四月廿日 (May 29, 107 CE) 永初元年七月十六日 (August 22, 107 CE)	86	0.91
Row 11, main trench	42	元初六年五月廿八日 (June 23, 119 CE) 元初六年六月五日 (July 29, 119 CE)	37	1.14
Row 10, main trench	36	元初六年八月廿六日 (October 17, 119 CE) 元初六年九月六日 (October 27, 119 CE)	11	3.27
Row 5, main trench	36	元初七年二月廿日 (April 5, 120 CE) 元初七年二月廿七日 (April 12, 120 CE)	8	4.50
Row 4, main trench	42	永寧元年五月十日 (June 23, 120 CE) 永寧元年五月十六日 (June 29, 120 CE)	7	6.00

than the brutal treatment of convict laborers during the Han and the harsh working conditions in mines and foundries outlined above and in chapter 3. Men who spend long days fashioning sharp tools and who do not fear death have already been given the means and the motivation for rebellion. It is probably no coincidence either that the rebellion took place in the dead of the North China winter, February 13 BCE. Though convicts were supposed to be given winter clothes and subsistence rations of food, suffering peasants and government conscripts were given first priority for such items.

Looking to regional triggers, it is clear that local conditions in the Shanyang area had been deteriorating for several decades. Shanyang Commandery was located in one of the most densely populated areas of Han China (on the Shandong Peninsula, near the course of the Yellow River), an area capable of tremendous agricultural production but also susceptible to droughts and floods that resulted in famines and bandit outbreaks. Since the time of Emperor Xuan (r. 74–49 BCE) until the moment of the rebellion, the Shanyang population had increased nearly 60 percent, straining the agricultural system.[151] A major break in the Yellow River dike system inundated nearly the entire lower course of the river in the autumn of 29 BCE and again two years later.[152] Subsequent floods ravaged the area in 23 and 17 BCE. The floods in 23 BCE were followed ten months later by a revolt of 180 convict laborers at an Iron Monopoly Office in Yingchuan Commandery.[153] The tremendous floods in 17 BCE, exacerbated by a botched dredging plan, struck primarily north and east of the Shanyang area, but the rising waters created a torrent of homeless vagrants searching for land and shelter.[154] These wandering mobs destabilized adjacent areas and compelled the government to give them tax relief or even relocate them to new land in other provinces.[155] All the disruptions may have triggered yet another serious rebellion, which broke out in a province neighboring Shanyang only twenty-one days before Su Ling's rebellion. In that incident, Fan Bing, the pupil of a famous scholar, murdered Zhuang Pu, the governor of Chenliu Commandery, and formed a rebel band.[156] It is reported that he was captured by a group of five convict laborers, who were subsequently made marquises.[157] The five could have been treacherous followers that Fan Bing had released from incarceration, or they could have been convicts released by the government specifically to apprehend the rebels. Such an expedient was common practice in Han China.[158] Perhaps, Su Ling and his men were also temporarily released from confinement to apprehend the Fan Bing rebels, only to mutiny for freedom themselves a couple weeks later.

Turning finally to systemic causes, it is apparent that extraordinary government corruption and imperial negligence had also put tremendous pressures on the fragile agrarian economy of China in the late Former Han period. The imperial bureaucratic state was founded on the premise of acceptable, moderate exploitation of the agrarian base, but the system was also prone to bouts of severe corruption and exploitation by local officials or imperial favorites. Emperor Cheng (r. 33–7 BCE) was not very interested in direct autocratic rule.[159] He spent much of the time late in his reign with the infamous Zhao sisters, who induced him to kill his only male heirs. He left the running of the empire mostly in the hands of his mother's family, the Wang clan. Five Wang men ran the country in succession during his reign, and according to critics, they garnished millions from imperial funds to live like kings. Sometimes, this favoritism had dangerous consequences, for in the course of yet another major rebellion of convict laborers in Guanghan Commandery in 17 BCE, suppression was delayed because the governor was an inexperienced weakling named Hu Shang, who just happened to be a nephew of the leader of the empire, Commander in Chief Wang Yin. Eventually, a newly appointed governor required thirty thousand government troops to put down the rebels, whose force had grown to ten thousand men.[160]

Local officials tried to remonstrate with the central government the only safe way they could, which was to report strange occurrences or portents that indicated warnings from Heaven that the earthly administration was amiss. Emperor Cheng received many of these warnings and often took them personally. It was reported that before the multiple rebellions broke out, a large boulder cried out in Tianshui Commandery (June 18 BCE), and strangely shaped, red atmospheric phenomena were spotted to the east and south of the capital (February to March 15 BCE).[161] These omens were interpreted as foreshadowing discontent among the populace and military strife.

But, enough of blame. Let us observe how Su Ling's rebellion unfolded to its end. When we last left our desperate convict laborers, they had risen up and killed their overseers, confiscated the weapons from the Shanyang arsenal (many of which they had probably cast themselves), and formed an armed band with Su Ling as their general. Their first move was apparently to go north into the Great Wild Marsh (Dayeze), which would have given them protection from government forces. They then crossed over the marsh into Dong Commandery, a sizable province along the course of the Yellow River, where they murdered the governor. This finally got the attention of the emperor and the rest of the central government. The state had been paralyzed by procedural issues, and apparently no one of sufficient rank was available or willing to investigate the matter. Finally, a magistrate of one of the capital counties was made Grand Master of Remonstrance (Jian Daifu) and given authority to investigate the extent of the revolt.[162] It was probably he who encouraged the emperor to send the Chief Aide of the Counselor in Chief (Chengxiang Zhangshi) and the Palace Aide to the Censor in Chief (Yushi Zhongcheng) to put down the revolt. The latter commanded the responsible Regional Inspectors (Cishi), who were supraprovincial authorities, and gave them the power to use military levies (*junxing*) and impose martial law to suppress the rebellion. By this time Su Ling and his band had created additional problems. Judging by reports of other bandit activity in the areas to the east of Shanyang around the same time, it appears that his brazen act encouraged others to take up arms against the state.[163]

Su Ling must have fared poorly against the newly raised government troops because he apparently left Dong Commandery and headed south. It was said that his army overran nineteen commanderies and princedoms of the empire, nearly one-fifth of the total number. Two other accounts make the improbable claim that the rebels overran forty commanderies and princedoms.[164] In the land just north of the Huai River, Su Ling made a foray into the sizable Runan Commandery (population 2,596,148) and killed the Defender (Duwei) in charge of Runan's military forces. He was not able to kill the governor, who was stationed ninety kilometers to the west. Moving ever westward, possibly toward the capital, he approached the border with Nanyang Commandery, a land full of angry peasants and oppressed convict iron-laborers like himself. It was here at the border that the government troops finally surrounded him. Sheriffs from Nanyang and the governor of Runan killed Su Ling, cut off his head, and rounded up his men.

The punishment of the surviving rebels was as swift and dramatic as the rewarding of their captors. The Han statutes were very clear that escaped convict laborers who kidnapped, pillaged, and killed were to be executed with one of the severest forms of the death penalty allowed by Han law, being quartered in the marketplace by chariots.[165] The government also encouraged rebels to turn each other in by offering turncoats commutation of this horrible sentence.[166] Occasionally, some elements of the rebel band would escape capture. For these, the government would issue an "all points bulletin" to every province of the empire, giving the names and physical descriptions of the men and offering rewards for capture.[167] There was no statute of limitations on such a heinous offense.

The men who eventually beheaded Su Ling and captured the bulk of his men were generously rewarded by Emperor Cheng. The *History of the Former Han* mentions that Zhuang Xin, the governor of Runan Commandery, who had directed the final capture of Su Ling, was elevated to the post of Chamberlain for the National Treasury (Dasinong), one of the highest positions in government. He was also given 100 *jin* of gold (equivalent to 24.5 kg).[168] Recently excavated documents from Yinwan allow us to uncover what happened to some of the lesser officials involved in the suppression.[169] A man surnamed Zhu was serving as clerk to the Regional Inspector of Yuzhou, one of the higher officials coordinating the suppression. Zhu was singled out for assisting in the capture of Su Ling himself and was made the new Vice Magistrate of Xiapi County, Donghai Commandery, a huge promotion of four levels in the bureaucracy. Zhang Chong and Ji Ji were both serving as local Neighborhood Heads (Tingzhang) in Nanyang Commandery, near where the rebels made their final stand. Their normal duties often involved the apprehension of criminals. Both were marked out for special distinction in the suppression and were promoted three levels to become County Defenders (Xianwei) of districts in Donghai Commandery. Several other men are mentioned in the Yinwan documents for having put down the smaller bandit uprisings in neighboring districts that were touched off by Su Ling's major rebellion. They were also given major promotions and increases in rank. The total number of officials rewarded after the suppression of Su Ling's rebellion is unclear since the Yinwan records inform us only about those men later transferred to Donghai, but the total may have been in the hundreds.

The Han system of convict labor, which was a continuation of the Qin system, was probably intended as a means of preventing rebellions, not instigating them. The jobs worked by the convict gangs were the most dangerous and backbreaking imaginable: mining, stoking blast furnaces, constructing cavernous imperial tombs and monumental city walls. If the state had exclusively employed regular conscripts in these jobs, farmer-citizens who were productive members of society, the harsh conditions and inevitable fatalities would have fostered great resentment in the general population. When convicts worked together with conscripts on large projects, such as on the walls of Han Chang'an, the conscripts went home after a month's work; the convicts did not. As we will see in the next section, government slaves were also a labor resource too skilled and too valuable to squander in hazardous mines and foundries. By utilizing convicts for the harshest jobs, the state thus hoped to stem popular resentment by working to death criminals who deserved to die anyway and who probably would have perished had it not been for the "mercy" of the emperor and his legal officials.

THE SLAVE ARTISAN

The wealth of the dynasty and state was based, both in revenue and labor, upon moderate exploitation of all the people rather than heavy exploitation of a minority.

C. MARTIN WILBUR, SLAVERY IN CHINA DURING THE FORMER HAN DYNASTY[170]

The final category of unfree labor to be treated in this chapter is the chattel slave (*nubei*), men and women owned by private citizens and by government offices. Having surveyed the dismal life and death of convict artisans during the Qin and Han, we have already, in a sense, seen the lowest extreme on our labor continuum in terms of working conditions and restricted movement. Though the slave artisan ranks at the bottom of our continuum in terms of freedom because he is *transferable property* and would probably never see freedom from bondage in his lifetime, his standard of living and freedom of movement were often superior to those of convicted-criminal laborers.

One would be hard-pressed to improve upon the comprehensive treatment of slavery in the Former Han period penned by C. Martin Wilbur in 1943.[171] The fruits of sixty years of modern archaeology in China have only served to bolster many of his arguments and flesh out additional details already predicted by him. However, one of his major conclusions does need to be altered somewhat at this time. What follows is a review of Wilbur's evidence, supplemented and emended by some recently discovered legal and artifactual material.

Male slaves during the Han were referred to as *nu*, whereas female slaves were called *bei*. Collectively, slaves were referred to by the compound term *nubei*. Slaves of all ages were also designated by the term *tong*, literally "youth" or "boy," with connotations not lost on the student of comparative slavery.[172] In Qin period legal texts and in some pre-Qin texts, male slaves are often called *chen*, while female slaves are called *qie*, words loaded with connotations of submission and sexual access.[173]

One could become a government-owned slave by several routes. The most common was enslavement as a family member of a convicted criminal.[174] The recently unearthed Han "Statute on Confiscation" (Shoulü) (ca. 186 BCE) states that those criminals convicted of a three-year hard-labor sentence or worse (see table 6.2), as well as those castrated for rape, would have their fields, residences, and other material property impounded by the government, along with their spouse and unmarried children.[175] This severe penalty grew out of the Chinese Legalist tradition of mutual responsibility for crimes. It acted not only to deter the potential criminal but also to reinforce the vigilance of family members mutually responsible for one another's conduct. In addition to this enslavement of the direct relations of criminals, the state also acquired numerous slaves formerly owned by convicted criminals, especially rich merchants guilty of tax evasion.[176] Children of government slaves were, of course, enslaved to the state from birth. It also appears from the textual sources that at least some of the thousands of non-ethnic-Han tribesmen captured in frontier battles were enslaved to the state.[177]

Enslavement to a private citizen followed slightly different paths. In times of economic distress, such as famine or civil war, heads of households would sell their children, their wives, and sometimes even themselves into slavery to survive. The practice was forbidden by the Han statutes and was penalized by tattooing and five years of hard labor (see table 6.2), though the practice was often overlooked and occasionally sanctioned by authorities.[178] Slave markets were also established that specialized in young foreign slaves captured in the areas of present-day Yunnan, Fujian, Vietnam, and other outlying regions.[179] Though it was a capital offense, slave traders were tempted to kidnap free ethnic-Han commoners right off the street and sell them as slaves.[180] The most common source of private-family slaves was probably from the wombs of other family slaves. Wilbur estimated that the total slave population probably numbered only 300,000–1,000,000 during the Former Han, or about 0.5–2 percent of the population.[181]

More than anything else, being a slave in early imperial China was a legal status. Slave status (*nubei*) was contrasted with commoner status (*shumin*). Slaves, of course, were property by definition, alienable for a contracted price. But this property aspect was complicated by the fact that they were also human beings, possibly former free citizens, and still contributing (and taxable) members of a constituted household in the empire. It also appears from some legal provisions that slaves were considered akin to subordinate members of the household, related in status to children or other family dependents.

A slave owner could beat his slave for insubordination, just as he could beat his own child or wife, but if the slave (or child) died within twenty days of the beating, the slave owner would be sentenced to "redeem" the death penalty, entailing a severe fine of 2 *jin* and 8 *liang* (approximately 620 g) of gold, equivalent to 25,000 copper coins.[182] A slave owner could not, however, wantonly execute a slave without first applying to local authorities for permission. Arbitrary murder of a slave was almost always a capital offense.[183]

Similar to later Chinese practice, and that of other slave-using cultures, slaves during the Qin and Han periods were often punished more severely than commoners accused of the same infraction.[184] For example, if a commoner struck another commoner of superior rank, he would be fined 4 *liang* (approximately 62 g) of gold, equivalent to 2,500 copper coins.[185] If a slave struck any commoner, he or she would be mutilated by being tattooed on the face and then returned to his or her owner.[186] Slaves had very few rights in court, for if any slave accused a member of his owner's household of a crime, his claim was ignored and he was executed in the marketplace for his trouble.[187] If he initiated baseless lawsuits against others, his left foot was cut off.[188]

The criminal punishment of slaves touches upon the conflict between the private property rights and legal jurisdiction of the household and the state's responsibility to prosecute crimes. If a slave committed a minor crime such as robbery, the state reserved the right to punish the infraction by tattooing the face of the slave but invariably returned him to his owner. If a slave committed a major crime, the state tried the slave and sentenced him to hard labor like any other convict. After the term was done, the slave was returned to the owner, if he survived his labor camp experience. If a slave killed someone, especially a member of the master's household, this canceled the private property rights of the household, and the state executed the slave. A slave who killed, or even only wounded, his owner was to be penalized with another of the harsher forms of the death sentence in Han law, public exposure of the severed head in the marketplace.[189] The same penalty was imposed on a child convicted of parricide.

The status of children resulting from the union of slave and commoner was another complicated matter involving overlapping property rights. The key factor seems to be whether the parties were engaged in illicit sex or were legally married. For example, if a commoner woman legally married a male slave and gave birth to a child, that child would have to be turned over to the male slave's owner because in the Chinese patrilineal system, the woman had legally married into the slave owner's "family."[190] However, if a commoner woman had *illicit* relations with a male slave, the resulting child would be free at birth and belong to the female commoner.[191] In a rare instance of mercy in the Han code, the law stated that if a slave committed a crime which normally would warrant confiscation of his commoner wife or children, they were not to be made slaves like himself.[192]

The state could manumit any or all government slaves by decree and instantly elevate their status to commoner, or even nobility.[193] On two occasions, slave women were elevated to become imperial consorts and, later, empresses.[194] Jin Midi, the captured son of a Xiongnu vassal king whom we met briefly in the last chapter, was enslaved as a horse groom in the imperial stables until he was freed by Emperor Wu and made a court gentleman. He subsequently rose to become one of the three most powerful ministers in the empire.[195] In 7 BCE, Emperor Ai freed slaves over fifty who were no longer of use to the state.[196] On two occasions, 160 BCE and 110 CE, emperors ordered the emancipation of every government-owned slave.[197]

The manumission of private slaves was a bit more complex. On a few occasions, the emperor ordered that people who had been sold into slavery or kidnapped by private individuals in times of crisis were to be freed immediately, though it is unclear if and how these edicts were enforced.[198] One text suggests that a slave could also purchase his freedom from his master.[199] If a slave owner wished to personally free one of his male or female slaves, the process was not so straightforward and could even be reversed. According to the Han statutes, if a slave owner so wished, he could *shenmian* (manumit) his slaves.[200] Female slaves could immediately be given *shuren* (commoner) status, but male slaves were to remain *sishu* (private retainers) of the master.[201] Both genders were still to be taxed by the government as slaves and employed in slave labor until the master's death. At that point, or when the master was convicted of a major crime, the male slaves would also be given commoner status and all were free to leave. At any point before his death, the master could change his mind and reenslave those whom he had previously manumitted. Thus, manumission while the owner was alive was provisional and removed only the legal status of "slave," with its harsher punishments, and not the bound labor of slavery. Since slaves were considered inheritable property of the entire household, the Han statutes also stipulated that only if a slave owner died without any official heirs would the family slaves *automatically* be made commoners upon his death.[202]

The living conditions of slaves varied considerably in early China. Some humble slaves lived miserable lives in poverty with their peasant owners, while a number of palace bond servants and slaves of wealthy men wore fine silks, rode armed on horseback, and even amassed great personal wealth. The life of a private slave often began in the slave market. Some polemical texts, actually some of the earliest documents in the world arguing for the abolition of slavery on moral grounds, decry the inhuman practice of selling slaves in the marketplace in the same pens used for horses and cattle.[203] One minister complained that, to attract buyers, slaves were sometimes dolled up in fine silk clothes before being put in the pens.[204]

The purchase of a slave required a written contract that stipulated the price and the duties a slave was to perform. This had to be approved (and taxed) by market officials.[205] Few statistics survive on prices, but it appears that during the Former Han period (206 BCE–8 CE), adolescent and older male slaves cost around 15,000 coins, whereas adult female slaves cost from 20,000 coins for a regular domestic slave to a reported 1,175,000 coins for a talented and beautiful one.[206] According to the inscription on an excavated stone that details the property value of several different households, the declared value of a male or female slave during the Latter Han (25–220 CE) period averaged 40,000 coins. Oxen were listed just after slaves in the same document, at 15,000 coins a head.[207]

It seems that most slaves were not physically restrained in any way, but there are references to some slaves wearing the same iron collars and fetters worn by hard labor convicts.[208] One can, to a certain degree, gauge the physical treatment of slaves by a curious absence. In all the annals of early imperial China, there is no record of any slave insurrection, of any size. Compare this to the enormous slave revolts (involving more than 100,000 slaves) in the Roman period in the West (ca. 135–70 BCE).[209] Yes, there are records of disobedient slaves who were disciplined by slave owners and government alike, but during the early empires in China, only the convict laborer was so ill treated, so cruelly worked, and so desperate as to stage serious rebellions.

One familiar with the institution of slavery in ancient Rome or in the antebellum American South might expect to find plentiful references in early China to slaves engaged in productive pursuits, either agricultural or industrial. But such references are rare indeed in Chinese texts, numbering fewer than a dozen brief passages. Most references to slave labor in Qin and Han period texts mention slaves engaged in domestic duties such as cleaning, cooking, mending, running errands, and tending animals. It is no wonder that these texts led Wilbur to characterize Han slavery as basically "domestic" in nature.[210] The scattered references to productive slaves were still compelling enough to suggest to him that something more was at work than he could see through the sources. Indeed, recently unearthed material and textual evidence does seem to contradict Wilbur's major conclusion and show that Han slaves were an important component of productive labor.

Let us first consider the few textual references and see how some slaves were used in artisan roles to make or decorate things for the state or for their private owners. Private production and state-sponsored production will be dealt with separately. For the use of slaves in private production, we are mostly screened from the actual situation by the bias of our sources. Workshops, both public and private, usually fly under the radar of the official historian, as was explained in chapter 1. All we can grasp at are one satirical literary treatment and two other scattered references.

The poet-official Wang Bao, who lived during the reign of Emperor Xuan (r. 74–49 BCE), once penned a mock slave contract called "The Contract for a Youth" (Tong yue), which comes across both as a comic satire and as an oblique criticism of slavery.[211] In the preamble to the contract (dated February 19, 59 BCE), the author is said to be visiting a widow on a business trip when he asks her deceased husband's male slave to fetch him some beer. When the slave refuses the request, the author offers to buy the recalcitrant slave from the widow. The parties agree to the price, but the slave, ironically named Bianliao (Conveniently Completed), insists that he will do no type of work unless it is specified in the contract. The author then proceeds to pen an extraordinarily long contract detailing every possible task a slave could ever perform. If fact, no one human being could ever accomplish all of the tasks Bianliao is contracted to perform. Though the treatment is comical and fictional, it does contain what appears to be an accurate depiction of what a domestic slave could do for a slave owner.

Much of what Bianliao is ordered to perform for the author would be expected of any hired farmhand or regular member of a peasant's family. He was expected to plant, weed, and harvest the crops, maintain the fields and facilities, guard the family, catch game, prepare meals, and serve guests. As for productive tasks, Bianliao is told he would be required to make brooms out of straw, carve wooden bowls, fashion bamboo rakes, weave shoes, tie fishing nets, carve dugout canoes for travel, cut wooden tablets and bamboo strips for writing, build retaining walls, erect huts, and hew lumber into cart shafts, sacrificial altars, benches, shoes, and feeding troughs. These are clearly artisan-related activities, but they are all for the domestic consumption of the owner's household. A few additional activities are listed as production for the market. Bianliao is told he will have to card hemp to trade in small roadside markets and fashion numerous knives and bows to exchange with the tribesmen in Yunnan for oxen and sheep. Thus, it appears that, for the minor slaveholder with only a few slaves, a private slave was merely a productive extension of his own household labor and marketing force. If the slave was clever at a craft, he could perhaps garner some additional cash for the family by selling his wares at market.

A much larger scale cottage industry was operated by a powerful minister living in the early part of the first century BCE. Zhang Anshi (d. 62 BCE) was the son of the infamous Chamberlain for Law Enforcement, Zhang Tang, who enforced the cruel letter of the law under Emperor Wu. Anshi was recommended to become an official because of his father's fame but soon rose through the ranks on his own merit. He held high government positions during the reigns of Emperor Zhao and Emperor Xuan and rivaled the regent Huo Guang in power and riches. His image was painted on the famous Unicorn Hall mural. His biography includes the following curious notice:

> Zhang Anshi was honored with a nobility and received the income from ten thousand households, yet he dressed himself in thick, black silk and his wife personally spun and wove fabric. All of his seven hundred household slaves had handicraft skills (*shouji*) and engaged in production. He supervised the production of goods within his household and saved up even the smallest things. Thus, he was able to multiply his capital. He was richer than General in Chief Huo Guang.[212]

The passage does not say what products Zhang Anshi's seven hundred slaves were making, but apparently they were profitable enough to make him richer than the most powerful man in the empire (Huo Guang).[213] Officials were not usually allowed to be merchants, so Zhang presumably marketed his products through middlemen to avoid being tainted with the stigma of selling things. Roman patricians frequently used business managers (who were often themselves slaves) to accomplish the same deception.[214]

Before the monopoly went into place shortly after 119 BCE, the form of private production that lent itself most readily to the mass exploitation of slave labor was the mining and smelting of iron. Several men who profited greatly in this enterprise are listed in the "Biographies of the Capital Accumulators" of the *Historical Records* and the *History of the Former Han*.[215] For instance, both texts record that:

> In Shu, the Zhuo family's ancestors were natives of Zhao. They were rich from iron smelting. When Qin defeated Zhao [228 BCE], [Qin] deported the Zhuo family to Shu. The husband and wife traveled along, pulling the cart together. [When the party was going toward the deportation place] all the deported captives who had a little extra wealth competed in begging the officials for a nearer place. These were placed at Jiameng. Only Mr. Zhuo said: "This land is restricted and poor. I have heard that below Min Mountain there are 'tubers'[216] under the rich soil, so that during a whole lifetime there will be no starving. The people engage in craft production and buy and trade in the marketplaces." Thereupon,

> he requested to be deported further, arrived at Linqiong, and was greatly delighted. He went to Iron Mountain (Tieshan), smelted and cast, manipulated the counting sticks, and traded with the peoples of Dian and Shu. He became rich to the extent of [possessing] eight hundred youths [or one thousand][217] and the pleasures of fields, ponds, and hunting [preserves] comparable to those of the rulers of men.[218]

Though the passage does not say specifically that Mr. Zhuo used his 800–1,000 slaves in his iron mines and foundries, Wilbur found it very doubtful that a major industrialist would own so many slaves without using them in his business.[219] Whereas the government had access to every source of free and unfree labor and could choose judiciously among them for each project and circumstance, private industrialists could not *convict* or *conscript* and thus were limited to using either wage labor, long-term indentures, or chattel slaves. It seems clear from this account that at least during the third to early second centuries BCE, private industrialists used slaves for those tasks in which the government would normally use convicts or a mixture of convicts and conscripts, activities such as iron mining and smelting. This must have reflected a perceived cost analysis on the part of the slave-owning industrialist. To Mr. Zhuo, buying and maintaining 800–1,000 slaves must have seemed more cost effective at the time than hiring the equivalent number of wage laborers, even though wage labor may have been more flexible.

This calculus apparently changed during and after the reign of Emperor Wu (r. 141–87 BCE). Seeking to refill the empty state treasury, Emperor Wu and his advisers devised several schemes to drain the wealth of rich industrialists and merchants. One scheme was to double the poll tax on slaves until it was twice the customary amount for other members of the family, amounting to as much as 380 coins per year per slave.[220] Merchants also had to pay this double poll tax. Emperor Wu further increased the burden of slave-owning industrialists and merchants by devising a new property and capital tax (*suanzi* or *suan minqian*), in which each person had to pay a percentage of all his capital wealth, including slaves (see chapter 4). If he failed to report his true net worth, all of his property would be confiscated by the state. As Lao Gan (b. 1907) noted, it is probably no coincidence that most of the references to wealthy industrialists employing large groups of slaves date to before the reign of Emperor Wu.[221] After that time, it appears the economic balance had shifted, and wage labor began to predominate in the industrial sector. The reason seems purely economic. Though long-term slaves could amass valuable skills on the job, they were now more expensive to buy and maintain, had to be supported well beyond their productive years, and could cause trouble. Wage labor was more flexible. The number of employees could be increased or downsized at will. The wage labor pool had also grown quickly in the first century BCE. General population growth and the increasing number of landless peasants swelled the labor force, thus lowering labor prices.

Despite the presence of slaves like Bianliao working down on the farm, Wilbur still resisted the idea that Han slaves were important to agricultural production. In addition to the lack of textual references, he viewed Han farming techniques as primitive, most suitable to cultivation of small plots by tenant farmers. However, during the 1970s a series of tombs belonging to lower-level officials were unearthed in Hubei, near the hill known as Fenghuangshan.[222] The tombs were provided with dozens of painted, wooden figurines meant to serve the tomb master in the afterlife. Accompanying the burials were inventories, recorded on bamboo strips, that listed each figurine, the named person it was supposed to represent, and that person's duty. Nearly all of the figurines represent slaves. Judging by the duties described in the inventories and on the hoes and spades held by the figurines, it appears that magistrate-level officials might have owned about forty to fifty slaves and that 25–43 percent of these were engaged in agricultural production.[223] Of this group, female slaves were the majority of the field laborers while men served as herders, stable hands, and field foremen. Clearly, slaves were a more important source of agricultural labor than Wilbur realized. For artisan production, the man buried in tomb M8 at Fenghuangshan employed just one slave/figurine in his household to *zuozao* (make things). Since this piece has never been published, perhaps we can picture this craftsman from his given name; he was called Xiong (Bear).[224]

Turning now to the use of government slaves, it appears that nearly every bureau in the Han government employed some slaves for messenger services, clerical work, or domestic duties. They were part of the physical property of the bureau, not owned by individual officials, and could even be sold as surplus to private citizens. But what about the vast and complex Han factory system? Did they employ slaves as well? The Qin and Han empires both operated more than one hundred individual factories, located in the capital and in the provinces, to produce weapons, tools, and luxury items for the state. These factories kept meticulous records of production and inscribed nearly every article with the names of the artisans employed to make the piece. Thousands of inscribed examples of this work survive thanks to the excavations of archaeologists. On some of the pieces from the Qin period, convict laborers are named alongside free artisans, but no surviving Qin or Han imperially produced object that I am aware of ever mentions a slave as the fabricator. Furthermore, according to all the official records of imperial tomb and palace construction, only the First Emperor of Qin seems to have employed slaves as a significant part of the workforce.

In a notorious example, and apparently an exception to normal legal practice, Wang Mang (r. 9–23 CE) enslaved tens of thousands of families implicated in counterfeiting coins. The men were loaded into cage carts, and the women and children wore iron collars and walked to the capital. Once they arrived, their jailors separated the families and gave them the ironic punishment of casting coins in the official government mint.[225] It was said that 60–70 percent died at this task. According to the remarks of Gong Yu quoted earlier (ca. 44 BCE), normally only conscripts and convicts worked in the mints. Such treatment of slaves, especially women and children, shocked the Han historian Ban Gu, whose comments drip with indignation at such inhumane treatment. Those government mint slaves who were still alive in 31 CE were freed by the first emperor of the Latter Han.[226]

One passage that might help us to understand the normal role of slaves within the Qin and Han factory system involves a technocrat named Zhao Guo. Around 87 BCE, Zhao Guo was named by Emperor Wu to be Commandant in Chief for Foraging (Sousu Duwei), a commission chartered to increase agricultural yields for the army. His great innovation was a perfected system of plowing, seeding, and fallowing called the *daitian fa* (alternating field system). Those who used his system diligently were said to have greatly increased their yields.[227] Part of the system incorporated a new plow design, accompanied by an automatic seeder.[228] Since only the government could cast iron agricultural tools under the iron monopoly, the Chamberlain for the National Treasury (Dasinong) established workshops to mass produce Zhao Guo's new tools for government use and sale to the public. These workshops were probably under the auspices of the Iron Monopoly Offices described above. At this point, the historian says that "skilled slaves along with minor officers made the farming implements." The key word here is *qiao*, which as I noted in chapter 2 could be translated "crafty," "clever," or "skilled." These *qiao* slaves were not unskilled laborers sent by the Chamberlain for the National Treasury to the iron foundries to stoke the furnaces or pump the bellows like convicts. They were actually going to *weizuo* (make) the new plowshares for Zhao Guo's innovative system. What I think this actually involved was that the experienced male slaves would design the intricate casting molds used in the production process. These men were sent by the parent organization of the Iron Monopoly Offices in the capacity of technical consultants to show the resident artisans how to retool the assembly line. This was a skilled position and a high-status assignment. Slaves of lower status may have populated the halls and kitchens of the imperial factories, providing logistical support to the artisans and officials, but we will probably never hear of them. A parallel practice can be seen in the Roman relief-pottery workshops of Arretium, in which experienced slaves created the master molds for the ware while lesser-skilled free craftsmen actually mass-produced the final product. As William Westermann argued, only slaves could provide the "continuity of employment" that maintained high standards of quality.[229]

THE ECONOMICS OF FREE AND UNFREE ARTISAN LABOR IN THE EARLY EMPIRES

During the early empires of China, the state had access to several pools of free and unfree labor to construct and manufacture things. These groups are enumerated in the *History of the Former Han* in a passage concerning imperial tomb construction as *zu, tu, gong, yong* 卒, 徒, 工, 庸 (conscripts, convicts, government artisans, and hired labor).[230] In this chapter, I have argued that high-level officials in charge of public-works projects in early China used a cost-benefit analysis when determining the number, season, work duration, and assigned tasks for these different labor pools. As a way of summarizing, let us reconstruct this economic thinking by envisioning a hypothetical construction project, Palace X, to be located just outside the capital.

To begin with, the work of preparing the foundation and the surrounding defense walls and moat will require large gangs of unskilled labor to move the earth and ram it into wooden forms. For this task, one would conscript about 100,000 unskilled peasants from the surrounding countryside for one month's labor. One could schedule this in the first month of spring, before the planting, possibly in midsummer, or in late fall after the harvest. The direct costs associated with this labor pool would include mainly food and temporary shelter. The indirect costs are more significant. One will not be able to conscript these men (and possibly women) for any other task, including tax-grain transport or local infrastructure repair, during this calendar year. When these jobs need to be done, replacements will have to be hired at two thousand coins per head, possibly resulting in 200 million coins in eventual outlay. Not having these ten myriads of men down on the farm for one month might also endanger the agricultural production of their region (and thus the tax base) or the stability of their nuclear families.

Once these peasants are released from service, one could bring in a large number of hard-labor convicts to continue the work year-round, until it is completed. One should only bring in about ten to twenty thousand of these men, since they will need to be guarded continually and kept in order. This group might work longer hours than the peasants but will be required to move about the same quota of earth. They can also perform dangerous work high in the air, deep underground, or near molten metal. The direct cost of acquiring this labor pool is negligible, involving their transportation from various regional jails, but their upkeep on site includes a subsistence level of food and appropriate clothing for the season. They will probably die at the rate of one to six men per day and will need to be replenished until the project is done. The indirect cost of convict labor is less tangible but more persistent. Once a man has been convicted and his family enslaved to the state, an entire productive household has been removed from the tax registers and the agricultural base. The minister Gong Yu recognized this pathology, but few emperors concurred with his opinion.

After the foundation and walls are complete, the Chamberlain for the Palace Buildings, who is a high-level public official, and the Court Architect, who is a professional artisan by necessity, would need to bring in professional carpenters, woodcarvers, metalsmiths, jade carvers, painters, and other artisans to erect the palace buildings and decorate them in lavish style. Some of these would be drawn from the permanent staff of court workshops like the Shangfang and the Yellow Gate that we encountered in the last chapter. A large number would probably be medium-skilled men and women conscripted from the ranks of the registered artisans of the empire. The direct cost of this group includes food, clothing, and housing, and possibly further remuneration in the form of monetary rewards for service. The indirect costs of the conscripted artisans stem from the labor exemption given to other members of their households. Perhaps two or three substitutes will need to be hired in their home county for each artisan employed by the state. Thus, two thousand conscripted artisans might indirectly cost the state eight to twelve million coins per year. A smaller group working on the project will consist of highly skilled master artisans hired directly by the Court Architect for the palace project. These men of great local reputation will be very well treated and paid according to their skills. They will probably also bring their apprentices and customary work crews. One or two palace master artisans, men like Ding Huan, whom we met in chapter 5, might also be used on the project to cast elaborate gilded-bronze lamps or to paint murals depicting great men of the past. They are *daizhao* artisans, at the beck and call of the emperor and fully supported by the state. Their materials probably cost more to acquire than their direct services, for their payments were more informal, in the guise of special rewards for a job well done and the prospect of future private commissions based on their enhanced reputations.

The last, and possibly least significant, labor pool that might work on this project is government slaves. Too valuable to waste on backbreaking foundation work or dangerous metal casting, a few senior members of this "pampered" group might have worked among the artisans, drawing on their experience from helping to build the last great palace. A larger number of government slaves would assist in logistical support for the project, male slaves to serve as couriers and clerks, female palace slaves to serve as cooks and maids.

The cost of each labor group would be weighted and combined to arrive at a grand total of person-days needed for the project. The standard quotas for each group were strictly codified in writing: a certain amount of work expected in spring as opposed to winter; one woman can embroider as much as one man; a free artisan can accomplish as much as four convict artisans on skilled tasks. We know from legal texts that all this was ideally taken into account. If the project went over budget, those responsible for these calculations were heavily fined.

As an imperial bureaucratic state, the early Chinese empire was ruled, not by autocrats waving royal scepters or by scholars brandishing moralizing texts, but by brush-pushing functionaries wielding information. Their databases consisted mostly of names attached to numbers: household registers, size and quality of land holdings, number of adult males liable for service, number of homeless migrants, etc. From this mountain of information, mind-boggling in its size and complexity for a precomputer age, grew the power to control the known world. In this light, the Han truly succeeded the Qin Empire in 207 BCE, not when the Han founder, Liu Bang, entered the Land within the Passes and accepted the surrender of the last Qin king, Ziying, nor when he finally killed his rival Xiang Yu at Gaixia, but when his future Counselor in Chief, Xiao He, entered the imperial archives of Qin and seized the law code, maps, and population registers of the Qin Empire.

EPILOGUE

If the original purpose of this book has been even partially achieved, you will never look at objects of early Chinese material culture housed in museums quite the same way again. What I urge is that, after you appreciate the formal and aesthetic qualities of an object, look beyond the *material* to see the very human *culture* that created it.

When you see a late Warring States or Han period lacquer vessel, after you appreciate the perfect bands and the swirling arabesques in red, hopefully you will think of Woman Ao and the mostly female work crews in the Xianyang lacquer workshops, deploying their highly efficient modular painting styles. Perhaps, you will then think of Mother Yi at the Western Workshop of Shu, working her way up the seniority ladder to the position of scribe, only to reach the "lacquer ceiling."

When you encounter a rubbing from a Han funerary monument, after your eyes have been intrigued by the iconography of gods and filial paragons, think of masons like Wang Shu, who worked on An Guo's funerary monument, or Bai Zhong, who was conscripted to work on the tombs of the Princes of Zhongshan and Rencheng, or Shi Juyi, who carved lavish monuments for an insignificant clerk near Beijing. Picture them sweating in their loincloths, wielding hammer and chisel, and perhaps thinking with each deafening crash of their hammers that they were akin to the servants of the Thunder God. Conjure up an image of Master Draftsman Dai Sheng, manipulating his stencils and pattern books to create seemingly original compositions, all with lightning speed.

When you come across an inscribed Han bronze mirror, pass quickly over the enigmatic geometric patterns (called TLV patterns by art historians) and instead envision the bustling markets of Chang'an, where artisans struggled to make a living despite government exactions, and merchants and customers filled the streets, sending up a deafening roar of unabashed commerce. Imagine the mirror peddlers on a hypothetical Bronze Mirror Lane, their hawkers promising you everything in this world, in the afterlife, and a good mirror to boot.

When you see an intricate Ordos-style bronze plaque, with its themes of animal combat, after you have paused to appreciate the energy and tension in the composition, think of Bronze Caster Cang, working in the area of the Qin capital of Xianyang, tailoring his products to suit the needs of both his Chinese clients, who wore silken caps and robes and lived in cities, and his Xiongnu clients, who wore felt and furs and roamed on horses with their flocks in the lands beyond the Great Wall.

When you hear of an ingenious early Chinese invention, perhaps invented hundreds of years before a similar device in the West, think of the great polymath Zhang Heng, whose devotion to empirical observation and to the perfection of instruments like his seismograph and armillary sphere hampered the advancement of his official career. Or perhaps you might think of the semilegendary craftsman Ding Huan, who applied physical and mechanical principles in unique ways to create moving fans, animated figurines, and self-leveling incense burners.

When you encounter a transcendent example of Chinese calligraphy that is preserved in the form of a rubbing taken from a stone stele, after you appreciate the grace and drama of the thickening and thinning strokes and have gained some insight into the nature of the master calligrapher's personality, think of Stone Carver Chen Xing, who was commissioned to carve the brush calligraphy of the illustrious scholar Cai Yong and his colleagues deeply and faithfully into stone.

If you ever have the opportunity to see a Han iron tool or agricultural implement in a museum, hopefully you will not now just dismiss it as a homely or inefficient relic of peasant life. Think instead of Su Ling and his thousands of convict brethren, toiling and dying in the satanic iron mills of the Han Empire, awaiting their opportunity to fight for their freedom.

It has not been a simple task to extract information from stubborn and biased sources in an effort to revive knowledge of an occupational class that was denigrated during its own day and forgotten when time passed it by. A few decades ago, before the recent finds of modern archaeology, the scanty available data had led scholars in the early China field to despair of ever being able to reconstruct a social history of artisans. While it is true that my harvest was not overly abundant, I hope that I have at least reclaimed some land in a new field and opened the way for future inquiries.

Since the ground of China is very fertile with undiscovered archaeological remains, I remain optimistic that more information about artisans from the early imperial period will continue to be unearthed and that, someday, scholars will produce an even more vivid and textured account of the lives of the women and men who truly "made" China.

NOTES

CHAPTER 1

1. Arthur Cotterell, *The First Emperor of China* (London: Macmillan, 1981), 28.

2. Lothar Ledderose, *Ten Thousand Things: Module and Mass Production in Chinese Art* (Princeton: Princeton University Press, 2000), chap. 3.

3. Yuan Zhongyi, *Qin bingmayong keng* (Beijing: Wenwu Chubanshe, 2003), 140–7; Ledderose, *Ten Thousand Things*, 70–4.

4. Ledderose, *Ten Thousand Things*, 72.

5. Ladislav Kesner, "Likeness of No One: (Re)presenting the First Emperor's Army," *Art Bulletin* 77, no. 1 (Mar. 1995): 120.

6. Ledderose, *Ten Thousand Things*, 72.

7. Qin Shihuang Ling Kaogudui, ed., "Qin Shihuang lingyuan K1006 peizangkeng diyi ci fajue jianbao," *Wenwu* (2002.3): 4–31.

8. Shaanxi Sheng Kaogu Yanjiusuo and Qin Shihuang Bingmayong Bowuguan, eds., *Qin Shi Huangdi lingyuan kaogu baogao 1999* (Beijing: Kexue Chubanshe, 2000), 166–99.

9. See Peter Hessler, "Rising to Life: Treasures of Ancient China," *National Geographic* 200, no. 4 (Oct. 2001): 52–5. James C. Y. Watt, in "Form and Space in Chinese Art" (public lecture at the Frick Art Museum, Pittsburgh, PA, May 8, 2005), suggested that the strongman

figure and the other entertainers were made by artisans from Central Asia working at the court of Qin Shihuang. Immigrant artisans are mentioned in later legends, such as those contained in the *Shiyi ji*. But these terracotta figures were made by a process similar to that used to construct the regimented army figures. At least one entertainer figure carries the name of the master potter who constructed it, and this name seems entirely Han Chinese. The extreme difference in style between the army figures and the entertainers can be plausibly explained without positing foreign assistance. Certainly, Qin artisans were capable of producing works of extreme naturalism, when the commission called for such a production. The recently unearthed life-size bronze cranes from the Mount Li necropolis are an excellent example. The rigid poses, generic appearance, and lack of unified vision of the human form among the terracotta army might simply be due to the fact that thousands of figures had to be constructed in a brief period of time, leading to modular techniques and a finer-than-usual division of labor among the craftsmen making the various body parts. The inclusion of water-pipe and tile makers on the work crew would not have been conducive to naturalism either. In contrast, it seems that each entertainer figure was a unique creation, or at least one of only a pair, and a single master potter may have fashioned one entire figure, giving him the opportunity to imbue his creation with more naturalism. Thus, each piece was a coherent human form. The difference in style may also have had something to do with the subject matter, as suggested to me by Katheryn Linduff. An imperial guard of clothed, ethnic-Han soldiers should look rigid and impassive, whereas nearly naked entertainers, most of whom were foreigners or men from border regions, called for a different artistic approach in order to convey their exotic nature.

10. Rubbings and transcriptions of the inscribed texts and stamps can be found in Shaanxi Sheng Kaogu Yanjiusuo and Shihuangling Qin Yongkeng Kaogu Fajuedui, eds., *Qin Shihuangling bingmayong keng: Yi hao keng fajue baogao 1974–1984* (Beijing: Wenwu Chubanshe, 1988), 1:194–207, 433–43. The analysis given here follows the interpretation of Yuan Zhongyi, "Qin ling bingmayong de zuozhe," *Wenbo* (1986.4): 52–62; Yuan Zhongyi, *Qin bingmayong keng*, 169–73.

11. Ledderose, *Ten Thousand Things*, 69.

12. For a table of these names, see Shaanxi Sheng Kaogu Yanjiusuo and Shihuangling Qin Yongkeng Kaogu Fajuedui, eds., *Qin Shihuangling bingmayong keng*, 1:203. We know that these names indicate artisans and not bureaucrats or some other noncraftsmen because occasionally a person will affix the word *gong* (artisan) in front of his or her name instead of the usual place-name.

13. The technical details of the candlestick can be found in the final excavation report, Zhongguo Shehui Kexueyuan Kaogu Yanjiusuo and Hebei Sheng Wenwu Guanlichu, eds., *Mancheng Han mu fajue baogao* (Beijing: Wenwu Chubanshe, 1980), 2:255–61.

14. Wen Fong, ed., *The Great Bronze Age of China: An Exhibition from the People's Republic of China* (New York: Metropolitan Museum of Art, 1980), no. 94.

15. Yang Xiaoneng, ed., *The Golden Age of Chinese Archaeology: Celebrated Discoveries from the People's Republic of China* (Washington, DC: National Gallery of Art, 1999), no. 137, quotation from 408.

16. *China Pictorial*, vol. 643, English ed., Jan. 2002, back cover.

17. The first school of thought holds that the Yangxin bronzes originally belonged to the household of Liu Jie, who was named the Yangxin Yi Marquis (Yangxin Yi Hou) in 179 BCE. His son succeeded to his fief in 165 BCE, but the marquisate was abolished in 151 BCE. The

argument goes that all their bronzes were confiscated by the emperor and apportioned to various palaces and imperial relatives. The original Mancheng report argues this view. See also Qin Jincai, "Han 'Yangxin Jia' tongqi de zuichu suoyouzhe wenti," *Kaogu yu wenwu* (1987.3): 84–6. The second school of thought (as followed here) believes that the Yangxin name indicates the Elder Yangxin Princess, eldest daughter of Emperor Jing. See Yuan Anzhi, "Tan 'Yangxin Jia' tongqi," *Wenwu* (1982.9): 18–20; Feng Zhou, "Zailun Han Maoling 'Yangxin Jia' tongqi suoyouzhe de wenti," *Kaogu yu wenwu* (1989.6): 86–9; Li Xueqin, "Handai qingtongqi de jige wenti-Mancheng, Maoling suochu jinwen de fenxi," *Wenwu yanjiu* 2 (1986): 101–5. The entire bibliography of the debate is summed up in Zhao Huacheng and Gao Chongwen, *Qin-Han kaogu* (Beijing: Wenwu Chubanshe, 2002), 164.

18. See Chen Zhi, ed., *Sanfu huangtu jiaozheng* (Xi'an: Shaanxi Renmin Chubanshe, 1980), 53. The Palace of Lasting Trust was located within the Palace of Lasting Joy (Changle Gong), one of the two main palace complexes within Han Chang'an. The post of Controller of the Imperial Bath of the Palace of Lasting Trust (Changxin Shangyu) is also seen in a list of official posts found at Zhangjiashan, where it holds a rank of 600 *shi*. See Zhangjiashan 247 Hao Mu Zhujian Zhengli Xiaozu, ed., *Zhangjiashan Han mu zhujian* (Beijing: Wenwu Chubanshe, 2001), 197 ("Ernian lüling," slip no. 462) (hereafter abbreviated *ZJS*). A related post existed already during the Qin. See the appropriate entries in Zhou Xiaolu and Lu Dongzhi, *Qin fengni ji* (Xi'an: San Qin Chubanshe, 2000).

19. Yuan Anzhi argues that Emperor Wu gave these articles to the Elder Yangxin Princess, who was his elder sister, in 136 BCE, in gratitude for helping him meet his future consort Wei Zifu. Thus, he takes the "seventh year" to indicate the seventh year of Emperor Wu's reign, not Emperor Jing's.

20. Lai Guolong, "Lighting the Way in the Afterlife: Bronze Lamps in Warring States Tombs," *Orientations*, Apr. 2002, 20–8.

21. This serial number is located on the upper candlestick support, a rather generic part. It may have indicated that this particular component was number 189 in a particular production run or that it was number 189 in a particular storage inventory. The other serial number is inscribed on the lower candlestick support and declares "number one" (*di yi*). This is a distinctive part, fitted into the hand of the figure, and this inscription also mentions the weight of the entire lamp. Thus, this serial number probably concerns the lamp as a whole. The fact that it is designated as number 1 suggests that more examples exist of this specific category or type of lamp.

22. Ban Gu, *Hanshu buzhu*, ed. Wang Xianqian (1900; repr., Taibei: Yiwen Yinshuguan, 1955), 24B:21a (hereafter abbreviated *HSBZ*); Ban Gu, *Hanshu* (Beijing: Zhonghua Shuju, 1962), 24B.1177 (hereafter abbreviated *HS*). The actual numbers listed in the text are "more than 28,000,000,000 five-*zhu* coins produced from 118 BCE to 1–5 CE," starting from when that denomination was first cast until Wang Mang began to alter the currency system. This is the most conservative interpretation of the passage. Certain ambiguities in the notation used to indicate large numbers in this text have led some scholars to an interpretation of 280 billion coins for this period (enlarged by a factor of ten) or even 280 trillion coins, an impossible number. The estimate of 600,000 coins per day assumes production 365 days a year, which is not very likely given the number of official holidays. Therefore, the daily production of coins was probably even greater. These incredibly high numbers are corroborated by other statements in the *Hanshu* listing the number of coins spent yearly by the imperial household and the number of coins in storage at the treasury, all numbered in the billions.

23. *HSBZ*, 72:13a–b; *HS*, 72.3075. These are the words of the high-ranking minister Gong Yu, who served Emperor Yuan and made this estimate in ca. 44 BCE.

24. For the original report, see Linyi Shi Bowuguan, ed., "Shandong Linyi jinqueshan Han huaxiangzhuan mu," *Wenwu* (1995.6): 72–8. The original position of these bricks in the tomb was not reported, nor whether the handprint faced to the inside or to the outside.

25. In 1994 I received a BA from the University of California at Santa Cruz in Asian history, with extensive coursework in anthropology. In 1997 I completed an MA in East Asian regional studies at Harvard, again with a dual emphasis in history and anthropology. Finally, in 2001 I received my PhD from Princeton University in Chinese art and archaeology.

26. Leonard H. Lesko, ed., *Pharaoh's Workers: The Villagers of Deir El Medina* (Ithaca, NY: Cornell University Press, 1994); Morris Bierbrier, *The Tomb-Builders of the Pharaohs* (Cairo: American University in Cairo Press, 1989).

27. Alison Burford, *Craftsmen in Greek and Roman Society* (Ithaca, NY: Cornell University Press, 1972).

28. James Cahill, *The Painter's Practice: How Artists Lived and Worked in Traditional China* (New York: Columbia University Press, 1994).

29. For an introduction to the Shuihudi discovery in English and some of the issues raised, see A. F. P. Hulsewé, "The Ch'in Documents Discovered in Hupei in 1975," *TP* 64, nos. 4–5 (1978): 175–218. The final site report, including transcriptions of all the slips (without notes), is found in Yunmeng Shuihudi Qin Mu Bianxiezu, ed., *Yunmeng Shuihudi Qin mu* (Beijing: Wenwu Chubanshe, 1981). The best transcription of the texts, with annotations, is found in Shuihudi Qinmu Zhujian Zhengli Xiaozu, ed., *Shuihudi Qinmu zhujian* (Beijing: Wenwu Chubanshe, 1990) (hereafter abbreviated *SHD*). All the legal texts are translated and annotated in A. F. P. Hulsewé, *Remnants of Ch'in Law: An Annotated Translation of the Ch'in Legal and Administrative Rules of the 3rd Century* B.C., *Discovered in Yün-Meng Prefecture, Hu-Pei Province, in 1975* (Leiden: E. J. Brill, 1985) (hereafter abbreviated *RCL*).

30. The initial find was reported in Jingzhou Diqu Bowuguan, "Jiangling Zhangjiashan san zuo Han mu chutu dapi zhujian," *Wenwu* (1985.1): 1–8; Zhangjiashan 247 Hao Mu Zhujian Zhengli Xiaozu, ed., "Jiangling Zhangjiashan Han jian gaishu," *Wenwu* (1985.1): 9–15. Sixteen years later, the final report of the slips from tomb 247 was published, which contains a complete transcription with notes; see *ZJS*. Some analysis and comparison to the Shuihudi texts is provided in Li Xueqin and Xing Wen, "New Light on the Early-Han Code: A Reappraisal of the Zhangjiashan Bamboo-Slip Legal Texts," *Asia Major*, 3d ser., 14, no. 1 (2001): 125–46. At present, no complete English translation of the texts is available. Regrettably, the great scholar of Chinese law A. F. P. Hulsewé, who translated the complete Shuihudi Qin legal texts, passed away while waiting for these bamboo slips to be published.

31. The digest of Han legal statutes found in tomb 247 carries an apparent title that reads "*ernian lüling*" (statutes and ordinances of the *second year*). Scholars are still divided as to which sovereign's reign that "second year" falls under. For the position taken by the majority of scholars, that the "second year" represents the second year of the personal reign of Empress Lü (186 BCE), see *ZJS* (introduction); Li Xueqin and Xing Wen, "New Light on the Early-Han Code," 125–46; Miyake Kiyoshi, "Chōkazan Kan kan (ninen ritsurei) kaidai," *Tōhō gakuhō* 76 (2004): 209–20. For the possibility that the "second year" represents the second year of the reign of Han Gaozu (205 BCE), see Zhang Jianguo, "Shixi Han chu 'yuefa san zhang' de falü

xiaoli—jiantan 'ernian lüling' yu Xiao He de guanxi," *Faxue yanjiu* 18, no. 1 (1996): 154–60; Cao Lüning, *Zhangjiashan Han lü yanjiu* (Beijing: Zhonghua Shuju, 2005), 1–12. Throughout this book, I will assume the date of this compilation to be 186 BCE.

32. Jingzhou Diqu Bowuguan, ed., "Jiangling Zhangjiashan liang zuo Han mu chutu dapi zhujian," *Wenwu* (1992.9): 1–11. In the report this tomb is called tomb 136. Other books call it tomb 336.

33. Craig Clunas, *Art in China* (Oxford: Oxford University Press, 1997).

34. Michael Rostovtzeff, *The Social and Economic History of the Roman Empire,* 2d ed., 2 vols. (Oxford: Clarendon Press, 1957).

35. Polanyi's positions are best summarized in his incomplete posthumous work, *The Livelihood of Man,* ed. Harry W. Pearson (New York: Academic Press, 1977).

36. This is in contrast to the *formalist* definition of the economy as the allocation of scarce resources among alternative ends.

37. M. I. Finley, *The Ancient Economy,* 2d ed. (London: Hogarth Press, 1985). Working in parallel to Finley, A. H. M. Jones (1904–70) sounded many of the same points in his collected essays, A. H. M. Jones, *The Roman Economy: Studies in Ancient Economic and Administrative History* (Totowa, NJ: Rowman and Littlefield, 1974).

38. Morris Silver, "Karl Polanyi and Markets in the Near East: The Challenge of the Evidence," *Journal of Economic History* 43, no. 4 (1983): 795–829.

39. Kevin Greene, *The Archaeology of the Roman Economy* (London: B. T. Batsford, 1986).

40. Michael E. Smith, "The Archaeology of Ancient State Economies," *Annual Review of Anthropology* 33 (2004): 73–102.

41. Douglass C. North, "Markets and Other Allocation Systems in History: The Challenge of Karl Polanyi," *Journal of European Economic History* 6 (1977): 703–16.

42. For a comprehensive overview of the Han period, with some reference to the Qin, see Michèle Pirazzoli-t'Serstevens, *The Han Civilization of China*, trans. Janet Seligman (New York: Rizzoli International Publications, 1982). For society and daily life, see Michael Loewe, *Everyday Life in Early Imperial China during the Han Period, 202 B.C.–A.D. 220* (London: Batsford, 1968; repr., Indianapolis, IN: Hackett Publishing Co., 2005). The standard scholarly work on the period is Denis Twitchett and Michael Loewe, eds., *The Cambridge History of China, vol. 1, The Ch'in and Han Empires, 221 B.C.–A.D. 220* (Cambridge: Cambridge University Press, 1986) (hereafter abbreviated *CHOC*). For comprehensive introductions to Chinese history and society, see Robert Murowchick, ed., *China: Ancient Culture, Modern Land* (Norman: University of Oklahoma Press, 1994); Patricia Buckley Ebrey, *Cambridge Illustrated History of China* (Cambridge: Cambridge University Press, 1996).

CHAPTER 2

1. Plutarch, *Life of Pericles,* trans. Robin Waterfield, in *Greek Lives* (Oxford: Oxford University Press, 1998), 145.

2. Xu Shen, *Shuowen jiezi zhu*, ed. and annotated by Duan Yucai (Shanghai: Shanghai Guji Chubanshe, 1981), 201. All translations are my own unless otherwise indicated.

3. Raymond Faulkner, *A Concise Dictionary of Middle Egyptian* (Oxford: Griffith Institute, 1962), 170; Rosemarie Drenkhahn, "Artisans and Artists in Pharaonic Egypt," in *Civilizations of the Ancient Near East*, ed. Jack M. Sasson (New York: Charles Scribner's Sons, 1995), 1:338.

4. Zhang Bingquan, *Yinxu wenzi bingbian,* in *Xiaotun,* ser. 2 (Taibei: Institute of History and Philology, Academia Sinica, 1957–72), no. 57. This is the same as Guo Moruo, ed., and Hu Houxuan, chief ed., *Jiaguwen heji* (n.p.: Zhonghua Shuju, 1978–82), no. 11484 (obverse). The uppermost inscription on the shell (across the top) can be translated as follows:

> Crackmaking on *jichou* day. Bin divined, "On the next *yiwei* day, [libation] and millet should be offered to Zu Yi . . ." [The king,] reading the cracks, prognosticated, saying, "There will be calamities . . . but we should not expect rain." On the evening of the sixth day [*jiawu*] the moon was eclipsed. On the day *yiwei* we offered libation. The *duogong* (many artisans) were dispatched in an orderly manner[?] [to carry out the ceremony].

Translation based on David N. Keightley, "Public Work in Ancient China: A Study of Forced Labor in the Shang and Western Chou" (PhD diss., Columbia University, 1969), 22 (with modifications suggested by Keightley, personal communication).

David Keightley argues that the *duogong* were practicing temple artisans with official status and not just government managers. He believes they personally made ritual objects like the famous Shang bronzes and participated in the rituals using these objects. See Keightley, "Public Work," 28–9. No Shang inscription actually mentions the *duogong* engaged in craft work or ordered to do such work. Nearly all scholars equate the *duogong* of the oracle bones with the *baigong* (hundred artisans) mentioned in Zhou texts. As a title, the *duogong* may refer to only one individual official, the person in charge of the many *gong.* Later texts compiled during the Han (*Shuoyuan, Kongzi jiayu*) refer to some of the diviners at the Shang court as being *gong* themselves.

5. One point that confused scholars for some while was that during the Anyang and Western Zhou periods the graph *gong* (artisan) was borrowed using the rebus principle to write several other homophones, including *gong* (merit), *gong* (to offer tribute), and *gong* (to attack). By the Late Bronze Age, determinatives were added to differentiate these words from the unadorned graph *gong*, increasing the clarity of the written script.

6. David Keightley explains this term by referring to the arithmetical text *Arithmetical Classic of the Gnomon and the Circular Paths of Heaven* (Zhoubi suanjing), in which it states that a carpenter's square could also be used as a compass if you turned the right-angle tool on its side to draw a circle. See Keightley, "Public Work," 15–6.

7. For all the various transcriptions and interpretations of this graph, see Matsumaru Michio and Takashima Ken'ichi, eds., *Kōkotsu moji jishaku sōran* (Tokyo: Tōkyō Daigaku Tōyō Bunka Kenkyūjo, 1993), 141.

8. See Li Xiaoding, *Jiagu wenzi jishi* (Nangang: Institute of History and Philology, Academia Sinica, 1965), 5:1589–94.

9. The earliest stage of the Chinese script has yet to be found. The *jiaguwen* script seen in the oracle bones from Anyang (ca. 1300–1045 BCE) is already quite advanced and probably represents a stage two or three hundred years removed from the origins of Chinese writing. Thus, we must hypothesize about the original intent of graphs whose meanings have already undergone evolution.

10. In some variants, the *gong* graph is placed within the box enclosure, suggesting the same meaning of a carpenter's tool inside a toolbox or perhaps inside a building enclosure.

11. Qu Tongzu [Ch'ü T'ung-tsu], *Han Social Structure,* ed. Jack L. Dull (Seattle: University of Washington Press, 1972), 63–4.

12. *HSBZ*, 24A:2a; *HS*, 24A.1117–8. Cf. the translation by Nancy Lee Swann, *Food and*

Money in Ancient China: The Earliest Economic History of China to A.D. *25, Han Shu 24, with Related Texts, Han Shu 91 and Shih-chi 129* (Princeton: Princeton University Press, 1950), 115.

13. See Derk Bodde, "The Idea of Social Class in Han and Pre-Han China," in *Thought and Law in Qin and Han China*, ed. W. L. Idema and E. Zürcher (Leiden: E. J. Brill, 1990), 26–41.

14. *Mengzi zhengyi, juan* 5, in *ZZJC*, 1:216–9; *SBCK*, 5:11a; translation from Bodde, "Idea of Social Class."

15. The analogy with the organs of the body is brought up in a parallel passage, *Mengzi zhengyi, juan* 11, in *ZZJC*, 1:467; *SBCK*, 11:14a.

16. Marcus Tullius Cicero, *De officiis*, 1.150–1. Passage translated by Finley in *Ancient Economy*, 41–2. Italics are my own. For a modern annotated translation of the whole work, see Marcus Tullius Cicero, *De officiis (On Duties)*, trans. E. M. Atkins, ed. M. T. Griffin (Cambridge: Cambridge University Press, 1991).

17. For a detailed account of Roman attitudes toward artisans, see Jean-Paul Morel, "The Craftsman," in *The Romans*, ed. Andrea Giardina, trans. Lydia G. Cochrane (Chicago: University of Chicago Press, 1993), 214–44; Burford, *Craftsmen in Greek and Roman Society.*

18. Morel, "Craftsman," 229.

19. The earliest economic writings that deliberately promoted agriculture as an important affair of state were those attributed to Li Kui, a minister to Marquis Wen of Wei (r. 403–387 BCE). Fragments of writings attributed to him are preserved in the *Historical Records* and the *History of the Former Han.* The word *ben* (root) is also used in the *Analects* to signify the fundamental, but Confucius refers to self-cultivation as the fundamental concept, not agriculture. The earliest use I could find of the *ben* and *mo* metaphor for occupations is in section 8 of the *Book of Lord Shang* (Shangjunshu). The *ben* there refers to both agriculture and warfare as fundamental to the welfare of the state. Section 8 probably does not belong to the oldest stratum of the *Book of Lord Shang.* It might date to around 275 BCE. The metaphor is used quite prominently in many third-century works, including *Master Xun* (Xunzi), *Spring and Autumn Annals of Mr. Lü* (Lüshi chunqiu), and *Master Han Fei* (Han Feizi).

20. In some usages of *ben*, it appears to signify the trunk of a tree rather than the roots.

21. For the memorial of Jia Yi, see *HSBZ*, 24A:10a–12a; *HS*, 24A.1127–30; translated in Swann, *Food and Money*, 152–8. Jia Yi encouraged the emperor to personally plow the sacred field as an example to the people. For the memorial of Chao Cuo, see *HSBZ*, 24A:12a–15a; *HS*, 24A.1130–4; translated in Swann, *Food and Money*, 158–70. Chao Cuo recommended that taxes on farmers should be lowered and that people should be allowed to use grain to commute punishments and buy honorary ranks.

22. Huan Kuan, *Yantielun jiaozhu*, ed. Wang Liqi (Beijing: Zhonghua Shuju, 1992), *juan* 1 (*pian* 1, "ben yi"), p. 1; *ZZJC*, 7:1; translated in Esson M. Gale, *"Discourses on Salt and Iron": A Debate on State Control of Commerce and Industry in Ancient China* (Leiden: E. J. Brill, 1931), 2–3. The debate that was the basis for *Discourses on Salt and Iron* (Yantielun) was held in 81 BCE, but the text was surely compiled some decades later by Huan Kuan.

23. Wang Fu, *Qianfu lun jian jiaozheng*, ed. Peng Duo (Beijing: Zhonghua Shuju, 1985), *juan* 3 (*pian* 12, "Fu chi"), p. 120; *ZZJC*, 8:50; passage translated in Etienne Balazs, *Chinese Civilization and Bureaucracy: Variations on a Theme*, trans. H. M. Wright, ed. Arthur F. Wright (New Haven: Yale University Press, 1964), 201.

24. For the textual history of the *Ritual System of the Zhou* (Zhouli) and the *Record of the Scrutiny of Crafts* (Kaogongji), see the appropriate entries in Michael Loewe, ed., *Early Chinese*

Texts: A Bibliographic Guide (Berkeley: Society for the Study of Early China, Institute of East Asian Studies, University of California, 1993), 24–32.

25. Harada Yoshito, "Shūkan kōkōki no seikaku to sono seisaku nendai to ni tsuite," in *Tōa kobunka setsuen* (Tokyo: Harada Yoshito Sensei Beiju Kinenkai, 1973), 240–52; Yoshida Mitsukuni, "Shūrai kōkōki no ikkōsatsu," *Tōhō gakuhō* 30 (1959): 167–226.

26. *Zhouli zhushu, juan* 39, in *SSJZS,* 9:1236–40. Cf. the French translation in Édouard Biot, *Le Tcheou-li, ou Rites des Tcheou* (Paris: Imprimerie Nationale, 1851; repr., Taibei: Chengwen, 1969), 2:457–8.

27. One can interpret the indirect object in the phrase regarding the merchants differently and conclude that the merchants were supplying the artisans, not the rulers, with materials (as suggested by Michael Loewe, personal communication).

28. Wang Fu, *Qianfu lun jian jiaozheng, juan* 1 (*pian* 2, "Wu ben"), pp. 14–15; *ZZJC,* 8:6–7.

29. Wang Fu, *Qianfu lun jian jiaozheng, juan* 3 (*pian* 12, "Fu chi"), p. 134; *ZZJC,* 8:56–7; Huan Kuan, *Yantielun jiaozhu, juan* 6 (*pian* 29, "san buzu"), p. 356.

30. *SJ,* 129.3254; translation from Burton Watson, trans., *Records of the Grand Historian: Han Dynasty II* (New York: Columbia University Press, 1993), 434.

31. *SJ,* 129.3274; translation from Burton Watson, *Records: Han Dynasty II,* 449 (with modification).

32. Anthony Barbieri-Low, "Carving Out a Living: Stone-Monument Artisans during the Eastern Han Period," in *Recarving China's Past,* ed. Cary Liu et al. (New Haven: Yale University Press, 2005).

33. Section 29 of the *Discourses on Salt and Iron* mentions that the wealthy of contemporary times all hire *minggong* (famous artisans) to make their elaborate, embroidered silk shoes (*Yantielun jiaozhu, juan* 6 [*pian* 29, "san buzu"], p. 355). Several stone monument inscriptions from the second century CE claim that *minggong* were hired to perform the commission.

34. *SJ,* 129.3272, 3283. The term *sufengzhe* (untitled nobility) seems to have been coined by Sima Qian, for it first appears in this passage. The word *su* is later used in the same sense by Wang Chong when he calls Confucius the "untitled king" (*su wang*) in *Lunheng, SBCK,* 13:17a. For a discussion of the term and the problem of translating it, see Yang Lien-sheng, "Notes on Dr. Swann's *Food and Money in Ancient China,*" *HJAS* 13, nos. 3–4 (1950): 529–30.

35. In chapter 91 of the *History of the Former Han,* Ban Gu repeats all of Sima Qian's wealthy men, then appends twelve more who lived after Sima Qian's time. None of these additional men were artisans or large-scale industrialists. For a more detailed analysis of the moneymakers, see Swann, *Food and Money,* 405–12.

36. The current editions of the *Historical Records* and the *History of the Former Han* write the surname Zhi with two different graphs (see my glossary).

37. See translation and references in chapter 3.

38. *Xijing zaji, SBCK* ed., 1:4b–5a. For the date and authorship of this work, see the references in note 44.

39. *Lunyu zhengyi,* in *ZZJC,* 1:5; cf. the translation by Arthur Waley, *The Analects of Confucius* (London: George Allen and Unwin, 1938), 84, no. 3. The use of this compound (*qiaoyan*) goes back well into the Zhou period.

40. *Laozi daodejing,* in *ZZJC,* 3:10; translated in Arthur Waley, trans., *The Way and Its Power: A Study of the Tao Te Ching and Its Place in Chinese Thought* (New York: Grove Press, 1958), 166.

41. *Xijing zaji, SBCK* ed., 2:1a.

42. This legend is contained in the *Record of Gleaned Remnants* (Shiyiji) of Wang Jia (d. 390 CE), which was revised and edited into the *Recording of Gleaned Remnants* (Shiyilu) by Xiao Qi of the Liang dynasty (ca. 502–58 CE). See Wang Jia, *Shiyiji*, vols. 1–8 of *Baibu congshu jicheng*, ser. 9, ed. Yan Yiping (Taibei: Yiwen Yinshuguan, 1966), 4:5a–b; Wang Jia, *Shiyiji*, ed. Qi Zhiping (Beijing: Zhonghua Shuju, 1981), 4.99–100; *Taiping yulan, juan* 752. The passage is translated in William R. B. Acker, trans., *Some T'ang and Pre-T'ang Texts on Chinese Painting* (Leiden: E. J. Brill, 1954–74), 2.1:4n3. Portions of this book of legends and historical tales are very similar in style to the anonymous *Miscellaneous Notes on the Western Capital* (Xijing zaji), which might help to date parts of that work to the fourth century CE.

43. *Han feizi jijie, juan* 11, in *ZZJC*, 5:202; *SBCK*, 11:4b; translation modified slightly from Susan Bush and Hsio-yen Shih, eds., *Early Chinese Texts on Painting* (Cambridge, MA: Harvard-Yenching Institute, 1985), 24. Cf. the different translation and interpretation by W. K. Liao, in *The Complete Works of Han Fei Tzu* (London: Probsthain, 1939), 2:40. The story later shows up in the *Lord of Huainan* and in the biography of Zhang Heng in *HHS*, 59.1912. The phrase "without form" could also be interpreted to mean "without a corporeal body of flesh and blood." The intent is the same.

44. Like many works that have come down to us from early China, the *Miscellaneous Notes on the Western Capital* (Xijing zaji) is a heterogeneous text containing diverse strata of different dates and origin. It purports to relate facts and events concerning the Western Han capital of Chang'an that were not recorded in the *Historical Records* or *History of the Former Han*. The stories from the *Miscellaneous Notes* were first excerpted by the Liang dynasty author Yin Yun (d. 529 CE) in his *Minor Tales* (Xiao shuo) in twelve passages that closely match the current text of the *Miscellaneous Notes*. The first mention of the *Miscellaneous Notes* in a bibliographic treatise is found in the *History of the Sui* (Suishu), where it is listed as an anonymous work in two *juan* (*Suishu*, 33.966). The *Old History of the Tang* (Jiu Tangshu) (46.1998, 2014) and the *New History of the Tang* (Xin Tangshu) (58.1474, 1502) both attributed it to the Jin dynasty author Ge Hong (ca. 283–363 CE) in one or two *juan*. Noted Tang authors like Liu Zhiji and Zhang Yanyuan all repeated this attribution, though the great commentator Yan Shigu believed the book to be anonymous "alley talk." By the Song, the work had swelled to six *juan*.

All of the oldest printed editions of the *Miscellaneous Notes* contain a colophon purportedly written by Ge Hong himself. In it, he claims that he culled the material for the *Miscellaneous Notes* from a *Hanshu* written by Liu Xin that supposedly also formed the principal source used by Ban Gu for his *History of the Former Han*. That claim is clearly nonsense, for not only is there no mention of Liu Xin writing such a history, but some of the events recorded in the *Miscellaneous Notes* directly contradict those found in the *History of the Former Han* of Ban Gu. It is accepted by most, though not all, scholars that the *History of the Former Han*'s source for the first century of the Han period is the *Historical Records* of Sima Qian.

Some material in the *Miscellaneous Notes* is clearly post-Han. There is at least one mention of a regulation that was codified only during the Eastern Jin period (317–420 CE). However, there is also clearly a stratum of original Han material in the *Miscellaneous Notes*, dating to as early as the first or second centuries CE. For example, the jade burial suit worn by Han Wudi is described in great detail in one section, but such artifacts were not used by later dynasties and their true form was revealed only by modern archaeology. Also, certain material-culture terms mentioned in the work match Han usage and not Sui-Tang practices. For instance, the word for "glass" is consistently *liuli* and not the *boli* often used in Sui and Tang works. Furthermore, the list of painters executed at the end of the famous story of Mao Yanshou (see my chap. 5) is far more detailed than would have been found in a completely fabricated legend. It appears to have been copied from some Han account of the executions.

In my opinion, the content, style, and language of the *Miscellaneous Notes* most closely resemble the *Record of Gleaned Remnants* (Shiyiji) written by Wang Jia (d. 390), who lived in a northern kingdom contemporary with the Jin dynasty. My conclusion would be that the *Miscellaneous Notes* was first compiled by Ge Hong, or someone of his generation, in the mid–fourth century CE from oral legends, from surviving Han books such as the *New Discourses* (Xinlun), *Old Observances of the Han* (Han jiuyi), and *Abstract of the Seven Bibliographic Categories* (Qilüe), and from third-century works like the *Old Events from the Three Capital Areas* (Sanfu jiushi). Between the fourth and ninth centuries, the work was probably padded with new material, resulting in the text that has been known since the late Tang.

For the colophons to the text and the pertinent bibliographic entries from the *Siku quanshu zongmu tiyao* and the *Siku tiyao bianzheng,* see Cheng Yizhong, ed., *Yandan zi: Xijing zaji* (Beijing: Zhonghua Shuju, 1987), 45–62. For a detailed discussion of the date and authorship of the *Miscellaneous Notes,* see Cao Haidong, trans., and Li Zhenxing, ed., *Xinyi Xijing zaji* (Taibei: Sanmin Shuju, 1995), 1–11; William H. Nienhauser, "Once Again, the Authorship of the *Hsi-Ching Tsa-Chi* (Miscellanies of the Western Capital)," *Journal of the American Oriental Society* 98, no. 3 (July–Sept. 1978): 219–36.

45. *Xijing zaji, SBCK* ed., 2:3a–3b. Cf. the translation by Acker, *Some T'ang and Pre-T'ang Texts* 2.1:15–6n5. The first mention of this story is probably in the *Old Events from the Three Capital Areas* (Sanfu jiushi), cited in the commentary to the *Selections of Refined Literature* (Wenxuan). The *Old Events* is probably the same as the *Old Incidents from the Three Capital Areas* (Sanfu gushi), believed by many to be a third- or early-fourth-century work. In that passage, the story is very plain and no dramatic details are given. The *Miscellaneous Notes* author probably used that story as a foundation and further elaborated the plot and the dramatis personae. The first part of this story is also recorded in the Tang geographic text *Kuodi zhi,* as quoted in a commentary to *SJ,* 8.387. That version does not include the mention of the builder or the quality of his replication either.

46. The *Historical Records* says that the name of the town where Gaozu's father lived near the capital was not changed to New Feng until after the father's death. The town was located within the fief Gaozu assigned to his father, near present-day Xi'an. See *SJ,* 8.387; translated in Burton Watson, *Records: Han Dynasty I,* 80.

47. See Acker, *Some T'ang and Pre-T'ang Texts,* 2.1:14–5. Cao Mao excelled in painting and calligraphy and came from a prominent line of rulers who were also artists and poets. He died when he was only twenty while trying to assert his authority over the Sima clan.

48. *Huainanzi, juan* 1, in *ZZJC,* 7:18; *SBCK,* 1:17b. The relevant passage is translated in Bush and Shih, *Early Chinese Texts,* 3–4, 19. The whole chapter has been translated by Evan Morgan, *Tao, the Great Luminant: Essays from "Huai-nan-tzu"* (Shanghai, 1935; repr., New York: Paragon Book Reprint Corp., 1969), 2–29.

49. *Huainanzi, juan* 16, in *ZZJC,* 7:281; *SBCK,* 16:10b; translation based on Bush and Shih, *Early Chinese Texts,* 28 (with modifications).

50. *Huainanzi, juan* 17, in *ZZJC,* 7:293; *SBCK,* 17:5b; translation from Bush and Shih, *Early Chinese Texts,* 28.

51. For an extensive discussion of the use of craft analogies in the Warring States period debates concerning artifice and the creation of culture, see Michael Puett, *The Ambivalence of Creation: Debates concerning Innovation and Artifice in Early China* (Stanford: Stanford University Press, 2001), especially chap. 2, "The Craft of Humanity."

52. *Lunyu zhengyi*, in *ZZJC*, 1:337; cf. the translation by Waley, *Analects*, 195.

53. For an anthology of these early works see Acker, *Some T'ang and Pre-T'ang Texts*.

54. *Zhouli zhushu*, *juan* 39, in *SSJZS*, 9:1242. Cf. the French translation in Biot, *Tcheou-li*, 2:460.

55. Ibid. Nearly the same argument, framed in terms of Yin-Yang, appears in the first book of the *Lord of Huainan*, *SBCK*, 1:7b; translated by Morgan, *Tao*, 10.

56. This and the following two anecdotes from *Master Zhuang* (Zhuangzi) belong to the so-called Outer Chapters of the text (nos. 8–22), a division made in the fourth century CE by Guo Xiang (d. 312 CE). These chapters do not seem to have been written by the same mystical poet who composed the famous Inner Chapters (nos. 1–7) but rather constitute essays and collections of fragments by later thinkers working in the same tradition. They probably range in date from the third century BCE to the third century CE. For a discussion, see Burton Watson, trans., *The Complete Works of Chuang-Tzu* (New York: Columbia University Press, 1968), 13–17.

57. *Zhuangzi jishi*, in *ZZJC*, 3:331; translation based on Burton Watson, *Complete Works of Chuang-Tzu*, 244–5 (with modifications). Cf. the translation by James Legge, trans., *The Sacred Books of China*, Sacred Books of the East, ed. F. Max Müller (Oxford: Clarendon Press, 1885; repr., Delhi: Motilal Banarsidass Publishers, 2001), 40:70. This same story is found in the *Lord of Huainan*, in *ZZJC*, 7:201; translated in Morgan, *Tao*, 124–5.

58. Woodworker Qing may have been a real historical personage in the state of Lu, as he is mentioned in *Mr. Zuo's Commentary on the Spring and Autumn Annals* (Zuozhuan) in the entry for Duke Xiang, fourth year (569 BCE), under the name Carpenter Qing. See James Legge, trans., *The Chinese Classics* (repr. of Oxford University Press ed.; Taibei: SMC Publishing, 2000), 5:421–3.

59. *Zhuangzi jishi*, in *ZZJC*, 3:289–90; translation based on Burton Watson, *Complete Works of Chuang-Tzu*, 205–6 (with modifications). Cf. the translation by Legge, *Sacred Books*, 40:22–3.

60. Michelangelo Buonarroti, *Complete Poems and Selected Letters of Michelangelo*, trans. Creighton Gilbert, ed. Robert N. Linscott (Princeton: Princeton University Press, 1980), no. 149.

61. *Zhuangzi jishi*, in *ZZJC*, 3:217–8; translation from Burton Watson, *Complete Works of Chuang-Tzu*, 152–3. Cf. the more literal translation of Legge in *Sacred Books*, 39:343–4. See also the slightly different version of this story in the *Lord of Huainan*, in *ZZJC*, 7:196; translated by Morgan, *Tao*, 114–5.

62. *Zhouli zhushu*, *juan* 39, in *SSJZS*, 9:1241–2. Cf. the French translation by Biot, *Tcheou-li*, 459–60. Michael Puett also translates this passage and places the author's view of the creation of culture into the context of Warring States debates concerning artifice. Puett places the rhetorical position of the *Record of the Scrutiny of Crafts* close to that of the Mohist critique of Confucius's argument concerning artifice. See Puett, *Ambivalence*, 76–7.

63. *HSBZ*, 8:25a; *HS*, 8.275; translation based on *HFHD*, 2:265, with modifications.

64. Translation based on that found in Bush and Shih, *Early Chinese Texts*, 6. For the original text and the translation of Legge, see *Chinese Classics*, 4:34.

65. *Han feizi jijie, juan* 19, in *ZZJC,* 5:350; *SBCK,* 19:7a; translation from Liao, *Complete Works of Han Fei Tzu,* 2:297.

66. *ZJS,* 168 ("Ernian lüling," slips 258–9). This law apparently applied only to regular silk fabric (*zeng*). The remainder of the clause lists the types and weaves of fabric to which the law did not apply.

67. *ZJS,* 168–9 ("Ernian lüling," slips 261–2). Those officials who apprehended the culprits were to be granted a two-year exemption from border garrison duty, an exemption that they could also transfer to someone else.

68. See *SHD,* 43–4 ("Qin lü shiba zhong," slip 100), where this article is translated into modern Chinese to suggest that artisans were allowed to inspect the weights and measures themselves. Cf. the English translation by Hulsewé, *RQL,* 57–58 (A54), where just the opposite interpretation is advanced.

69. Yan Kejun, comp., *Quan shanggu sandai Qin Han Sanguo Liuchao wen* (Beijing: Zhonghua Shuju, 1958), 1:724 ("Quan Hou Han wen," *juan* 46:6b).

70. *Shanyu* was the title of the king of the Xiongnu; *yanzhi* was the title of his queen.

71. *Xijing zaji, SBCK* ed., 2:1a. Cf. the translation of this story in Nienhauser, "Once Again," 227, and the *Lidai minghua ji* version in Acker, *Some Tang and Pre-Tang Texts,* 2.1:4–6. Paul Pelliot argued that, since the painters' involvement with Wang Zhaojun's exit from court is not recorded in any contemporary Han source and since her tale becomes more elaborate with time, it did not actually happen. William Nienhauser argues that, since the painters do not appear in the *History of the Latter Han* version of Wang Zhaojun's tale (*HHS,* 89.2941) but do appear in early-sixth-century poetry, their tale was fabricated from oral legends sometime between the writing of the *History of the Latter Han* (425–45 CE) and the earliest poetic versions (500–20 CE). William Acker argues, on the other hand, that the very detailed nature of the list of executed artisans would be entirely out of place in a fanciful tale and probably records some truth about a real court scandal involving these court painters. See Acker, *Some Tang and Pre-Tang Texts,* 2.1:5–6n1.

72. *Xijing zaji, SBCK* ed., 1:7a; translated in Anthony Barbieri-Low, "The Organization of Imperial Workshops during the Han Dynasty" (PhD diss., Princeton University, 2001), 456.

73. Lydia Thompson, "Ritual, Art, and Agency: Consecrating the Burial Ground" (paper presented at the international symposium "Recarving China's Past: Art, Archaeology, and Architecture of the 'Wu Family Shrines,'" Princeton, NJ, April 30–May 1, 2005), 9–10.

74. Ibid., 9.

75. As cited in Gerald D. Berreman and Adrian C. Mayer, "Caste," in *International Encyclopedia of the Social Sciences,* ed. David L. Sills (New York: Macmillan, 1968), 1:333.

76. Ibid., 334–5.

77. Satō Taketoshi, *Chūgoku kodai kōgyōshi no kenkyū* (Tokyo: Yoshikawa Kōbunkan, 1962), 10–24; K. C. Chang, *Shang Civilization* (New Haven: Yale University Press, 1980), 159–64, 230–3.

78. Anthony Barbieri-Low, "Occupational Clans and Artisan Families in Ancient China" (presentation at the symposium "The Family Model in Chinese Art and Culture," Tang Center for East Asian Art, Princeton University, Nov. 6, 2004); Keightley, "Public Work," 29–39; Eugenia Herbert, *Iron, Gender, and Power: Rituals of Transformation in African Societies* (Bloomington: Indiana University Press, 1993), 26.

79. *Guanzi, pian* 20, in *ZZJC,* 5:121–2; *SBCK,* 8:5a–7a; translated in W. Allyn Rickett, trans.,

Guanzi: Political, Economic, and Philosophical Essays from Early China (Princeton: Princeton University Press, 1985), 1:325–8. The "Xiao kuang" chapter of the *Master Guan* is closely related to the "Qi yu" chapter of the *Discourses of the States* (Guoyu), which contains an almost-identical passage. Rickett dates both chapters to about 300–250 BCE. The *Master Xun*, which is also dated to the third century BCE, contains a variation on this maxim: "Of the sons of artisans, there is none that does not continue the profession." See *Xunzi jijie, pian* 8, in *ZZJC,* 2:92.

80. Xu Zhuoyun [Hsu Cho-yun], *Ancient China in Transition* (Stanford: Stanford University Press, 1965).

81. Pu Muzhou [Poo Mu-chou], *In Search of Personal Welfare: A View of Ancient Chinese Religion* (Albany, NY: SUNY Press, 1998), chap. 4.

82. To my knowledge, there is no complete translation into English of either Shuihudi daybook. For an introduction to the texts in English, with excerpts, see Michael Loewe, "The Almanacs (*jih-shu*) from Shui-hu-ti," *Asia Major*, 3d ser., 1, no. 2 (1988): 1–28. A complete transcription into modern Chinese graphs, with photographs and annotations, can be found in *SHD.* Commentaries and analysis of the daybooks can also be found in Liu Lexian, *Shuihudi Qin jian rishu yanjiu* (Taibei: Wenjin Chubanshe, 1994), and in Wu Xiaoqiang, *Qin jian rishu jishi* (Changsha: Yuelu Shushe, 2000).

83. For the official transcription and annotation of the text, see *SHD,* 202–5 ("Rishu jia," slips 140–9). For translations into modern Chinese, along with additional annotation and analysis, see Liu Lexian, *Shuihudi,* 179–86, and Wu Xiaoqiang, *Qin jian rishu,* 100–6. The "Giving Birth to Children" section is contained in Daybook Text A. A nearly identical, though abbreviated, version is found in Daybook Text B and is often used by scholars to emend words in Text A. A few dozen other birth outcome predictions are scattered throughout the remainder of Daybook Texts A and B from Shuihudi. These outcomes are tabulated in Wu Xiaoqiang, *Qin jian rishu,* 334–46.

84. Michael Loewe (personal communication) wonders if the dates in the text refer to the time of conception of the child ("when the parents caused it to be born") and not to the date of birth.

85. The Daybook Text B edition of this text leaves out the word "filial" and just says "crafty."

86. The Daybook Text B version of this passage places a negative in front of the first predicate: "will not be skilled at martial arts and will be a crafty artisan."

87. Wu Xiaoqiang has tabulated all the birth outcomes mentioned in the Shuihudi daybooks and determined that in Daybook Text A, sixty-three birth outcomes are positive, fifty are clearly negative, and fifteen are either neutral or impossible to determine. In Daybook Text B, fifty of the outcomes are positive, thirty-seven are negative, and eight are neutral or indeterminate. For marriages, the outcomes are negative approximately 60 percent of the time. See Wu Xiaoqiang, *Qin jian rishu,* 314.

88. For example, one of the two artisan birthdays mentioned above was *dinghai.* It has been argued that the *ding* graph in this cyclical-date compound might have originally (in oracle-bone script) been a pictograph of a nail. The element *hai* is the phonetic portion of the graph for "child," *hai.* Thus, the entire date compound might be a pun on *dinghai* (nail child), a boy destined to be a carpenter perhaps. This is all speculation, of course.

89. The *Classic of Obstetrics* (Chanjing) is a lost work, written by De Zhenchang sometime during the Six Dynasties period. It is recorded in the bibliographic treatise of the *History of the*

Sui (Suishu). Portions of the *Classic of Obstetrics* were preserved in Japan within the tenth-century medical encyclopedia *Ishinpō* by Tanba Yasuyori. For the sixty-day-cycle birth outcome text, see Tanba Yasuyori, *Ishinpō*, trans. Maki Sachiko (Tokyo: Chikuma Shobō, 1994), 24:106–14.

90. *SHD*, 55 ("Qin lü shiba zhong," slip 156); translated in *RCL*, 83 A9. There seem to have been two types of bondservant (*lichen, liqie*) in the Qin period. One type appears to have served a short-term labor sentence, possibly for three years. The other type, probably the type referred to in this statute, seems to have been hereditary state serfs, who were liable for service in government industries. See Hulsewé, "Ch'in Documents," 211–4.

91. See his biography in *SJ*, 57.2065–73; translated in Burton Watson, *Records: Han Dynasty I*, 369–80; *HSBZ*, 40:20a–25a; *HS*, 40.2050–7.

92. The subjects of some of the biographies of this type include the following:

Wei Li, who worked for a time as a hired laborer, later became a model commandery governor in a very difficult southern province. See *HHS*, 76.2458–9; *HHSJJ* 76:2a–b.

Cheng Gong (*HHSJJ*, 27:11a–b; *HHS*, 27.944–5) lost his father as a child and herded pigs as a hired laborer. He later became a noted scholar and a high-ranking official.

Hou Jin (*HHSJJ*, 80B:13a; *HHS*, 80B.2649) was a native of Dunhuang who also lost his father as a child. He worked as a hired laborer to survive and to support his studies. He was later summoned to fill many posts but always refused. He eventually became a mountain recluse.

Diwu Fang (*HHSJJ*, 76:12a; *HHS*, 76.2475–6) was orphaned as a child. He worked as a hired farm laborer to support his family and his studies. Later he was nominated as Filial and Incorrupt and eventually rose to the post of commandery governor.

Wu You (*HHSJJ*, 64:1a–3a; *HHS*, 64.2099–102) lost his father (who was a governor) at twenty. He herded pigs to earn a living and read books while he worked. He was later summoned to office and attained the post of chancellor of a princedom.

Liu Liang (*HHSJJ*, 80B:5b–8a; *HHS*, 80B.2635–40) lost his father in childhood. He supported himself by selling books in the market. He was later nominated for office in the capital.

93. *HHSJJ*, 53:9b–11b; *HHS*, 53.1750–4.

94. Satō, *Chūgoku kodai kōgyōshi no kenkyū*, 286–90. The money was supposedly paid at the end of the period of servitude. Indentured laborers stood on a slippery slope and could easily fall into permanent slavery.

95. The Great Proscription (*danggu*) 166–84 CE was a time during the Latter Han when men who opposed the eunuch faction at court were barred from holding office. Their family members (to the third-cousin) and protégés were also forbidden from holding government posts. It was lifted when the Yellow Turban Rebellion caused a greater crisis for the bureaucracy.

96. Hong Gua, *Li xu*, in *Shike shiliao congshu*, ser. A, ed. Yan Gengwang (Taibei: Yiwen Yinshuguan, 1966), 19:3b–5a. The cyclical dates in the inscription are not possible in the month listed for the death of Master Guo.

97. There is the possibility that the "work of a blacksmith" phrase in this inscription might be an allegorical reference to some kind of personal cultivation and not a reference to actual metallurgy.

98. Yamada Katsuyoshi, "Shinkandai shukōgyō no tenkai—Shinkandai kōkan no hensen kara kangaeru," *Tōyōshi kenkyū* 56, no. 4 (1998): 26–9.

99. A. H. M. Jones, "The Caste System in the Later Roman Empire," *Eirene* 8 (1970): 88–96.

100. *ZJS*, 203 ("Ernian lüling," slips 474–6). Foreman Clerks (Lingshi) on the staff of the Palace Aid to the Censor in Chief (Yushi Zhongcheng) during the Former Han had to pass a test of nine thousand written characters. See Hans Bielenstein, *The Bureaucracy of Han Times* (Cambridge: Cambridge University Press, 1980), 9.

101. *HSBZ*, 19A:31a–b; *HS*, 19A.743. The figure of 120,285 given in these two editions is emended to 130,285 by Bielenstein, *Bureaucracy*, 156, 205–6n1.

102. William V. Harris, *Ancient Literacy* (Cambridge, MA: Harvard University Press, 1989), 7–8.

103. Ibid., 22.

104. Hebei Sheng Wenhuaju Wenwu Gongzuodui, ed., "Hebei Ding xian beizhuang Han mu fajue baogao," *Kaogu xuebao* (1964.2): 127–94.

105. The Cangshan inscription (151 CE) is riddled with the same problems. See Li Falin, *Shandong Han huaxiangshi yanjiu* (Ji'nan: Qi-Lu Shushe, 1982), 100–1. Li Falin concurs that these epitaphs must have been composed and written by the craftsmen.

106. This same loan is seen in several pre-Han texts but rarely in texts composed during the Latter Han and afterward. The loan seems to have become unacceptable around the time of the composition of the dictionary *Shuowen jiezi* (121 CE).

107. See Lin Suqing, "Liang-Han jingming chutan," *Zhongyang yanjiuyuan, Lishi yuyan yanjiusuo jikan*, 63, no. 2 (1993): 345–9.

108. Earlier texts and documents (Warring States to Qin) seem to have more phonetic loans than Han documents. For a standard list of loan characters in Classical texts, see Bernhard Karlgren, "Loan Characters in Pre-Han Texts," *BMFEA* 35 (1963): 1–128. For phonetic loans and determinative swaps in Qin legal texts, see *RCL*, 241–2. While Han administrative material, such as that found at Dunhuang, Juyan, and Yinwan, is usually written more accurately than craftsmen's inscriptions, documents written or copied by local clerks on the frontiers of the empire sometimes contain more nonstandard features than documents drawn up by the central government.

109. William Boltz, *The Origin and Early Development of the Chinese Writing System* (New Haven: American Oriental Society, 1994), 168–77.

110. A similar conclusion is reached by Li Falin, *Shandong*, 100–1, and by Wu Hung, "Beyond the 'Great Boundary': Funerary Narrative in the Cangshan Tomb," in *Boundaries in China*, ed. John Hay (London: Reaktion Books, 1994), 92–3, 98.

111. For model legal forms for divorce, property division, etc., see Yamamoto Tatsuro and Ikeda On, eds., *Tun-huang and Turfan Documents concerning Social and Economic History* (Tokyo: Committee for the Studies of the Tun-huang Manuscripts, Tōyō Bunko, 1978), 3:150(71) no. 487, 156(65) no. 495, 151(70) no. 488.

CHAPTER 3

1. *HSBZ*, 10:1b; *HS*, 10.301; translated in *HFHD*, 2:373–4.

2. *SHD*, 43–4 ("Qin lü shiba zhong," slip 100); translated in *RCL*, A54; Yamada Katsuyoshi, "Offices and Officials of Works, Markets and Lands in the Ch'in Dynasty," *Acta Asiatica*

58 (1990): 4–5. Numerous Qin workshop names are preserved on sealing clays; see Zhou Xiaolu and Lu Dongzhi, *Qin fengni ji*, 27–43.

3. One of the main imperial workshops in the Han capital was the Kaogongshi. In 104 BCE, its name was officially shortened to Kaogong. See *HSBZ*, 19A:15a, 16b; *HS*, 19A.731–2; Bielenstein, *Bureaucracy*, 51.

4. For a comprehensive history of this factory and its organization, see Barbieri-Low, "Organization."

5. Rong Geng, *Han jinwen lu* (Beiping [Beijing]: Institute of History and Philology, Academia Sinica, 1931), no. 2; Wu Rongzeng, "Xi-Han guqian zhong suojian de gongguan," *Kaogu* (2000.9): 62–3.

6. Luoyang Bowuguan, ed., "Luoyang Jianxi qilihe Dong-Han mu fajue jianbao," *Kaogu* (1975.2): 116–24, 134.

7. Lucy Lim, ed., *Stories from China's Past: Han Dynasty Pictorial Tomb Reliefs and Archaeological Objects from Sichuan Province, People's Republic of China* (San Francisco: Chinese Culture Foundation of San Francisco, 1987), pls. 16–8.

8. See the original report in Luoyang Shi Wenwu Gongzuo Dui, ed., "Luoyang jingu zhan 11 hao Han mu fajue jianbao," *Wenwu* (1983.4): 15–28. See also Henan Bowuyuan, ed., *Henan chutu Handai jianzhu mingqi* (Zhengzhou: Daxiang Chubanshe, 2002), pls. 58–60. The authors of *Henan chutu Handai jianzhu mingqi* do not give the exact reasons for their suggestion that these models represent dye shops, but one can assume that they based their interpretation on the location of the models in the tomb, their structure, and the items found within them. Also, although most of the containers in the tomb held grains or other foodstuffs, two jars found near the models were labeled *jin* (gold), which might indicate that they once contained a yellow dye.

9. The stone was discovered in 1930 near Tengzhou City, Shandong, and was published in Ye Zhaohan, "Handai shike yetie gufeng lutu," *Wenwu* (1959.1): 20–1. For a reconstruction of the bellows seen on the stone, see Wang Zhenduo, "Handai yetie gufeng fengji de fuyuan," *Wenwu* (1959.5): 43–4. The most complete reproduction of the whole scene is found in Shandong Sheng Bowuguan and Shandong Sheng Wenwu Kaogu Yanjiusuo, eds., *Shandong Han huaxiangshi xuanji* ([Ji'nan]: Qi-Lu Shushe, 1982).

10. Luo Fuyi, "Xiang Tajun shi citing tizi jieshi," *Gugong bowuyuan yuankan* 2 (1960): 179.

11. For an inscription in which master and disciple are listed in descending order of rank, see note 60.

12. Zhao Mingcheng (1081–1129 CE) reads the first name as Meng Ji and the second name as Ji di Mao; see *Jinshi lu*, vols. 7–11 of *Shike shiliao congshu*, ser. B, ed. Yan Gengwang (Taibei: Yiwen Yinshuguan, 1966), 14:8a. The Qing scholar Weng Fanggang (1733–1818) reads the first name as Meng Fu and the second name as Li di Mao; see *Liang-Han jinshi ji*, vols. 12–19 of *Shike shiliao congshu*, ser. A, ed. Yan Gengwang (Taibei: Yiwen Yinshuguan, 1966), 15:53a; Jiang Yingju and Wu Wenqi (*Handai Wu shi muqun*, 11) follow Weng. The best extant rubbings (Academia Sinica set) seem to affirm Zhao's suggestion that the second and third graphs are probably the same, though it is unclear whether Li or Ji is intended.

13. For the adaptation of Roman motifs in Han China, see Anthony Barbieri-Low, "Roman Themes in a Group of Eastern Han Lacquer Vessels," *Orientations*, May 2001, 52–8.

14. *Xijing zaji, SBCK* ed., 1:6a–b; Xiang Xinyang and Liu Keren, eds., *Xijing zaji jiaozhu* (Shanghai: Shanghai Guji Chubanshe, 1991), 41–4, 59–61. Translations of these passages can be found in chapter 5 below.

15. *ZJS*, 171 ("Ernian lüling," slips 278–80); *SHD*, 46 ("Qin lü shiba zhong," slip 112); translated in *RCL*, A61. See also Wu Rongzeng, "Qin de guanfu shougongye," in *Yunmeng Qinjian yanjiu*, ed. Zhonghua Shuju Bianjibu (Beijing: Zhonghua Shuju, 1981), 40–1.

16. Wu Rongzeng, "Qin de guanfu shougongye," 39–40; Barbieri-Low, "Organization," 315–6.

17. Zhang Jiuling et al., eds., *Da Tang liudian* (Taibei: Wenhai Chubanshe, 1962), 392–3; Ouyang Xiu et al., eds., *Xin Tangshu* (Beijing: Zhonghua Shuju, 1975), 1268–9; translated by Robert des Rotours, *Traité des fonctionnaires et Traité de l'armée, tr. de la Nouvelle histoire des T'ang (chap. XLVI–L)* (Leiden: E. J. Brill, 1947), 1:459–60.

18. For studies and translations, see the entry in Loewe, *Early Chinese Texts*, 16–23, 33–8. For the *Zhoubi suanjing*, see Christopher Cullen, *Astronomy and Mathematics in Ancient China: The "Zhoubi suanjing"* (Cambridge: Cambridge University Press, 1996).

19. Translation from Shen Kangshen, John N. Crossley, and Anthony W.-C. Lun, *The Nine Chapters on the Mathematical Arts* (Oxford: Oxford University Press, 1999), 340–1 (with minor modifications). See the similar problem in *ZJS*, 265 ("Suanshu shu," slip 131).

20. For a detailed study of these methods, see Barbieri-Low, "Organization."

21. Satō, *Chūgoku kodai kōgyōshi no kenkyū*, 329–59; Yang Kuan, *Zhanguo shi*, 3d ed. (Shanghai: Renmin Chubanshe, 1998), 188–212.

22. This article is found in the "Statute on Passes and Markets" (Guanshi lü) from the Jin law code, as cited in *Imperial Overview of the Taiping Era* (Taiping yulan) (*juan* 756:2a). Since the Jin law code was largely based on the Qin and Han law codes, it is likely that the now-fragmentary "Statute on Passes and Markets" from these two codes was the progenitor of this Jin article. For the text of the article, see Cheng Shude, *Jiuchao lükao* (Taibei: Taiwan Shangwu Yinshuguan, 1965), 2:354.

23. The *Yueling* is a book in the current text of the *Record of Ceremonial* (Liji). For this passage, see *SSJZS*, 13:640–1. This same passage occurs in the *Spring and Autumn Annals of Mr. Lü* (Lüshi chunqiu) and has traditionally been thought to have been copied from this work to the *Record of Ceremonial*. The situation may be more complex than that. Compare the translation of this quotation in Legge, *Sacred Books*, 27:299.

24. Cui Shi, "Zhenglun," in Yan Kejun, *Quan Shanggu*, 1:725 ("Quan Hou Han wen," *juan* 46:7a).

25. Excerpted from "Shu Capital Rhapsody" (Shudu fu), attributed to Yang Xiong, in Zhang Zhenze, ed., *Yang Xiong ji jiaozhu* (Shanghai: Shanghai Guji Chubanshe, 1993), 35–8.

26. Huan, *Yantielun jiaozhu*, *juan* 6 (*pian* 29, "San buzu"), p. 351; for a translation of this passage, see Barbieri-Low, "Organization," 402.

27. A 1,200-coin platter is published in Harada Yoshito and Tazawa Kingo, *Rakurō* (Tokyo: Tōkō-shoin, 1930), 42–3, pls. 56–9. See also the discussion in chapter 4 below. A price recorded on a wooden slip from the site of Juyan was five red cups for 250 coins; see Yu Huaqing, "Qin-Han qiqi jiage kaobian," *Zhongguo shi yanjiu* (1984.4): 97–104; Fu Juyou, "Zhongguo qiqi de dianfeng shidai—Handai qi gongyi meishu zonglun," in *Han*, ed. Fu Juyou, vol. 3 of *Zhongguo qiqi quanji*, ed. Zhongguo Qiqi Quanji Bianji Weiyuanhui (Fuzhou: Fujian Meishu Chubanshe, 1998), 48. The price for chickens (39–40 coins) comes from the "Chicken Register" (dated 62 BCE) found at the site of Dunhuang, Xuanquan. See Hu Pingsheng and Zhang Defang, eds., *Dunhuang Xuanquan Han jian shicui* (Shanghai: Shanghai Guji Chubanshe, 2001), 77–80.

28. A lively and detailed eyewitness account of the collection and processing of lacquer

fluid in mid-eighteenth-century China is contained in a letter written to the French Academy of Sciences by the Jesuit missionary Père d'Incarville; see an edited version of the letter in "Mémoire sur le vernis de la Chine," in *L'art de peinture, doreur, vernisseur*, ed. Jean-Felix Watin (1772; repr., Paris: Leonce Laget, 1975), 310–27. The original letter can be found in the collection *Lettres édifiantes et curieuses, écrites des missions étrangères*, 26 vols. (Paris: Chez J. G. Merigot, 1780–3).

29. For a review of technical analyses of the core supports used in Chinese lacquerware, see Barbieri-Low, "Organization," 268–82.

30. Huan, *Yantielun jiaozhu*, *juan* 6 (*pian* 29, "San buzu"), p. 356; translated in Barbieri-Low, "Organization," 403.

31. This type of production strategy is often called flow-line production.

32. *SHD*, 43 ("Qin lü shiba zhong," slip 98); *RCL*, A52.

33. Barbieri-Low, "Organization," 173–6.

34. Ledderose, *Ten Thousand Things*; see especially his discussion of bronze casting in chapter 2 and export porcelain in chapter 4.

35. For a dated sequence of examples showing this degeneration, see Barbieri-Low, "Organization," figs. 31, 33–9, 47, 49.

36. See the examples from Mawangdui tomb 1, in Hunan Sheng Bowuguan and Zhongguo Shehui Kexueyuan Kaogu Yanjiusuo, eds., *Changsha Mawangdui yihao Han mu* (Beijing: Wenwu Chubanshe, 1973), 2: pls. 117–8, 141–3; Ledderose, *Ten Thousand Things*, 156–8.

37. Translation based on Wu Hung, *Monumentality in Early Chinese Art and Architecture* (Stanford: Stanford University Press, 1995), 194 (with slight modifications).

38. The concentrated cluster of dated monuments in Shandong begins around 83–7 CE and disappears soon after the Yellow Turban Rebellion ravaged the area (184 CE). There is some evidence for a stone monument tradition after this date, much of it in the way of reused materials from earlier monuments. For a comprehensive list of dated monuments, see Jiang Yingju and Yang Aiguo, *Handai huaxiangshi yu huaxiangzhuan* (Beijing: Wenwu Chubanshe, 2001), 36–42.

39. Based on regional stylistic analysis, Xin Lixiang lays out five stone-carving traditions: (1) Shandong Peninsula and northern Jiangsu and Anhui, (2) the area around Han period Nanyang Commandery in present-day Henan, (3) western Shanxi and northern Shaanxi, (4) Sichuan and northern Yunnan, and (5) the immediate area around the Latter Han capital at Luoyang. See Xin Lixiang, *Handai huaxiangshi zonghe yanjiu* (Beijing: Wenwu Chubanshe, 2000), 13–7.

40. Ibid., 13–4.

41. Seminar presentation by Professor Lothar von Falkenhausen, University of California at Los Angeles, Mar. 2002.

42. The three inscriptions I have used to help reconstruct this process are the following:

1. The inscribed doorpost from the offering hall of Xiang Tajun; see transcription and notes in Luo Fuyi, "Xiang Tajun," 178–81. This post, now in the Palace Museum, Beijing, was found accidentally in 1934, seventy kilometers southwest of Donge County, Shandong. Suspicions have been raised about the long inscription, which skirts damaged areas of the stone. Numerous errors and phonetic loans in the inscription have also raised doubts, but these only support the authenticity of the inscription (see my section on literacy in chap. 2). On a recent visit to the Palace Museum, I was not able to see the original post, but only a rubbing.

2. The inscribed stones from An Guo's offering hall; see transcription and notes in Li Falin, *Shandong*, 101–8. A more recent, improved transcription (without notes) can be found in *ZHQ*, 2: nos. 108–9. These two stones were part of a set of floral-decorated slabs found at Songshan that may have been originally intended as ceiling stones but were instead probably used to form the walls of an offering hall. Later, they were all reused in a belowground tomb. The dates within the inscription contain some errors. The *taisui* position for the year is erroneously given as *guiyou*, when it should be *dingyou*. The "twenty-sixth day" at the start of the inscription should read "sixteenth day," as it does at the end. Such errors are not uncommon on Han stone monuments.

3. The long-lost stele of Wu Liang; see transcriptions in Zhao Mingcheng, *Jinshi lu*, 14:10b; Hong Gua, *Li shi*, 6:13b–15a; see partial English translation in Wilma Fairbank, "The Offering Shrines of 'Wu Liang Tz'u,'" *HJAS* 6, no. 1 (1941): 8. Since this object no longer exists, and received transcriptions vary, I have used this inscription very sparingly, only in places where it is corroborated by the other two.

43. Most recently, Xin Lixiang, building on the work of Nagahiro Toshio and others, has laid out the process quite clearly in his book *Handai huaxiangshi zonghe yanjiu*, 22–6. He bases his reconstruction largely on the same three inscriptions.

44. Bierbrier, *Tomb-Builders of the Pharaohs*, 43–64; Drenkhahn, "Artisans and Artists in Pharaonic Egypt," 336–7; Christopher J. Eyre, "Work and Organisation of Work in the New Kingdom," in *Labor in the Ancient Near East*, ed. Marvin Powell (New Haven: American Oriental Society, 1987), 167–222.

45. Some monuments appear to have been carved from an even harder, recrystallized limestone called dolomite. Further south into Jiangsu, sandstone monuments become more prevalent.

46. The exact phrases used are *nanshan*, *nanshan zhi yang*, *xian xi'nan xiaoshan yangshan*. See glossary for the Chinese characters.

47. Wang Xueli, *Qin Shihuang ling yanjiu* (Shanghai: Shanghai Renmin Chubanshe, 1994), 200–1; Henan Sheng Wenwu Kaogu Yanjiusuo, ed., *Yongcheng Xi-Han Liang Guo wangling yu qinyuan* (Zhengzhou: Zhongzhou Guji Chubanshe, 1996), 74–80.

48. Shandong Sheng Jining Shi Wenwuju, ed., *Han Rencheng Wang mu keshi jingxuan* ([Ji'nan]: Shandong Meishu Chubanshe, 1998), 12.

49. See the An Guo inscription transcribed in Li Falin, *Shandong*, 105. Li interprets the phrases *luanshi* and *lianju* as being names of artisans. If so, they would be rather ironic names for masons and quarry workers. Taken literally, they are verb-object compounds meaning "bind up the stones" and "connect together the carts" and thus more likely are the predicates of the previously mentioned subjects, the artisans Wang Shu, Wang Jian, and Jiang Hu. The fact that the final syllable in the name Jiang Hu (*GSR*, 49a': *g'o/γuo) happens to rhyme with the last syllable of *lianju* (*GSR*, 74a: *kio/kiwo) supports this interpretation. See the translation of this passage by Klaas Ruitenbeek, *Chinese Shadows: Stone Reliefs, Rubbings, and Related Works of Art from the Han Dynasty (206 BC–AD 220) in the Royal Ontario Museum* (Toronto: Royal Ontario Museum, 2002), 17.

50. Heze Diqu Bowuguan and Liangshan Xian Wenhuaguan, eds., "Shandong Liangshan Dong-Han jinian mu," *Kaogu* (1988.11): 982.

51. Tan Qixiang, ed., *Zhongguo lishi ditu ji* (Beijing: Zhongguo Ditu Chubanshe, 1982–7), 2:44–5.

52. For the interpretation of these phrases in the An Guo inscription, see Li Falin, *Shandong,* 105.

53. Shandong Sheng Jining Shi Wenwuju, ed., *Han Rencheng Wang,* 44–5.

54. Heze Diqu Bowuguan and Liangshan Xian Wenhuaguan, "Shandong Liangshan." The notation reads *ci biao fan you* X (all of the X on this exposed surface). It might have been a note from one literate craftsman to another, indicating that the former had completed the carving of all the figures on that surface. The excavators, however, suggest that the term *biao* might instead indicate that the stone was a grave marker (*mu biao*). The stone in question (dated 167 CE) is difficult to reconstruct but might have been a partition gable in an aboveground offering hall.

55. The artisan listed just after Dai Sheng, a man named Shao Qiangsheng, might also have been a master draftsman. Traces of initial sketches have been found on some stones from Shaanxi; see Dai Yingxin and Wei Suizhi, "Shaanxi Suide huangjiata Dong-Han huaxiangshi muqun fajue jianbao," *Kaogu yu wenwu* (1988.5–6): 251–61; Xin Lixiang, *Handai,* 25.

56. Li Falin, *Shandong,* 105; Hong Gua, *Li shi,* 6:14a. Cf. the translation of Wilma Fairbank (following Chavannes) as "engraved the text (*wen*)" and "carved the designs," in "Offering Shrines of 'Wu Liang Tz'u,'" 8.

57. Traces of final painting have been found on stones from Shanxi, Shaanxi, Henan, and Sichuan. See references in Xin Lixiang, *Handai,* 26. For color plates of some of these stones and chemical analyses of the pigments, see Shaanxi Sheng Kaogu Yanjiusuo and Yulin Shi Kaogu Guanli Weiyuanhui Bangongshi, eds., *Shenmu Dabaodang: Handai chengzhi yu muzang kaogu baogao* (Beijing: Kexue Chubanshe, 2001), pls. 2–23.

58. Xin Lixiang, *Handai,* 26; Shandong Sheng Bowuguan and Shandong Sheng Wenwu Kaogu Yanjiusuo, *Shandong Han huaxiangshi xuanji,* 15–6.

59. Eyre, "Work and Organisation of Work in the New Kingdom," 173.

60. The titles of master and apprentice appear in sequence in an inscription dated 142 CE, but only one name is given. See Sishui Xian Wenguansuo, ed., "Shandong Sishui nanchen Dong-Han huaxiangshi mu," *Kaogu* (1995.5): 390–5.

61. Luo Fuyi, "Xiang Tajun," 178–9.

62. Li Falin, *Shandong,* 106. For the characters of *lianyue* (numerous months) and *gongfu wuji* (incalculable labor), see the glossary. *ZHQ,* 2: no. 108, transcribes the second phrase as *gongfu wukao* (unending labors).

63. Li Falin, *Shandong,* 103.

64. Shandong Sheng Bowuguan and Shandong Sheng Wenwu Kaogu Yanjiusuo, *Shandong Han huaxiangshi xuanji,* 14, pl. 1; *ZHQ,* 2: no. 52. Li Falin (*Shandong,* 47) transcribes his name as Huan Sangzhong.

65. Shandong Sheng Bowuguan and Shandong Sheng Wenwu Kaogu Yanjiusuo, *Shandong Han huaxiangshi xuanji,* no. 159.

66. Hebei Sheng Wenhuaju Wenwu Gongzuodui, "Hebei Ding Xian," 127–94.

67. Martin J. Powers, *Art and Political Expression in Early China* (New Haven: Yale University Press, 1991), 142–55.

68. Xin Lixiang, *Handai,* 45–7.

69. Shaanxi Sheng Kaogu Yanjiusuo and Yulin Shi Kaogu Guanli Weiyuanhui Bangongshi, *Shenmu Dabaodang,* 121.

70. See examples in Käte Finsterbusch, *Verzeichnis und Motivindex der Han-Darstellungen* (Wiesbaden: Otto Harrassowitz, 1966–2004), 2: nos. 381–2, 418–9, 425–8.

71. Dai Yingxin and Wei Suizhi, "Shaanxi," 260–1.

72. See *ZHQ*, 1: nos. 90–92; Zhu Xilu, *Jiaxiang Han huaxiangshi* (Ji'nan: Shandong Meishu Chubanshe, 1992), no. 45.

73. See Xin Lixiang, *Handai*, 83–102. For a review of other theories concerning this scene, see Wu Hung, *The Wu Liang Shrine* (Stanford: Stanford University Press, 1989), 193–213.

74. For one widow, see Zhu, *Jiaxiang*, pls. 28, 64–5, 78; *ZHQ*, 1: nos. 66, 84. Two widows, Zhu, *Jiaxiang*, pls. 3, 62, 87; *ZHQ*, 1: no. 51; Finsterbusch, *Verzeichnis*, 2: no. 270. Three widows, Zhu, *Jiaxiang*, pls. 64, 106. Four widows, Zhu, *Jiaxiang*, pls. 7, 31, 86, 90, 138. Five widows, Finsterbusch, *Verzeichnis*, 2: no. 269. Six widows, Finsterbusch, *Verzeichnis*, 2: no. 373.

75. Qu, *Han Social Structure*, 44–8.

76. A popular motif on Han stones is a depiction of Confucius and his numerous disciples, often in the context of Confucius meeting the Daoist sage Laozi. Frequently, a scene label was cleared next to each figure, but rarely are any men except Laozi, Kongzi, or Kongzi's disciple Zi Lu individually identified in the scene; see *ZHQ*, 1: nos. 57, 59–60, 228.

77. The process of carving the captions is reconstructed by Lai Fei, "Shandong Handai huaxiangshi bangti," *Meishushi yanjiu* (1994.2): 27–8.

78. See *ZHQ*, 1: no. 230. On this stone two stories are incorrectly captioned. The story of Dong Yong is mislabeled as the Zhao Xun story, and the story of the filial son Xing Qu is incorrectly identified as that of the filial son Ding Lan. The compositions for depicting these stories are similar, and only someone who really knew the details of the stories could distinguish them.

79. Yang Liansheng, "Schedules of Work and Rest in Imperial China," *HJAS* 18 (1955): 302. The Han statute for this holiday is quoted in *Chuxueji, juan* 20.

80. The La New Year was the commonly accepted New Year festival and the ancestor of many modern-day New Year rituals. It was celebrated over several days, sometime between January 16 and 27. The Day of Concealment fell in the sixth lunar month and was a time for staying at home to rest, presumably to avoid contact with extreme heat and evil spirits. For references to all these holidays, see Derk Bodde, *Festivals in Classical China* (Princeton: Princeton University Press, 1975), 49–74, 317–25; Yang, "Work and Rest," 303–5; Pu, *In Search of Personal Welfare*, 125–34; *ZJS*, 223 ("Zouyanshu," slip 128); *HS*, 65.2846.

81. *SHD*, 45 ("Qin lü shiba zhong," slip 108); Zhang Jiuling et al., *Da Tang liudian*, 234.

82. Yang, "Work and Rest," 315–6.

83. *SHD*, 83–4 ("Qin lü zachao," slips 17–8); *RCL*, C11. For more examples, see also *RCL*, C12–C14 and B22.

84. *RCL*, C12.

85. *SHD*, 97 ("Qin lü dawen," slip 13); *RCL*, D12.

86. *ZJS*, 147 ("Ernian lüling," slip 92).

87. Yang, "Work and Rest," 320–5.

88. *SJ*, 6.265; translated in William H. Nienhauser, ed., *The Grand Scribe's Records* (Bloomington: Indiana University Press, 1994), 1:155. See also *HSBZ*, 36:23b–24a; *HS*, 36.1954. A fanciful legend retold in the *Shiyiji* relates that when the tomb was opened at the beginning of the Han period, the artisans were still alive. While underground they had continued to work at

making objects and carving a stele of grievances. See Wang Jia, *Shiyiji* (Beijing: Zhonghua Shuju, 1981), 5.119–20.

89. For the last decade, more than 6,000 men have died each year in China from coal-mining accidents alone. See Audra Ang, "China Says More than 6,000 Miners Killed Last Year," *Associated Press Worldstream*, Jan. 17, 2005.

90. *SJ*, 49.1973; *HSBZ*, 97A:7b–8a; *HS*, 97A.3944; translated in C. Martin Wilbur, *Slavery in China during the Former Han Dynasty, 206 B.C.–A.D. 25* ([Chicago]: Field Museum of Natural History, [1943]; repr., New York: Russell and Russell, 1967), 275–7.

91. See *HSBZ*, 10:5b, 27A:13b; *HS*, 10.309, 27A.1334; *HFHD*, 2:385. A similar incident occurred at the Iron Monopoly Office of Zhuo Commandery in 91 BCE. The molten iron there was said to have "all flown up and out of the furnace." See *HSBZ*, 27A:13a–b; *HS*, 27A.1334; *HFHD*, 2:385n5.9. Both incidents are also translated and discussed in Donald B. Wagner, *The State and the Iron Industry in Han China* (Copenhagen: Nordic Institute of Asian Studies, 2001), 46–7.

92. *GSR*, 1015f: *gliông/liung.

93. Wagner, *State and Iron Industry*, 47.

94. Brendon Williams, Nicola Porter, and Jason Lamport, "Corus Inferno; Tragedy as Steelworks Rocked by Horror Explosions," *The Mirror*, Nov. 9, 2001; "Blame Put on Coolant, Call for Steel-Rules Review," *Western Mail*, July 12, 2002; "Blast Horror Revealed," *South Wales Evening Post*, Apr. 20, 2002.

95. For the technical aspects of this process, see Kilian Anheuser, "Cold and Hot Mercury Gilding of Metalwork in Antiquity," *Bulletin of the Metals Museum* 26, no. 2 (1996): 48–52; Peter Northover and Kilian Anheuser, "Gilding in Britain: Celtic, Roman, and Saxon," in *Gilded Metals: History, Technology, and Conservation*, ed. Terry Drayman-Weisser (London: Archetype Publications, 2000), 109–21. Through replication experiments, Anheuser was able to determine the optimum temperature for the process and was also able to disprove the long-held misconception that the mercury could evaporate at room temperature without roasting.

96. For the scientific analysis of early gilded pieces from the British Museum, see P. A. Lins and W. A. Oddy, "The Origins of Mercury Gilding," *Journal of Archaeological Science* 2 (1975): 365–73. The earliest Western pieces date from Celtic contexts in the first century BCE; see Anheuser, "Cold and Hot," 48; Northover and Anheuser, "Gilding in Britain," 111.

97. Joseph Needham et al., *Science and Civilisation in China* (Cambridge: Cambridge University Press, 1954–), 5.2:240–9.

98. Barbieri-Low, "Organization," 301.

99. Botanists sometimes classify the lacquer tree as *Toxicodendron verniciflua*, placing it in the same genus as plants like poison oak (*T. diversilobum*) and poison sumac (*T. vernix*). In some older publications, it is classed *Rhus vernicifera*, a term no longer sanctioned by modern botanical usage. See Sir Harry Garner, *Chinese Lacquer* (London: Faber and Faber, 1979), 19–20; A. Burmester, "Technical Studies of Chinese Lacquer," in *Urushi: Proceedings of the Urushi Study Group, June 10–27, 1985*, ed. N. S. Brommelle and Perry Smith (Marina del Rey, CA: Getty Conservation Institute, 1988), 165.

100. Robert L. Rietschel and Joseph F. Fowler, "Toxicodendron Plants and Spices," in *Fisher's Contact Dermatitis*, 4th ed. (Baltimore: Williams and Wilkins, 1995).

101. Zhou Yimou and Xiao Zuotao, eds., *Mawangdui yishu kaozhu* (Tianjin: Tianjin Kexue Jishu Chubanshe, 1988); translation in Donald J. Harper, *Early Chinese Medical Literature: The Mawangdui Medical Manuscripts* (London: Kegan Paul International, 1998), 293–5.

102. Garner, *Chinese Lacquer*, 22.

103. Preya Kullavanijaya and Suwirakorn Ophaswongse, "A Study of Dermatitis in the Lacquerware Industry," *Contact Dermatitis* 36 (1997): 244–6; Kawai Keiichi et al., "Hyposensitization to Urushiol among Japanese Lacquer Craftsmen: Results of Patch Tests on Students Learning the Art of Lacquerware," *Contact Dermatitis* 25 (1991): 290.

104. See d'Incarville, "Memoire sur le vernis de la Chine," 317–9.

105. Satō, "Chūgoku kodai no shikki kōgyō," *Jimbun kenkyū* 9, no. 11 (1958): 41–3.

106. Pu, *In Search of Personal Welfare*.

107. See Herbert, *Iron, Gender, and Power*, chaps. 1–3. For the sexualized rites and mythology associated with primitive metallurgy worldwide, see Mircea Eliade, *The Forge and the Crucible: The Origins and Structures of Alchemy*, 2d ed., trans. Stephen Corrin (Chicago: University of Chicago Press, 1978).

108. For the textual history of the *Wu-Yue chunqiu*, see the appropriate entry in Loewe, *Early Chinese Texts*, 473–6. For the original passage, see *Wu-Yue chunqiu*, *SBCK* ed., 4:3a–4a; Zhao Ye, *Wu-Yue chunqiu* (Taibei: Shijie Shuju, 1962), 76–8. See translation in Donald B. Wagner, *Iron and Steel in Ancient China* (Leiden: E. J. Brill, 1993), 113–4. Extant versions of the story vary slightly. In the version printed in the *Imperial Overview of the Taiping Era* (Taiping yulan), both Ganjiang and Moye contribute hair and nails. This seems more fitting within the context of the story, so I have emended the *Wu-Yue chunqiu* version to reflect this tradition. See Li Fang et al., eds., *Taiping yulan*, *SBCK* ed. (Shanghai: Commercial Press, 1935; repr., 7 vols., Taibei: Commercial Press, 1968), *juan* 343:2a–b, p. 1704. Other legends of sword smiths are recounted in Lionello Lanciotti, "Notes on Ancient Chinese Metallurgy: Sword Casting and Related Legends in China," *East and West* 6, no. 2 (1955): 106–14.

109. The story is recorded in a letter written by the French Jesuit missionary Père François Xavier d'Entrecolles (1664–1741), who was living in Jiangxi. See *Lettres édifiantes et curieuses*; translated in William Burton, *Porcelain, Its Nature, Art, and Manufacture* (London: B. T. Batsford, 1906), 107–8.

110. According to five-elements (*wuxing*) theory, each dynasty flourished by virtue of one of the elements (water, fire, wood, metal, earth). When one element declined, another was in ascendancy, signaling a change in dynastic rule. The order of the elements varies according to different schools of thought. In one Han interpretation of the theory, the Zhou dynasty flourished under the element of wood, while the Han flourished under the element of fire. This passage leaves the Qin, who took water as their patron element, completely out of the legitimate succession of dynasties.

111. Ouye was a legendary sword smith of Yue who was also mentioned in the story of Ganjiang and Moye related earlier.

112. Wang Jia, *Shiyiji*, 5.110–3. Portions of the sword description emulate passages in a literary piece about virtuous ministers by Wang Bao in *Wenxuan*, *juan* 47. The final paragraph of the story, which involves the sword's subsequent history in palace storage, has been omitted.

113. Shaanxi Sheng Qianbi Xuehui, ed., *Qin-Han qianfan* (Xi'an: San-Qin Chubanshe, 1992), 147. Since this mold was found in Anhui, far beyond the capital area where all legitimate casting took place, it may be a mold used by a private workshop for counterfeiting coins. It might also have been made specifically for burial, to allow the deceased to cast his own coins in the afterlife.

114. Hosea Ballou Morse, *The Gilds of China* (London: Longmans, Green, and Co., 1909); John Stewart Burgess, *The Guilds of Peking* (New York: Columbia University Press, 1928), 91–102, chap. 11.

115. For a story in the *Mozi* text concerning Lu Ban and the construction of siege engines, see Needham et al., *Science and Civilisation,* 5.6:446–7, 450; *Mozi jiangu,* in *ZZJC,* 4:292–6 (*pian* 50, "Gongshu"); *SBCK,* 13:12a–14a; also translated in Yi-pao Mei, trans., *The Ethical and Political Works of Motse* (London: Probsthain, 1929), 255–9. See also the references in *Liji zhengyi,* in *SSJZS,* 3:346–7.

116. Chang Qu, *Huayang guozhi jiaozhu,* ed. Liu Lin (Chengdu: Ba-Shu Shushe, 1984), 244; Chang Qu, *Huayang guozhi jiaobu tuzhu,* ed. Ren Naiqiang (Shanghai: Shanghai Guji Chubanshe, 1987), 157.

117. *HSBZ,* 28A:68a–b; *HS,* 28A.1598; *HHSJJ, zhi* 23A.13b–14a; *HHS, zhi* 23.3509. This location is now in Qionglai County, Sichuan. According to Wagner, iron products from this factory were marked with the inscription "Shu jun Chengdu." See Wagner, *State and Iron Industry,* 95, entry 32.

118. As cited in Chang Qu, *Huayang guozhi jiaobu tuzhu,* 161n19, and Liu Lin ed., 247–8n6.

119. The attribution of the invention of metal weapons to Chi You was not universally accepted. It is here cited from the *zuopian* section of the *Shiben.* See Song Zhong, *Shiben,* in *Baibu congshu jicheng,* ser. 38, ed. Yan Yiping (Taibei: Yiwen Yinshuguan, 1968), 25:1b–2a.

120. See note 101.

121. In tomb texts and other tracts of the Han period, the Heavenly Thearch is also known as the Yellow Thearch (Huangdi) or the Yellow God (Huangshen). For his role in the popular conception of the underworld and/or heavenly bureaucracy, see Anna Seidel, "Traces of Han Religion in Funerary Texts Found in Tombs," in *Taoism and Religious Culture,* ed. Akizuki Kan'ei (Tokyo: Hirakawa Shuppan, 1987), 21–57.

122. Michael Loewe also points out that in rituals for rain in early China, gods could be either punished or worshiped. See Michael Loewe, *Divination, Mythology, and Monarchy in Han China* (Cambridge: Cambridge University Press, 1994), 419.

123. Qu, *Han Social Structure,* 49–62.

124. See chap. 6, under "The Slave Artisan."

125. Several anecdotes about this type of situation are related in Qu, *Social Structure,* 54.

126. *HSBZ,* 84:1a–b; *HS,* 84.342.

127. *HSBZ,* 91:6a; *HS,* 91.3686; Swann, *Food and Money,* 431. The text is ambiguous as to whose business she was continuing. It merely says that her forebears had monopolized the cinnabar mines for generations. This could refer either to her natal family or to her husband's family.

128. See Finsterbusch, *Verzeichnis,* 2: no. 271; *ZHQ,* 2: no. 94; Zhu, *Jiaxiang,* fig. 101. For an analysis of the wheel technology represented by this scene, see Needham et al., *Science and Civilisation,* 4.2:80–2. This stone is now in the National Museum of Chinese History in Beijing. The stone shown in figure 3.15a was found in the same general area during the last century and is published in Édouard Chavannes, *La sculpture sur pierre en Chine au temps des deux dynasties Han* (Paris: E. Leroux, 1893), pl. 43; Zhu, *Jiaxiang,* fig. 1.

129. This story is found in *Zhuangzi* and *Huainanzi.*

130. *ZJS,* 171 ("Ernian lüling," slip 278).

131. For a survey of these different factories, see Barbieri-Low, "Organization," 61–5, 87–9.

132. *HSBZ*, 28A:79a–80a; *HS*, 28A.1583.

133. *HSBZ*, 72:10a–b; *HS*, 72.3070, 3073.

134. *HSBZ*, 11:3a; *HS*, 11.336; *HFHD*, 3:23 and note 3.3. Emperor Jing promulgated a similarly worded edict in 142 BCE. See *HSBZ*, 5:9a; *HS*, 5.151; *HFHD*, 1:328 and note 9.4. The phrase *hai nü hong* (*gong*) might also be read, "harmful to the female artisans."

135. *SHD*, 46 ("Qin lü shiba zhong," slip 110); *RCL*, A60.

136. Yunmeng Shuihudi Qin Mu Bianxiezu, *Yunmeng Shuihudi Qin mu*; Hubei Sheng Bowuguan, ed., "Yunmeng Dafentou yihao Han mu," *Wenwu ziliao congkan* 4 (1981): 1–28; Satō Taketoshi, "Shin-Kan sho no shikki no seisan ni tsuite," *Koshi shunjū* 4 (1987): 3–16.

137. *SHD*, 32 ("Qin lü shiba zhong," slips 51–2). This statute classified convict females, but the distinction was probably the same for other labor conscription definitions. Under Han regulations, girls were divided into preservice females (*weishi nü*), who were one to six years old, and serviceable females (*shi nü*), who were seven to fourteen. Adult females (*da nüzi*) were fifteen or older.

138. For photos and drawings of the inscriptions, see Yunmeng Shuihudi Qin Mu Bianxiezu, *Yunmeng Shuihudi Qin mu*, 104–38, pls. 47–9.

139. Hubei Sheng Bowuguan, "Yunmeng Dafentou," 1–28.

140. Satō, "Shin-Kan sho no shikki," 10–12.

141. For the most complete tables of these names, see Barbieri-Low, "Organization," 318–21.

142. For the original object and transcription issues, see Umehara Sueji, *Shina Kandai kinenmei shikki zusetsu* (Kyoto: Kuwana Bunseidō, 1943; repr., Kyoto: Dohōsha, 1984), Former Han, no. 4, pl. 1; Rakurō Kanbo Kankōkai, ed., *Rakurō Kanbo*, 2 vols. (Nara: Rakurō Kanbo Kankōkai, 1974), no. 97, pl. 29.2. This piece was excavated in 1924 from Sekiganri (Korean: Sogamri) tomb 194 in North Korea. The fragmentary inscription is translated in Barbieri-Low, "Organization," 402.

143. *Wenwu* (1991.10): 51, figs. 35–6, pls. 6.1–2; excavated in 1985 from tomb 104 at Baonüdun, Jiangsu. See the translation in Barbieri-Low, "Organization," 412.

144. Stevan Harrel, Bamo Qubumo, and Ma Erzi, *Mountain Patterns: The Survival of Nuosu Culture in China* (Seattle: University of Washington Press, 2000), 31–2.

145. Umehara, *Shina Kandai kinenmei shikki zusetsu*, Former Han, no. 1.

146. Bielenstein, *Bureaucracy*, 9, 19.

CHAPTER 4

1. Zhang Heng, "Western Metropolis Rhapsody," translated in David R. Knechtges, *Wen xuan, or Selections of Refined Literature*, 3 vols. to date (Princeton: Princeton University Press, 1982–96), 1:203.

2. For a survey of Warring States economic and social developments, see Yang Kuan, *Zhanguo shi*, chap. 3; Xu Zhuoyun [Hsu Cho-yun], *Ancient China in Transition*. For a recent survey of the archaeology of Warring States period cities, see Sahara Yasuo, *Kandai toshi kikō no kenkyū* (Tokyo: Kyūko Shoin, 2002).

3. G. William Skinner, "Regional Urbanization in Nineteenth-Century China" and "Cities and the Hierarchy of Local Systems," in *The City in Late Imperial China: Studies in Chinese Society*, ed. G. William Skinner and Hugh D. R. Baker (Stanford: Stanford University Press,

1977), 211–52, 275–352. I would never presume that my cursory analysis of the Han macroregions even approaches the exhaustive study of Skinner, who analyzed the population and marketing patterns of thousands of Chinese towns and cities from the late imperial period. The fact that several of the macroregions of the Han remained regional economic units until late imperial times strongly bolsters Skinner's analysis. Skinner based his division primarily on natural watersheds, but he also took into consideration population densities, extent of rural peripheries, and differential distribution of economic resources.

4. *SJ*, 129.3253 ff.

5. One could argue that the final regional layout of the last seven of the Warring States had evolved organically from the sixth to the third centuries BCE, from the arbitrary boundaries of their original enfeoffments to a closer match with the natural determinants of geography and waterborne trading networks. Qin's final dominance of the other states was mostly due to its greater agricultural and administrative efficiency, but even in ancient times it was also recognized that Qin had benefited from an ideal defensive location "within the passes" (*guanzhong*). Sima Qian appears to have been one of the first to perceive that this area was dominant also because it straddled multiple trade routes.

6. Even though Sima Qian's description covers the period from ca. 200 to 100 BCE, many of these cities continued to be great marketing centers for many decades to come. In 10 CE, when Wang Mang changed the titles of market officials, he chose the markets of Chang'an, Luoyang, Handan, Linzi, Yuan, and Chengdu as the most important metropolitan markets. See *HSBZ*, 24B:23b–24a; *HS*, 24B.1180; translated in Swann, *Food and Money*, 336–7.

7. The figure of two million was arrived at by adding up the populations of the counties in the immediate vicinity of the capital, including the Three Metropolitan Districts (Sanfu), based on the census of 2 CE contained in chapter 28 of the *History of the Former Han*.

8. The population figures for the Yangzi River valley area during the Han were not as comprehensive or accurate as those figures collected for regions closer to the capital; thus, a certain amount of underreporting was inevitable. Han officials had not penetrated deeply into the most mountainous or swampy areas, completely ignoring large numbers of the indigenous population. Nevertheless, malaria was endemic in many of these areas, and it is unlikely that they supported extremely large populations at this time.

9. Ban Gu, "Liang du fu," in *Wen xuan*, comp. Xiao Tong, annotated by Li Shan (Hong Kong: Shangwu Yinshuguan, 1973), *juan* 1, p. 4, translated in Knechtges, *Wen xuan*, 1:105. The hyperbolic descriptions of the Han rhapsodic genre (*fu*) must certainly be used with caution, since they were meant to glorify the Han or to criticize profligate consumption, but archaeological surveys and other textual sources have confirmed many of their claims regarding the size and organization of the capital marketplaces.

10. For an analysis of the markets of Chengdu and Chang'an based on textual records and pictorial sources, see Liu Zhiyuan, "Handai shijing kao: Shuo Dong-Han shijing huaxiangzhuan," *Wenwu* (1973.3): 52–7. For a more comprehensive study of Han markets, see Sahara Yasuo, "Kandai no ichi ni tsuite," *Shirin* 68, no. 5 (1985): 33–71.

11. For a synthesis of the ongoing Han Chan'an excavations, see Liu Qingzhu, "Han Chang'an cheng de kaogu faxian ji xiangguan wenti yanjiu," *Kaogu* (1996.10): 1–14. For a slightly out-of-date treatment in English, see Wang Zhongshu, *Han Civilization*, trans. K. C. Chang (New Haven: Yale University Press, 1982), chap. 1. For a diachronic narrative of the building of Chang'an, see Wu Hung, *Monumentality*, chap. 3.

12. The remains of the bridge foundation have been found but have not yet been published.

13. The Yong Gate was also known as the Tu Gate and possibly also the Guang Gate, but these alternate names are sometimes bestowed on the Heng Gate as well. The Chucheng Gate led into the imperial kitchens, ideally situated near the Eastern Market. For a detailed identification of the gates of Han Chang'an, see Chen Zhi, *Sanfu huangtu,* 21–8.

14. The "Edict concerning Kingly Staffs," found at Wuwei, Gansu, states that, from the time of Emperor Xuan onward, men over eighty (later lowered to seventy) who had received a staff with a bird finial from the state were allowed to travel on the *chidao* (speedway), the central lane of imperial roads. Another version of this same edict, found at the site of Mozuizi, says that the honored seniors could travel just to the side of the *chidao.* See Wuwei Xian Bowuguan, ed., "Wuwei xinchu wangzhang zhaoling ce," in *Han jian yanjiu wenji,* ed. Gansu Sheng Wenwu Gongzuodui and Gansu Sheng Bowuguan (Lanzhou: Gansu Renmin Chubanshe, 1984), 36, strip 10. See the discussion in A. F. P. Hulsewé, "Qin and Han Legal Manuscripts," in *New Sources of Early Chinese History: An Introduction to the Reading of Inscriptions and Manuscripts,* ed. Edward L. Shaughnessy (Berkeley: Society for the Study of Early China and the Institute of East Asian Studies, University of California, 1997), 197n11.

15. Wang, *Han Civilization,* 3. According to some sources, the two sectors were divided into nine different markets, of which the Western Market housed six and the Eastern Market housed three. Chen Zhi and Sahara Yasuo contend that the Western and Eastern Markets were only two of the nine markets mentioned, and that the others were located elsewhere around the city. See Chen Zhi, *Sanfu huangtu,* 29–31; Sahara, "Kandai no ichi," 35–40.

16. *SJ,* 22.1120.

17. A survey revealed that the wall around the Eastern Market measured 780 meters from east to west and 650–700 meters from north to south. See Liu Qingzhu, "Xi'an Shi Han Chang'an cheng dongshi he xishi yizhi," *Zhongguo kaoguxue nianjian,* 1987, 264. The Mall of America encloses 390,193 square meters of store and entertainment space; the total leasable area in the mall is 232,258 square meters (http://www.mallofamerica.com/about_the_mall/mallfacts.aspx, accessed Jan. 22, 2004).

18. *HSBZ,* 5:4a, 49:24a; *HS,* 5.142, 49.2302. For a brief summary of the Rebellion of the Seven Kingdoms, see *HFHD,* 1:292–7.

19. *HSBZ,* 2:6a; *HS,* 2.91; *HFHD,* 1:184.

20. Zhongguo Shehui Kexueyuan Kaogu Yanjiusuo Hanchengdui, ed., "Han Chang'an cheng yaozhi fajue baogao," *Kaogu xuebao* (1994.1): 99–129. For color pictures of some of the molds and figurines, see Ōsaka Shiritsu Bijutsukan and Yomiuri Shinbun Ōsaka Honsha, eds., *Yomigaeru Kan ōchō: 2000-nen no toki o koete* (Osaka: Yomiuri Shinbun Ōsaka Honsha, 1999), pls. 20–2.

21. Li Yufang, "Han Chang'an cheng hongfan yao he zhubi yizhi," *Zhongguo kaoguxue nianjian,* 1993, 245–6.

22. Zhongguo Shehui Kexueyuan Kaogu Yanjiusuo Hancheng Gongzuodui, ed., "1992 nian Han Chang'an cheng yezhu yizhi fajue jianbao," *Kaogu* (1995.9): 792–807.

23. Zhongguo Shehui Kexueyuan Kaogu Yanjiusuo Hancheng Gongzuodui, ed., "Han Chang'an cheng yihao yaozhi fajue jianbao," *Kaogu* (1991.1): 18–22; Zhongguo Shehui Kexueyuan Kaogu Yanjiusuo Hancheng Gongzuodui, ed., "Han Chang'an cheng 23–27 yaozhi fajue jianbao," *Kaogu* (1994.11): 986–95.

24. Wang Jiayou and Jia Ke, "Dong-Han Xinfan huaxiangzhuan shijingtu shi," in *Zhongguo gudai ditu ji,* ed. Cao Wanru et al. (Beijing: Wenwu Chubanshe, 1990–7), 1:18.

25. Xu Shen, *Shuowen,* 588. See also Liu Zhiyuan, "Handai shijing," 54; Sahara, "Kandai no ichi," 48–9.

26. Wang Jiayou and Jia Ke, "Dong-Han Xinfan," explain this by saying that the southern edge of the Blue Ram Market abutted onto a river, so no wall was necessary.

27. Liu Qingzhu, "Xi'an Shi."

28. Ibid.

29. For textual references to terms referring to the layout and composition of markets, see Liu Zhiyuan, "Handai shijing," 54–5.

30. *SJ,* 127.3216; translated in Burton Watson, *Records: Han Dynasty II,* 425–6.

31. See Li Xueqin, "Shi fa jiang shu," in *Jianbo yiji yu xueshushi* (Taibei: Shibao Chuban, 1994), 380–7. The so-called *Market Laws* text, excavated from the Yinqueshan site in Shandong, does not contain actual legal regulations but is an idealizing text describing the role of markets in the ideal world and how they should be structured. It is related to sections of the *Guanzi* text. One suspects that, when the *Market Laws* text was written, quite the opposite situation may have existed in contemporary markets (i.e., gem sellers had enormous stalls), and thus the author was arguing for how stalls should ideally be handed out.

32. Liu Zhiyuan, "Handai shijing," 56.

33. Liu Qingzhu, "Han Chang'an cheng buju jiegou bianxi," *Kaogu* (1987.10): 942.

34. Sahara, "Kandai no ichi," 58n4. The Tang market was opened at high noon with three hundred beats of the drum and closed a little over an hour and a half before sunset with three hundred clangings of a bell; see Zhang Jiuling et al., *Da Tang liudian, juan* 20, p. 373.

35. See references in Liu Zhiyuan, "Handai shijing," 55.

36. See Zuo Si (ca. 250–305 CE), "Shu du fu," in Xiao Tong, *Wen xuan, juan* 4, p. 89; translated in Knechtges, *Wen xuan,* 1:361.

37. These references are brought together in Sahara, "Kandai no ichi," 35–40.

38. Xu Zhuoyun [Hsu Cho-yun], *Han Agriculture: The Formation of Early Chinese Agrarian Economy, 206 B.C.–A.D. 220, ed.* Jack L. Dull (Seattle: University of Washington Press, 1980), 67–80, 130.

39. Sahara, "Kandai no ichi," 40–4.

40. Ibid.; Utsunomiya Kiyoyoshi, *Kandai shakai keizaishi kenkyū,* rev. ed. (Tokyo: Kōbundō, 1967), chap. 9.

41. Katō Shigeru, "Kandai ni okeru kokka zaisei to teishitsu zaisei to no kubetsu," in *Shina keizaishi kōshō* (Tokyo: Tōyō Bunko, 1952–3), 1:58–60; Yu Yingshi [Yü Ying-shih], *Trade and Expansion in Han China: A Study in the Structure of Sino-Barbarian Economic Relations* (Berkeley and Los Angeles: University of California Press, 1967), 95.

42. Yu Yingshi, *Trade,* chap. 5.

43. Ōba Osamu, "The Ordinances on Fords and Passes Excavated from Han Tomb Number 247, Zhangjiashan," *Asia Major,* 3d ser., 14, no. 2 (2001): 123–4.

44. Satō, *Chūgoku kodai kōgyōshi no kenkyū,* 25–49.

45. Yang Kuan, *Zhanguo shi,* chap. 3.

46. For the Han taxes, see *HSBZ,* 24B:13b; *HS,* 24B.1166; translated in Swann, *Food and Money,* 282. For the Sui regulation, see Wei Zheng, *Suishu* (Beijing: Zhonghua Shuju, 1973),

2.41. This edict proclaimed a law that artisans were no longer allowed to become officials, just as merchants had usually been prohibited from entering the bureaucracy.

47. Qu, *Han Social Structure*, 117–8.

48. J. J. L. Duyvendak, *The Book of Lord Shang* (London: Probsthain, 1928), 48–50, 177–84.

49. *SJ*, 6.253; translated in Burton Watson, *Records: Qin Dynasty*, 53.

50. *HSBZ*, 24B:4a; *HS*, 24B.1153; translated in Swann, *Food and Money*, 231–2. A more detailed list of the restrictions, probably closer to the original edict, is found in *HSBZ*, 1B:13a–b; *HS*, 1B.65; *HFHD*, 1:120–1.

51. Nishijima Sadao, "The Economic and Social History of Former Han," in *CHOC*, 576.

52. *HSBZ*, 6:35a; *HS*, 6.205 (commentary of Zhang Yan, ca. 3d century); *HFHD*, 2:108n35.2; *HSBZ*, 49:12b–13a; *HS*, 49.2284; Swann, *Food and Money*, 50nE.1; Qu, *Han Social Structure*, 118, 328n21.

53. For textual references, see Katō, "Kandai ni okeru," 56–60; Liu Zhiyuan, "Handai shijing," 55.

54. *HSBZ*, 86:1a–1b; *HS*, 86.3482. In this incident, He Xian, He Wu's younger brother, was not paying his market tax and his family was arrested and detained by the authorities until his powerful brother intervened.

55. This was a staff with a little carved dove on the end. It was also called a kingly staff (*wangzhang*); see *HHSJJ*, *zhi* 4:8b and comm., *zhi* 5:6b and comm.; *HHS*, *zhi* 4.3109, *zhi* 5.3124; Wuwei Xian Bowuguan, "Wuwei xinchu," 34–61. For pictures of an actual kingly staff, see Gansu Sheng Bowuguan, ed., "Gansu Wuwei Mozuizi Han mu fajue," *Kaogu* (1960.9), pls. 7.4–7.5. According to the census records of Donghai Commandery, ca. 13 BCE, 2,823 people over seventy in Donghai (out of a total population of close to 1.4 million) had received a kingly staff from the government; see Lianyungang Bowuguan, ed., *Yinwan Han mu jiandu* (Beijing: Zhonghua Shuju, 1997), 78.

56. Katō, "Kandai ni okeru," 58. Before 120 BCE, the market tax revenue from within fiefdoms was retained by the prince or marquis; see *HSBZ*, 24A:9b–10a; *HS*, 24A.1127; translated in Swann, *Food and Money*, 150–1, 371.

57. *SJ*, 52.2008; *HSBZ*, 38:9b; *HS*, 38.2000.

58. *HSBZ*, 2:6a; *HS*, 2.91. This is quoted from the Han statutes in the commentary by Ying Shao.

59. For the poll tax on slaves, see ibid. The adult poll tax fluctuated throughout the Former Han period, from as high as 190 coins during the reign of Emperor Wu to as low as 40 coins under Emperor Wen, but 120 coins seems to have been the fixed amount from 31 BCE until the end of the Latter Han and may have been the initial amount established by Liu Bang. The poll tax on children seems to have begun around 120 BCE under Emperor Wu with 20 coins per child of three to fourteen years of age. The amount was soon raised to 23 coins, with the extra three coins going to the army. In 79 BCE, the amount was lowered again to 20 coins, and around 44 BCE, the bottom age was raised to seven. See discussions in Nishijima, "Economic and Social History," 598; Katō, "Kandai ni okeru," 60–4; Katō Shigeru, "A Study on the *Suanfu*, the Poll Tax of the Han Dynasty," *Memoirs of the Research Department of the Tōyō Bunko* 1 (1926): 51–68; Swann, *Food and Money*, 366–9.

60. *HSBZ*, 24B:13a–b; *HS*, 24B.1166–7; translated in Swann, *Food and Money*, 279–82. The

amount is listed as one *suan* on each two thousand coins for the first category. Since the *suan* (poll tax unit) during Wudi's time has been reconstructed by Katō Shigeru to be 190 cash at its height, this tax amounted to 9.5 percent. Other scholars have used the traditional interpretation of one *suan* as always amounting to 120 cash in their differing calculations. Xu Zhuoyun [Hsu Cho-yun] uses 127 cash, based on a commentary by Fu Qian.

61. *HSBZ*, 24B:13a–b; *HS*, 24B.1167; Swann, *Food and Money*, 278–83; Nishijima, "Economic and Social History," 599; Xu Zhuoyun, *Han Agriculture*, 75–6. It is unclear when, if ever, these onerous property taxes were repealed. An undated bamboo slip from the site of Xuanquan in Gansu quotes the property tax regulation from a statute on military laws. See Hu and Zhang, *Dunhuang Xuanquan*, 11–2.

62. *ZJS*, 192 ("Ernian lüling," slips 436–8). This is part of the "Statute on Currency" (Jinbu lü).

63. *ZJS*, 168–9 ("Ernian lüling," slip 260). A similar Qin statute can be found in *SHD*, 36–7 ("Qin lü shiba zhong," slip 68); *RCL*, A45.

64. *SSJZS*, 8:449; translated in Biot, *Tcheou-li*, 1:325. Most scholars now agree that the *Zhouli* text was composed sometime during the middle to late Warring States period. For the Yinqueshan text, see Li Xueqin, "Shi fa jiang shu."

65. From the Qin "Statute on Currency"; see *SHD*, 37 ("Qin lü shiba zhong," slip 69); *RCL*, A46.

66. From the Qin "Statute on Passes and Markets"; see *SHD*, 42–3 ("Qin lü shiba zhong," slip 97); *RCL*, A51. Also see the similar passage from the Han statutes in *ZJS*, 190–1 ("Ernian lüling," slips 429–30).

67. From the Qin "Statute on Currency"; see *SHD*, 35–7 ("Qin lü shiba zhong," slips 65, 68); *RCL*, A42, A45.

68. *SSJZS*, 8:443–4; translated in Biot, *Tcheou-li*, 1:317–9.

69. See chapter 6, under the heading "The Slave Artisan."

70. *ZJS*, 135 ("Ernian lüling," slips 14–5).

71. A. F. P. Hulsewé, "'Contracts' of the Han Period," in *Il diritto in Cina*, ed. Lionello Lanciotti (Florence: Leo S. Olschki, 1978), 11–38.

72. *ZJS*, 178 ("Ernian lüling," slips 334–6).

73. Yangzhou Bowuguan, ed., "Jiangsu Yizheng Xupu 101 hao Xi-Han mu," *Wenwu* (1987.1): 1–19. See translation and analysis in Bret Hinsch, "Women, Kinship, and Property as Seen in a Han Dynasty Will," *TP* 84, nos. 1–3 (1998): 1–21.

74. For how the bureaucracy at imperial factories paralleled the territorial administration, see Barbieri-Low, "Organization," chap. 5.

75. For this title, see *HSBZ*, 19A:20b–21b, 24B:23b–24a; *HS*, 19A.736, 24B.1180; Swann, *Food and Money*, 336–7; Liu Zhiyuan, "Handai shijing," 56n11; Bielenstein, *Bureaucracy*, 87. In 186 BCE this was still a single post, ranked at 600 *shi*; see *ZJS*, 197 ("Ernian lüling," slips 461, 464).

76. The capital area during the Qin and early Han was under the control of the Chamberlain for the Capital (Neishi). In 155 (or 135) BCE, the Han split the position into (east) Zuo Neishi and (west) You Neishi. In 104 BCE, the You Neishi was renamed You Fufeng, while the Zuo Neishi was renamed Zuo Pingyi. The capital city itself (and its markets) was put under the jurisdiction of a third official, the Metropolitan Governor (Jingzhao Yin). The smaller suburban markets of Chang'an remained under the jurisdiction of the east division (Zuo Neishi/Zuo Pingyi). See *HSBZ*, 19A:20b–21a; *HS*, 19A.736; Bielenstein, *Bureaucracy*, 87–8.

77. Bielenstein, *Bureaucracy,* 88–9.

78. *HSBZ,* 19A:21a, 24B:23b–24a; *HS,* 19A.736, 24B.1180; Swann, *Food and Money,* 336–7; Bielenstein, *Bureaucracy,* 87.

79. Luo Fuyi, "Xiang Tajun," 179.

80. *HSBZ,* 86:1a–1b; *HS,* 86.3482.

81. Wei Hong, *Han jiu yi,* in Sun Xingyan et al., comps., *Han guan liu zhong* (Beijing: Zhonghua Shuju, 1990), 92.

82. Beijing Wenwu Gongzuodui, ed., "Beijing xijiao faxian Handai shique qingli jianbao," *Wenwu* (1964.11): 13–22; Shao Mingsheng, "Han Youzhou shuzuo Qin Jun shique shiwen," *Wenwu* (1964.11): 23–4; Beijing Wenwu Jingcui Daxi Bianweihui and Beijing Shi Wenwu Shiye Guanliju, eds., *Beijing wenwu jingcui daxi, shidiao juan* (Beijing: Beijing Chubanshe, 2000), p. 35, fig. 1, p. 49, pl. 8.

83. Hebei Sheng Wenhuaju Wenwu Gongzuodui, "Hebei Ding Xian," 127–94. Based on internal evidence from inscriptions, the tomb itself was most likely begun between 84 and 88 CE and expanded after Liu Yan's death in 90 CE.

84. This practice of inscribing the blocks of a royal mortuary complex seems to have begun in the Former Han period; see Henan Sheng Wenwu Kaogu Yanjiusuo, *Yongcheng Xi-Han Liang Guo wangling yu qinyuan,* 151–86.

85. *HHSJJ,* 42:20a; *HHS,* 42.1450.

86. Liu Zhong, the contemporary Prince of Dongping, and Liu Chang, the contemporary Prince of Liang, were nephews of Liu Yan, and Liu Chang was also the son of Emperor Ming.

87. Hebei Sheng Wenhuaju Wenwu Gongzuodui, "Hebei Ding Xian," 156 (no. 41), 158 (no. 155). The two stone rubbings recorded with his name appear identical, though they are published as two separate inscriptions.

88. Liu Shang's brief biography can be found in *HHSJJ,* 42:15b–16a; *HHS,* 42.1443. For a more complete publication of the stone inscriptions, see Shandong Sheng Jining Shi Wenwuju, *Han Rencheng.*

89. See Shandong Sheng Jining Shi Wenwuju, *Han Rencheng,* 111, 118. *Yuan* means "primary" and is sometimes used for the given name of an eldest son in lieu of the more common name Bo. Zhong is the standard name for the second-eldest son in early Chinese families.

90. See ibid., 118, 120.

91. See Hebei Sheng Wenhuaju Wenwu Gongzuodui, "Hebei Ding Xian," 188, rubbing 19.

92. *Xijing zaji, SBCK* ed., 2:1a; Xiang and Liu *Xijing zaji jiaozhu,* 67–71. For a translation of this whole story, see chapter 2 above. For the historical mention of Wang Zhaojun, see *HSBZ,* 9:12b–13a; *HS,* 9.297; translated in *HFHD,* 2:334–5.

93. Shaanxi Sheng Kaogu Yanjiusuo, ed., "Xi'an beijiao Zhanguo zhutong gongjiang mu fajue jianbao," *Wenwu* (2003.9): 4–14; Yue Lianjian, "Xi'an beijiao Zhanguo wanqi zhutong gongjiang mu chulun," *Kaogu yu wenwu* (supplement), 2002.

94. Joseph Hackin, *Nouvelles recherches archéologiques à Begram, ancienne Kâpicî, 1939–1940: Rencontre de trois civilisations, Inde, Grèce, Chine,* 2 vols. (Paris: Imprimerie Nationale, 1954).

95. R. Pfister, *Textiles de Palmyre découverts par le Service des antiquités du Haut-commissariat de la République française dans la nécropole de Palmyre* (Paris: Les Editions d'Art et d'Histoire, 1934); Otto Maenchen-Helfen, "From China to Palmyra," *Art Bulletin* 25, no. 4 (Dec. 1943): 358–62; Lothar von Falkenhausen, "Die Seiden mit chinesischen Inschriften," in

Die Textilien aus Palmyra: Neue und alte Funde, ed. Andreas Schmidt-Colinet, Anne-Marie Stauffer, and Khaled Al As'ad (Mainz: Philipp von Zabern, 2000), 58–81; Lothar von Falkenhausen, "Inconsequential Incomprehensions: Some Instances of Chinese Writing in Alien Contexts," *Res* 35 (1999): 42–69.

96. Manfred Raschke, "New Studies in Roman Commerce with the East," *Aufstieg und Niedergang der römischen Welt im Spiegel der neueren Forschung* II, 9.2 (1978): 604–1361.

97. *SJ*, 123.3164–6; translated in Burton Watson, *Records: Han Dynasty II*, 235–6. See parallel text in *HSBZ*, 61:2b–3a; *HS*, 61.2689; translated in A. F. P. Hulsewé and Michael Loewe, *China in Central Asia: The Early Stage, 125 B.C.–A.D. 23; An Annotated Translation of Chapters 61 and 96 of the "History of the Former Han Dynasty"* (Leiden: E. J. Brill, 1979), 211. The exact dates of Zhang Qian's journey are uncertain.

98. The disruptions culminated in the so-called Yellow Turban Rebellion. See *CHOC*, 1:324–6, 338–41.

99. A representative selection of these finds are referenced in the following notes. Also see Xuzhou Bowuguan, ed., "Jiangsu Xuzhou damiao Jin-Han huaxiangshi mu," *Wenwu* (2003.4): 61–70. For a Han tomb reused in the tenth century, see Nanjing Bowuyuan, "Xuzhou Mao cun huaxiangshi mu," *Kaogu* (1980.4): 347–52; Nanyang Shi Wenwu Gongzuodui, ed., "Nanyang Shi yaocai shichang huaxiangshi mu fajue jianbao," *Zhongyuan wenwu* (1994.1): 96–100. Three more recycled tombs were reported in the 1985.3 issue of *Zhongyuan wenwu*. For a *que* pillar-gate stone reused inside a tomb, see Su Zhaoqing et al., *Juxian wenwu zhi* (Ji'nan: Qi-Lu Shushe, 1993), 127–33.

100. See text and notes in Li Falin, *Shandong*, 107. Compare the partial translations of An Guo's inscription by Ruitenbeek, *Chinese Shadows*, 16–18, and by Powers, *Art and Political Expression*, 52. A complete translation can be found in Wu Hung, *Monumentality*, 193–4. A similar warning can be found at the end of the inscription carved on a doorpost of Xiang Tajun's shrine. See Luo Fuyi, "Xiang Tajun," 180.

101. It is ironic that the stones of An Guo's shrine also appear to have been reused ceiling stones from a belowground tomb.

102. Jiaxiang Xian Wushici Wenguansuo, ed., "Shandong Jiaxiang Songshan faxian Han huaxiangshi," *Wenwu* (1979.9): 1–6; Jining Diqu Wenwuzu and Jiaxiang Xian Wenguansuo, eds., "Shandong Jiaxiang Songshan 1980 nian chutu de Han huaxiangshi," *Wenwu* (1982.5): 60–70; Zhu Xilu and Jiaxiang Xian Wenguansuo, eds., "Jiaxiang Wulaowa faxian yipi Han huaxiangshi," *Wenwu* (1982.5): 71–8.

103. In some cases, we get the impression that the post-Han tomb builders did not want to completely escape the influence of the recycled imagery. In one apparent husband-wife burial near Tengzhou, Shandong, the dividing wall between the coffins was made from the recycled western and eastern walls of an aboveground offering hall. Yet their placement seems to have been intentionally gendered. The stone depicting the Queen Mother of the West (Xiwangmu) faced toward one spouse, while the stone depicting the King Father of the East (Dongwanggong) kept watch over the other. Sadly, the state of skeletal preservation prevents us from knowing for certain the gender of either skeleton. See *Kaogu* (2002.10): 87–93.

104. Nicholas Reeves, *Akhenaten: Egypt's False Prophet* (London: Thames and Hudson, 2001), 26, 91–5.

105. For a Henan example, see Henan Sheng Wenhuaju Wenwu Gongzuodui and Nanyang Shi Wenwu Guanli Weiyuanhui, eds., "Henan Nanyang dongguan Jin mu," *Kaogu* (1963.1):

25–7. For Shandong, see Wang Sili, "Shandong Feicheng Han huaxiang mu diaocha," *Wenwu cankao ziliao* (1958.4): 34–6.

106. Nanyang Shi Bowuguan, ed., "Nanyang faxian Dong-Han Xu Aqu muzhi huaxiangshi," *Wenwu* (1974.8): 73–5, 41. I am thankful for the suggestions of Hsu Cho-yun in reading difficult portions of this epitaph.

107. See the original report in Harada and Tazawa, *Rakurō*.

108. Though the two words sounded very similar during the Han, the substitution of *zhi* (to make, to regulate) (*GSR*, 976z: *diəg/d'i) for *zhi* (value) (*GSR*, 919h: *d'iəg/d'i) is not commonly seen as a phonetic loan in inscriptions dated to the Han period. The equivalence is seen in texts like the *Explication of Names* (Shiming). If taken literally, the graph *zhi* would allow this passage to be translated "made 1,200 pieces" or "underwent 1,200 manufacturing and inspection processes." Because of the common practice of listing the value (*zhi*) on bronze vessels at this time, I would still argue for the substitution.

109. The word *lao* could also mean "diligent and careful," as in "carefully made by diligent artisans" or "carefully submitted."

110. For the stylistic history of Western Workshop lacquers, see Barbieri-Low, "Organization," chap. 3.

111. For the other platter, see Harada and Tazawa, *Rakurō*, 43–4, pl. 60.

112. Ibid., 36–40, pls. 43–4.

113. The Lu as in Lu family (archaic *lwo or *lwag) did not rhyme in Han times with the *lu* meaning "deer," which was pronounced something more like *luk (*GSR*, 1209a).

114. For a general introduction to the inscriptions on Han mirrors, see Lin Suqing, "Liang-Han jingming chutan," 325–70; Bernhard Karlgren, "Early Chinese Mirror Inscriptions," *BMFEA* 6 (1934): 9–79. Several of the more poetic inscriptions are translated in Michael Loewe, *Ways to Paradise: The Chinese Quest for Immortality* (London: George Allen and Unwin, 1979), 60–85, 158–202. Large compilations of mirror inscriptions (without addressing issues of authenticity) can be found in Wang Shilun, "Lidai jingming xuanlu," in *Zhejiang chutu tongjing* (Beijing: Wenwu Chubanshe, 1987); and Fu Kaisen [John Calvin Ferguson], *Lidai zhulu jijin mu* (Peking, 1939; repr., Taibei: Taiwan Shangwu Yinshuguan, 1971), 1279–1331.

115. For a description and history of the Shangfang, see Barbieri-Low, "Organization," 65–7.

116. Chen Zhi, "Guanyu Liang-Han de shougongye," in *Liang-Han jingji shiliao luncong* (Xi'an: Shaanxi Renmin Chubanshe, 1958), 110.

117. The reading and accuracy of this date are greatly suspect. The first graph in the reign date is hard to read. It could indicate the [Yong]jia era (145 CE), the [Yang]jia era (132–5 CE), or the [Yuan]jia era (151–2 CE), which are all fairly close in time. As to the reading of the specific month and day, Michael Loewe points out that a large number of dated Han mirrors claim that they were cast on the *bingwu* day. According to the *Discourses Weighed* (Lunheng) of Wang Chong, that particular day was auspicious for metallurgy. See Michael Loewe, "Dated Inscriptions on Certain Mirrors (A.D. 6–105): Genuine or Fabricated?" *Early China* 26–7 (2001–2): 237.

118. For an explanation of the *sanyang* phrase on bronze mirrors, see Karlgren, "Early Chinese Mirror Inscriptions," no. 120.

119. Umehara Sueji, *Kan Sangoku Rikuchō kinenkyō zusetsu* (Kyoto: Kuwana Bunseidō, 1943), Han period no. 8. The mirror was reportedly found near Luoyang. The current where-

abouts of this mirror are unknown, and we have only a rubbing. A bronze mirror, dated May 14, 181 CE, was recovered by authorities in 1986 from looters in Hubei. Its inscription begins with a very similar mix of the same three imperial factory names and incorporates many of the same phrases. The design is also of the same general type. See *Kaogu* (2004.7): 71.

120. Kyōto Kokuritsu Hakubutsukan, ed., *Moriya kōzō shūshū hōkaku kiku shijin kyō zuroku* (Kyoto: Kyōto Kokuritsu Hakubutsukan, 1969), no. 30.

121. I have modified my translation somewhat to force the rhyme in English. I have also drawn on the earlier translation of Loewe, *Ways to Paradise,* 200–1.

122. See transcription and translation in ibid., 203 (mirror X2006).

123. For the pronunciation of the final syllable of line 5, see *GSR,* 947a: *məg/məu. The final voiced-guttural g appears to have been lost between Archaic and Ancient Chinese, by the Han at least.

124. Lin Suqing, "Liang-Han jingming suojian jiyu yanjiu," in *Handai wenxue yu sixiang xueshu yantaohui lunwenji,* ed. Guoli Zhengzhi Daxue Zhongwen Xisuo (Taibei: Wenshizhe Chubanshe, 1991), 174, no. 87.

125. Wang Shilun, "Lidai," no. 130; Lin Suqing, "Liang-Han jingming chutan," nos. 97–105.

126. Wang Shilun, "Lidai," no. 90; Lin Suqing, "Liang-Han jingming chutan," nos. 73, 85, 87.

127. Wang Shilun, "Lidai," nos. 110, 134.

128. Ibid., nos. 136–7; Lin Suqing, "Liang-Han jingming chutan," nos. 102, 106.

129. Many of these "advertising" mirrors can be found in Lin Suqing, "Liang-Han jingming suojian jiyu yanjiu," 177–8.

130. Wang Shilun, "Lidai," no. 127. It has been suggested by Lai Guolong (personal communication) that some of these family-branded mirrors may be copies made during the Song dynasty.

131. Henan Sheng Wenwu Yanjiusuo and Zhenping Xian Wenhuaguan, eds., "Henan Zhenping chutu de Handai jiaocang tiefan he tieqi," *Kaogu* (1982.3): 243–51.

132. The two final graphs in the couplet, *gang* (bushing) and *zhong* (middle), began with different initials and ended with different finals but still belonged to the same general rhyming group (*dong*). Leaving off the metal determinative on the final character of the first line may have also been an intentional pun, since the unadorned graph is just *gong* (artisan). Thus, the line could also be read as "The Wang family are big strong artisans."

133. The phrase *minggong* (famous artisan) is found in the An Guo inscription in reference to Wang Shu, Wang Jian, and Jiang Hu from Gaoping. The phrase *mingshi* (famous stones) is found in the Wu Liang stele inscription. For references, see chapter 3. The phrase *qiaogong* (skillful artisan) is mentioned in an epitaph within the tomb of a governor of Liaodong Commandery, dated 90 CE, found in Suide County, Shaanxi. It is used to refer to a mason surnamed Wang who fashioned the tomb. See Wu Zhenfeng, "Qin Jin liang sheng Dong-Han huaxiangshi tiji jishi," *Kaogu yu wenwu* (2006.1): 53.

134. For the original report, see Wang Sili, "Shandong Feicheng," 34–6. The reading presented here follows that of Li Falin, *Shandong,* 46. A very different reading is presented in Shandong Sheng Bowuguan and Shandong Sheng Wenwu Kaogu Yanjiusuo, *Shandong Han huaxiangshi xuanji,* no. 472. The final few words are mostly effaced and difficult to read.

135. See the bilingual German-Chinese report in Susanne Greiff and Yin Shenping, *Das Grab des Bin Wang: Wandmalereien der Östlichen Han Zeit in China* (Mainz: Verlag des Römisch-Germanischen Zentralmuseums in Kommission bei Harrassowitz Verlag, Wiesbaden, 2002). For the significance of the artist's self-presentation, see the review by Martin Kern, *China Review International* 10, no. 2 (Fall 2003): 389–93.

136. Greiff and Yin, *Grab des Bin Wang,* fig. 28a–b.

137. Ibid., fig. 32a–b.

CHAPTER 5

1. *Xijing zaji, SBCK* ed., 1:1b.

2. *SJ,* 8.385–6; translation from Burton Watson, *Records: Han Dynasty I,* 79.

3. Wang Yanshou, "Rhapsody on the Hall of Spiritual Light" (Lu Lingguangdian fu), translated in Arthur Waley, *The Temple and Other Poems* (New York: A. A. Knopf, 1923), 95–7, with modification and additional translation by author.

4. *HSBZ,* 54:23a–b; *HS,* 54.2468–9; translated in Burton Watson, trans., *Courtier and Commoner in Ancient China: Selections from the History of the Former Han by Pan Ku* (New York: Columbia University Press, 1974), 44–5.

5. See a commentary by Zhang Yan (third century) in *HSBZ,* 54:23a notes; *HS,* 54.2469n1. The unicorn capture may have been the one that occurred in 122 BCE (*SJ,* 28.1387) (Emperor Wu reigned from 141 to 87 BCE). In Han and later sources there is mention of both a Qilin Ge (Unicorn Hall) and a Qilin Dian (Unicorn Palace Hall). They were both said to be part of the Weiyang Palace complex. It is unclear if these names refer to the same building. See Zhang Yonglu, ed., *Handai Chang'an cidian* (Xi'an: Shaanxi Renmin Chubanshe, 1993), 148; Chen Zhi, *Sanfu huangtu,* 37, 39.

6. Cai Zhi, *Han guan dianzhi yishi xuanyong,* in Sun Xingyan et al., *Han guan liu zhong,* 204; cf. the translation in Wu Hung, *Wu Liang Shrine,* 193.

7. The Xiongnu were a confederation of nomadic pastoralists who lived to the north of the Great Wall. During most of the Former Han period, they were the principal military opponent of the dynasty.

8. Wang Chong, "Xu song pian," in *Lunheng, ZZJC,* 7:197; cf. the translation in A. Forke, *Lun-Heng: Philosophical Essay by Wang Ch'ong* (New York: Paragon Book Gallery, 1962), 2:223.

9. *HSBZ,* 54:23a; *HS,* 54.2468.

10. Zhang Yanyuan, *Lidai minghua ji* (Beijing: Renmin Meishu Chubanshe, 1983), 74.

11. *HSBZ,* 69:16b–17a; *HS,* 69.2994–5. The text of the eulogy is also recorded in Xiao Tong, *Wen xuan,* 2:1032–4.

12. Julia F. Andrews, *Painters and Politics in the People's Republic of China* (Berkeley and Los Angeles: University of California Press, 1994), 65, 75–86, figs. 29–31, pl. 1. See the original work in color in *China Pictorial* (1953.10), 20–21. The restored original painting is housed in the Museum of Revolutionary History, Beijing.

13. Hans Bielenstein, "Lo-Yang in Later Han Times," *BMFEA* 48 (1976): 26–7. The Cloud Terrace was a great platform on which the Guangde Palace Hall rested.

14. *HHSJJ,* 22:13b–14a; *HHS,* 22.789–91.

15. See Bielenstein, "Lo-yang," 26–7; *HHSJJ*, 24:17a; *HHS*, 24.851. When asked by a royal relative why Ma Yuan was excluded from the mural, Emperor Ming just laughed and said nothing.

16. See the Chinese text and a different translation in Acker, *Some T'ang and Pre-T'ang Texts*, 1:72.

17. *HHSJJ*, 44:12a–13a and comm.; *HHS*, 44.1511. Hu Guang (91–172 CE) had died just five years previously. The other man, Huang Qiong, had died in 164 CE.

18. Cao Zhi, "Preface to Eulogies on Painting" (Huazan xu) (written ca. 214 CE); translation based on Acker, *Some T'ang and Pre-T'ang Texts*, 1:73 (with modifications). The text can also be found in *Taiping yulan*, 751:2b–3a; Cao Zhi, *Cao Zhi ji jiaozhu*, ed. Zhao Youwen (Beijing: Renmin Minxue Chubanshe, 1984), 67–9. The surviving eulogies can be found in *Cao Zhi ji jiaozhu*, 69 ff. The structure of these eulogies is remarkably similar to the eulogy texts seen on the upper register of the west wall of the Wu Liang Shrine and undoubtedly come from the same tradition. That similarity strengthens the view that the Wu Liang Shrine images were directly descended from palace cycles of exemplary illustrations.

19. This is a reference to the words of Zigong in the *Analects* (19.20).

20. This is a reference to the Lord of Wei (Weizi), a noble at the Shang court and a stepbrother of the last Shang king. He admonished Zhou about his indulgence in alcohol and then left the court.

21. *HSBZ*, 100:3b–4a; *HS*, 100.4200–1. Wu Hung discusses this incident in *Wu Liang Shrine*, 172, where he inexplicably dates the incident to the reign of Emperor Wu. Wu then builds on this incorrect date to argue for the existence of didactic screens at court during the second century BCE.

22. *HSBZ*, 66:10a; *HS*, 66.2891; translation from Acker, *Some T'ang and Pre-T'ang Texts*, 1:112 (modified); cf. the different translation in Wu Hung, *Wu Liang Shrine*, 164.

23. *HSBZ*, 30:33b; *HS*, 30.1727.

24. Wu Hung, *Wu Liang Shrine*, 171.

25. See Yao Zhenzong, comp., *Qilüe bielu yiwen*, in *Xuxiu siku quanshu* (Shanghai: Guji Chubanshe, 1995), 916:567; cf. the different translation in Wu Hung, *Wu Liang Shrine*, 171.

26. See *HSBZ*, 97B:8a–b; *HS*, 97B.3985–6; translation from Burton Watson, *Courtier and Commoner*, 263. This poem is very likely authentic, since it was allegedly penned by the great-aunt of Ban Gu, the man who wrote the *History of the Former Han*.

27. *HSBZ*, 97B:7a–b; *HS*, 97B.3983–4.

28. Ban Jieyu's biography is now included in *juan* 8 of the *Old Arrayed Biographies of Women* (Gu lienü zhuan). Most of the text of her biography is derived from the *History of the Former Han* account by Ban Gu.

29. Shanxi Sheng Datong Shi Bowuguan and Shanxi Sheng Wenwu Gongzuo Weiyuanhui, eds., "Shanxi Datong shijiazhai Bei Wei Sima Jinlong mu," *Wenwu* (1972.3): 20–33.

30. *HHSJJ*, 8:7b; *HHS*, 8.340–1.

31. For the details of the Hongdumen Xue, see Michael Nylan, "Calligraphy, the Sacred Text, and the Test of Culture," in *Character and Context in Chinese Calligraphy*, ed. Cary Y. Liu et al. (Princeton: Art Museum, Princeton University, 1999), 74n98; Bielenstein, "Lo-yang," 27–8; the commentary in *HHSJJ*, 8:7b also gives some further details.

32. *HHSJJ*, 77:7b–8a; *HHS*, 77.2499.

33. *HHSJJ*, 60B:12b–13a; *HHS*, 60B.1996–7. This memorial was submitted in the late summer of 177 CE, before the actual establishment of the Hongdumen Xue. It is translated in Mark

Laurent Asselin, "The *Hou Han Shu* Biography of Cai Yong" (MA thesis, University of Washington, 1991), 130–56.

34. See Nylan, "Calligraphy," 51; *HHSJJ,* 60B:13b; *HHS,* 60B.1998; translated in Asselin, "*Hou Han Shu* Biography," 157.

35. *HHSJJ,* 60B:17a–b; *HHS,* 60B.2000–2.

36. *HHSJJ,* 60B:19ab–20a; *HHS,* 60B.2006; translated in Asselin, "*Hou Han Shu* Biography," 199.

37. Zhang Yanyuan, *Lidai minghua ji,* 74.

38. *HSBZ,* 68:1b; *HS,* 68.2932; translation from Burton Watson, *Courtier and Commoner,* 123.

39. *HSBZ,* 68:19a; *HS,* 68.2960; translation from Burton Watson, *Courtier and Commoner,* 153 (with modifications). Nearly the same story is recorded in *pian* 32, "Luanlong," of Wang Chong's *Discourses Weighed* (Lunheng), in *ZZJC,* 7:158. In the *Lunheng* version, the ritual motions of Jin Midi are recorded differently. Jin is said to "kneel down and pay his respects, [then] rising, he would stand facing it and weep so that he moistened his sleeves; only after a long time would he go away." Cf. the different translation by Forke, *Lun-Heng,* 2:354.

40. Figural illustrations without text are often called *hua* (pictures). Maps and charts that contain illustrations and explanatory captions are usually called *tu* (captioned images).

41. Since this section of the stone has suffered heavy damage, the caption next to the mother's image is mostly obliterated. The text of this caption was recorded in the Song dynasty. There has been some confusion as to whether the caption originally referred to an image of Jin Midi's father or of his mother. See the discussion in Wu Hung, *Wu Liang Shrine,* 296–8.

42. *HSBZ,* 10:1a–1b; *HS,* 10.301. The event is also recorded in *HSBZ,* 98:3a; *HS,* 98.4016, where the building is referred to as Jiaguan Huatang (2) (see my glossary for the characters). The name recorded in the annals is probably the correct one.

43. Liu Xiang, *Gu lienüzhuan, SBCK* ed., 1:24a–25a; translated in A. R. O'Hara, *The Position of Women in Early China* (Washington, DC: Catholic University of America Press, 1945), 43–4.

44. She is known under various names (Nüqi, Qimu, Jiuying) and references to her can be found in the *Elegies of Chu, Lord of Huainan, Spring and Autumn Annals of Mr. Lü,* and the *Classic of Mountains and Seas* (Shanhaijing). Like Xiwangmu and Nüwa, she was originally a fearsome deity, possibly associated with disaster. Her name was also used for a mountain and for a constellation in which her nine sons were a trailing tail of stars. See the discussion in Wen Yiduo, *Tianwen shuzheng* (Beijing: Sanlian Shudian, 1980), 11–14; Zhao Bangyan, "Jiuzimu kao," *Zhongyang yanjiuyuan, Lishi yuyan yanjiusuo jikan,* 2, no. 3 (1931): 261–74; Li Liansheng, "Xiyouji, Guizimu yu Jiuzimu," *Zhongguo dianji yu wenhua* (2002.4): 33–40.

45. "Tianwen," in *Chuci, SBCK* ed., 3:5a. In his translation of the "Heavenly Questions," David Hawkes translates the name Nüqi as Mother Star when referring to the goddess, focusing on her aspect as a constellation. See David Hawkes, trans., *The Songs of the South: An Ancient Chinese Anthology of Poems by Qu Yuan and Other Poets* (London: Penguin Books, 1985), 127, line 19; 130, lines 83–90. There are actually two female figures called Nüqi in the current text of the "Heavenly Questions." The commentator Wang Yi remarks that one (*Chuci,* 3:19a) is actually a sister-in-law to Jiao, a legendary strongman from the Xia dynasty, while the other is the female goddess with nine offspring.

46. Hārītī's name was translated into Chinese through both sound-transcriptions and

meaning-translations. By sound, it became Helidi or Gelidi, written with various characters. The original Sanskrit word apparently means "green" or "stealing," but in China the content of her story was used to give her the name Guizimu (Mother of Demon Children), which would have sounded roughly similar to the word "Jiuzimu" in ancient pronunciation (*gui*, *GSR*, 569a: *kiwər/kjwei; *jiu*, *GSR*, 992a: *kiûg/kiəu—they have the same initial but a different final). This confusing translation was probably intentional. Later, the names Jiuzimu and Guizimu were interchangeable for this deity.

47. The current text of the *Record of the Seasonal Observances of the Jing-Chu Region* does not contain this passage. It is quoted from now-lost portions of the original text by Tang and Song encyclopedias. See Zhao Bangyan, "Jiuzimu kao," 265.

48. Zhang Yanyuan's *Record of the Famous Painters of Successive Dynasties* records a painting of Jiuzimo (Hārītī) by Jie Qian of the Liang dynasty, who was famous for painting wall murals in monasteries. See Acker, *Some T'ang and Pre-T'ang Texts,* 2.1:182–3; 2.2:92.

49. Xu Meiling [Mei-ling Hsu], "The Qin Maps: A Clue to Later Chinese Cartographic Development," *Imago Mundi* 45 (1993): 90–100; Cao Wanru et al., eds., *Zhongguo gudai ditu ji* (Beijing: Wenwu Chubanshe, 1990–7), vol. 1. Some of these maps indicate the location of timber resources and may have been economic in nature. The wooden boards overlap in area coverage and represent the territory near modern Tianshui City in Gansu.

50. Rafé de Crespigny, "Maps from Mawangdui," *Cartography* 11, no. 4 (1980): 211–22; Anneliese Gutkind Bulling, "Ancient Chinese Maps: Two Maps Discovered in a Han Dynasty Tomb from the Second Century B.C.," *Expedition* 20, no. 2 (1978): 16–25. The same tomb also contained a military garrison map that depicted the frontier defenses of the Changsha Princedom. On this map, the mountains are depicted with decorative flourishes that borrow much from the tradition of lacquer painting and textile decoration.

51. *HSBZ*, 54:11a; *HS*, 54.2451. For example, we know that copies of maps were immediately sent back to Emperor Wu for his perusal.

52. *HSBZ*, 30:59a–64b; *HS*, 30.1762.

53. J. J. L. Duyvendak, "An Illustrated Battle-Account in the History of the Former Han Dynasty," *TP* 34 (1939): 249–64; 35 (1940): 211–5.

54. *HSBZ*, 70:7a–10b; *HS*, 70.3012–4. Most of the narrative is translated in the article by Duyvendak, "Illustrated Battle-Account," 258–61.

55. In an article published in 1943, Homer Dubs was even more adventurous in his follow-up to Duyvendak's article and reconstructed the contents of each scene from the textual account. See Homer H. Dubs, "A Roman Influence upon Chinese Painting," *Classical Philology* 38, no. 1 (Jan. 1943): 13–9. Furthermore, Dubs took up Duyvendak's suggestion that the battle illustrations of the punishment of Zhizhi Shanyu might have been painted by a non-Chinese artist captured during the battle in far-off Sogdiana, someone who might have been more familiar with sequential narrative illustration than the Chinese mapmakers accompanying Chen Tang's troops. Earlier, Dubs had argued in a controversial thesis that the battle tactics and fortifications employed by Zhizhi during this battle suggested that he was using Roman troops, possibly some of Crassus's legionaries who had been captured during the disastrous battle with the Parthians at Carrhae in 53 BCE. See Homer H. Dubs, "An Ancient Military Contact between Romans and Chinese," *American Journal of Philology* 62, no. 3 (July 1941): 322–30; Homer H. Dubs, *A Roman City in Ancient China* (London: China Society, 1957).

In his 1943 article, Dubs suggested that Chen Tang's victory painting was modeled on the practice of using illustrated props during the Roman victory procession known as the *triumphus,* in which the Roman army displayed models and pictures of captured cities and the battles fought over them. Dubs argued that because Chen Tang was in grave trouble for forging an imperial edict, he needed something very flashy and innovative to trumpet his victory and convince the emperor not to execute him. Thus, Dubs is arguing that complex narrative illustration in Chinese art was stimulated by a single contact with Roman soldiers. Dubs tells a vivid story, but ultimately his theory is unconvincing. There is no compelling proof for any part of his argument. Each piece of speculation is built upon a previous speculation until the entire façade consists of nothing but inference and imagination. In recent years, archaeologists have begun to uncover evidence of an earlier Chinese tradition of narrative illustration that formed the foundation for the type of scenes envisioned by Duyvendak. See Wu Hung, "The Origins of Chinese Painting," in *Three Thousand Years of Chinese Painting,* ed. Richard Barnhart et al. (New Haven: Yale University Press, 1977), 20–1. It seems clear that no Parthian or Roman artist was ever needed to show the Han Chinese how to tell a story in pictures.

56. Duyvendak, "Illustrated Battle-Account," 258, 261.

57. *HSBZ,* 9:11b; *HS,* 9.295; translated in *HFHD,* 2:331–2. Duyvendak suggests that this practice of offering illustrated victory accounts to the ancestors was practiced continually in China for two thousand years. He cites two pieces of evidence, including the Qianlong Emperor's famous illustrations of his victories of 1759 CE. See Duyvendak, "Illustrated Battle-Account," 256–7. Michael Loewe (personal communication) reads this passage differently and argues that the report in the Imperial Shrine was only a verbal report (*gao*), unrelated to the written or visual materials presented at the banquet.

58. Duyvendak, "Illustrated Battle-Account," 256–7.

59. Ibid., 257.

60. A useful guide to reading this scene is found in Ruitenbeek, *Chinese Shadows,* 67–85.

61. This is not to preclude the possibility that many decorative images in the palace were also imbued with religious or political meanings.

62. For the full report of the excavations and color plates of the mural fragments, see Shaanxi Sheng Kaogu Yanjiusuo, ed., *Qindu Xianyang kaogu baogao* (Beijing: Kexue Chubanshe, 2004). Later texts record that the First Emperor preferred to build his newer palaces south of the Wei River.

63. "Large Ancient Basement Unearthed in Shaanxi," *Xinhuanet,* English ed., Jan. 10, 2004; "2000-Year-Old Imperial Palace Unearthed in Xi'an," *Xinhuanet,* English ed., Apr. 4, 2004; "Zai Han Chang'an cheng Changlegong shouci fajue chutu Handai gongdian bihua," *Xinhuanet,* Chinese ed., Feb. 3, 2004.

64. Ying Shao, *Han guan yi,* in Sun Xingyan et al., *Han guan liu zhong,* 174.

65. Cai Zhi, *Han guan dianzhi yishi xuanyong,* in Sun Xingyan et al., *Han guan liu zhong,* 204. This passage was reconstructed from a quotation found in *Record of Elementary Learning* (Chuxueji). A similar passage occurs in Ying Shao, *Han guan yi,* in Sun Xingyan et al., *Han guan liu zhong,* 115, 143. The two fragmentary works share several passages in common.

66. *Hu-fen* was also a term used to refer to the white-lead cosmetic used by women during the Han and by male courtiers who wished to attract the sexual attention of the emperor.

67. Based on archaeological remains, wall frescoes were certainly common in northern India and Chinese Turkestan throughout the period. Until the earlier history of plaster murals in China is made clear, the issue will remain unresolved.

68. Shaanxi Sheng Kaogu Yanjiusuo, *Qindu Xianyang*, 565.

69. Ying Shao, *Han guan yi*, in Sun Xingyan et al., *Han guan liu zhong*, 174.

70. See Chen Zhi, *Sanfu huangtu*, 57–9.

71. *HSBZ*, 97B:10a–b; *HS*, 97B.3989. See the translation in Burton Watson, *Courtier and Commoner*, 266. The *Miscellaneous Notes* account may have been a fictional embellishment on the original *History of the Former Han* text, or both texts may have been copied from the same original, and the *History of the Former Han* version may represent an abridgement. Another description can be found in Chen Zhi, *Sanfu huangtu*, 58–9. That account says that Zhao Feiyan herself resided in the hall. It may be that both sisters lived there together for a while.

72. The *History of the Former Han* description says that the hall was painted in black lacquer in contrast to the red courtyard.

73. My translation, based on the critical text and notes in Xiang and Liu, *Xijing zaji jiaozhu*, 41–4.

74. *Xijing zaji, SBCK* ed., 1:6b–7a.

75. Sun Ji, *Handai wuzhi wenhua ziliao tushuo* (Beijing: Wenwu Chubanshe, 1991), 358–64.

76. Xianyang Diqu Wenguanhui and Maoling Bowuguan, eds., "Shaanxi Maoling yihao wumingzhong yihao congzangkeng de fajue," *Wenwu* (1982.9): 1–16.

77. The Palace Servant Bureau (Neizhe) was a group of twenty eunuchs who were in charge of the clothing and personal effects of the imperial family.

78. The Palace Managers (Neiguan) was an office run by two chief eunuchs, operating under the Privy Treasurer. The office was apparently in existence only after 144 BCE, corroborating the interpretation of the dates in the inscription as belonging to Emperor Wu's reign.

79. Cf. the English translation in Ledderose, *Ten Thousand Things*, 81, which is in turn based on the French translation in Michèle Pirazzoli-t'Serstevens, "Ateliers, patronage et collections princières en Chine à l'époque Han," *Comptes rendus des séances de l'Académie des inscriptions et belles-lettres*, Apr.–June 1990, 522.

80. The Attendant Workshop was a palace workshop that was under the control of the Privy Treasurer during Emperor Wu's reign. It was known for making lamps, censers, weapons, and other bronze objects. We might suppose that since two different workshop names are mentioned the lid and base of this piece were made in two different shops. It is curious that two different totals are given for the combined weight. Because the production serial numbers of the lid and base are sequential, however, I doubt that the two subassemblies were made in different workshops. The Attendant Workshop and the Palace Managers both operated under the Privy Treasury during Emperor Wu's reign, and the former may have actually been under the control of the latter. The two different scribes who wrote the lid and base inscriptions were probably just referring to the same workshop by different bureaucratic levels of reference.

81. For the identification of this tomb with the Elder Yangxin Princess, see Liu Qingzhu and Li Yufang, *Xi-Han shiyi ling* (Xi'an: Shaanxi Renmin Chubanshe, 1987), 63–6. Liu and Li argue that her body may have been reburied with that of her second husband, the great Han general Wei Qing, in a tomb closer to Maoling at a later date.

82. For the role of Penglai and its representations, see Loewe, *Ways to Paradise*, 16, 37–9. Kiyohiko Munakata argues differently, saying that the *boshanlu* censers represent "a complete

image of a sacred mountain (Kunlun or Mt. Hua) as a cosmic pillar, connected with heaven above and, through the water, with the netherworld below." See Kiyohiko Munakata, *Sacred Mountains in Chinese Art* (Champaign: Krannert Art Museum, University of Illinois Press, 1991), 28–34.

83. The spiritual quests of Emperor Wu are described in *SJ*, 28.1355–1404; translated in Burton Watson, *Records: Han Dynasty II*, 3–52.

84. This censer has been published many times, but the most detailed analysis in English can be found in Wen Fong, *Great Bronze Age of China*, no. 95.

85. For the history and organization of these factories, see Barbieri-Low, "Organization."

86. Sun Ji, *Handai wuzhi wenhua*, 313–4; Fang Guojin, "Liujin tong hu," *Wenwu cankao ziliao* (1958.9): 69–70. A similar palace vessel (dated 48 CE) from the same factory was published in *Wenwu* (1995.10): 80–3.

87. The source of this definition is the *Solitary Judgments* (Duduan), written by Cai Yong. The term seems to have originally referred to the imperial carriage. It was later extended to refer to other articles for imperial use and then to the person of the emperor himself. The recent discovery of an armory inventory from Yinwan, in Jiangsu, casts some doubt on this interpretation, however. So many items in the armory were classified as *shengyu* that the term might indicate only a high level of quality and not restricted use.

88. Kayamoto Tojin and Machida Akira, "Kandai kinenmei shikki shūsei," in *Rakurō Kanbo*, ed. Rakurō Kanbo Kankōkai (Nara: Rakurō Kanbo Kankōkai, 1974), no. 49. The platter was looted from a tomb in the Lelang cemetery.

89. Umehara Sueji, *Shina Kandai kinenmei shikki zusetsu*, Wang Mang, no. 3, pl. 35; Kayamoto and Machida, "Kandai shūsei," no. 54.

90. Carol Michaelson, *Gilded Dragons: Buried Treasures from China's Golden Ages* (London: British Museum, 1999), no. 48. For the Heavenly Horses, see Hulsewé and Loewe, *China in Central Asia*, 132–4n332. The Ferghana Valley is presently divided among the modern states of Uzbekistan, Tajikistan, and Kyrgyzstan.

91. See *HSBZ*, 58:4a; *HS*, 58.2617 comm.; *HHSJJ*, 24:10a–b and comm.; *HHS* 24.840; Chen Zhi, *Sanfu huangtu*, 62.

92. Chen Zhi, *Sanfu huangtu*, 127; Biclenstein, "Lo-yang," 90.

93. *HHSJJ*, 24:10a–b; *HHS*, 24.840–1. See discussion in Bielenstein, "Lo-yang," 25–6.

94. Translation loosely based on Bielenstein, "Lo-yang," 26, with modifications and expansion based on the fuller text in Yan Kejun, *Quan Shanggu*, 1:561 ("Quan Hou Han wen," *juan* 17:6a–b); *Taiping yulan*, 896:6a. The translation is tentative because of numerous obscure technical terms. A good deal of horse physiognomy lore is contained in *juan* 6 of the *Essential Techniques for the Peasantry* (Qimin yaoshu) (sixth century CE). Some of the technical terms are glossed in Shi Shenghan's modern Chinese annotated translation; see Shi Shenghan, *Qimin yaoshu jinshi* (Beijing: Kexue Chubanshe, 1957–8), 351–91.

95. The First Emperor of Qin cast several colossal bronze human statues from the melted weapons of the conquered states. These survived for centuries until they were melted down.

96. *HSBZ*, 6:27b comm.; *HS*, 6.194 comm.; *HFHD*, 2:129–31. See detailed discussions of the *juedi* games in Bodde, *Festivals*, 206; Michael Loewe, "The *Chüeh-ti* Games: A Re-enactment of the Battle between Ch'ih-yu and Hsüan-yüan?" in *Thought and Law in Qin and Han China*, ed. W. L. Idema and E. Zürcher (Leiden: E. J. Brill, 1990), 140–57; reprinted in Loewe, *Divina-*

tion, 236–48. The games were suspended in 44 BCE to cut costs, but they seem to have been revived under the Latter Han under a different name.

97. In 105 BCE, the games were held in Shanglin Park. See *HSBZ*, 6:31a; *HS*, 6.198; *HFHD*, 2:98.

98. Xiao Tong, *Wen xuan*, 1:42–44; passage translated by David R. Knechtges in Gong Kechang, *Studies on the Han Fu*, trans. and ed. David R. Knechtges et al. (New Haven: American Oriental Society, 1997), 302–5. I have abridged and modified Knechtges's translation.

99. The current received text of the *Happenings from the Reign of Han Emperor Wu* is attributed to Ban Gu, the man who wrote the *History of the Former Han*, but this attribution appears quite late. The book appears in the bibliographic treatise of the *History of the Sui* as an anonymous work in two *juan*. The current text in one *juan* contains several passages extracted from the *History of the Former Han* and *Historical Records* and does not always accord with quotations from this work from Tang and Song encyclopedias. The original book was probably composed during the Six Dynasties period, possibly as early as the fourth century CE. It comes from the same literary genre as works like the *Miscellaneous Notes on the Western Capital*. Dubs (*HFHD*, 2:129–31) proposed that it was written by Wang Jian (452–89 CE).

100. The description I have translated is a quotation from the *Happenings from the Reign of Han Emperor Wu* as found in the *Yiwen leiju*, *juan* 41, *Taiping yulan*, 755:5b. This and other quotations from the original text of the *Happenings* can be found in Hong Yixuan, comp., *Han Wu gushi*, vol. 15 of *Baibu congshu jicheng*, ser. 38, part 2, ed. Yan Yiping (Taibei: Yiwen Yinshuguan, 1968). See also Michael Sullivan, *The Birth of Landscape Painting in China* (Berkeley and Los Angeles: University of California Press, 1962), 36.

101. Before 104 BCE, the New Year's court audience was held on the first day of the tenth month, which was regarded as the beginning of the year.

102. Cai Zhi was the uncle of Cai Yong. He was arrested along with Yong in 178 CE. Yong's death sentence was commuted to hard labor, but it appears that Zhi's sentence was carried out.

103. This enigmatic term is explained in Bodde, *Festivals*, 154–5. It was an auspicious animal whose name was probably derived from a Sanskrit word.

104. Cai Zhi, *Han guan dianzhi yishi xuanyong*, quoted in the commentary to *HHSJJ*, *zhi* 5:12a–b; *HHS*, *zhi* 5.3131; my translation, with suggestions based on Bodde, *Festivals*, 151–2.

105. Anhui Sheng Wenwu Kaogu Yanjiusuo and Ma'anshan Shi Wenwuju, eds., "Anhui Ma'anshan Dong-Wu Zhu Ran mu fajue jianbao," *Wenwu* (1986.3): 1–15. The tray-table was clearly made in Chengdu, as were many of the pieces from Zhu Ran's tomb. Some theorize that the pieces belonged to the rulers or nobles of the Kingdom of Shu and were captured by Zhu Ran in battle. They may have also once belonged to Sun Quan, the ruler of the Kingdom of Wu.

106. I am uncertain which emperor is represented in this scene. Further research into the titles mentioned in the captions might prove helpful in resolving this issue. The mention of the generic noble title Marquis of the Metropolitan Residence (Duting Hou) suggests that the scene must take place during the second half of the Latter Han or early Three Kingdoms period, when that title was in use. One of the figures on the dais is identified as Pingle Hou, which was a title held by Gongsun Yuan, the stalwart of the Cao Wei dynasty, who once tricked Sun Quan into thinking he might defect. See *Sanguo zhi*, Zhonghua ed., 1138–9. Since Gongsun Yuan apparently held the title of Pingle Hou around 227–32 CE, the scene might thus be a mocking portrayal of Emperor Ming of the Wei dynasty (r. 227–39 CE).

107. Barbieri-Low, "Organization," chap. 1.

108. For the history of this office, see Yonezawa Yoshio, "Kandai ni okeru kyūtei sakuga kikō no hattatsu," *Kokka* 48, no. 6 (1938): 148–51.

109. Ibid., 148.

110. Ying Shao, *Han guan yi,* in Sun Xingyan et al., *Han guan liu zhong,* 139.

111. *HHSJJ, zhi* 26:5b; *HHS, zhi* 26.3594; Bielenstein, *Bureaucracy,* 53, 64.

112. Bielenstein, *Bureaucracy,* 53, 64; Ying Shao, *Han guan yi,* in Sun Xingyan et al., *Han guan liu zhong,* 139. The man who controlled this office was ranked at 400 *shi.*

113. See note 38.

114. Yonezawa Yoshio, "Kandai ni okeru kyūtei sakuga kikō no hattatsu," *Kokka* 48, no. 9 (1938): 263–7.

115. Zhang Zongxiang, ed., *Jiaozheng sanfu huangtu* (Shanghai: Gudian Wenxue Chubanshe, 1958), 55; Zhongguo Shehui Kexueyuan Kaogu Yanjiusuo, ed., *Han Chang'an cheng Weiyang Gong 1980–1989 nian kaogu fajue baogao* (Beijing: Zhongguo Da Baike Quanshu, 1996), 1:7–14.

116. *HSBZ,* 19A:15a; *HS,* 19A.731.

117. Bielenstein, *Bureaucracy,* 52.

118. *HHSJJ, zhi* 26:7b; *HHS, zhi* 26.3596; Bielenstein, *Bureaucracy,* 61–2, 67.

119. Bielenstein, *Bureaucracy,* 61–2, 67.

120. Zhang Yanyuan, *Lidai minghua ji,* 77–8. This passage is quoted in slightly different forms in other Tang and Song texts, but the author and source are not clear. The historicity of the event can be doubted, but the ideology behind the division of labor is quite believable. See Yonezawa, "Kandai ni okeru kyūtei sakuga kikō no hattatsu," *Kokka* 48, no. 6 (1938): 150–1.

121. See translation in Acker, *Some T'ang and Pre-T'ang Texts,* 2.1:14.

122. *HHSJJ,* 77:7b–8a; *HHS,* 77.2499.

123. A clue to when the Ding Huan stories were first written down might lie in certain editions' avoidance of the character *heng* (eternal). Since this was the personal name of Emperor Wen (Liu Heng), it was sometimes replaced during the two Han dynasties with the graph *chang* (perpetual). I would speculate that the Ding Huan stories were first recorded during the second or early third centuries CE.

124. Needham et al., *Science and Civilisation,* 1:53, 4.1:123, 4.2:233. Needham then reverses his course and supposes that, since the poet Sima Xiangru (d. 117 BCE) refers in a poem to a device similar to one of Ding Huan's creations, Ding Huan may have lived in the second century BCE instead (4.2:234).

125. Yin Yun, *Xiaoshuo* (Shanghai: Guji Chubanshe, 1984), 11.

126. *Xijing zaji, SBCK* ed., 1:6a; Yin Yun, *Xiaoshuo,* 11; *Taiping yulan,* 752:3a–b, 870:1b. Cf. the translation in Needham et al., *Science and Civilisation,* 4.2:233.

127. Needham et al., *Science and Civilisation,* 4.2:233 note c.

128. *Xijing zaji, SBCK* ed., 1:6b; Yin Yun, *Xiaoshuo,* 11; *Taiping yulan,* 752:3b; cf. the translation in Needham et al., *Science and Civilisation,* 4.1:123.

129. Needham et al., *Science and Civilisation,* 4.1:123.

130. *Xijing zaji, SBCK* ed., 1:6a–b; Yin Yun, *Xiaoshuo,* 11; *Taiping yulan,* 752:3b; translation from Joseph Needham et al., *Science and Civilisation,* 4.2:151. The *Taiping yulan* version says that the fans were only one *chi* across. This seems a bit small, though ten-*chi* fans would be enormous.

131. Needham et al., *Science and Civilisation,* 4.2:151.

132. *Xijing zaji, SBCK* ed., 1:6a–b; Yin Yun, *Xiaoshuo,* 11; *Taiping yulan,* 752:3b. Cf. the translation by Needham et al., *Science and Civilisation,* 4.2:233.

133. *Chuxueji, juan* 19, Zhonghua ed., p. 456. Some scholars doubt the authenticity of the "Meiren fu." See the complete account of the Cardan suspension in Needham et al., *Science and Civilisation,* 4.2:228–36; Berthold Laufer, "Cardan's Suspension in China," in *Anthropological Essays Presented to William Henry Holmes in Honor of His Seventieth Birthday* (Washington, DC: J. W. Bryan, 1916; repr., New York: AMS Press, 1977), 288–92.

134. Michaelson, *Gilded Dragons,* no. 73. Similar Tang examples are in the Carl Kempe Collection and the Shōsō-in repository in Nara, Japan.

135. For Ma Jun, see Needham et al., *Science and Civilisation,* 4.1:39–42.

136. *Taiping yulan,* 750:10b. For information about Sun Changzhi and his writings, see Erik Zürcher, "Recent Studies in Chinese Painting," *TP* 51, nos. 4–5 (1964): 401–3.

137. Zürcher, "Recent Studies in Chinese Painting," 401–3. See also Acker, *Some T'ang and Pre-T'ang Texts,* 2.1:10–1, 2.2:60. The poem "Milky Way" is about a drought sent by Heaven. "North Wind" is a love poem set in deep winter. Both are in the *Book of Songs* (Shijing).

138. For Zhao Qi's brief biography, see *HHSJJ,* 64:14a–18a; *HHS* 64.2121–5.

139. *HHSJJ,* 64:17b; *HHS,* 64.2124; translation after Acker, *Some T'ang and Pre-T'ang Texts,* 2.1:9 (with modifications). See also Wu Hung, *Monumentality,* 223–24.

140. In a very influential article, Paul Pelliot once argued that Zhao Qi's role as a great painter had been greatly inflated by Zhang Yanyuan. Pelliot even argued that the *History of the Latter Han* passage just translated could be interpreted to mean that Zhao Qi hired *someone else* to paint his tomb and did not execute the paintings himself. William Acker rebutted Pelliot, arguing that the *History of the Latter Han* text clearly states that Zhao Qi painted the images himself. See Paul Pelliot, "Notes sur quelques artistes des Six Dynasties et des T'ang," *TP* 22 (1923): 221–3; Acker, *Some T'ang and Pre-T'ang Texts,* 2.1:8–10.

141. Li Daoyuan, *Shuijing zhu jiao,* ed. Wang Guowei (Shanghai: Renmin Chubanshe, 1984), *juan* 34, p. 1084; *HHSJJ,* 64:17b comm.

142. For Zhang Heng's official biography, see *HHSJJ,* 59:1a–26b; *HHS,* 59.1897–1951.

143. Xiao Tong, *Wen xuan,* 1:25–72; translated in Knechtges, *Wen xuan,* 1:311–36.

144. Needham et al., *Science and Civilisation,* 3:537–43.

145. Ibid., 99–100. Zhang Heng's value was 3.1622.

146. Ibid., 338–43, 355–9.

147. Ibid., 359–61.

148. See the poem "Song of Like Sound" (Tongsheng ge) in Zhang Heng, *Zhang Heng shiwen ji jiaozhu,* ed. Zhang Zhenze (Shanghai: Guji Chubanshe, 1986), 7–9; translation in R. H. van Gulik, *Sexual Life in Ancient China: A Preliminary Survey of Chinese Sex and Society from ca. 1500 BC till 1644 AD* (Leiden: E. J. Brill, 1961), 73.

149. For a description of this seismograph, see *HHSJJ,* 6:7a, 59:8a–b; *HHS,* 6.260, 59.1909–10; Li Fang et al., *Taiping yulan, juan* 752:1b. For analysis and translation, see Needham et al., *Science and Civilisation,* 3:626–35; Robert Temple, *The Genius of China: 3000 Years of Science, Discovery, and Invention* (New York: Simon and Schuster, 1986), 162–6.

150. The exact details of the internal mechanism are hotly debated among historians of scientific instruments. See Needham and Temple references in previous note.

151. *HHSJJ*, 59:1b; *HHS*, 59.1897.

152. *HHSJJ*, 59:3a–b; *HHS*, 59.1899.

153. Translation from Acker, *Some T'ang and Pre-T'ang Texts*, 2.1:13.

154. The story of Lu Ban is recorded in the *Fengsu tongyi* of Ying Shao, quoted in *Taiping yulan*, 750:10a. The Qin story is recorded in the *San Qi lüeji*. In that tale the artist is drowned in the sea when the monster becomes angry at being depicted. For a comparison of the original texts, see Yonezawa Yoshio, "Kandai kaiga shiryō shū," *Kokka* 98, no. 9 (1993): 33, nos. 41–2.

155. Yin Yun, *Xiaoshuo*, 80. Of course, this legend sounds ridiculous to us, since Zhang Heng died in 139 CE and Cai Yong was born at least six or seven years earlier in 132 or 133 CE. It seems from this persistent legend, though, that people of later centuries who were not so scrupulous about absolute dates considered Cai Yong to be the reincarnation of Zhang Heng. The two men were even said to have a similar physical appearance.

156. See Cai Yong's biography in *HHSJJ*, 60B:1a–21b; *HHS*, 60B.1979–2008; translated and annotated in Asselin, "*Hou Han Shu* Biography." For further analysis, see Mark Laurent Asselin, "'A Significant Season' Literature in a Time of Endings: Cai Yong and a Few Contemporaries" (PhD diss., University of Washington, 1997); Gong Kechang, "A Critical Biography of Cai Yong," in *Studies on the Han Fu*, 339–89. For the dispute about his year of birth, see Asselin, "Significant Season," 74n1.

157. *HHSJJ*, 60B:1b–2a; *HHS*, 60B.1980.

158. Cai Yong writes this in a memorial to the throne protesting his arrest in 178 CE. See *HHSJJ*, 60B:16b; *HHS*, 60B.2001. In other editions of this memorial, the words used are *xingming tuxiang* (apply names to portraits). See Asselin, "*Hou Han Shu* Biography," 174n377.

159. See note 17. The other man portrayed in the mural was Huang Qiong. The full text of the encomium to both men was preserved in the now-lost *History of the Latter Han* (Hou Hanshu) of Xie Cheng (third century CE), quoted in the commentary to *HHSJJ*, 44:12a–13a; *HHS*, 44.1511–2n1.

160. Acker, *Some T'ang and Pre-T'ang Texts*, 2.1:12, 2.2:60–1.

161. See references to the original fragmentary text and a partial translation by Asselin, "Significant Season," 513–4. In some texts this work is called *Instructions for Women* (Nü xun) instead.

162. *Taiping yulan, juan* 750:10a, quoting the *Notes in Exposition of Painting* (Shuhua ji) of Sun Changzhi; also found in *Lidai minghua ji*, translation from Acker, *Some T'ang and Pre-T'ang Texts*, 2.1:11–2, 2.2:61. The two texts are similar, though Sun Changzhi's is more detailed and is clearly the source of Zhang Yanyuan's summary notice. The *Notes in Exposition of Painting* was still extant in the Northern Song.

163. Gong, "Critical Biography," in *Studies on the Han Fu*, 367n106; Asselin, "*Hou Han Shu* Biography," 242, no. 63.

164. Yang Ci and Yang Biao both worked with Cai Yong on the Stone Classics project. Cai Yong would later write a funerary epitaph for Yang Ci as well. The biographies of all the five generations can be found in *HHSJJ*, 54:1a–22b; *HHS*, 54.1759–96.

165. *HHSJJ*, 53:9a; *HHS*, 53.1749–50 (biography of Jiang Gong). Emperor Huan wanted to see what the reclusive Jiang Gong (96–173 CE) looked like, so he had the local government send out portrait painters to capture his likeness. Jiang Gong hid under the bedcovers and said he

could not come out because of dizziness. The portraitists were unable to get a look at him to paint him.

166. For the scholarly and political background of this project, see Nylan, "Calligraphy," 48–9; Bielenstein, "Lo-Yang," 69–70.

167. The "Annals of Emperor Ling" state that there were only five Classics inscribed on stone (*HHSJJ,* 8:5b; *HHS,* 8.336). The *Commentary on the Classic of Waterways* (Shuijingzhu) agrees with this figure. Cai Yong's biography translated here says six. The bibliographic treatise in the *History of the Sui* indicates seven. Qian Cunxun (following Ma Heng) explains away this discrepancy and argues that archaeological remains support the presence of seven different texts: *Book of Changes* (Yijing), *Book of Documents* (Shangshu), *Book of Songs* (Shijing), *Book of Etiquette and Ceremonial* (Yili), *Spring and Autumn Annals* (Chunqiu), *Gongyang Commentary* (Gongyang zhuan), and *Confucian Analects* (Lunyu). See Qian Cunxun [Tsien Tsuen-hsuin], *Written on Bamboo and Silk: The Beginnings of Chinese Books and Inscriptions,* 2d ed. (Chicago: University of Chicago Press, 2004), 80, table 2.

168. *HHSJJ,* 60B:7b–8b; *HHS,* 60B.1990; translation from Asselin, "*Hou Han Shu* Biography," 117–20 (with modifications). For the identities of the other compilers mentioned in this passage, see the notes in Asselin, "*Hou Han Shu* Biography," 117–20. For a different translation of most of this passage, see Qian, *Written on Bamboo and Silk,* 79–80.

169. Li Daoyuan, *Shuijing zhu jiao,* 548–9, records the date of completion as 183 CE. See also *HHSJJ,* 8:5b comm. Li Daoyuan also says that the stelae name Cai Yong *and others.* Li Daoyuan (d. 527 CE) had been an official in Luoyang and would have had access to the surviving fragments of the Stone Classics. According to the "Annals of Emperor Ling," sometime between January 12 and February 9, 183 CE, just before the New Year, Emperor Ling visited the Imperial Academy. Perhaps, this was to inspect the work before the final unveiling of the newly completed Stone Classics.

170. See Qian, *Written on Bamboo and Silk,* 80; Bielenstein, "Lo-yang," 70. This information is from the now-lost *History of the Latter Han* (Hou Hanshu) of Xie Cheng (fl. ca. 222 CE).

171. The largest collection of rubbings of extant fragments of the Stone Classics can be found in Ma Heng, *Han Shijing jicun,* 2 vols. (Beijing: Kexue Chubanshe, 1957; repr., Taibei: Yiwen Yinshuguan, 1976).

172. For the history of the stones, see Qian, *Written on Bamboo and Silk,* 81–3; Ma Heng, "Han *Shijing* gaishu," *Kaogu xuebao* (1955.10): 4.

173. For the textual problems with the word *dan* (vermilion) in this passage, see Asselin, "*Hou Han Shu* Biography," 118n224.

174. See Cai Yong's essays "Power of the Clerical Script" and "Power of the Seal Script," in Yan Kejun, *Quan Shanggu,* 1:900 ("Quan Hou Han wen," *juan* 80:1a–b).

175. See Nylan, "Calligraphy," 49–52.

176. Hong Gua, *Li shi,* 14:13a.

177. Ma Heng, "Han *Shijing* gaishu," 2.

178. Hong Gua, *Li shi,* 14:14a–b.

179. Ten men are recorded in various chapters of the *History of the Latter Han.* A further fifteen names are found on stone fragments found during the Song and the early part of the twentieth century. For the names and ranks of these men, see Ma Heng, "Han *Shijing* gaishu," 3. In 175 CE, Cai Yong was serving as a Court Gentleman for Consultation (Yilang) with a rank of 600 *shi*, the same rank as Grand Astrologer Shan Yang, who also served on the project. They

were significantly outranked by Tangxi Dian, Leader of the Gentlemen of the Interior for Miscellaneous Uses, and Yang Ci, Grand Master for Splendid Happiness, who both ranked at fully 2,000 *shi.*

180. Ma Heng, "Han *Shijing* gaishu," 4.

181. Hong Gua, *Li shi,* 14:14a–b; Qian, *Written on Bamboo and Silk,* 81.

182. As quoted in the commentary to *HHSJJ,* 60B:8a; *HHS,* 60B.1990. The text refers to this classic as the *Record of Ceremonial* (Liji), a name that during Han times actually indicated the *Yili* text and not the text currently referred to as the *Liji.*

CHAPTER 6

1. Stanley L. Engerman, introduction to *Terms of Labor: Slavery, Serfdom, and Free Labor,* ed. Stanley L. Engerman (Stanford: Stanford University Press, 1999), 1–24; M. I. Finley, "Slavery," in *International Encyclopedia of the Social Sciences,* ed. David L. Sills (New York: Macmillan, 1968), 14:307–13.

2. Translated in Arthur Waley, *The Analects,* 84.

3. Yang Liansheng [Lien-sheng Yang], *Excursions in Sinology* (Cambridge, MA: Harvard University Press, 1969), 191–248; A. F. P. Hulsewé, "Some Remarks on Statute Labour during the Ch'in and Han Period," *Orientalia Venetiana* 1 (1984): 195–204.

4. Keightley, "Public Work."

5. Wilbur, *Slavery,* 244–52.

6. The term "corvée" derives from medieval French feudal law and referred to the labor service rendered to feudal lords by peasants. Later, it was extended to refer to the French monarchy's practice of conscripting peasants to work on roads and other projects during the seventeenth and eighteenth centuries.

7. Michael Loewe, *Records of Han Administration* (Cambridge: Cambridge University Press, 1967), 1:79–81, 162–4.

8. *HSBZ,* 5:3b; *HS,* 5.141; *HFHD,* 1:312; Swann, *Food and Money,* 50–1; Wilbur, *Slavery,* 223.

9. Hulsewé, "Statute Labour," 198; *SHD,* 6 ("Bian nian ji," slip 8.2); Chen Zhi, *Liang-Han jingji shiliao luncong* (Xi'an: Shaanxi Renmin Chubanshe, 1958), 15–6; Robin D. S. Yates, "Social Status in the Ch'in: Evidence from the Yun-meng Legal Documents, Part One, Commoners," *HJAS* 47, no. 1 (1987): 203–17; Cao Lüning, *Zhangjiashan Han lü yanjiu* (Beijing: Zhonghua Shuju, 2005), 206–8.

10. A person or his parents had to declare his age to officials, who were charged with verifying the information. If the age was incorrectly reported and was three or more years off the mark, the individual or his parent was prosecuted. See *ZJS,* 177 ("Erning lüling," slips 325–7). Calendar age in early China was marked in *sui,* which included the year of birth as year 1.

11. *SHD,* 32 ("Qin lü shiba zhong," slips 49–52); *RCL,* A12, A13n1.

12. *HSBZ,* 1A:34a; *HS,* 1A.37 (commentary of Ru Shun); *HFHD,* 1:80n2; *ZJS,* 182 ("Ernian lüling," slip 363).

13. Huan, *Yantielun jiaozhu, juan* 3 (*pian* 15, "Wei tong"), p. 192; Gale, *Discourses on Salt and Iron,* 97.

14. Based on *ZJS,* 182 ("Ernian lüling," slips 364–5).

15. Nishijima, "Economic and Social History," 552–3.

16. *ZJS,* 188 ("Ernian lüling," slip 413).

17. *HSBZ*, 5:3b; *HS*, 5.141l; *HFHD*, 1:312.

18. Huan, *Yantielun jiaozhu, juan* 3 (*pian* 15, "Wei tong"), p. 192; Gale, *Discourses on Salt and Iron*, 97.

19. *ZJS*, 181 ("Ernian lüling," slip 356).

20. Wei Hong, *Han jiuyi*, in Sun Xingyan et al., *Han guan liu zhong*, 85. Wei represents this as the Qin system, but it more likely describes the system in place at the end of the Former Han.

21. *ZJS*, 181, 187–8 ("Ernian lüling," slips 357, 407). The word "*huan*" suggests the onset of cataracts and reduced vision. See Zhongwen Da Cidian Bianzuan Weiyuanhui, ed., *Zhongwen da cidian*, 4th ed., 10 vols. (Taibei: Huagang Chuban Youxian Gongsi, 1979), entry 23875.

22. The same partial exemption was granted to men who were sick due to old war wounds; see *ZJS*, 188 ("Ernian lüling," slip 408).

23. These criticisms of the Qin were voiced by the great Confucian essayist Jia Yi (201–169 BCE) in his tract "Faulting the Qin" (Guo Qin lun), inserted by Sima Qian into *SJ*, 6.276–84; translated in Burton Watson, *Records: Qin Dynasty*, 74–83; and Nienhauser, *Grand Scribe's Records*, 1:163–9. Sima Qian puts similar accusations into the mouths of Qin officials working under the Second Emperor; see *Shiji*, 6.271; Burton Watson, *Records: Qin Dynasty*, 68–9. Dong Zhongshu (ca. 179–104 BCE) also criticized the Qin labor requirements as too high and maintained that the Han were wrong for following them; see *HSBZ*, 24A:16a–17a; *HS*, 24A.1137; Swann, *Food and Money*, 179–83.

24. *HSBZ*, 24A:16a–17a; *HS*, 24A.1137; Swann, *Food and Money*, 50–1, 179–83.

25. Yan Gengwang, *Qin-Han difang xingzhi zhidu*, vol. 1 of *Zhongguo difang xingzhi zhidu shi* (Taibei: Institute of History and Philology, Academia Sinica, 1961), 1:237–9; *HSBZ*, 19A:30a; *HS*, 19A.742; Bielenstein, *Bureaucracy*, 103.

26. *RCL*, A64; *SHD*, 47–8 ("Qin lü shiba zhong," slips 122–4).

27. Hulsewé, "Statute Labour," 196.

28. Translated in Shen, Crossley, and Lun, *Nine Chapters*, 310–9. This is assuming that only one man from each household is managing a cart by himself. If, as other problems in the book suggest, as many as six men might be needed on a grain cart, the annual percentages of conscripted men increase dramatically.

29. *SHD*, 89 ("Qin lü zachao," slip 9); *RCL*, C25. The fine was valued at two suits of armor, the cash value of which is unknown.

30. *ZJS*, 189 ("Ernian lüling," slip 16).

31. An identical text is found on two different boards from well no. 1 at the site [J1 (16) 5, J1 (16) 6]. For the original text of these boards and a preliminary report of the Liye finds, see Hunan Sheng Wenwu Kaogu Yanjiusuo et al., eds., "Hunan Longshan Liye: Zhanguo Qin dai gucheng yihao jing fajue jianbao," *Wenwu* (2003.1): 33–4. For a preliminary assessment of the Liye finds, see Robin D. S. Yates, "Law in the Making of the Empire: Evidence from the Newly Discovered Qin Slips from Liye, Hunan" (paper presented at the annual meeting of the Association for Asian Studies, Chicago, IL, Apr. 1, 2005).

32. Only the first eight ranks were available to commoners. Rank 9 and above were reserved for officials and aristocrats. See Michael Loewe, "The Orders of Aristocratic Rank of Han China," *TP* 48, nos. 1–3 (1960): 145, 149–50, 157–8; Swann, *Food and Money*, 31, 169, 273.

33. *HSBZ*, 29:15b comm.; *HS*, 29.1690 comm.; *HSBZ*, 7:8b–9a; *HS*, 7.230, commentary of Ru

Shun; *HFHD*, 2:176–7; Loewe, *Records of Han Administration*, 1:81, 162–4. For a different interpretation of *jian geng*, see commentary of Fu Qian (fl. 169–89 CE) in *HSBZ*, 35:5b; *HS*, 35.1905 comm. At present, there appears to be no way to completely reconcile these conflicting commentaries.

34. Many of these remissions are quoted in Xu Tianlin, *Xi-Han huiyao* (Shanghai: Shanghai Renmin Chubanshe, 1976), *juan* 47, pp. 550–5; Xu Tianlin, *Dong Han huiyao* (Taibei: Shijie Shuju, 1960), *juan* 29, pp. 313–4; *HHSJJ*, 4:10a; *HHS*, 4.183, 6.260–9.

35. *RCL*, D143, D144; *SHD*, 131–2 ("Qin lü dawen," slips 163–4). See also the piece of case law in *RCL*, E6; *SHD*, 163–4 ("Fengzhen shi," slips 97–8).

36. *ZJS*, 188 ("Ernian lüling," slips 413–4).

37. *RCL*, A64; *SHD*, 47–8 ("Qin lü shiba zhong," slips 115–24). See also the parallel rule for military conscripts in *SHD*, 90 ("Qin lü zachao," slips 40–2); *RCL*, C26.

38. Shen, Crossley, and Lun, *Nine Chapters*, 254–61; *RCL*, A58; *SHD*, 45 ("Qin lü shiba zhong," slip 108).

39. Hulsewé, "Statute Labour," 202.

40. *RCL*, A8, A39, A57, D109; *SHD*, 23–4, 38–9, 45 ("Qin lü shiba zhong," slips 15, 77–8, 104–7), 124 ("Qin lü dawen," slip 131); *ZJS*, 191 ("Ernian lüling," slip 434).

41. *RCL*, D178; *SHD*, 141 ("Qin lü dawen," slip 199).

42. Yang Liansheng, "Economic Aspects," in *Excursions in Sinology*, 231–48.

43. *HSBZ*, 7:2a; *HS*, 7.219; *HFHD*, 2:154; *HSBZ*, 97A:17a; *HS*, 97A.3957.

44. *HSBZ*, 11:5a; *HS*, 11.339; *HFHD*, 3:29.

45. Shen, Crossley, and Lun, *Nine Chapters*, 310–2; *ZJS*, 188 ("Ernian lüling," slips 411–5).

46. *HSBZ*, 24A:19a; *HS*, 24A.1141; Swann, *Food and Money*, 192–3.

47. *HSBZ*, 72:13a–b; *HS*, 72.3075.

48. *HSBZ*, 10:5a; *HS*, 10.308–9; *HFHD*, 2:383–4; *HSBZ*, 29:14b–15b; *HS*, 29.1688–9; translated in Needham et al., *Science and Civilisation*, 4.3:329–31.

49. *HSBZ*, 1A:23a; *HS*, 1A.27; *HFHD*, 1:64.

50. *HSBZ*, 1B:7a; *HS*, 1B.58; *HFHD*, 1:108.

51. Chen Zhi, *Sanfu huangtu*, 33.

52. *HSBZ*, 1B:7b: *HS*, 1B.58; *HFHD*, 1:109. The complex took nearly a year and a half to renovate. A description of this complex can be found in Wu Hung, *Monumentality*, 150.

53. *HSBZ*, 1B:12a–b; *HS*, 1B.64; *HFHD*, 1:118. Though Xiao He is given the lion's share of the credit for building the palaces, it was probably Yangcheng Yan who deserves the real credit. He had experience building siege engines and fortifications during the civil war. According to the *History of the Former Han*, Yangcheng Yan was made Privy Treasurer (Shaofu) in 202 BCE. This title might be an error for Jiangzuo Shaofu, the title of the lead architect of the empire, which was later changed to Jiangzuo Dajiang in 144 BCE. This was the highest bureaucratic position for a craftsman in the empire and more suitable for Yangcheng Yan than the purely economic position of Privy Treasurer. Yangcheng Yan is said to have built the Changle Gong, the Weiyang Palace, and the Chang'an city walls. He was enfeoffed by Empress Lü in 187 BCE and apparently held his post for twenty-one years until his death in 181 BCE. See *HSBZ*, 16:63a; *HS*, 16.619; *HSBZ*, 19B:2a; *HS*, 19B.747.

54. *SJ*, 6.251; Burton Watson, *Records: Qin Dynasty*, 52.

55. *HSBZ*, 1B:7b: *HS*, 1B.59; *HFHD*, 1:109.

56. Wang Zhongshu, *Han Civilization*, 1–2; Stephen James Hotaling, "The City Walls of

Han Ch'ang-an," *TP* 64, nos. 1–3 (1978): 1–46; Carl Whiting Bishop, "An Ancient Chinese Capital," *Antiquity* 12 (1938): 68–78.

57. If it was 16 meters wide at the base, 12 meters wide at the top, 12 meters high, and 25,700 meters in circumference, the wall would have contained approximately 4.32 million cubic meters of rammed earth. According to the ratios given in *Nine Chapters on the Mathematical Arts,* this would be multiplied by 4/3 to arrive at the volume of excavated earth. See Shen, Crossley, and Lun, *Nine Chapters,* 254.

58. For a photo, see Wang Zhongshu, *Han Civilization,* pl. 3.

59. *HSBZ,* 2:4a (and comm. of Wang Xianqian); *HS,* 2.48; *HFHD,* 1:179. Overall, the *History of the Former Han* provides much more detail of the construction of the Chang'an walls than do the corresponding chapters in the *Historical Records* of Sima Qian. The *Historical Records* says that the wall was begun in earnest in the third year of Emperor Hui's reign, thus 192 BCE; see *SJ,* 9.398. For a detailed discussion of the construction accounts of the Chang'an walls, see Wu Hung, *Monumentality,* 156–60.

60. In comparison, according to the *History of the Sui,* two million male peasants were called up each month for nearly a year to construct the monumental walls of the Sui dynasty's eastern capital at Luoyang in the years 605–6 CE. See Yang Liansheng, *Excursions in Sinology,* 202–3; *Suishu,* 24.686.

61. This probably took place in the first month of the lunar year, which contained thirty days that year. The second month contained only twenty-nine days that year.

62. The emperor at this time was technically still a minor, since he had not undergone his capping ceremony. At this time, and for most of the remainder of his reign, he was entirely dominated by his mother, Empress Lü. She probably issued the edict in his name.

63. *HSBZ,* 2:4b and comm.; *HS,* 2.89; *HFHD,* 1:180–1.

64. *HSBZ* 2:5a; *HS,* 2.89; *HFHD,* 1:181. Lien-sheng Yang [Yang Liansheng] demonstrated that the presence of the graph *li* in this compound does not mean that slaves were included in this labor source. As a compound, it clearly means "convict bondsmen" or simply "convicts." See Yang Liansheng, *Excursions in Sinology,* 205–6. For varying translations of this term, see *HFHD,* 1:181; Wilbur, *Slavery,* 224; A. F. P. Hulsewé, *Remnants of Han Law* (Leiden: E. J. Brill, 1955), 130.

65. *SJ,* 9.398.

66. *HSBZ,* 2:5b: *HS,* 2.90; *HFHD,* 1:183.

67. *HSBZ,* 2:5b: *HS,* 2.90–1; *HFHD,* 1:183.

68. Translated in Xu Zhuoyun, *Han Agriculture,* 215–28.

69. It appears that a special class of convicts who were working just to pay off monetary fines or redemption fees did not have to work year-round but were excused for twenty-day periods during the planting season and for weeding of the crops. See *RCL,* A67; *SHD,* 53 ("Qin lü shiba zhong," slip 144).

70. Wu Hung comes to the same conclusions in *Monumentality,* 156.

71. The circle would have extended east only into Henan Commandery and southwest into Hanzhong Commandery, but it would not have incorporated the well-populated Shandong Peninsula nor the Sichuan Basin.

72. *ZJS,* 188 ("Ernian lüling," slips 412–3).

73. Yang Liansheng, *Excursions in Sinology,* 213–4.

74. Shen, Crossley, and Lun, *Nine Chapters,* 254–5.

75. Ibid., 258–9.

76. Yang Liansheng, *Excursions in Sinology,* 213.

77. Huang Shengzhang, "Qin bingqi fenguo, duandai, yu youguan zhidu yanjiu," *Guwenzi yanjiu* 21 (2001): 245–6.

78. *RCL*, A36; *SHD*, 37 ("Qin lü shiba zhong," slip 71).

79. *ZJS*, 171 ("Ernian lüling," slips 278–80). The first two graphs of slip 278, where the passage quoted in the text begins, are damaged and unreadable. I have interpolated the phrase "For those who are recruited for" to stand in their place. Decipherment of those two words might significantly change the interpretation of this passage. Other legal and economic terms in the passage are also problematic and subject to widely varying interpretations.

80. Barbieri-Low, "Organization," 290–3, 318 (table 3).

81. For the destruction of the shrines dedicated to Emperor Wu and Emperor Zhao, see *HSBZ*, 99C:12a; *HFHD,* 3:408. For the ritual desecration and occupation of Gaozu's shrine, see *HSBZ*, 99C:13b; *HS*, 99C.4169; *HFHD,* 3:412–3. For the destruction of the tomb complexes of Emperors Yuan and Cheng as sympathetic magic, see *HSBZ,* 99C:24a–b; *HS*, 99C.4186; *HFHD,* 3:454–5.

82. In conscious emulation of the Duke of Zhou's divining the best location for Chengzhou (Luoyang), the eastern capital of the Zhou dynasty.

83. *HSBZ*, 99C:8b–9a; *HS*, 99C.4161; *HFHD*, 3:397.

84. Reeves, *Akhenaten*, 26, 91–5; *HSBZ*, 99C:9a–b; *HS*, 99C.4162; *HFHD*, 3:398.

85. *HSBZ*, 99C:9b; *HS*, 99C.4162; *HFHD,* 3:399–400.

86. *HSBZ*, 99C:10a; *HS*, 99C.4162; *HFHD*, 3:400.

87. *HSBZ*, 99C:16b; *HS*, 99C.4174; *HFHD*, 3:422.

88. *HSBZ*, 99C:26b, 28a; *HS*, 99C.4190, 4192; *HFHD* 3:462, 466–7.

89. See reports in *Kaogu Tongxun* (1957.6): 26–30, pl. 8; *Kaogu xuebao* (1959.2): 45–54; *Kaogu* (1960.7): 38; *Kaogu* (1960.9): 53–8; *Kaogu* (1963.9): 501–15; *Kaogu* (1989.3): 261–8; *Kaogu yu wenwu* (1992.4): 96–106; Wang Zhongshu, *Han Civilization*, 9–10, figs. 29–32.

90. Yang Liansheng, *Excursions in Sinology,* 191–215. For the Han period, there is evidence that conscripted servicemen built and repaired portions of the western defense line and engaged in conscripted agricultural work. See Loewe, *Records of Han Administration.*

91. The words are those of Mei Fu, a critic of the policies of Emperor Cheng. See *HSBZ,* 67:8b; *HS,* 67.2918.

92. Hulsewé, *Remnants of Han Law*, 53–4; *HSBZ*, 23:15b; *HS*, 23.1101, translated in Hulsewé, *Remnants of Han Law*, 338. The *History of the Latter Han* lists 610 crimes punishable by death in 94 CE (*HHS*, 46.1554).

93. The table is based upon the Han statutes found at Zhangjiashan, dated 186 BCE. For the traditional understanding of these punishments, see *Han jiuyi*, 85; Hulsewé, *Remnants of Han Law,* 128–32, 335–6; *HSBZ*, 2:3a–b and comm., 23:13b–14b and comm.; *HS,* 2.85, 87 and comm., 23.1099–1100 and comm.; *HFHD*, 1:177n1; Qu, *Han Social Structure*, 330n28; Nishijima, "Economic and Social History," 532–3; Wilbur, *Slavery,* 81–3; *RCL*, 14–8.

94. In fact, the harshest hard-labor penalty was often referred to as the death penalty reduced by one degree. See Hulsewé, *Remnants of Han Law,* 129.

95. Ibid., 71–101.

96. One is the *Models for Sealing and Investigating* (Fengzhen shi) from Shuihudi tomb 11.

See *SHD*, 145–64; translated by Hulsewé in *RCL*, 183–207, and by Katrina C. D. McLeod and Robin D. S. Yates in "Forms of Ch'in Law: An Annotated Translation of the *Feng-chen shih*," *HJAS* 41, no. 1 (1981): 111–63. The other is the *Book of Submitted Doubtful Cases* (Zouyan shu) from Zhangjiashan tomb 247. See *ZJS*, 213–31; analyzed by Miyake Kiyoshi in "Shin-Kan jidai no saiban seido," *Shirin* 81, no. 2 (Mar. 1988): 35–68; Ikeda Yūichi 池田雄一, ed., *Sōgensho—Chūgoku kodai no saiban kiroku* 奏讞書—中國古代の裁判記錄 [*Book of Submitted Doubtful Cases*—a record of judicial process from ancient China] (Tokyo: Tōsui Shobō, 2002).

97. *ZJS*, 149 ("Ernian lüling," slips 114–7).

98. There are a few recorded cases of successful appeals. In one case from the Qin state (246–245 BCE), a man successfully appealed his hard-labor sentence for stealing a cow. The authorities determined that he had been wrongly convicted because both the accusation against him and his confession were elicited by excessive torture. The state made some monetary compensation to the man, but he was not entirely set free. His convict-laborer status was merely commuted to a different form of government service. See *ZJS*, 221–3 ("Zouyan shu," slips 99–123).

99. *HSBZ*, 23:14b–15a; *HS*, 23.1099–1100; Hulsewé, *Remnants of Han Law*, 336–7.

100. For details of these reforms, and the further reforms of 156 and 144 BCE, see Hulsewé, *Remnants of Han Law*, 124–6; *HSBZ*, 23:12b–15a; *HS*, 23.1098–1100, translated in Hulsewé, *Remnants of Han Law*, 333–7. Castration was clearly retained as a mutilating punishment, despite these reforms.

101. See textual references in Hulsewé, *Remnants of Han Law*, 131–2; Chen Zhi, "Guanyu Liang-Han de tu," in *Liang-Han jingji shiliao luncong* (Xi'an: Shaanxi Renmin Chubanshe, 1958), 259–70.

102. Hulsewé, *Remnants of Han Law*, 132.

103. Chen Zhi, "Guanyu Liang-Han de tu," 259–60.

104. *SJ*, 6.256, 265, 270; Burton Watson, *Records: Qin Dynasty*, 56, 63, 68; *HSBZ*, 31:4b; *HS*, 31.1790; Wilbur, *Slavery*, 261. Some commentators believe that the convicts toiled with the children of private household slaves, not the children of government-owned slaves.

105. Sumiya Sadatoshi, "Shin ni okeru seidō kōgyō no ikkōsatsu—kōkan o chūshin ni," *Sundai shigaku* 55 (1982): 66–8; Huang Shengzhang, "Qin bingqi."

106. *RCL*, A62; *SHD*, 46 ("Qin lü shiba zhong," slip 113). Part of the difficulty with this passage stems from the interpretation of the term "*lichen*" (bond servant) in the Shuihudi slips. At times it seems to represent a labor punishment, but in other instances it seems to describe a hereditary servitude closer to government serfdom. See Hulsewé, "Ch'in Documents," 211–4; Robin D. S. Yates, "Slavery in Early China: A Socio-cultural Approach," *Journal of East Asian Archaeology* 3, nos. 1–2 (2001): 304, 312–4.

107. *RCL*, A35; *SHD*, 35 ("Qin lü shiba zhong," slip 62). For the ambiguity of the social status of these women, see previous note.

108. *RCL*, A58, A59; *SHD*, 45–6 ("Qin lü shiba zhong," slip 109).

109. Iron tools were apparently made in at least two foundries in Shanyang. Archaeologists have recovered iron tools inscribed with the characters *shan-yang er*, signifying Facility 2 of the Shanyang Iron Monopoly Office. This facility was still in operation under the Wang Mang regime; see Li Jinghua, "Handai tie nongqi mingwen shishi," *Kaogu* (1974.1): 61–6.

110. Barbieri-Low, "Organization," 77–83; Kageyama Tsuyoshi, *Chūgoku kodai no shukō-*

gyō to senbaisei (Tokyo: Tōkyō Daigaku Shuppankai, 1984), chaps. 6, 8. For a thorough account in English of the history and technology of this system, see Wagner, *State and Iron Industry.*

111. *SJ,* 30.1428–9; Burton Watson, *Records: Han Dynasty II,* 69–71; *HSBZ,* 24B:12a–13a; *HS,* 24B.1165–6; Swann, *Food and Money,* 271, 275–8. For the disputed chronology of the monopoly system, see Wagner, *State and Iron Industry,* 1n2, 8–12.

112. Yang Yuan, "Xi-Han yan tie gongguan de dili fenbu," *Xianggang zhongwen daxue, Zhongguo wenhua yanjiusuo xuebao* 9 (1978): 219–46; Wagner, *State and Iron Industry,* 89–99. The situation during the Latter Han is somewhat less clear. The *History of the Latter Han* lists thirty-six localities that "have iron," and this is presumed by Wagner to mean that some sort of government iron production also took place in these areas. See Wagner, *State and Iron Industry,* 16–7, 33–5.

113. See note 47 above.

114. Barbieri-Low, "Organization," 82–3.

115. Henan Sheng Wenhuaju Wenwu Gongzuodui, ed., *Gong Xian tieshenggou* (Beijing: Wenwu Chubanshe, 1962); Zhao Qingyun et al., eds., "Gongxian tieshenggou Handai yezhu yizhi zai tantao," *Kaogu xuebao* (1985.2): 157–83. Further references can be found in Wagner, *State and Iron Industry,* 102, table 1, no. 7.

116. Zhengzhou Shi Bowuguan, ed., "Zhengzhou Guxingzhen Handai yetie yizhi fajue jianbao," *Wenwu* (1978.2): 28–47, 27. An excellent translation by Donald Wagner is available in Albert E. Dien, Jeffrey K. Riegel, and Nancy T. Price, eds., *Chinese Archaeological Abstracts,* vol. 3, *Eastern Zhou to Han* (Los Angeles: Institute of Archaeology, University of California, 1985), 1040–65. Further studies can be found in Wagner, *State and Iron Industry,* 107–8, table 1, no. 26.

117. Henan Sheng Wenhuaju Wenwu Gongzuodui, ed., "Nanyang Handai tie gongchang fajue jianbao," *Wenwu* (1960.1): 58–60. After thirty years, the full report was finally published in *Huaxia kaogu* (1991.1): 1–110. See also Li Jinghua and Chen Changshan, *Nanyang Handai yetie* (Zhengzhou: Zhongzhou Guji Chubanshe, 1995). Further studies can be found in Wagner, *State and Iron Industry,* 103–4, table 1, no. 16.

118. Sun Ji, *Handai wuzhi wenhua,* 35–50; Wang Zhongshu, *Han Civilization,* chap. 6; Huangshi Shi Bowuguan, *Tonglüshan gu kuangye yizhi* (Beijing: Wenwu Chubanshe, 1999).

119. Li Jinghua and Chen Changshan, *Nanyang,* 11; Huangshi Shi Bowuguan, *Tonglüshan,* 253.

120. Henan Sheng Bowuguan, Shijingshan Gangtie Gongsi Liantiechang, and Zhongguo Yejin Shi Bianxiezu, eds., "Henan Handai yetie jishu chutan," *Kaogu xuebao* (1978.1): 9.

121. Wang Zhenduo, "Handai yetie gufeng fengji de fuyuan," 43–4.

122. For this number, see the incident recorded in *HSBZ,* 27A:13b; *HS,* 27A.1334; *HFHD,* 2:385n5.9.

123. Lianyungang Bowuguan, ed., *Yinwan Han mu jiandu,* 84; partially translated in Wagner, *State and Iron Industry,* 40–2.

124. See note 120.

125. Wagner, *State and Iron Industry,* 73.

126. Charles K. Hyde, *Technological Change and the British Iron Industry, 1700–1870* (Princeton: Princeton University Press, 1977), appendix A.

127. Wilbur, *Slavery*, 83; *RCL*, A68, A70; *SHD*, 51–4 ("Qin lü shiba zhong," slips 133–40, 147).

128. *RCL*, A49, A50, A65, A68; *SHD*, 41–2, 51–2 ("Qin lü shiba zhong," slips 90–6, 133–42).

129. *RCL*, A12, A15, A16, A17, A18; *SHD*, 32–5 ("Qin lü shiba zhong," slips 49–52, 55–60). These figures were the legal norms under the Qin and should be taken as ideal maximums. It is doubtful whether the convicts received this quantity of rations on a regular basis.

130. *RCL*, A70. *SHD*, 53–4 ("Qin lü shiba zhong," slip 148) states that if a convict broke a pot or a tool, he was to be caned ten strokes for each coin of value of the object. For a broken tool or other object valued over twenty coins, he was to be beaten until "ripe." This beating could have been fatal. See also *ZJS*, 140, 150 ("Ernian lüling," slips 48, 119).

131. *ZJS*, 147 ("Ernian lüling," slips 90–1).

132. Hulsewé, *Remnants of Han Law*, 225–50.

133. For amnesties of convict laborers who had worked on imperial tombs, see *HSBZ*, 5:7a, 10:8b; *HS*, 5.147, 10.316; *HFHD*, 1:321, 2:394.

134. Hu and Zhang, *Dunhuang Xuanquan*, 14–5.

135. Hulsewé, *Remnants of Han Law*, 240; *HSBZ*, 8:1b comm.; *HS*, 8.235–6n8; *HFHD*, 2:200n1.4.

136. Shihuangling Qin Yongkeng Kaogu Fajuedui, ed., "Qin Shihuang ling xice Zhaobeihu cun Qin xingtu mu," *Wenwu* (1982.3): 1–11; Ledderose, *Ten Thousand Things*, 57.

137. See note 104. Apparently a smaller labor force had worked on the necropolis since the King of Qin first took the throne in 246 BCE. After 221 BCE, the project took on grander dimensions.

138. Qin Zhonghang, "Han Yangling fujin qiantu mu de fajue," *Wenwu* (1972.7): 51–3. Wang Zhongshu, *Han Civilization*, 212–3; Peter Hessler, "Rising to Life: Treasures of Ancient China," *National Geographic*, Oct. 2001, 48–67.

139. The Luoyang graveyard was first discovered in 1907 during railway construction. It was not formally excavated until 1964. A preliminary survey appeared in Huang Shibin, "Han Wei Luoyang cheng xingtu fenchang diaocha ji," *Kaogu tongxun* (1958.6): 40–4. The preliminary excavation report can be found in Zhongguo Kexueyuan Kaogu Yanjiusuo Luoyang Gongzuodui, ed., "Dong-Han Luoyang cheng nanjiao de xingtu mudi," *Kaogu* (1972.4): 2–19. To my knowledge the full report of this excavation has never been published. See also Hulsewé, *Remnants of Han Law*, 132; Wagner, *State and Iron Industry*, 51n46.

140. The Luoyang bones have been studied in great detail in Pan Qifeng and Han Kangxin, "Luoyang Dong-Han xingtu mu rengu jianding," *Kaogu* (1988.3): 277–83. This study contradicts some of the findings of the preliminary excavation report. The studied sample included 422 partial or complete skeletons, of which 397 could be sexed with certainty.

141. Pan and Han, "Luoyang Dong-Han," 279–82.

142. *HHSJJ*, 7:4b; *HHS*, 7.294.

143. Pan and Han, "Luoyang Dong-Han," 278. Nearly 43 percent of the skeletons suitable for study showed some form of advanced dental disease.

144. Sun Ji, *Handai wuzhi wenhua*, 402.

145. Zhongguo Kexueyuan Kaogu Yanjiusuo Luoyang Gongzuodui, "Dong-Han Luoyang," 9.

146. Yan Kejun, *Quan shanggu*, 1:852 ("Quan Hou Han wen," *juan* 69:1b–2a). See also Chen Zhi, "Guanyu Liang-Han de tu," 261–2.

147. Yan Kejun, *Quan shanggu*, 1:924 ("Quan Hou Han wen," *juan* 83:11a).

148. We have no way of knowing what percentage of men died from overwork, disease, and accidents in Han mining, but if gold mines in Ptolemaic Egypt and Roman silver mines in Spain (both worked by slaves) can provide any useful analogy, the mortality rate may have been as high as 100 percent. See Diodorus Siculus, *Bibliotheca historica,* trans. C. H. Oldfather (Cambridge, MA: Harvard University Press, 1976), bk. 3.

149. *HSBZ,* 5:5a, 7a; *HS,* 5.143, 7.147; *HFHD,* 1:315, 321–2.

150. Emperor Cheng lamented the fact that so many men died building his "new" tomb at Changling. The site was low and damp but the Court Architect pushed the project forward, leading to many deaths and great expense. The unfortunate architect was banished to the deserts of the northwest (Dunhuang), and the former tomb site was redesignated. See *HSBZ,* 10:11a–b, 12a–b; *HS,* 10.320, 322; *HFHD,* 2:401–5.

151. *HSBZ,* 28A(2):34a comm.; *HS,* 28A.1570. The population went from more than 500,000 (given in round numbers) in ca. 66 BCE to 801,288 by 2 CE, shortly after Su Ling's rebellion. See also *HSBZ,* 76.14a.

152. See note 48.

153. *HSBZ,* 10:7a–b; *HS,* 10.313–4; *HFHD,* 2:389, 391.

154. *HSBZ,* 29:15b–16a; *HS,* 29.1690–1.

155. *HSBZ,* 10:10b; *HS,* 10.318–9; *HFHD,* 2:399–400.

156. *HSBZ,* 10:12b; *HS,* 10.323; *HFHD,* 2:406.

157. The enfeoffments of four of these men are recorded in *HSBZ,* 17:31b–32b, and *HS,* 17.674–5, and took place about six months after the rebellion began. Thus, the Fan Bing and Su Ling rebellions overlapped for much of their duration.

158. *ZJS,* 152 ("Ernian lüling," slips 140–3).

159. *HFHD,* 2:356–72.

160. *HSBZ,* 10:10b; *HS,* 10.318; *HFHD,* 2:399–400; *HSBZ,* 77.

161. *HSBZ,* 27A:18b, 26:58b; *HS,* 27A.1341, 26.1311.

162. *HSBZ,* 86:7b; *HS,* 86.3490–1.

163. Lianyungang Bowuguan, *Yinwan,* 86–9.

164. *HSBZ,* 27A:18b, 26:58b; *HS,* 27A.1341, 26.1311. It has been suggested that the word "forty" may have been a copyist's error for "fourteen" or "ten" and that "commanderies and princedoms" may have been a copyist's error for the smaller unit of "counties." Commanderies and princedoms in that part of Han China were not very large. It is not inconceivable that the band could have passed through nineteen of them. The *Qian Han ji* (26:11a) records nineteen commanderies and princedoms as well.

165. *ZJS,* 143 ("Ernian lüling," slips 65–6).

166. This occurred in the suppression of the convict rebellion led by Zheng Gong in Guanghan Commandery in 17 BCE; see *HSBZ,* 10:10b; *HS,* 10.319; *HFHD,* 2:400. The legal statutes from Zhangjiashan stipulate not only that the turncoat must notify the officials of the location of the rebels but that the information must also lead to the capture of the majority of the band; see *ZJS,* 152.

167. Several of these APBs have been found in Han period documents excavated in the far northwest; see Hu and Zhang, *Dunhuang Xuanquan,* 20–1; Loewe, *Records of Han Administration,* 1:68–9.

168. *HSBZ,* 10:13a; *HS,* 10.323–4; *HFHD,* 2:407.

169. Lianyungang Bowuguan, *Yinwan,* 85–95.

170. Wilbur, *Slavery*, 248.

171. Ibid. See also the synthesis of the same materials in a broader social analysis by Qu Tongzu in *Han Social Structure*, 135–59, 322–92. See also Yates, "Slavery in Early China."

172. Wilbur, *Slavery*, 64–71.

173. *RCL*, A11, A68, D4, D43, D60, D89, D149, D150, D153, E3, E15, E16.

174. Wilbur, *Slavery*, 72–9.

175. *ZJS*, 156–7 ("Ernian lüling," slips 174–81). This statute was apparently abrogated by Emperor Wen in 179 BCE, but it seems to have been reinstated later, at least for capital cases like rebellion. See *HSBZ*, 4:5b, 5:4a; *HS*, 4.110–11n1, 5.142; *HFHD*, 1:233, 313; Li Junming, "Zhangjiashan Han jian 'shou lü' yu jiazu lianzuo," *Wenwu* (2002.9): 60–3.

176. *HSBZ*, 24B:16a–17a; *HS*, 24B.1170; Swann, *Food and Money*, 294–300.

177. Wilbur, *Slavery*, 98–117.

178. Ibid., 85–90. For the recently discovered Han laws against selling people, see *ZJS*, 143–4 ("Ernian lüling," slip 67).

179. Wilbur, *Slavery*, 92–7.

180. Ibid., 90–2; *ZJS*, 142–5 ("Ernian lüling," slips 66–9, 71–3).

181. Wilbur, *Slavery*, 174–7. In another publication, Wilbur puts this estimate at between 1 and 5 percent of the population. See C. Martin Wilbur, "Industrial Slavery in China during the Former Han Dynasty (206 *BC–AD* 25)," *Journal of Economic History* 3, no. 1 (May 1943): 56–69.

182. *ZJS*, 139, 150 ("Ernian lüling," slips 39, 119). This same fine was imposed on prison guards who beat convicts to death; see *ZJS*, 140 ("Ernian lüling," slip 48). This is a large sum of money, out of the reach of most commoners. It represents more than half the yearly salary of a district magistrate during the Han. If one could not pay off redemption fines for punishment, they had to be worked off in the same convict labor camps described above. See *RCL*, A68; *SHD*, 51–2 ("Qin lü shiba zhong," slips 133–40). The Qin epitaph in table 6.3 records just such a laborer working off fines.

183. See Wilbur, *Slavery*, 151–6. Also see *RCL*, E15, and *SHD*, 154 ("Fengzhen shi," slips 37–41), for a request by an owner to have an insubordinate slave sold to the government as a convict laborer, and *RCL*, E16, and *SHD*, 155 ("Fengzhen shi," slips 42–5), for an appeal from an owner to have an insubordinate slave mutilated.

184. It appears that in the Han slaves were given penalties one degree more severe for the same crime. During the Tang, this was raised to two degrees of increased severity. See Wilbur, *Slavery*, 147–51; *Tang lü shu yi*, *juan* 22, 24; translated in Wallace Johnson, *The T'ang Code*, 2 vols. (Princeton: Princeton University Press, 1979).

185. *ZJS*, 138 ("Ernian lüling," slip 28).

186. Ibid., slip 30.

187. *ZJS*, 151 ("Ernian lüling," slip 133). The same penalty applied to children accusing their parents and to wives accusing their mothers-in-law. See also Wilbur, *Slavery*, 156–7.

188. *ZJS*, 152 ("Ernian lüling," slip 135).

189. *ZJS*, 139 ("Ernian lüling," slip 34).

190. *ZJS*, 158 ("Ernian lüling," slip 188).

191. Ibid., slip 189.

192. *ZJS*, 157 ("Ernian lüling," slip 180).

193. See the complete discussion of manumission in Wilbur, *Slavery,* 129–39; Qu, *Han Social Structure*, 156–9.

194. Their biographies are translated in Wilbur, *Slavery,* 298–9, 418–9.

195. *HSBZ,* 68; *HS,* 68.2959–69; translated in Wilbur, *Slavery,* 323–4, and Burton Watson, *Courtier and Commoner,* 151–7.

196. *HSBZ,* 11:3b; *HS,* 11.336; *HFHD,* 3:24; Wilbur, *Slavery,* 133, 438–9; Qu, *Social Structure,* 361.

197. For 160 BCE, see *HSBZ,* 4:17b; *HS,* 4.130; *HFHD,* 1:265; Wilbur, *Slavery,* 134, 293. For 110 CE, see *HHSJJ,* 5:7b; *HHS,* 5.215; Qu, *Han Social Structure,* 379. One cannot know how completely these manumission edicts were carried out.

198. Wilbur, *Slavery,* 134–9.

199. *HSBZ,* 17:25b; *HS,* 17.665; Wilbur, *Slavery,* 135, 419.

200. *ZJS,* 155 ("Ernian lüling," slips 162–3).

201. The term "private retainer" was later used by Wang Mang when he attempted to make slaves inalienable in 9 CE. By trying to convert all slaves into the private retainers of their former masters, he hoped to change their legal status and make them illegal to buy or sell. See *HSBZ,* 99B:8b; *HS,* 99B.4111; Wilbur, *Slavery,* 452–5; *HFHD,* 3:286.

202. *ZJS,* 184 ("Ernian lüling," slip 382). The family's other material property would be confiscated by the state. If the master possessed many slaves and only one family member would take over his household status, then the disposition of the slaves would be according to length of service, presence of children, or the final wishes of the master.

203. The claim was made by Wang Mang; see *HSBZ,* 99B:8a–b; *HS,* 99B.4110; translated in Wilbur, *Slavery,* 452–5; *HFHD,* 3:285. Dong Zhongshu had earlier (ca. 100 BCE) argued that slavery should be abolished, apparently because it allowed for extragovernmental executions by slave owners; see *HSBZ,* 24A:17a; *HS,* 24A.1133; translated in Wilbur, *Slavery,* 312–3, and in Swann, *Food and Money,* 183.

204. Jia Yi (ca. 201–169 BCE), a minister to Emperor Wen, made this claim around 177–174 BCE. See *HSBZ,* 48:17b–18a; *HS,* 48.2242; translated in Wilbur, *Slavery,* 279–80.

205. Wilbur, *Slavery,* 121–6.

206. The old male slave Bianliao in Wang Bao's mock slave contract (see below) was sold for 15,000 cash. Two adolescent male slaves recorded in an inventory from Juyan in Gansu were valued at 30,000 for the pair. An adult female slave from the same record was valued at 20,000 coins. The Prince of Jibei once boasted that he paid 4.7 million coins for four female slaves skilled in different arts. See Wilbur, *Slavery,* 122n1, 288–90; Loewe, *Records of Han Administration,* 1:72; Xu Zhuoyun, *Han Agriculture,* 230–1; *SJ,* 105.2805.

207. The property record was engraved sometime toward the end of the Han period on a recycled stone slab that may have once been part of a funerary monument. This document may have served to record a property division among members of a wealthy landlord household. The property record stone itself was later recycled as the door of a Three Kingdoms period tomb in Sichuan. See a rubbing and full references in Nagata Hidemasa, *Kandai sekkoku shūsei* (Kyoto: Dōhōsha, 1994), no. 144.

208. *HSBZ,* 37:1a–b; *HS,* 37.1975; Wilbur, *Slavery,* 267–8.

209. Finley, "Slavery," 311.

210. Wilbur, *Slavery,* 240–4.

211. The original text as found in the 1598 edition of the encyclopedia *Record of Elementary Learning* (Chuxueji) can be found in Wilbur, *Slavery*, 382–6. For translations, see Wilbur, *Slavery*, 383–92; Xu Zhuoyun, *Han Agriculture*, 231–4. The most detailed study of the "Tong yue" is Utsunomiya, *Kandai shakai keizaishi kenkyū*, chap. 9.

212. *HSBZ*, 59:7b–11a; *HS*, 59.2652; partially translated in Wilbur, *Slavery*, 365; Qu, *Han Social Structure*, 355–6.

213. Though this account claims that Zhang Anshi was richer than Huo Guang, Huo Guang's marquisate (the source of real, steady income) was eventually increased to 17,000 households, nearly twice the size of Zhang Anshi's enfeoffment.

214. Jean-Jacques Aubert, "Workshop Managers," in *The Inscribed Economy: Production and Distribution in the Roman Empire in the Light of "Instrumentum Domesticum,"* ed. W. V. Harris (Ann Arbor: University of Michigan, 1993), 171–81; Morel, "Craftsman," 214–44.

215. *SJ*, 129; translated in Burton Watson, *Records: Han Dynasty II*, 450; *HSBZ*, 91:8b–9a; *HS*, 91.3690–1. Both chapters are translated and analyzed in Swann, *Food and Money*, 405–64. The passage on the Zhuo family is also translated in Wagner, *Iron and Steel*, 251.

216. Donald Wagner (*Iron and Steel*, 251) took the term "*qunchi*" (tubers) to possibly refer to "bog iron" under the marshy ground.

217. The *Historical Records* account says 1,000 youths here.

218. *HSBZ*, 91:8b–9a; *HS*, 91.3690; my translation follows Wilbur, *Slavery*, 259–60, with some modifications.

219. Wilbur, *Slavery*, 218.

220. This is from a quotation from the Han legal statutes, found in the commentary of Ying Shao (ca. 140–204 CE) to *HSBZ*, 2:6a; *HS*, 2.91; *HFHD*, 1:184n1. Ying Shao implies that double the poll tax was always charged for slaves, but according to other commentators, it was Emperor Wu who raised the amount. See Wilbur, *Slavery*, 461n1. The maximum figure presented here assumes a poll tax of 190 coins under Emperor Wu, as reconstructed by Katō Shigeru, "Study on the *Suan-fu*."

221. Lao Gan, "Handai de guyong zhidu," *Lishi yuyan yanjiusuo jikan* 23 (1951): 77–87.

222. Original reports can be found in *Wenwu* (1974.6): 41–53, and *Wenwu* (1976.6): 69–75.

223. For an analysis of the roles of slaves as indicated by these figurines, see Yu Weichao, "Gushi fenqi wenti de kaoguxue guancha," in *Xianqin Lian-Han kaoguxue lunji* (Beijing: Wenwu Chubanshe, 1985), 11–6.

224. The names inscribed on the funerary figurines from Fenghuangshan are almost our only evidence for the names of slaves during the Former Han period. The names seem to be a mixture of pejorative names like Disrespectful, Bear, Panther, Drunkie, Girlie, Captured, Bound, Carrier, and Round and names of virtuous personality traits like Gentleman, Lucky, Worthy, Trust, Stalwart, Appropriateness, and Contemplation. The names in the second category were common in the general population. A common name for female slaves seems to have been Increase (i.e., fertility).

225. *HSBZ*, 24B:26b, 99C:12b–13a; *HS*, 24B.1184, 99C.4167; Wilbur, *Slavery*, 464–5; Swann, *Food and Money*, 352–3; *HFHD*, 3:410–1.

226. *HHSJJ*, 1A:2b; *HHS*, 1B.50; Wilbur, *Slavery*, 466. The edict specifically says that those enslaved during Wang Mang's regime "not in accordance with the former laws" were to be freed.

227. *HSBZ*, 24A:17a–19a; *HS*, 24A.1138–9; Swann, *Food and Money*, 184–91; Xu Zhuoyun,

Han Agriculture, 112–7, 295–9. For contemporary records of the *daitian fa* in practice, see Loewe, *Records of Han Administration,* 1:70, 2:319. A lost book called the *Five Fascicles of Mr. Zhao* (Zhaoshi wupian), recorded with other agricultural manuals in the "Bibliographic Treatise" (Yiwen zhi) of the *History of the Former Han,* might have been penned by Zhao Guo himself to describe his method; see entry in *HSBZ,* 30:49a (and comm.); *HS,* 30.1743.

228. Xu Zhuoyun, *Han Agriculture,* 300, quoting the *Discourse on Administration* (Zhenglun) of Cui Shi.

229. William Linn Westermann, "Industrial Slavery in Roman Italy," *Journal of Economic History* 2 (1942): 156–7, 161–2.

230. *HSBZ,* 70:16b; *HS,* 70.3024.

GLOSSARY OF CHINESE CHARACTERS

Ai (emperor) 哀帝
an 案
An Guo (fiefdom) 安國
An Guo (person's name) 安國
Anling 安陵
Anyi 安邑
Ao 驁
Aqu 阿瞿
Bai (eldest son) 伯
Bai (surname) 柏
Bai Hua 柏華
Bai Yuan 柏元
Bai Yuan Zhong Hua 柏元仲華
Bai Zhong 柏仲
baigong 百工
Baiguan zhi 百官志
Baihu 百虎
Ban Bo 班伯
Ban Gu 班固
Ban Jieyu 班婕妤
banliang 半兩
bei 婢
beizhong xianglu 被中香鑪
ben 本
Bianliao 便了
biao 表
biezhi 別治
biezuo 別作
Bin Wang 邠王
Bing Ji 丙吉
bingshu 兵書
bocan 白粲
bushi 逋事
Busi 卜肆
Cai Yong 蔡邕
Cai Zhi 蔡質

Cang 蒼
cao 曹
Cao Mao 曹髦
Cao Yi 操義
Cao Zhi 曹植
Chang 常
chang (perpetual) 常
Chang Qu 常璩
Chang'an 長安
Changle Gong 長樂宮
Changle Shi 常樂室
changman deng 常滿燈
Changshan Commandery 常山郡
Changxin Gong 長信宮
Chanjing 產經
Chao Cuo 晁錯
chen 臣
Chen Chang 陳敞
Chen Tang 陳湯
Chen Xing 陳興
cheng 丞
Cheng (emperor) 成帝
Cheng Gong 承宮
chengdan 城旦
Chengdu 成都
Chengxiang 丞相
Chengxiang Zhangshi 丞相長史
chi 翅
Chi You 蚩尤
chidao 馳道
Chucheng Gate 廚城門
chui 錘
Chunyu Zhang 淳于長
Chuxueji 初學記
ci 賜
ci biao fan you X 此表凡有X
Cishi (Regional Inspector) 刺史
cishi (sacrificial chamber) 司(祠)室
citang 祠堂
Cui Shi 崔寔
Da Ji 妲己
da nüzi 大女子
da nüzi Ao 大女子鰲
da she 大赦
Dafentou 大墳頭
Dai Sheng 代盛
daitian fa 代田法
Dan 旦
dan (vermilion) 丹
dani budao 大逆不道
Daodejing 道德經
Daolü 盜律
Dashi 大市
Dasinong 大司農
Daxia 大夏
Dayeze 大野澤
De (Acquire) 得
de qi zhen 得其真
De Zhenchang 德貞常
di (apprentice) 弟
di (younger brother) 弟
dian 殿
diao 調
diaowen 調(雕)文(紋)
Dilizhi 地理志
ding 丁
Ding County 定縣
Ding Hu 丁護
Ding Huan 丁緩
Ding Lan 丁蘭
ding nüzi 丁女子
Ding Shou 丁綬
Ding Shuan 丁諼
Ding Yuan 丁媛
dinghai (day 24 in sexagenary cycle) 丁亥
dinghai ("nail child") 釘孩
dingyou 丁酉
Diwu Fang 第五訪
dizi 弟子
Dong Commandery 東郡
Dong Guan 東觀
Dong Xiwen 董希文
Dong Yong 董永
Dong Zhishi-Xi Zhishi 東織室-西織室
Dong Zhongshu 董仲舒
Dong Zhuo 董卓
Donge County 東阿縣
Donghai Commandery 東海郡
Dongmen Jing 東門京
Dongping Princedom 東平國

Dongshi 東市
Dongshi ling-Xishi ling 東市令–西市令
Dongwanggong 東王公
Dongyuan Jiang 東園匠
dou 斗
Dou Guangguo 竇廣國
Dou Taihai 竇太后
Dou Wan 竇綰
Dou Xian 竇憲
doulai 鬥來
Du Yannian 杜延年
duhui 都會
Dujiang 都匠
Duling 杜陵
Duting Hou 都亭侯
Duwei 都尉
Erjing fu 二京賦
fa 法
Fan Bing 樊並
Fan Yu 樊育
Fang Feng 房風
fangji 方技
fangshi 方士
fangzhong 房中
fayao 乏傜
Feilian 非廉
Feng 豐
Feng-zhen shi 封診式
Fu (Day of Concealment) 伏
fu (registration) 傅
fu (rhapsody) 賦
Fu Qian 服虔
fu zuo 復作
fuchu 復除
Fulü 復律
Fuxi 伏羲
Gan Yanshou 甘延壽
gang 釭
Ganjiang 干將
Ganquan Gong 甘泉宮
Gaoping 高平
geng 更
Geng Shouchang 耿壽昌
gong (artisan) 工
gong (attack) 攻
gong (factory) 工
gong (merit) 功
gong (offer tribute) 貢
gong (palace) 宮
Gong Kuan 龔寬
gong lichen 工隸臣
gong liqie 工隸妾
Gong Yu 貢禹
Gongcao 功曹
gongfu wuji 功扶(夫)無極
gongfu wukao 功扶(夫)無攷(考)
Gonggeng Zhang 工更長
Gonggong 供工
gongren 工人
gongshi (fabrication chamber) 工室
Gongshi (Master of Artisans) 工師
Gongshi (type of rank) 公士
Gongshu Lu Ban 公輸魯班
Gongshui 宮水
Gongsun Yuan 公孫淵
gongxian 工獻
Gongzu 公卒
Gu (given name) 古
gu (merchant) 賈
guan 官
Guan Zhong 管仲
Guang Gate 光門
Guanghan Commandery 廣漢郡
Guanglu Daifu 光祿大夫
Guangluxun 光祿勳
Guangwu (emperor) 光武
guanzhong 關中
gui 規
guixin 鬼薪
guiyou 癸酉
Guizimu 鬼子母
guo 郭
Guo Qin lun 過秦論
Guo Tai 郭泰
Guxingzhen 古滎鎮
hai (child) 孩
hai (cyclical branch) 亥
hai nü gong (harming women artisans) 害女紅(工)
hai nü gong (harming women's work) 害女紅(功)

Han Fei 韓非
Han Feizi 韓非子
Han guan dianzhi yishi xuanyong 漢官典職儀式選用
Han guan yi 漢官儀
Han jiuyi 漢舊儀
Han lin'ge tu 漢麟閣圖
Han Yue 韓說
Han Zeng 韓增
hang 行
haowu 好物
He Jin 何進
He Wu 何武
He Xian 何顯
Hedong Commandery 河東郡
Hefei 合肥
Helidi 訶利底
Henan 河南
heng (eternal) 恆
Heng Gate 横門
he-san 河三
he-yi 河一
Hongdumen Xue 洪(鴻)都門學
Hou Jin 侯瑾
hou mai ci jing 後買此鏡
houfeng didong yi 候風地動儀
hu (household) 戶
hu (northern barbarian) 胡
Hu Guang 胡廣
Hu Kuan 胡寬
Hu Shang 扈商
Hu Wang 胡王
huagong 畫工
huan (dim-sighted) 晥
Huan (Duke of Qi) 齊桓公
Huan (emperor) 桓帝
huan (market wall) 闤
Huan Chan 桓孱
Huan Sangzhong 桓桑終
Huan Village 宦里
Huang Ba 黃霸
Huang Qiong 黃瓊
Huangdi 黃帝
Huangdi Taichuzu Miao 黃帝太初祖廟
Huanghou 皇后
Huangmen 黃門
Huangmen Ling 黃門令
Huangshen 黃神
huangtu 黃塗
huanlao 晥老
huashi 畫師
huashi gong 畫師工
Huashi Shu 畫室署
Huayang Avenue 華陽街
hufen 胡粉
Huhanye Shanyu 呼韓邪單于
hui 闠
Hui (emperor) 惠帝
Huo Guang 霍光
Huozhi liezhuan 貨殖列傳
ji (auspicious) 吉
Ji (given name) 季
ji (minor contract) 劑
ji (skill) 技
Ji di Mao 季弟卯
Ji Ji 幾級
Jia Kui 賈逵
Jia Yi 賈誼
Jiaguan Huatang (1) 甲觀畫堂
Jiaguan Huatang (2) 甲館畫堂
jiamiao 家廟
jian 監
Jian Daifu 諫大夫
jian geng 踐更
jiang (architect, carpenter) 匠
Jiang (Frontier) 彊
Jiang Gong 姜肱
Jiang Lan 江覽
Jiang Yingju 蔣英炬
Jiangling 江陵
Jiangxue tu 講學圖
Jiangzuo Dajiang 將作大匠
Jie Qian 解倩
jin 金
Jin Midi 金日磾
Jinbu lü 金布律
Jing (emperor) 景帝
Jing (Respect) 敬
Jing Chu suishi ji 荊楚歲時記

Jingdezhen 景德鎮
Jingzhao Yin 京兆尹
Jining 濟寧
Jinma Men 金馬門
Jiuzhang suanshu 九章算術
jiuzi zhi mu 九子之母
Jiuzimo 九子魔
Jiuzimu 九子母
ju 矩
juan (scroll of book) 卷
juan (iron wedge) 鐫
jue 絕
juedi 角抵, 觳抵
jun 均
junxing 軍興
Juyan 居延
Kaiguo Dadian 開國大典
Kaogong 考工
Kaogongji 考工記
Kaogongshi 考工室
kehua 刻畫
Keqing 客卿
Kong Rong 孔融
Kongzi 孔子
Kuodizhi 括地志
La New Year 臘日
Lai Fei 賴非
Langzhong 郎中
lao 牢
Lao Gan 勞幹
Laozi 老子
Lei Gong 雷公
Lelang 樂浪
li (slave, convict bondsman) 隸
Li (surname, given name) 李
Li di Mao 李弟卯
Li Ju 李菊
Li Kui 李悝
Li Ling 李陵
Li Yannian 李延年
Liang Princedom 梁國
Liangqiu He 梁丘賀
lianju 連車
lianyue 連月
lichen 隸臣
lie 列
Lie Yi 烈裔
Lienü tu 列女圖
Lienüzhuan 列女傳
Lienüzhuan songtu 列女傳頌圖
liezhang 列長
Ling 令
Lingshi 令史
Linjin 臨晉
Linqiong 臨邛
Linzi 臨淄
liqie 隸妾
lishu 隸書
Liu Bang 劉邦
Liu Bao 劉褒
Liu Bo 劉白
Liu Chang 劉暢
Liu Dan 劉旦
Liu De 劉德
Liu Fuling (Emperor Zhao) 劉弗陵
Liu Haiyang 劉海陽
Liu He 劉賀
Liu Ji 劉季
Liu Jie 劉揭
Liu Liang 劉梁
Liu Shang 劉尚
Liu Sheng 劉勝
Liu Shi 劉奭
Liu Xiang 劉向
Liu Xin 劉歆
Liu Yan 劉焉
Liu Zhong 劉忠
liujin 鎏金
Long (surname) 龍
long-long 隆隆
lu (deer) 鹿
lu (income) 祿
Lu (surname of lacquer makers) 盧氏
Lü (surname) 呂
Lu Ban 魯班
Lü Buwei 呂不韋
Lu Ji 陸機
Lu Princedom 魯國
luanshi 孿石
Lunheng 論衡

Luoyang 洛陽
Luoyang ji 洛陽記
Ma Jun 馬鈞
Ma Midi 馬日磾
Ma Yuan 馬援
mai ci jingzhe 買此鏡者
maidi quan 買地卷
maizhe 買者
Mangliu 芒柳
Mao Yanshou 毛延壽
Maoling 茂陵
mashi 馬式
Meng Ao 蒙驁
Meng Ben 孟賁
Meng Fu 孟孚
Meng Ji 孟季
mianlao 免老
miao ci 廟祠
minggong 名工
mingshi 名石
minqian 緡錢
mo 末
modou 墨斗
mozhi 磨治
Mu Fang 母放
Mu Yi 母夷
mubiao 墓表
mugong 木工
nai li chen 耐隸臣
nai li qie 耐隸妾
nai sikou 耐司寇
nanshan 南山
nanshan zhi yang 南山之陽
Nanyang Commandery 南陽郡
Nanyue 南越
Neiguan 內官
Neishi 內史
Neizhe 內者
niaozhuan 鳥篆
nu 奴
nubei 奴婢
Nüjie 女誡
Nüqi 女歧（岐）
Nüwa 女媧
Nüxun 女訓
Panyu 番禺
Pei Commandery 沛郡
pian 篇
Ping 平
pingfeng 屛風
pingjia 平價
Pingle Guan 平樂觀
pingman 平慢
Poo Mu-chou 蒲慕州
Prince Jian of Zhongshan 中山簡王
Prince Xiao of Rencheng 任城孝王
qi (number 7) 七
qi (vital energy) 氣
Qi Commandery 齊郡
Qi San Fuguan 齊三服官
qian 鉗
qianxiang 錢鉐
qiao 巧
qiao bu cheng 巧不成
qiaoyan 巧言
qie 妾
qilin 麒麟
Qilin Dian 麒麟殿
Qilin Ge 麒麟閣
Qi-Lu 齊魯
Qin Ershi 秦二世
Qin Jun 秦君
Qing 清
qing (rank 10) 卿
qing chengdan 黥城旦
qing chong 黥舂
Qinglong 青龍
Qingyangsi 青羊肆
qiting 旗亭
Qiu Yan 仇延
Qiwang 漆王
qiyun 氣韻
quanshu 券書
quanyue 券約
que 闕
qunchi 踆（蹲）鴟
ren 仁
Rencheng Princedom 任城國
rishu 日書
ronggong 冗工

rouxing 肉刑
Runan Commandery 汝南郡
ruo zhen 若真
Shandong 山東
Shang (dynasty) 商
shang (merchant trader) 商
Shang Yang 商鞅
Shangdang Commandery 上黨郡
Shangfang 尚方
Shangfang zuojing 尚方作鏡
Shangjunshu 商君書
Shangshu Ling 尚書令
Shangyu 尚浴
Shanyang Commandery 山陽郡
shan-yang er 山陽二
shanyu 單于
shanzhong 善終
Shao (emperor) 少帝
Shao Qiangsheng 邵強生
Shaofu 少府
Shaofu Cheng 少府丞
shen 神
Shen Nong 神農
shengyu 乘輿
Shengzi 生子
shenmian 身免
shenqi 神器
Shentu Pan 申屠蟠
shi (chamber) 室
shi (marketplace) 市
shi (master) 師
shi (picul of rank) 石
shi (technocrat, scholar) 士
shi (scribe) 史
shi (time, season) 時
shi (to commission) 使
shi furen 師夫人
Shi Juyi 石巨宜
shi zai ci xia 死(屍)在此下
shichan 市廛
shigong 石工
Shihuozhi 食貨志
Shiji (Historical Records) 史記
shiji (market register) 市籍
Shijing 詩經
shilie 市列
shilou 市樓
shinü 使女
Shisefu 市嗇夫
shishi 石室
shisi 市肆
shitang 食堂
Shiyilu 拾遺錄
Shiyuan 市掾
Shizhang 市長
shizu 市租
Shouchun 壽春
shouji 手技
Shoulü 收律
shu (knack) 數(術)
Shu Commandery 蜀郡
shu fazuo 戍罰作
Shu Jun Xigong 蜀郡西工
Shuhua ji 述畫記
shuhui 輸會
Shuihudi 睡虎地
shumin 庶民
shuren 庶人
si 似
Sigong 寺工
Sima Qian 司馬遷
Sima Xiangru 司馬相如
simin 四民
Simin yueling 四民月令
sishu 私屬
Song Hong 宋弘
Songshan 宋山
Sousu Duwei 騪粟都尉
Su Ling 蘇令
Su Wu 蘇武
suan 算
suan minqian 算緡錢
suanfu 算賦
suanshu shu 算術書
suanzi 算訾
sufengzhe 素封者
sugong 素工
sui 隧
Sun Changzhi 孫暢之
Sun Zhongyang 孫仲陽

Tai Xue 太學
Taichang 太常
Taiguan 太官
Taishanghuang 太上皇
Taishi Ling 太史令
taisui 太歲
tang 堂
Tang liudian 唐六典
Tangxi Dian 堂谿典
Tiandi 天帝
tianma 天馬
Tianshui Commandery 天水郡
Tianwen 天問
tianzu 田租
Tieguan 鐵官
Tieshan 鐵山
Tieshanmiao 鐵山廟
Tieshenggou 鐵生溝
Tiezu 鐵祖
ting 亭
Tingwei 廷尉
Tingyuan 廷掾
Tingzhang 亭長
tong 僮（童）
Tong yue 僮約
Tonglüshan 銅綠山
Tongma xiangfa 銅馬相法
Tongsheng ge 同聲歌
tou 頭
tu 徒
Tu Gate 突門
tuhua 圖畫
tuli 徒隸
Wafangzhuang 瓦房莊
wan (ten thousand) 萬
wan chengdan 完城旦
wan chong 完舂
wang 王
Wang Bao 王褒
Wang Cheng 王成
Wang Chong 王充
Wang Fu 王符
Wang Jia 王嘉
Wang Jiling 王季陵
Wang Mang 王莽
Wang Xu 王盱
Wang Yanshi 王延世
Wang Yin 王音
wang zhang 王杖
Wang Zhaojun 王昭君
Wang Zhengjun 王政君
Wang Ziya 王子雅
Wei Hong 衛宏
Wei Li 衛颯
Wei Qiao 渭橋
Wei Xiang 魏相
weishi nü 未使女
Weiyang Gong 未央宮
weizuo 為作
Wen (emperor) 文帝
Wen Shuyang 文叔陽
Weng Fanggang 翁方綱
Wheelwright Pian 輪扁
Woodworker Qing 梓慶
Wu (ancient state, territory) 吳
Wu (emperor) 武帝
Wu Kuan 吳寬
Wu Liang 武梁
Wu You 吳祐
wudu 五蠹
Wulaowa 五老洼
Wushier bingfang 五十二病方
xi (asemantic verbal pause) 兮
Xi (Connected) 係
Xi (Happy) 喜
Xiadu 下杜
Xiahou Sheng 夏候生
Xi'an 西安
Xian ling 縣令
Xian ting 咸亭
xian xinan xiaoshan yangshan 縣西南小山陽山
Xiang (Administrator) 相
Xiang Sefu 鄉嗇夫
Xiang Tajun 鄉他君
Xiang Yu 項羽
xianglu 香爐
xianling quanshu 先令券書
Xianwei 縣尉
Xianyang 咸陽

Xiao He 蕭何
xiao jue 小爵
Xiao kuang 小匡
xiao nan 小男
xiao nanzi 小男子
xiao nüzi 小女子
Xiao Qi 蕭綺
Xiao Wangzhi 蕭望之
xiaolian 孝廉
Xiaqiu County 瑕丘縣
Xie Cheng 謝承
Xijing zaji 西經雜記
xin (anoint with blood) 釁
Xin (dynasty) 新
xin (heart, mind) 心
Xin Feng (New Feng) 新豐
xin gong 新工
Xinfeng fang jiquan tu 新豐放雞犬圖
xing 形
Xing Qu 邢渠
Xingle Gong 興樂宮
xingming maozhuang 姓名貌狀
xingming tuxiang 姓名圖象
xingsi 形似
Xingyang 滎陽
Xiong (given name) 熊
Xiongnu 匈奴
Xishi (famous beauty) 西施
Xishi (Western Market) 西市
xiu 髹
Xiuchu King 休屠王
xiugong 髹工
xiumu 休沐
Xiwangmu 西王母
Xu (surname) 許
Xu County 許縣
Xu Shen 許慎
Xuan (emperor) 宣帝
Xuande Dian 宣德殿
xunlu 熏爐
yan (speech) 言
Yan (territory near Beijing) 燕
Yang Biao 楊彪
Yang Ci 楊賜
Yang Lu 楊魯
Yang Qiu 陽球
Yang Wang 陽望
Yang Xiong 楊(揚)雄
Yang Yuan 楊遠
Yang Yun 楊惲
Yangcheng Yan 陽成延
Yangling 陽陵
Yangxin jia 陽信家
Yangxin Yi Hou 陽信夷侯
Yangxin Zhang Gongzhu 陽信長公主
yang-yi 陽一
yao yi 徭役
Ye (Wilderness) 野
Yi (ethnonym) 夷
Yi Wan 姨綰
yi zi sun 宜子孫
Yilang 議郎
Ying Shao 應劭
Yingchuan Commandery 潁川郡
yinguan gong 隱官工
Yiwen zhi 藝文志
Yiyang 宜陽
yizhong 邑中
yong (indenture, hire for wages) 傭
Yong Gate 雍門
You Fufeng 右扶風
you gong 尤工
You Neishi 右內史
Yu Dingguo 于定國
Yuan (city) 宛
Yuan (emperor) 元帝
Yuan (given name) 元
Yue Song 樂松
Yueling 月令
Yueyang 櫟陽
Yun Tai 雲臺
yunjiu 醞酒
Yunmeng County 雲夢縣
Yushi Daifu 御史大夫
Yushi Zhongcheng 御史中丞
Yuzhou 豫州
zan (eulogy) 贊
zan (chisel) 鏨
zao (early) 早
zao (flea) 蚤

zaogong 造工
Zeilü 賊律
zeng 繒
Zhai Fangjin 翟方進
Zhang (surname on tomb brick) 張
Zhang Anshi 張安世
Zhang Chang 張敞
Zhang Chong 張崇
Zhang Fang 張放
Zhang Heng 張衡
Zhang Kan 張堪
Zhang Qian 張騫
Zhang Tang 張湯
Zhang Wensi 張文思
Zhang Xun 張 馴
Zhang Yan 張晏
Zhangjiashan 張家山
Zhao (emperor) 昭帝
Zhao Chongguo 趙充國
Zhao Feiyan 趙飛燕
Zhao Guo 趙過
Zhao Qi 趙岐
Zhao Xun 趙苟 (徇)
Zhao Zhaoyi 趙昭儀
Zhaoshi wupian 趙氏五篇
Zhaoyang Dian 昭陽殿
zhen 真
zhenbao 珍寶
zheng 徵
Zheng Gong 鄭躬
Zheng Xuan 鄭玄
Zhenglun 政論
Zhenping 真平
zhi (long contract) 質
Zhi (surname of mirror makers) 至
Zhi (surname of knife sharpeners in *HS*) 質
Zhi (surname of knife sharpeners in *SJ*) 郅
zhi (to make, to regulate) 治
zhi (to pawn) 質
zhi (value) 值
zhishi 治石
Zhizhi Shanyu 郅支單于
Zhong (given name for second son) 仲
Zhong (Heavy) 重
Zhong Shangfang 中尚方
Zhou (last Shang king) 紂
Zhou, Duke of 周公
Zhou Bo 周勃
Zhoubi suanjing 周髀算經
Zhouli 周禮
Zhu (surname) 朱
Zhuang Pu 莊普
Zhuang Xin 莊訢
Zhuangzi 莊子
zhuanshu 篆書
zhubu 主簿
zhuhou wang 諸侯王
Zhuo (surname) 桌
Zhuo Commandery 涿郡
Zhuo Wangsun 卓王孫
Zhuo Wenjun 卓文君
zishu 貲戍
Zong Lin 宗懍
Zouyan shu 奏讞書
zu 卒
zun 尊
zuo 作
Zuo Neishi 左內史
Zuo Pingyi 左馮翊
zuo ru sikou 作如司寇
zuofu 作府
zuoshi 作室
Zuoshimen 作室門
zuozao 作造

ABBREVIATIONS

BMFEA	*Bulletin of the Museum of Far Eastern Antiquities.*
CHOC	*Cambridge History of China. Vol. 1, The Ch'in and Han Empires, 221 B.C.–A.D. 220.* Ed. Denis Twitchett and Michael Loewe. Cambridge: Cambridge University Press, 1986.
GSR	Bernhard Karlgren. *Grammata Serica Recensa.* Stockholm: Museum of Far Eastern Antiquities, 1964.
HFHD	Homer H. Dubs. *History of the Former Han Dynasty.* 3 vols. Baltimore: Waverly Press, 1938–55.
HHS	Fan Ye. *Hou Hanshu.* 18 vols. Beijing: Zhonghua Shuju, 1965.
HHSJJ	Fan Ye. *Hou Hanshu jijie.* Ed. Wang Xianqian. 1915. Reprint, Beijing: Zhonghua Shuju, 1984.
HJAS	*Harvard Journal of Asiatic Studies.*
HS	Ban Gu. *Hanshu.* 12 vols. Beijing: Zhonghua Shuju, 1962.
HSBZ	Ban Gu. *Hanshu buzhu.* Ed. Wang Xianqian. 1900. Reprint, Taibei: Yiwen Yinshuguan, 1955.
RCL	A. F. P. Hulsewé. *Remnants of Ch'in Law: An Annotated Translation of the Ch'in Legal and Administrative Rules of the 3rd Century B.C., Discovered in Yün-Meng Prefecture, Hu-Pei Province, in 1975.* Leiden: E. J. Brill, 1985.

SBCK	*Sibu congkan.*
SHD	Shuihudi Qinmu Zhujian Zhengli Xiaozu, ed. *Shuihudi Qinmu zhujian.* Beijing: Wenwu Chubanshe, 1990.
SJ	Sima Qian. *Shiji.* 2d ed. 10 vols. Beijing: Zhonghua Shuju, 1982.
SSJZS	Li Xueqin et al., eds. *Shisanjing zhushu.* Rev. ed. 26 vols. Beijing: Beijing Daxue Chubanshe, 2000.
TP	*T'oung pao.*
ZHQ	Zhongguo Huaxiangshi Quanji Bianji Weiyuanhui, ed. *Zhongguo huaxiangshi quanji.* Ji'nan: Shandong Meishu Chubanshe, 2000.
ZJS	Zhangjiashan 247 Hao Mu Zhujian Zhengli Xiaozu, ed. *Zhangjiashan Han mu zhujian.* Beijing: Wenwu Chubanshe, 2001.
ZZJC	Zhonghua Shuju Bianjibu, ed. *Zhuzi jicheng.* 8 vols. Beijing: Zhonghua Shuju, 1954.

BIBLIOGRAPHY

WORKS IN WESTERN LANGUAGES

Acker, William R. B., trans. *Some T'ang and Pre-T'ang Texts on Chinese Painting.* 2 vols. Leiden: E. J. Brill, 1954–74.

Akademiia Nauk SSSR, ed. *Kratkie otchety ekspeditsii po issledovaniiu Severnoi Mongolii v sviazi s Mongolo-Tibetskoi ekspeditsiei P. K. Kozlova* [Short report of the expedition on the investigation of northern Mongolia in connection with the Mongolian-Tibetan Expedition of P. K. Kozlov]. Leningrad, 1925.

Andrews, Julia F. *Painters and Politics in the People's Republic of China.* Berkeley and Los Angeles: University of California Press, 1994.

Anheuser, Kilian. "Cold and Hot Mercury Gilding of Metalwork in Antiquity." *Bulletin of the Metals Museum* 26, no. 2 (1996): 48–52.

Ashton, T. S. *An Economic History of England: The 18th Century.* London: Methuen, 1961.

———. *The Industrial Revolution, 1760–1830.* London: Oxford University Press, 1954.

Asselin, Mark Larent. "The *Hou Han Shu* Biography of Cai Yong." MA thesis, University of Washington, 1991.

———. "'A Significant Season' Literature in a Time of Endings: Cai Yong and a Few Contemporaries." PhD diss., University of Washington, 1997.

Aubert, Jean-Jacques. “Workshop Managers.” In *The Inscribed Economy: Production and Distribution in the Roman Empire in the Light of “Instrumentum Domesticum,”* ed. W. V. Harris, 171–81. *Journal of Roman Archaeology* Supplementary Series, no. 6. Ann Arbor: University of Michigan, 1993.

Bagley, Robert W. “Replication Techniques in Eastern Zhou Bronze Casting.” In *History from Things*, ed. Steven Lubar and W. David Kingery, 231–41. Washington: Smithsonian Institution Press, 1993.

———. *Shang Ritual Bronzes in the Arthur M. Sackler Collections.* Cambridge, MA: Harvard University Press, 1987.

———. “What the Bronzes from Hunyuan Tell Us about the Foundry at Houma.” *Orientations*, January 1995, 46–54.

Baines, John. “On the Status and Purposes of Ancient Egyptian Art.” *Cambridge Archaeological Journal* 4, no. 1 (1994): 67–94.

Balazs, Etienne. *Chinese Civilization and Bureaucracy: Variations on a Theme.* Trans. H. M. Wright. Ed. Arthur F. Wright. New Haven: Yale University Press, 1964.

Barbieri-Low, Anthony. “Carving Out a Living: Stone-Monument Artisans during the Eastern Han Period.” In *Recarving China’s Past: Art, Archaeology, and Architecture of the “Wu Family Shrines,”* ed. Naomi Noble Richard, 485–512. Princeton: Princeton University Art Museum; New Haven: Yale University Press, 2005.

———. “Occupational Clans and Artisan Families in Ancient China.” Paper presented at the symposium “The Family Model in Chinese Art and Culture,” Tang Center for East Asian Art, Princeton University, November 6, 2004.

———. “The Organization of Imperial Workshops during the Han Dynasty.” PhD diss., Princeton University, 2001.

———. “Roman Themes in a Group of Eastern Han Lacquer Vessels.” *Orientations*, May 2001, 52–8.

Berreman, Gerald D., and Adrian C. Mayer. “Caste.” In *International Encyclopedia of the Social Sciences*, ed. David L. Sills, 1:333–44. New York: Macmillan, 1968.

Bielenstein, Hans. *The Bureaucracy of Han Times.* Cambridge: Cambridge University Press, 1980.

———. “The Census of China during the Period 2–742 A.D.” *BMFEA* 19 (1947): 125–63.

———. “Lo-Yang in Later Han Times.” *BMFEA* 48 (1976): 1–142.

———. “The Restoration of the Han Dynasty [I]: With Prolegomena on the Historiography of the Hou Han Shu.” *BMFEA* 26 (1954): 1–209.

———. “The Restoration of the Han Dynasty II: The Civil War.” *BMFEA* 31 (1959): 1–287.

———. “The Restoration of the Han Dynasty III: The People.” *BMFEA* 39 (1967): 1–198.

———. “The Restoration of the Han Dynasty IV.” *BMFEA* 51 (1979): 1–300.

Bierbrier, Morris. *The Tomb-Builders of the Pharaohs.* Cairo: American University in Cairo Press, 1989.

Biot, Édouard. *Le Tcheou-li, ou Rites des Tcheou* [The ritual system of the Zhou]. 3 vols. Paris: Imprimerie Nationale, 1851. Reprint, Taibei: Chengwen, 1969.

Bishop, Carl Whiting. “An Ancient Chinese Capital.” *Antiquity* 12 (1938): 68–78.

Bodde, Derk. *Festivals in Classical China.* Princeton: Princeton University Press, 1975.

———. “The Idea of Social Class in Han and Pre-Han China.” In *Thought and Law in Qin and Han China*, ed. W. L. Idema and E. Zürcher, 26–41. Leiden: E. J. Brill, 1990.

Boltz, William. *The Origin and Early Development of the Chinese Writing System.* New Haven: American Oriental Society, 1994.
Brandt, Klaus, Jr., and A. Burmester. "Beitrag zur Archäometrie organischer Materialien—ostasiatischer Lack" [Contribution to the archaeometry of organic materials: East Asian lacquer]. *Berliner Beiträge zur Archäometrie* 7 (1982): 216–51.
Brandt, Klaus, Jr., and Jean-Paul Desroches. *Laques chinois du Linden-Museum de Stuttgart* [Chinese lacquers in the Linden Museum, Stuttgart]. Paris: Musée Guimet, 1986.
Bulling, Anneliese Gutkind. "Ancient Chinese Maps: Two Maps Discovered in a Han Dynasty Tomb from the Second Century B.C." *Expedition* 20, no. 2 (1978): 16–25.
Buonarroti, Michelangelo. *Complete Poems and Selected Letters of Michelangelo.* Trans. Creighton Gilbert. Ed. Robert N. Linscott. Princeton: Princeton University Press, 1980.
Burford, Alison. *Craftsmen in Greek and Roman Society.* Ithaca, NY: Cornell University Press, 1972.
Burgess, John Stewart. *The Guilds of Peking.* New York: Columbia University Press, 1928.
Burmester, A. "Technical Studies of Chinese Lacquer." In *Urushi: Proceedings of the Urushi Study Group, June 10–27, 1985*, ed. N. S. Brommelle and Perry Smith, 163–88. Marina del Rey, CA: Getty Conservation Institute, 1988.
Burton, William. *Porcelain, Its Nature, Art, and Manufacture.* London: B. T. Batsford, 1906.
Bush, Susan, and Hsio-yen Shih, eds. *Early Chinese Texts on Painting.* Cambridge, MA: Harvard-Yenching Institute, 1985.
Cahill, James. *The Painter's Practice: How Artists Lived and Worked in Traditional China.* New York: Columbia University Press, 1994.
Capon, Edmund, and William MacQuitty. *Princes of Jade.* New York: E. P. Dutton, 1973.
Chang, K. C. *See* Zhang Guangzhi.
Chase, W. T., and P. Jett. "Gilding of Metals in China." In *Gilded Metals: History, Technology, and Conservation*, ed. Terry Drayman-Weisser, 145–55. London: Archetype Publications, 2000.
Chavannes, Édouard. *Mission archéologique dans la Chine septrionale* [Archaeological mission in North China]. 2 vols. of text, 4 vols. of plates. Paris: Imprimerie Nationale, 1913–5.
———. *La sculpture sur pierre en Chine au temps des deux dynasties Han* [Sculpture on stone in China during the two Han dynasties]. Paris: E. Leroux, 1893.
Chen Qiyun [Chen Chi-yun]. "Han Dynasty China: Economy, Society, and State Power—a Review of Cho-Yun Hsü, *Han Agriculture: The Formation of Early Chinese Agrarian Economy.*" *TP* 70, nos. 1–3 (1984): 127–48.
Ch'ü T'ung-tsu. *See* Qu Tongzu.
Cicero, Marcus Tullius. *De officiis (On Duties).* Trans. E. M. Atkins. Ed. M. T. Griffin. Cambridge: Cambridge University Press, 1991.
Clunas, Craig. *Art in China.* Oxford: Oxford University Press, 1997.
Cotterell, Arthur. *The First Emperor of China.* London: Macmillan, 1981.
Cullen, Christopher. *Astronomy and Mathematics in Ancient China: The "Zhoubi suanjing."* Cambridge: Cambridge University Press, 1996.
Davies, Norman de Garis. *The Rock Tombs of El Amarna.* Vol. 7, part 3, *The Tombs of Huya and Ahmes.* London: Egypt Exploration Fund, 1905.
———. *The Tomb of Rekh-mi-re at Thebes.* 2 vols. New York: [Plantin Press], 1943.
de Crespigny, Rafé. "Maps from Mawangdui." *Cartography* 11, no. 4 (1980): 211–22.

———. *Official Titles of the Former Han Dynasty.* Canberra: Australian National University Press, 1967.
des Rotours, Robert. *Traité des fonctionnaires et Traité de l'armée, tr. de la Nouvelle histoire des T'ang (chap. XLVI–L)* [Treatise on the bureaucracy and Treatise on the army, translated from *The New History of the Tang*]. 2 vols. Leiden: E. J. Brill, 1947.
Desroches, Jean-Paul, and Hélène Fromentin. *Asie Extrême: Chine, Coré, Japon, Viêtnam* [Far East: China, Korea, Japan, Vietnam]. Paris: Musée Guimet, 1993.
Dien, Albert E., Jeffrey K. Riegel, and Nancy T. Price, eds. *Chinese Archaeological Abstracts.* Vol. 3, *Eastern Zhou to Han.* Los Angeles: Institute of Archaeology, University of California, 1985.
d'Incarville, Père L. "Mémoire sur le vernis de la Chine" [Account of the lacquer varnish of China]. In *L'art de peinture, doreur, vernisseur* [The art of painting, gilding, and lacquering], ed. Jean-Felix Watin, 310–27. 1772. Reprint, Paris: Leonce Laget, 1975.
Diodorus Siculus. *Bibliotheca historica.* Trans. C. H. Oldfather. Cambridge, MA: Harvard University Press, 1976.
Drayman-Weisser, Terry, ed. *Gilded Metals: History, Technology, and Conservation.* London: Archetype Publications, 2000.
Drenkhahn, Rosemarie. "Artisans and Artists in Pharaonic Egypt." In *Civilizations of the Ancient Near East*, vol. 1, ed. Jack M. Sasson, 331–43. New York: Charles Scribner's Sons, 1995.
Dubs, Homer H. "An Ancient Military Contact between Romans and Chinese." *American Journal of Philology* 62, no. 3 (July 1941): 322–30.
———. *The History of the Former Han Dynasty.* 3 vols. Baltimore: Waverly Press, 1938–55.
———. *A Roman City in Ancient China.* London: China Society, 1957.
———. "A Roman Influence upon Chinese Painting." *Classical Philology* 38, no. 1 (January 1943): 13–9.
Duyvendak, J. J. L. *The Book of Lord Shang.* London: Probsthain, 1928.
———. "An Illustrated Battle-Account in the History of the Former Han Dynasty." *TP* 34 (1939): 249–64; 35 (1940): 211–5.
Ebrey, Patricia. *The Aristocratic Families of Early Imperial China: A Case Study of the Po-Ling Ts'ui Family.* Cambridge: Cambridge University Press, 1978.
———. *Cambridge Illustrated History of China.* Cambridge: Cambridge University Press, 1996.
———. "The Economic and Social History of Later Han." In *CHOC*, 608–48.
Eliade, Mircea. *The Forge and the Crucible: The Origins and Structures of Alchemy.* 2d ed. Trans. Stephen Corrin. Chicago: University of Chicago Press, 1978.
Ellsworth, Robert Hatfield. *Later Chinese Painting and Calligraphy, 1800–1950.* 2 vols. New York: Random House, 1987.
Engerman, Stanley L. Introduction to *Terms of Labor: Slavery, Serfdom, and Free Labor*, ed. Stanley L. Engerman, 1–24. Stanford: Stanford University Press, 1999.
Eyre, Christopher J. "Work and Organisation of Work in the New Kingdom." In *Labor in the Ancient Near East*, ed. Marvin Powell, 167–222. New Haven: American Oriental Society, 1987.
———. "Work and Organisation of Work in the Old Kingdom." In *Labor in the Ancient Near East*, ed. Marvin Powell, 5–48. New Haven: American Oriental Society, 1987.
Fairbank, Wilma. "The Offering Shrines of 'Wu Liang Tz'u.'" *HJAS* 6, no. 1 (1941): 1–36.

Falkenhausen, Lothar von. "Inconsequential Incomprehensions: Some Instances of Chinese Writing in Alien Contexts." *Res* 35 (1999): 42–69.

———. "Die Seiden mit chinesischen Inschriften." In *Die Textilien aus Palmyra: Neue und alte Funde*, ed. Andreas Schmidt-Colinet, Anne-Marie Stauffer, and Khaled Al As'ad, 58–81. Mainz: Philipp von Zabern, 2000.

Faulkner, Raymond. *A Concise Dictionary of Middle Egyptian.* Oxford: Griffith Institute, 1962.

Finley, M. I. *The Ancient Economy.* 2d ed. London: Hogarth Press, 1985.

———. "Slavery." In *International Encyclopedia of the Social Sciences*, ed. David L. Sills, 14:307–13. New York: Macmillan, 1968.

Finsterbusch, Käte. *Verzeichnis und Motivindex der Han-Darstellungen* [Directory and motif-index of Han representations]. 4 vols. Wiesbaden: Otto Harrassowitz, 1966–2004.

Fong, Wen, ed. *The Great Bronze Age of China: An Exhibition from the People's Republic of China.* New York: Metropolitan Museum of Art, 1980.

Forke, A. *Lun-Heng: Philosophical Essay by Wang Ch'ong.* 2 vols. New York: Paragon Book Gallery, 1962.

Frank, Tenney, ed. *An Economic Survey of Ancient Rome.* Vol. 5, *Rome and Italy of the Empire.* Baltimore: Johns Hopkins Press, 1940.

Gale, Esson M. *"Discourses on Salt and Iron": A Debate on State Control of Commerce and Industry in Ancient China.* Leiden: E. J. Brill, 1931.

Gale, Esson M., Peter A. Boodberg, and T. C. Lin. "Discourses on Salt and Iron (*Yen T'ieh Lun:* chaps. xx–xxviii)." *Journal of the North China Branch of the Royal Asiatic Society* 65 (1934): 73–110.

Garner, Sir Harry. *Chinese Lacquer.* London: Faber and Faber, 1979.

———. "Technical Studies of Oriental Lacquer." *Studies in Conservation* 8, no. 1 (1963): 84–98.

Giles, Herbert A. *A Chinese-English Dictionary.* 2d ed. Shanghai, 1912. Reprint, Taibei: Ch'eng Wen Publishing Co., 1972.

Gong Kechang. *Studies on the Han Fu.* Trans. and ed. David R. Knechtges et al. New Haven: American Oriental Society, 1997.

Greene, Kevin. *The Archaeology of the Roman Economy.* London: B. T. Batsford, 1986.

Greiff, Susanne, and Yin Shenping. *Das Grab des Bin Wang: Wandmalereien der Östlichen Han Zeit in China* [The Tomb of Bin Wang: Painted murals of the Eastern Han in China]. Mainz: Verlag des Römisch-Germanischen Zentralmuseums in Kommission bei Harrassowitz Verlag, Wiesbaden, 2002.

Gulik, R. H. van. *Sexual Life in Ancient China: A Preliminary Survey of Chinese Sex and Society from ca. 1500 BC till 1644 AD.* Leiden: E. J. Brill, 1961.

Hackin, Joseph. *Nouvelles recherches archéologiques à Begram, ancienne Kâpicî, 1939–1940: Rencontre de trois civilisations, Inde, Grèce, Chine* [New archaeological research on Begram, ancient Kapisa, 1939–1940: The meeting of three civilizations, India, Greece, and China]. 2 vols. Paris: Imprimerie Nationale, 1954.

Hamada Kōsaku. "On the Painting of the Han Period: Newly Discovered Materials in Korea and in South Manchuria." *Memoirs of the Research Department of the Tōyō Bunko* 8 (1936): 31–44.

Harper, Donald J. *Early Chinese Medical Literature: The Mawangdui Medical Manuscripts.* London: Kegan Paul International, 1998.

Harrel, Stevan, Bamo Qubumo, and Ma Erzi. *Mountain Patterns: The Survival of Nuosu Culture in China*. Seattle: University of Washington Press, 2000.
Harris, William V. *Ancient Literacy*. Cambridge, MA: Harvard University Press, 1989.
Hawkes, David, trans. *The Songs of the South: An Ancient Chinese Anthology of Poems by Qu Yuan and Other Poets*. London: Penguin Books, 1985.
Herbert, Eugenia. *Iron, Gender, and Power: Rituals of Transformation in African Societies*. Bloomington: Indiana University Press, 1993.
Hessler, Peter. "Rising to Life: Treasures of Ancient China." *National Geographic* 200, no. 4 (October 2001): 48–67.
Hinsch, Bret. *Passions of the Cut Sleeve: The Male Homosexual Tradition in China*. Berkeley and Los Angeles: University of California Press, 1990.
———. *Women in Early Imperial China*. Lanham, MD: Rowman and Littlefield Publishers, 2002.
———. "Women, Kinship, and Property as Seen in a Han Dynasty Will." *TP* 84, nos. 1–3 (1998): 1–21.
Hirth, Friedrich. *China and the Roman Orient: Researches into Their Ancient and Medieval Relations as Represented in Old Chinese Records*. Shanghai and Hong Kong: Kelly and Walsh, 1885. Reprint, Chicago: Ares Publishers, 1975.
Hotaling, Stephen James. "The City Walls of Han Ch'ang-an." *TP* 64, nos. 1–3 (1978): 1–46.
Hsu Cho-yun. *See* Xu Zhuoyun.
Hua Jueming. "The Mass Production of Iron Castings in Ancient China." *Scientific American* 348, no. 1 (1983): 120–8.
Hucker, Charles O. *A Dictionary of Official Titles in Imperial China*. Stanford: Stanford University Press, 1985.
Hulsewé, A. F. P. "The Ch'in Documents Discovered in Hupei in 1975." *TP* 64, nos. 4–5 (1978): 175–218.
———. "'Contracts' of the Han Period." In *Il diritto in Cina* [The law in China], ed. Lionello Lanciotti, 11–38. Florence: Leo S. Olschki, 1978.
———. "Han-Time Documents: A Survey of Recent Studies Occasioned by the Finding of Han-Time Documents in Central Asia." *TP* 45 (1957): 1–50.
———. "The Influence of the 'Legalist' Government of Qin on the Economy as Reflected in the Texts Discovered in Yunmeng County." In *The Scope of State Power in China*, ed. S. R. Schram, 211–36. London: St. Martin's Press, 1985.
———. "Notes of the Historiography of the Han Period." In *Historians of China and Japan*, ed. William G. Beasley and Edwin G. Pulleyblank, 31–43. London: Oxford University Press, 1961.
———. "The Problem of the Authenticity of *Shih-chi* ch. 123, the Memoir on Ta Yuan." *TP* 61, nos. 1–3 (1975): 83–147.
———. "Qin and Han Legal Manuscripts." In *New Sources of Early Chinese History: An Introduction to the Reading of Inscriptions and Manuscripts*, ed. Edward L. Shaughnessy, 193–221. Berkeley: Society for the Study of Early China and the Institute of East Asian Studies, University of California, 1997.
———. *Remnants of Ch'in Law: An Annotated Translation of the Ch'in Legal and Administrative Rules of the 3rd Century B.C., Discovered in Yün-Meng Prefecture, Hu-Pei Province, in 1975*. Leiden: E. J. Brill, 1985.

———. *Remnants of Han Law.* Leiden: E. J. Brill, 1955.
———. "Some Remarks on Statute Labour during the Ch'in and Han Period." *Orientalia Venetiana* 1 (1984): 195–204.
———. "Weights and Measures in Ch'in Law." In *State and Law in East Asia*, ed. Dieter Eikemeier and Herbert Franke, 25–39. Wiesbaden: Otto Harrassowitz, 1981.
Hulsewé, A. F. P., and Michael Loewe. *China in Central Asia: The Early Stage, 125 B.C.–A.D. 23; An Annotated Translation of Chapters 61 and 96 of the "History of the Former Han Dynasty."* Leiden: E. J. Brill, 1979.
Hyde, Charles K. *Technological Change and the British Iron Industry, 1700–1870.* Princeton: Princeton University Press, 1977.
Idema, W. L., and E. Zürcher, eds. *Thought and Law in Qin and Han China.* Leiden: E. J. Brill, 1990.
Jacobson, Esther. "Beyond the Frontier: A Reconsideration of Cultural Interchange between China and the Early Nomads." *Early China* 13 (1988): 201–40.
———. "Mountains and Nomads: A Reconsideration of the Origins of Chinese Landscape Representation." *BMFEA* 57 (1985): 133–79.
James, Jean M. "Interpreting Han Funerary Art: The Importance of Context." *Oriental Art* 31, no. 3 (1985): 283–92.
———. "Some Rules of Composition for Figural Art during the Han Dynasty and the Emergence of Landscape." *Oriental Art* 33, no. 3 (1987): 261–7.
Jenyns, Soame, and William Watson. "Lacquer." In *Chinese Art: The Minor Arts*, 2:272–85. New York: Universe Books, 1963.
Johnson, Wallace. *The T'ang Code.* 2 vols. Princeton: Princeton University Press, 1979.
Jones, A. H. M. "The Caste System in the Later Roman Empire." *Eirene* 8 (1970): 79–96.
———. *The Roman Economy: Studies in Ancient Economic and Administrative History.* Totowa, NJ: Rowman and Littlefield, 1974.
Kalinowski, Marc. "Les traités de Shuihudi et l'hémérologie Chinoise à la fin des Royaumes-Combattants" [The treatises from Shuihudi and Chinese divination at the end of the Warring States]. *TP* 72 (1986): 175–228.
Kamiya Masakazu. "The Staffing Structure of Commandery Offices and County Offices and the Relationship between Commanderies and Counties in the Han Dynasty." *Acta Asiatica* 58 (1990): 59–88.
Karlgren, Bernhard. "Early Chinese Mirror Inscriptions." *BMFEA* 6 (1934): 9–79.
———. *Grammata Serica Recensa.* Stockholm: Museum of Far Eastern Antiquities, 1964.
———. "Loan Characters in Pre-Han Texts." *BMFEA* 35 (1963): 1–128.
Katō Shigeru. "A Study on the *Suan-fu*, the Poll Tax of the Han Dynasty." *Memoirs of the Research Department of the Tōyō Bunko* 1 (1926): 51–68.
Kawai Keiichi, Nakagawa Mikio, Kawai Kyozo, Foo-min Liew, and Hirokazu Yasuno. "Hyposensitization to Urushiol among Japanese Lacquer Craftsmen: Results of Patch Tests on Students Learning the Art of Lacquerware." *Contact Dermatitis* 25 (1991): 290–5.
Kayamoto Tojin. "Han Tombs of Lo-Lang—Their Studies by Japanese Scholars." *Memoirs of the Research Department of the Tōyō Bunko* 21 (1962): 97–124.
Keightley, David N. "Public Work in Ancient China: A Study of Forced Labor in the Shang and Western Chou." PhD diss., Columbia University, 1969.

Kesner, Ladislav. "Likeness of No One: (Re)presenting the First Emperor's Army." *Art Bulletin* 77, no. 1 (March 1995): 115–32.

Kiyohiko Munakata. *Sacred Mountains in Chinese Art.* Champaign: Krannert Art Museum, University of Illinois Press, 1991.

Knechtges, David R. *The Han Rhapsody: A Study of the Fu of Yang Hsiung, 53 B.C.–A.D. 18.* Cambridge: Cambridge University Press, 1976.

———, trans. *Wen xuan, or Selections of Refined Literature.* 3 vols to date. Princeton: Princeton University Press, 1982–96.

Knight, Michael John. "Bronze to Lacquer: Changes in Preferred Media in the Arts of the Kingdom of Chu." PhD diss., Columbia University, 1992.

Koga Noboru. "A Brief History of Ch'in and Han Studies in Japan." *Acta Asiatica* 58 (1990): 89–119.

Kullavanijaya, Preya, and Suwirakorn Ophaswongse. "A Study of Dermatitis in the Lacquerware Industry." *Contact Dermatitis* 36 (1997): 244–6.

Kwang-chih Chang. *See* Zhang Guangzhi.

Lai Guolong. "Lighting the Way in the Afterlife: Bronze Lamps in Warring States Tombs." *Orientations*, Apr. 2002, 20–8.

Lanciotti, Lionello. "Notes on Ancient Chinese Metallurgy: Sword Casting and Related Legends in China." *East and West* 6, no. 2 (1955): 106–14.

Lao Gan [Lao Kan]. "Population and Geography in the Two Han Dynasties." In *Chinese Social History*, ed. E-Tu Zen Sun and John De Francis, 83–102. New York: Octagon Books, 1966.

Lao Kan. *See* Lao Gan.

Lau, D. C., trans. *The Analects.* London: Penguin Books, 1979.

———, trans. *Mencius.* Rev. bilingual ed. Hong Kong: Chinese University Press, 2003.

Laufer, Berthold. "Cardan's Suspension in China." In *Anthropological Essays Presented to William Henry Holmes in Honor of His Seventieth Birthday.* Washington, DC: J. W. Bryan, 1916. Reprint, New York: AMS Press, 1977.

Ledderose, Lothar. "Module and Mass Production." In *International Colloquium on Chinese Art History*, vol. 2. Taibei: Guoli Bowuyuan, 1992.

———. *Ten Thousand Things: Module and Mass Production in Chinese Art.* Princeton: Princeton University Press, 2000.

Legge, James, trans. *The Chinese Classics.* 5 vols. Reprint of Oxford University Press ed., Taibei: SMC Publishing, 2000.

———, trans. *The Sacred Books of China.* Sacred Books of the East, ed. F. Max Müller, vols. 3, 16, 27–28, 39–40. Oxford: Clarendon Press, 1885. Reprint, Delhi: Motilal Banarsidass Publishers, 2001.

Lesko, Leonard H., ed. *Pharaoh's Workers: The Villagers of Deir El Medina.* Ithaca, NY: Cornell University Press, 1994.

Leslie, D. D., and K. J. H. Gardiner. "'All Roads Lead to Rome': Chinese Knowledge of the Roman Empire." *Journal of Asian History* 29, no. 1 (1995): 61–81.

———. *The Roman Empire in Chinese Sources.* Rome: Bardi, 1996.

Lettres édifiantes et curieuses, écrites des missions étrangères. 26 vols. Paris: Chez J. G. Merigot, 1780–3.

Li Xueqin and Xing Wen. "New Light on the Early-Han Code: A Reappraisal of the Zhangjiashan Bamboo-Slip Legal Texts." *Asia Major*, 3d ser., 14, no. 1 (2001): 125–46.

Liao, W. K., trans. *The Complete Works of Han Fei Tzu.* 2 vols. London: Probsthain, 1939.
Lim, Lucy, ed. *Stories from China's Past: Han Dynasty Pictorial Tomb Reliefs and Archaeological Objects from Sichuan Province, People's Republic of China.* San Francisco: Chinese Culture Foundation of San Francisco, 1987.
Lins, P. A., and W. A. Oddy. "The Origins of Mercury Gilding." *Journal of Archaeological Science* 2 (1975): 365–73.
Liu, Cary Y., et al., eds. *Character and Context in Chinese Calligraphy.* Princeton: Art Museum, Princeton University, 1999.
Loehr, Max. *Ritual Vessels of Bronze Age China.* New York: Asia Society.
Loewe, Michael. "The Almanacs (*jih-shu*) from Shui-hu-ti." *Asia Major,* 3d ser., 1, no. 2 (1988): 1–28.
———. "Attempts at Economic Co-ordination during the Western Han Dynasty." In *The Scope of State Power in China*, ed. S. R. Schram, 237–68. London: St. Martin's Press, 1985.
———. "The Authority of the Emperors of Ch'in and Han." In *State and Law in East Asia*, ed. Dieter Eikemeier and Herbert Franke, 80–111. Wiesbaden: Otto Harrassowitz, 1981.
———. *A Biographical Dictionary of the Qin, Former Han, and Xin Periods (221 BC–AD 24)* Leiden: E. J. Brill, 2000.
———. "The *Chüeh-ti* Games: A Re-enactment of the Battle between Ch'ih-yu and Hsüan-yüan?" In *Thought and Law in Qin and Han China,* ed. W. L. Idema and E. Zürcher, 140–57. Leiden: E. J. Brill, 1990.
———. *Crisis and Conflict in Han China.* London: George Allen and Unwin, 1974.
———. "Dated Inscriptions on Certain Mirrors (A.D. 6–105): Genuine or Fabricated?" *Early China* 26–7 (2001–2): 233–56.
———. *Divination, Mythology, and Monarchy in Han China.* Cambridge: Cambridge University Press, 1994.
———, ed. *Early Chinese Texts: A Bibliographic Guide.* Berkeley: Society for the Study of Early China, Institute of East Asian Studies, University of California, 1993.
———. *Everyday Life in Early Imperial China during the Han Period, 202 B.C.–A.D. 220.* London: Batsford, 1968. Reprint, Indianapolis, IN: Hackett Publishing Co., 2005.
———. "Han Administrative Documents: Recent Finds from the North-West." *TP* 72 (1986): 291–314.
———. "The Imperial Tombs of the Former Han Dynasty and Their Shrines." *TP* 80 (1993): 302–40.
———. "Manuscripts Found Recently in China: A Preliminary Survey." *TP* 63, nos. 2–3 (1977): 99–136.
———. "The Orders of Aristocratic Rank of Han China." *TP* 48, nos. 1–3 (1960): 97–174.
———. "Recent Archaeological Discoveries of the Ch'in and Han Periods." In *Zhongguo kaoguxue yu lishixue zhi zhenghe yanjiu* [Synthetic research into Chinese archaeology and history], ed. Cang Zhenhua, 605–50. Taibei: Institute of History and Philology, Academia Sinica, 1997.
———. *Records of Han Administration.* 2 vols. Cambridge: Cambridge University Press, 1967.
———. *Ways to Paradise: The Chinese Quest for Immortality.* London: George Allen and Unwin, 1979.
Maenchen-Helfen, Otto. "From China to Palmyra." *Art Bulletin* 25, no. 4 (December 1943): 358–62.

Maspero, Henri. “La vie privée en Chine à l’époque des Han” [Private life in China during the Han period]. *Revue des arts asiatiques* 7 (1932): 185–201.
Mattusch, Carol C. “The Berlin Foundry Cup: The Casting of Greek Bronze Statuary in the Early Fifth Century B.C.” *American Journal of Archaeology* 84, no. 4 (1980): 435–44.
———. *The Fire of Hephaistos: Large Classical Bronzes from North American Collections.* Cambridge, MA: Harvard University Art Museums, 1996.
———. *Greek Bronze Statuary: From the Beginnings through the Fifth Century B.C.* Ithaca, NY: Cornell University Press, 1988.
McKendrick, Neil. “Josiah Wedgwood and Factory Discipline.” *Historical Journal* 4, no. 1 (1961): 30–55.
———. “The Role of Science in the Industrial Revolution: A Study of Josiah Wedgwood as a Scientist and Industrial Chemist.” In *Changing Perspectives in the History of Science: Essays in Honour of Joseph Needham*, ed. Mikulás Teich and Robert M. Young, 274–319. Boston: D. Reidel, 1973.
McLeod, Katrina C. D., and Robin D. S. Yates. “Forms of Ch’in Law: An Annotated Translation of the *Feng-chen shih*.” *HJAS* 41 no. 1 (1981): 111–63.
Michaelson, Carol. *Gilded Dragons: Buried Treasures from China’s Golden Ages.* London: British Museum, 1999.
———. “Mass Production and the Development of the Lacquer Industry during the Han Dynasty.” *Orientations*, November 1992, 60–5.
Morel, Jean-Paul. “The Craftsman.” In *The Romans*, ed. Andrea Giardina, trans. Lydia G. Cochrane, 214–44. Chicago: University of Chicago Press, 1993.
Morgan, Evan. *Tao, the Great Luminant: Essays from “Huai-nan-tzu.”* Shanghai, 1935. Reprint, New York: Paragon Book Reprint Corp., 1969.
Morse, Hosea Ballou. *The Gilds of China*. London: Longmans, Green, and Co., 1909
Murowchick, Robert, ed. *China: Ancient Culture, Modern Land.* Norman: University of Oklahoma Press, 1994.
Musée national des arts asiatiques-Guimet, ed. *Visiteurs de l’empire céleste* [Visitors from the celestial empire]. Paris: Réunion des musées nationaux, 1994.
Needham, Joseph, et al. *Science and Civilisation in China.* 7 vols. to date. Cambridge: Cambridge University Press, 1954–.
Nienhauser, William H., ed. *The Grand Scribe’s Records.* 9 vols planned. Bloomington: Indiana University Press, 1994–.
———. “Once Again, the Authorship of the *Hsi-Ching Tsa-Chi* (Miscellanies of the Western Capital).” *Journal of the American Oriental Society* 98, no. 3 (July–September 1978): 219–36.
Nishijima Sadao. “The Economic and Social History of Former Han.” In *CHOC*, 551–607.
North, Douglass C. “Markets and Other Allocation Systems in History: The Challenge of Karl Polanyi.” *Journal of European Economic History* 6 (1977): 703–16.
Northover, Peter, and Kilian Anheuser. “Gilding in Britain: Celtic, Roman, and Saxon.” In *Gilded Metals: History, Technology, and Conservation*, ed. Terry Drayman-Weisser, 109–21. London: Archetype Publications, 2000.
Nylan, Michael. “Calligraphy, the Sacred Text, and the Test of Culture.” In *Character and Context in Chinese Calligraphy*, ed. Cary Y. Liu et al., 16–77. Princeton: Art Museum, Princeton University, 1999.

Ōba Osamu. "The Ordinances on Fords and Passes Excavated from Han Tomb Number 247, Zhangjiashan." *Asia Major,* 3d ser., 14, no. 2 (2001): 119–41.
Oddy, Andrew. "A History of Gilding with Particular Reference to Statuary." In *Gilded Metals: History, Technology, and Conservation*, ed. Terry Drayman-Weisser, 1–19. London: Archetype Publications, 2000.
O'Hara, A. R. *The Position of Women in Early China.* Washington, DC: Catholic University of America Press, 1945.
O'Neil, P. J. *Japanese Names: A Comprehensive Index by Characters and Headings.* New York: Wetherhill, 1972.
Pelliot, Paul. "Notes sur quelques artistes des Six Dynasties et des T'ang" [Notes on several artists from the Six Dynasties and the Tang]. *TP* 22 (1923): 215–91.
Pfister, R. *Textiles de Palmyre découverts par le Service des antiquités du Haut-commissariat de la République française dans la nécropole de Palmyre.* Paris: Les Editions d'Art et d'Histoire, 1934.
Pirazzoli-t'Serstevens, Michèle. "The Art of Dining in the Han Period: Food Vessels from Tomb No. 1 at Mawangdui." *Food and Foodways* 4, nos. 3–4 (1991): 209–19.
———. "Ateliers, patronage et collections princières en Chine à l'époque Han" [Workshops, patronage, and princely collections in China during the Han period]. *Comptes rendus des séances de l'Académie des inscriptions et belles-lettres,* April–June 1990, 521–36.
———. *The Han Civilization of China.* Trans. Janet Seligman. New York: Rizzoli International Publications, 1982.
———. "Cultural Contributions of the Outside World to China: Interaction and Assimilation." In *"Yingjie Ershiyi Shiji De Zhongguo Kaoguxue" Guoji Xueshu Taolunhui Wenji* ["Greeting twenty-first century Chinese archaeology," collected papers of the international symposium], ed. Beijing Daxue Kaoguxuexi, 381–403. Beijing: Kexue Chubanshe, 1998.
———. "Pour une archéologie des échanges: Apports étrangers en Chine—transmission, réception, assimilation" [Toward an archaeology of exchanges: Foreign contributions in China—transmission, reception, assimilation]. *Arts Asiatiques* 49 (1994): 21–33.
Plutarch. *Greek Lives: A Selection of Nine Greek Lives.* Trans. Robin Waterfield. Oxford: Oxford University Press, 1998.
Polanyi, Karl. *The Livelihood of Man.* Ed. Harry W. Pearson. New York: Academic Press, 1977.
Pollard, Sidney. *The Genesis of Modern Management: A Study of the Industrial Revolution in Great Britain.* Cambridge, MA: Harvard University Press, 1965.
Poo Mu-chou. *See* Pu Muzhou.
Powers, Martin J. *Art and Political Expression in Early China.* New Haven: Yale University Press, 1991.
———. "Unit Style and System Style: A Preliminary Exploration." In *Zhongguo kaoguxue yu lishixue zhi zhenghe yanjiu* [Synthetic research into Chinese archaeology and history], ed. Cang Zhenhua, 743–92. Taibei: Institute of History and Philology, Academia Sinica, 1997.
Prüch, Margarete. *Die Lacke der Westlichen Han-Zeit (206 V.–6. N. Chr.): Bestand und Analyse* [The lacquers of the Western Han: Inventory and analysis]. Frankfurt am Main: Peter Lang, 1997.
Pu Muzhou [Poo Mu-chou]. *In Search of Personal Welfare: A View of Ancient Chinese Religion.* Albany, NY: SUNY Press, 1998.

Puett, Michael. *The Ambivalence of Creation: Debates Concerning Innovation and Artifice in Early China.* Stanford: Stanford University Press, 2001.

Qian Cunxun [Tsien Tsuen-hsuin]. "A Study of the Book Knife in Han China (206 BC–AD 220)." *Chinese Culture* 12 (1971): 87–101.

———. *Written on Bamboo and Silk: The Beginnings of Chinese Books and Inscriptions.* 2d ed. Chicago: University of Chicago Press, 2004.

Qu Tongzu [Ch'ü T'ung-tsu]. *Han Social Structure.* Ed. Jack L. Dull. Seattle: University of Washington Press, 1972.

Raschke, Manfred. "New Studies in Roman Commerce with the East." *Aufstieg und Niedergang der römischen Welt im Spiegel der neueren Forschung* II, 9.2 (1978): 604–1361.

Rawson, Jessica. *Chinese Ornament: The Lotus and the Dragon.* London: British Museum Publications, 1984.

———. "Strange Creatures." *Oriental Art* 44, no. 2 (1998): 44–7, 90.

Reeves, Nicholas. *Akhenaten: Egypt's False Prophet.* London: Thames and Hudson, 2001.

Rickett, W. Allyn, trans. *Guanzi: Political, Economic, and Philosophical Essays from Early China.* 2 vols. Princeton: Princeton University Press, 1985–98.

Rietschel, Robert L., and Joseph F. Fowler. "Toxicodendron Plants and Spices." In *Fisher's Contact Dermatitis.* 4th ed. Baltimore: Williams and Wilkins, 1995.

Rostovtzeff, Michael. *The Social and Economic History of the Roman Empire.* 2d ed. 2 vols. Oxford: Clarendon Press, 1957.

Ruitenbeek, Klaas. *Chinese Shadows: Stone Reliefs, Rubbings, and Related Works of Art from the Han Dynasty (206 BC–AD 220) in the Royal Ontario Museum.* Toronto: Royal Ontario Museum, 2002.

Schottenhammer, Angela. "Slaves and Forms of Slavery in Late Imperial China (Seventeenth to Early Twentieth Centuries)." *Slavery and Abolition* 24, no. 2 (2003): 143–54.

Schuessler, Axel. *A Dictionary of Early Zhou Chinese.* Honolulu: University of Hawaii Press, 1987.

Seidel, Anna. "Traces of Han Religion in Funerary Texts Found in Tombs." In *Taoism and Religious Culture,* ed. Akizuki Kan'ei, 21–57. Tokyo: Hirakawa Shuppan, 1987.

Shaughnessy, Edward L., ed. *New Sources of Early Chinese History: An Introduction to the Reading of Inscriptions and Manuscripts.* Berkeley: Society for the Study of Early China and the Institute of East Asian Studies, University of California, 1997.

———. *Sources of Western Zhou History.* Berkeley and Los Angeles: University of California Press, 1991.

Shen Kangshen, John N. Crossley, and Anthony W.-C. Lun. *The Nine Chapters on the Mathematical Arts.* Oxford: Oxford University Press, 1999.

Silver, Morris. "Karl Polanyi and Markets in the Near East: The Challenge of the Evidence." *Journal of Economic History* 43, no. 4 (1983): 795–829.

Singer, Charles, E. J. Holmyard, A. R. Hall, and Trevor Williams, eds. *A History of Technology.* 7 vols. Oxford: Clarendon Press, 1954–8, 1978.

Skinner, G. William, and Hugh D. R. Baker, eds. *The City in Late Imperial China.* Stanford: Stanford University Press, 1977.

Smith, Michael E. "The Archaeology of Ancient State Economies." *Annual Review of Anthropology* 33 (2004): 73–102.

So, Jenny. *Eastern Zhou Ritual Bronzes from the Arthur M. Sackler Collections.* New York: Arthur M. Sackler Foundation, 1995.
Stein, Aurel. *Serindia: Detailed Report of Explorations in Central Asia and Westernmost China, Carried Out and Described under the Orders of H. M. Indian Government.* Oxford: Clarendon Press, 1921.
Sullivan, Michael. *The Birth of Landscape Painting in China.* Berkeley and Los Angeles: University of California Press, 1962.
Svistunova, Natalia. "State-Run Workshops in the Tang Period (7th–10th Centuries)." In *China: State and Society,* ed. Social Sciences Today Editorial Board, 64–93. Moscow: USSR Academy of Sciences, 1984.
Swann, Nancy Lee. *Food and Money in Ancient China: The Earliest Economic History of China to A.D. 25, Han Shu 24, with Related Texts, Han Shu 91 and Shih-chi 129.* Princeton: Princeton University Press, 1950.
Temple, Robert. *The Genius of China: 3000 Years of Science, Discovery, and Invention.* New York: Simon and Schuster, 1986.
Thompson, Lydia. "Ritual, Art, and Agency: Consecrating the Burial Ground." Paper presented at the international symposium "Recarving China's Past: Art, Archaeology, and Architecture of the 'Wu Family Shrines,'" Princeton, NJ, April 30–May 1, 2005.
Thote, Alain. "Innovations techniques et diversification des commandes: L'artisanat du laque en Chine aux ve–ive siècles avant J.-C." [Technical innovations and division of labor: The craft industry of lacquer in China during the 5th and 4th centuries before Christ]. *Arts Asiatiques* 45 (1990): 76–89.
Tichane, Robert T. *Ching-te-chen: Views of a Porcelain City.* Painted Post, NY: New York State Institute for Glaze Research, 1983.
Tomita Kojiro. "A Han Lacquer Dish and a Koryo Silver Ewer from Korea." *Bulletin of the Museum of Fine Arts, Boston* 33 (1935): 64–9.
Trever, Camilla. *Excavations in Northern Mongolia (1924–1925).* Leningrad: Academy of History of Material Culture, 1932.
Tsien Tsuen-hsuin. *See* Qian Cunxun.
Twitchett, Denis, and Michael Loewe, eds. *The Cambridge History of China, vol. 1.* Cambridge: Cambridge University Press, 1986.
Wagner, Donald B. *Iron and Steel in Ancient China.* Leiden: E. J. Brill, 1993.
———. *The State and the Iron Industry in Han China.* Copenhagen: Nordic Institute of Asian Studies, 2001.
Waley, Arthur, trans. *The Analects of Confucius.* London: George Allen and Unwin, 1938.
———, trans. *The Temple and Other Poems.* New York: A. A. Knopf, 1923.
———, trans. *The Way and Its Power: A Study of the Tao Te Ching and Its Place in Chinese Thought.* New York: Grove Press, 1958.
Wang Yü-ch'üan. *See* Wang Yuquan.
Wang Yuquan [Wang Yü-ch'üan]. "An Outline of the Central Government of the Former Han Dynasty." *HJAS* 12 (1949): 134–87.
Wang Zhongshu. *Han Civilization.* Trans. K. C. Chang. New Haven: Yale University Press, 1982.
Watson, Burton, trans. *The Complete Works of Chuang-Tzu.* New York: Columbia University Press, 1968.

———, trans. *Courtier and Commoner in Ancient China: Selections from the History of the Former Han by Pan Ku.* New York: Columbia University Press, 1974.
———, trans. *Records of the Grand Historian.* 3 vols. New York: Columbia University Press, 1993.
Watson, William. "Chinese Lacquered Wine-Cups." *British Museum Quarterly* 21, no. 1 (1957): 21–5.
———. "The Sources and Development of Style in Pre-Han and Han Lacquer Ornament." In *Studies in Chinese Archaeology and Art.* London: Pindar Press, 1998.
Watt, James C. Y., and Barbara Brennan Ford. *East Asian Lacquer: Selections from the Florence and Herbert Irving Collection.* New York: Metropolitan Museum of Art, 1991.
Westermann, William Linn. "Industrial Slavery in Roman Italy." *Journal of Economic History* 2 (1942): 149–63.
Wilbur, C. Martin. "Industrial Slavery in China during the Former Han Dynasty (206 BC–AD 25)." *Journal of Economic History* 3, no. 1 (May 1943): 56–69.
———. *Slavery in China during the Former Han Dynasty, 206 B.C.–A.D. 25.* [Chicago]: Field Museum of Natural History, [1943]. Reprint, New York: Russell and Russell, 1967.
Wild, Henri. *Le tombeau de Ti: La chapelle* [The tomb of Ti: Chapel]. Cairo: Imprimerie de l'Institut français d'archéologie orientale, 1966.
Wilkinson, Endymion. *Chinese History: A Manual.* Cambridge, MA: Harvard University Press, 1998.
Willetts, William. *Chinese Art.* 2 vols. [Harmondsworth]: Penguin Books, [1958].
———. *Foundations of Chinese Art: From Neolithic Pottery to Modern Architecture.* London: Thames and Hudson, 1965.
Wu Hung. "Beyond the 'Great Boundary': Funerary Narrative in the Cangshan Tomb." In *Boundaries in China,* ed. John Hay, 81–104. London: Reaktion Books, 1994.
———. "Buddhist Elements in Early Chinese Art (2nd and 3rd Centuries A.D.)" *Artibus Asiae* 47 (1986): 253–316.
———. *Monumentality in Early Chinese Art and Architecture.* Stanford: Stanford University Press, 1995.
———. "The Origins of Chinese Painting." In *Three Thousand Years of Chinese Painting,* ed. Richard Barnhart et al., 15–86. New Haven: Yale University Press, 1977.
———. *The Wu Liang Shrine.* Stanford: Stanford University Press, 1989.
Xu Meiling [Mei-ling Hsu]. "The Qin Maps: A Clue to Later Chinese Cartographic Development." *Imago Mundi* 45 (1993): 90–100.
Xu Zhuoyun [Hsu Cho-yun]. *Ancient China in Transition.* Stanford: Stanford University Press, 1965.
———. *Han Agriculture: The Formation of Early Chinese Agrarian Economy, 206 B.C.–A.D. 220.* Ed. Jack L. Dull. Seattle: University of Washington Press, 1980.
Yamada Katsuyoshi. "Offices and Officials of Works, Markets and Lands in the Ch'in Dynasty." *Acta Asiatica* 58 (1990): 1–23.
Yamamoto Tatsuro and Ikeda On, eds. *Tun-huang and Turfan Documents concerning Social and Economic History.* Tokyo: Committee for the Studies of the Tun-huang Manuscripts, Tōyō Bunko, 1978.
Yang, Lien-sheng. *See* Yang Liansheng.

Yang Boda and Weng Wan-go. *The Palace Museum, Peking: Treasures of the Forbidden City.* New York: Harry Abrams, 1982.
Yang Liansheng [Yang, Lien-sheng]. *Excursions in Sinology.* Cambridge, MA: Harvard University Press, 1969.
———. "Great Families of the Eastern Han." In *Chinese Social History*, ed. E-Tu Zen Sun and John De Francis, 103–34. New York: Octagon Books, 1972.
———. *Money and Credit in China, a Short History.* Cambridge, MA: Harvard University Press, 1952.
———. "Notes on Dr. Swann's *Food and Money in Ancient China.*" *HJAS* 13, nos. 3–4 (December 1950): 524–57.
———. "Schedules of Work and Rest in Imperial China." *HJAS* 18 (1955): 301–25.
———. *Studies in Chinese Institutional History.* Cambridge, MA: Harvard University Press, 1961.
Yang Xiaoneng, ed. *The Golden Age of Chinese Archaeology: Celebrated Discoveries from the People's Republic of China.* Washington, DC: National Gallery of Art, 1999.
Yates, Robin D. S. "Law in the Making of the Empire: Evidence from the Newly Discovered Qin Slips from Liye, Hunan." Paper presented at the annual meeting of the Association of Asian Studies, Chicago, IL, April 1, 2005.
———. "Slavery in Early China: A Socio-cultural Approach." *Journal of East Asian Archaeology* 3, nos. 1–2 (2001): 283–331.
———. "Social Status in the Ch'in: Evidence from the Yun-meng Legal Documents, Part One, Commoners." *HJAS* 47, no. 1 (1987): 197–237.
Yetts, Perceval. "Chinese Lacquer." *Burlington Magazine*, May 1926, 258–63.
———. "Discoveries of the Kozlov Expedition." *Burlington Magazine*, April 1926, 168–84.
Yi-pao Mei, trans. *The Ethical and Political Works of Motse.* London: Probsthain, 1929.
Yu Yingshi [Yü Ying-shih]. *Trade and Expansion in Han China: A Study in the Structure of Sino-Barbarian Economic Relations.* Berkeley and Los Angeles: University of California Press, 1967.
Yü Ying-shih. *See* Yu Yingshi.
Zhang Guangzhi [Kwang-chih Chang]. *Shang Civilization.* New Haven: Yale University Press, 1980.
Zhou Baozhong. "The Protection of Ancient Chinese Lacquerware." In *Urushi: Proceedings of the Urushi Study Group, June 10–27, 1985*, ed. N. S. Brommelle and Perry Smith, 71–8. Marina del Rey, CA: Getty Conservation Institute, 1988.
Zürcher, Erik. "Recent Studies in Chinese Painting." *TP* 51, nos. 4–5 (1964): 377–422.

WORKS IN CHINESE

An Zuozhang 安作璋 and Xiong Tieji 熊鐵基. *Qin Han guanzhi shi gao* 秦漢官制史稿 [A draft history of the Qin and Han bureaucracy]. Ji'nan: Qi-Lu Shushe, 1985.
Anhui Sheng Wenwu Kaogu Yanjiusuo and Ma'anshan Shi Wenwuju, eds. "Anhui Ma'anshan Dong-Wu Zhu Ran mu fajue jianbao" 安徽馬鞍山東吳朱然墓發掘簡報 [Preliminary excavation report of the Eastern Wu tomb of Zhu Ran at Ma'anshan in Anhui]. *Wenwu* (1986.3): 1–15.
Anhuisheng Wenwu Gongzuodui, ed. "Fuyang Shuanggudui Xi-Han Ruyin Hou mu fajue

jianbao" 阜陽雙古堆西漢汝陰侯墓發掘簡報 [Preliminary excavation report of the Western Han tomb of the Marquis of Ruyin at Shuanggudui, Fuyang]. *Wenwu* (1978.8): 12–31.

Ban Gu 班固. *Hanshu* 漢書 [History of the Former Han dynasty]. 12 vols. Beijing: Zhonghua Shuju, 1962.

———. *Hanshu buzhu* 漢書補注 [History of the Former Han dynasty with corrections and annotations]. Ed. Wang Xianqian 王先謙. 1900. Reprint in 2 vols., Taibei: Yiwen Yinshuguan, 1955.

Beijing Wenwu Gongzuodui, ed. "Beijing xijiao faxian Handai shique qingli jianbao" 北京西郊發現漢代石闕清理簡報 [Preliminary report on cleaning up the Han stone pillar-gates found in the western suburbs of Beijing]. *Wenwu* (1964.11): 13–22.

Beijing Wenwu Jingcui Daxi Bianweihui and Beijing Shi Wenwu Shiye Guanliju, eds. *Beijing wenwu jingcui daxi* 北京文物精粹大系 [The great tradition of the cream of Beijing's cultural relics]. 16 vols. to date. Beijing: Beijing Chubanshe, 2000–.

Cai Yonghua 蔡永華. "Jiefang hou Xi'an fujian faxian de Xi-Han, Xin-Mang qianfan" 解放後西安附近發現的西漢新莽錢範 [Western Han and Wang Mang period coin molds found after liberation near Xi'an]. *Kaogu* (1978.2): 122–9.

Cao Haidong 曹海東, trans., and Li Zhenxing 李振興, ed. *Xinyi Xijing zaji* 新譯西京雜記 [New translation of the *Miscellaneous Notes on the Western Capital*]. Taibei: Sanmin Shuju, 1995.

Cao Lüning 曹旅寧. *Zhangjiashan Han lü yanjiu* 張家山漢律研究 [Research into the Han legal statutes from the Zhangjiashan site]. Beijing: Zhonghua Shuju, 2005.

Cao Wanru 曹婉如. "Dong-Han chengshi jubu ditu de yanjiu: Chengdu shi xijiao Dong-Han mu chutu shijing huaxiang zhuan" 東漢城市局部地圖的研究: 成都市西郊東漢墓出土市井畫像磚 [Research on the plan of Eastern Han cities: The pictorial brick with marketplace scene found in an Eastern Han tomb in the western suburbs of Chengdu]. *Ziran kexueshi yanjiu* 4, no. 2 (1985): 159–62.

Cao Wanru 曹婉如 et al., eds. *Zhongguo gudai ditu ji* 中國古代地圖集 [An atlas of ancient maps of China]. 3 vols. Beijing: Wenwu Chubanshe, 1990–7.

Cao Zhi 曹植. *Cao Zhi ji jiaozhu* 曹植集校注 [Critical annotated edition of the collected works of Cao Zhi]. Ed. Zhao Youwen 趙幼文. Beijing: Renmin Wenxue Chubanshe, 1984.

Chang Qu 常璩. *Huayang guozhi jiaobu tuzhu* 華陽國志校補圖注 [Annotated and illustrated critical edition of the *Account of the States South of Mount Hua*]. Ed. Ren Naiqiang 任乃強. Shanghai: Shanghai Guji Chubanshe, 1987.

———. *Huayang guozhi jiaozhu* 華陽國志校注 [Annotated critical edition of the *Account of the States South of Mount Hua*]. Ed. Liu Lin 劉琳. Chengdu: Ba-Shu Shushe, 1984.

Chen Mingda 陳明達. "Handai de shique" 漢代的石闕 [Stone pillar-gates of the Han period]. *Wenwu* (1961.12): 9–23.

Chen Ping 陳平. "Shilun Zhanguo xing Qin bing de niandai ji youguan wenti" 試論戰國型秦兵的年代及有關問題 [Discussion of the date of Qin weapons of Warring States–type and other associated problems]. In *Zhongguo kaoguxue yanjiu lunji* 中國考古學研究論集, ed. Feng Huifu 馮慧福, 310–35. Beijing: Sanqin Chubanshe, 1987.

Chen Zhenyu 陳振裕. "Qindai qiqi zonglun" 秦代漆器綜論 [Comprehensive discussion of Qin lacquerware]. In *Zhongguo qiqi quanji* 中國漆器全集 [Complete collection of Chinese lacquerware], vol 2. Fuzhou: Fujian Meishu Chubanshe, 1998.

———. "Shilun Hubei Zhanguo Qin-Han qiqi de niandai fenqi" 試論湖北戰國秦漢漆器的

年代分期 [A trial periodization of lacquer vessels of the Warring States, Qin, and Han periods from Hubei]. *Jiang-Han kaogu* (1980.2): 37–50.
———. "Xian-Qin qiqi gaishu" 先秦漆器概述 [General description of pre-Qin lacquerware]. In *Xian-Qin* 先秦, ed. Chen Zhenyu 陳振裕, vol. 1 of *Zhongguo qiqi quanji* 中國漆器全集 [Complete collection of Chinese lacquerware], ed. Zhongguo Qiqi Quanji Bianji Weiyuanhui. Fuzhou: Fujian Meishu Chubanshe, 1998.
———. "Yunmeng Xi-Han mu chutu mufang chushi" 雲夢西漢墓出土木方初釋 [Preliminary translation of the wooden board unearthed from the Western Han tomb at Yunmeng]. *Wenwu* (1973.9): 37–9, 44.
Chen Zhi 陳直. "Cong Qin-Han shiliao zhong kan tuntian, caikuang, zhuqian sanzhong zhidu" 從秦漢史料中看屯田採礦鑄錢三種制度 [Looking at the three systems of garrison farming, mining, and coin casting from Qin and Han historical data]. *Lishi yanjiu* (1955.6): 89–110.
———. "Gu qiwu wenzi congkao" 古器物文字叢考 [Investigation of inscriptions on ancient objects]. *Kaogu* (1963.2): 80–86.
———. "Guanyu liang-Han de shougongye" 關於兩漢的手工業 [Concerning the handicraft industries of the two Han dynasties]. In *Liang-Han jingji shiliao luncong* 兩漢經濟史料論叢. Xi'an: Shaanxi Renmin Chubanshe, 1958.
———. "Guanyu Xi'an Sanqiao Gaoyaocun Xi-Han tongqi mingwen de jidian yijian" 關於西安三橋高窯村西漢銅器銘文的幾點意見 [A few opinions on the inscriptions found on bronze vessels from Sanqiao Gaoyaocun near Xi'an]. *Kaogu* (1963.8): 436.
———. "Guizhou Qingzhen Xian Han mu faxian qierbei qipan huikao" 貴州清鎮縣漢墓發現漆耳杯漆盤匯考 [Collected investigations of the lacquer platters and cups found in the Han tombs at Qingzhen County, Guizhou]. *Guizhou wenshi congkan* (1983.3): 59–62.
———. "Handai renmin de richang shenghuo" 漢代人民的日常生活 [Daily life of people of the Han period]. *Xibei daxue xuebao* (1957.4): 79–84.
———. "Handai yan tie zhuqian san da shougongye" 漢代鹽鐵鑄錢三大手工業 [The three great Han industries of salt, iron, and coin-casting]. *Renwen zazhi* (1957.1): 11–23.
———. "Liang-Han fangzhi qiqi shougongye" 兩漢紡織漆器手工業 [Textile and lacquerware industries of the two Han dynasties]. *Xibei daxue xuebao* (1957.2): 1–20.
———. *Liang-Han jingji shiliao luncong* 兩漢經濟史料論叢 [Collected writings on the economic historical data of the two Han dynasties]. Xi'an: Shaanxi Renmin Chubanshe, 1958.
———, ed. *Sanfu huangtu jiaozheng* 三輔黃圖校正 [Critical edition of the *Yellow Plan of the Three Capital Districts*]. Xi'an: Shaanxi Renmin Chubanshe, 1980.
———. *Wenshi kaogu luncong* 文史考古論叢 [Collected discussions on literature, history, and archaeology]. Tianjin: Tianjin Guji Chubanshe, 1988.
Cheng Lin 成林 and Cheng Zhangcan 程章燦, eds. *Xijing zaji quanyi* 西京雜記全譯 [Complete translation of *Miscellaneous Notes on the Western Capital*]. Guiyang: Guizhou Renmin Chubanshe, 1993.
Cheng Shude 程樹德. *Jiuchao lükao* 九朝律考 [Investigation of the laws of nine dynasties]. 2 vols. Taibei: Taiwan Shangwu Yinshuguan, 1965.
Cheng Yizhong 程毅中, ed. *Yandan zi: Xijing zaji* 燕丹子:西京雜記 [Prince Dan of Yan: Miscellaneous notes on the Western Capital]. Beijing: Zhonghua Shuju, 1987.
Cui Shi 崔寔. *Simin yueling jiaozhu* 四民月令校注 [Critical annotated edition of *Monthly*

Ordinances for the Four Peoples]. Ed. Shi Shenghan 石聲漢. Beijing: Zhonghua Shuju, 1965.
Dai Xiaobei 戴曉北 and Bo Hua 柏樺. "Xi-Han san gongguan zhiyi" 西漢三工官志疑 [Doubts concerning the Three Offices of Workmen of the Western Han]. *Xibei daxue xuebao* (1984.2): 44.
Dai Yingxin 戴應新 and Li Zhongxuan 李仲烜. "Shaanxi Suide Xian yanjiacha Dong-Han huaxiangshi mu" 陝西綏德縣延家岔東漢畫像石墓 [Eastern Han pictorial tomb at Yanjiacha, Suide County, Shaanxi]. *Kaogu* (1983.3): 233–7.
Dai Yingxin 戴應新 and Wei Suizhi 魏遂志. "Shaanxi Suide huangjiata Dong-Han huaxiangshi muqun fajue jianbao" 陝西綏德黃家塔東漢畫像石墓群發掘簡報 [Preliminary excavation report of the Eastern Han pictorial tombs at Huangjiata, Suide County, Shaanxi]. *Kaogu yu wenwu* (1988.5–6): 251–61.
Dan Xianjin 單先進 and Feng Yuhui 馮玉輝. "Chongyang Shi faxian Zhanguo jinian mingwen tongge" 衡陽市發現戰國紀年銘文銅戈 [Inscribed, dated, Warring States era bronze halberd found in Chongyang City]. *Kaogu* (1977.5): 357–8.
Dong Zuobin 董作賓. *Zhongguo nianli zongpu* 中國年曆總譜 [Comprehensive Chinese chronological tables]. 2 vols. Hong Kong: Hong Kong University Press, 1960.
Du Naisong 杜迺松. "Xian-Qin liang-Han qingtong zhuzao gongyi yanjiu" 先秦兩漢青銅鑄造工藝研究 [Research on the bronze-casting art of the pre-Qin, Qin, and Han periods]. *Gugong bowuyuan yuankan* (1989.3): 38–57.
Fan Ye 范曄. *Hou Hanshu* 後漢書 [History of the Latter Han]. 18 vols. Beijing: Zhonghua Shuju, 1965.
———. *Hou Hanshu jijie* 後漢書集解 [Collected explanations to the *History of the Latter Han*]. Ed. Wang Xianqian 王先謙. 1915. Reprint in 2 vols., Beijing: Zhonghua Shuju, 1984.
Fang Guojin 方國錦. "Liujin tong hu" 鎏金銅斛 [Gilded-bronze grain measure]. *Wenwu cankao ziliao* (1958.9): 69–70.
Fang Shiming 方詩銘. "Cong chutu wenwu kan Handai 'gong guan' de yixie wenti" 從出土文物看漢代工官的一些問題 [Using unearthed relics to look at several problems concerning Han period Offices of Workmen]. *Shanghai bowuguan jikan* (1982): 136–45.
Feng Zhengao 逢振鎬. "Liang-Han shiqi Shandong yetie shougongye de fazhan" 兩漢時期山東冶鐵手工業的發展 [The development of iron metallurgy in Shandong during the Han period]. *Dongyue luncong* (1983.3): 103–7.
———. "Qin-Han shiqi Shandong zhitongye de fazhan" 秦漢時期山東製銅業的發展 [Development of bronze fabrication in Shandong during the Qin and Han periods]. *Dongyue luncong* (1985.6): 58–64.
Feng Zhou 豐州. "Zailun Han Maoling 'Yangxin Jia' tongqi suoyouzhe de wenti" 再論漢茂陵陽信家銅器所有者的問題 [Renewed discussion of the ownership of the 'House of Yangxin' bronzes from the Han period Maoling complex]. *Kaogu yu wenwu* (1989.6): 86–9.
Fu Juyou 傅舉有. "Zhongguo qiqi de dianfeng shidai—Handai qi gongyi meishu zonglun" 中國漆器的巔峰時代—漢代漆工藝美術總論 [The pinnacle of Chinese lacquerware: A comprehensive discussion of Han era lacquer art and craft]. In *Han* 漢, ed. Fu Juyou 傅舉有, 1–56, vol. 3 of *Zhongguo qiqi quanji* 中國漆器全集 [Complete collection of Chinese lacquerware], ed. Zhongguo Qiqi Quanji Bianji Weiyuanhui. Fuzhou: Fujian Meishu Chubanshe, 1998.

———, ed. *Mawangdui Han mu wenwu* 馬王堆漢墓文物 [Cultural relics from the Han tombs at Mawangdui]. Changsha: Hunan Chubanshe, 1992.
Fu Kaisen 福開森 [John Calvin Ferguson]. *Lidai zhulu jijin mu.* 歷代著錄吉金目 [Catalog of auspicious metal artifacts recorded in successive ages] Peking, 1939. Reprint, Taibei: Taiwan Shangwu Yinshuguan, 1971.
Fu Zhufu 傅築夫. "Chunqiu Zhanguo shiqi de guan-si shougongye" 春秋戰國時期的官私手工業 [Private and state-run handicraft industries of the Spring and Autumn and Warring States periods]. *Nankai xuebao* (1980.4): 1–14.
Gansu Sheng Bowuguan, ed. "Gansu Wuwei Mozuizi Han mu fajue" 甘肅武威磨嘴子漢墓發掘 [Excavation of Han tombs at Mozuizi, Wuwei County, Gansu]. *Kaogu* (1960.9): 15–28.
———. "Wuwei Mozuizi sanzuo Han mu fajue jianbao" 武威磨嘴子三座漢墓發掘簡報 [Preliminary excavation report of three Han tombs at Mozuizi, Wuwei County]. *Wenwu* (1972.12): 9–23.
Gansu Sheng Bowuguan and Chu Shibin 初師賓, eds. "Gansu Jingyuan xinchu Dong-Luoma liujin yinpan lüekao" 甘肅靖遠新出東羅馬鎏金銀盤略考 [Brief study of the recently unearthed Eastern Roman Empire gilded silver platter from Jingyuan, Gansu]. *Wenwu* (1990.5): 1–9.
Guizhou Sheng Bowuguan, ed. "Guizhou Qingzhen Pingba Han mu fajue baogao" 貴州清鎮平壩漢墓發掘報告 [Excavation report of the Han tombs at Pingba, Qingzhen, in Gansu]. *Kaogu xuebao* (1959.1): 85–102.
Guizhou Sheng Wenwu Guanli Weiyuanhui, ed. "Guizhou Qingzhen Pingba Han zhi Song mu fajue jianbao" 貴州清鎮平壩漢至宋墓發掘簡報 [Preliminary excavation report of the Han to Song period tombs at Pingba, Qingzhen, in Guizhou]. *Kaogu* (1961.4): 207–11.
Guo Moruo 郭沫若. *Liang-Zhou jinwenci daxi tulu kaoshi* 兩周金文辭大系圖錄攷釋 [The great tradition of inscribed vessels from the two Zhou dynasties, illustrated and explained]. 1957. 2d rev. ed. 2 vols. Shanghai: Shanghai Shudian, 1999.
Guo Moruo 郭沫若, ed., and Hu Houxuan 胡厚宣, ed.-in-chief. *Jiaguwen heji* 甲骨文合集 [Collection of shell and bone inscriptions]. 13 vols. N.p.: Zhonghua Shuju, 1978–82.
Guo Yong 郭勇. "Shanxi Sheng Shiyu Xian chutu de Xi-Han tongqi" 山西省石玉縣出土的西漢銅器 [Western Han bronze articles unearthed at Shiyu county, Shanxi]. *Wenwu* (1963.11): 4–12.
Guoli Gugong Bowuyuan, ed. "Shijing jiusi" 市井酒肆 [Marketplaces and wine-seller lanes]. *Gugong wenwu yuekan* 78 (1989): 72–5.
Han Kongyue 韓孔樂 and Wu Dianqing 武殿卿. "Ningxia Guyuan faxian Han chu tong-ding" 寧夏固原發現漢初銅鼎 [Early Han bronze cauldron discovered in Guyuan County, Ningxia]. *Wenwu* (1982.12): 35.
He Benxing 郝本性. "Xinzheng Zheng-Han gu cheng faxian yipi Zhanguo tong bingqi" 新鄭鄭韓故城發現一批戰國銅兵器 [A set of Warring States era bronze weapons found at the ancient city site of the Zheng and Han states at Xinzheng]. *Wenwu* (1972.10): 32–40.
He Zicheng 賀梓城. "Xi'an Han cheng yizhi fujin faxian Handai tongding shi kuai" 西安漢城遺址附近發現漢代銅錠十塊 [Ten Han period copper ingots found near the site of the Han city at Xi'an]. *Wenwu cankao ziliao* (1956.3): 82.
Hebei Sheng Wenhuaju Wenwu Gongzuodui, ed. "Hebei Ding Xian beizhuang Han mu fajue baogao" 河北定縣北莊漢墓發掘報告 [Excavation report of the Han tomb at Beizhuang, Ding County, Hebei]. *Kaogu xuebao* (1964.2): 127–94.

Henan Bowuyuan, ed. *Henan chutu Handai jianzhu mingqi* 河南出土漢代建築明器 [Han period architectural *mingqi* unearthed in Henan]. Zhengzhou: Daxiang Chubanshe, 2002.

Henan Sheng Bowuguan, Shijingshan Gangtie Gongsi Liantiechang, and Zhongguo Yejin Shi Bianxiezu, eds. "Henan Handai yetie jishu chutan" 河南漢代冶鐵技術初探 [Preliminary investigation of Han era iron metallurgical techniques in Henan]. *Kaogu xuebao* (1978.1): 1–24.

Henan Sheng Bowuguan and Zhongguo Yejin Shi Bianxiezu, eds. *Handai diezhu* 漢代疊鑄 [Han period stack-casting]. Beijing: Wenwu Chubanshe, 1978.

Henan Sheng Wenhuaju Wenwu Gongzuodui, ed. "Cong Nanyang Yuan cheng yizhi chutu Handai lihuamo he zhufan kan lihua de zhuzao gongyi guocheng" 從南陽宛城遺址出土漢代犁鏵模和鑄範看犁鏵的鑄造工藝過程 [Casting processes for plowshares, through an examination of the Han period plowshares and molds found at the city site of Yuan, in Nanyang]. *Wenwu* (1965.7): 1–11.

———. *Gong Xian tieshenggou* 鞏縣鐵生溝 [Site of Tieshenggou in Gong County]. Beijing: Wenwu Chubanshe, 1962.

———. "Nanyang Handai tie gongchang fajue jianbao" 南陽漢代鐵工廠發掘簡報 [Preliminary excavation report of the Han period iron facility at Nanyang]. *Wenwu* (1960.1): 58–60.

Henan Sheng Wenhuaju Wenwu Gongzuodui and Nanyang Shi Wenwu Guanli Weiyuanhui, eds. "Henan Nanyang dongguan Jin mu" 河南南陽東關晉墓 [Jin tomb at Dongguan in Nanyang County, Henan]. *Kaogu* (1963.1): 25–7.

Henan Sheng Wenwu Kaogu Yanjiusuo, ed. *Yongcheng Xi-Han Liang Guo wangling yu qinyuan* 永城西漢梁國王陵與寢園 [Royal tombs and surrounding necropolis of the Western Han Princes of Liang at Yongcheng]. Zhengzhou: Zhongzhou Guji Chubanshe, 1996.

Henan Sheng Wenwu Yanjiusuo and Zhenping Xian Wenhuaguan, eds. "Henan Zhenping chutu de Handai jiaocang tiefan he tieqi" 河南鎮平出土的漢代窖藏鐵範和鐵器 [Iron articles and molds for iron casting found in the Han period hoard unearthed at Zhenping, Henan]. *Kaogu* (1982.3): 243–51.

Heze Diqu Bowuguan and Liangshan Xian Wenhuaguan, eds. "Shandong Liangshan Dong-Han jinian mu" 山東梁山東漢紀年墓 [Dated Eastern Han tomb at Liangshan, Shandong]. *Kaogu* (1988.11): 975–82.

Hong Gua 洪适. *Li shi* 隸釋 [Explication through clerical script]. Vols. 1–8 of *Shike shiliao congshu* 石刻史料叢書 [Collection of historical data from stone inscriptions], ser. A, ed. Yan Gengwang 嚴耕望. Taibei: Yiwen Yinshuguan, 1966.

———. *Li xu* 隸續 [Continuation of *Explication through clerical script*]. Vols. 9–11 of *Shike shiliao congshu* 石刻史料叢書 [Collection of historical data from stone inscriptions], ser. A, ed. Yan Gengwang 嚴耕望. Taibei: Yiwen Yinshuguan, 1966.

Hong Yixuan 洪頤烜, comp. *Han Wu gushi* 漢武故事. Vol. 15 of *Baibu congshu jicheng* 百部叢書集成, ser. 38, part 2, ed. Yan Yiping 嚴一萍. Taibei: Yiwen Yinshuguan, 1968.

Hu Pingsheng 胡平生 and Zhang Defang 張德芳, eds. *Dunhuang Xuanquan Han jian shicui* 敦煌懸泉漢簡釋粹 [Explanation of the highlights of Han bamboo strips from Xuanquan, Dunhuang]. Shanghai: Shanghai Guji Chubanshe, 2001.

Hua Jueming 華覺明. "Zhongguo gudai de diezhu jishu" 中國的古代疊鑄技術 [Stack-casting techniques of ancient China]. In *Zhongguo yezhu shi lunji* 中國冶鑄史論集 [Collected writings on the history of Chinese metallurgy], 247–77. Beijing: Wenwu Chubanshe, 1986.

Huan Kuan 桓寬. *Yantielun jiaozhu* 鹽鐵論校注 [Annotated critical edition of the *Discourses on Salt and Iron*]. Ed. Wang Liqi 王利器. 2 vols. Beijing: Zhonghua Shuju, 1992.

Huang Huixian 黃惠賢, ed. *Ershiwushi renming da cidian* 二十五史人名大辭典 [Great dictionary of personal names found in the twenty-five official histories]. 2 vols. Zhengzhou: Zhongzhou Guji Chubanshe, 1997.

Huang Shengzhang 黃盛璋. "Qin bingqi fenguo, duandai, yu youguan zhidu yanjiu" 秦兵器分國,斷代與有關制度研究 [Research into the periodization, geographic distribution, and other related rules and regulations concerning Qin weaponry]. *Guwenzi yanjiu* 21 (2001): 227–85.

———. "Sigong xinkao" 寺工新考 [New examination of the Attendant Workshop]. *Kaogu* (1983.9): 829–33.

Huang Shibin 黃士斌. "Han Wei Luoyang cheng xingtu fenchang diaocha ji" 漢魏洛陽城刑徒墳場調查記 [Record of the archaeological survey of the convict burial ground near the Luoyang City site of the Han and Wei dynasties]. *Kaogu tongxun* (1958.6): 40–4.

Huang Zhanyue 黃展岳. "Guanyu Wang Mang jiumiao de wenti" 關於王莽九廟的問題 [Concerning the problem of Wang Mang's Nine Ancestral Shrines]. *Kaogu* (1989.3): 261–8.

———. "Han Chang'an cheng nanjiao lizhi jianzhu de weizhi ji qi youguan wenti" 漢長安城南郊禮制建築的位置及其有關問題 [Placement of the ritual structure in the southern suburbs of Han period Chang'an and related issues]. *Kaogu* (1960.9): 53–8, 52.

———. "Xi'an Sanqiao Gaoyaocun Xi-Han tongqiqun mingwen bushi" 西安三橋高窯村西漢銅器群銘文補釋 [Corrected transcriptions of the Western Han bronze inscriptions from Gaoyaocun, Sanqiao, Xi'an Municipality]. *Kaogu* (1963.4): 198–200.

Huangshi Shi Bowuguan. *Tonglüshan gu kuangye yizhi* 銅綠山古礦冶遺址. Beijing: Wenwu Chubanshe, 1999.

Hubei Sheng Bowuguan, ed. "Yunmeng Dafentou yihao Han mu" 雲夢大墳頭一號漢墓 [Han tomb 1 at Dafentou, Yunmeng]. *Wenwu ziliao congkan* 4 (1981): 1–28.

———. *Zeng Hou Yi mu* 曾侯乙墓 [Tomb of Marquis Yi of Zeng]. 2 vols. Beijing: Wenwu Chubanshe, 1989.

Hubei Sheng Bowuguan, Xiaoxian Diqu Wenjiaoju, and Yunmeng Xian Wenhuaguan, eds. "Hubei Yunmeng Xi-Han mu fajue jianbao" 湖北雲夢西漢墓發掘簡報 [Preliminary excavation report of the Western Han tombs at Yunmeng, Hubei]. *Wenwu* (1973.9): 23–33.

Hubei Sheng Jingzhou Diqu Bowuguan, ed. *Jiangling Mashan yihao Chu mu* 江陵馬山一號楚墓 [Chu tomb 1 at Mashan, Jiangling]. Beijing: Wenwu Chubanshe, 1985.

———. *Jiangling Yutaishan Chu mu* 江陵雨臺山楚墓 [Chu tomb at Yutaishan, Jiangling]. Beijing: Wenwu Chubanshe, 1984.

Hunan Sheng Bowuguan and Zhongguo Shehui Kexueyuan Kaogu Yanjiusuo, eds. *Changsha Mawangdui yihao Han mu* 長沙馬王堆一號漢墓 [Han tomb 1 at Mawangdui, near Changsha]. 2 vols. Beijing: Wenwu Chubanshe, 1973.

Hunan Sheng Wenwu Kaogu Yanjiusuo et al., eds. "Hunan Longshan Liye: Zhanguo Qin dai gucheng yihao jing fajue jianbao" 湖南龍山里耶:戰國—秦代古城一號井發掘簡報 [Preliminary excavation report of well no. 1 at the Warring States to Qin period walled town site at Liye, Longshan County, Hunan]. *Wenwu* (2003.1): 4–35.

Ji Annuo 紀安諾 [Giele, Enno]. "Yinwan xin chutu xingzheng wenshu de xingzhi yu Handai difang xingzheng” 尹灣新出土行政文書的性質與漢代地方行政 [The nature of the recently unearthed administrative documents from Yinwan and Han era regional administration]. *Dalu zazhi* 95, no. 3 (1997): 21–45.

Jiang Yingju 蔣英炬. “Guanyu Han huaxiangshi chansheng beijing yu yishu gongneng de sikao” 關于漢畫像石產生背景與藝術功能的思考 [Investigation into the background of Han pictorial brick production and their artistic function]. *Kaogu* (1998.11): 90–6.

———. “Handai de xiao citing: Jiaxiang Songshan Han huaxiangshi de jianzhu fuyuan” 漢代的小祠堂:嘉祥宋山漢畫像石的建築復原 [Small Han period shrines: Architectural reconstruction of the Han pictorial stones from Songshan, Jiaxiang County]. *Kaogu* (1983.8): 741–51.

———. “Linyi Yinqueshan Xi-Han mu qiqi mingwen kaoshi” 臨沂銀雀山西漢墓漆器銘文考釋 [Investigation and transcription of the lacquer inscriptions from the Western Han tomb at Yinqueshan, Linyi City]. *Kaogu* (1975.6): 349–51.

Jiang Yingju 蔣英炬 and Wu Wenqi 吳文琪. *Handai Wu shi muqun shike yanjiu* 漢代武氏墓群石刻研究 [Research on the stone carvings from the Han period Wu family cemetery]. Ji’nan: Shandong Meishu Chubanshe, 1995.

Jiang Yingju 蔣英炬 and Yang Aiguo 楊愛國. *Handai huaxiangshi yu huaxiangzhuan* 漢代畫像石與畫像磚 [Han period pictorial stones and bricks]. Beijing: Wenwu Chubanshe, 2001.

Jiaxiang Xian Wushici Wenguansuo, ed. “Shandong Jiaxiang Songshan faxian Han huaxiangshi” 山東嘉祥宋山發現漢畫像石 [Han pictorial stones found at Songshan, Jiaxiang County, Shandong]. *Wenwu* (1979.9): 1–6.

Jin Huai 金槐. “Henan Zheng Xian faxian yichu Handai zhuqian yizhi” 河南鄭縣發現一處漢代鑄錢遺址 [Han period coin-casting site discovered in Zheng County, Henan]. *Wenwu* (1963.12): 42.

Jingzhou Diqu Bowuguan, ed. “Jiangling Zhangjiashan liang zuo Han mu chutu dapi zhujian” 江陵張家山兩座漢墓出土大批竹簡 [Large cache of bamboo slips unearthed from two Han tombs at Zhangjiashan, Jiangling]. *Wenwu* (1992.9): 1–11.

———. “Jiangling Zhangjiashan san zuo Han mu chutu dapi zhujian” 江陵張家山三座漢墓出土大批竹簡 [Large cache of bamboo slips unearthed from three Han tombs at Zhangjiashan, Jiangling]. *Wenwu* (1985.1): 1–8.

Jinian Cheng Fenghuangshan Yiliuba Hao Han Mu Fajue Zhenglizu, ed. “Hubei Jiangling Fenghuangshan yiliuba hao Han mu fajue jianbao” 湖北江陵鳳凰山一六八號漢墓發掘簡報 [Preliminary excavation report of Han tomb 168 at Fenghuangshan, Jiangling, Hubei]. *Wenwu* (1975.9): 1–19, 28.

Jining Diqu Wenwuzu and Jiaxiang Xian Wenguansuo, eds. “Shandong Jiaxiang Songshan 1980 nian chutu de Han huaxiangshi” 山東嘉祥宋山 1980 年出土的漢畫像石 [Han pictorial stones unearthed in 1980 at Songshan, Jiaxiang County, Shandong]. *Wenwu* (1982.5): 60–70.

Ju Qingyuan 鞠清遠. “Handai de guanfu gongye” 漢代的官府工業 [Han period state-run industries]. *Shihuo* 1 (1934): 1–5.

Kaogu Yanjiusuo Han Cheng Fajuedui, ed. “Han Chang’an cheng nanjiao lizhi jianzhuqun fajue jianbao” 漢長安城南郊禮制建築群發掘簡報 [Preliminary excavation report of the ritual structures in the southern suburbs of the Han Chang’an city]. *Kaogu* (1960.7): 36–9.

Lai Fei 賴非. “Shandong Handai huaxiangshi bangti” 山東漢代畫像石榜題 [Captions on Han period pictorial stones from Shandong]. *Meishushi yanjiu* (1994.2): 23–8.

Lao Gan 勞幹. “Handai de guyong zhidu” 漢代的雇傭制度 [The labor system of the Han period]. *Lishi yuyan yanjiusuo jikan* 23 (1951): 77–87.
Li Daoyuan 酈道元. *Shuijing zhu jiao* 水經注校 [Critical edition of *Commentary on the Classic of Waterways*]. Ed. Wang Guowei 王國維. Shanghai: Renmin Chubanshe, 1984.
Li Falin 李發林. *Shandong Han huaxiangshi yanjiu* 山東漢畫像石研究 [Research on Han period pictorial stones from Shandong]. Ji'nan: Qi-Lu Shushe, 1982.
Li Fang 李昉 et al., eds. *Taiping yulan* 太平御覽 [Imperial overview of the Taiping era]. *SBCK* ed., Shanghai: Commercial Press, 1935. Reprint, 7 vols., Taibei: Commercial Press, 1968.
Li Guangjun 李光軍. “Liang-Guang chutu Xi-Han qiwu mingwen guanming kao” 兩廣出土西漢器物銘文官名考 [Investigation of the official titles seen in inscriptions on Western Han articles unearthed from Guangdong and Guangxi]. *Wenbo* (1987.3): 32–8.
———. “Qin ‘gongshi’ kao” 秦工師考 [Investigation into the Qin ‘Master of Artisans’]. *Wenbo* (1992.3): 59–64.
Li Jinghua 李京華. “Handai tie nongqi mingwen shishi” 漢代鐵農器銘文試釋 [Trial translation of inscriptions on Han period agricultural tools]. *Kaogu* (1974.1): 61–6.
Li Jinghua 李京華 and Chen Changshan 陳長山. *Nanyang Handai yetie* 南陽漢代冶鐵 [Han period iron metallurgy at Nanyang]. Zhengzhou: Zhongzhou Guji Chubanshe, 1995.
Li Junming 李均明. “Zhangjiashan Han jian ‘shou lü’ yu jiazu lianzuo” 張家山漢簡收律與家族連坐 [The “Statute on Confiscation” from Zhangjiashan and the implication of family members]. *Wenwu* (2002.9): 60–3.
Li Liansheng 李連生. “Xiyouji, Guizimu yu Jiuzimu” 西游記,鬼子母與九子母 [*The Journey to the West,* Hariti, and the Mother of Nine Sons]. *Zhongguo dianji yu wenhua* (2002.4): 33–40.
Li Rusen 李如森. “Zhanguo Qin-Han qiqi zongshu” 戰國秦漢漆器綜述 [Comprehensive description of Warring States, Qin, and Han lacquer]. *Shixue jikan* (1987.4): 72–5.
Li Xiaoding 李孝定. *Jiagu wenzi jishi* 甲骨文字集釋 [Collected explanations of oracle-bone characters]. 14 vols. Nangang: Institute of History and Philology, Academia Sinica, 1965.
Li Xueqin 李學勤. “Handai qingtongqi de jige wenti-Mancheng, Maoling suochu jinwen de fenxi” 漢代青銅器的幾個問題滿城茂陵所出金文的分析 [Several problems associated with Han bronzes: An analysis of the inscriptions from Mancheng and Maoling]. *Wenwu yanjiu* 2 (1986): 101–5.
———. *Jianbo yiji yu xueshushi* 簡帛佚籍與學術史 [Lost books on silk and bamboo and the history of their scholarship]. Taibei: Shibao Chuban, 1994.
———. “Zhanguo shidai de Qin guo tongqi” 戰國時代的秦國銅器 [Qin bronzes from the Warring States period]. *Wenwu cankao ziliao* (1957.8): 38–40, 53.
———. “Zhanguo timing gaishu” (xia) 戰國題銘概述 (下) [General description of Warring States period inscriptions (second part)]. *Wenwu* (1959.9): 58–61.
Li Xueqin 李學勤 et al., eds. *Shisanjing zhushu* 十三經注疏 [Annotated *Thirteen Classics*]. Rev. ed. 26 vols. Beijing: Beijing Daxue Chubanshe, 2000.
Li Yufang 李毓芳. “Han Chang'an cheng hongfan yao he zhubi yizhi” 漢長安城烘範窯和鑄幣遺址 [Coin casting and mold-baking kiln sites at Han Chang'an]. *Zhongguo kaoguxue nianjian,* 1993, 245–6.
Li Zhaohe 李昭和. “‘Ba-Shu’ yu ‘Chu’ qiqi chutan” 巴蜀與楚漆器初探 [Preliminary investigation of Ba-Shu and Chu lacquer]. In *Zhongguo kaogu xuehui dierci nianhui lunwenji*

中國考古學會第二次年會論文集 [Papers from the second annual meeting of the Chinese Archaeological Society], ed. Zhongguo Kaogu Xuehui, 93–9. Beijing: Wenwu Chubanshe, 1980.
Lianyungang Bowuguan, ed. *Yinwan Han mu jiandu* 尹灣漢墓簡牘 [Wooden boards and slips from the Han tomb at Yinwan]. Beijing: Zhonghua Shuju, 1997.
Lianyungang Shi Bowuguan, ed. "Jiangsu Donghai Xian Yinwan Han muqun fajue jianbao" 江蘇東海縣尹灣漢墓群發掘簡報 [Preliminary excavation report of the Han cemetery at Yinwan, in Donghai County, Jiangsu]. *Wenwu* (1996.8): 4–25.
———, ed. "Yinwan Han mu jiandu shiwen xuan" 尹灣漢墓簡牘釋文選 [Select transcription of the wooden boards and bamboo strips from the Han tomb at Yinwan]. *Wenwu* (1996.8): 26–31.
Lianyungang Shi Bowuguan, Donghai Xian Bowuguan, Jianbo Yanjiu Zhongxin, Zhongguo Shehui Kexueyuan, and Zhongguo Wenwu Yanjiusuo, eds. "Yinwan Han mu jiandu chutan" 尹灣漢墓簡牘初探 [Preliminary investigation of the wooden boards and bamboo slips from the Han tomb at Yinwan]. *Wenwu* (1996.10): 68–71.
Liao Boyuan [Liu Pak-yuen] 廖佰源. *Jiandu yu zhidu: Yinwan Hanmu jiandu guan wenshu kaozheng* 簡牘與制度：尹灣漢墓簡牘官文書考證 [Slips, boards, and institutions: An investigation into the administrative documents from the Han tomb at Yinwan]. Taibei: Wenjin Chubanshe, 1998.
———. "Yinwan Han mu jiandu yu Handai junxian shuli zhidu" 尹灣漢墓簡牘與漢代郡縣屬吏制度 [The wooden boards and bamboo slips from the Han tomb at Yinwan and the system of subordinate officials in Han commanderies and counties]. *Dalu zazhi* 95, no. 3 (1997): 14–20.
Lin Suqing 林素清. "Liang-Han jingming chutan" 兩漢鏡銘初探 [Preliminary inquiry into Han period mirror inscriptions]. *Zhongyang yanjiuyuan, Lishi yuyan yanjiusuo jikan,* 63, no. 2 (1993): 325–70.
———. "Liang-Han jingming suojian jiyu yanjiu" 兩漢鏡銘所見吉語研究 [Research into auspicious phrases seen in Han period mirror inscriptions]. In *Handai wenxue yu sixiang xueshu yantaohui lunwenji* 漢代文學與思想學術研討會論文集 [Collected papers of the academic conference on Han literature and thought], ed. Guoli Zhengzhi Daxue Zhongwen Xisuo, 161–88. Taibei: Wenshizhe Chubanshe, 1991.
Lin Yeqiang 林業強 and You Xuehua 游學華, eds. *Hubei chutu Zhanguo Qin-Han qiqi* 湖北出土戰國秦漢漆器 [Warring States, Qin, and Han lacquer unearthed in Hubei]. Hong Kong: Xianggang Zhongwen Daxue Wenwuguan, 1994.
Linyi Shi Bowuguan, ed. "Shandong Linyi jinqueshan Han huaxiangzhuan mu" 山東臨沂金雀山漢畫像磚墓 [Han period pictorial-brick tomb at Jinqueshan, Linyi City, Shandong]. *Wenwu* (1995.6): 72–8.
Liu Lexian 劉樂賢. *Shuihudi Qin jian rishu yanjiu* 睡虎地秦簡日書研究 [Research into the Qin 'day books' from Shuihudi]. Taibei: Wenjin Chubanshe, 1994.
Liu Qingzhu 劉慶柱. "Han Chang'an cheng buju jiegou bianxi" 漢長安城佈局結構辨析 [Analysis of the layout and structure of Han period Chang'an]. *Kaogu* (1987.10): 937–44.
———. "Han Chang'an cheng de kaogu faxian ji xiangguan wenti yanjiu" 漢長安城的考古發現及相關問題研究 [The archaeological discovery of Han period Chang'an and research into related problems]. *Kaogu* (1996.10): 1–14.
———. "Han Chang'an cheng Weiyang Gong buju xingzhi chulun" 漢長安城未央宮佈局形

制初論 [Preliminary discussion of the layout of the Weiyang Palace within Han period Chang'an City]. *Kaogu* (1995.12): 1115–24.
———. "Handai guqian yu Handai gongguan yanjiu" 漢代骨簽與漢代工官研究 [Han period bone tags and research into the Han period Office of Workmen]. *Shaanxi lishi bowuguan guankan* (1997.4): 1–12.
———. "Xi'an Shi Han Chang'an cheng dongshi he xishi yizhi" 西安市漢長安城東市和西市遺址 [The eastern and western market sites at Han period Chang'an, Xi'an City]. *Zhongguo kaoguxue nianjian,* 1987, 264.
———. "Zailun Han Chang'an cheng buju jiegou jiqi xiangguan wenti" 再論漢長安城佈局結構及其相關問題 [Another discussion of the layout and structure of Han period Chang'an and related problems]. *Kaogu* (1992.7): 632–8.
Liu Qingzhu 劉慶柱 and Li Yufang 李毓芳. *Xi-Han shiyi ling* 西漢十一陵 [The eleven imperial mausoleums of the Western Han]. Xi'an: Shaanxi Renmin Chubanshe, 1987.
Liu Tizhi 劉體智. *Xiaojiao jing'ge jinshi wenzi* 小校經閣金石文字 [Characters on bronze and stone from the Pavilion of the Classics]. 18 vols. N.p., 1935.
Liu Xinjian 劉心健 and Liu Zichang 劉自強. "Shandong Cangshan Zuo cheng yizhi chutu Dong-Han tongqi" 山東蒼山柞城遺址出土東漢銅器 [Eastern Han bronzes unearthed from the city site of Zuo at Cangshan, Shandong]. *Wenwu* (1983.10): 75–7.
Liu Xinjian 劉心健 and Zhang Mingxue 張鳴雪. "Shangdong Junan faxian Handai shique" 山東莒南發現漢代石闕 [Han era stone pillar-gates discovered in Junan, Shandong]. *Wenwu* (1965.5): 16–19.
Liu Yunyong 劉運勇. "Zailun Xi-Han Chang'an buju ji xingcheng yuanyin" 再論西漢長安佈局及形成原因 [Another discussion of the reasons behind the layout of Han Chang'an]. *Kaogu* (1992.7): 640–5, 639.
Liu Zhiyuan 劉志遠. "Handai shijing kao: Shuo Dong-Han shijing huaxiangzhuan" 漢代市井考:說東漢市井畫像磚 [Investigation of Han era markets: Explaining the Eastern Han pictorial-brick market scene]. *Wenwu* (1973.3): 52–7.
Lu Shuxun 陸樹勛. "Han kouqi kao" 漢釦器考 [Investigation of metal-rimmed Han lacquer]. *Guxue congkan* (1939.1).
Lu Zhaoyin 盧兆蔭. "Guanyu Mancheng Han mu qipan mingwen ji qita" 關於滿城漢墓漆盤銘文及其它 [Concerning the inscription on the lacquer platter from the Han tomb at Mancheng and other issues]. *Kaogu* (1974.1): 67–8.
Lu Zhuomin 呂桌民. "Cong kaogu ziliao kan Qin-Han shiqi Xianyang de zhitaoye" 從考古資料看秦漢時期咸陽的製陶業 [Looking at Qin and Han pottery production at Xianyang from archaeological data]. *Wenbo* (1989.3): 51–5.
Luo Fuyi 羅福頤, "Xiang Tajun shi citing tizi jieshi" 鄉他君石祠堂題字解釋 [Transcription and explanation of the stone shrine inscription of Xiang Tajun]. *Gugong bowuyuan yuankan* (1960.2): 178–81.
Luo Ping 羅平. "Hebei Chengde zhuanqu Handai kuangye yizhi de diaocha" 河北承德專區漢代礦冶遺址的調查 [Survey of the Han period mining and smelting site in the Chengde special region, Hebei]. *Kaogu tongxun* (1957.1): 22–6.
Luoyang Bowuguan, ed. "Luoyang jianxi qilihe Dong-Han mu fajue jianbao" 洛陽澗西七里河東漢墓發掘簡報 [Preliminary excavation report of the Eastern Han tomb at Qilihe, Jianxi]. *Kaogu* (1975.2): 116–24, 134.
Luoyang Shi Wenwu Gongzuo Dui, ed., "Luoyang jingu zhan 11 hao Han mu fajue jianbao"

洛陽金谷站11號漢墓發掘簡報 [Preliminary excavation report of Han tomb no. 11 at the Jingu station, Luoyang City]. *Wenwu* (1983.4): 15–28.

Ma Feibai 馬非百. "Qin-Han jingji shi ziliao (1) shougongye" 秦漢經濟史資料(1)手工業 [Qin and Han economic history data (1): manufacturing]. *Shihuo* 2, no. 8 (1935): 22–33.

———. "Qin-Han jingji shi ziliao (2) shangye" 秦漢經濟史資料(2)商業 [Qin and Han economic history data (2): commerce]. *Shihuo* 2, no. 10 (1935): 7–32.

———. "Qin-Han jingji shi ziliao (3) nongye" 秦漢經濟史資料(3)農業 [Qin and Han economic history data (3): agriculture]. *Shihuo* 3, no. 1 (1935): 9–31.

———. "Qin-Han jingji shi ziliao (4) huobi zhidu" 秦漢經濟史資料(4)貨幣制度 [Qin and Han economic history data (4): currency system]. *Shihuo* 3, no. 2 (1935): 2–25.

———. "Qin-Han jingji shi ziliao (5) renkou ji tudi" 秦漢經濟史資料(5)人口及土地 [Qin and Han economic history data (5): population and land]. *Shihuo* 3, no. 3 (1936): 8–38.

———. "Qin-Han jingji shi ziliao (6) nuli zhidu" 秦漢經濟史資料(6)奴隸制度 [Qin and Han economic history data (6): slave system]. *Shihuo* 3, no. 8 (1936): 37–52.

———. "Qin-Han jingji shi ziliao (7) zushui zhidu" 秦漢經濟史資料(7)租稅制度 [Qin and Han economic history data (7): taxation]. *Shihuo* 3, no. 9 (1936): 9–33.

Ma Heng 馬衡. "Han *Shijing* gaishu" 漢石經概述 [General description of the Han *Stone Classics*]. *Kaogu xuebao* (1955.10): 1–9.

———. *Han Shijing jicun* 漢石經集存 [Collection of surviving fragments of the Han *Stone Classics*]. 2 vols. Beijing: Kexue Chubanshe, 1957. Reprint, Taibei: Yiwen Yinshuguan, 1976.

Ma Xianxing 馬先醒, ed. *Hanshi wenxian leimu: Zengding ban* 漢史文獻類目:增訂版 [Categorized index of Han historical writings: Revised and expanded edition]. Yangming Shan: Jiandu She, 1976.

Nan Bo 南波. "Jiangsu Lianyungang Shi haizhou Xi-Han Shi Qiyao mu" 江蘇連雲港市海州西漢侍其繇墓 [The Western Han tomb of Shi Qiyao at Haizhou, Lianyungang City, Jiangsu]. *Kaogu* (1975.3): 169–77.

Nanjing Bowuyuan, ed. "Xuzhou Mao cun huaxiangshi mu" 徐州茅村畫像石墓 [Pictorial-stone tomb at Maocun, Xuzhou]. *Kaogu* (1980.4): 347–52.

Nanyang Shi Bowuguan, ed. "Nanyang faxian Dong-Han Xu Aqu muzhi huaxianshi" 南陽發現東漢許阿瞿墓志畫像石 [Discovery of the Eastern Han pictorial-stone epitaph of Xu Aqu at Nanyang]. *Wenwu* (1974.8): 73–5, 41.

Nanyang Shi Wenwu Gongzuodui, ed. "Nanyang Shi yaocai shichang huaxiangshi mu fajue jianbao" 南陽市藥材市場畫像石墓發掘簡報 [Preliminary excavation report of the pictorial-stone tomb found at the herbal market in Nanyang City]. *Zhongyuan wenwu* (1994.1): 96–100.

Ouyang Xiu 歐陽修 et al., eds. *Xin Tangshu* 新唐書 [The new history of the Tang]. 10 vols. Beijing: Zhonghua Shuju, 1975.

Pan Qifeng 潘其風 and Han Kangxin 韓康信. "Luoyang Dong-Han xingtu mu rengu jianding" 洛陽東漢刑徒墓人骨鑒定 [Appraisal of the bones from the Eastern Han convict cemetery at Luoyang]. *Kaogu* (1988.3): 277–83.

Qin Jincai 秦進才. "Han 'Yangxin Jia' tongqi de zuichu suoyouzhe wenti" 漢'陽信家'銅器的最初所有者問題 [The question of the original owner of the Han period Yangxin bronzes]. *Kaogu yu wenwu* (1987.3): 84–6.

Qin Shihuang Ling Kaogudui, ed. "Qin Shihuang lingyuan K1006 peizangkeng diyi ci fajue

jianbao" 秦始皇陵園 K1006 陪葬坑第一次發掘簡報 [Preliminary report of the first excavation of attendant pit K1006 at the Qin Shihuang mausoleum]. *Wenwu* (2002.3): 4–31.
Qin Yong Keng Kaogudui, ed. "Lintong Zhengzhuang Qin shiliao jiagongchang yizhi diaocha jianbao" 臨潼鄭莊秦石料加工場遺址調查簡報 [Preliminary survey report of the Qin stone-dressing site at Zhengzhuang in Lintong County]. *Kaogu yu wenwu* (1981.1): 39–43.
Qin Zhaofen 秦照芬. "Handai zhengfu dui tiegongye de jingying" 漢代政府對鐵工業的經營 [The management of the iron industry by the Han government]. *Jiandu xuebao* 13 (1990): 135–62.
Qin Zhonghang 秦中行. "Han Yangling fujin qiantu mu de fajue" 漢陽陵附近鉗徒墓的發掘 [Excavation of the shackled convicts' cemetery near the Han Yangling mausoleum]. *Wenwu* (1972.7): 51–3.
Rong Geng 容庚. *Han jinwen lu* 漢金文錄 [Record of Han inscriptions on metal]. Beiping [Beijing]: Institute of History and Philology, Academia Sinica, 1931.
———. *Jinwen bian* 金文編 [Compilation of bronze inscriptional forms]. Rev. and enl. ed. Beijing: Zhonghua Shuju, 1985.
———. "Lelang yiji chutu zhi qiqi mingwen kao" 樂浪遺蹟出土之漆器銘文考 [Study of the lacquer inscriptions unearthed from the Lelang site]. *Beida guoxue yuekan* 1, no. 1 (1926): 39–42.
Rong Wenku 榮文庫. "Handai guanying tongtieye zhong de laodongzhe jiegou" 漢代官營銅鐵業中的勞動者結構 [Organization of the laborers in Han period, government-run bronze and iron industries]. *Liaoning daxue xuebao* (1990.2): 8–12.
———. "Handai zhongyang tongqi shengchan gongguan jigou kaoshi" 漢代中央銅器生產工官機構考釋 [Explanation of the structure of the Office of Workmen for Han period centrally controlled bronze production]. *Liaoning daxue xuebao* (1987.5): 83–5.
Shaanxi Sheng Bowuguan, ed. "Chang'an Wotouzhai Handai qianfan yizhi diaocha" 長安窩頭寨漢代錢範遺址調查 [Investigation of the Han period coin-casting site at Wotouzhai, near Han Chang'an]. *Kaogu* (1972.5): 31–32, 55.
Shaanxi Sheng Kaogu Yanjiusuo, ed. *Qindu Xianyang kaogu baogao* 秦都咸陽考古報告 [Archaeological report of the Qin capital of Xianyang]. Beijing: Kexue Chubanshe, 2004.
———. "Xi'an beijiao Zhanguo zhutong gongjiang mu fajue jianbao" 西安北郊戰國鑄銅工匠墓發掘簡報 [Preliminary excavation report of the Warring States period tomb of a bronzecaster from the northern suburbs of Xi'an]. *Wenwu* (2003.9): 4–14.
Shaanxi Sheng Kaogu Yanjiusuo and Qin Shihuang Bingmayong Bowuguan, eds. *Qin Shi Huangdi lingyuan kaogu baogao 1999* 秦始皇帝陵園考古報告 1999 [Archaeological report for the First Emperor of Qin's necropolis, 1999]. Beijing: Kexue Chubanshe, 2000.
Shaanxi Sheng Kaogu Yanjiusuo and Shihuangling Qin Yongkeng Kaogu Fajuedui, eds. *Qin Shihuangling bingmayong keng: Yi hao keng fajue baogao 1974–1984* 秦始皇陵兵馬俑坑: 一號坑發掘報告 *1974–1984* [The pits with the terracotta army in the necropolis of the First Emperor of Qin: Excavation report of pit no. 1, 1974–1984]. 2 vols. Beijing: Wenwu Chubanshe, 1988.
Shaanxi Sheng Kaogu Yanjiusuo and Yulin Shi Kaogu Guanli Weiyuanhui Bangongshi, eds. *Shenmu Dabaodang: Handai chengzhi yu muzang kaogu baogao* 神木大保當: 漢代城址与墓葬考古報告 [Dabaodang site in Shenmu County: Archaeological report of the Han period city site and burials]. Beijing: Kexue Chubanshe, 2001.

Shaanxi Sheng Qianbi Xuehui, ed. *Qin-Han qianfan* 秦漢錢範 [Qin and Han coin molds]. Xi'an: San-Qin Chubanshe, 1992.

Shaanxi Sheng Wenguanhui and Dengcheng Xian Wenhuaguan Zhihe Fajuedui, eds. "Shaanxi Potoucun Xi-Han zhuqian yizhi fajue jianbao" 陝西坡頭村西漢鑄錢遺址發掘簡報 [Preliminary excavation report of the Western Han coin-casting site at Potoucun, Shaanxi]. *Kaogu* (1982.1): 23–30.

Shandong Sheng Bowuguan and Shandong Sheng Wenwu Kaogu Yanjiusuo, eds. *Shandong Han huaxiangshi xuanji* 山東漢畫像石選集 [A collection of selected Han pictorial stones from Shandong]. [Ji'nan]: Qi-Lu Shushe, 1982.

Shandong Sheng Jining Shi Wenwuju, ed. *Han Rencheng Wang mu keshi jingxuan* 漢任城王墓刻石精選 [Prime selections among the stone carvings from the Han Prince of Rencheng's tomb]. [Ji'nan]: Shandong Meishu Chubanshe, 1998.

Shanxi Sheng Datong Shi Bowuguan and Shanxi Sheng Wenwu Gongzuo Weiyuanhui, eds. "Shanxi Datong shijiazhai Bei Wei Sima Jinlong mu" 山西大同石家寨北魏司馬金龍墓 [The Northern Wei tomb of Sima Jinlong at Shijiazhai, Datong County, Shanxi]. *Wenwu* (1972.3): 20–33.

Shanxi Sheng Kaogu Yanjiusuo, ed. "Shanxi Xia Xian Yuwang cheng Handai zhutie yizhi shijue jianbao" 山西夏縣禹王城漢代鑄鐵遺址試掘簡報 [Preliminary report of the test excavation of a Han period iron-casting site at Yuwangcheng, Xia County, Shanxi]. *Kaogu* (1994.8): 685 91.

Shao Mingsheng 邵茗生. "Han Youzhou shuzuo Qin Jun shique shiwen" 漢幽州書佐秦君石闕釋文 [Transcription of the inscription on the Han period pillar-gate of the clerk Master Qin at Youzhou]. *Wenwu* (1964.11): 23–4.

Shenchou Bowuguan, ed. *Zhongguo Handai huaxiangshi huaxiangzhuan wenxian mulu* 中國漢代畫像石畫像磚文獻目錄 [Index to literature on Han period Chinese pictorial stones and pictorial bricks]. Beijing: Wenwu Chubanshe, 1995.

Shi Shenghan 石聲漢. *Qimin yaoshu jinshi* 齊民要術今釋 [Modern translation of *Essential Techniques for the Common People*]. 4 vols. Beijing: Kexue Chubanshe, 1957–8.

Shi Shuqing 史樹青. "Wo guo gudai de jincuo gongyi" 我國古代的金錯工藝 [Our country's ancient craft of metal inlay]. *Wenwu* (1973.6): 66–72.

Shihuangling Qin Yongkeng Kaogu Fajuedui, ed. "Qin Shihuang ling xice Zhaobeihu cun Qin xingtu mu" 秦始皇陵西側趙背戶村秦刑徒墓 [Convict laborer graves at Zhaobeihu village on the western side of the mausoleum of the First Emperor of Qin]. *Wenwu* (1982.3): 1–11.

Shuihudi Qinmu Zhujian Zhengli Xiaozu, ed. *Shuihudi Qinmu zhujian* 睡虎地秦墓竹簡 [Bamboo slips from the Qin tomb at Shuihudi]. Beijing: Wenwu Chubanshe, 1978.

———. *Shuihudi Qinmu zhujian* 睡虎地秦墓竹簡 [Bamboo slips from the Qin tomb at Shuihudi]. Beijing: Wenwu Chubanshe, 1990.

Sibu congkan 四部叢刊 [Reprint collection of the four branches of literature]. 504 titles in 3,112 bound *ce*. Shanghai: Shangwu Yinshuguan, 1919–36.

Sichuan Sheng Bowuguan and Qingchuan Xian Wenhuaguan, eds. "Qingchuan Xian chutu Qin geng xiu tianlü muban—Sichuan Qingchuan Xian Zhanguo mu fajue jianbao" 青川縣出土秦更修田律木版—四川青川縣戰國墓發掘簡報 [The wooden board with the Qin *gengxiu* agricultural statute unearthed from Qingchuan County: Preliminary excavation report on the Warring States period tomb in Qingchuan County, Sichuan]. *Wenwu* (1982.1): 1–21.

Sima Qian 司馬遷. *Shiji* 史記 [Historical records]. 2d ed. 10 vols. Beijing: Zhonghua Shuju, 1982.
Sishui Xian Wenguansuo, ed. “Shandong Sishui nanchen Dong-Han huaxiangshi mu” 山東泗水南陳東漢畫像石墓 [Eastern Han pictorial-stone tomb from Nanchen Village, near the Si River, Shandong]. *Kaogu* (1995.5): 390–5.
Song Boyin 送伯胤 and Li Zhongyi 李忠義. “Cong Han huaxiangshi tansuo Handai zhiji gouzao” 從漢畫像石探索漢代織機構造 [An inquiry into the structure of Han period looms from depictions on Han pictorial stones]. *Wenwu* (1962.3): 25–8, 44.
Song Jie 宋杰. “Handai guyong jiage bianxi” 漢代雇傭價格辨析 [Analysis of labor prices during the Han period]. *Beijing shiyuan xuebao* (1988.2): 77–83.
Song Zhimin 宋治民. “Handai de qiqi zhizao shougongye” 漢代的漆器製造手工業 [Han period lacquer manufacture]. *Sichuan daxue xuebao* (1982.2): 84–9.
———. “Handai de tongqi zhuzao shougongye” 漢代的銅器鑄造手工業 [Han period bronze-casting industry]. *Zhongguo shi yanjiu* (1985.2): 13–26.
———. “Handai mingke suojian zhiguan xiaoji” 漢代銘刻所見職官小記 [Minor notes on the official titles seen in Han period inscriptions]. *Kaogu* (1979.5): 459–60.
———. *Handai shougongye* 漢代手工業 [Han period manufacturing]. Chengdu: Ba-Shu Shushe, 1992.
———. *Zhanguo, Qin-Han kaogu* 戰國秦漢考古 [Warring States, Qin, and Han archaeology]. Chengdu: Sichuan Daxue Chubanshe, 1994.
Song Zhong 宋衷. *Shiben* 世本 [Genealogical origins]. In *Baibu congshu jicheng*, ser. 38, ed. Yan Yiping. Taibei: Yiwen Yinshuguan, 1968.
Su Zhaoqing 蘇兆慶 et al. *Juxian wenwu zhi* 莒縣文物志 [Record of cultural relics in Ju County]. Ji’nan: Qi-Lu Shushe, 1993.
Sun Ji 孫機. *Handai wuzhi wenhua ziliao tushuo* 漢代物質文化資料圖說 [Illustrated descriptions of Han period material culture]. Beijing: Wenwu Chubanshe, 1991.
Sun Weizu 孫慰祖 and Xu Gufu 徐谷甫, eds. *Qin-Han jinwen huibian* 秦漢金文匯編 [Collection of Qin and Han inscriptions on metal]. Shanghai: Shanghai Shudian, 1997.
Sun Xingyan 孫星衍 et al., comps. *Han guan liu zhong* 漢官六種 [Six examples of Han writings on official posts]. Beijing: Zhonghua Shuju, 1990.
Suo Yuming 索予明. “Handai de jingmi gongye” 漢代的精密工業 [The precision of Han period industry]. In *Zhongguo qi gongyi yanjiu lunji* 中國漆工藝研究論集. Taibei: Guoli Gugong Bowuyuan, 1990.
———. “Qin-Han qiwen quanci” 秦漢桼文詮次 [Periodization of Qin and Han lacquer inscriptions]. In *Zhongguo qi gongyi yanjiu lunji* 中國漆工藝研究論集. Taibei: Guoli Gugong Bowuyuan, 1990.
———, ed. *Qiqi pian* 漆器篇 [Lacquer volume]. A volume in *Zhonghua wu qiannian wenwu jikan* 中華五千年文物輯刊 [Compilation of five thousand years of Chinese cultural relics]. Taibei: Zhonghua Wuqiannian Wenwu Jikan Bianji Weiyuanhui, 1984.
———. *Zhongguo qi gongyi yanjiu lunji* 中國漆工藝研究論集 [Collected writings on Chinese lacquer craft]. Taibei: Guoli Gugong Bowuyuan, 1990.
Tan Qixiang 譚其驤, ed. *Zhongguo lishi ditu ji* 中國歷史地圖集 [Collection of Chinese historical maps]. 8 vols. Beijing: Zhongguo Ditu Chubanshe, 1982–7.
Tang Jinyu 唐金裕. “Xi’an Shi beijiao Handai zhuanwa yaozhi” 西安市北郊漢代磚瓦窯址 [Han period brick and tile kiln site in the northern suburbs of Xi’an]. *Kaogu* (1964.4): 180–1.

Tang Wenxing 湯文興. "Cong gudai zhuqian kan woguo diezhu jishu de qiyuan yu fazhan" 從古代鑄錢看我國疊鑄技術的起源與發展 [The origin and development of our country's stack-casting technology from an examination of ancient coin casting]. *Zhongyuan wenwu*, special issue, 1981, 12–9.

———. "Woguo gudai jizhong huobi de zhuzao jishu" 我國古代幾種貨幣的鑄造技術 [Several of our country's ancient coin-casting techniques]. *Zhongyuan wenwu* (1983.2): 74–8.

Teng Zhaozong 滕昭宗. "Yinwan Han mu jiandu gaishu" 尹灣漢墓簡牘概述 [General description of the bamboo slips and wooden boards from the Han tomb at Yinwan]. *Wenwu* (1996.8): 32–6.

Tong Shuye 童書業. "Zhanguo Qin-Han shidai de shougongye yu shangye" 戰國秦漢時代的手工業與商業 [Warring States, Qin, and Han period manufacturing and commerce]. *Wenshizhe* (1958.2): 27–38.

Wang Fu 王符. *Qianfu lun jian jiaozheng* 潛夫論箋校正 [Annotated critical edition of *Criticisms of a Hidden Man*]. Ed. Peng Duo 彭鐸. Beijing: Zhonghua Shuju, 1985.

———. *Xinyi qianfu lun* 新譯潛夫論 [New translation of *Criticisms of a Hidden Man*]. Trans. and annotated by Peng Bingcheng 彭丙成. Ed. Chen Manming 陳滿銘. Taibei: Sanmin Shuju, 1998.

Wang Jia 王嘉. *Shiyiji* 拾遺記 [Record of gleaned remnants]. Vols. 1–8 of *Baibu congshu jicheng* 百部叢書集成, ser. 9, ed. Yan Yiping 嚴一萍. Taibei: Yiwen Yinshuguan, 1966.

———. *Shiyiji* 拾遺記 [Record of gleaned remnants]. Ed. Qi Zhiping 齊治平. Beijing: Zhonghua Shuju, 1981.

Wang Jiayou 王家佑 and Jie Ke 賈克. "Dong-Han Xinfan huaxiangzhuan shijing tushi" 東漢新繁畫像磚市井圖釋 [Explanation of the map of a marketplace on a brick relief of the Eastern Han dynasty, found at Xinfan]. In *Zhongguo gudai ditu ji*, ed. Cao Wanru et al., 1:18. Beijing: Wenwu Chubanshe, 1990–7.

Wang Qinjin 王勤金, Li Jiuhai 李久海, and Xu Liangyu 徐良玉. "Yangzhou chutu de Handai mingwen tongjing" 揚州出土的漢代銘文銅鏡 [Inscribed Han bronze mirrors unearthed from Yangzhou]. *Wenwu* (1985.10): 90–6.

Wang Shilun 王士倫. "Lidai jingming xuanlu" 歷代鏡銘選錄 [Record of selected mirror inscriptions from various dynasties]. In *Zhejiang chutu tongjing* 浙江出土銅鏡 [Bronze mirrors unearthed from Zhejiang]. Beijing: Wenwu Chubanshe, 1987.

Wang Shiren 王世仁. "Han Chang'an cheng nanjiao lizhi jianzhu (Datumen cun yizhi) yuanzhuang de tuice" 漢長安城南郊禮制建築(大土門村遺址)原狀的推測 [A hypothesis concerning the original appearance of the ritual structure in the southern suburbs of Han period Chang'an (Datumen village site)]. *Kaogu* (1963.9): 501–15.

Wang Shixiang 王世襄. "Dui xipi qiqi de zai renshi" 對犀皮漆器的再認識 [A new understanding of 'rhinoceros skin' lacquer]. *Wenwu* (1986.3): 25–7.

———. *Zhongguo gudai qiqi* 中國古代漆器 [Ancient Chinese lacquer]. Beijing: Wenwu Chubanshe, 1987.

———. "Zhongguo gudai qiqi gongyi" 中國古代漆器工藝 [Ancient Chinese lacquer-craft]. In vol. 8 of *Zhongguo meishu quanji: Gongyi meishu bian*. Beijing: Wenwu Chubanshe, 1989.

Wang Sili 王思禮. "Shandong Feicheng Han huaxiang mu diaocha" 山東肥城漢畫像墓調查 [Investigation of the Han pictorial tomb at Feicheng, Shandong]. *Wenwu cankao ziliao* (1958.4): 34–6.

Wang Xiantang 王獻唐. "Qi guo zhuqian de sange jieduan" 齊國鑄錢的三個階段 [Three stages in coin casting of the Qi state]. *Kaogu* (1963.11): 623–9.
Wang Xueli 王學理. *Qin Shihuang ling yanjiu* 秦始皇陵研究 [Research on Qin Shihuang's mausoleum]. Shanghai: Shanghai Renmin Chubanshe, 1994.
———. "Qindai jungong shengchan biaozhunhua de chubu kaocha" 秦代軍工生產標準化的初步考察 [Preliminary investigation into the standardization of Qin weapons production]. *Kaogu yu wenwu* (1987.5): 57–67.
Wang Yunwu 王雲五, ed. *Han liqi zhidu ji qita wuzhong* 漢禮器制度及其他五種 [The Han system of ritual vessels and five other varieties (of texts)]. Shanghai: Shangwu Yinshuguan, 1939.
Wang Zhenduo 王振鐸. "Handai yetie gufeng fengji de fuyuan" 漢代冶鐵鼓風風機的復原 [Reconstruction of the bellows of a Han period blast furnace]. *Wenwu* (1959.5): 43–4.
Wang Zhongshu 王仲殊. "Han Chang'an cheng kaogu gongzuo de chubu shouhuo" 漢長安城考古工作的初步收獲 [Preliminary results from the archaeological work at the Han period Chang'an City]. *Kaogu tongxun* (1957.5): 102–10.
———. "Han Chang'an cheng kaogu gongzuo shouhuo xuji" 漢長安城考古工作收獲續記 [Follow-up report on the results of archaeological work at the Han period Chang'an City]. *Kaogu tongxun* (1958.4): 23–32.
———. *Handai kaoguxue gaishuo* 漢代考古學概說 [General discussion of Han archaeology (*Han civilization*)]. Beijing: Zhonghua Shuju, 1984.
———. "Handai wuzhi wenhua lüeshuo" 漢代物質文化略說 [General sketch of Han material culture]. *Kaogu tongxun* (1956.1): 57–76.
———. "Zhongguo gudai ducheng gaishuo" 中國古代都城概說 [General discussion of ancient Chinese cities]. *Kaogu* (1982.5): 505–15.
Wei Zheng 魏徵. *Suishu* 隋書 [History of the Sui]. 6 vols. Beijing: Zhonghua Shuju, 1973.
Wen Yiduo 聞一多. *Tianwen shuzheng* 天問疏證 [Critical commentary on the *Heavenly Questions*]. Beijing: Sanlian Shudian, 1980.
Weng Fanggang 翁方綱. *Liang-Han jinshi ji* 兩漢金石記 [Record of inscriptions on stone from the two Han dynasties]. Vols. 12–19 of *Shike shiliao congshu* 石刻史料叢書, ser. A, ed. Yan Gengwang 嚴耕望. Taibei: Yiwen Yinshuguan, 1966.
Wenwu Bianji Weiyuanhui, ed. *Wenwu kaogu gongzuo shinian* 文物考古工作十年 [Ten years of cultural relics and archaeology]. Beijing: Wenwu Chubanshe, 1990.
Wu Kerong 武可榮. "Shixi Donghai Yinwan Han mu zengxiu de neirong yu gongyi" 試析東海尹灣漢墓繒繡的內容與工藝 [Test analysis of the subject matter and technology of the embroidered silk from the Han tomb at Yinwan, Donghai County]. *Wenwu* (1996.10): 64–7.
Wu Rongzeng 吳榮曾. "Qin de guanfu shougongye" 秦的官府手工業 [Qin state-run manufacturing]. In *Yunmeng Qin jian yanjiu* 雲夢秦簡研究 [Research on Qin bamboo slips from Yunmeng], ed. Zhonghua Shuju Bianjibu, 39–52. Beijing: Zhonghua Shuju, 1981.
———. "Xi-Han guqian zhong suojian de gongguan" 西漢骨簽中所見的工官 [Offices of Workmen seen on Western Han bone tags]. *Kaogu* (2000.9): 60–8.
Wu Wenqi 吳文祺. "Cong Shandong Han huaxiangshi tuxiang kan Handai shougongye" 從山東漢畫像石圖像看漢代手工業 [Looking at Han period manufacturing using scenes on pictorial stones from Shandong]. *Zhongyuan wenwu* (1991.3): 33–41.
Wu Xiaoqiang 吳小強. *Qin jian rishu jishi* 秦簡日書集釋 [Collected explanations of Qin almanacs found on bamboo slips]. Changsha: Yuelu Shushe, 2000.

Wu Zhenfeng 吳鎮烽. "Qin Jin liang sheng Dong-Han huaxiangshi tiji jishi" 秦晉兩省東漢畫像石題記集釋 [Transcription and explanation of the collected captions from Eastern Han pictorial stones from the two provinces of Qin and Jin]. *Kaogu yu wenwu* (2006.1): 53–69.

Wuwei Xian Bowuguan, ed. "Wuwei xinchu wangzhang zhaoling ce" 武威新出王仗詔令冊 [The newly discovered decree concerning kingly staffs from Wuwei]. In *Han jian yanjiu wenji* 漢簡研究文集 [Collected essays of research into Han bamboo slips], ed. Gansu Sheng Wenwu Gongzuodui and Gansu Sheng Bowuguan, 34–61. Lanzhou: Gansu Renmin Chubanshe, 1984.

Xia Nai 夏鼐. "Woguo gudai can, sang, sichou de lishi" 我國古代蠶桑絲綢的歷史 [Our country's ancient history of silkworms, mulberry trees, and silk]. *Kaogu* (1972.2): 12–27.

Xi'an Shi Wenwu Guanli Weiyuanhui, ed. "Xi'an Sanqiaozhen Gaoyaocun chutu de Xi-Han tongqi qun" 西安三橋鎮高窯村出土的西漢銅器群 [Group of Han period bronzes unearthed from Gaoyao Village, Sanqiaozhen, Xi'an City]. *Kaogu* (1963.2): 62–70.

Xiang Xinyang 向新陽 and Liu Keren 劉克任, eds. *Xijing zaji jiaozhu* 西京雜記校注 [Annotated critical edition of the *Miscellaneous Notes on the Western Capital*]. Shanghai: Shanghai Guji Chubanshe, 1991.

Xianyang Diqu Wenguanhui and Maoling Bowuguan, eds. "Shaanxi Maoling yihao wumingzhong yihao congzangkeng de fajue" 陝西茂陵一號無名冢一號從葬坑的發掘 [Excavation of accompanying pit no. 1 near unnamed tomb no. 1 at the Maoling complex in Shaanxi]. *Wenwu* (1982.9): 1–16.

Xiao Kangda 蕭亢達. "Yunmeng Shuihudi Qin mu qiqi zhenke mingji tanxi: Jian tan Qindai 'ting' 'shi' difang guanying shougongye" 雲夢睡虎地秦墓漆器針刻銘記探析:兼談秦代'亭''市'地方官營手工業 [Investigation into the needle-incised inscriptions on the lacquers from Qin tombs at Yunmeng, Shuihudi: Discussing the officially sponsored regional "neighborhood" and "marketplace" production of the Qin period]. *Jianghan kaogu* (1984.2): 67–72.

Xiao Tong 蕭統, comp. *Wen xuan* 文選 [Selections of refined literature]. Annotated by Li Shan 李善. 2 vols. Hong Kong: Shangwu Yinshuguan, 1973.

Xie Guihua 謝桂華. "Yinwan Han mu jiandu he Xi-Han difang xingzheng zhidu" 尹灣漢墓簡牘和西漢地方行政制度 [The bamboo slips and wooden boards from the Han tomb at Yinwan and the Western Han system of regional administration]. *Wenwu* (1997.1): 42–8.

Xin Lixiang 信立祥. *Handai huaxiangshi zonghe yanjiu* 漢代畫像石綜合研究 [Comprehensive research into Han period pictorial stones]. Beijing: Wenwu Chubanshe, 2000.

Xing Yitian 邢義田. "Yinwan Han mu mudu wenshu de mingcheng he xingzhi—Jiangsu Donghai Xian Yinwan Han mu chutu jiandu duji zhiyi" 尹灣漢墓木牘文書的名稱和性質—江蘇東海縣尹灣漢墓出土簡牘讀記之一 [The name and character of the documents on wooden boards from the Han tomb at Yinwan—reading notes on one of the boards unearthed from the Han tomb at Yinwan in Donghai County, Jiangsu]. *Dalu zazhi* 95 (1997.3): 1–13.

Xu Daoling 許道齡 and Liu Zhiping 劉致平. "Guanyu Xi'an xijiao faxian de Handai jianzhu yizhi shi mingtang huo biyong de taolun" 關於西安西郊發現的漢代建築遺址是明堂或辟雍的討論 [A discussion concerning whether the Han structure found in the western suburbs of Xi'an is the Bright Hall or the Circular Moat]. *Kaogu* (1959.4): 193–6.

Xu Shen 許慎. *Shuowen jiezi zhu* 說文解字注 [Annotated edition of *Explaining the Graphs and Analyzing the Characters*]. Ed. and annotated by Duan Yucai 段玉裁. Shanghai: Shanghai Guji Chubanshe, 1981.

Xu Tianlin 徐天麟. *Dong Han huiyao* 東漢會要 [Collected essentials of the Eastern Han]. Taibei: Shijie Shuju, 1960.

———. *Xi-Han huiyao* 西漢會要 [Collected essentials of the Western Han]. Shanghai: Shanghai Renmin Chubanshe, 1976.

Xuzhou Bowuguan, ed. "Jiangsu Xuzhou damiao Jin-Han huaxiangshi mu" 江蘇徐州大廟晉漢畫像石墓 [Jin and Han pictorial-stone tomb at Damiao in Xuzhou, Jiangsu]. *Wenwu* (2003.4): 61–70.

Yan Gengwang 嚴耕望. *Qin-Han difang xingzhi zhidu* 秦漢地方行政制度 [The Qin and Han systems of regional administration]. Vol. 1 of *Zhongguo difang xingzhi zhidu shi* 中國地方行政制度史 [History of Chinese regional administration]. Taibei: Institute of History and Philology, Academia Sinica, 1961.

Yan Kejun 嚴可均, comp. *Quan shanggu sandai Qin Han Sanguo Liuchao wen* 全上古三代秦漢三國六朝文 [Complete prose of the ancient past, the Three Dynasties, Qin, Han, Three Kingdoms, and Six Dynasties periods]. 4 vols. plus index. Beijing: Zhonghua Shuju, 1958.

Yang Cong 楊琮. "Henei gongguan de shezhi jiqi nuji shengchan niandai kao" 河內工官的設置及其弩機生產年代考 [Investigation into the establishment of the Henei Office of Workmen and the time period of its crossbow mechanism production]. *Wenwu* (1994.4): 60–4.

Yang Hong 楊泓. "Sanguo kaogu de xin faxian" 三國考古的新發現 [New discovery for Three Kingdom period archaeology]. *Wenwu* (1986.3): 16–24.

Yang Jiandong 楊建東. "Weishan chutu Dong Han Yonghe yuannian huaxiang shi" 微山出土東漢永和元年畫像石 [Eastern Han pictorial stone with a Yonghe 1 reign date unearthed in Weishan County]. *Zhongguo wenwu bao*, May 27, 1998.

Yang Jianhong 楊劍虹. "Cong Yunmeng Qin jian kan Qindai shougongye he shangye de ruogan wenti" 從雲夢秦簡看秦代手工業和商業的若干問題 [A few issues concerning manufacturing and commerce during the Qin period seen through the Qin bamboo slips from Yunmeng]. *Jianghan kaogu* (1989.2): 87–92.

———. "Qin-Han shiqi jiangnan de shougongye shengchan" 秦漢時期江南的手工業生產 [Qin and Han period manufacturing in the Jiangnan region]. *Jiangxi shifan daxue xuebao* (1988.3): 21–5.

Yang Kuan 楊寬. "Xi'an Chang'an buju jiegou de zai tantao" 西安長安佈局結構的再探討 [Another discussion of the layout and structure of the Han Chang'an city near Xi'an]. *Kaogu* (1989.4): 348–56.

———. *Zhanguo shi* 戰國史 [History of the Warring States]. 3d ed. Shanghai: Renmin Chubanshe, 1998.

Yang Shusen 陽樹森. "Chunqiu Zhanguo shidai jingji zhi yanjiu" 春秋戰國時代經濟之研究 [Economic research on the Spring and Autumn and Warring States periods]. *Zhongguo lishi xuehui shixue jikan* 8 (1976): 255–82.

Yang Yuan 陽遠. "Xi-Han yan tie gongguan de dili fenbu" 西漢鹽鐵工官的地理分佈 [Geographic distribution of the Western Han Salt and Iron Offices and Offices of Workmen]. *Xianggang zhongwen daxue, Zhongguo wenhua yanjiusuo xuebao* 9 (1978): 219–46.

Yangzhou Bowuguan, ed. "Jiangsu Hanjiang xian yaozhuang 102 hao Han mu" 江蘇邗江縣姚莊 102 號漢墓 [Han tomb 102 at Yaozhuang, Hanjiang County, Jiangsu]. *Kaogu* (2000.4): 50–65.

———, ed. "Jiangsu Hanjiang yaozhuang 101 hao Xi-Han mu" 江蘇邗江姚莊 101 號西漢墓 [Western Han tomb 101 at Yaozhuang, Hanjiang County, Jiangsu]. *Wenwu* (1988.11): 19–43.

———, ed. "Jiangsu yizheng xupu 101 hao Xi-Han mu" 江蘇儀征胥浦 101 號西漢墓 [Western Han tomb 101 at Xupu, Yizheng, Jiangsu]. *Wenwu* (1987.1): 1–19.

Yangzhou Bowuguan and Hanjiang Wenhuaguan, eds. "Yangzhou Hanjiang xian huchang Han mu" 揚州邗江縣胡場漢墓 [Han tomb at Huchang, Hanjiang County, Jiangsu]. *Wenwu* (1980.3): 1–10.

Yangzhou Bowuguan and Hanjiang Xian Tushuguan, eds. "Jiangsu Hanjiang xian yangshouxiang baonüdun Xin Mang mu" 江蘇邗江縣楊壽鄉寶女墩新莽墓 [Wang Mang period tomb at Baonüdun, Yangshouxiang, Hanjiang County, Jiangsu]. *Wenwu* (1991.1): 39–61.

Yao Zhenzong 姚振宗, comp. *Qilüe bielu yiwen* 七略別錄佚文 [Reconstructed text of *The Alternative Recording of the Seven Bibliographic Categories*]. In *Xuxiu siku quanshu* 續修四庫全書 [Continuation of the complete book of the four treasuries]. Shanghai: Guji Chubanshe, 1995.

Ye Xiaoyan 葉小燕. "Xi-Han shiqi de huangjin" 西漢時期的黃金 [Gold during the Western Han period]. In *Qingzhu Su Bingi kaogu wushiwunian lunwenji* 慶祝蘇秉琦考古五十五年論文集 [Collected papers celebrating Su Bingqi's fifty-five years in archaeology], ed. Su Bingi Kaogu Wushiwunian Lunwenji Bianjizu, 473–81. Beijing: Wenwu Chubanshe, 1989.

Ye Zhaohan 葉照涵. "Handai shike yetie gufeng lutu" 漢代石刻冶鐵鼓風爐圖 [The illustration of a blast furnace on a Han period pictorial stone carving]. *Wenwu* (1959.1): 20–1.

Yin Xiande 尹顯德. "Sichuan Qingzhou chutu jiunian Lü Buwei ji" 四川青州出土九年呂不韋戟 [The ninth-year Lü Buwei halberd unearthed from Qingzhou, Sichuan]. *Kaogu* (1991.1): 16–7, 15.

Yin Yun 殷芸. *Xiaoshuo* 小說 [Minor tales]. Shanghai: Guji Chubanshe, 1984.

Yingjing Gumu Fajue Xiaozu, ed. "Sichuan Yingjing guchengping Qin-Han muzang" 四川滎經古城坪秦漢墓葬 [Qin and Han period burials from Guchengping, Yingjing County, Sichuan]. *Wenwu ziliao congkan* 4 (1981): 70–4.

Yu Haoliang 于豪亮. "Sichuan fuling de Qinshihuang ershiliu nian tong ge" 四川涪陵的秦始皇二十六年銅戈 [The bronze halberd made in the twenty-sixth year of the First Emperor of Qin unearthed from Fuling, Sichuan]. *Kaogu* (1976.1): 22–3.

Yu Huaqing 余華青. "Lüeshu Qin-Han shiqi de zhou che zhizao ye" 略述秦漢時期的舟車制造業 [A brief description of boat and vehicle construction during the Qin and Han periods]. *Qinghai shehui kexue* (1985.1): 92–7.

———. "Qin-Han qiqi jiage kaobian" 秦漢漆器價格考辨 [Determination of the price of lacquer during the Qin and Han periods]. *Zhongguo shi yanjiu* (1984.4): 97–104.

Yu Weichao 俞偉超. "Gushi fenqi wenti de kaoguxue guancha" 古史分期問題的考古學觀察 [Archaeological investigation into the problem of historical periodization]. In *Xian-Qin liang-Han kaoguxue lunji* 先秦兩漢考古學論集 [Collected writings on pre-Qin, Qin, and Han archaeology]. Beijing: Wenwu Chubanshe, 1985.

Yu Weichao 俞偉超 and Li Jiahao 李家浩. "Mawangdui yihao mu chutu qiqi zhidi zhu wenti" 馬王堆一號墓出土漆器制地諸問題 [Several problems regarding the place of fabrication of the lacquers unearthed from Mawangdui tomb 1]. In *Xian-Qin liang-Han kaoguxue lunji* 先秦兩漢考古學論集 [Collected writings on pre-Qin, Qin, and Han archaeology]. Beijing: Wenwu Chubanshe, 1985.

———. "Qin-Han de 'ting,' 'shi,' taowen" 秦漢的'亭','市'陶文 [The Qin and Han period pottery inscriptions of "neighborhood" and "market"]. In *Xian-Qin liang-Han kaoguxue lunji* 先秦兩漢考古學論集. Beijing: Wenwu Chubanshe, 1985.

Yuan Anzhi 員安志. "Tan 'Yangxin Jia' tongqi" 談'陽信家'銅器 [Discussing the House of Yangxin bronzes]. *Wenwu* (1982.9): 18–20.

Yuan Zhongyi 袁仲一. *Qin bingmayong keng* 秦兵馬俑坑 [Pits of Qin terracotta warriors and horses]. Beijing: Wenwu Chubanshe, 2003.

———. "Qin ling bingmayong de zuozhe" 秦陵兵馬俑的作者 [The makers of the terracotta army in the Qin necropolis]. *Wenbo* (1986.4): 52–62.

———. "Qin minying zhitao zuofang de taowen" 秦民營製陶作坊的陶文 [Pottery inscriptions from privately run Qin workshops]. *Kaogu yu wenwu* (1981.1): 95–101.

———, ed. *Qin Shihuang bingmayong bowuguan* 秦始皇兵馬俑博物館 [Museum of the terracotta army of Qin Shihuang]. Beijing: Wenwu Chubanshe, 1999.

———. "Qin zhongyang duzao de bingqi keci zongshu" 秦中央督造的兵器刻辭綜述 [Comprehensive discussion of the inscriptions on Qin weapons made under government-supervised production]. *Kaogu yu wenwu* (1984.5): 101–12, 100.

Yuan Zhongyi 袁仲一 and Cheng Xuehua 程學華. "Qin Shihuang ling xice xingtu mudi chutu de wawen" 秦始皇陵西側刑徒墓地出土的瓦文 [Pottery inscriptions unearthed from the convict cemetery west of Qin Shihuang's mausoleum]. In *Zhongguo kaogu xuehui dierci nianhui lunwenji* 中國考古學會第二次年會論文集 [Collected papers from the second annual conference of the Society for Chinese Archaeology], ed. Zhongguo Kaogu Xuehui, 186–95. Beijing: Wenwu Chubanshe, 1980.

———. "Qindai zhongyang guanshu zhitaoye de taowen" 秦代中央官署製陶業的陶文 [Qin period ceramic inscriptions from government-run pottery production]. *Kaogu yu wenwu* (1980.3): 83–92.

Yue Lianjian 岳連建. "Xi'an beijiao Zhanguo wanqi zhutong gongjiang mu chulun" 西安北郊戰國晚期鑄銅工匠墓初論 [Preliminary discussion of the late Warring States era bronze caster's tomb from the northern suburbs of Xi'an]. *Kaogu yu wenwu* (supplement), 2002.

Yunmeng Shuihudi Qin Mu Bianxiezu, ed. *Yunmeng Shuihudi Qin mu* 雲夢睡虎地秦墓 [Qin tombs at Shuihudi, Yunmeng]. Beijing: Wenwu Chubanshe, 1981.

Zang Lihe 臧勵龢, ed. *Zhongguo renming da cidian* 中國人名大辭典 [Great biographical dictionary of Chinese names]. Shanghai: Shangwu Yinshuguan, 1934.

Zeng Yong 曾庸. "Handai de shougongye" 漢代的手工業 [Han period manufacturing]. *Lishi jiaoxue* (1957.7): 19–22.

Zhang Bingquan 張秉權. *Yinxu wenzi bingbian* 殷墟文字丙編 [Third fascicle of inscriptions from the ruins of Yin]. In *Xiaotun* 小屯, ser. 2. Taibei: Institute of History and Philology, Academia Sinica, 1957–72.

Zhang Chuanxi 長傳璽, ed. *Zhanguo Qin-Han shi lunwen suoyin 1900–1980* 戰國秦漢史論文索引 1900–1980 [Index to historical essays on the Warring States, Qin, and Han periods, 1900–1980]. Beijing: Beijing Daxue Chubanshe, 1983.

———. *Zhanguo Qin-Han shi lunzhu suoyin xubian* 戰國秦漢史論著索引續编: 論文 1981–1990 專著 1900–1990 [Index to historical essays and books on the Warring States, Qin,

and Han periods (continuation): Essays, 1981–1990, specialist monographs, 1900–1990]. Beijing: Beijing Daxue Chubanshe, 1992.
Zhang Heng 張衡. *Zhang Heng shiwen ji jiaozhu* 張衡詩文集校注 [Annotated critical edition of the collected poetry and prose of Zhang Heng]. Ed. Zhang Zhenze 張震澤. Shanghai: Guji Chubanshe, 1986.
Zhang Jianguo 張建國. "Shixi Han chu 'yuefa san zhang' de falü xiaoli—jiantan 'Ernian Lüling' yu Xiao He de guanxi" 試析漢初"約法三章"的法律效力—兼談"二年律令"與蕭何的關係 [A trial analysis of the legal effectiveness of the "reforming the laws in three chapters" at the beginning of the Han—along with a discussion of the relationship between the "Statutes and Ordinances of the Second Year" and Xiao He]. *Faxue yanjiu* 18, no. 1 (1996): 154–60.
Zhang Jingguo 張敬國, Li Zhongda 李仲達, and Hua Jueming 華覺明. "Guichi Dong-Zhou tongding de fenxi yanjiu" 貴池東周銅錠的分析研究 [Analysis of the Eastern Zhou copper ingots from Guichi]. *Ziran kexueshi yanjiu* 4, no. 2 (1985): 168–71.
Zhang Jiuling 張九齡 et al., eds. *Da Tang liudian* 大唐六典 [Six statutes of the Great Tang]. Taibei: Wenhai Chubanshe, 1962.
Zhang Limeng 張理萌. "Handai qiqi chutan" 漢代漆器初探 [Preliminary inquiry into Han period lacquer]. *Gugong bowuyuan yuankan* (1989.3): 24–31.
Zhang Yanyuan 張顏遠. *Lidai minghua ji* 歷代名畫記 [Record of the famous painters of successive dynasties]. Beijing: Renmin Meishu Chubanshe, 1963.
Zhang Yonglu 張永祿, ed. *Handai Chang'an cidian* 漢代長安詞典 [Dictionary of Han period Chang'an]. Xi'an: Shaanxi Renmin Chubanshe, 1993.
Zhang Zhenglang 張政烺. "Handai de tieguan tu" 漢代的鐵官徒 [Convict laborers at the Iron Monopoly Offices during the Han]. *Lishi jiaoxue* (1951.1): 17–22.
Zhang Zhenze 張震澤, ed. *Yang Xiong ji jiaozhu* 揚雄集校注 [Annotated critical edition of Yang Xiong's collected writings]. Shanghai: Shanghai Guji Chubanshe, 1993.
Zhang Zigao 張子高 and Yang Gen 楊根. "Cong Houma taofan he xinglong tiefan kan Zhanguo shidai de yezhu jishu" 從候馬陶範和興隆鐵範看戰國時代的冶鑄技術 [Warring States period casting technology seen from the iron molds from Xinglong and the ceramic molds from Houma]. *Wenwu* (1973.6): 62–5.
Zhang Zongxiang 張宗祥, ed. *Jiaozheng sanfu huangtu* 校正三輔黃圖 [Critical edition of the *Yellow Plan of the Three Capital Districts*]. Shanghai: Gudian Wenxue Chubanshe, 1958.
Zhangjiashan 247 Hao Mu Zhujian Zhengli Xiaozu, ed. "Jiangling Zhangjiashan Han jian gaishu" 江陵張家山漢簡概述 [General description of the Han bamboo slips from the site of Zhangjiashan at Jiangling]. *Wenwu* (1985.1): 9–15.
———, ed. *Zhangjiashan Han mu zhujian* 張家山漢墓竹簡 [Bamboo slips from the Han tomb at Zhangjiashan (tomb 247)]. Beijing: Wenwu Chubanshe, 2001.
Zhao Bangyan 趙邦彥. "Jiuzimu kao" 九子母攷 [Investigation into the "Mother of Nine Sons"]. *Zhongyang yanjiuyuan, Lishi yuyan yanjiusuo jikan*, 2, no. 3 (1931): 261–74.
Zhao Huacheng 趙化成 and Gao Chongwen 高崇文. *Qin-Han kaogu* 秦漢考古 [Qin and Han archaeology]. Beijing: Wenwu Chubanshe, 2002.
Zhao Mingcheng 趙明成. *Jinshi lu* 金石錄 [Record of inscriptions on metal and stone]. Vols. 7–11 of *Shike shiliao congshu* 石刻史料叢書 [Collection of historical data from stone inscriptions], ser. B, ed. Yan Gengwang 嚴耕望. Taibei: Yiwen Yinshuguan, 1966.

Zhao Qingyun 趙青云 et al., eds. “Gongxian tieshenggou Handai yezhu yizhi zai tantao” 鞏縣鐵生溝漢代冶鑄遺址再探討 [A reinvestigation of the Han period iron smelting and casting site at Tieshenggou in Gong County, Henan]. *Kaogu xuebao* (1985.2): 157–83.
Zhao Ye 趙曄. *Wu-Yue chunqiu* 吳越春秋 [The chronicle of Wu and Yue]. Taibei: Shijie Shuju, 1962.
Zheng Shaozong 鄭紹宗. “Hebei Sheng faxian Xi-Han jinbing he Yuandai yinding” 河北省發現西漢金餅和元代銀錠 [Yuan era silver ingots and Former Han period gold ingots discovered in Hebei]. *Wenwu* (1981.4): 91–2.
———. “Hebei Xingtang faxian de liangjian Handai rongqi” 河北行唐發現的兩件漢代容器 [Two Han period containers found at Xingtang, Hebei]. *Wenwu* (1976.12): 89.
———. *Mancheng Han mu* 滿城漢墓 [Han tombs at Mancheng]. Beijing: Wenwu Chubanshe, 2003.
Zheng Shi 鄭實. “Sefu kao” 嗇夫考 [Study of the office of overseer]. *Wenwu* (1978.2): 55–7.
Zhengzhou Shi Bowuguan, ed. “Zhengzhou Guxingzhen Handai yetie yizhi fajue jianbao” 鄭州古滎鎮漢代冶鐵遺址發掘簡告 [Preliminary excavation report of the Han period iron-smelting site at Guxingzhen near Zhengzhou]. *Wenwu* (1978.2): 28–47, 27.
Zhongguo Huaxiangshi Quanji Bianji Weiyuanhui, ed. *Zhongguo huaxiangshi quanji* 中國畫像石全集 [Complete collection of Chinese pictorial stones]. 8 vols. Ji’nan: Shandong Meishu Chubanshe, 2000.
Zhongguo Kexueyuan Kaogu Yanjiusuo Luoyang Gongzuodui, ed. “Dong Han Luoyang cheng nanjiao de xingtu mudi” 東漢洛陽城南郊的刑徒墓地 [Convict laborer cemetery in the southern suburbs of Eastern Han Luoyang]. *Kaogu* (1972.4): 2–19.
Zhongguo Qingtongqi Quanji Bianji Weiyuanhui, ed. *Zhongguo qingtongqi quanji* 中國青銅器全集 [Complete collection of Chinese bronzes]. 16 vols. Beijing: Wenwu Chubanshe, 1993–8.
Zhongguo Qiqi Quanji Bianji Weiyuanhui, ed. *Zhongguo qiqi quanji* 中國漆器全集 [Complete collection of Chinese lacquer]. 6 vols. to date. Fuzhou: Fujian Meishu Chubanshe, 1997–.
Zhongguo Shehui Kexueyuan Kaogu Yanjiusuo, ed. *Xin Zhongguo de kaogu faxian he yanjiu* 新中國的考古發現和研究 [Archaeological discoveries and research in new China]. Beijing: Wenwu Chubanshe, 1984.
———. *Han Chang’an cheng Weiyang Gong 1980–1989 nian kaogu fajue baogao* 漢長安城未央宮1980–1989年考古發掘報告 [Excavation report of the 1980–1989 seasons at the Weiyang Palace of Han period Chang’an City]. 2 vols. Beijing: Zhongguo Da Baike Quanshu, 1996.
Zhongguo Shehui Kexueyuan Kaogu Yanjiusuo and Hebei Sheng Wenwu Guanlichu, eds. *Mancheng Han mu fajue baogao* 滿城漢墓發掘報告 [Excavation report of the Han tombs at Mancheng]. 2 vols. Beijing: Wenwu Chubanshe, 1980.
Zhongguo Shehui Kexueyuan Kaogu Yanjiusuo Han Chang’an Cheng Gongzuodui, ed. “Han Chang’an cheng Bei Gong de tantan ji qi nanmian zhuanwa yao de fajue” 漢長安城北宮的勘探及其南面磚瓦窯的發掘 [Survey of the Northern Palace of Han period Chang’an City and the excavation of the brick and tile kiln at its southern edge]. *Kaogu* (1996.10): 23–32.
———, ed. “Han Chang’an cheng Weiyang Gong xi’nan jiaolou yizhi fajue jianbao” 漢長安

城未央宮西南角樓遺址發掘簡報 [Preliminary excavation report of the turret tower site at the southwestern corner of the Weiyang Palace of Han period Chang'an City]. *Kaogu* (1996.3): 19–27.
Zhongguo Shehui Kexueyuan Kaogu Yanjiusuo Hancheng Gongzuodui, ed. "Han Chang'an cheng faxian Xi-Han yaocang tongqi" 漢長安城發現西漢窯藏銅器 [Former Han period bronze hoard found in kiln of Chang'an City]. *Kaogu* (1985.5): 400–3.
———. "Han Chang'an cheng 2–8 hao yaozhi fajue jianbao" 漢長安城2–8號窯址發掘簡報 [Preliminary excavation report of kiln sites 2–8 at the Han period Chang'an City]. *Kaogu* (1992.2): 138–42.
———. "Han Chang'an cheng 23–27 hao yaozhi fajue jianbao" 漢長安城23–27號窯址發掘簡報 [Preliminary excavation report of kiln sites 23–27 at the Han period Chang'an City]. *Kaogu* (1994.11): 986–95.
———. "Han Chang'an cheng Weiyang Gong dierhao yizhi fajue jianbao" 漢長安城未央宮第二號遺址發掘簡報 [Preliminary excavation report of site 2 at the Weiyang Palace within Han period Chang'an City]. *Kaogu* (1992.8): 724–32.
———. "Han Chang'an cheng Weiyang Gong disan jianzhu yizhi fajue jianbao" 漢長安城未央宮第三建築遺址發掘簡報 [Preliminary excavation report of structure 3 at the Weiyang Palace of the Han period Chang'an City]. *Kaogu* (1989.1): 33–43, 19.
———. "Han Chang'an cheng Weiyang Gong disihao jianzhu fajue jianbao" 漢長安城未央宮第四號建築發掘簡報 [Preliminary excavation report of structure 4 at the Weiyang Palace within Han period Chang'an City]. *Kaogu* (1993.11): 1002–11.
———. "Han Chang'an cheng wuku yizhi fajue de chubu shouhuo" 漢長安城武庫遺址發掘的初步收獲 [Preliminary results from the excavation of the armory site of Han period Chang'an City]. *Kaogu* (1978.4): 261–9.
———. "Han Chang'an cheng yihao yaozhi fajue jianbao" 漢長安城一號窯址發掘簡報 [Preliminary excavation report of kiln site 1 at the Han period Chang'an City]. *Kaogu* (1991.1): 18–22.
———. "1992 nian Han Chang'an cheng yezhu yizhi fajue jianbao" 1992 年漢長安城冶鑄遺址發掘簡報 [Preliminary report of the 1992 excavation of the casting site at Han period Chang'an City]. *Kaogu* (1995.9): 792–807.
———. "1996 nian Han Chang'an cheng yezhu yizhi fajue jianbao" 1996 年漢長安城冶鑄遺址發掘簡報 [Preliminary report of the 1996 excavation of the casting site at Han period Chang'an City]. *Kaogu* (1997.7): 5–12.
Zhongguo Shehui Kexueyuan Kaogu Yanjiusuo Hanchengdui, ed. "Han Chang'an cheng yaozhi fajue baogao" 漢長安城窯址發掘報告 [Excavation report of the kiln sites of Han period Chang'an City]. *Kaogu xuebao* (1994.1): 99–129.
Zhongguo Wenwu Jinghua Bianji Weiyuanhui, ed. *Zhongguo wenwu jinghua* 中國文物精華 [The cream of Chinese cultural relics]. Beijing: Wenwu Chubanshe, 1990.
———. *Zhongguo wenwu jinghua* 中國文物精華 [The cream of Chinese cultural relics]. Beijing: Wenwu Chubanshe, 1997.
Zhonghua Shuju Bianjibu, ed. *Zhuzi jicheng* 諸子集成 [Compilation of the writings of the various philosophers]. 8 vols. Beijing: Zhonghua Shuju, 1954.
Zhongwen Da Cidian Bianzuan Weiyuanhui, ed. *Zhongwen da cidian* 中文大辭典 [Encyclopedic dictionary of the Chinese language]. 4th ed. 10 vols. Taibei: Huagang Chuban Youxian Gongsi, 1979.

Zhou Xiaolu 周曉陸 and Lu Dongzhi 路東之, eds. *Qin fengni ji* 秦封泥集 [Collection of Qin sealing clays]. Xi'an: San Qin Chubanshe, 2000.
Zhou Xiaolu 周曉陸, Lu Dongzhi 路東之, and Pang Rui 龐睿. "Qindai fengni de zhongda faxian: Meng Zhai cang Qin fengni de chubu yanjiu" 秦代封泥的重大發現：夢齊藏秦封泥的初步研究 [Major discovery of Qin period sealing clays: Preliminary research into the Qin sealing clays kept by Mengzhai]. *Kaogu yu wenwu* (1997.1): 33–47.
Zhou Yimou 周一謀 and Xiao Zuotao 蕭左桃, eds. *Mawangdui yishu kaozhu* 馬王堆醫書考注 [An annotated study of the medical manuscripts from Mawangdui]. Tianjin: Tianjin Kexue Jishu Chubanshe, 1988.
Zhu Xilu 朱錫祿. *Jiaxiang Han huaxiangshi* 嘉祥漢畫像石 [Han pictorial stones from Jiaxiang County, Shandong]. Ji'nan: Shandong Meishu Chubanshe, 1992.
———. *Wushi ci Han huaxianshi* 武氏祠漢畫像石 [Han pictorial stones from the Wu family shrines]. Ji'nan: Shandong Meishu Chubanshe, 1986.
Zhu Xilu 朱錫祿 and Jiaxiang Xian Wenguansuo, eds. "Jiaxiang Wulaowa faxian yipi Han huaxiangshi" 嘉祥五老洼發現一批漢畫像石 [A group of Han pictorial stones discovered at Wulaowa, Jiaxiang County]. *Wenwu* (1982.5): 71–8.
Zhuang Huiming 庄揮明. "Handai guyong laodongzhe shenfen tedian de zai tantao" 漢代雇傭勞動者身分特點的再探討 [Another inquiry into the special features of the social status of hired laborers during the Han period]. *Zhongguo shehui jingjishi yanjiu* (1990.10): 1–8.
Zhucheng Xian Bowuguan, ed. "Shandong Zhucheng Han mu huaxiangshi" 山東諸城漢墓畫像石 [Pictorial stones from the Han tomb at Zhucheng, Shandong]. *Wenwu* (1981.10): 14–21.
Zi Xi 梓溪. "Tan jizhong guqiwu de fan" 談幾種古器物的範 [Discussion of molds for several types of ancient objects]. *Wenwu cankao ziliao* (1957.8): 45–8.
Zuo Decheng 左德承, ed. *Yunmeng Shuihudi chutu Qin-Han qiqi tulu* 雲夢睡虎地出土秦漢漆器圖錄 [Catalog of Qin and Han lacquers unearthed from Shuihudi, Yunmeng]. Wuhan: Hubei Meishu Chubanshe, 1986.
Zuo Ming 作銘. "Zuijin Changsha chutu Lü Buwei ge de mingwen" 最近長沙出土呂不韋戈的銘文 [The inscription on the Lü Buwei halberd recently unearthed at Changsha]. *Kaogu* (1959.9): 458.

WORKS IN JAPANESE

Adachi Kiroku 足立喜六. *Chōan shiseki no kenkyū* 長安史跡の研究 [Research into the historic site of Chang'an]. Tokyo: Tōyō Bunko, 1933.
Chōsen Koseki Kenkyūkai, ed. *Rakurō Ō Kō bo* 楽浪王光墓 [Tomb of Wang Guang at Lelang]. Keijō [Seoul]: Chōsen Koseki Kenkyūkai, 1935.
———, ed. *Rakurō saikyō tsuka* 楽浪彩篋塚 [The tomb of the painted basket at Lelang]. Kyoto: Benridō, 1934.
Fukushuku Takao 福宿孝夫. "Kandai no shikkimei ni kansuru kōsatsu" 漢代の漆器銘に関する考察 [An investigation into Han period lacquer inscriptions]. *Miyazaki daigaku kyōiku gakubu kiyō* 74, no. 1 (1993): 23–48.
Gao Min 高敏. "Shin Kan jidai no kanshi shukōgyō" 秦漢時代の官私手工業 [State-sponsored and private handicraft production during the Qin and Han periods]. *Chūgoku* 4 (1989): 103–22.

Hamaguchi Shigekuni 浜口重国. *Shin Kan Zui Tō shi no kenkyū* 秦漢随唐史の研究 [Research into Qin, Han, Sui, and Tang history]. Tokyo: Tōkyō Daigaku Shuppankai, 1966.

Harada Yoshito 原田淑人. "Futatabi Rakurō shutsudo shikki meibunchū no shūji ni tsuite narabi ni rō no ji ni tsuite" 再び楽浪出土漆器銘文中の洀字に就いて並びに牢の字に就いて [Once again, concerning the "*zhou*-artisan" seen in lacquer inscriptions unearthed from Lelang, and also the "lao" character]. *Shigaku zasshi* 38, no. 6 (1927): 25–8.

———. "Rakurō shutsudo shikki meibunchū ni miyuru shūkō ni tsuite" 楽浪出土漆器銘文中見ゆる洀工に就いて [Concerning the "*zhou*-artisan" seen in lacquer inscriptions unearthed from Lelang]. *Shigaku zasshi* 37, no. 8 (1926): 67–70.

———. "Shina hai no kikei to yōto to ni tsuite" 支那杯の器形と用途とに就いて [The form and function of the cup in China]. In *Tōa kobunka kenkyū* 東亜古文化研究 [Research in ancient East Asian culture], 469–75. Tokyo: Zauhō Kankōkai, 1940.

———. "Shūkan kōkōki no seikaku to sono seisaku nendai to ni tsuite" 周官考工記の性格とその年代とについて [The dating and character of the *Record of the Scrutiny of Crafts* found in the *Ritual System of the Zhou*]. In *Tōa kobunka setsuen* 東亜古文化説苑 [Discussion of ancient East Asian culture], 240–52. Tokyo: Harada Yoshito Sensei Beiju Kinenkai, 1973.

Harada Yoshito 原田淑人 and Tazawa Kingo 田沢金吾. *Rakurō* 楽浪 [Lelang: The tomb of Wang Xu]. Tokyo: Tōkō-shoin, 1930.

Hayashi Minao 林巳奈夫, ed. *Kandai no bunbutsu* 漢代の文物 [Han period cultural relics]. Kyoto: Kyōto Daigaku Jinbun Kagaku Kenkyūjo, 1976.

Huang Xiaofen 黄曉芬. "Kanbo to Kanbo kenkyū" 漢墓と漢墓研究 [Han tombs and Han tomb research]. *Kodai bunka* 49, no. 7 (1997): 1–19.

Ikeda Yūichi 池田雄一 ed. *Sōgensho—Chūgoku kodai no saiban kiroku* 奏讞書—中國古代の裁判記錄 [*Book of Submitted Doubtful Cases*—a record of judicial process from ancient China]. Tokyo: Tōsui Shobō, 2002.

Kageyama Tsuyoshi 影山剛. *Chūgoku kodai no shukōgyō to senbaisei* 中国古代の手工業と専売制 [Ancient Chinese manufacturing and monopolies]. Tokyo: Tōkyō Daigaku Shuppankai, 1984.

———. "Chūgoku kodai no shōgyō to shōnin" 中国古代の商業と商人 [Merchants and commerce in ancient China]. In *Kodaishi kōza* 古代史講座 [Seminar in ancient history], vol. 9. Tokyo: Gakuseisha, 1963.

Kamada Shigeo 鎌田重雄. "Kandai gunkoku no jōkei" 漢代郡国の上計 [The forwarding of accounts in Han period commanderies and princedoms]. In *Kandai shi kenkyū* 漢代史研究 [Han history research]. Tokyo: Kawata Shobō, 1949.

Katō Shigeru 加藤繁. "Kandai ni okeru kokka zaisei to teishitsu zaisei to no kubetsu" 漢代に於ける国家財政と帝室財政との区別 [The differentiation between the financial administration of the imperial house and the state finances during the Han period]. In *Shina keizaishi kōshō* 支那経済史考証, 1:35–156. Tokyo: Tōyō Bunko, 1952–3.

———. "Senshin no chūzō kahei ni tsuite" 先秦の鋳造貨幣に就いて [Pre-Qin coin casting]. In *Shina keizaishi kōshō* 支那経済史考証, 2:733–58. Tokyo: Tōyō Bunko, 1952–3.

———. *Shina keizaishi kōshō* 支那経済史考証 [Investigation of Chinese economic history]. 2 vols. Tokyo: Tōyō Bunko, 1952–3.

Kayamoto Tojin 榧本杜人 and Machida Akira 町田章. "Kandai kinenmei shikki shūsei" 漢

代紀年銘漆器聚成 [Collection of dated Han lacquer inscriptions]. In *Rakurō Kanbo* 楽浪漢墓 [Han tombs at Lelang], ed. Rakurō Kanbo Kankōkai, 96–122. Nara: Rakurō Kanbo Kankōkai, 1974.
Kudō Motoo 工藤元男. "Suikochi Shinbo chikkan ni mieru dainai to shōnai" 睡虎地秦墓竹簡に見える大内と少内 [The terms *danei* and *shaonei* seen in the bamboo slips from the Qin tomb at Shuihudi]. *Shikan* 105 (1981): 19–34.
Kusuyama S. 楠山修作 "Kandai ni okeru kokka zaisei ni tsuite" 漢代における国家財政について [Government fiscal administration during the Han]. *Shirin* 69, no. 3 (1986): 106–22.
Kyōto Kokuritsu Hakubutsukan, ed. *Moriya kōzō shūshū hōkaku kiku shijin kyō zuroku* 守屋孝蔵蒐集方格規矩四神鏡図録 [TLV and directional-animal mirrors from the Moriya Kōzō collection]. Kyoto: Kyōto Kokuritsu Hakubutsukan, 1969.
Machida Akira 町田章. "Shikki" 漆器 [Lacquer]. In *Kandai no bijutsu* 漢代の美術 [Han art], ed. Ōsaka Shiritsu Bijutsukan, 211–24. Tokyo: Heibonsha, 1975.
Masuda Koh, ed. *Kenkyusha's New Japanese-English Dictionary.* 4th ed. Tokyo: Kenkyūsha, [1974].
Matsumaru Michio 松丸道雄 and Takashima Ken'ichi 高島謙一, eds. *Kōkotsu moji jishaku sōran* 甲骨文字字釈綜覧 [Comprehensive catalog of oracle-bone character transcriptions and interpretations]. Tokyo: Tōkyō Daigaku Tōyō Bunka Kenkyūjo, 1993.
Matsuzaki Tsuneko 松崎つね子. "Shikki rakuin moji ni miru Shin Kan kyūshitsu kōgei" 漆器烙 印文字に見る秦漢髹漆工芸 [Qin and Han lacquer craft as seen through branded inscriptions on lacquer vessels]. In *Chūgoku kodai no kokka to minshū* 中国古代の国家と民衆 [People and state of ancient China], ed. Chūgoku kodai no kokka to minshū Henshu Iinkai, 93–109. Tokyo: Kyūko Shoin, 1995.
Miyake Kiyoshi. 宮宅潔. "Chōkazan Kan kan (ninen ritsurei) kaidai" 張家山漢簡《二年律令》解題 [Bibliographic notes on the "Statutes and Ordinances of the Second Year" from the Han bamboo strips from Zhangjiashan]. *Tōhō gakuhō* 76 (2004): 209–20.
———. "Shin-Kan jidai no saiban seido" 秦漢時代の裁判制度 [Judicial process during the Qin and Han periods]. *Shirin* 81, no. 2 (March 1988): 35–68.
Momiyama Akira 籾山明. "Shutsudo moji shiryō nōto" 出土文字資料ノート [Notes on excavated inscriptional data]. *Koshi shunjū* 6 (1989): 69–80.
Morohashi Tetsuji 諸橋轍次. *Dai Kan-Wa jiten* 大漢和辞典 [Great Chinese-Japanese dictionary]. 13 vols. Tokyo: Taishūkan, 1955–60.
Nagahiro Toshio 長広敏雄, ed. *Kandai gazō no kenkyū* 漢代画像の研究 [Research on Han period pictorial images]. Tokyo: Chūō Kōron Bijutsu Shuppan, 1965.
Nagata Hidemasa 永田英正. *Kandai sekkoku shūsei* 漢代石刻集成 [Collection of Han period inscriptions on stone]. 2 vols. Kyoto: Dōhōsha, 1994.
Naitō Konan 内藤湖南. "Futatabi Rakurō shutsudo no shikki meibun ni tsuite" 再び楽浪出土の漆器銘文に就て [Once again, concerning inscriptions on lacquers unearthed from the Lelang site]. In *Naitō Konan zenshū* 内藤湖南全集, vol. 7. Tokyo: Chikuma Shobō, 1969. (Originally published 1926.)
———. "Rakurō iseki shutsudo shikki no meibun" 楽浪遺跡出土漆器の銘文 [Inscriptions on lacquers unearthed from the Lelang site]. In *Naitō Konan zenshū* 内藤湖南全集 [Complete collection of the writings of Naitō Konan], vol. 7. Tokyo: Chikuma Shobō, 1969. (Originally published 1926.)

———. "Shina kaigashi kōwa" 支那絵画史講話 [Discussion of the history of Chinese painting]. In *Naitō Konan zenshū* 内藤湖南全集, vol. 13. Tokyo: Chikuma Shobō, 1969.

Nakayama Shigeru 仲山茂. "Kandai no enshi" 漢代の掾史 [The office of bureau clerk during the Han]. *Shirin* 81, no. 4 (1998): 67–100.

Ōba Osamu 大庭修. "Kan no shokufu" 漢の嗇夫 [The office of overseer during the Han]. *Tōyōshi kenkyū* 14, nos. 1–2 (1955): 61–80.

Okazaki Takashi 岡崎敬. *Tōzai kōshō no kōkogaku* 東西交渉の考古学 [Archaeology of East-West interactions]. Tokyo: Heibonsha, 1973.

Ōkushi Atsuhiro 大櫛敦弘. "Kandai no tetsu senbai to tekki seisan" 漢代の鉄専売と鉄器生産 [Han period iron monopoly and iron production]. *Tōhō gaku* 78 (1989): 29–40.

Ōsaka Shiritsu Bijutsukan and Yomiuri Shinbun Ōsaka Honsha, eds. *Yomigaeru Kan Ōchō: 2000-nen no toki o koete* よみがえる漢王朝一 2000 年の時をこえて [Bringing the Han dynasty back to life: Overcoming the distance of 2,000 years]. Osaka: Yomiuri Shinbun Ōsaka Honsha, 1999.

Ōshima Toshikazu 大島利一. "Chūgoku kodai no shukōgyō" 中国古代の手工業 [Ancient Chinese handicrafts]. In *Kodaishi kōza* 古代史講座 [Seminar in ancient history], vol. 9. Tokyo: Gakuseisha, 1963.

Rakurō Kanbo Kankōkai, ed. *Rakurō Kanbo* 楽浪漢墓 [Han tombs at Lelang]. 2 vols. Nara: Rakurō Kanbo Kankōkai, 1974.

Sahara Yasuo 佐原康夫. "Kan Chōanjō miōkyū sangō kenchiku yishi ni tsuite" 漢長安城未央宮三号建築遺址について [Concerning structure 3 at the Weiyang Palace of Han Chang'an]. *Shirin* 74, no. 1 (1991): 102–17.

———. "Kandai gunken no zaisei kikō ni tsuite" 漢代郡県の財政機構について [The structure of Han period commandery and county financial administration]. *Tōhō gakuhō* 62 (1990): 1–29.

———. "Kandai no ichi ni tsuite" 漢代の市について [Han period markets]. *Shirin* 68, no. 5 (1985): 33–71.

———. *Kandai toshi kikō no kenkyū* 漢代都市機構の研究 [Research into the structure of Han cities and markets]. Tokyo: Kyūko Shoin, 2002.

———. "Nanyō gabōjō Kandai seitetsu iseki no gijutsushiteki kentō" 南陽瓦房荘漢代製鉄遺跡の技術史的検討 [Technical investigation into the iron production site at Wafangzhuang in Nanyang]. *Shirin* 76, no. 1 (1993): 121–34.

———. "Senkoku jidai no fu-ko ni tsuite" 戦国時代の府庫について [Treasuries and depots during the Warring States period]. *Tōyōshi kenkyū* 43, no. 1 (1984): 31–59.

Sanae Yoshio 早苗良雄. *Kandai kenkyū bunken mokuroku: hōbun-hen* 漢代研究文献目録邦文編 [Index of Japanese writings on the Han period]. Kyoto: Hōyū Shoten, 1979.

Satō Taketoshi 佐藤武敏. *Chōan* 長安 [Chang'an]. Tokyo: Kondō Shuppansha, 1971.

———. *Chūgoku kodai kōgyōshi no kenkyū* 中国古代工業史の研究 [Research on the history of ancient Chinese craft production]. Tokyo: Yoshikawa Kōbunkan, 1962.

———. "Chūgoku kodai no asaorimono seisan" 中国古代の麻織物生産 [Production of hemp textiles in ancient China]. *Tōyōshi kenkyū* 19, no. 1 (1960): 1–23.

———. "Chūgoku kodai no kinuorimono gyō no keiei keitai" 中国古代の絹織物業の経営形態 [Organization and management of ancient Chinese silk production]. *Shūkan tōyōgaku* 4 (1960): 63–79.

———. "Chūgoku kodai no shikki kōgyō" 中国古代の漆器工業 [Ancient Chinese lacquer craft]. *Jimbun kenkyū* 9, no. 11 (1958): 23–64.
———. "Chūgoku kodai no urushi jihai" 中国古代の漆耳杯 [Lacquered eared cups of ancient China]. *Museum* (1987.6): 4–13.
———. "Kandai Chōan no ichi" 漢代長安の市 [The markets of Han period Chang'an]. In *Chūgoku kodaishi kenkyū* 中国古代史研究 [Research on ancient Chinese history], vol. 2, ed. Chūgoku kodaishi kenkyū Kai, 225–52. Tokyo: Yoshikawa Kōbunkan, 1965.
———. "Kandai ni okeru tetsu no seisan—toku ni seitetsu iseki o chūshin ni" 漢代における鉄の生産一とくに製鉄遺跡を中心に [Han period iron production—especially focusing on iron production sites]. *Jimbun kenkyū* 15, no. 5 (1958): 1–20.
———. "Shin Kan sho no shikki no seisan ni tsuite" 秦漢初の漆器の生産について [Lacquer production in the Qin and early Han periods]. *Koshi shunjū* 4 (1987): 3–16.
———. "Xiushilu ni tsuite" 髹飾録について [On the text *Record of Lacquer Decoration*]. *Museum* (1988.11): 15–24.
Sekino Tadashi 関野貞. *Rakurō-gun jidai no iseki* 楽浪郡時代の遺跡 [The site of Lelang Commandery]. 2 vols. Keijō [Seoul]: Chōsen Sōtokufu, 1927.
Shōsōin Jimusho, ed. *Shōsōin no shikkō* 正倉院の漆工 [Lacquer craft in the Shōsōin collection]. Tokyo: Heibonsha, 1975.
Sumiya Sadatoshi 角谷定俊. "Shin ni okeru seidō kōgyō no ikkōsatsu—kōkan o chūshin ni" 秦における青銅工業の一考察一工官を中心に [Investigation of Qin bronze production, focusing on the Office of Workmen]. *Sundai shigaku* 55 (1982): 52–86.
Sumiya Tsuneko 角谷常子. "Shin Kan jidai no kantoku kenkyū" 秦漢時代簡牘の研究 [Research into bamboo slips and wooden boards of the Qin and Han periods]. *Tōyōshi kenkyū* 55, no. 1 (1996): 211–24.
Tanba Yasuyori 丹波康頼. *Ishinpō* 医心方 [Medical methods]. Vol. 24. Trans. Maki Sachiko 槇佐知子. Tokyo: Chikuma Shobō, 1994.
Tani Toyonobu and Hiroshi Sobukawa, eds. *Shin Kan* 秦漢 [Qin and Han]. Vol. 2 of *Sekai bijutsu daizenshū: Tōyō hen* 世界美術大全集：東洋編 [Great collection of world art: East Asia], ed. Sekai Bijustsu Henshūbu. Tokyo: Shōgakukan, 1998.
Tōkyō Kokuritsu Hakubutsukan, ed. *Urushi de egakareta shinpi no seikai: Chūgoku kodai shikkiten* 漆で描かれた神秘の世界：中国古代漆器展 [Mysterious world of lacquer designs: Exhibition of ancient Chinese lacquer]. [Tokyo]: Toyota Zaidan, 1998.
Umehara Sueji 梅原末治. "Chūgoku kodai shikki no moji" 中国古代漆器の文字 [Graphs on ancient Chinese lacquers]. *Bokubi* 53 (1956): 2–18.
———. *In bo hakken mokki in'ei zuroku* 殷墓発見木器印影図録 [Pictorial record of the impressions of wooden articles found at the Yin tombs]. Kyoto: Benridō, 1959.
———. *Kan Sangoku Rikuchō kinenkyō zusetsu* 漢三国六朝紀年鏡図説 [Illustrated catalog of dated Han, Three Kingdoms, and Six Dynasties mirrors]. Kyoto: Kuwana Bunseidō, 1943.
———. "Kandai shikki kinen meibun shūroku" 漢代漆器紀年銘文集録 [Collection of Han period dated lacquer inscriptions]. *Tōhō gakuhō* 5 (1934): 207–22.
———. "Kandai shikki kinen meibun shūroku hoi" 「漢代漆器紀年銘文集録」補遺 [Collection of Han period dated lacquer inscriptions: Addendum and corrections]. *Tōhō gakuhō* 6 (1936): 315–8.

———. "Kandai shikki kinen meibun shūroku hoi (dai ni)" 「漢代漆器紀年銘文集録」補遺（第二）[Collection of Han period dated lacquer inscriptions: Addendum and corrections, no. 2]. *Tōhō gakuhō* 11, no. 4 (1941): 74–90.
———. *Mōko Noin-Ura hakken no ibutsu* 蒙古ノインウラ発見の遺物 [Artifacts found at the Noin-Ula site in Mongolia]. Tokyo: Tōyō Bunko, 1960.
———. "Ō Mō jidai no shikki meibun" 王莽時代の漆器銘文 [Wang Mang period lacquer inscriptions]. *Tōyōshi kenkyū* 3, no. 3 (1938): 62–6.
———. "Shina hakken kodai shikki no atarashi shiryō" 支那発見古代漆器の新資料 [Discovery in China of new data on ancient lacquer]. In *Shina kōkogaku ronkō* 支那考古学論考. Tokyo: Kōbundō, 1938.
———. "Shina hakken no Kandai no shitsuren" 支那発見の漢代の漆匳 [Han period lacquer toiletry boxes discovered in China]. In *Shina kōkogaku ronkō* 支那考古学論考. Tokyo: Kōbundō, 1938.
———. *Shina Kandai kinenmei shikki zusetsu* 支那漢代記年銘漆器図説 [Illustrated catalog of dated Han lacquers]. Kyoto: Kuwana Bunseidō, 1943. Reprint, Kyoto: Dohōsha, 1984.
———. "Shina Kandai no hari" 支那漢代の玻璃 [Han period Chinese glass]. In *Shina kōkogaku ronkō* 支那考古学論考. Tokyo: Kōbundō, 1938.
———. *Shina kōkogaku ronkō* 支那考古学論考 [Writings on Chinese archaeology]. Tokyo: Kōbundō, 1938.
Utsunomiya Kiyoyoshi 宇都宮清吉. *Kandai shakai keizaishi kenkyū* 漢代社会経済史研究 [Research into Han period social and economic history]. Rev. ed. Tokyo: Kōbundō, 1967.
Yamada Katsuyoshi 山田勝芳. "Shinkandai shukōgyō no tenkai—Shinkandai kōkan no hensen kara kangaeru" 秦漢代手工業の展開ー秦漢代工官の変遷から考える [Development of handicraft industries during the Qin and Han—investigating the evolution of the Office of Workmen institution]. *Tōyōshi kenkyū* 56, no. 4 (1998): 1–32.
Yamaguchi Kenritsu Hagi Bijutsukan and Uragami Kinenkan, eds. *Chūgoku sennin no furusato: Santōshō bunbutsuten* 中国仙人のふるさと：山東省文物展 [Homeland of Chinese immortals: Exhibition of cultural relics from Shandong]. Ōsaka-fu Izumi-shi: Ōsaka-furitsu Yayoi bunka hakubutsukan, 1996.
Yonezawa Yoshio 米沢嘉圃. "Kandai ni okeru kyūtei sakuga kikō no hattatsu" 漢代に於ける宮廷作画機構の発達（上） [Development of the structure of court painting during the Han, part 1]. *Kokka* 48, no. 6 (1938): 145–51.
———. "Kandai ni okeru kyūtei sakuga kikō no hattatsu" 漢代に於ける宮廷作画機構の発達（中）[Development of the structure of court painting during the Han, part 2]. *Kokka* 48, no. 9 (1938): 263–7.
———. "Kandai ni okeru kyūtei sakuga kikō no hattatsu" 漢代に於ける宮廷作画機構の発達（下の一） [Development of the structure of court painting during the Han, part 3a]. *Kokka* 48, no. 10 (1938): 293–6.
———. "Kandai ni okeru kyūtei sakuga kikō no hattatsu" 漢代に於ける宮廷作画機構の発達（下の二）[Development of the structure of court painting during the Han, part 3b]. *Kokka* 48, no. 11 (1938): 301–5.
———. "Kandai ni okeru kyūtei sakuga kikō no hattatsu" 漢代に於ける宮廷作画機構の発達（下の三）[Development of the structure of court painting during the Han, part 3c]. *Kokka* 48, no. 12 (1938): 331–5.

———. "Kandai kaiga shiryō shū" 漢代絵画史料集 [Compilation of historical references to Han period painting]. *Kokka* 98, no. 9 (1993): 31–4.
Yoshida Mitsukuni 吉田光邦. "Shūrai kōkōki no ikkōsatsu" 周礼考工記の一考察 [Investigation into the *Record of the Scrutiny of Crafts* in the *Ritual System of the Zhou*]. *Tōhō gakuhō* 30 (1959): 167–226.

INDEX

Photos and illustrations are indicated with **bold** type.